Tomb Families

Tomb Families

Private Tomb Distribution in the New Kingdom Theban Necropolis

Katherine Slinger

Archaeopress Egyptology 40

Archaeopress Publishing Ltd
Summertown Pavilion
18-24 Middle Way
Summertown
Oxford OX2 7LG

www.archaeopress.com

ISBN 978-1-80327-036-4
ISBN 978-1-80327-037-1 (e-Pdf)

Table of Contents

List of Figures

List of Tables

Acknowledgements

Firstly, I would like to thank my PhD supervisors, Dr Steven Snape and Professor Chris Eyre for all their help and guidance over the years. I would also like to thank Dr Matthew Fitzjohn for helping me get to grips with the QGIS software.

I would like to thank the University of Liverpool for awarding me the Sir Joseph Rotblat Alumni Scholarship which funded this research project, and for granting me the Peet Travel Award on two occasions, which enabled me to travel to Luxor to complete my GPS surveying. Thank you also to Dr Shirley for her correspondence regarding her own research into the Theban tombs, and to Dr Ángeles Jimenez-Higueras for allowing me to consult her then unpublished thesis.

I would also like to thank the many friends I have made along the way, particularly my friends in Egypt for inspiring my love of Egyptology in the first place, always showing such interest in my research, and for looking after me when I am there.

Finally, I would like to thank my amazing parents, for their support and for making it possible for me to follow my dreams and pursue Egyptology – a lifelong dream of mine. None of this would have been possible without them and their constant support and encouragement. Also, Shannon, Millie and Bella who kept me sane and always reminded me that there was life outside the PhD!

Abbreviations

Abbreviations for Publications used in References and Appendices

KRI: Kitchen, K.A., 1969-1990, *'Ramesside Inscriptions, Historical and Biographical,* Volumes I-VIII. Oxford.
LAe: Helck, W. & Otto, E. (eds.), 1972-1995, *Lexikon der Ägyptologie,* Volumes I-VII. Wiesbaden.
LD: Lepsius, K.R. (ed.), 1849-1859, *Denkmäler aus Ägypten und Äthiopien.* Volumes I-VI. Berlin.
PM I: Porter, B. & Moss, R., 1960, *Topographical Bibliography of Ancient Egyptian Hieroglyphic Texts, Statues, Reliefs and Paintings I: The Theban Necropolis: Part 1: Private Tombs: 2nd Edition.* Oxford.
Urk. IV: Sethe, K., 1906-1909, *Urkunden der 18. Dynastie IV. Abteilung Band II.* Heft 1-16. Leipzig, continued by Helck, W., 1955-1958, *Urkunden der 18. Dynastie IV. Abteilung Band II.* Heft 17-22. Berlin.

Abbreviations for Specific Periods

Dyn - Dynasty
FIP – First Intermediate Period
MK – Middle Kingdom
OK - Old Kingdom
Ram – Ramesside Period (Nineteenth/Twentieth Dynasty)
SIP – Second Intermediate Period

Abbreviations for King's Reigns

A – Amenhotep
Ah – Ahmose
Ame – Amenmessu
Amen – Amenemhat
Ay – Ay
Hat – Hatshepsut
Hor – Horemheb
Mer – Merenptah
Mon – Montuhotep
R – Ramesses
S – Seti
Sen – Senwosret
Set – Setnakhte
Sip – Siptah
STII – Seqenenre Tao
T – Tuthmosis
Tau - Tausert
Tut – Tutankhamun

Abbreviations for Common Titles

HPA – High Priest of Amun
2PA – 2nd Priest of Amun
3PA – 3rd Priest of Amun
4PA – 4th Priest of Amun
OP – Overseer of Priests

Miscellaneous Abbreviations

BFV – Beautiful Festival of the Valley
BM - British Museum
DEM – Digital Elevation Modelling
GIS - Geographical Information Software
GPS - Geographic Positioning System
K-n- -- Kampp numbered tomb
KML - Keyhole Markup Language
O - Ostraca
QGIS - Quantum Geographical Information Software
TCX - Training Center XML
TT – Theban Tomb (original number)

Conventions

Translation of Texts

[ ] words lost in the original text and restored.

... Part of translation not included in the extract.

QGIS

Screenshots of the QGIS projects used for this research have been used as maps throughout this publication, in addition to those from Google Earth Pro importing the same GPS co-ordinates, and Google My Maps. Unless otherwise stated in the List of Figures, all maps are from the QGIS.

The key to be used in conjunction with all QGIS maps showing TTs organised by date is opposite on page xxi and online at https://doi.org/10.32028/9781803270364-online. QGIS maps showing the TTs distributed by occupational groupings have individual legends included within the maps.

https://doi.org/10.32028/9781803270364-online

Abstract

The Theban Necropolis contains hundreds of tombs belonging to elite individuals, dating from the end of the Old Kingdom through to the Ptolemaic Period, with the vast majority dating to the New Kingdom (*c.* 1550-1077 BC). These tombs are scattered across the landscape at the edge of the desert between the Valley of the Kings to the west, and the row of royal mortuary temples along the edge of the cultivation to the east. This research project focuses on New Kingdom private tomb distribution and investigates this apparently random arrangement of tombs by focusing on factors which may have influenced tomb location. GPS surveying and further analysis of tomb distribution using QGIS software is used to enable these tombs to be categorised in several different ways, demonstrating that specific areas of the necropolis were popular at different times and among particular groups of people. By investigating the evolution of the necropolis and spatial analysis of the tombs considering the date they were built, it has been possible to identify clusters and patterns between tombs built during the same reign(s).

A complete database of the tomb owners has been compiled using original source material to transliterate and translate their titles, enabling a detailed investigation into different occupational groups, in order to identify if these groupings are reflected by tomb distribution. Familial connections between tomb owners have been compared to tomb distribution to identify potential family groupings, and the proximity and orientation of the tombs in relation to royal mortuary temples and festival processional routes is also considered. The earliest tombs in the necropolis dating to the Old and Middle Kingdoms have also been included, to compare their distribution to that of their New Kingdom neighbours and to ascertain if their presence influenced later tomb location. Tomb reuse and the use of shared courtyards have also been analysed, in order to establish periods and areas of the necropolis where these practices were most common. This research provides a deeper understanding of the necropolis as a whole, and how the tomb linked to the wider sacred landscape of Thebes.

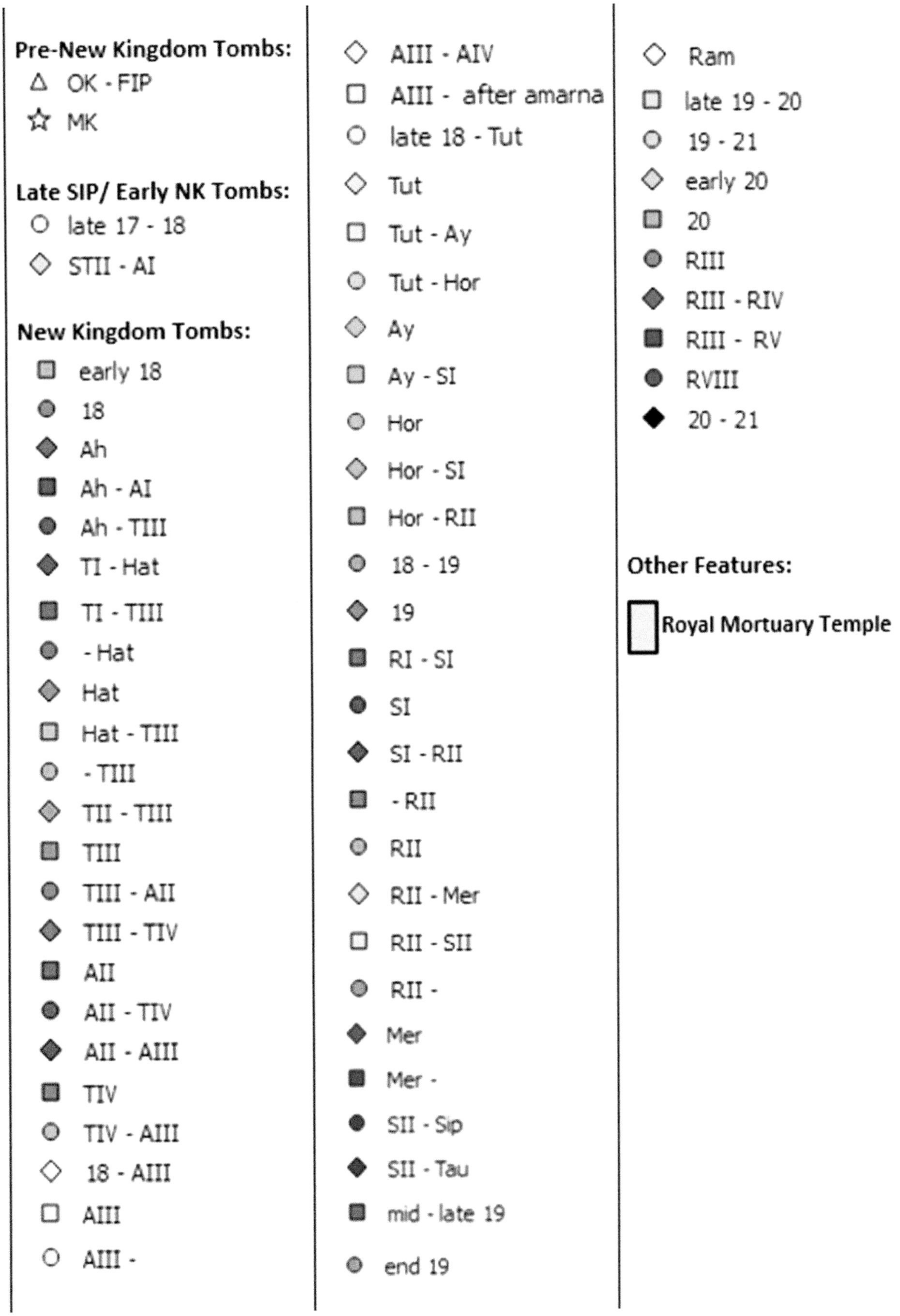

QGIS Legend

https://doi.org/10.32028/9781803270364-online

Chapter 1: Introduction

This publication considers the organisation of the New Kingdom Theban necropolis, focusing on factors influencing the distribution of these tombs. The necropolis is surveyed systematically, from north to south, focusing on one area at a time, considering why tombs were built in particular locations or in distinct clusters.

The geographical location of each tomb within the necropolis is defined using GPS information gathered in the field, imported into QGIS software within the much larger area known generally as the 'Theban Necropolis'. The tombs are then analysed for patterns in their distribution by reign, and geographical and spatial alignment. The tomb owners themselves are explored by examining their titles and familial relationships where inscriptional evidence survives. Tombs organised by broader occupational groupings are also identified. The proximity of the tombs to other features, both natural (such as the pyramid shaped Qurn mountain) and built (royal mortuary temples and tombs) is also taken into consideration to understand the wider sacred landscape of Western Thebes. No such comprehensive study exists so this research is a necessary and crucial investigation to allow a fuller understanding of this vast and very important archaeological site.

This innovative combination and approach to the primary evidence combined with insights of previous research provides a deeper understanding of the necropolis itself, how it was organised, and the importance placed on specific areas at particular times or to certain groups of people. It will ultimately clarify to what degree tomb location was allocated or chosen, and what additional factors drove this location. This study is therefore pioneering as these questions have not been directly addressed before when considering the entire necropolis. This type of research permits Egyptologists to consider the mortuary landscape of Thebes in a new way, allowing us a greater understanding of how the necropolis was organised. The tomb distribution patterns which have emerged during this study will provide a focus for future excavations in the area, attempting to locate as yet undiscovered or 'lost' tombs, with potentially exciting implications.

Area

The Theban Necropolis is located on the west bank of the modern-day city of Luxor (see Figure 1). It consists of the Valley of the Kings, the Valley of the Queens, the royal mortuary temples, the workmen's village of Deir el-Medina and the so-called 'Tombs of the Nobles' which this study considers. This private necropolis contains hundreds of non-royal tombs, and spreads along the edge of the cultivation, parallel with the River Nile. It is bordered to the west by the Theban Mountains, beyond which lies the Valley of the Kings, and to the east by the row of royal mortuary temples. The New Kingdom cemetery stretches from the area of el-Tarif in the north to the modern road to Deir el-Medina in the south and is divided into in several geographical areas. From north to south they are Dra Abu el-Naga, Deir el-Bahri, el-Asasif, el-Khokha, Sheikh Abd el-Qurna, and Qurnet Murai (see Figure 2). An enclosed cemetery also exists at Deir el-Medina. The tombs are located between 160m and 80m above sea level, at which height the flatter floodplain begins.

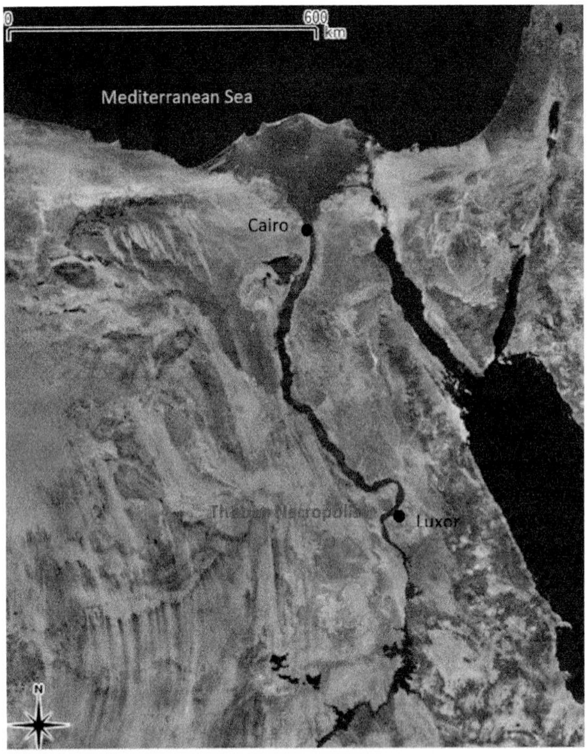

Figure 1: Location of the Theban Necropolis (Author's own using Google Earth)

Data Set

A Microsoft Access database has been created of the 414 original Theban Tombs (TTs), officially numbered by the Antiquities Service (see Figure 3). The tombs numbered later by Kampp (1996) have been excluded from this initial data set as the names and titles of the majority of

Figure 2: Areas of the Theban Necropolis (Author's own using Google My Maps)

the owners of these tombs are not available due to the poor preservation of these tombs. As a result of this lack of inscriptional information these Kampp tombs could not be analysed in the same way as the original tombs, as they cannot be grouped by occupation or affiliation. The 'Theban Necropolis' database contains: the TT number; the date or specific reign(s) to which the tomb was dated; the name of the tomb owner(s); the complete transliterated and translated title(s) of the tomb owner; the category or categories of occupation of the tomb owner; any affiliation of the individuals, for example to a specific deity; any spatial connection between the tombs, such as shared courtyards or entrances; any known familial connection to other tombs in the necropolis. In cases where the tomb has been reused, the details of each occupant have been included, with the order of occupation denoted numerically. Tombs built or reused after the end of the New Kingdom have not been included as they are not relevant to this study.

QGIS

This database has been joined to Quantum Geographical Information Software (QGIS), in order to create a layered map of the necropolis. These interchangeable layers include tombs of different dates, dates of reuse, occupational groups, and specific titles, thus allowing the analysis of tomb distribution to identify potential patterns and trends. In order to join the database to the QGIS software, the database needed a spatial data component. Despite the apparent commencement of a number of projects to provide Geographic Positioning System (GPS) co-ordinates for the Theban tombs, no such complete resource exists in the public domain, and requests to the relevant bodies for access to GPS or GIS data for the area have not been successful. Due to the lack of a professionally available topographic map of the area of a scale and quality appropriate for this project, or a comprehensive map of the area's tombs and surrounding structures, the existing plans and plates by Porter Moss (1960) and Kampp (1996) were consulted as the most complete and recent maps available for this purpose. As a result of the lack of publicly available spatial data, these plans have been attached to the GIS software using a method of geo-referencing fixed geographical landmarks identifiable on both the maps and satellite imagery. This time-consuming process allowed the plates to be attached to a map of Egypt using a Google Earth plug-in to provide satellite imagery. However, in order to test the accuracy of both the maps and the geo-referencing process, a survey was undertaken by the author, of key tombs and features in the necropolis using a handheld Garmin GPS device, in order to obtain GPS data to compare to the QGIS image. GPS readings were taken at the entrance of all accessible tombs in the necropolis, and at a number of additional locations identifiable from satellite imagery, such as mortuary temples, processional paths and modern landmarks, in order to enhance the accuracy of the geo-referencing.

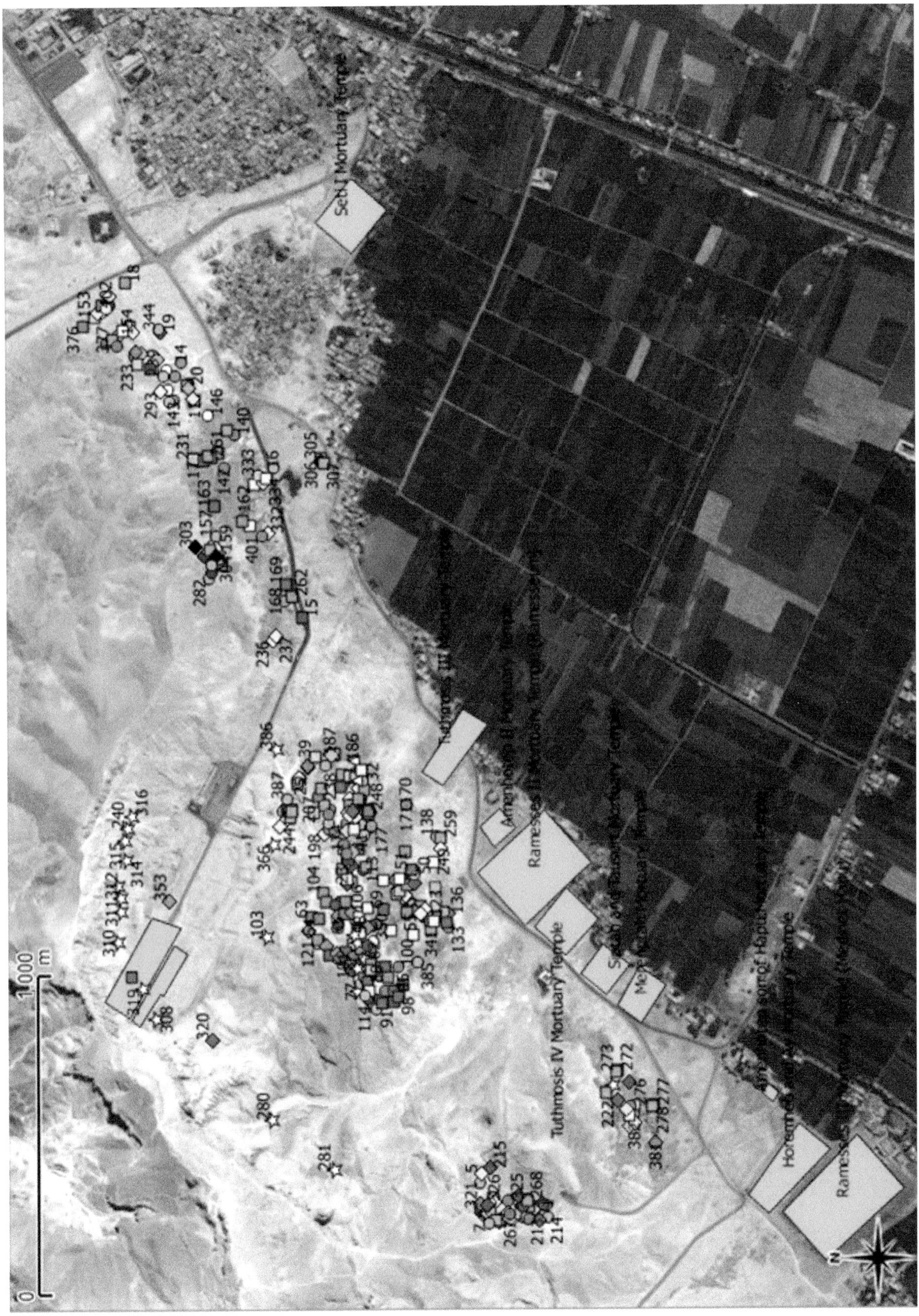

Figure 3: Theban Tombs in relation to the rest of the Theban Necropolis (Author's own using QGIS)

This GPS data was imported into QGIS software, allowing geo-referencing of the relevant plans and plates, using the waypoints taken in the field to ensure an accuracy of within five metres. Once the plates were geo-referenced they were used to digitise and number each Theban Tomb, providing latitude and longitude co-ordinates using the plans to locate them. Once this data had been obtained, the simplified Theban Tombs database could be joined to the 'Tombs shapefile' using the tomb number. This joining allows the creation of layers within the GIS to illustrate patterns using different criteria. An additional layer was created in 'Google My Maps' and imported into the QGIS software, digitising major mortuary temples visible on the satellite imagery on the eastern edge of the necropolis to ascertain proximity and orientation in relation to the tombs. Digital Elevation Modelling (DEM) has also been performed using 'Google Earth Pro' to create a KML (Keyhole Markup Language) file, which was imported into a TCX (Training Center XML) converter to obtain altitude data and convert it into a TCX file. This was then imported into the QGIS and saved as a 'shapefile'. This allows a layer to ascertain the elevation of the tomb and the contours of the entire necropolis to identify potential reasons for distributional patterns.

Subsequent trips were then made to the Theban Necropolis to take further GPS readings in order to ascertain the accuracy of this method. These calculations have shown that the locations of tombs visible on the QGIS are accurate to within five metres in open sky conditions, which is accurate enough for the purposes of this study.

Sources

The information in the database is based on Porter and Moss (1960), Kampp (1996a and b) and individual tomb publications where available. Theban Tomb dates are primarily based on Kampp's (1996) dating criteria as the most recent and comprehensive available, but also considering dating by Porter and Moss (1960), and individual tomb publications where necessary. Other evidence for the dating of individual tombs, where relevant, has also been considered.

The titles are primarily derived from translating the hieroglyphic inscriptions from each individual tomb, the majority of which have been reproduced in the *Urkunden* IV (Sethe 1906-09, and Helck 1955-58) for the Eighteenth Dynasty tombs, and Kitchen's *Ramesside Inscriptions* (1969-1990) for the Nineteenth and Twentieth Dynasty tombs. Individual tomb publications have also been consulted wherever possible. The hieroglyphic transcription of titles by Gardiner and Weigall (1913) have been used as a source for otherwise unpublished tombs. As many of the tomb owners possessed multiple titles, priority has been given to functional rather than honorary titles, with the most important titles listed first. This field of the database is limited by the number of tombs which have not been fully published, as well as inaccessible or poorly preserved tombs. A comprehensive publication of New Kingdom titles is lacking, so the index of Al-Ayedi (2006) has been used for reference purposes. Quirke (2004), Ward (1982) and Fischer (1997) have also been useful, as although they pertain to the Middle Kingdom still contain some relevant information

Only titles listed within tombs have been included in this study, while further titularies from additional inscriptional evidence have been excluded, as the translation of all available sources is beyond the scope of this research project. This is limiting in some cases where a more definite affiliation or additional titles are known for some individuals from other sources, but it seems sensible that any titles affecting tomb placement would be included within the tomb itself, and not solely be known from other sources.

Occupational Groupings

All tomb owners listed their titularies within their tombs, which can be used to identify and differentiate between them. Their occupations have been categorised into several groups, based on those used by Gardiner and Weigall (1913: 41-44), with some tomb owners with multiple titles falling into multiple categories.

The first of these groups is the priesthood, which includes different classes of priest, along with those with esoteric knowledge, such as 'Chief of the Brazier Burners', 'Scribe of Divine Records', and 'Head of the Master of Ceremonies'. The second group consists of those individuals who were affiliated to the temple estate in an administrative capacity rather than a religious one. This included those with roles in the temple such as 'Stewards', 'Overseers' of various departments of the temple, such as the treasury, granary or storehouse, the 'Overseer of Works', 'Temple Scribes', and those responsible for otherwise provisioning the temple.

The third group includes those individuals with a royal administrative title, affiliated to the palace or court. These individuals directly served the king and royal family, including 'Royal Stewards', 'Heralds', 'Butlers', 'Royal Physicians' and 'Nurses', along with those possessing administrative titles such as 'Royal Scribes', 'Overseers of the Treasury' or 'Overseer of the Granary' of the King, and 'Overseers of the Royal Harem'. Members of the royal family form a small separate group, consisting of royal sons, wives and daughters.

Another group is the general centralised administration of the country. These national roles include the 'Viziers', 'Chancellors', 'Overseers' of the state treasury and granary, and important agricultural titles. The local administration forms another distinct group, consisting of individuals with regional rather than national power. These include 'Mayors', local governors, harbour-masters, and those with provincial titles such as 'King's Son of Kush', and 'Eyes of the King' in foreign lands. Military titles are also differentiated, with this group including 'Overseers of the Army', 'Lieutenant Commanders', 'Captain of Troops', 'Chief of Horses' and 'Military Scribes'. The final group is made up of those tomb owners for whom we only have honorary court titles, such as 'Sole Companion' or 'Child of the Nursery'. When an honorary title occurs in conjunction with a functional title, the functional title has been used to categorise the occupation of the tomb owner.

Spatial Analysis

Using firstly date and then titles, the distribution of tombs has been analysed in order to identify potential clusters. The QGIS has been filtered to show the stages of development of each area of the necropolis, allowing groupings of contemporary tombs to be identified. The titles of each tomb owner have then been analysed within their occupational groupings, in order to identify any trends or spatial connections between tombs belonging to individuals who had similar titles. Familial connections have been identified, where evidence permits, to look for relationships of tombs belonging to family members. Shared tombs have also been considered, to explore the connection between the individuals who were buried there.

Research Questions

- **How did the Theban Necropolis evolve over time?**

The New Kingdom tombs are analysed to ascertain if there is evidence of a gradual spread of tombs from a single original occupied area as the necropolis expanded. Another theory is that the most desirable locations were filled first and later tombs filled in the gaps. This seems to be a generalised rather simplistic way to look at the evolution of the necropolis, so trends during specific reigns are also considered to look for spatial connections between tombs and the rest of the funerary landscape.

- **Were individuals buried near their family or contemporaries – or perhaps even in friendship groups?**

Any known familial relationships are considered in relation to the placement of their tombs to see if relations are buried in the vicinity of each other. The occupation and affiliation of tomb owners is also considered to see if there is evidence of colleagues who lived and worked together being buried close to each other.

- **Is there evidence of occupational clusters?**

When the titles of tomb owners are organised into groups according to their occupation, their tombs are considered in relation to other individuals who held the same or similar title(s) or had the same affiliation, to see if trends between certain occupations can be observed that might be indicative of areas of the necropolis allocated to specific professions or groups.

- **Were lower ranking individuals buried in the vicinity of their superior(s)?**

Middle Kingdom cemeteries such as Beni Hassan were organised by the high officials being buried on the upper slopes, and the lower officials on the lower slopes. In the Old and Middle Kingdom the royal tomb acted as a focal point for clusters of tombs belonging to officials who served them. In the New Kingdom when the king's burial had been removed to the Valley of the Kings, did the tombs of the most important officials act as a similar focus? By studying the tombs of the Viziers and the High Priests of Amun, the two most important New Kingdom officials, and those buried in close proximity, it is possible to see if their colleagues or subordinates were spatially connected to them after death.

- **Was tomb distribution influenced by proximity to the royal mortuary temple of the reigning king?**

In the Old and Middle Kingdom, officials were buried in close proximity to the tomb of their king. The isolated nature of the royal tomb in the New Kingdom meant that this was now impossible, but it was still possible to be buried relatively close to the more accessible royal mortuary temple of the reigning king, or at least orientated towards it. The location of contemporary mortuary temples will be considered alongside the evolution of the necropolis.

- **Was tomb location influenced by the processional routes of the Beautiful Festival of the Valley and other festivals?**

The evolving processional route of the BFV is considered alongside the evolution of the necropolis, to see there is evidence of tombs being located along or orientated towards the processional route, in order to participate in the festival after death. Additional processions and cultic activity in the necropolis may also have influenced tomb distribution.

- **Who was buried in the most desirable locations? Were they reserved for the**

wealthiest or most important individuals or those closest to the king?

It seems likely that positions on the upper slopes with superior views, or in close proximity to important elements of the funerary landscape such as mortuary temples and processional routes, would have been reserved for high-ranking individuals. The analysis of the titles of those buried for example in Upper Qurna reveal if there is evidence for this, or if it was a case of first come first served.

- **Were certain locations popular during certain periods for a reason?**

When the evolution of the necropolis is studied, can the popularity of specific areas during certain periods be identified and linked to other factors, such as the titles of those buried there, or proximity to other elements of the funerary landscape at that time? Or does it appear to have been more of a natural expansion due to areas becoming too full to be a viable option for rock-cut tombs, so a different area was chosen to allow new tomb building?

- **Does this tell us anything about mortuary beliefs at different times?**

Does tomb distribution inform our knowledge of important factors when choosing a plot for tomb building during specific periods? For example is it possible to identify periods when spatial connections to tombs belonging to individuals with the same title, potential colleagues or family members seemed to have driven tomb distribution, or when connections with specific mortuary temples or processional routes were a more important factor, perhaps showing a change in tomb distribution as in tomb architecture and decoration between the Eighteenth Dynasty and the Ramesside Period.

- **Why were some tombs located around a shared courtyard, or with shared access?**

The use of shared architectural features may have allowed contemporary individuals to conveniently share resources to create an impressive façade or entrance for their tombs, while familial or titular links between tomb owners may be indicative of a desire to spend eternity in close proximity by spatially linking their tombs in this way. Later tombs may have been added onto existing features to establish a link with an esteemed ancestor, or simply taking advantage of an existing courtyard by cutting a subsidiary tomb. An analysis of shared courtyards reveals more about this practice.

- **Which tombs were reused and who reused them? To what extent was this practice a result of lack of space and resources, or is there evidence of links between occupants of the same tomb?**

By mapping reused tombs, chronological patterns can be identified, potentially indicating whether this was a case of necessity, simply reusing any suitable tomb, or if it was more prevalent in specific areas, suggesting that location was the driving factor behind the decision. Links between the various occupants of a tomb and those of nearby tombs may also reveal a connection, such as the reuse of tombs by members of the same profession or a tomb close to that of a family member.

- **What does all this information tell us about how tomb plots were allocated?**

The issue of New Kingdom private tomb allocation is not well understood, so any evidence of a centralised organisation of the necropolis may be indicative of state involvement in tomb allocation. If the necropolis evolved more naturally then this would suggest more of an element of personal choice when choosing a location to build a tomb.

Shared Courtyards

A number of tombs opened onto a courtyard which was shared with other tombs, while others shared access. These connections are analysed to try and explain why these tombs were linked, and whether this was intentional or accidental. These tombs have been identified from the plans by Kampp (1996), Google Earth satellite imagery, and confirmed by visits to as many shared courtyards as accessible. Those tombs containing a breakthrough into another tomb which is clearly identifiable as an accidental occurrence during the construction of the later tomb, or a deliberate attempt by tomb robbers to gain access, have been excluded as they are irrelevant to this study. This information has been incorporated at the end of each chapter.

Tomb Reuse

A number of tombs were reused (some multiple times) during the New Kingdom. A separate QGIS map has been created by filtering the attached attribute table to show only reused tombs, with the key equating to the date of (first in the case of multiple reuses) reuse. The dates of occupation, in conjunction with the titles of original and secondary owners are then analysed, to attempt to draw conclusions about the reasons for reuse, investigating potential connections between the tomb owners, or whether it was reusing a prime location to site a tomb, or simply a matter of convenience. These factors help to explain why certain areas of the necropolis were reused more than others, and why reuse was more popular during certain periods than others.

Problems and Limitations

Preservation and Publication of the Theban Tombs

The amount of data available for each tomb varies greatly, thus affecting the accuracy of dating and full titles of the tomb owner. This is partly as a result of the nature of Egyptian tombs, with poor preservation and a lack of accurate recording of the inscriptions, in addition to a number of tombs being inaccessible. Many TTs are not fully published and not included in the source material, thus limiting the titles included in the database. The number of titles available for each tomb owner depends on their availability for the aforementioned reasons, but also on the space available within the tomb to record them.

Tomb Construction

When identifying tomb patterns according to date, tombs dated to a specific reign may not provide an accurate reflection of the date when construction began. In those cases where a definitive reign is given, it was usually towards the end of an official's career when he attained his highest office, and not necessarily at the time when construction on the tomb began, and therefore its location was chosen. This depended on the lifespan of the tomb owner and how early in his career he began work on his tomb. If tomb construction was begun early in a career, which seems likely, its location might have been chosen one or two reigns prior to the reign of the last king served (Roth 1988: 202), or it may have been begun later in his career when he had sufficient resources to complete it. Manniche (1987: 11) estimates 70 days as potentially the length of time taken to carve and decorate a private New Kingdom Theban tomb, but without specific textual evidence this is speculation. This needs to be considered when identifying chronological patterns.

Several publications deal with the construction and decoration of New Kingdom private Theban tombs, and who was responsible for it. Although many elements of these arguments are not relevant to this study, they provide information about the rate of tomb building, and may also inform the issue of tomb allocation. Romer (1988: 211-232) claims that the workmen at Deir el-Medina were only responsible for the construction of tombs within the village and not the wider necropolis. He also conducts a statistical analysis of the private Theban Tombs throughout the New Kingdom, concluding that approximately eight tombs were built every ten years in the Theban Necropolis, so almost one a year (Romer 1988: 212). He states that private tomb production was reasonably consistent, suggesting a permanent workforce, directed by a single authority, to which he links the workmen at Deir el-Medina, although he finds no evidence that texts from Deir el-Medina referred to private tomb production outside the village.

Cooney (2008: 79-115) examines this theory by considering the textual evidence from Western Thebes. She convincingly argues that Romer's conclusions are based on outdated reign dates, and the tomb building patterns mirror periods of prosperity and recession, which would have influenced the entire Western Theban population, and thus the rate of tomb production, whether organised privately or by the state (Cooney 2008: 81-82). She provides textual evidence from the Ramesside Period, proving that Deir el-Medina craftsmen were involved in the decoration of the tombs of certain high officials in the wider necropolis, but not the actual tomb construction (Cooney 2008: 96-101). She concludes that these were not rare examples, but rather there was a private sector market for funerary goods, driven by the demands of highly placed Theban officials and the craftsmen themselves (Cooney 2008: 112). This then begs the question were these highly placed Theban officials responsible for choosing their own tomb and allocating others to lower officials, or was this element organised by the state.

Tomb Allocation

Very little is known about private New Kingdom tomb allocation. We do not know if individuals chose the location of the tomb themselves or whether it was allocated. Ikram (2003: 150-151) concludes that from the Middle Kingdom onwards, non-royal tomb owners financed their own tombs and were responsible for the construction and decoration rather than the king, but that the local government may have sold simple shaft tombs to potential tomb owners. Taylor (2003: 170-171) agrees that non-royal individuals in the New Kingdom were responsible for constructing their own tombs, but there is no mention of how tomb plots were allocated.

Literature Review

Many scholars refer to the organisation of the Theban necropolis with different agendas, but a detailed comprehensive study of the entire New Kingdom necropolis has never been completed previously. This literature review provides an overview of only those works which are most relevant to this research in terms of the basic core data they contain, and those that have been particularly useful when considering specific research questions relating to tomb distribution.

Core Data

The most complete and useful publications discussing the tombs of the Theban Necropolis are the reference works of Porter and Moss (1960), and Kampp (1996). Both systematically discuss each Theban Tomb, providing dating, names, and in the case of Porter and Moss, the main titles of tomb owners. The dating of Porter and Moss is based on inscriptional evidence such as regnal dates and royal cartouches for precise dating, in addition to artistic conventions when exact dating is not possible. The more recent dating by Kampp uses Porter and Moss's dating as a starting point but attempts to clarify and in some cases refine these dates by categorising the tombs on the basis of the architectural development of the tombs themselves, from 'Houses of the Dead' in the Middle Kingdom and early New Kingdom, into 'private mortuary temples' in the Ramesside Period (Kampp-Seyfried 2003: 10). The chronological and topographical distribution of tombs is considered in terms of their architectural type, rather than by an analysis of the relationship between the individuals who built the tombs, but this research has been invaluable to inform my work through this improved dating criteria. Both publications provide plans of tombs and maps of major areas of the necropolis (although Kampp excludes tombs in Deir el-Medina, Deir el-Bahri and several outlying tombs). These volumes remain the best source of general information about the dates and locations of the Theban tombs.

Gardiner and Weigall (1913) and Engelbach (1924) list the names and major titles of each tomb owner, from TT1 to TT252 in the original publication, and TT253 to TT334 in the supplement. Hieroglyphic inscriptions of the main titles are also included. The titles are grouped by affiliation, such as royal family, royal officials, general administration, local administration, military charges, priesthoods, temple administration, and members of the Place of Truth. This is a useful starting point when considering occupational groups, but some titles are omitted, so these groupings are somewhat simplified, while some are confusingly in multiple categories. These publications are incomplete as they do not include all Theban Tombs and only list the major titles of each tomb owner.

The best source for the complete set of titles in each tomb varies depending on the date of the tomb. '*Urkunden der 18. Dynastie*' (Sethe, 1905-09: Heft 1-16 and Helck 1955-61: *Heft* 17-22) is the best and most complete source for the original hieroglyphic inscriptions for most Eighteenth Dynasty tombs, while Kitchen's '*Ramesside Inscriptions*' (1969-90: Volumes I-VIII) is invaluable for the majority of Nineteenth and Twentieth Dynasty tombs. A combination of these sources has been used to compile the database for this research, supplemented by additional publications for individual tombs wherever available.

Necropolis Development

The earliest useful reference to the organisation of the necropolis as a whole is that of Rhind (1862: 50-51), who concludes that there is no progressive order of tombs according to date, and no strict groups according to the importance of the rank of their owners. He finds that those decorated tombs on the upper slopes, particularly in Qurna and Dra Abu el-Naga, were almost all owned by priests, the government or the army, with some lower-class individuals in undecorated tombs among them.

One of the most relevant papers considering the development of the private Theban Necropolis is that of Helck (1962: 225-243), who demonstrates the connection between social position and tomb location. He describes the general evolution of the Theban necropolis from its earliest tombs, and throughout the New Kingdom, but also crucially identifies a connection between the orientation and location of officials' tombs and the contemporary mortuary temples in the Eighteenth Dynasty. He suggests that the necropolis evolved from north to south, linked to the movement south of the royal mortuary temples, but that this trend only applied to '*sozial hochgestellter*', such as the Viziers, high priests, treasurers and mayors, while less important members of society filled in the gaps after the most important burials had moved southwards. He also identifies that the placement of Amenhotep III's mortuary temple further south than previous Eighteenth Dynasty temples relieved the overcrowding of some areas of the necropolis (i.e., Upper Qurna), as it led to the expansion of the cemetery onto the lower slopes. Helck credits the increased tomb building in Qurnet Murai after the Amarna Period as a result of the connection with the late Eighteenth Dynasty mortuary temples built in this southern area.

Kampp (1996: 120-22) further expands upon and challenges some of Helck's deductions by arguing against the connection between tomb orientation in Dra Abu el-Naga (specifically that of the Ramesside group including TT35, TT157 and TT158) and Karnak temple, citing the relatively small size of the necropolis in relation to the relatively long distance to the east bank, as Karnak can be observed from almost all regions of the necropolis. She acknowledges this as a factor but also relates this dense group of tombs to the identification of Seventeenth and early Eighteenth Dynasty royal tombs in this area. She identifies a preference for el-Khokha and el-Asasif, relative to their size, during the Ramesside Period, which should be considered in addition to the popularity of Dra Abu el-Naga at this time. She enhances Helck's conclusions by referring to the '*Nekropolenstraßen*' or 'Necropolis Roads' in relation to the development of the individual areas of the necropolis. As it would not have been possible in all areas to orientate every tomb towards the mortuary temples used during the Beautiful Festival of the Valley, she suggests that tombs are orientated instead towards the processional routes and festival grounds, which explains the semi-circular orientation of the tombs in Lower Qurna, and the use of two sides of the valley in el-Khokha, and similarly in Dra Abu el-Naga East. She states that the natural paths leading through necropolis hardly differ today from the ancient paths, so can be used to help divide the necropolis into areas. This premise has been used in this thesis when reassessing the boundaries between some areas. She notes that the ideal east-west tomb orientation is dependent on geographical conditions where the tomb is built, but the most successful cases in achieving this are observed in those tombs built during the reign of Amenhotep III and post-Amarna (presumably as they had expanded into other areas of the necropolis, where there was more space and less rock to dictate orientation). The natural terrain and desired orientation towards the tombs of high-ranking officials were responsible for the development of the necropolis during the Eighteenth Dynasty, but it is not clear to what extent the paths though the necropolis were used to access individual tombs or whether they were included in the festival processions (Kampp 1996: 120-122). These theories are all relevant to my research and as such will be returned to later in this thesis (see Chapter 14).

Abdul-Qader Muhammad (1966: 3-4) describes the initial use of el-Khokha, Deir el-Bahri and the northern slope of Qurna facing Deir el-Bahri for the earliest tombs, before TT60 became the first tomb on the eastern slope of Qurna. He discusses the organisation of the New Kingdom necropolis in more detail, stating that Dra Abu el-Naga was used at the beginning of the reign of Ahmose, before Qurna became the sole location for all tombs from Amenhotep I to Hatshepsut. From Tuthmosis III the tombs were scattered throughout the necropolis. Another pattern he observes was that high officials were buried on the upper slopes, less important officials on the lower slopes, and minor officials at Dra Abu el-Naga and other sites. He notes that the upper slopes were full by the end of the reign of Tuthmosis IV, so the high officials of Amenhotep III had to use the lower slopes (for example TT55 and TT57) or find new sites such as el-Khokha (TT48) or el-Asasif (TT192) with better quality limestone. He states that the only important tomb of Amenhotep III in Upper Qurna is Ramose (TT46), with any Ramesside tombs in the area reusing early Eighteenth Dynasty structures. He considers the 'most important' Ramesside tombs to be those concentrated in Lower Qurna (TT106, TT23, TT41) and southern Dra Abu el-Naga (TT157, TT35, TT156, TT148), with the 'less important' also at Dra Abu el-Naga, and Deir el-Medina. While some interesting general patterns have been observed, they are too broad to be of much use, as there are exceptions to these generalisations which need to be considered.

Dodson (1991: 33-42) notes that the earliest Eighteenth Dynasty tombs were at Dra Abu el-Naga, with later ones at Qurna, and those dating to Tuthmosis IV and Amenhotep III cut on the lower slopes of Qurna and Khokha as a result of the superior rock quality for fine carving on the lower slopes. He suggests that the presence of fewer Theban tombs dated to the late Eighteenth Dynasty onwards was as a result of the elite then being buried at Saqqara, with a few notable exceptions. Space constraints at Thebes are explained, with the upper slopes of Sheikh Abd el-Qurna filling up by the end of the reign of Tuthmosis IV, leading high officials of Amenhotep III to build their tombs on the lower slopes, or in alternative areas such as Qurnet Murai (Dodson and Ikram 2008: 217).

Social Status of Tomb Owners connected to Tomb Distribution

The significance of the location of a tomb within a cemetery is recognised as a means of indicating the economic and social status of the deceased, rather than making a religious statement (Ikram 2003: 141-143; Dodson and Ikram 2008: 23-30). Ikram concludes that in non-royal cemeteries the most important people were buried higher up the cliff, and less important, less wealthy individuals were buried lower down the slopes, with the poorest located at the desert edge. The later tombs would then squeeze in wherever they could find space. She refers to how rock quality could reverse this hierarchy, citing Thebes as an exception to this rule, as the best rock lies on the lower slopes and valley floor, so a choice had to be made between a prominent location on the upper slopes and carved decoration (Ikram 2003: 150-151). The clustering of family tombs is observed, as are some groups of tombs belonging to people sharing the same major position (Dodson and Ikram 2008: 27). The sacred power of Deir el-Bahri, as both the centre of the Hathor cult and a place of royal affiliation, is described as an attraction to tomb builders, to itself and the adjacent Khokha and Asasif. Areas along the processional route of the Beautiful Festival of the Valley would also have been favoured for burials as they would have received divine blessings as the procession passed (Dodson and Ikram 2008: 27-29).

Taylor (2003: 139-141) makes some broad comments on the location of tombs and spatial layout of cemeteries. He discusses how social hierarchy was maintained beyond death by the positioning of tombs, that within a cemetery the graves of important people occupied the most prominent locations, which acted as focal points around which the graves of people of lower rank were grouped. He mentions the grouping of officials' tombs specifically within the Theban Necropolis, and how some tombs were positioned in a relationship to royal monuments such as the royal mortuary temples on the west bank. He suggests that areas of a cemetery were allotted to different social groups (without providing any examples) but explains that these patterns changed over time as the use of the site progressed, with the majority of graves only dug when required. These statements are generalised and require further analysis to prove or disprove them in relation to this study (see Chapter 14).

Auenmüller's research into the significance of provincial tomb location and factors affecting this (2014: 171-193), are also relevant to this study. He considers the ideological significance of the location chosen for New Kingdom elite tombs, and what spatial and social relations were indicated by a tomb's location. This research does not however focus on the significance of a tomb's location within a given necropolis, but rather the choice to be buried in a particular necropolis and what this reveals about the status and provenance of the tomb owner. There are relevant observations, for example the potential reasons why some provincial mayors, from places such as Thebu, Thinis, the Fayum and the oases, chose to be buried at Thebes rather than their place of office (the owners of TT20, TT63, TT109 and TT155), with potential factors including their origin, and functional connections to Theban institutions (Auenmüller 2014: 179-180). He concludes that the highest members of the administrative elite, for example those with titles connected them to the king or cult of Amun, were buried in major city necropoli such as Thebes, while the lower members, for example those with purely provincial titles, such as mayor of a specific town, were buried in the cemetery of their hometown or place of office. There are however exceptions to this rule as the study of the titles of tomb owners in this study reveals a range of officials, not only high-ranking. This would suggest that the lower-ranking inhabitants of the necropolis must have either originated from Thebes or had an occupational connection to the area.

Use of Different Regions of the Necropolis

There is some relevant research into specific areas of the necropolis, rather than considering it as a whole entity. The research conducted by Winlock (1924: 217-277), Miniaci (2009: 19-25) and Polz (2007: 172-197) into identifying Seventeenth and early Eighteenth Dynasty royal burials in Dra Abu el-Naga has been very informative when considering this area. Polz's work in particular (2007: 172-197), identifying the double tomb complex of Amenhotep I and Ahmose Nefertari to be Kampp numbered tombs -130- and -131-, now designated K93.11 and K93.12, and the archaeological evidence of cultic activity in this area from the early Eighteenth Dynasty into the Ramesside Period, has had a direct influence on my arguments concerning tomb placement in this area.

The dissertation of Jimenez-Higueras (2016) addresses some similar research questions to this project but focuses solely on two groups of private tombs in Dra Abu el-Naga. This scientific analysis attempts to reconstruct the ancient landscape by considering aspects such as rock quality, 'viewshed' and 'line of sight' from the tomb, and reconstruction of paths between them. The emphasis here is on connections between tombs and the wider funerary landscape by conducting visibility surveys and links to processional activity in the area, and there is also some analysis of distribution by date, kinship and occupation. The conclusions made are sound and those relevant assertions are pertinent to my research (Chapter 5). It differs from my research in terms of methodology, and it only focuses on two case studies within this one area, rather than the entire necropolis - indeed the author suggests the need to conduct research across the entire Theban Necropolis in order to understand it better.

The research of Shirley (2010: 73-113) into the connections between the offices of 'Viceroys, Viziers, and the Amun Precinct' considers tomb placement in specific areas. She identifies that the late Seventeenth Dynasty tombs are at Dra Abu el-Naga, with new areas such as Asasif and Qurna explored in the early Eighteenth Dynasty. Factors influencing tomb location included rock quality, visibility from the plain and relation to royal mortuary temples, but in the early New Kingdom presumably they were placed at particular spots for specific reasons, although these are not elaborated on here. She focuses on a 'family precinct' of tombs in Upper Qurna (TT81, TT83, TT61, TT131, TT122, TT228 and TT100), using natural pathways, contour levels and direct distances between the tombs to supporting the concept of planned topographical positioning of this group. During the reigns of Hatshepsut and Tuthmosis III, additional tombs were built in this area belonging to priests or administrators connected to the Estate of Amun, who would have served alongside members of this group. She identifies Qurna as the chosen spot for burial of the high elite during this period, while the other areas of the necropolis, with a few exceptions, are used by the mid and lower-level officials connected to the Estate of Amun and funerary temples (Shirley 2010: 98-109). While thorough and comprehensive concerning the tombs it considers, this study is of limited use here due to the relatively short time-span and single area of the necropolis that is dealt with.

The organisation and reasons behind the use of Qurnet Murai are discussed by Gabolde (1995: 155-165), who concludes that this area was chosen for two reasons, to maintain proximity to the mortuary temple of the king they served in life, or to construct vast tombs at a time when the necropolis was becoming crowded. These conclusions are referred to when discussing this area (see Chapter 10).

Tomb Distribution during Specific Periods

The most relevant publications covering the earliest uses of the Theban Necropolis are those of Winlock (1947) and Soliman (2009). Winlock (1947) provides a commentary of the rulers of Thebes and their monuments from the First Intermediate Period, throughout the Middle Kingdom and into the Second Intermediate Period. There is little information regarding the location of these tombs, or those of their officials, so while interesting background information about the region, this publication does not influence this thesis. The Theban Tombs from the Old Kingdom up to the end of the Second Intermediate Period, both royal and private, are considered by Soliman (2009), who provides a history of the pre-New Kingdom Necropolis, together with detailed description of individual tombs and titles of their owners (although neither hieroglyphic text nor transliteration are included). This information is useful when considering the relationship between these and later burials, but there is no discussion relating to why these early tombs were located in these specific areas of the necropolis.

Rummel's research (2013: 207-232) considers the Theban ritual landscape, focusing on Western Thebes in the Twentieth Dynasty, and the topographical connection between private tombs and the Beautiful Festival of the Valley. The relationship between private tombs, local temples and processional ways is studied, as well as the manner of their inclusion into the Valley Festival. This research addresses similar concepts to this project, but earlier tombs are not investigated, nor the necropolis as a whole.

Bács (2011: 1-46) addresses the modern misconception that very few new tombs were made in the late Ramesside Period, with reuse envisaged as the norm, arguing instead that this is a result of the poor preservation and lack of secure dating of these tombs. He attributes approximately sixty tombs to the Twentieth Dynasty, on the basis of royal names present in their decoration, or on stylistic grounds, with more to be added which are currently designated 'Ramesside' in date. He notes that the distributional pattern of these tombs extends across the entire necropolis, with a preference for Dra Abu el-Naga. He makes the distinction that the Theban Necropolis at this time was no longer a court cemetery, but rather that of a single community centred around Karnak temple and the vast Estate of Amun. This meant that these tomb owners were associated with the various Theban cults, as priests or officials. The choice of tomb site was dependant on a number of factors. Dra Abu el-Naga was desirable as it was near the contemporary royal mortuary temple and the processional route of the Beautiful Festival of the Valley. It was also an ancient royal cemetery, and the burial ground of the High Priests of Amun from the early Nineteenth Dynasty onwards.

The Theban Necropolis has inspired a range of individual tomb publications, too many to list here, but those used can be found in the individual references for each tomb (see Appendix 1–14). The majority of these include a paragraph discussing the tomb's location, orientation, its proximity to neighbouring tombs where relevant, and some useful illustrations. While informative these observations are of limited use to this study as they focus on individual tombs rather than the necropolis as a whole. The lack of these publications for the majority of tombs also limits their usefulness in the context of this project.

This review of existing research has revealed a lack of analysis of the organisation and tomb distribution in the New Kingdom Theban Necropolis as a whole.

Chapter 2:
Topography of the Theban Necropolis

Physical Topography of Western Thebes

Geological Landscape

The natural landscape surrounding the Theban Necropolis consists of the River Nile lying approximately 4km to the east, bordered by an area of flat floodplain at an altitude of 80m above sea level. To the north-west of the floodplain lies a rock formation of undulating cliffs, known as the Theban Mountains, which rise gradually at first to an altitude of 100m above sea level before rising more steeply to a maximum altitude of 463m above sea level at the peak of Gebel el-Qurn (see Digital Elevation Model – Figure 4).

The Theban Mountains were deposited in a pelagic and shallow marine environment. The underlying geology of the Theban Necropolis is made up of lower Paleocene to early Eocene bedrock consisting of three formations: the Tarawan, Esna and Thebes Formation (see Figure 5). The Tarawan Formation is the lowest and is comprised of chalk. This soft chalk bedrock is found between 0m and 85m above sea level and has been identified as the bedrock of some of the lower private tombs and in the vicinity of Deir el-Bahri (see Chapter 6). The Esna Formation is composed of shale and marl layers, found between 85m and 190m above sea level, while the Theban Formation consists of a marl layer from 190m to 235m above sea level, with limestone layers of varying quality from 235m to 463m above sea level (see Figure 6; Wüst and McLane 2000: 163-190). These different layers of bedrock explain why quality of the bedrock is superior on the lower slopes, particularly in Sheikh Abd el-Qurna where tomb decoration can be carved directly into the bedrock rock, whereas on the upper slopes it is necessary to plaster the walls before painting onto the plaster as the limestone is not stable enough to carve into.

Natural Features

The natural feature which dominates this landscape is the line of Theban Mountains which lie directly to the north-west of the necropolis itself, forming a natural boundary between this cemetery and the royal cemeteries of the Valley of the Kings and the Valley of the Queens. The highest point of this rock formation is Gebel el-Qurn, which naturally resembles the shape of

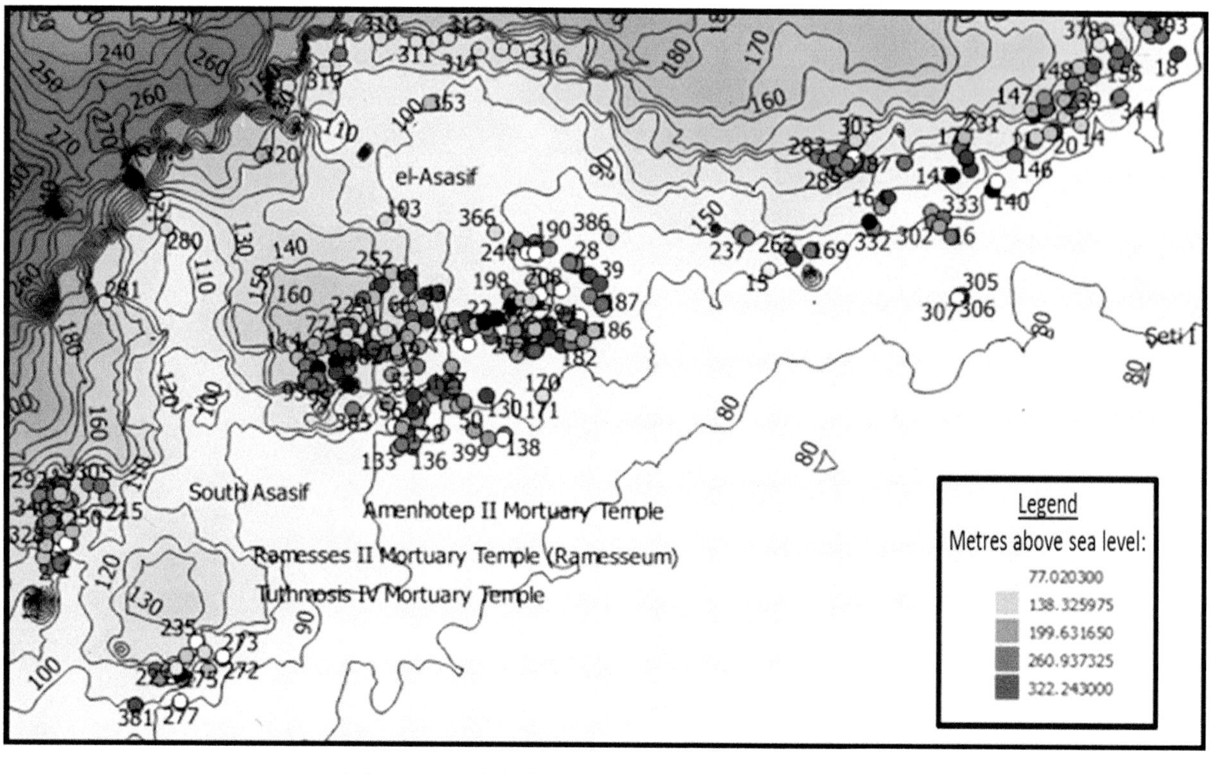

Figure 4: Digital Elevation Model of the Theban Necropolis (Author's own using QGIS)

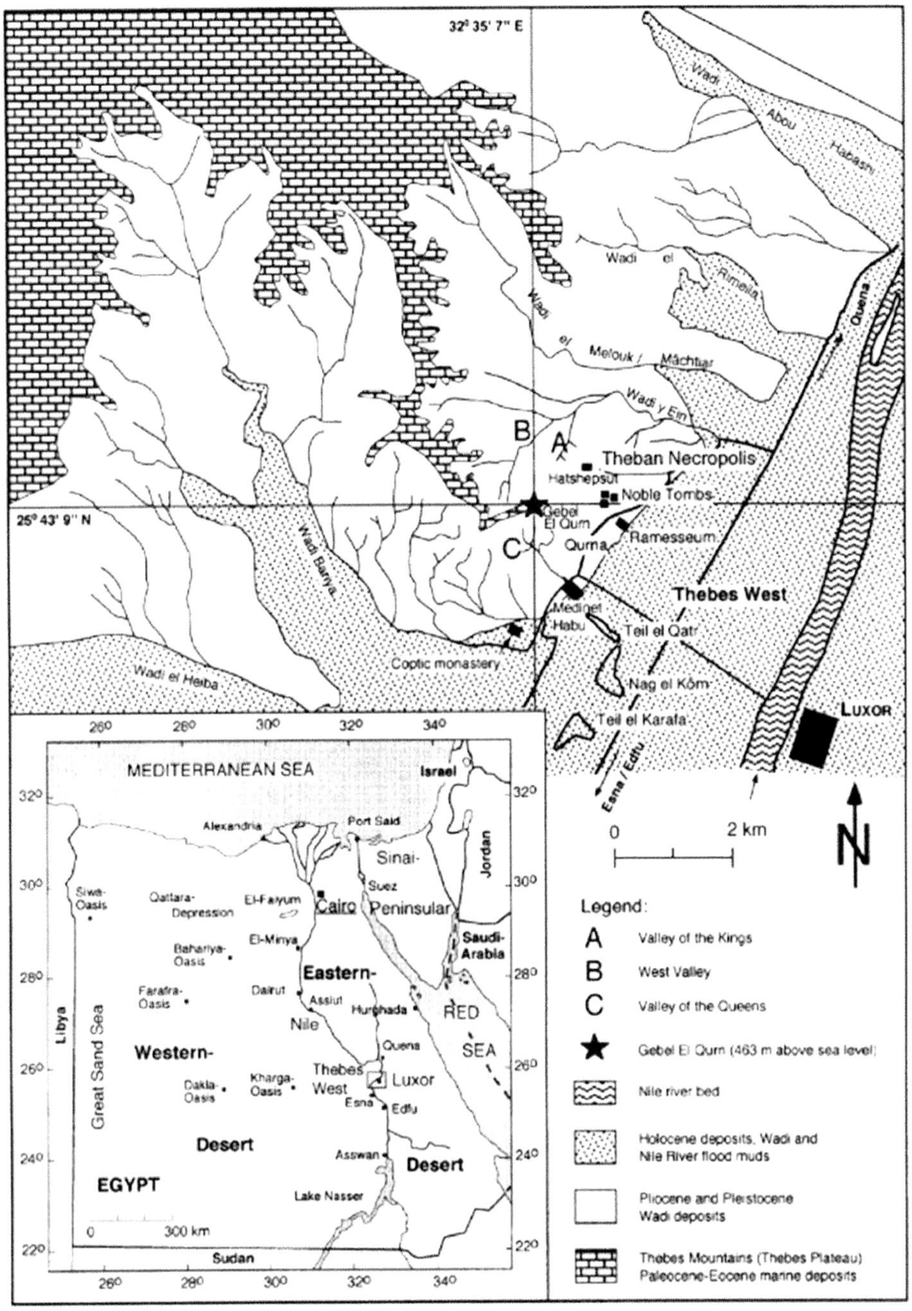

Figure 5: The Geology of the Theban Necropolis (Wüst and McLane 2000: 165 – Courtesy of Dr Raphael Wüst)

a pyramid (see Figure 7). It is believed that the shape of this peak symbolised the royal symbol of a pyramid and inspired the Egyptians to be buried beneath this structure, in a similar way to how the Old and Middle Kingdom officials were buried in the shadow of the pyramid of the king they served. The Ancient Egyptians believed that this 'Peak of the West' was not only the home but the personification of the cobra goddess Meretseger, 'She who Loves Silence' (Pinch 2004: 164) as evidenced by the shrine set up to her on the path between Deir el-Medina and the Valley of the Queens and the numerous stele dedicated to her. The Theban Mountains also naturally form a bay of steep cliffs in a semi-circular shape in the area of Deir el-Bahri (see Figure 8), which was associated with the cow goddess Hathor, as evidenced by the Hathor chapel with Hatshepsut's mortuary temple (see Figures 9 and 10) This area became an area of cultic significance as a result of its connections with Hathor and royal structures built in this area (see Chapter 2).

A number of wadis and ancient pathways criss-cross through the necropolis (see Figure 6) which have hardly changed since antiquity (Kampp 1996: 121). These

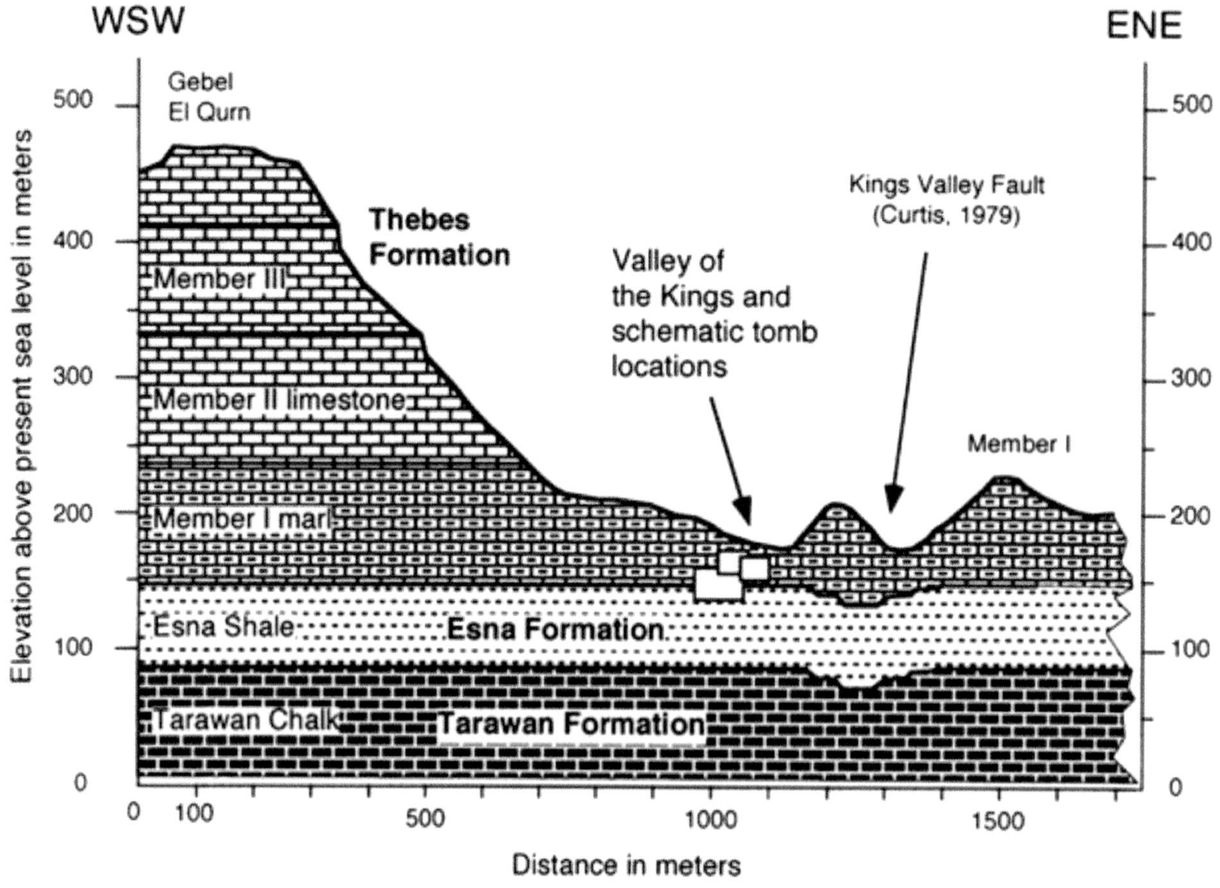

Figure 6: Stratigraphic and lithological composition of the Thebes West area showing the three flat-lying rock formations: Tarawan, Esna and Thebes Formation (Wüst and McLane 2000: 169 - Courtesy of Dr Raphael Wüst)

Figure 7: Examples of Natural Features of the Theban Necropolis (Author's own)

Figure 8: The bay of cliffs at Deir el-Bahri (Author's own)

Figure 9: The Hathor Chapel within Hatshepsut's Mortuary Temple (Author's own)

Figure 10: The goddess Hathor depicted within Hatshepsut's Mortuary Temple (Author's own)

routes provided necessary access to the necropolis for the purpose of tomb construction, so were a factor when the necropolis was expanding but were also crucial for processional and cultic activity and to allow relatives to visit the tombs during the Beautiful Festival of the Valley. These features influenced tomb location and orientation as tombs were built to overlook cultic areas such as the 'Forecourt of Amun' in Dra Abu el-Naga and processional routes. These localised features will be discussed further in each relevant chapter.

Built Features

Aside from the tombs themselves, a number of other structures were built in the Theban Necropolis and also on the east bank which also influenced tomb distribution. The royal mortuary temples and their associated processional routes had a huge influence on tomb location and orientation (see Chapter 2). The position of Karnak Temple on the east bank, directly opposite the southern end Dra Abu el-Naga also influenced tomb position (see Figure 11).

Division of the Necropolis

For the purpose of this research the necropolis has been divided into sections using the modern place names for different areas of the necropolis. These sections are from north to south: Dra Abu el-Naga, Deir el-Bahri, el-Asasif, Sheikh Abd el-Qurna, Qurnet Murai and Deir el-Medina (see Figure 12). This approach has been chosen in order to make this vast area and large dataset manageable, whilst basing these divisions as much as possible on ancient pathways, notable areas of land between these areas which are not used for tomb building, thus implying a break in the cemetery, to allow relevant conclusions to be drawn by looking a more focused group of tombs. Whilst the tomb owners themselves would not have used these modern names or perhaps even differentiated between each different area of the necropolis, there are clearly patterns and trends visible in the majority of these areas which allow them to be treated as separate groups. For some areas the division is less than ideal, necessitating the study of each area as distinct from the adjacent area, whereas in reality this may not have been the case. Ideally the necropolis should be studied as a body of tombs, but certainly the central area, including Qurna and el-Khokha appears to be distinct from Qurnet Murai, Deir el-Medina and Dra Abu el-Naga due to the distance between the tombs and in some cases physical boundaries between areas. A number of modern roads intersect the necropolis. They do not influence tomb distribution, but they do divide the necropolis into its specific cemeteries and appear to follow the route of ancient paths. One such modern road runs parallel to the eastern boundary of

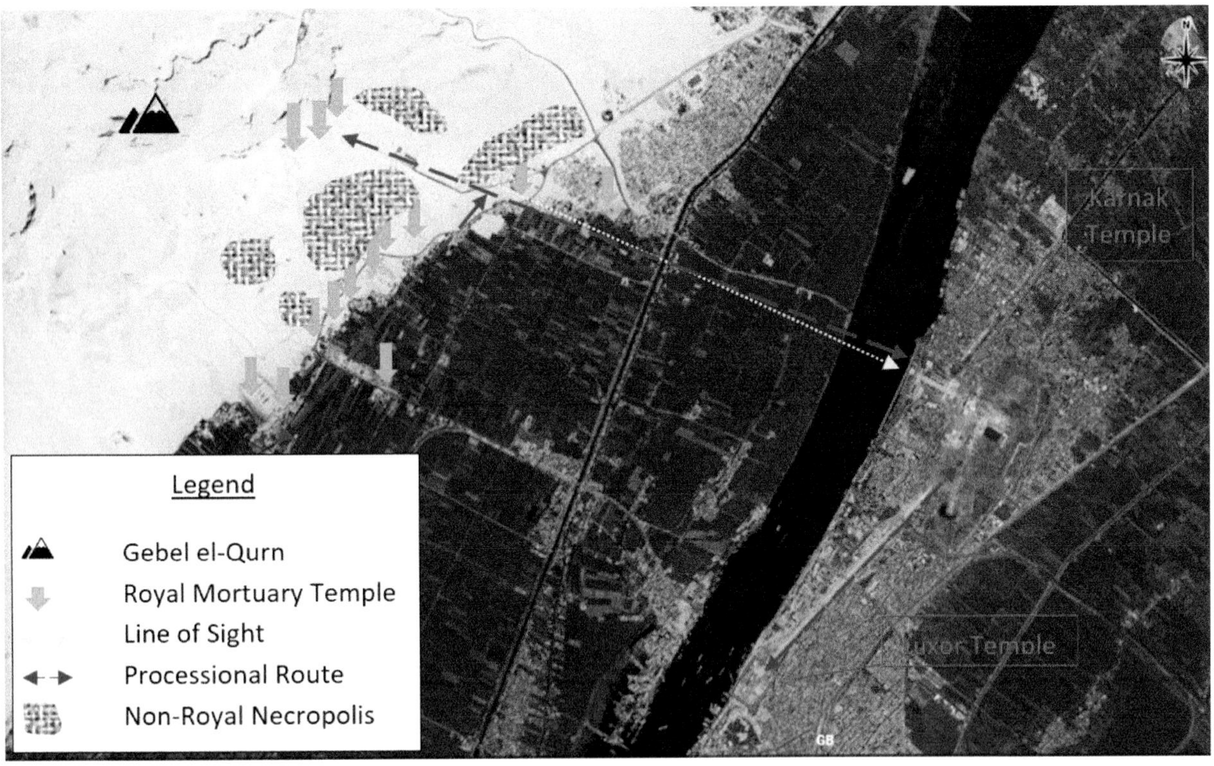

Figure 11: Natural and Built Features influencing the Theban Necropolis (Author's own using Google Earth)

the necropolis from the direction of New Qurna in the north towards Medinet Habu in the south, dividing the cemetery from the row of royal mortuary temples. This road is bisected by several additional modern roads westwards from this road to allow tourists to access the major sites in the necropolis. One such road lies at the northern boundary of Dra Abu el-Naga and leads to the Valley of the Kings, another at the south of Dra Abu el-Naga leads to Deir el-Bahri, and a third to the south of Qurnet Murai leads to Deir el-Medina.

Two of these areas have been sub-divided into smaller groups due to the size of these areas and the number of tombs they hold. Dra Abu el-Naga has been divided into Dra Abu el-Naga East and West, each area containing a small hill, with the division based on the ancient wadi, Shig el-Ateyat, which crosses the centre of the area. Sheikh Abd el-Qurna has also been sub-divided into Upper and Lower Qurna. The tomb owners on the upper slopes have distinct characteristics from those on the lower slopes, while the evolution of this area implies that there was a distinction between the upper and lower slopes in antiquity. The division has been made based on ancient pathways and the presence of a clear space between these two groups of tombs which is empty of tombs so forms a convenient boundary. These divisions are discussed further within their respective chapters.

Cultic Topography of Western Thebes

Royal Temples

Traditionally royal burials were made up of two parts, the temple where the cult of the deceased king was perpetuated, and the tomb as the place of burial. From early in the New Kingdom the tombs themselves were hidden in the Valley of the Kings, so the visible royal mortuary temples fulfilled the cultic element of the royal burial (Strudwick and Strudwick 1999: 72-73). The majority of these mortuary temples lay along the edge of the cultivation, to the east of the necropolis, with others at Deir el-Bahri within the bay of cliffs at the end of a causeway. The QGIS includes only those mortuary temples easily identifiable on satellite imagery, in order to ensure accurate placement of those temples using GPS co-ordinates, as the other temples were not included on any of the plans used for geo-referencing. A number of other mortuary and cult temples existed, and formed part of the funerary landscape of Western Thebes, so were relevant in terms of tomb placement (see Figure 13).

Processional Routes

The deceased desired a view of the festival processional routes and royal mortuary temples in order to symbolically participate eternally in the necropolis

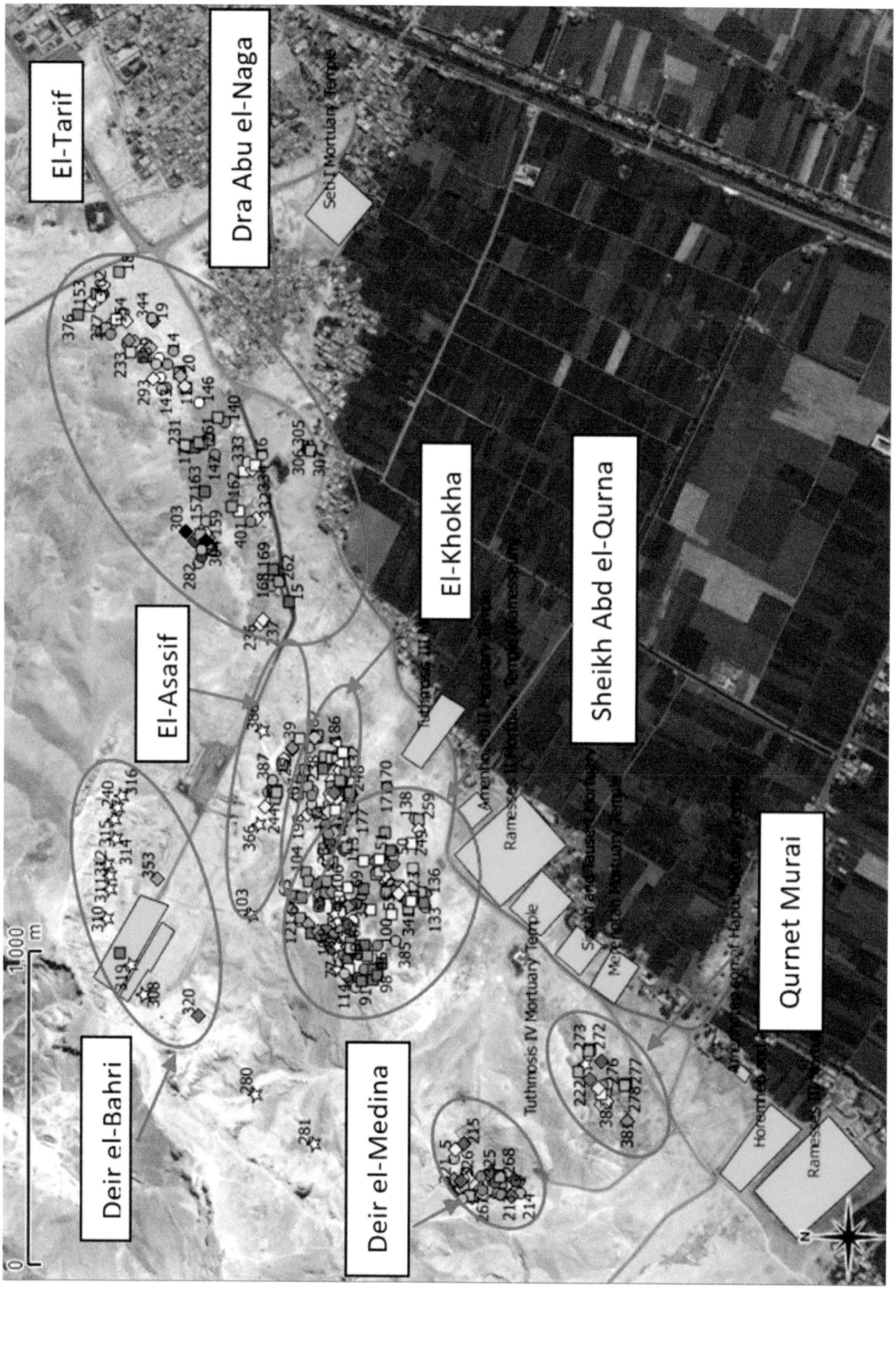

Figure 12: The Division of the Theban Necropolis (Author's own using QGIS)

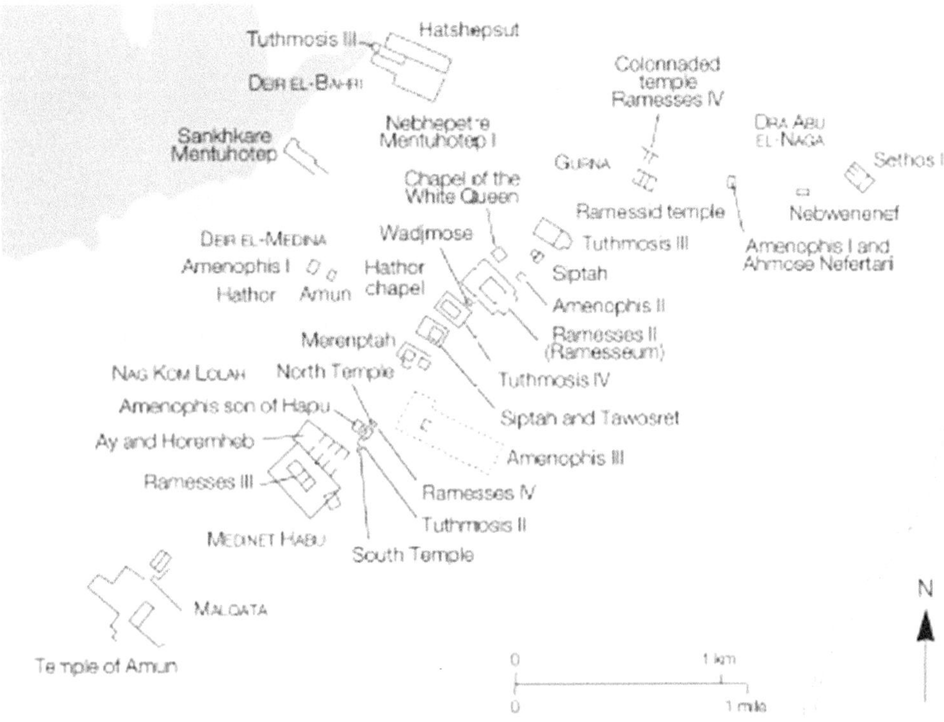

Figure 13: The Temples of Western Thebes (Wilkinson 2000: 172; Copyright owned by Robert Partridge, Ancient Egyptian Picture Library)

festivals after their death, and to receive associated offerings. The view would also have benefited visitors to the tombs, as friends and family of the deceased would spend festivals within the tomb chapel and observe the festivities. Similarities can be drawn with the 'Terrace of the Great God' at Abydos, where *mahat*-chapels, usually containing stelae, were set up along the processional route, in order for the deceased to partake in the Osiris festivals (Simpson 1974: 3; O'Connor 2009: 95). The presence of Middle Kingdom tombs along the causeway at Deir el-Bahri also appears to be linked to processional activity. The view would therefore have been necessary from the entrance or courtyard of the tomb, so would have influenced its orientation.

The necropolis witnessed a range of cultic activity, the most important of which was the annual 'Beautiful Festival of the Valley' (BFV). The cult statue of the god Amun would travel west across the Nile by barge, and be carried in procession along the processional route to the mortuary temple of the reigning king. Amun would spend the night on the west bank, continuing the procession the following day before returning to Karnak. The processional route evolved throughout the New Kingdom as more mortuary temples were built, influencing tomb placement as tombs overlooked the route. The barque was transported from the riverbank towards Deir el-Bahri by means of a canal (now disappeared), and a system of land-routes and waterways was used to move the divine barque to its various stops, as attested in textual and pictorial references to the festival, from tombs and temples, in conjunction with the archaeological record (Graham *et al.* 2012: 135). Onlookers could watch the procession from the tomb terraces, particularly those on higher ground. To determine if this function was a factor when determining the location of the tomb, a processional way must be established based on the importance of particular temples at various times throughout the New Kingdom.

The earliest temples in Western Thebes were the Middle Kingdom temple of Montuhotep II at Deir el-Bahri, and the unfinished temple of Montuhotep III and IV within the cliffs to the south (see Figure 14). The BFV is attested from the late Middle Kingdom, visiting the temple of Montuhotep II. This enclosed bay set back into the desert cliffs was orientated towards Karnak temple on the opposite side of the river, establishing a visual connection between the two sites. The site was also connected with the goddess Hathor, personified by the western mountain. The route from the landing stage to Deir el-Bahri was marked by a monumental processional way, and the area remained the sacral focus of the procession until the late New Kingdom (Cabrol 2001: 550).

At the beginning of the Eighteenth Dynasty the divine barque would have disembarked in the vicinity of what now remains of the Seti I temple. Cabrol (2001:

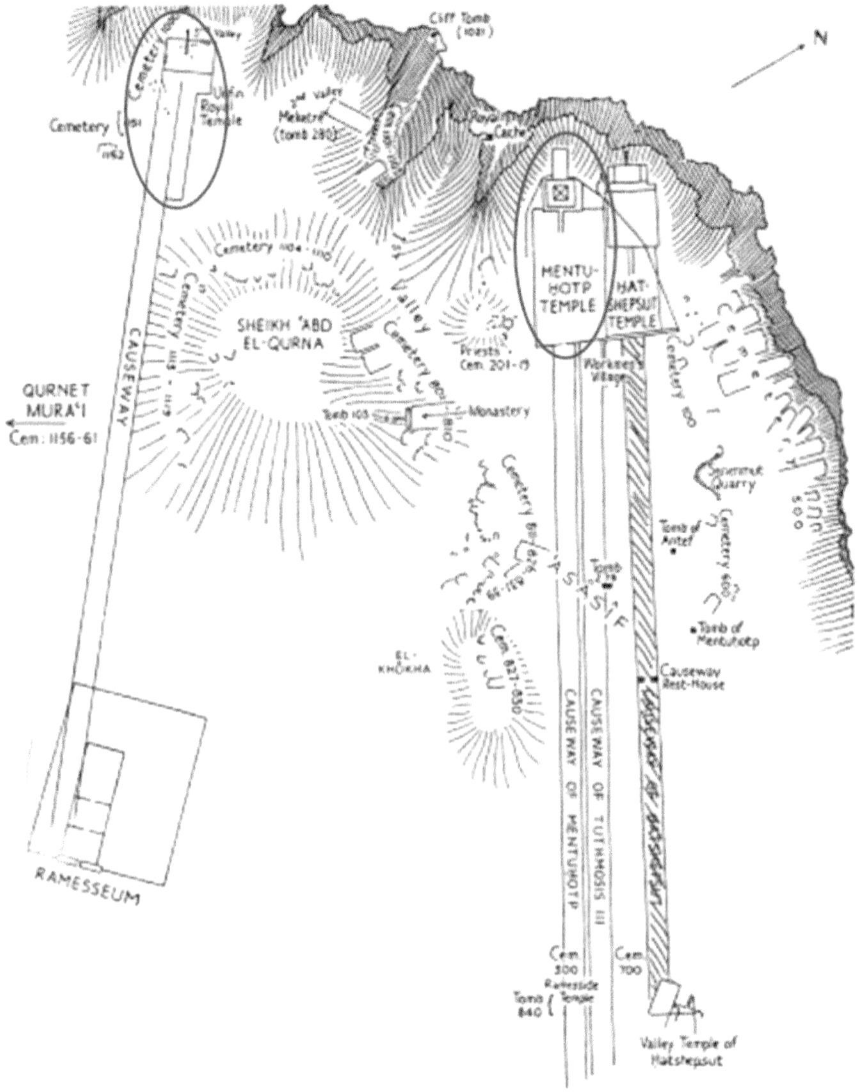

Figure 14: Map showing location of Middle Kingdom temples, shown in blue (PM I: Pl. V - Courtesy of the Griffith Institute)

544) speculates that there may have been an earlier royal building on the site but the lack of textual or iconographical evidence from this period at the site makes it impossible to include this building in the processional route with any certainty. From the landing stage the barque would have passed by *Mn-swt*, the temple of Amenhotep I and Ahmose-Nefertari at the southern corner of Dra Abu el-Naga (see Figure 15). There may have been additional funerary temples of Amenhotep I at Deir el-Bahri, north of the Seti I temple at the southern end of Dra Abu el-Naga, and a third with uncertain location south of his tomb (Cabrol 2001: 545), however the lack of archaeological evidence makes the role of these early temples unclear, so they have not been included. Certainly, the processional route in use at the beginning of the Eighteenth Dynasty still had Deir el-Bahri as its destination.

The mortuary temple of Tuthmosis I, '*Ḫnmt-ꜥnḫ*', or 'United with Life', is referred to in private tombs as a destination of the barque, and textual records show it was still functioning in the Twentieth Dynasty. Inscriptional evidence from TT49, probably dating to the reign of Ay, refers to Amun resting at this earlier temple 'according to former customs' (Davies 1933: Pl. LIII), suggesting that it acted as a way station at the end of the Eighteenth Dynasty, so it is reasonable to assume that the mortuary temples of previous rulers had similar functions in the festivals of their successors. It is unclear if this temple was part of the procession during Tuthmosis I's reign due to the lack of textual evidence. Potential sites for this temple include the Medinet Habu area (Otto 1952: 91), or near Deir el-Bahri, but the lack of definitive archaeological evidence makes it impossible to include it in this study (Cabrol 2001: 558).

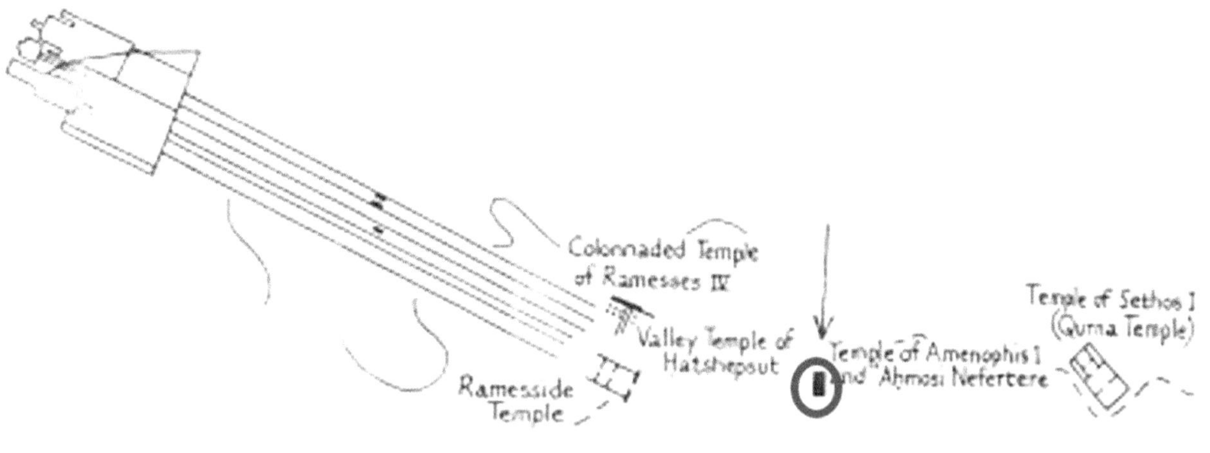

Figure 15: Location of the Temple of Amenhotep I and Ahmose-Nefertari: Menisut (PM II: Pl. XXXIII - Courtesy of the Griffith Institute)

A number of blocks found north of Medinet Habu were inscribed with the name of Tuthmosis II, suggesting that this was the site of his mortuary temple, referred to as *Šspt-ʿnḫ*, or 'Seizing Life', although it is unclear if this was completed during his reign or later. The earliest version may not have contained a chapel for the divine barque, but it was later refurbished by Tuthmosis III to accommodate the god, possibly as part of the development of the royal ancestor cult under the co-rulers. This temple is not attested after Tuthmosis III, so it is unclear if it remained part of the processional route (Cabrol 2001: 559-560).

Eighteenth Dynasty structures also existed at Medinet Habu. The small temple now enclosed within the Ramesside enclosure wall is ascribed to Hatshepsut and Tuthmosis III, called *Ḏsr-st* or 'Holy Place', which was not a mortuary temple but dedicated to a local form of Amun. This was possibly built on the site of an earlier structure from the reign of Tuthmosis I (Hölscher 1939: 6). The presence of Eighteenth Dynasty building activity in the area may suggest that the procession also processed southwards to this area (Cabrol 2001: 562). It is unclear prior to the reign of Hatshepsut if the procession visited the mortuary temples of other rulers or went directly to Deir el-Bahri. After her reign it visited every royal mortuary temple whose cult was still maintained, which may have lasted for a few generations (Arnold 1992: 35) or even longer. Cabrol (2001: 553) finds it likely that every structure along the route between Deir el-Bahri and Medinet Habu was a stop for the festival procession.

Hatshepsut built *Ḏsr-ḏsrw* or 'Holy of Holies' at Deir el-Bahri, adjacent to the Middle Kingdom temple, replacing it as the processional destination. A monumental causeway, lined with red granite sphinxes, ran parallel to the earlier processional way, its eastern end marked with a valley temple, destroyed in antiquity, where the divine barque would have been received (see Figure 16). The focus of this complex was the sanctuary of Amun, where the sacred barque spent the night. The temples of Tuthmosis I, Tuthmosis II, along with that of her co-ruler, Tuthmosis III, acted as waystations during her reign, as attested on the reliefs at her mortuary temple (Cabrol 2001: 551). The Red Chapel shows the procession visiting the temple of Tuthmosis II en-route to Deir el-Bahri, and Tuthmosis I's temple on the return journey to Karnak, in either Hatshepsut's reign or that of her successor, depending on the dating of the scenes (Karkowski 1992: 162).

Tuthmosis III built his Qurna temple, *Ḥnkt-ʿnḫ* or 'Offering Life', during Hatshepsut's co-regency, which was accessed by canal from the river (Cabrol, 2001: 554). Only functioning as a waystation during Hatshepsut's reign, this was the most attested western temple of this king in private tomb inscriptions, showing that the temple functioned as a key stop for the divine barque until the Nineteenth Dynasty (Helck 1962: 96). After Hatshepsut's death, Tuthmosis III built a second temple at Deir el-Bahri, *Ḏsr-3ḫt*, or 'Sacred Horizon', between 9sr-Dsrw and the earlier Middle Kingdom temple (Lipinska 1977: 62-64). This temple replaced *Ḏsr-ḏsrw* as the god's resting place, as evidenced by scenes of both river and overland processions on the upper register of the northern wall of the hypostyle hall (Dolińska 2010: 57), and contemporary private tomb inscriptions.

The mortuary temple of Amenhotep II lay to the north-east of the Ramesseum. Its name is unclear, as contemporary inscriptions refer to it as *Šspt-ʿnḫ* (as Tuthmosis II) and *Iʿbt-3ḫt* or 'Joining the Horizon' (TT95 and TT56). This could possibly refer to two distinct temples but only one has been identified (Haeny 1997: 100). To the south, the mortuary temple of Tuthmosis

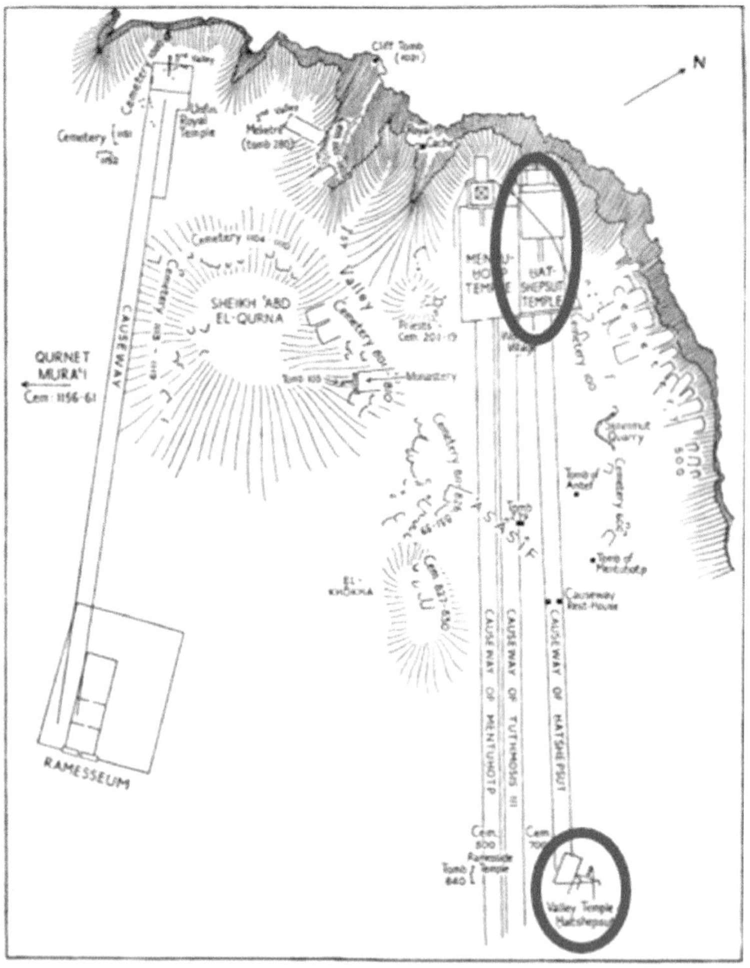

Figure 16: Plan of Deir el-Bahri showing the mortuary temple and valley of Hatshepsut, shown in blue (PM I: Pl. V - Courtesy of the Griffith Institute)

IV (of unknown name) was also discovered (Petrie 1896: 3-9). Both temples remained active until the Ramesside period, so would have been visited during the festival. Amenhotep III built the largest mortuary temple in Western Thebes, named *Šspt-Ỉmn-wṯst-nfrw=f*, or 'Receiving Amun and Exalting his Beauty', located to the south-east of the Ramesseum, on the edge of the cultivation. This would certainly have dominated the mortuary landscape as a result of its colossal size, so would have been visible from some distance away. Inscriptions on a re-used contemporary stela (Cairo Museum 34025: recto: 9), reveal that this temple was explicitly built to be 'a resting place of the Lord of the Gods at his festival of the valley' (*Urk.* IV: 1650) and remained in use until at least the reign of Ramesses II. The temple does not form part of the relatively straight line of mortuary temples, but is situated further to the east, affecting its position as part of a possible network of canals between the temples. It is also possible that by the end of the reign of Amenhotep III the procession visited an Amun temple at the complex at Malkata (Cabrol 2001: 556).

There are no archaeological remains for a mortuary temple of Amenhotep IV/ Akhenaten, as he intended to be buried at el-Amarna, and the BFV was not attested during his reign, so there would have been no contemporary processional route. One further royal mortuary temple has been identified to the north of Medinet Habu, 'Enduring is the Memorial in the Place of Eternity'. It was built by Ay, but subsequently usurped by Horemheb, and is thought to have incorporated an earlier chapel of Tutankhamun, who reinstated the festival. This temple would have been visited by the procession from at least the reign of Ay onwards and remained in use until at least the reign of Ramesses III (Haeny 1997: 106).

At the beginning of the Nineteenth Dynasty, Ramesses I's reign was too short to build a mortuary temple. His son, Seti I, built his mortuary temple, *Sty-mry-n-ptḥ ꜣḫ* or 'Glorious is Seti-Merenptah' to the east of Dra Abu el-Naga, to act as the landing stage of the festival, as shown by the scenes of Seti offering incense to the barque of the god (Haeny 1997: 112). This temple replaced the old landing stage and was in use until the end of the New Kingdom (Wilkinson 2000: 173-174). Ramesses II built his vast mortuary temple, *Ḫnmt wꜣst* or 'United with Thebes', between the temples of Amenhotep II and Tuthmosis IV temple, and inscriptions within the hypostyle hall state that it was a resting place for the barque of Amun during the BFV (Haeny 1997: 115-116). This temple was also attested until the end of the New Kingdom, so remained part of the BFV. His successor, Merenptah, built his to the south of the temple of Tuthmosis IV which is now largely destroyed (Haeny 1997: 119). Amenmessu and Seti II have no known temple in Western Thebes (Haeny 1997: 119). The mortuary temple of Tausert and Siptah was built between those of Tuthmosis IV and Merenptah. Ramesses III built a large mortuary temple named *Ḫnmt-nḥḥ* or 'United with Eternity' at the southern end of the necropolis at Medinet Habu. This temple contains three rooms where the barques of Amun, Mut and Khonsu were received during the BFV. There is also a depiction of Ramesses III offering incense to the barque of Ramesses II, suggesting that processional activity also took place between the temples (Haeny 1997: 109 and 120-121). This is also attested until the end of the New Kingdom so would have remained part of the BFV procession.

There is little evidence of the mortuary temples of the Ramesside kings who succeeded Ramesses III. Archaeological evidence suggests that Ramesses IV built a colonnaded temple to the north of Hatshepsut's valley temple at the entrance to Deir el-Bahri and began a second temple just to the south which was never completed (Wilkinson 2000: 181). A smaller structure near Medinet Habu served his mortuary cult instead (see Figure 17). The Deir el-Bahri temple seems likely to have been continued by Ramesses V, and later usurped by Ramesses VI, but it is unclear whether it was ever completed, as the temple was systematically quarried away in later periods. No evidence survives of the mortuary establishments of Ramesses VII and VIII, although it is reasonable to assume that they existed. One single source, P. Abbott, relates to a mortuary temple of Ramesses IX, and there appears to have been construction activity at Medinet Habu during his reign (Bács 2011: 4-5).

Throughout the New Kingdom the procession travelled directly across the Nile and along the canal to the landing stage at the eastern end of the Deir el-Bahri causeway, then headed south to the active mortuary temples along the desert edge (see Figures 18 and 19), before returning to Deir el-Bahri to spend the night. The next day it processed east along the causeway via various waystations, to the landing stage for the return trip to Karnak (see Figure 20). The barque was transported between these temples by means of a canal system, which may have existed as early as the

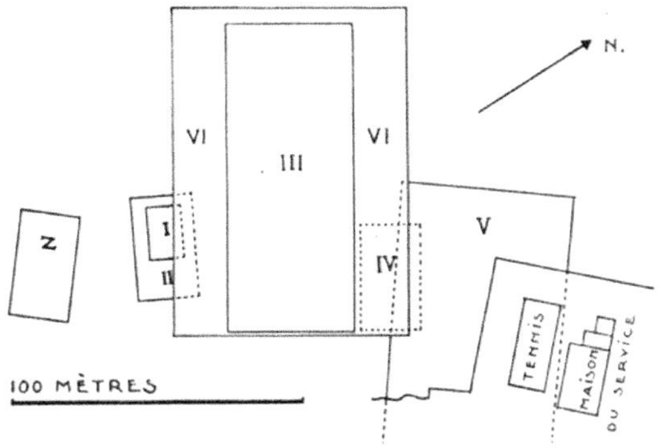

Figure 17: The temple of Ramesses IV at Medinet Habu (No. V) (Bács 2011: Figure 1 – Courtesy of Dr Tamás A. Bács)

Eighteenth Dynasty. Canals of Tuthmosis I and III are listed on Hatshepsut's Red Chapel, linking their mortuary temples with the Nile, but their existence has not yet been archeologically verified (Karkowski 1992: 160-162). This suggests the procession may have been partially water-based and partially via land at this time. Prior to the reign of Tuthmosis II there is no archaeological evidence of the processional route, but from the reign of Tuthmosis III there is evidence of a waterway leading from Deir el-Bahri towards the south, as the position of *Ḥnkt-ꜥnḫ* attests. Over time foundations were laid along this southern canal, until the line of mortuary temples reached as far as Medinet Habu. An examination of the north-south channel within the cultivated land parallel to the Nile shows evidence of a main waterway leading to the south. The temple of Amenhotep III, located much further to the east than the other temples, must have been served by its own individual canal (Cabrol 2001: 653-656).

Initial results from the Theban Harbours and Waterscapes Project's surveys in 2012 and 2013 of the area in front of the mortuary temples of Tuthmosis III (*Ḥnkt-ꜥnḫ*), Amenhotep II and III, suggested the presence of secondary canals leading to the landing stages in front of each mortuary temple, and a processional way joining the temple to the landing stage in the case of Tuthmosis III. These results require further study before definite conclusions regarding an intra-temple canal system can be reached (Graham *et al.* 2013: 35-52). There is further evidence of the existence of a minor branch of the Nile to the east of the mortuary temples, which silted up at the end of the New Kingdom (see Figure 21). The presence of this waterway would have connected the royal mortuary temples and facilitated easy transport between them (Toonen *et al.* 2017: 273-290).

Dolińska (2007: 75) suggests that all existing temples were visited during the course of a single day, but logistical and time constraints as the New Kingdom

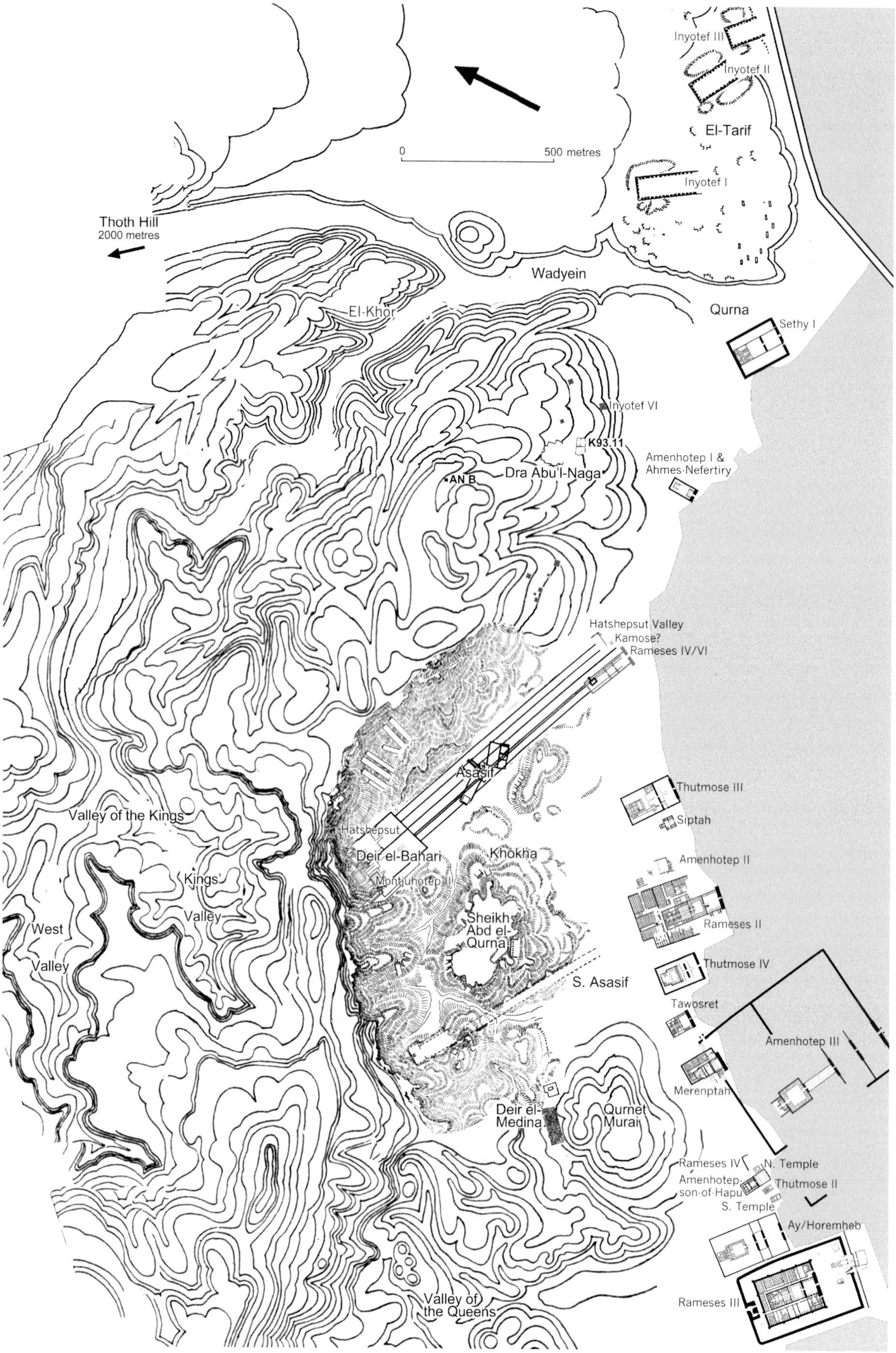

Figure 18: Thebes West at the end of the New Kingdom (Courtesy of Professor Aidan Dodson)

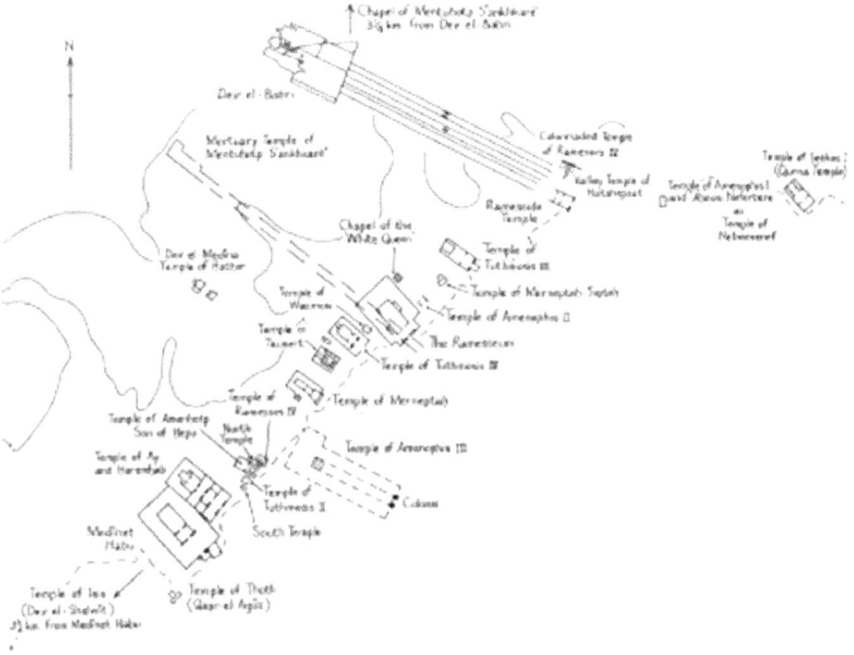

Figure 19: Plan of Western Thebes (PM II: Pl. XXXIII – Courtesy of the Griffith Institute)

progressed must be considered. Although we cannot be certain exactly which previous temples were included, we know that Deir el-Bahri remained crucial, along with contemporary structures and other important temples where the cult of the deceased king was maintained (see Figure 22).

The Estate of Amun

The 'Estate of Amun' covered a vast area of land on both banks of the Nile. It included Karnak and Luxor temples on the east bank, and a large area of the west bank opposite, containing the royal mortuary temples, demarcated by the perimeter of the processional routes (see Figure 23). When the 'Estate of Amun' is referred to within the titulary of a tomb owner, it could refer to any of this area and not a specific temple.

Figure 20: Map of Western Thebes – original edited to highlight processional routes (Dodson and Ikram 2008: 330 – Courtesy of Professor Aidan Dodson)

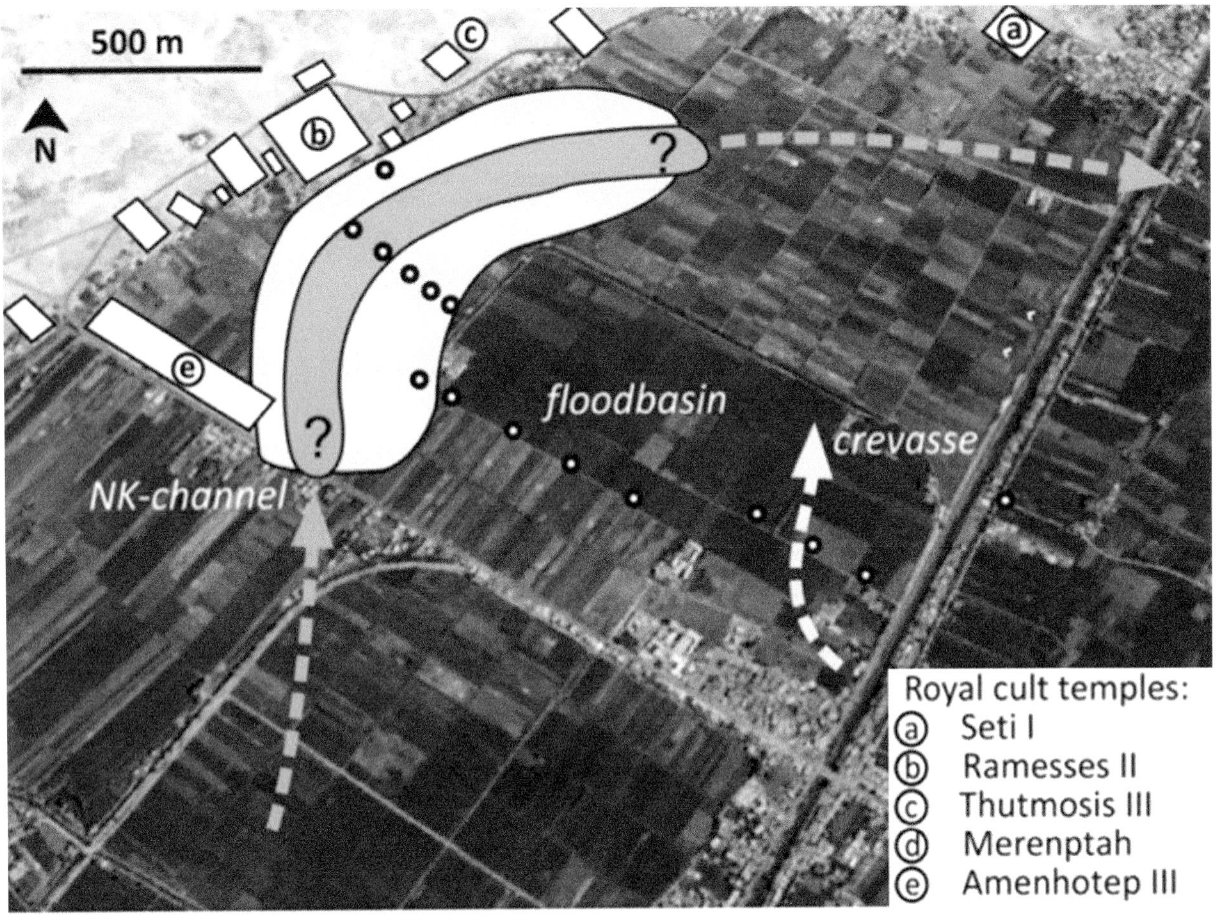

Figure 21: Reconstruction of the New Kingdom fluvial landscape with suggested upstream and downstream locations of the New Kingdom Nile branch (Blue colours suggest the maximum open channel width) (Toonen et al. 2012: Figure 6 - Courtesy of the Theban Harbours and Waterscapes Project, EES)

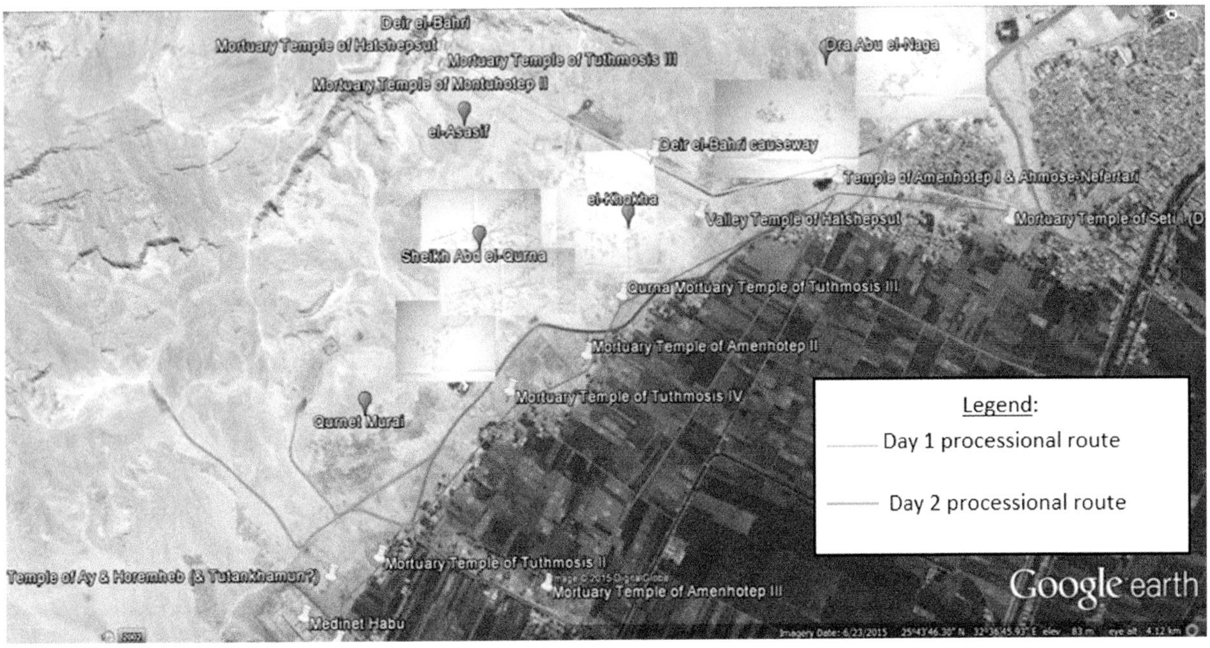

Figure 22: Satellite image of the necropolis showing processional routes in relation to the wider landscape (Author's own using Google Earth)

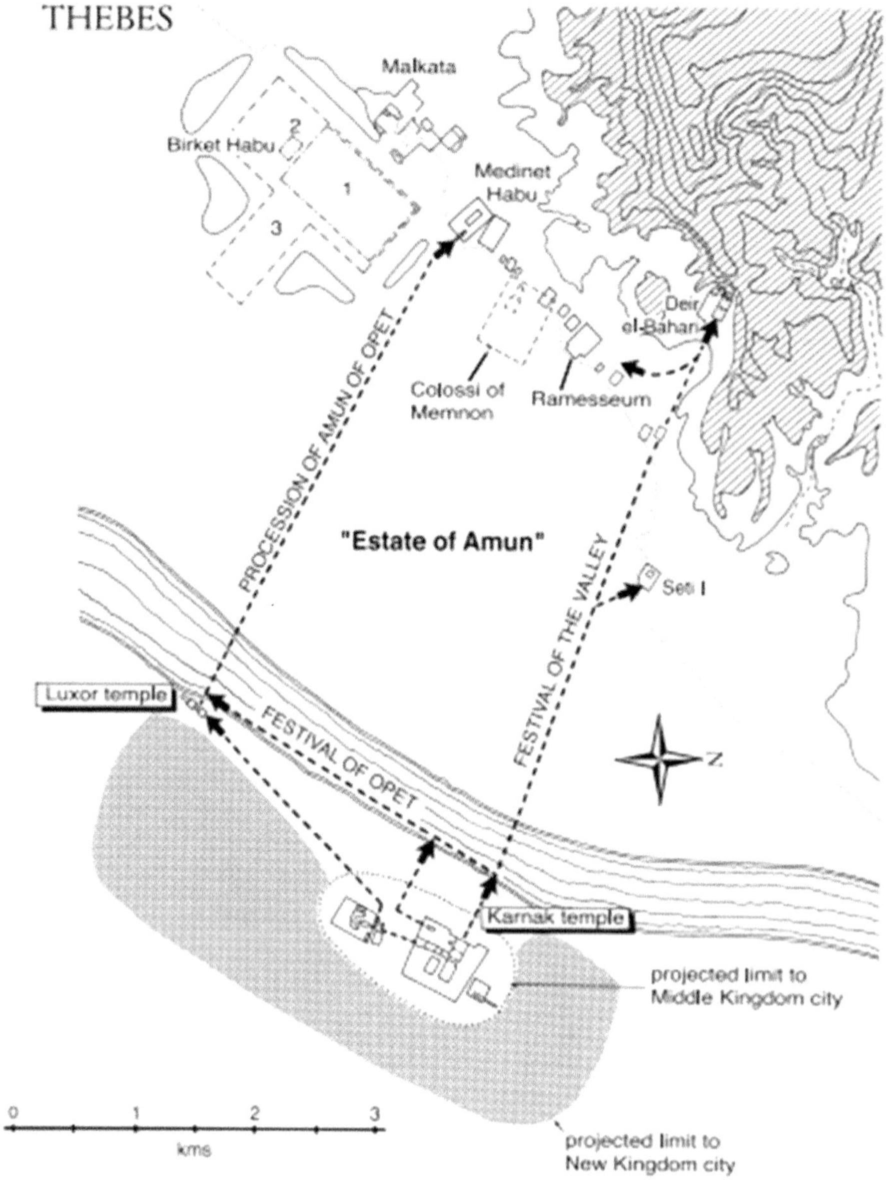

Figure 23: Map of the 'Estate of Amun' in the New Kingdom, showing main temples and processional routes (Kemp 1989: 203, Figure 71 – Courtesy of Professor Barry Kemp)

Chapter 3:
The Earliest Tombs

Old Kingdom and First Intermediate Period Tombs

(See Appendix 1)

The Theban Necropolis was already in use as early as the Old Kingdom. The oldest known Theban tombs are two large mastabas dating to the Fourth Dynasty. They are located in el-Tarif, north of Dra Abu el-Naga, opposite the Old Kingdom settlement at Karnak (see Figure 24). The names and titles of their owners do not survive, but it seems likely that a larger Old Kingdom cemetery existed in this area (Soliman 2009: 3).

During the Sixth Dynasty there was an increase in tomb building in the provinces by the *ḥry-tp-ˁ3*, translated as 'Great Chieftains' or nomarchs (Dodson and Ikram 2008: 177). This trend was reflected at Thebes by a cluster of rock-cut tombs at el-Khokha (Figure 25) dated to the late Old Kingdom (Saleh 1977: 10, 14 and 17), or First Intermediate Period (Kampp 1996: 140-143) The tomb of Khenu has not yet been numbered and as such is not shown on the GIS image, but is located 15m north-west of TT186 (Saleh 1977: 10). This cemetery was opposite the east bank settlement of Luxor, and these tombs were built close together within a 50m radius (see Figures 26 and 27).

These early Khokha tombs date between the late Fifth or early Sixth Dynasty and the First Intermediate Period. A familial connection has been established between two of the tomb owners, as Iky-TT186, was the father of Khenti-TT405 (Saleh 1977: 27; Fábián 2011: 44). These tombs also shared a courtyard and were connected by both chapels and burial chambers (Saleh 1977: 19). The chronology and precise dating of these five tombs has not yet been established satisfactorily (Fábián 2011: 44). Further Old Kingdom and First Intermediate tombs may have existed in this area, but they are likely to have been reused (Soliman 2009: 11), or not yet excavated (Saleh 1977: 11).

The tombs in this cluster were all owned by high officials, most of whom were local governors, with the exception of Senyiker-TT185 (see Appendix 1), explaining their decision to be buried in the provinces. Their titles and burial here suggest that the Theban nome was important and enjoying a period of prosperity at the end of the Old Kingdom, allowing a few individuals to receive the royal permission necessary to be buried here. The scarcity of these early burials makes this difficult to prove, with later generations potentially damaging any contemporary tombs when building their own (Saleh 1977: 11). The provincial titles of some of the tomb owners suggest that although Thebes was growing in importance, it was not yet an important administrative centre, although the owners of TT186, TT413 and TT405 all reference the king in their titles, suggesting royal interest in the area. If some of the

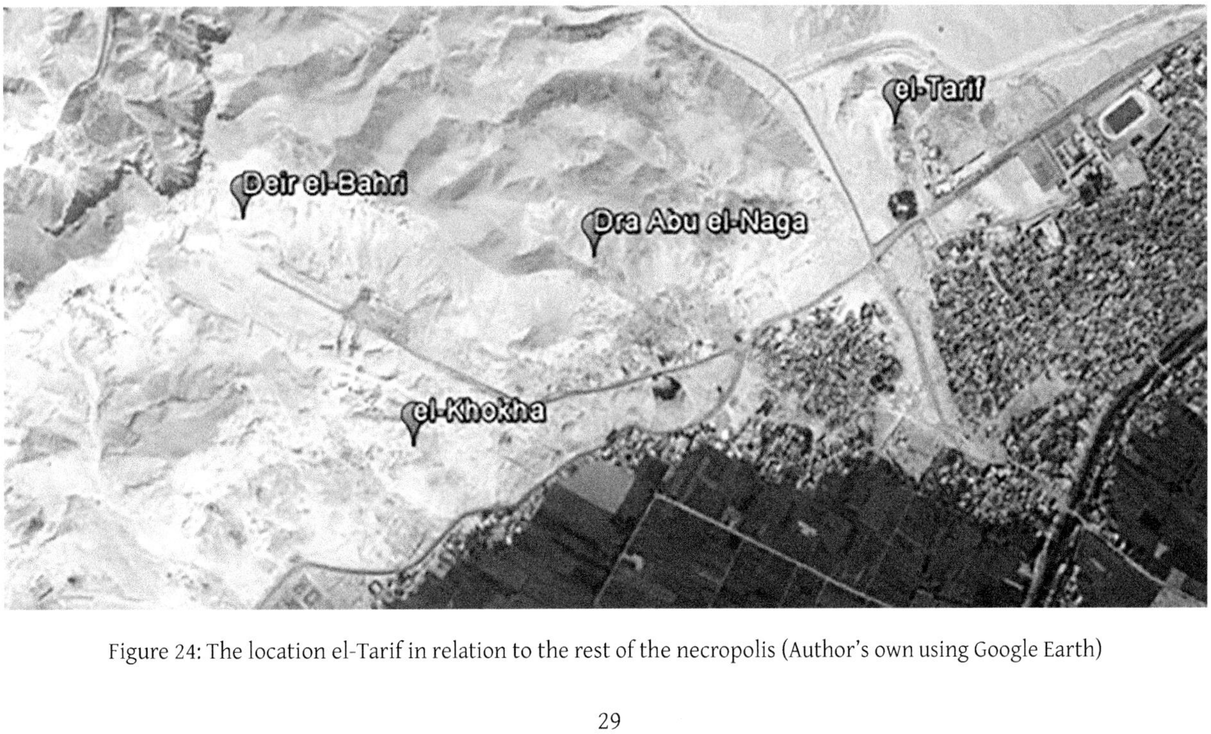

Figure 24: The location el-Tarif in relation to the rest of the necropolis (Author's own using Google Earth)

Figure 25: Old Kingdom/ First Intermediate Period TTs (Author's own using QGIS)

Figure 26: The el-Khokha hillock from the south (marked) where these earliest tombs are located (Fábián 2011: 43 – Courtesy of Dr Zoltan Fábián. György Csáki's photos from 1989)

Figure 27: The south slope of el-Khokha from the north. From right to left TT413, TT185, and TT186 and TT405 (Fábián 2011: 44 - Courtesy of Dr Zoltan Fábián. György Csáki's photos from 1989)

that the proximity to earlier tombs in the necropolis was a factor when locating tombs. Perhaps as space on the upper slopes was at a premium, these individuals instead chose the Khokha tombs to associate themselves with their Old Kingdom ancestors.

Other later neighbours date from the reign of Ramesses II in addition to those datable only as Ramesside. The later date of these tombs at a time when the necropolis was densely populated, such a long time after these Old Kingdom and First Intermediate Period tombs were

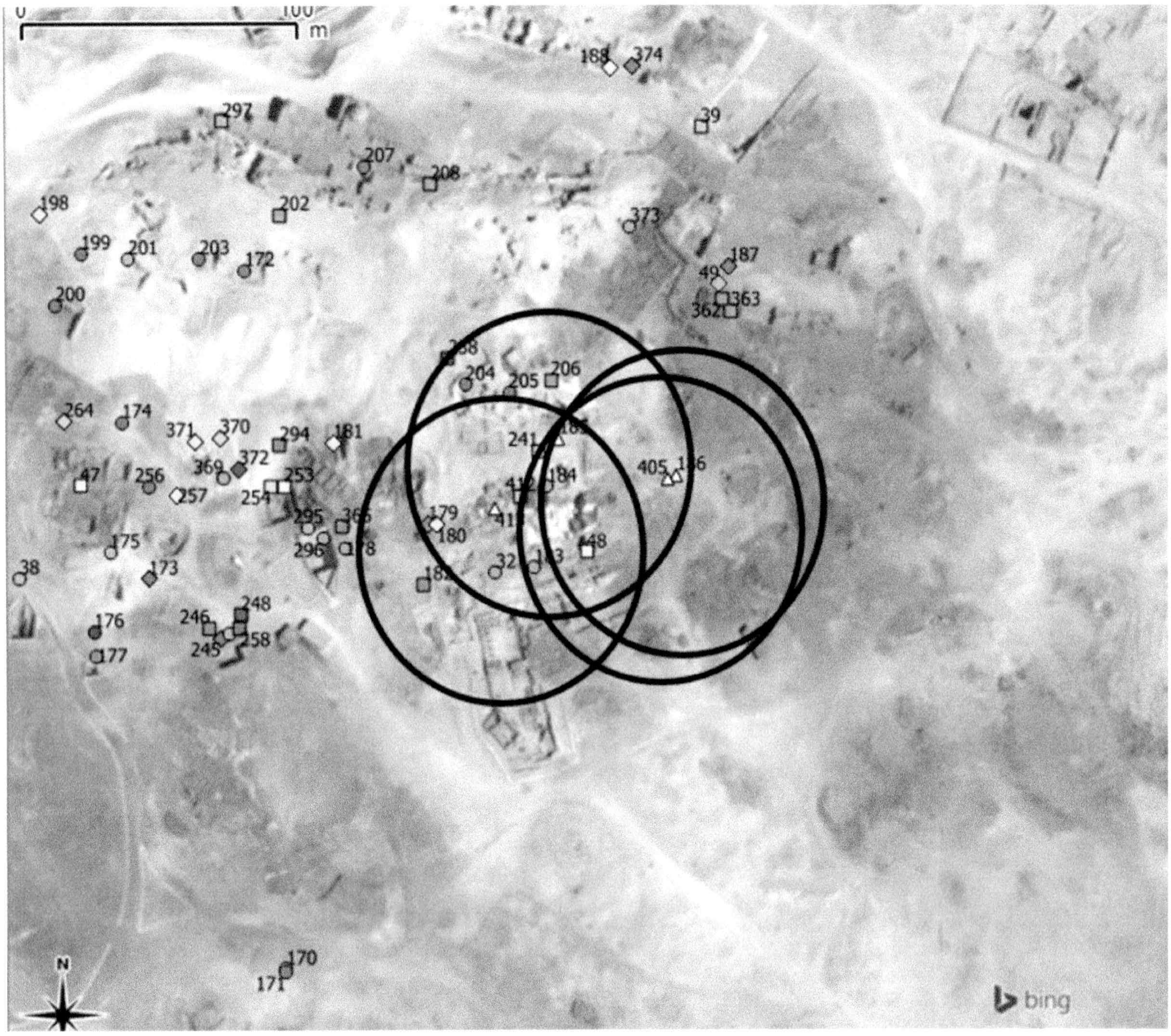

Figure 28: OK/FIP TTs and their New Kingdom neighbours within a 50m radius (Author's own using QGIS)

Table 1: Dates of New Kingdom TTs within a 50m radius of OK-FIP group

Dynasty	Reign	TT
18	_	TT204
18	Hat	TT179
18	Hat-TIII	TT241, TT412
18	TIII	TT182
18	TIII-AII	TT205
18	AII	TT238
18	AIII	TT48
19	RII	TT32, TT183, TT184
19/20	Ram	TT180
20	_	TT206

tombs do indeed date to the First Intermediate Period, this could also be explained by the local Theban ruler declaring himself king.

Later Neighbours of the Old Kingdom/First Intermediate Period TTs

Eight of the 13 New Kingdom neighbours within a 50m radius of the OK-FIP tombs at el-Khokha date to the Eighteenth Dynasty, between the reigns of Hatshepsut and Amenhotep III (see Figure 28 and Table 1). As the majority of the early tomb owners held provincial titles it makes a link with New Kingdom titles problematic. Any familial relationship between the New Kingdom tomb owners and the earlier occupants is unlikely and impossible to establish due to the length of time between these occupations. The apparently deliberate attempt, particularly by officials dating to the reigns of Hatshepsut and Tuthmosis III, to site their tombs close to Middle Kingdom predecessors (see below), shows

built, makes a deliberate attempt to associate the tomb owners with these earlier tombs unlikely. The most likely reason for this is a lack of space on the upper slopes resulting in tombs spilling into the el-Khokha area.

Trends can be observed when analysing the New Kingdom neighbours of the el-Khokha group (see Appendix 9). Seven New Kingdom neighbours held titles connecting them to the Estate of Amun (TT32, TT48, TT179, TT183, TT184, TT204 and TT241). The rise to prominence of the cult of local Theban god Amun in the early Eighteenth Dynasty explains the shift in titles from local governors and administrators in the late Old Kingdom and First Intermediate Period, to those employed by the Estate of Amun in the early New Kingdom. Perhaps these individuals were associating themselves with these early local rulers as a result of the connection between local god Amun and the Theban area. Eight of the New Kingdom tomb owners have a royal affiliation, suggesting a link between royal connection and burial here, while the Old Kingdom owner of TT186 was the 'Royal Chamberlain of the Great House'. Five later neighbours were 'Royal Scribes' (TT32, TT48, TT183, TT184 and TT412), although the prevalence of this title in the New Kingdom make any conclusions difficult to draw. Two were 'Royal Butlers' (TT205 and TT238) and there was also a 'Child of the Nursery' (TT241).

Before the New Kingdom, the only TTs were those dated to the end of the Old Kingdom or FIP, distributed in a cluster at el-Khokha, and those dating to the Middle Kingdom. The Middle Kingdom tombs are found predominantly along the northern edge of the causeway at Deir el-Bahri, with a cluster in Upper Qurna, a few examples at el-Asasif, and isolated examples elsewhere (see Figure 29).

El-Tarif

An Eleventh Dynasty cemetery was located at el-Tarif. *Saff* tombs belonging to local rulers Intef I, II and III were located here, along with the smaller, mostly anonymous, tombs of their officials (Soliman, 2009: 29-31). Only limited excavations have taken place in this area as a result of modern habitation. This movement of cemeteries from el-Tarif to el-Khokha, and later back

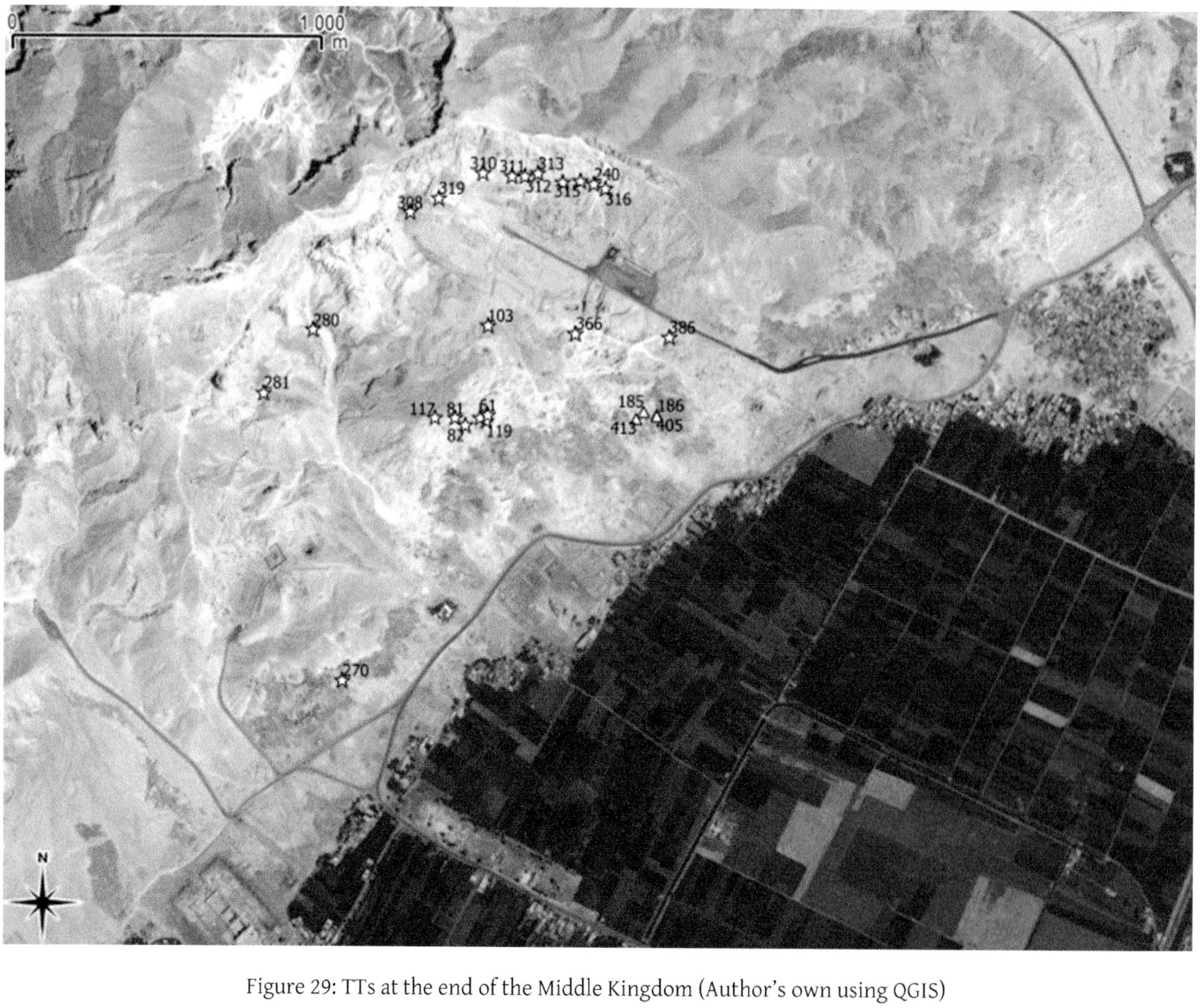

Figure 29: TTs at the end of the Middle Kingdom (Author's own using QGIS)

to el-Tarif, reflected the desire to be buried opposite the east bank settlement where the tomb owners would have lived, at Karnak and Luxor respectively (Rzepka, 2003: 383).

Middle Kingdom Tombs

(See Appendix 2)

The focus of elite burials moved southwards from el-Tarif to Deir el-Bahri at the beginning of the Middle Kingdom, as many early Middle Kingdom tombs were built in the northern hills overlooking the mortuary temple and tomb of Nebhepetre Montuhotep II. Another group of Middle Kingdom burials is located in Upper Qurna, with several isolated tombs appearing in other areas of the necropolis (see Figure 30). More were discovered under the sites of the New Kingdom mortuary temples of Seti I and Ramesses II, indicating the existence of a larger Middle Kingdom cemetery at Thebes (Soliman 2009: 42-43). The majority of these Middle Kingdom Theban tombs date to the Eleventh Dynasty. A number of additional unfinished, unused Middle Kingdom tombs have been identified in the southern and western faces of the hill of Sheikh Abd el-Qurna (Winlock 1915: 34-36, see Figure 31). However, as these tombs were not used and are not numbered as TTs, they are not mentioned further here.

Of the 21 Middle Kingdom tombs (excluding TT281 which is an unfinished temple), seven have owners with unknown titles. Of the 14 tomb owners with surviving titles, there were three 'Viziers and Governors of the Town', two 'Mayors', four 'Chancellors' and three 'Royal Seal-bearers' (some individuals held more than one of these titles). From these recurring titles, and the royal affiliation attested in the majority of them, the importance of Thebes as an administrative centre and capital city can be confirmed. The lack of religious titles (in contrast to New Kingdom tomb owners) also demonstrates that Thebes was not yet the religious centre it would become in the New Kingdom.
There were several royal women buried at Deir el-Bahri, including Queen Neferu II-TT319, who was the mother of Montuhotep I and wife of Montuhotep II (Winlock 1942: 101-104), and Kemsit-TT308, the 'Sole Royal Concubine' and 'Priestess of Hathor' (Engelbach 1924: 22). The temple of Montuhotep II also included funerary chapels for six female members of his family (Dodson and Ikram 2008: 190), reinforcing the link

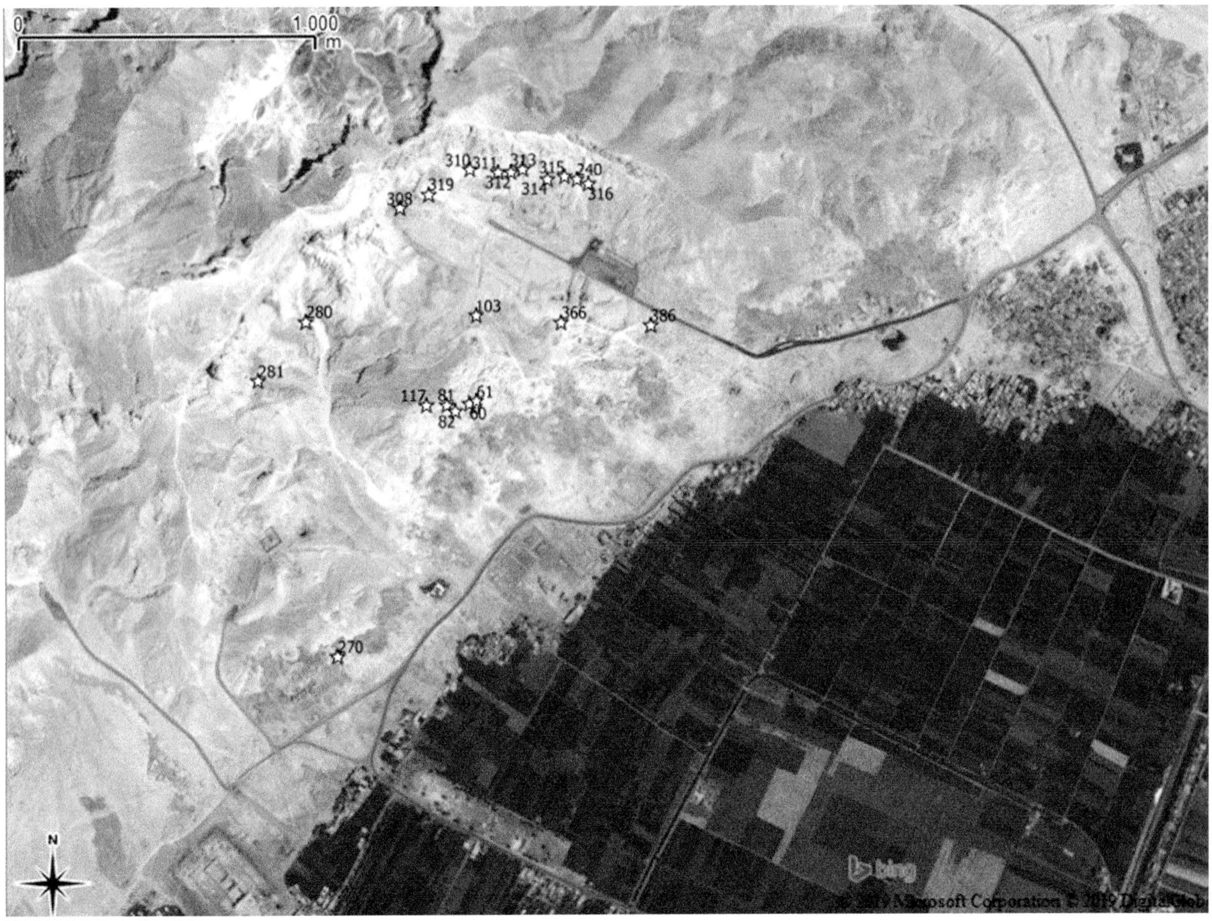

Figure 30: Middle Kingdom TTs (Author's own using QGIS)

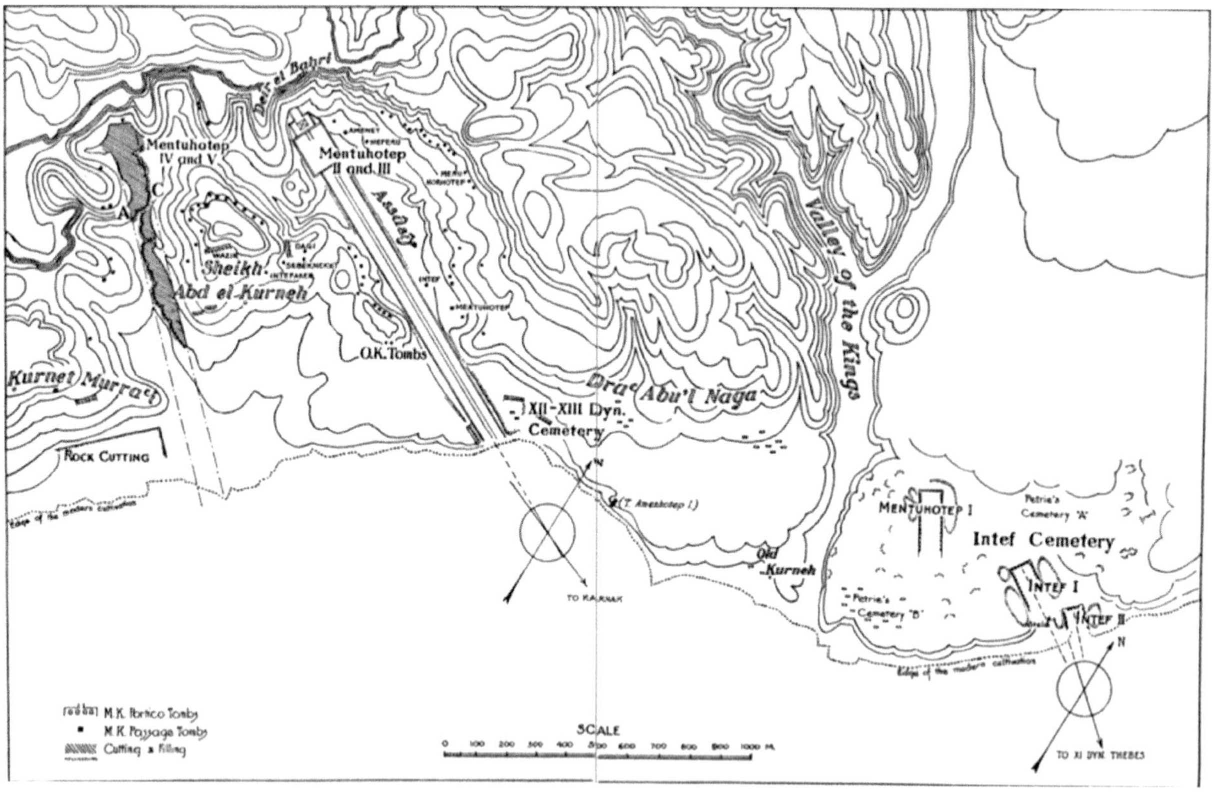

Figure 31: Sketch Map of the Middle Kingdom Theban Necropolis (Winlock 1915: Figure 1 – Out of Copyright)

between this area and the royal women of this period, potentially due to the link between the goddess Hathor and Deir el-Bahri (Winlock 1915: 5).

When the royal capital moved to Iti-Tawy in the Twelfth Dynasty, the royal family and officials moved with it, aspiring to burial close to the royal pyramids instead. There were still a number of administrative officials living at Thebes, but there is a lack of Twelfth Dynasty tombs at Thebes compared to regional centres in Middle Egypt. This may be as a result of the specific topography of Western Thebes, which does not provide the same cliff-terraces for tomb building, as found at Beni Hassan (Snape 2011: 171).

Middle Kingdom TT Reuse

Five Middle Kingdom tombs were reused during the New Kingdom, four during the Eighteenth Dynasty and one in the Nineteenth Dynasty. All four Eighteenth Dynasty usurpations took place around the reign of Tuthmosis III, suggesting a possible interest in the Middle Kingdom during this period. The tombs were reused by individuals with a range of titles, but there is a potential link between Viziers and the Middle Kingdom burials (see Chapter 12). Four of these reused tombs were located in Qurna, and one in Qurnet Murai. None of the Deir el-Bahri tombs were reused (see Chapter 6), possibly as a result of the poor rock quality necessitating the use of a limestone lining to the walls before decoration (Dodson and Ikram 2008: 190-191), or this could reinforce the idea that special permission was required to be buried in this area. The visibility of these tombs with their monumental causeways may also have ensured their ongoing protection (see Figures 32 and 33).

Later Neighbours of the Middle Kingdom TTs

The Old Kingdom and First Intermediate Period tombs formed a distinct cluster in el-Khokha, while the Middle Kingdom tombs formed two main groups, in addition to several more isolated burials. The Deir el-Bahri tombs lined the causeway overlooking the temple, whereas the Qurna tombs formed a cluster. There is no obvious connection between these two groups, other than their proximity to Deir el-Bahri and their elevated positions (see Figure 34).

The Middle Kingdom tombs on the northern hills overlooking the causeway at Deir el-Bahri (TT316, TT240, TT315, TT314, TT313, TT312, TT311, TT310) and those located under the mortuary temples (Neferu and Iah-TT319 and Kemsit-TT308) do not have any neighbouring tombs within a 50m radius (see Figure 35). Ahmose-Meritamen-TT358 was a member of the royal family, buried behind the mortuary temple of Hatshepsut, during the reign of Tuthmosis III or

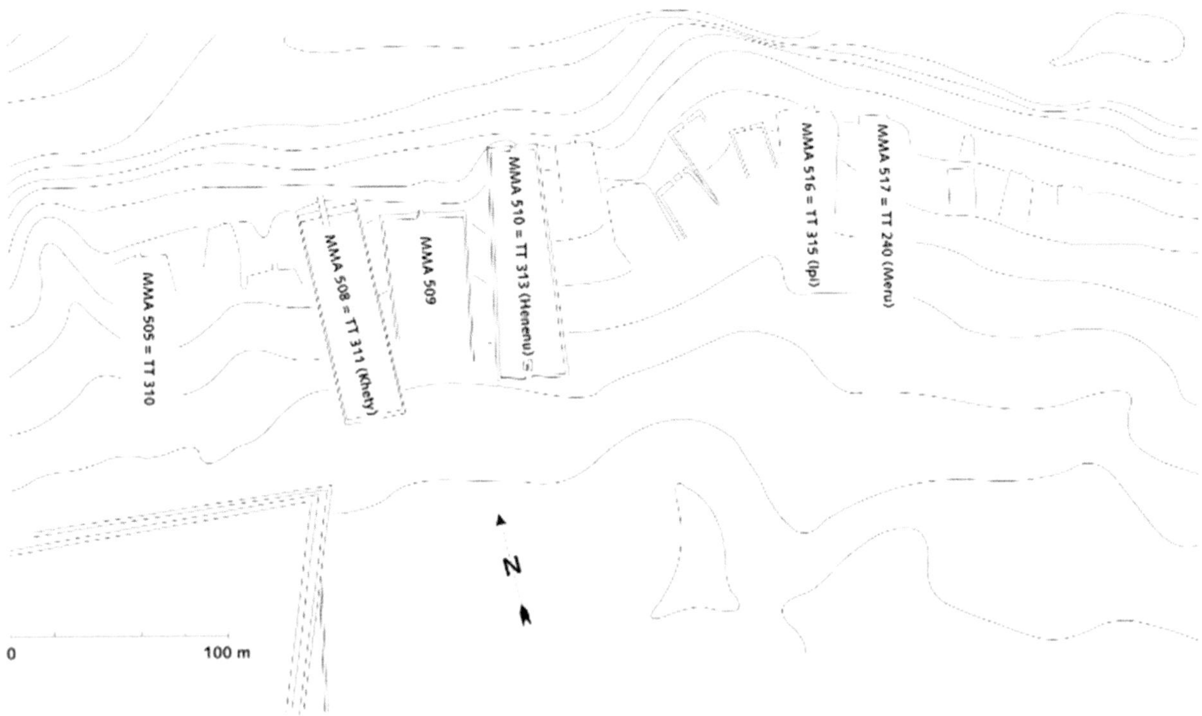

Figure 32: Middle Kingdom tombs along the northern edge of the causeway at Deir el-Bahri (Allen 1996a: 4 – Courtesy of Professor James Allen)

Figure 33: Middle Kingdom tombs at Deir el-Bahri (Author's own)

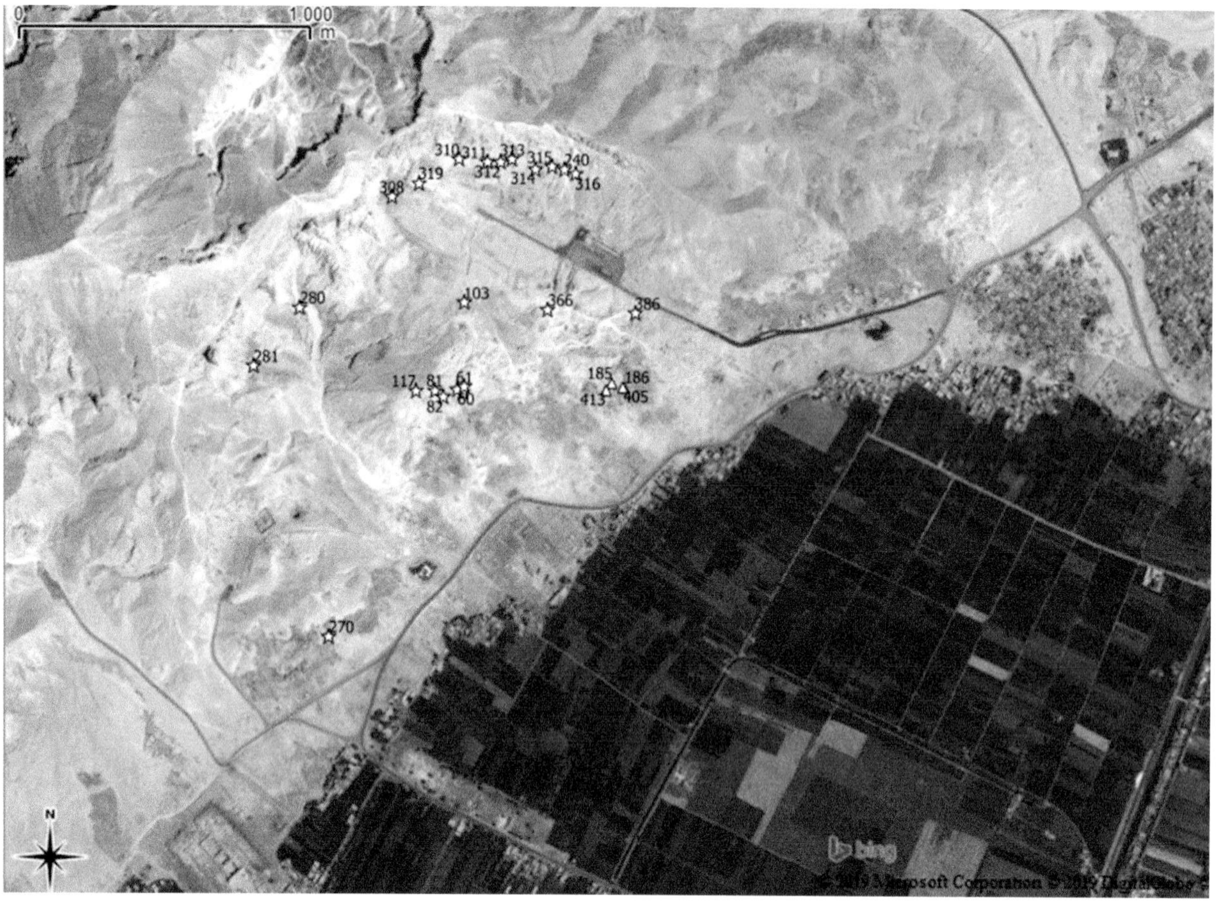

Figure 34: TTs prior to the New Kingdom (Author's own using QGIS)

Amenhotep II (Kampp 1996: 588). Meketre-TT280 (and the unfinished Middle Kingdom temple, TT281) are isolated on the western edge of the necropolis, south of Deir el-Bahri, with no neighbouring tombs. The closest neighbour to TT280 is Inhapi-TT320, another isolated tomb over 100m away, located between TT308 and TT280 along the edge of the western cliffs (see Figure 36). Inhapi was possibly the wife of Ahmose, and TT320 is dated to his reign (Kampp 1996: 574). The tomb was re-used in the Twentieth Dynasty as a royal cachette. The existence of another early Eighteenth Dynasty royal burial suggests that prior to the establishment of the Valley of the Queens, this site was chosen as a suitable cemetery for royal women, as it was close to the Middle Kingdom royal cemetery where Montuhotep II and his queens had been buried, and close to this king's mortuary temple. The lack of New Kingdom burials or usurpations in the Deir el-Bahri area reinforces the idea that building in this part of the necropolis must have been restricted (see Chapter 6). The lack of later burials in the area south of Deir el-Bahri where TT280 is located can be explained by the lack of New Kingdom activity in this area and its secluded nature at some distance from the more populated areas of the necropolis.

Dagi-TT103 lies closer to the rest of the necropolis; to the north of the Upper Qurna cluster of Middle Kingdom tombs, but the closest tomb still lies over 100m away. Djar-TT366 and Intef-TT386 also lie on the outskirts of a populated area of el-Asasif close to the causeway to Deir el-Bahri, but there are no neighbouring tombs within a 50m radius of each of them respectively. Six Middle Kingdom tombs are arranged in a cluster on the upper slopes of Sheikh Abd el-Qurna, and a number of New Kingdom tombs are situated within a 50m radius of them (see Figure 37).

Of the 27 New Kingdom tombs lying within a 50m radius of these Middle Kingdom tombs, 26 date to the Eighteenth Dynasty, prior to the Amarna period (see Table 2), as do the majority of those located close to the earlier el-Khokha group. The location of these tombs may indicate a deliberate desire by later tomb owners to associate themselves with their ancestors. The position of the Middle Kingdom cluster in a desirable location on the upper slopes, with excellent views towards the east bank, made this a popular position in which to site a tomb, so a definite attempt to locate a tomb close to their Middle Kingdom predecessors cannot be proved. A link between certain individuals and professions,

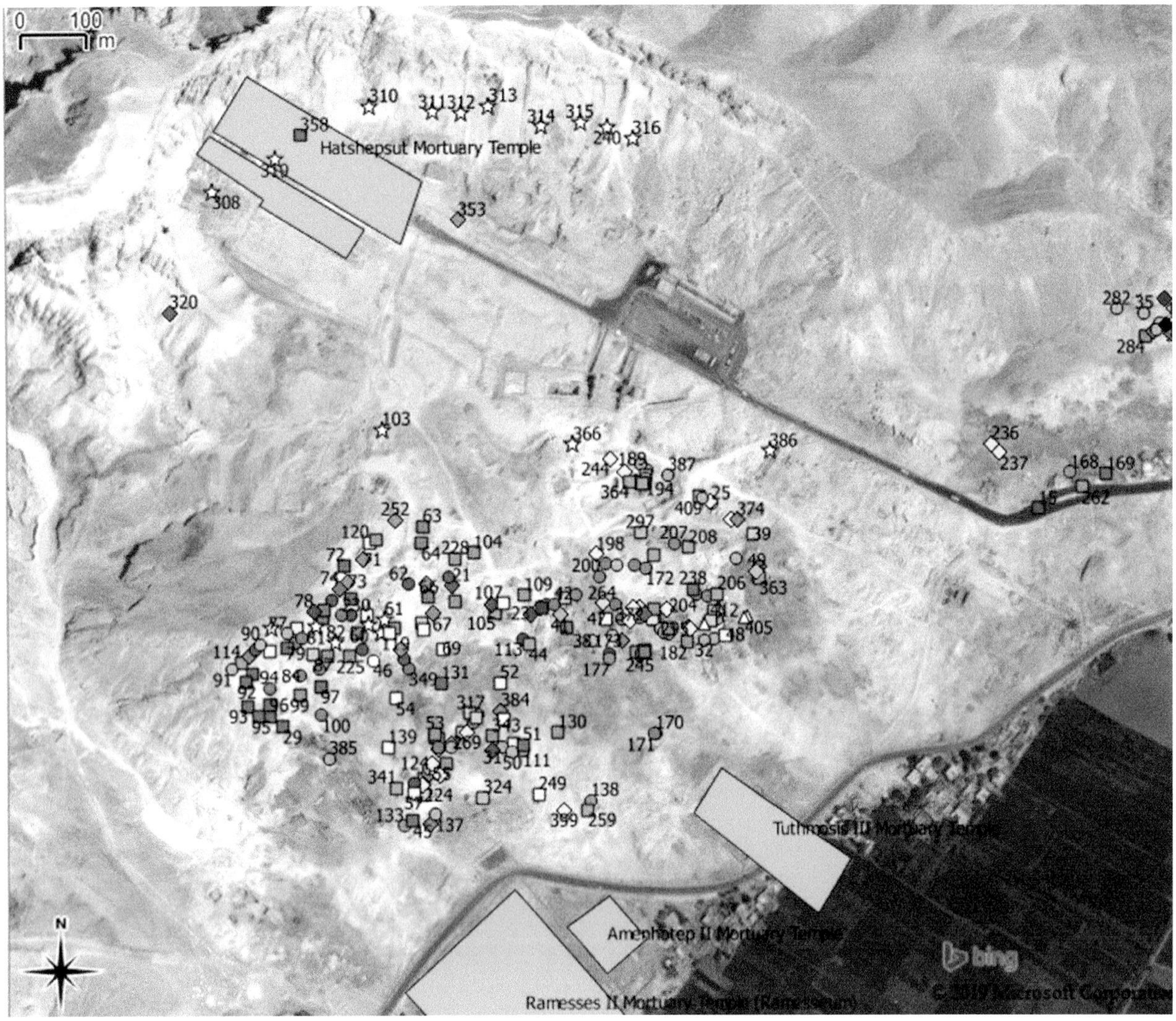

Figure 35: Middle Kingdom TTs (excluding TT270) and their New Kingdom neighbours (Author's own using QGIS)

Figure 36: Aerial view of TT320 (Author's own)

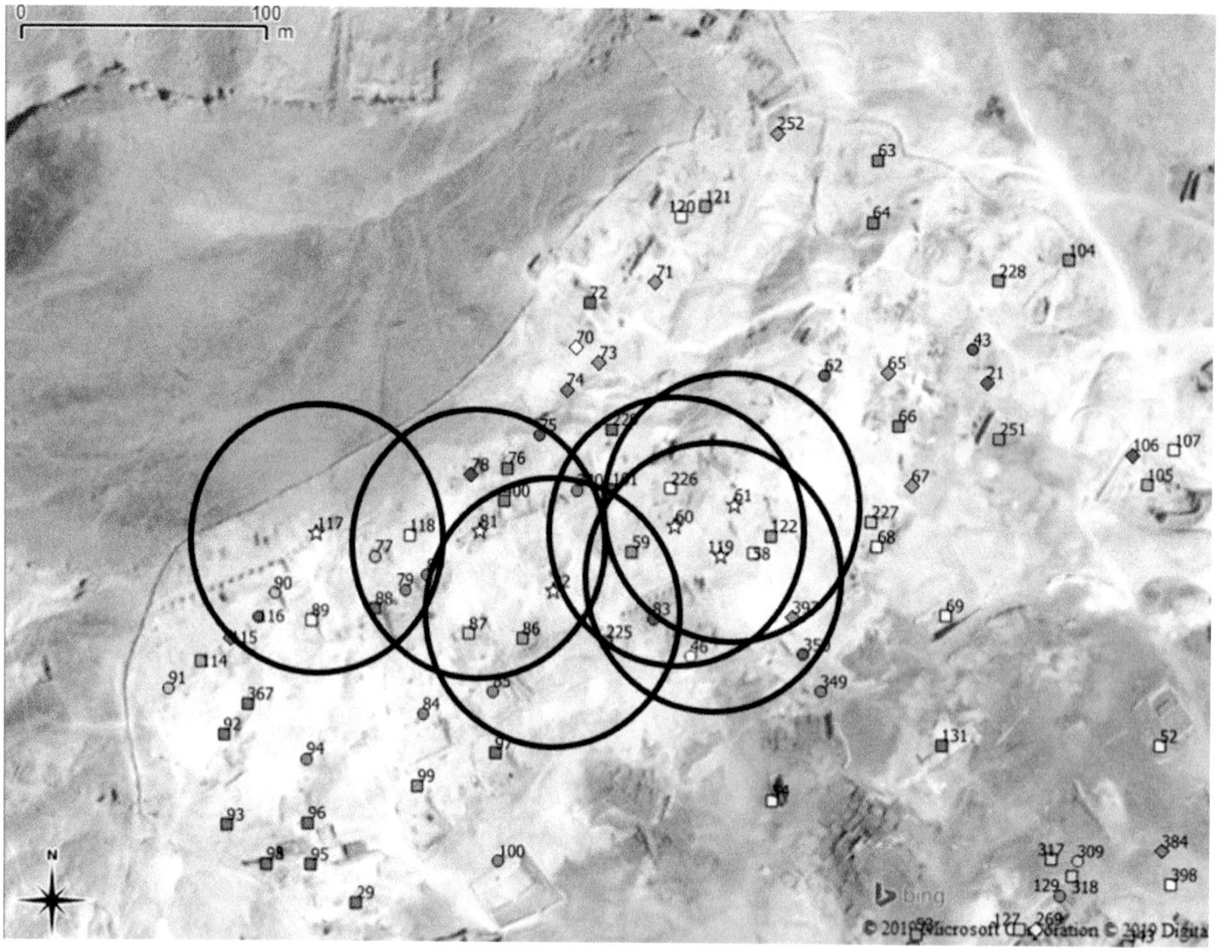

Figure 37: Qurna Middle Kingdom TTs and New Kingdom TTs within a 50m radius (Author's own using QGIS)

Table 2: Date of New Kingdom TTs within a 50m radius of Qurna Middle Kingdom TTs

Dynasty	Reign	TT
18	_	TT230
18	Ah-TIII	TT83
18	Hat	TT397
18	Hat-TIII	TT87, TT227
18	TIII	TT59, TT86, TT122, TT225
18	TIII-AII	TT79, TT80
18	AII	TT88, TT229
18	AII-TIV	TT75, TT101, TT116, TT350
18	AII-AIII	TT78
18	TIV	TT76, TT400
18	TIV-AIII	TT90, TT77
18	AIII	TT58, TT89, TT118, TT226
19	_	TT115

such as the link between Viziers and this area, and in particular Middle Kingdom and Eighteenth Dynasty Viziers, will be discussed (see Chapter 12). A range of titles were held by the New Kingdom tomb owners in this area, but with only limited Middle Kingdom titles surviving (see Appendix 2), with the exception of the Viziers, it is difficult to establish any link between Middle Kingdom and New Kingdom tomb owners by title.

The neighbouring New Kingdom tomb owners included several 'High Priests' (TT59, TT86, TT225) and 'Overseers of Priests' of different deities (the third occupant of TT58, and owners of TT78 and TT86), in addition to a number of lower-ranking priests. There were also a number of temple administrators, including two 'Overseers of the Works of Amun' (TT78 and TT86), two 'Overseers of the Cattle of Amun' (TT76 and TT78) and an 'Overseer of the Granary of Amun' (TT86). The largest group was those connected to the royal administration, including 'Royal Seal-bearers' (TT75, TT76, TT78, TT86, TT88, TT89), 'Stewards' (TT76, TT89, TT226) and 'Fan-bearers' (TT77, TT78, TT88, TT118 and TT226). Among the general administration there were

Figure 38: TT270 and its New Kingdom TT neighbours within a 50m radius (Author's own using QGIS)

Table 3: Dates of New Kingdom TTs within a 50m radius of TT270

Dynasty	Reign	TT
19	Mer	TT274
20	RIII-RIV	TT222
20	-	TT235, TT272, TT273

two 'Overseers of the Treasury' (TT80 and TT86), two 'Overseers of the Granary (TT79 and TT87) and even a 'Vizier' (TT83). The range of important titles found amongst the tomb owners here suggests that either this area was popular amongst the highest members of the elite as a result of its desirable location, or that these most important members of society deliberately chose this site in order to be buried close to their Middle Kingdom predecessors.

TT270 is located some distance away from the other Middle Kingdom tombs, in the southern area of the necropolis at Qurnet Murai. This area is not densely populated but five tombs lie within 50m of TT270 (see Figure 38), all of which date to the Nineteenth and

Twentieth Dynasties, in contrast to the neighbours of the other Middle Kingdom tombs which predominantly date to the Eighteenth Dynasty (see Table 3). This sparsely populated southern area of the necropolis was a less desirable location to site a tomb due to its lower slopes and distance from Deir el-Bahri. This area was more popular in the Ramesside period as a result of the lack of space at Qurna and its proximity to Ramesside mortuary temples. The lack of tombs makes analysis of these neighbouring tombs of limited use. The proximity to a Middle Kingdom tomb seems likely to have been coincidental rather than deliberate.

Conclusions

The majority of these early tombs were located in contemporary clusters, suggesting a deliberate decision to be buried in the vicinity of each other. The Old Kingdom/ First Intermediate Period tombs are clustered together at el-Khokha, while the majority of Middle Kingdom tombs either border the causeway to Deir el-Bahri or are clustered in Upper Qurna. The early el-Khokha tombs all belonged to provincial governors, which was presumably a hereditary title suggesting a familial link in addition to an occupational one. The limited survival of the titles of the Middle Kingdom tomb owners makes further analysis of the relationship between these individuals problematic.

There is a potential link between tombs dated to the Middle Kingdom and the early Eighteenth Dynasty in Upper Qurna, where a substantial number of Eighteenth Dynasty tombs are located within 50m of a Middle Kingdom tomb, while a large proportion of these tombs are reused during the Eighteenth Dynasty. Several further Middle Kingdom tombs have no New Kingdom tombs built nearby and do not appear to have been reused, due either to their positioning on the outskirts of the necropolis, or apparent restrictions on where New Kingdom officials could be buried. These links will be discussed further when analysing specific areas of the necropolis, and trends among occupational groups.

Chapter 4:
The New Kingdom Evolution of the Theban Necropolis

The Eighteenth Dynasty

Seven tombs date to the late Seventeenth or early Eighteenth Dynasty (see Figure 39), while a number date to the early Eighteenth Dynasty, prior to the reign of Hatshepsut (see Figure 40). Six of these tombs are located in Dra Abu el-Naga East, close to the royal tombs of the Seventeenth (Miniaci 2009: 19-25; Winlock 1924: 237-243) and early Eighteenth Dynasty, including Amenhotep I and Ahmose-Nefertari (Polz 2007: 172-197), and the mortuary temple of Amenhotep I and Ahmose Nefertari. There are five examples elsewhere in the necropolis, namely the outlying royal tomb close to Deir el-Bahri (TT320), two located in Qurna (TT46 and TT398), one in el-Khokha (TT297), and one along the causeway at Dra Abu el-Naga West (TT15).

The New Kingdom brought about the promotion of Amun to state deity, so royal cemeteries moved to Thebes, allowing kings to be buried within the Estate of Amun. This in turn led to officials being buried nearby, but the hidden nature of the Valley of the Kings made burial in close proximity to their king impossible, leading to the increased popularity of the Theban Necropolis for non-royal burials. Being buried here allowed individuals to be buried close to the religious capital of Thebes, where many of them worked, within the Estate of Amun, and in relative proximity to the royal tombs.

A number of tombs are imprecisely dated between various reigns, but during the reigns of Hatshepsut and Tuthmosis III there are a large number of more accurately dated burials. The majority of these tombs are located in Qurna and el-Khokha, with a significant number still found in Dra Abu el-Naga (see Figures 41, 42 and 43). This shift from Dra Abu el-Naga to the central area of the necropolis during these reigns may have been due to several reasons. Those in Upper Qurna are in particularly close proximity to the Middle Kingdom

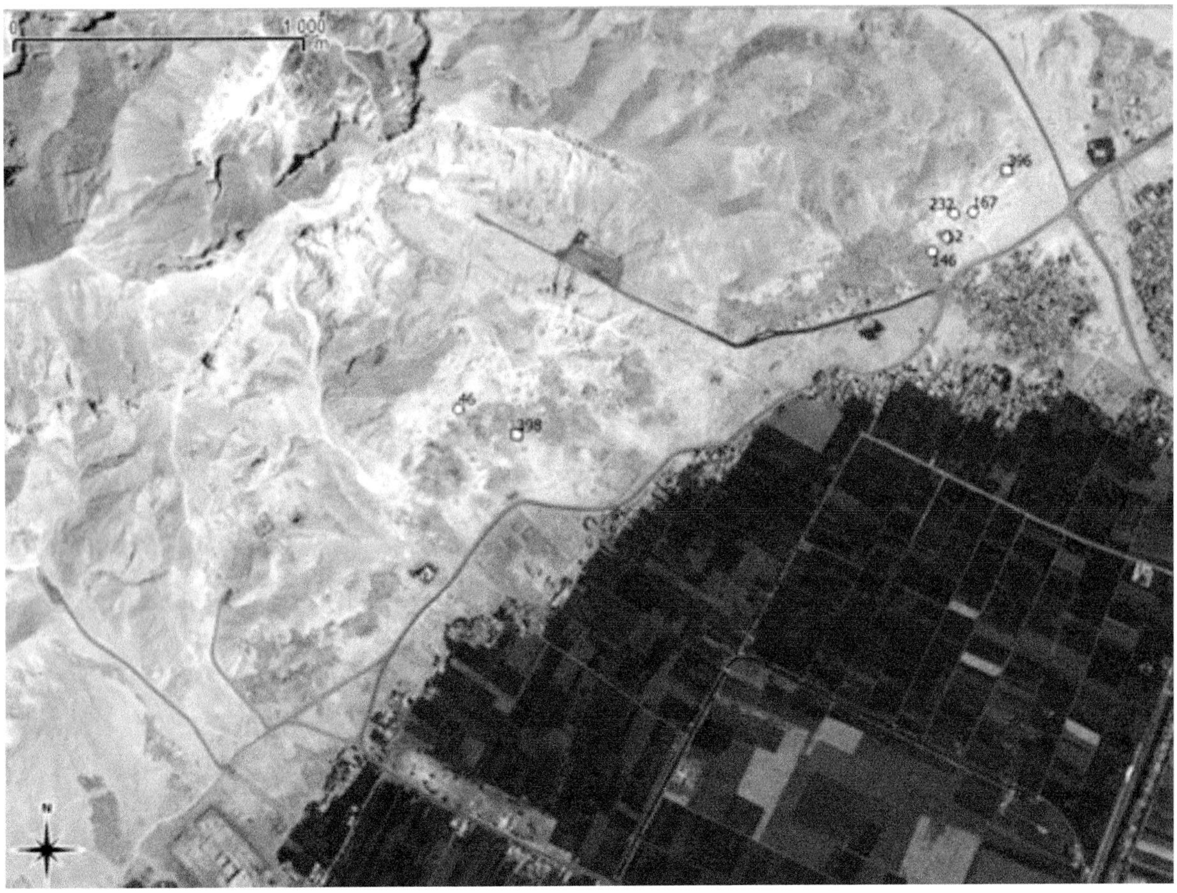

Figure 39: TTs dated to the late Seventeenth or early Eighteenth Dynasty (Author's own using QGIS)

Figure 40: TTs in the early Eighteenth Dynasty (prior to the reign of Hatshepsut) (Author's own using QGIS)

tombs in the area, and had the benefit of an elevated position, with the resulting visibility and presence these tombs would have had from the cultivation. They would also have had views towards the Qurna mortuary temple of Tuthmosis III, and the processional route of the BFV. This choice of location may also replicate the concerns of the long-reigning, powerful rulers, Hatshepsut and Tuthmosis III, as rather than locating their tombs close to the early Eighteenth Dynasty rulers at Dra Abu el-Naga, the nobles who served them instead may have made the decision to locate their tombs here in order to associate themselves with the Middle Kingdom nobles. This reflects the way in which their monarchs were keen to establish a link between themselves and their influential Middle Kingdom predecessors, such as Nebhepetre Montuhotep II, whose Deir el-Bahri mortuary temple lies adjacent to the site of their own temples (see Chapter 6). A number of these Middle Kingdom tombs were also reused during this specific period (see Chapter 9). The proximity to the Qurna mortuary temple of Tuthmosis III also seems to have been a contributory factor to this choice of location, with tombs to the north and west directly overlooking the temple.

The continued use of Dra Abu el-Naga may have been continuity of tradition from the early New Kingdom, linked to the earlier royal burials in the area. The tombs sited here were also positioned along the processional route of the BFV as it headed towards Deir el-Bahri (see Figure 44). The lack of burials along the causeway to Deir el-Bahri, or at el-Asasif seems strange as this must have been a desirable location, particularly during these reigns. This suggests that at this time it was not appropriate for individuals to be buried close to Deir el-Bahri, or that it required special permission as in the case of TT353 (see Chapter 6). If this was the case, Dra Abu el-Naga West and Upper Qurna would have been closest to Deir el-Bahri which may explain the orientation of some of these Qurna tombs (see Chapter 9).

During the reign of Amenhotep II, tomb building was concentrated in the north-west of Upper Qurna (see Figure 45), with a distinct cluster of 11 tombs built in close proximity here by the officials of Amenhotep II (see Chapter 9). Other areas of the necropolis were only in occasional use at this time.

This pattern continued into the reign of Tuthmosis IV, with Upper Qurna remaining the most popular area for tomb building, but there is not such a clearly defined cluster of tombs as those dating to Amenhotep II. Instead, tomb building gradually spread eastwards, and tombs became more densely packed (see Figures 45, 46 and 47). The mortuary temples of Amenhotep

Figure 41: TTs dated to the reign of Hatshepsut (Author's own using QGIS)

Figure 42: TTs dated to the reign of Tuthmosis III (Author's own using QGIS)

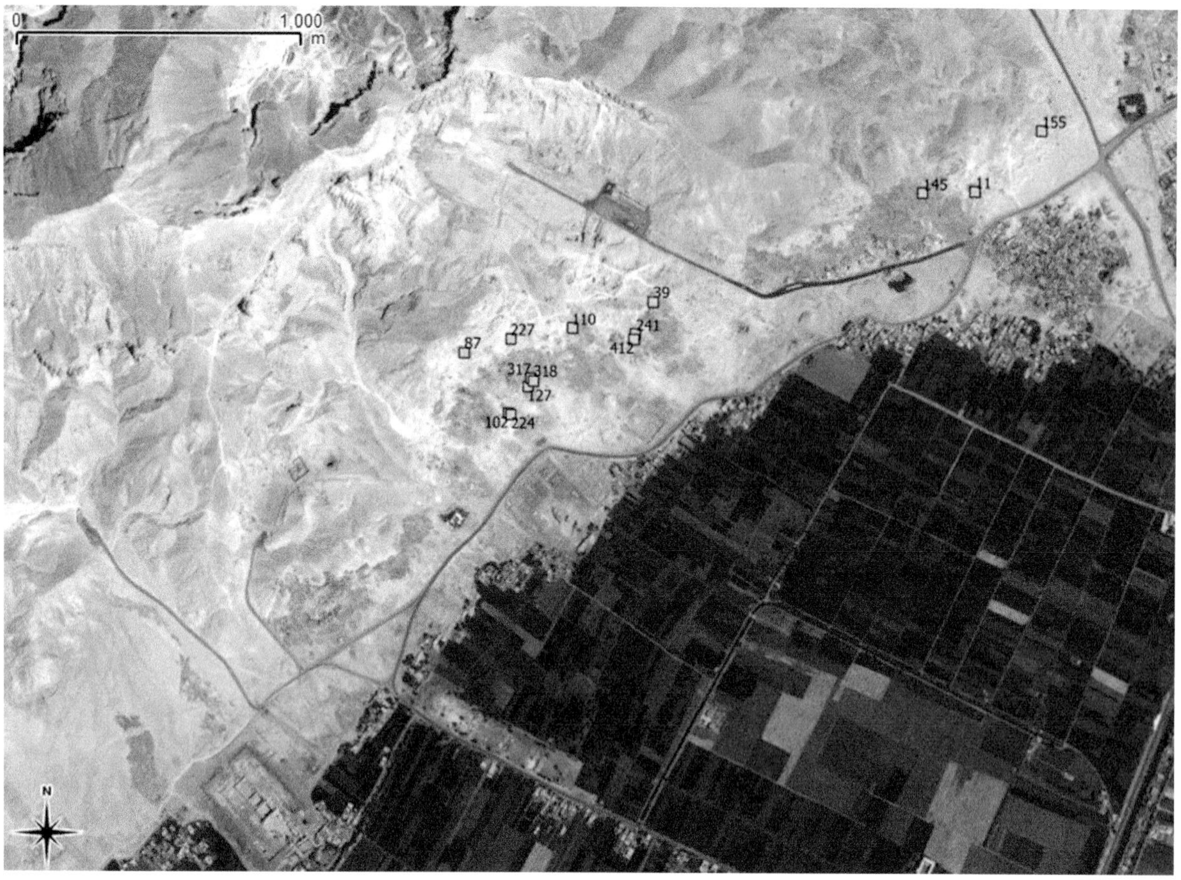

Figure 43: TTs datable only to the reign of Hatshepsut or Tuthmosis III (Author's own using QGIS)

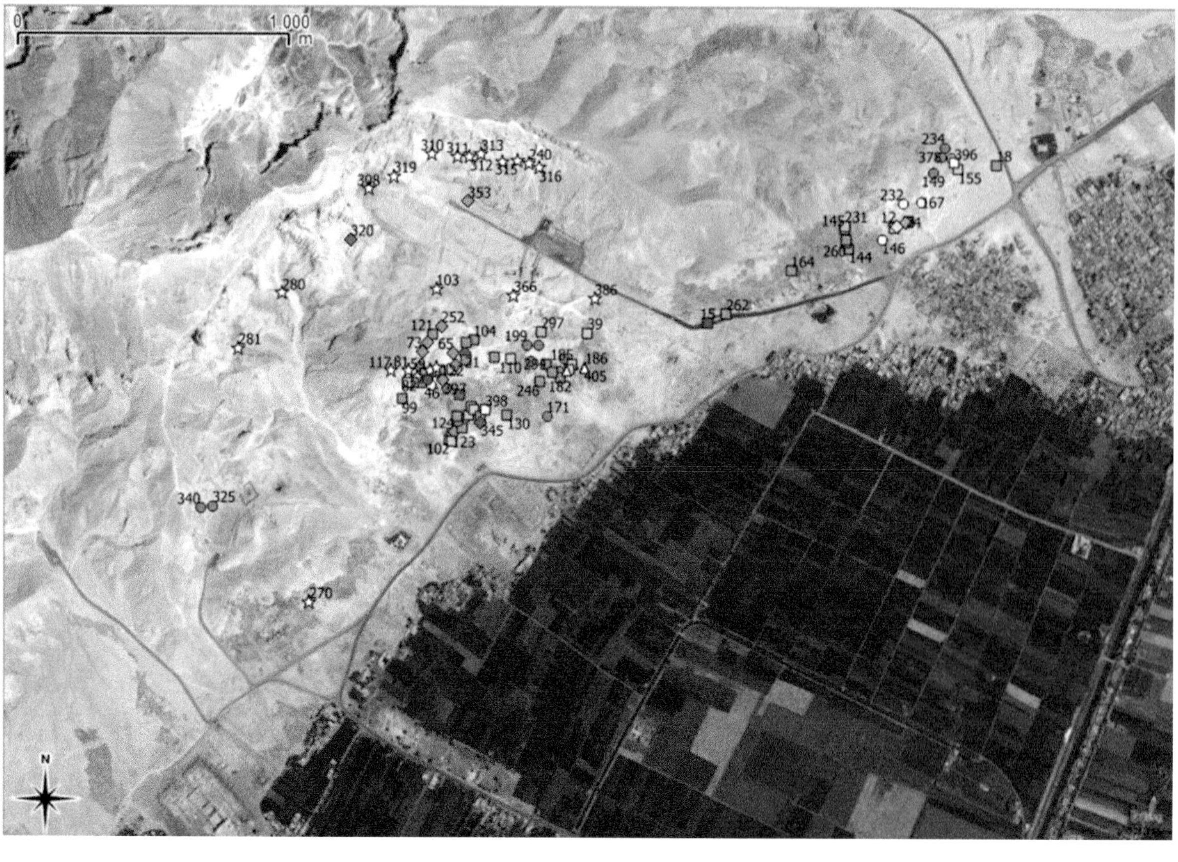

Figure 44: TTs at the end of the reign of Tuthmosis III (Author's own using QGIS)

Figure 45: TTs dated to the reign of Amenhotep II (Author's own using QGIS)

Figure 46: TTs dated to the reign of Tuthmosis IV (Author's own using QGIS)

Figure 47: TTs datable only to the reign of Amenhotep II or Tuthmosis IV (Author's own using QGIS)

II and Tuthmosis IV were located to the south of the Qurna temple of Tuthmosis III, and while tombs were built close to or overlooking the temple of Amenhotep II they were not located as far south as the Tuthmosis IV mortuary temple, despite an empty area of the necropolis lying opposite these temples (see Figure 48). This may suggest a change in permission required to build in the vicinity of a royal mortuary temple, as from this reign onwards private tombs no longer directly overlooked royal mortuary temples, potentially indicating the importance of a clear path from the royal mortuary temple to the western cliffs. Dra Abu el-Naga continued to be used (albeit less frequently), presumably as a result of lack of space in Qurna, positions overlooking the BFV processional route, and proximity to earlier royal tombs (see Chapter 5).

During the reign of Amenhotep III, Qurna and el-Khokha were still the most popular areas for tomb-building, with a few still being built at Dra Abu el-Naga (see Figure 49). The lower slopes of Qurna became more popular, due to the overcrowding of the upper slopes, and better rock quality and more space available on the lower slopes. The mortuary temple of Amenhotep III lay some distance to the south-east of the other mortuary temples, closest to Qurnet Murai, yet this southern area of the necropolis was only used for one tomb (TT383) during this reign. This may be due to the fact that although Qurnet Murai is the closest area to this temple, it was still such a distance away to make this irrelevant. The colossal nature of the Amenhotep III temple made it visible from more central areas of the necropolis too, explaining the use of these areas during this period as they were more conveniently located for festival processions and making offerings. Tomb owners may have chosen areas overlooking the mortuary temples of earlier rulers instead due to the isolated location of the Amenhotep III temple, or this lack of movement may suggest that proximity to the current royal mortuary temple was not the primary concern at this time, perhaps in favour of being buried adjacent to other individuals in the necropolis.

During the Amarna Period, the Theban Necropolis was vacated in favour of the cemetery at Amarna, with a few exceptions in Lower Qurna and el-Asasif dated between Amenhotep III or early in the reign of Akhenaten before the move to Amarna (see Figure 50). After Amarna was abandoned and the nobles returned to Thebes for burial, there was an increase in the popularity of Qurnet Murai, presumably as a result of its proximity to the mortuary temple of these late Eighteenth Dynasty

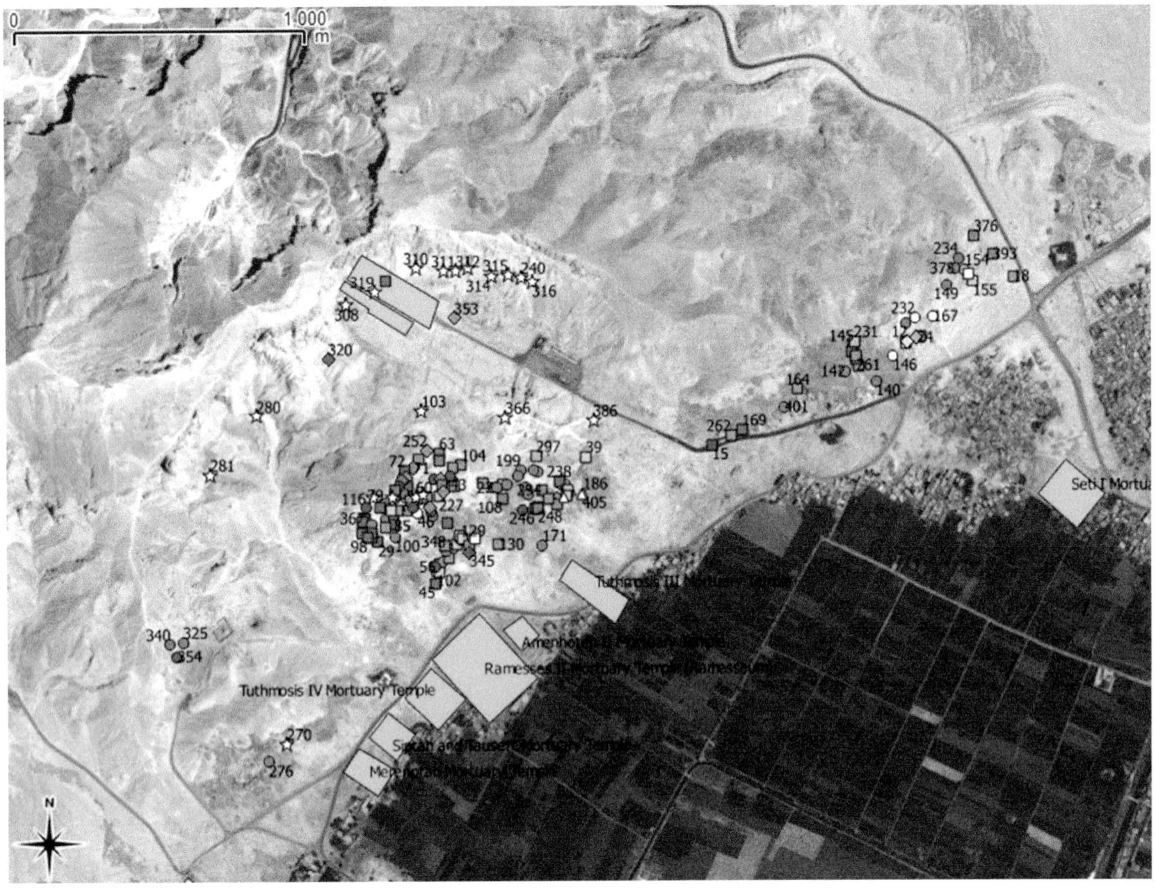

Figure 48: TTs at the end of the reign of Tuthmosis IV (Author's own using QGIS)

Figure 49: TTs dated to the reign of Amenhotep III (Author's own using QGIS)

Figure 50: TTs datable only to the reign of Amenhotep III or Akhenaten (Author's own using QGIS)

Figure 51: TTs dated to the Eighteenth Dynasty- after Amarna (Author's own using QGIS)

Figure 52: TTs in the Theban Necropolis at the end of the Eighteenth Dynasty (Author's own using QGIS)

kings close to Medinet Habu, in addition to the lack of space in other areas (see Figure 51). There were a few tombs still built in the northern areas of the necropolis.

By the end of the Eighteenth Dynasty, the central necropolis (including Upper and Lower Qurna, and the adjoining area of el-Khokha spreading into el-Asasif) was clearly the most popular and crowded area to locate tombs and had remained so throughout the dynasty. Tombs were tightly packed into this central area, with the highest concentration on the upper slopes close to the Middle Kingdom tombs. These upper slopes filled up before the populated area expanded northwards into el-Khokha and towards the Deir el-Bahri causeway, and southwards towards the cultivation. It could not expand to the west due to the summit of the hill. Dra Abu el-Naga also remained consistently in use to a lesser extent with a less concentrated distribution of tombs, dispersed all along the area, parallel to the modern road. Other clusters of tombs emerged at Qurnet Murai and Deir el-Medina (see Figure 52).

The Nineteenth and Twentieth Dynasties

Only three TTs can be dated precisely to the early Nineteenth Dynasty prior to the reign of Ramesses II (see Figure 53), with several more datable only to the late Eighteenth or early Nineteenth Dynasty. There does not seem to be a link between these early Nineteenth Dynasty tombs and the mortuary temple of Seti I, which is located further to the east than other mortuary temples, close to the landing stage used during the BFV. The closest area of the necropolis to this temple is Dra Abu el-Naga East, but no tombs in this area can be definitively dated to the reign of Seti I. Even Dra Abu el-Naga East is some 500m to the north of the temple, suggesting that the distance between the necropolis and the mortuary temple of Seti I rendered any link with tomb distribution irrelevant, as the temple cannot be overlooked from the necropolis due to the flat ground to the west (see Chapter 5).

There was a peak in tomb building during the reign of Ramesses II. These tombs were not built in one specific area, but distributed between Lower Qurna, el-Khokha, Asasif and Dra Abu el-Naga West, in areas where space remained. Upper Qurna and Dra Abu el-Naga East were densely populated with Eighteenth Dynasty tombs, leaving little space for later tombs to be built in these areas (see Figure 54). A number of tombs were also built during this period at Deir el-Medina. The mortuary temple of Ramesses II is located close to Lower Qurna (see Figure 55), and while some tombs dating to this reign are located in the area adjacent to the temple, there were more located in the northern areas of el-Asasif and el-Khokha. This suggests that proximity

Figure 53: TTs dated to the early Nineteenth Dynasty prior to the reign of Ramesses II (Author's own using QGIS)

to the royal mortuary temple was not a primary concern when siting a tomb at this time. The area of the necropolis located directly behind the Ramesseum remained clear of tombs throughout the New Kingdom, with no tombs built between Qurnet Murai and Lower Qurna. This may suggest that this area was deliberately left empty of tombs, in a manner similar to the area surrounding the temples at Deir el-Bahri, as this area was closest to the Ramesseum and other royal mortuary temples from the reign of Tuthmosis IV onwards, so was perhaps treated as sacred ground under royal prescription to allow a spatial connection and clear line of sight between the mortuary temple and the western cliffs. Another explanation is the presence of an abandoned Middle Kingdom causeway, which led from the south-western corner of where the Ramesseum now stands towards the Theban Mountains (Winlock 1915: 29-33; see Chapter 3).

Eight TTs are dated to the Nineteenth Dynasty, after the reign of Ramesses II. There are no obvious clusters, with new tombs fitted between the existing Eighteenth Dynasty tombs (see Figure 56).

By the end of the Nineteenth Dynasty, the necropolis had expanded south and east in Lower Qurna, northwards towards the Deir el-Bahri causeway in el-Asasif and included the upper slopes of Dra Abu el-Naga West (see Figures 57 and 58). The Deir el-Medina cemetery also grew significantly during this period. The distinct Nineteenth Dynasty cluster in Dra Abu el-Naga West, the majority of which date between the reigns of Seti I and Ramesses II, could potentially be a result of the view from this area towards the processional route from the Seti I mortuary temple to Deir el-Bahri, or other cultic activity in the area (see Chapter 5).

A large number of tombs are datable only to the Ramesside Period, rather than to a specific reign, so these tombs have been treated as a separate group. These tombs are scattered fairly evenly across the necropolis, with a cluster in Lower Qurna, in relatively close proximity to the Ramesseum. There were also a number of Ramesside tombs built at Deir el-Medina, el-Khokha and el-Asasif, while Dra Abu el-Naga West and East continued to be used (see Figure 59).

The majority of Twentieth Dynasty TTs are not datable to a specific reign (see Figure 60). There was a cluster of six Twentieth Dynasty TTs built at Qurnet Murai, as a result of available space or proximity to late Ramesside mortuary temples in this southern area of the necropolis. There were also a significant number built at Deir el-Medina, and several in Lower Qurna.

Figure 54: TTs dated to the reign of Ramesses II (Author's own using QGIS)

Figure 55: TTs in the Theban Necropolis at the end of the reign of Ramesses II (Author's own using QGIS)

Figure 56: Nineteenth Dynasty TTs dated after the reign of Ramesses II (Author's own using QGIS)

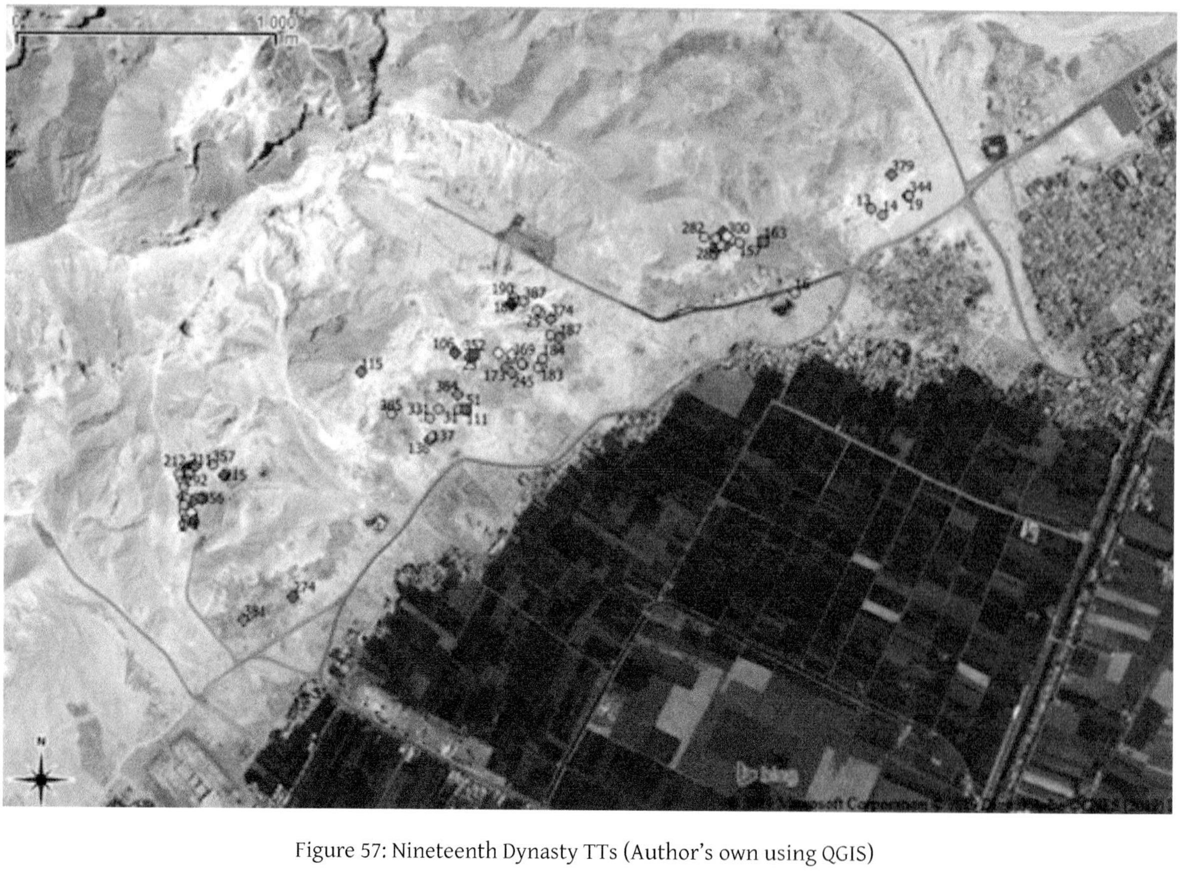

Figure 57: Nineteenth Dynasty TTs (Author's own using QGIS)

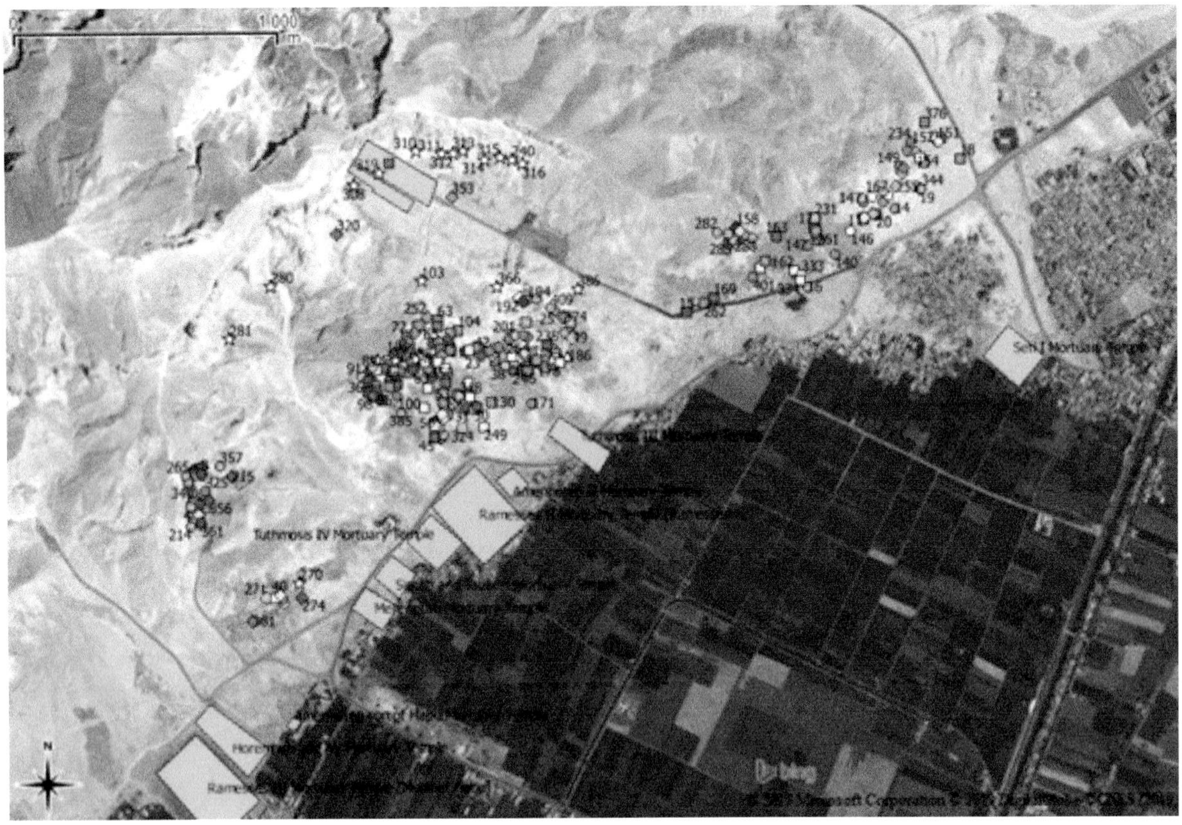

Figure 58: TTs in the Theban Necropolis at the end of the Nineteenth Dynasty (Author's own using QGIS)

Figure 59: Non-reign-specific Ramesside TTs (Author's own using QGIS)

Figure 60: Twentieth Dynasty TTs (Author's own using QGIS)

El-Asasif and el-Khokha remained popular, again probably as a result of space being available. There were relatively few Twentieth Dynasty TTs built at Dra Abu el-Naga, although the number of Ramesside tombs here suggests this area remained popular throughout the New Kingdom. The mortuary temple of Ramesses III at Medinet Habu was located some distance to the south of the southern extent of the necropolis, in an area where the desert edge is wider, and the high cliffs are located some distance to the west of the temple. This makes this area unsuitable for siting private tombs, and it would be difficult to build private tombs in this area to overlook the temple (see Figure 61).

The distribution of tombs during the Nineteenth and Twentieth Dynasties reflects an expansion of the existing Eighteenth Dynasty necropolis, utilising available space, particularly in el-Khokha and Dra Abu el-Naga (see Figures 62 and 63). All areas used for tomb-building during the Eighteenth Dynasty remained popular, with the exception of Upper Qurna which had become saturated with tombs due to its desirable location and elevated position. Lower Qurna remained popular throughout the New Kingdom, expanding southwards and eastwards towards the line of royal mortuary temples. There would have been no distinction between el-Khokha and Qurna in antiquity, so the increase in popularity of northern Khokha in the later New Kingdom is again a result of this natural expansion. There may have been an additional factor in the shortage of new tombs in Upper Qurna in the Ramesside Period. A path once existed leading east to west, connecting el-Khokha to Upper Qurna, so tombs were originally laid out on either side of the road, aligned with this path. However after the Amarna Period, TT41 (Hor-SI) was built at the end of the path, followed by TT106 (SI-RII) and TT23 (Mer), resulting in the lack of connection between el-Khokha and Upper Qurna, and thus reducing the use of Upper Qurna during the Ramesside Period to only two new tombs (TT114-Dyn 20, and TT115-Dyn 19), and three reused tombs (TT65, TT68 and TT71- all reused Dyn 20) (Kampp 1996: 122).

El-Asasif increased in popularity later in the New Kingdom, which may indicate a change in permission required to be buried in this desirable location, as it seems unlikely that this would not have been the burial site of choice for Eighteenth Dynasty tomb owners, when cultic and building activity at Deir el-Bahri was at its peak. This could be as a result of the natural expansion northwards of the necropolis as other areas became full. Dra Abu el-Naga was never as densely populated with tombs as Qurna, but it did remain in constant,

Figure 61: Aerial view of Medinet Habu showing flat plain to the west (Author's own)

steady use throughout the New Kingdom, reflecting its proximity to the early New Kingdom royal burials and associated cultic activity, and the processional route of the BFV. The cemetery at Deir el-Medina expanded significantly throughout the New Kingdom.

From the end of the reign of Ramesses II onwards, particularly towards the end of the Nineteenth Dynasty and throughout the Twentieth Dynasty, fewer elite tombs were built at Thebes, potentially due to a shift of power to the north with the move of the Ramesside capital to the delta. This would have led to the elite being buried in Pi-Ramesses near where they worked, as indicated by discovery of a number of burials dating from the reign of Ramesses II, later in the Ramesside Period, and some more precisely dated to the reign of Ramesses III (Bietak and Forstner-Müller 2011: 47-49). There have however been relatively few tombs and funerary objects discovered at Pi-Ramesses, none of which can be linked with certainty to burials of members of the local, regional, or country-wide elite. Considering that most Egyptian cities, not to mention royal residences such as Pi-Ramesses, had cemeteries in their vicinities, serving at least the local elite, this

Figure 62: Nineteenth and Twentieth Dynasty TTs (Author's own using QGIS)

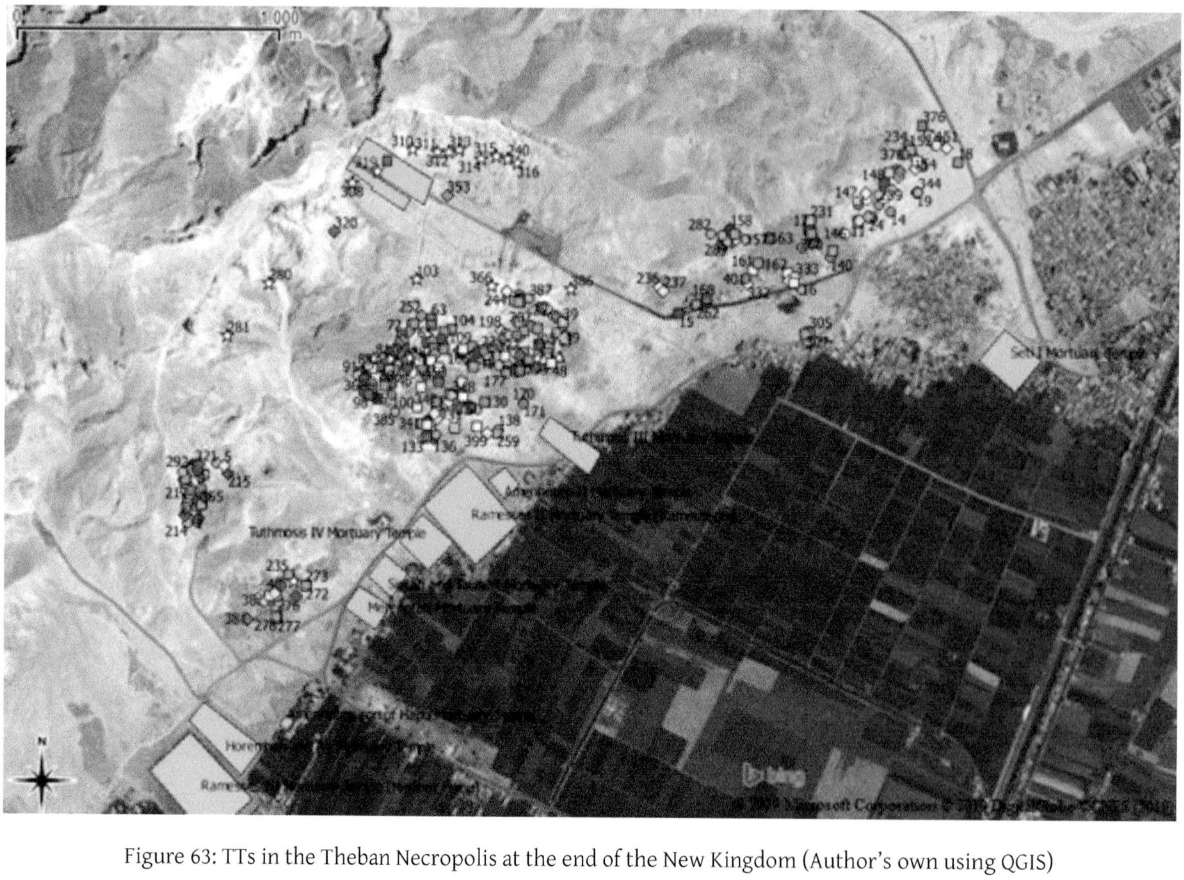

Figure 63: TTs in the Theban Necropolis at the end of the New Kingdom (Author's own using QGIS)

Figure 64: Part of the New Kingdom necropolis at Saqqara (Author's own)

finding is striking, suggesting that these burials might have never been located there. This apparent absence may be at least partly due to the poor preservation of the site and the construction of modern settlements over potential cemeteries (Franzmeier and Moje 2018: 114-120).

There were also numerous elite burials at Saqqara from the mid-Eighteenth Dynasty until the early Twentieth Dynasty (see Figure 64), due to its proximity to the administrative capital of Memphis, although relatively few have yet been found (Martin 1991: 31-33 and 194-197; Zivie 2007: 17-20 and 139-141; Staring 2015: 9-13; Strudwick and Strudwick 1999: 142). A large number of these burials date to the Ramesside Period, and the Nineteenth Dynasty in particular (Franzmeier and Moje 2018: 120), however the number and quality of Ramesside tombs at Saqqara declined rapidly after the reign of Ramesses II (Raven 2018: 246). No tombs from the late Twentieth Dynasty have yet been found at Saqqara, although textual evidence suggests that they exist and are waiting to be found (Martin 1991: 189). There were also a number of Ramesside officials buried at Sedment and Tell Basta (Franzmeier and Moje 2018: 120-121), and in provincial cemeteries (Auenmüller 2013: 466-468; Raven 2018: 247). There is however a shortage of good quality tombs from the Memphite region from the second half of the Twentieth Dynasty, suggesting a failing funerary economy by the end of the New Kingdom (Cooney 2018: 63), with new tombs being constructed only scarcely throughout the country.

Certainly, by the Twentieth Dynasty, there were fewer resources available for tomb-building (Cooney 2014: 16-28), and a lack of space for new burials (Cooney 2008: 79-115; Cooney 2014: 22). There also appears to have been a preference by the mid-Twentieth Dynasty for larger undecorated tomb caches containing hundreds of coffins, rather than smaller decorated tombs constructed earlier in the New Kingdom (Cooney 2008: 99; Cooney 2018: 67-68). This suggests another potential reason for the decline in tomb building in the Twentieth Dynasty. The wide-spread tomb robbery detailed in Papyrus Abbott (P. BM EA 10221), suggests that the majority of elite tombs had been violated by Year 19 of the reign of Ramesses IX (Peet 1930: 37-42), which may also have influenced a potential change in burial practice. By the reign of Ramesses XI, state-sanctioned, systematic looting of tombs, as detailed in P. BM EA 10375, was commonplace (Taylor 2001: 182), even being perpetrated by the guardians of the tombs (Cooney 2014: 22). Evidence of strikes among the workmen from Deir el-Medina from the reign of Ramesses III is also suggestive of a failing economy, such as those detailed in the Turin Strike Papyrus.

Patterns of Tomb Reuse

A number of TTs were reused throughout the New Kingdom (see Figure 65 and Table 4). The highest concentration is found in Upper Qurna, where the earliest examples of tomb reuse occurred, with a number dating to the early Eighteenth Dynasty. A number of tombs were reused in Lower Qurna and el-Khokha, but there are only four confirmed and two possible cases of reuse in Dra Abu el-Naga East, and two in Dra Abu el-Naga West. There is only evidence of one reused tomb in Qurnet Murai, and there is no evidence of tomb reuse in Deir el-Medina or el-Asasif. Each example is discussed individually within the chapter relating to its location.

The majority of reuse occurred towards the end of the New Kingdom (see Figure 66), as a necessity when the lack of resources due to the failing economy and socio-political instability made it difficult to construct new tombs. Other cases of reuse occur within living memory, and during periods of prosperity when tomb building was flourishing. Some of these examples appear to be as a result of family connections or to commemorate the deceased, as suggested by Strudwick (2010: 254), to associate the later occupant(s) of the tomb deliberately with the original owner. This was not always with a family member, but often an illustrious colleague or superior. Other examples of a quick re-use cannot be easily explained by this theory but may just be as a result of a desirable location or view.

The reuse of tombs in the Twentieth Dynasty is viewed in different ways. Many scholars believe that tombs were reused at this time due to a lack of funds, resources and space (see above), while others believe that it was an attempt at continuity by connecting with the local past, as a result of lack of space alone. This problem was solved by cutting new tombs into the side wall of existing sunken courtyards in the flatter areas of the necropolis, or by cutting into the façade on the steeper slopes, to create new Ramesside style tombs. Abandoned or unfinished older tombs were considered neutral spaces to be adapted, but the scale of work and labour this took, for example in TT30, is often overlooked, and not to be confused with a lack of resources (Bács 2011: 4-10).

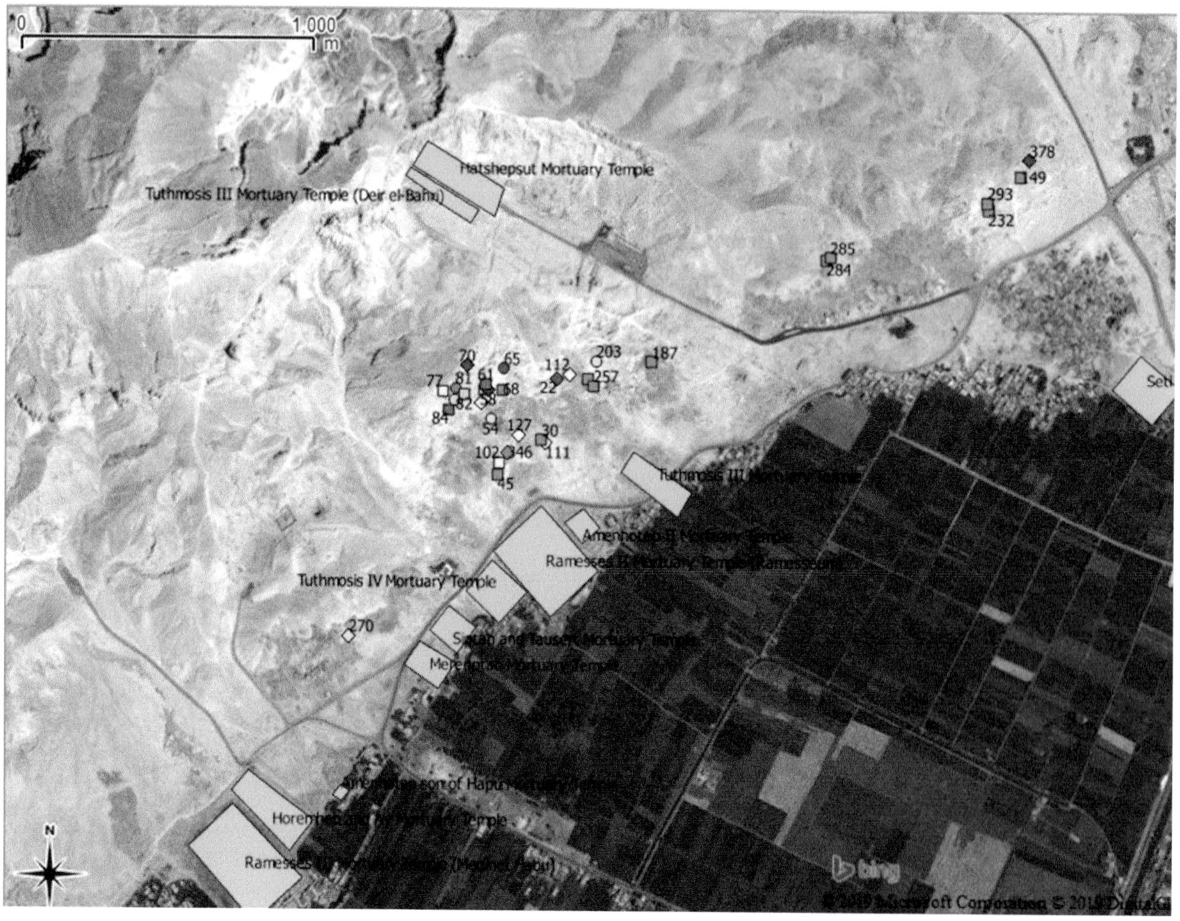

Figure 65: Reused TTs in Theban Necropolis at the end of the New Kingdom (shown by date of first reuse) (Author's own using QGIS)

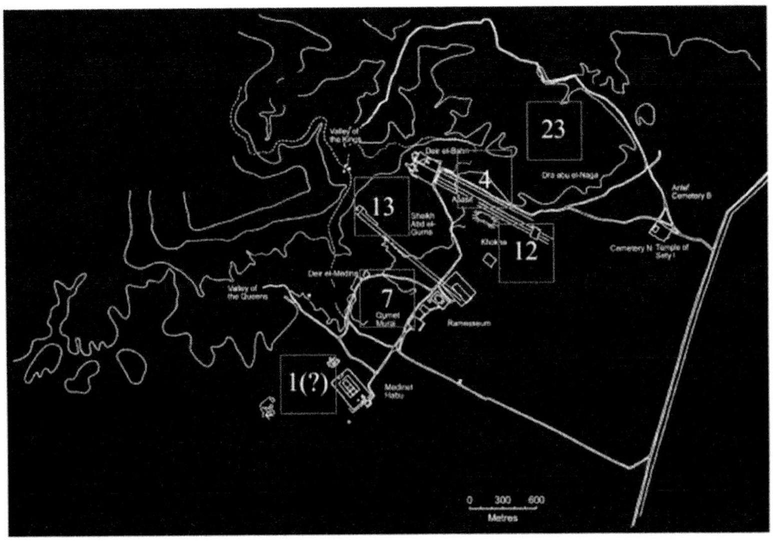

Figure 66: Distributional patterning of Twentieth Dynasty tombs, with numbers indicating the number of tombs attributed to the Twentieth Dynasty in each area (Bács 2011: Figure 5 - Courtesy of Dr Tamás A. Bács)

Table 4: New Kingdom TT Reuse

Area	Reused Tombs	Original Date	Date(s) of Reuse
Qurnet Murai	TT270	MK	Ram
Upper Qurna	TT46 TT54 TT58 TT61 TT65 TT68 TT70 TT77 TT81 TT82 TT84 TT87 TT119	End Dyn 17-Dyn 18 AIII AIII MK Hat AIII Dyn 18 - AIII TIV-AIII MK MK TIII-AII Hat-TIII MK	AIII-AIV RII Dyn 19 and Dyn 20 TI-TIII RIX Dyn 20 Dyn 20/21 AIII Ah - Hat Hat-TIII AII TIV-end Dyn18 Hat-TIII
Lower Qurna	TT30 TT45 TT102 TT111 TT127 TT346	AIII AII Hat-TIII RII Hat-TIII Dyn 18- AIII	Dyn 20 Dyn 20 AIII Ram Ram RIV
El-Khokha	TT22 TT112 TT174 TT187 TT203 TT257 TT294	TIII/AII TIII/AII Dyn 18 Dyn 19 Dyn 18 AIII/AIV TIII	AII/AIII Ram Dyn 20 Dyn 20 RII Dyn 20 Ram
Dra Abu el-Naga West	TT284 TT285	Dyn 19 Dyn 19	Dyn 20 Dyn 20
Dra Abu el-Naga East	TT149 TT152? TT232 TT293? TT378	Dyn 18 AIII-Amarna Late Dyn 17/Dyn 18 Ram Dyn 18	Dyn 20 Ram Dyn 20 Dyn 20 Dyn 19

Chapter 5: Dra Abu el-Naga

(See Appendices 3 and 4)

Location

Dra Abu el-Naga is situated at the north-eastern end of the Theban necropolis, enclosed by the northern edge of the Deir el-Bahri causeway to the south, and the modern road leading to the Valley of the Kings, the wadi of Biban el-Moluk to the north (see Figure 67). The tombs in this area are located between 80m and 140m above sea level, with the flood-plain in this area beginning at 80m above sea level (see Figure 68). Most tombs are scattered in a relatively narrow band along the southern and eastern slopes of the hill, with some located in the relatively flat area close to the cultivation, before the ground level rises steeply into the Theban hills. There are 84 TTs in this area, all dating to the New Kingdom, with the exception of four (TT12, TT167, TT232 and TT396) which may date to either the late Seventeenth or early Eighteenth Dynasty.

There are no earlier tombs among these TTs, although earlier structures do exist in this area as Dra Abu el-Naga was used as a cemetery from the First Intermediate Period onwards. The Middle Kingdom Intef cemetery at el-Tarif (Arnold 1976; Snape 2011: 166-167; Winlock 1915: 13-24 and Winlock 1947: 8-57) seems likely to have extended further south into Dra Abu el-Naga during the Eleventh Dynasty had not Montuhotep II transferred the royal cemetery to Deir el-Bahri during his reign (Winlock 1915: 24-29; Winlock 1947: 25-27 and 38-44). After this shift, Dra Abu el-Naga was used occasionally for burials, either facing Deir el-Bahri or en-route between el-Tarif and Deir el-Bahri. During the Twelfth and Thirteenth Dynasty a number of burials took place in Dra Abu el-Naga, spreading northwards from the end of the Deir el-Bahri causeway all the way to the Intef cemetery at el-Tarif (Winlock 1915: 36-37).

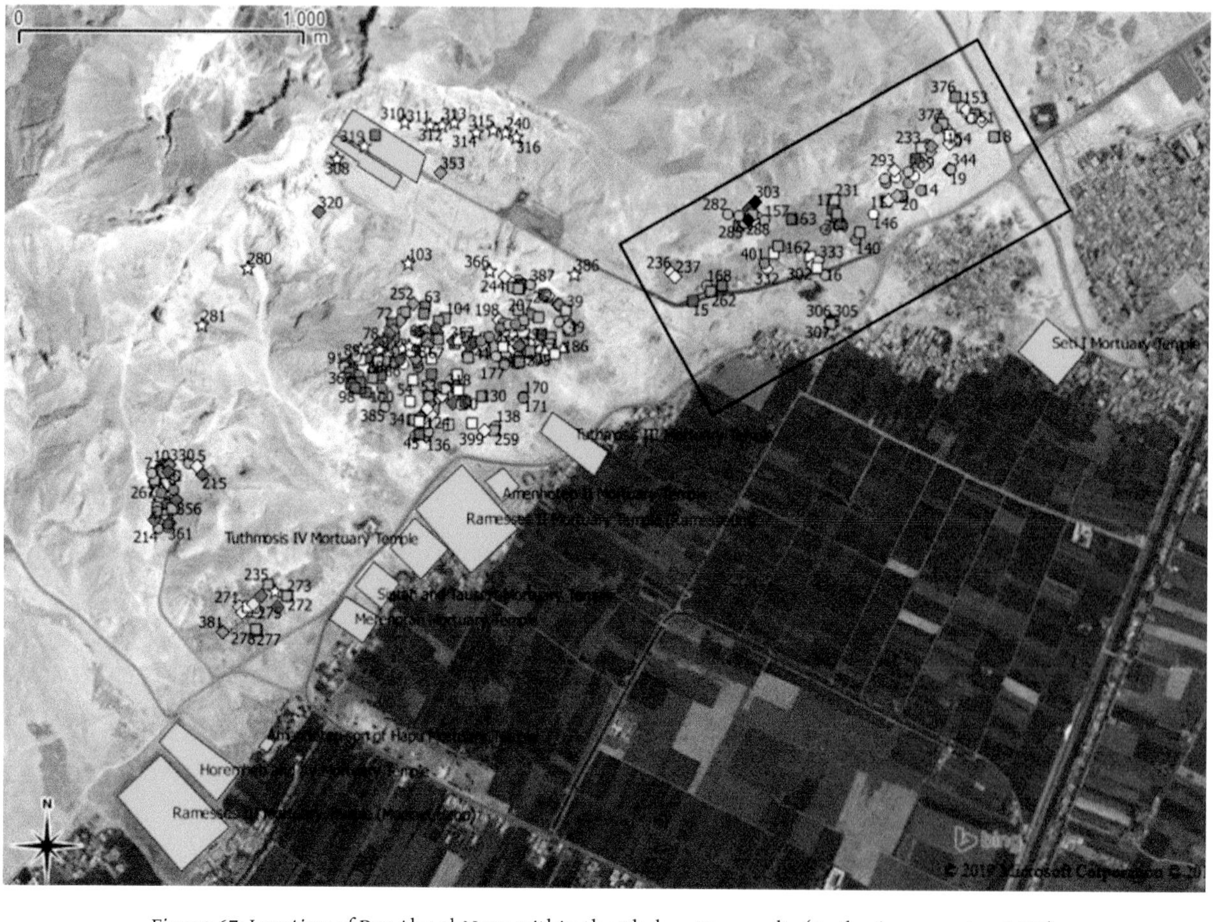

Figure 67: Location of Dra Abu el-Naga within the Theban Necropolis (Author's own using QGIS)

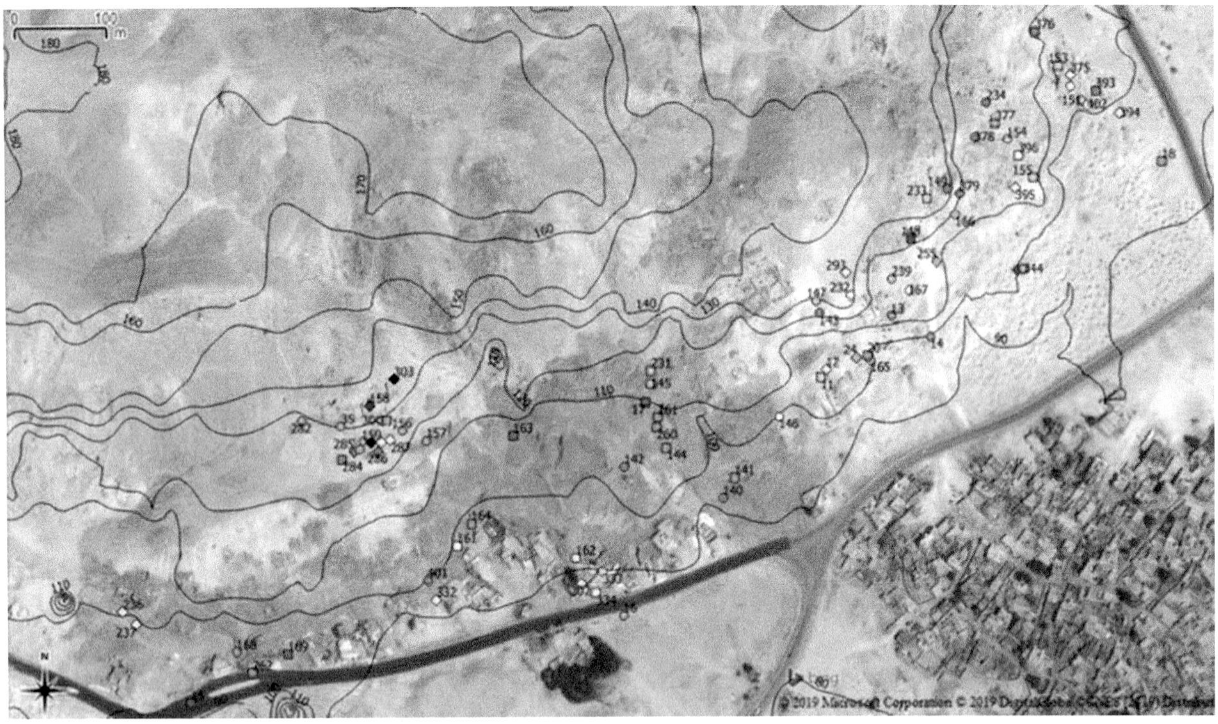

Figure 68: Landscape of Dra Abu el-Naga (Author's own using QGIS)

It was not until the Sixteenth and Seventeenth Dynasties that Dra Abu el-Naga was used as a royal cemetery, with the royal pyramids being arranged chronologically from north to south, according to Papyrus Abbott (Winlock 1947: 105-08). Two of these tombs were discovered at Dra Abu el-Naga in the early Nineteenth century but have since been lost so cannot be precisely located (Winlock 1924: 240). Winlock discovered a mud-brick pyramid which he attributed to a further royal tomb (Winlock 1924: 237-243), and the location of one tomb is now known, that of Nubkheperra Intef, in addition to a number of funerary objects which have been identified from as yet undiscovered tombs (Miniaci 2009: 19-25). It seems likely that this area held a number of Second Intermediate Period royal burials, and the associated private burials located close to the resting place of their king, of which a number have been discovered, but are numbered separately to the Theban Tomb numbering system so are not included here.

The popularity of this area in the late Seventeenth Dynasty continued into the early Eighteenth Dynasty, when several members of the royal family and high officials continued to be buried in this area (Miniaci 2009: 25-26), although from the reign of Tuthmosis I the kings themselves were buried in the Valley of the Kings. The tombs of Amenhotep I and Ahmose-Nefertari (K93.11 and K93.12) are also believed to have been situated in Dra Abu el-Naga East (Polz 2012: 115) (see Figure 69). This site was used sporadically throughout the New Kingdom, but the next relatively large concentration of burials was dated to the Ramesside period, when a number of tombs were built at the western end of Dra Abu el-Naga.

The Division between Dra Abu el-Naga West and East

For the purpose of this study this area has been divided into two areas, Dra Abu el-Naga West and Dra Abu el-Naga East, with three of the tombs classified as outlying tombs. This division follows that made by Kampp (1996) when she divided the area into Dra Abu el-Naga I (Plan VI), here referred to as Dra Abu el-Naga West, and Dra Abu el-Naga II (Plan VII), here referred to as Dra Abu el-Naga East. The division also falls along the path of a natural wadi, providing a topographical break between the areas (see Figure 69).

The Evolution of Dra Abu el-Naga

Six TTs date to the late Seventeenth or early Eighteenth Dynasty, prior to the reign of Hatshepsut, in addition to K93.11 and K93.12. They are all located between the centre and eastern end of Dra Abu el-Naga, between 100m and 120m above sea level. With the exception of TT396, they form a loose cluster around K93.11 and K93.12 (see Figure 70), which have been identified as the tomb complex of Amenhotep I and Ahmose-Nefertari (Polz 2007: 172-197). The presence of these royal burials with monumental pylons, in addition to the Seventeenth Dynasty royal tombs, explain the preference for this eastern area of Dra Abu el-Naga

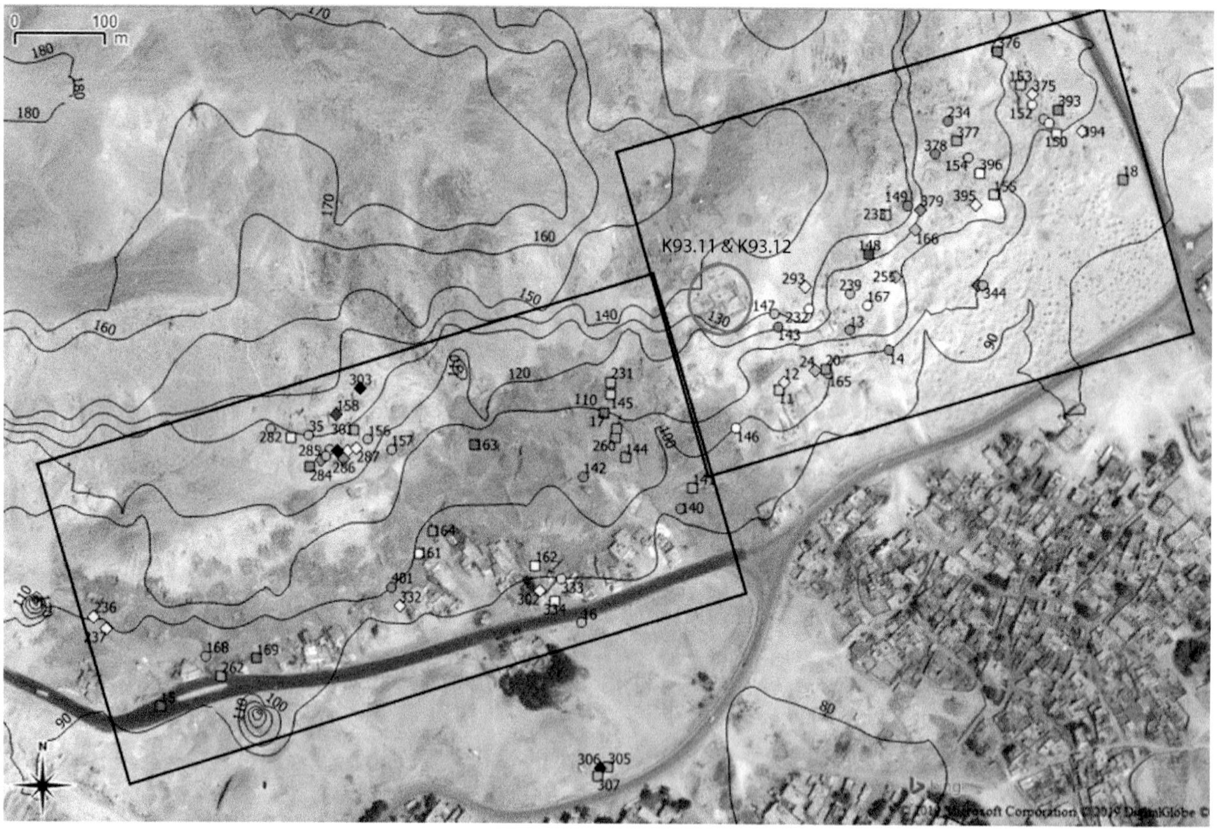

Figure 69: Dra Abu el-Naga TTs (indicating location of K93.11 and K93.12) (Author's own using QGIS)

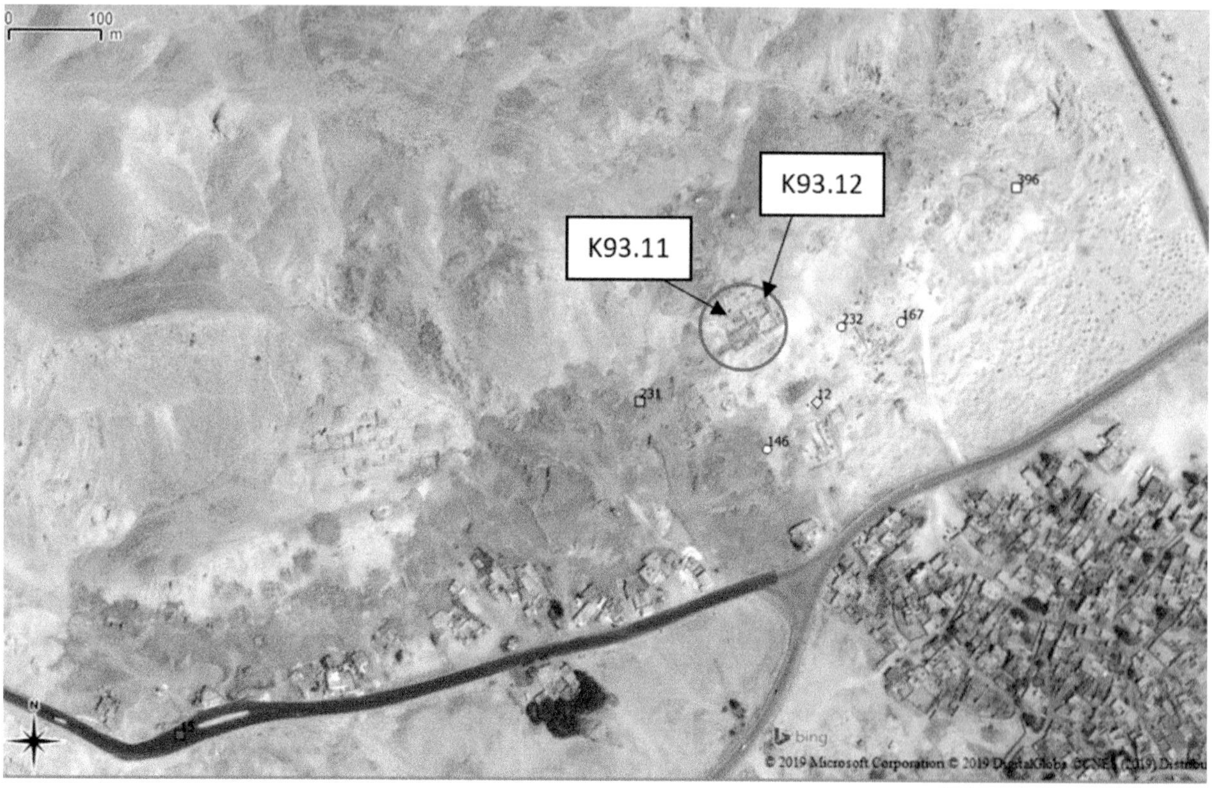

Figure 70: TTs in Dra Abu el-Naga prior to the reign of Hatshepsut (indicating location of K93.11 and K93.12) (Author's own using QGIS)

Figure 71: TTs in Dra Abu el-Naga at the end of the reign of Tuthmosis III (indicating location of K93.11 and K93.12) (Author's own using QGIS)

during this period. This area is also in close proximity to the el-Tarif Intef cemetery, the mortuary temple of Menisut, and the *wadi* leading to the Valley of the Kings (from Tuthmosis I onwards). There is also evidence of cultic activity from the early Eighteenth Dynasty onwards in the area of K93.11 and K93.12, and the Intef tombs (Polz 2007: 172-197), which would influence later tomb placement.

None of the TTs in Dra Abu el-Naga are datable to a specific reign between that of Ahmose and Tuthmosis II. There are three tombs that can only be dated to either Hatshepsut or Tuthmosis III, one dating up to the reign of Hatshepsut, and a further seven tombs dating to Tuthmosis III. By the end of the reign of Tuthmosis III the tombs had spread westwards, closer to the Deir el-Bahri causeway where the temples of Hatshepsut and Tuthmosis III were located, and the Qurna temple of Tuthmosis III. These tombs generally follow the natural contours of the area, but they are also located slightly further down the slopes as they range from 90m and 120m above sea level (see Figure 71). A defined cluster of four tombs, side by side, can be identified at the east of the area (TT154, TT155, TT234 and TT396). Another cluster of four tombs are located several hundred metres to the west in two adjacent pairs (TT11 and TT12, TT20 and TT24), all within 60m of each other. TT12 is the earliest of these tombs, dating to the late Seventeenth or early Eighteenth Dynasty, while the other three date between Tuthmosis II and III. Close to this cluster are another three of the late Seventeenth or early Eighteenth Dynasty tombs (TT146, TT167 and TT232). In the centre of Dra Abu el-Naga there are five tombs in close proximity (TT144, TT145, TT231, TT260 and TT261) along the *wadi* (see below). TT231 is the earliest, datable only to the early Eighteenth Dynasty, while the others are close in date, dating to either Hatshepsut or Tuthmosis III (TT145) or to Tuthmosis III (TT144, TT260 and TT261). TT164 (TIII) lies to the south of the other tombs at the mouth of another *wadi*. Tombs dating to the early Eighteenth Dynasty, and to Hatshepsut or Tuthmosis III in particular, are arranged on either side of the 'Forecourt of Amun' and the processional approach to K93.11 and K93.12 (see below).

By the end of the Amarna Period the tombs in Dra Abu el-Naga continued to spread westwards towards the Deir el-Bahri causeway, and also northwards along the modern road to the Valley of the Kings (see Figure 72). There were two additions at the east of the area dating to Tuthmosis IV (TT376 and TT393), and a further two tombs dating between Amenhotep III and the Amarna Period (TT150 and TT152). There were a further three in the west, all dating to Amenhotep III (TT161, TT162 and TT334). Both groups were not in particularly close proximity but show some evidence of clustering by reign.

By the end of the Eighteenth Dynasty, the east of Dra Abu el-Naga had a higher concentration of tombs than

Figure 72: TTs in Dra Abu el-Naga at the end of the Amarna Period (indicating location of K93.11 and K93.12) (Author's own using QGIS)

the west, but both ends were still in use (see Figure 73). Throughout the dynasty the cemetery at Dra Abu el-Naga had expanded slightly both eastwards and westwards, and while the tombs generally remained in a line parallel to the modern road, the band of land in use had widened in the eastern and central areas to include the lower slopes.

In the late Eighteenth or early Nineteenth Dynasty, TT166 and TT255 were built in close proximity within the eastern half of this area. TT19 (SI-RII) and TT344 (RII) were located adjacent to each other on the lower slopes at the eastern end of Dra Abu el-Naga. A larger cluster emerged in the west of Dra Abu el-Naga where seven new tombs were built, all dating to the reign of Ramesses II (TT35, TT156, TT157, TT282, TT284, TT288 and TT289). This is a clear example of clustering by date and was also the first time the necropolis here had expanded into the upper slopes in this western area (see Figure 74). During this reign, TT16 was built at the lowest point of the area, so Dra Abu el-Naga expanded both northwards, and to a lesser extent, southwards.

By the end of the dynasty, the western cluster of tombs initially dating to the reign of Ramesses II had grown significantly. This cluster now included twelve tombs, as five tombs had been built adjacent to the existing seven (TT158, TT283, TT285, TT286 and TT300) with another in close proximity (TT163) (see Figures 75 and 76). Several other tombs had been built across Dra Abu el-Naga during the Nineteenth Dynasty, but this large cluster was the most significant development.

Relatively few tombs were built in the Theban necropolis during the Twentieth Dynasty. In Dra Abu el-Naga these later tombs were again distributed across the area in both the west and east. The necropolis expanded slightly further to the west as two tombs were built adjacent to each other, close to the Deir el-Bahri causeway (TT236 and TT237). There were also two outlying tombs (TT305 and TT307), which formed an isolated cluster to the south, with TT306 which dated to the Twentieth or Twenty First Dynasty. There are a number of Ramesside, and Twentieth Dynasty tombs located at the eastern end of Dra Abu el-Naga, but without precise dating to a specific reign(s), a date connection cannot be proven. The other Twentieth Dynasty tombs were scattered across the area and show no evidence of clustering by date (see Figure 77). The aforementioned western cluster of tombs on the upper slopes also expanded further to include 17 tombs (see Figure 78), while the area to the south of them remained unoccupied.

Figure 73: TTs in Dra Abu el-Naga at the end of the Eighteenth Dynasty (indicating location of K93.11 and K93.12) (Author's own using QGIS)

Figure 74: TTs in Dra Abu el-Naga at the end of reign of Ramesses II (indicating location of K93.11 and K93.12) (Author's own using QGIS)

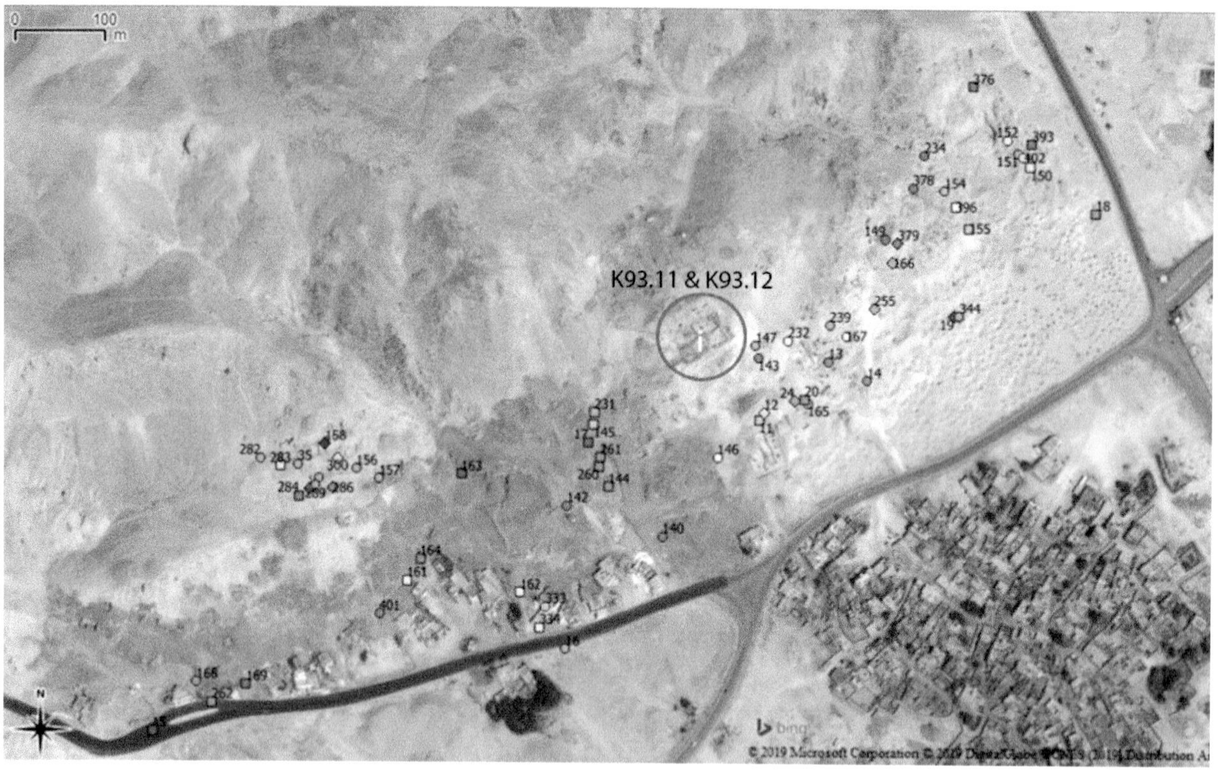

Figure 75: TTs in Dra Abu el-Naga at the end of the Nineteenth Dynasty (indicating location of K93.11 and K93.12) (Author's own using QGIS)

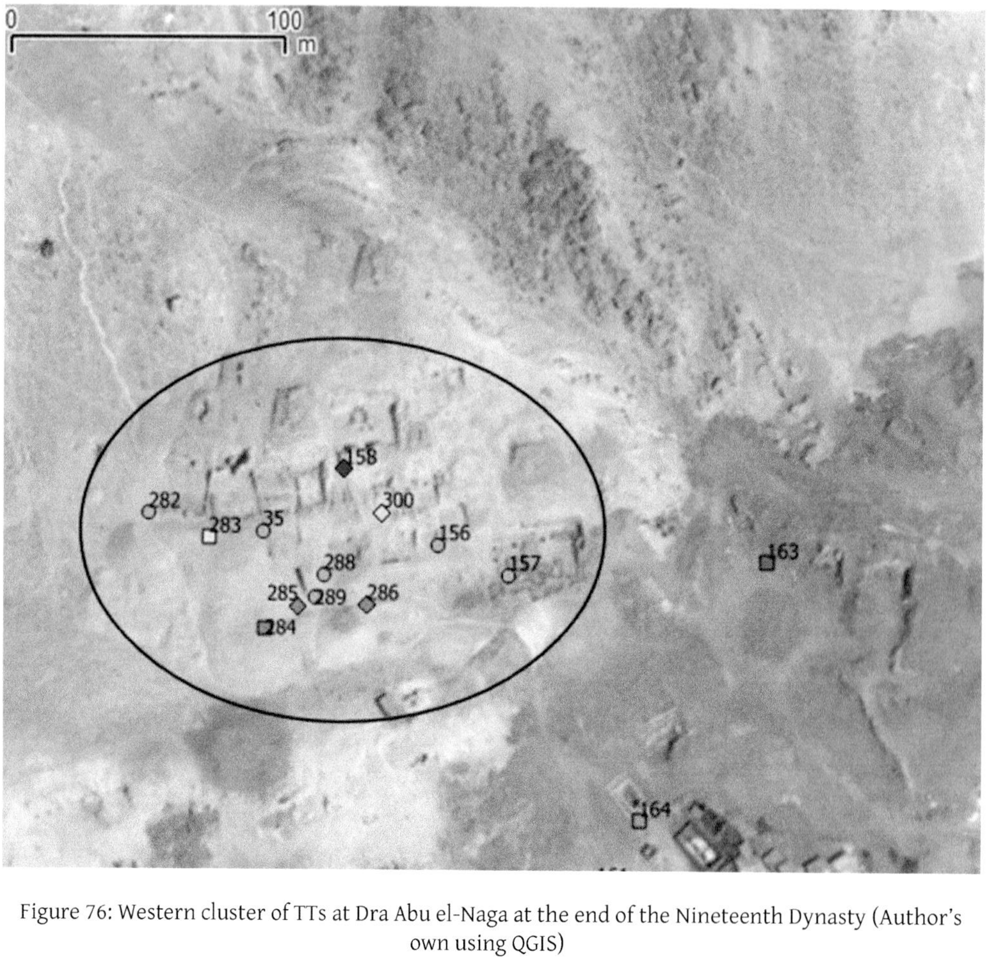

Figure 76: Western cluster of TTs at Dra Abu el-Naga at the end of the Nineteenth Dynasty (Author's own using QGIS)

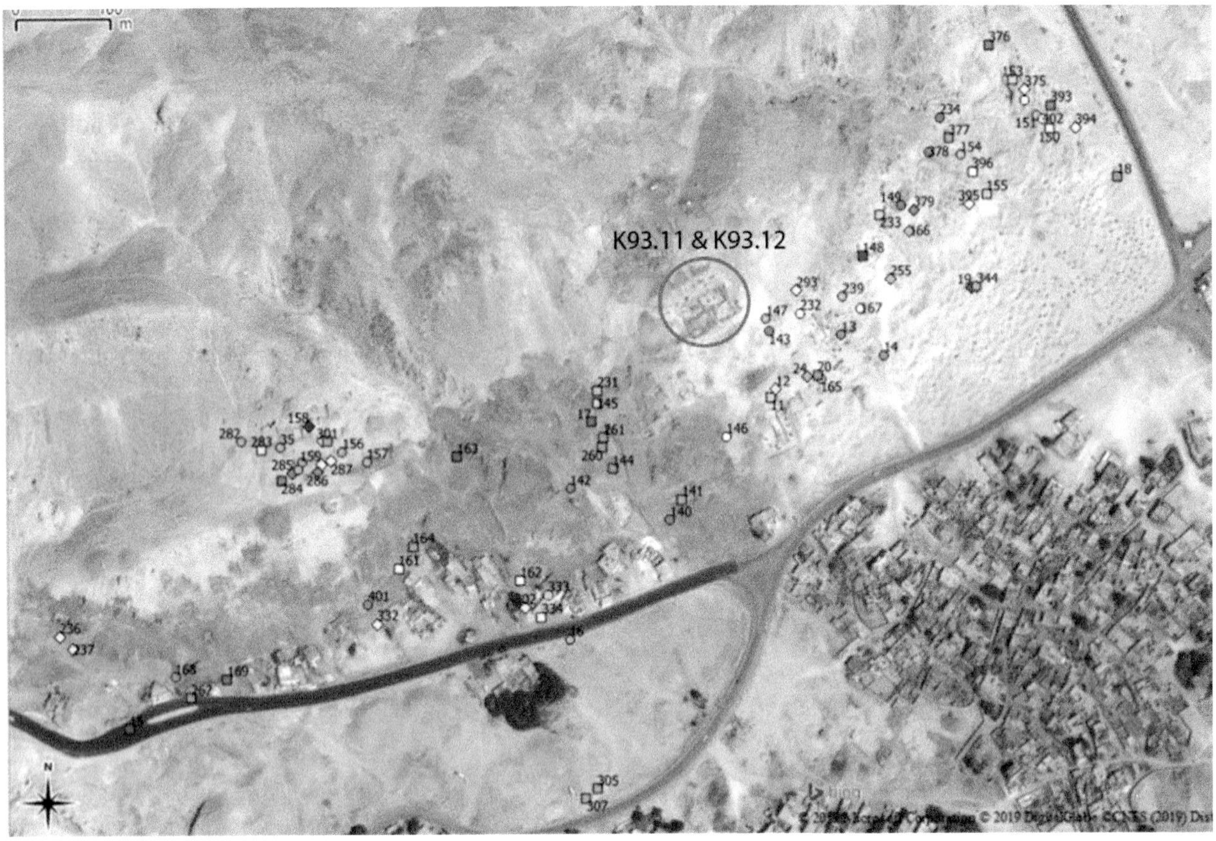

Figure 77: TTs in Dra Abu el-Naga at the end of the New Kingdom (indicating location of K93.11 and K93.12) (Author's own using QGIS)

Figure 78: Western cluster of TTs in Dra Abu el-Naga at the end of the New Kingdom (Author's own using QGIS)

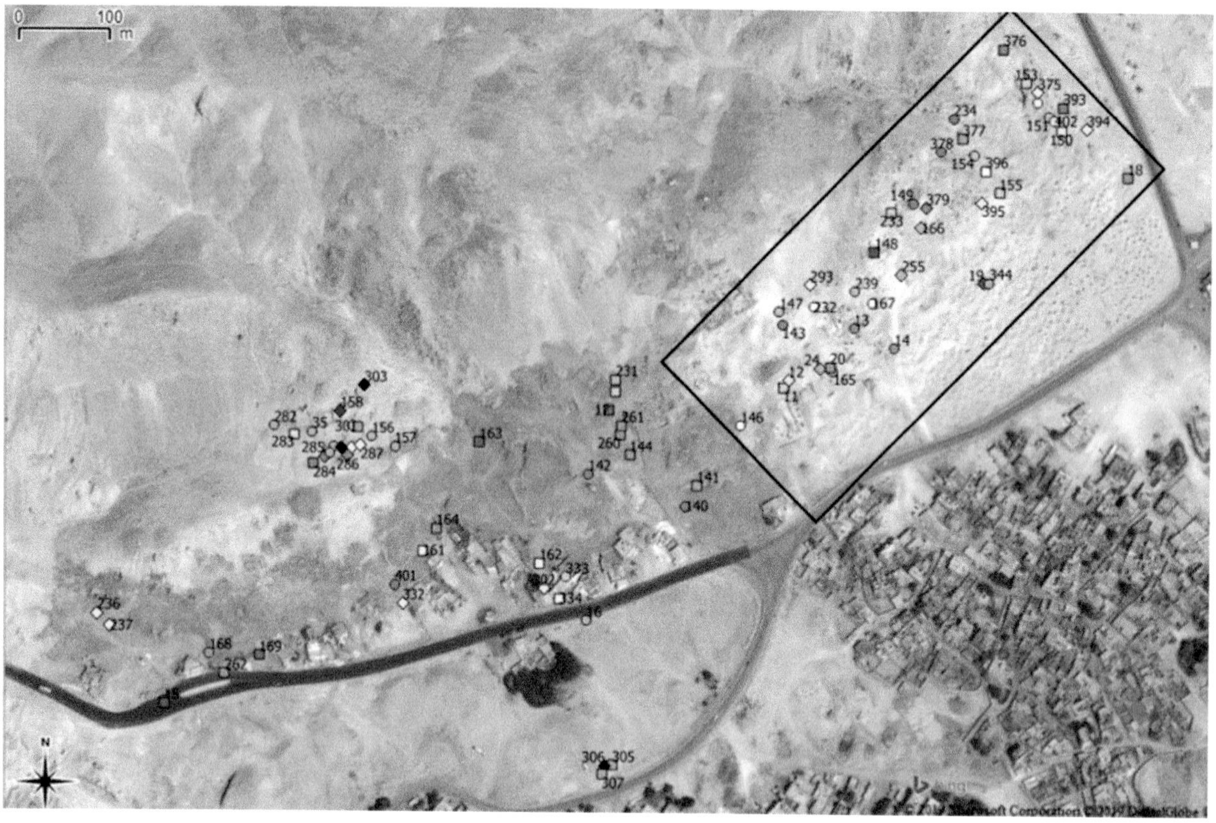

Figure 79: Location of Dra Abu el-Naga East (Author's own using QGIS)

Dra Abu el-Naga East

(See Appendix 3)

Location

Dra Abu el-Naga East is bordered by two modern roads, one to the south leading eastwards towards el-Tarif, and one to the east, leading northwards towards the Valley of the Kings (see Figure 79). Dra Abu el-Naga East contains 39 TTs, again distributed along the edge of the modern road, between 90m and 130m above sea level. The height of the floodplain in this area begins at 80m above sea level (see Figure 80). The tombs in this area are more uniformly distributed than in Dra Abu el-Naga West, with no immediately obvious clustering (see Figure 81). The band of tombs is wider and sits along the natural contours of these slopes.

Date of Use

Dra Abu el-Naga East was in use as a cemetery earlier in the New Kingdom than Dra Abu el-Naga West. The majority of tombs in this eastern area date to the beginning of the New Kingdom, as 27 of the 39 tombs here were built during the Eighteenth Dynasty (or possibly even the late Seventeenth Dynasty in the case of five). This is a far greater percentage of earlier tombs than in Dra Abu el-Naga West, where the majority of tombs date to the Nineteenth and Twentieth Dynasties (see Table 5). The popularity of eastern area of the site at this time is explained by the proximity of the Intef cemetery and the presence of a number of Seventeenth Dynasty and early Eighteenth Dynasty royal burials in this area, as mentioned above.

Five tombs in Dra Abu el-Naga East date to the late Seventeenth or early Eighteenth Dynasty (TT12, TT146, TT167, TT232 and TT396). These early tombs are all located in the western section of Dra Abu el-Naga East, close to K93.11 and K93.12 (apart from TT396 which lies further to the east), but do not form a distinct cluster. Mapping the Seventeenth Dynasty royal tombs in the area would be helpful to establish a pattern here. Dra Abu el-Naga East was used as a cemetery consistently throughout the Eighteenth Dynasty, with a peak in usage between the reigns of Tuthmosis IV and Amenhotep III, when eight tombs were built here (TT147, TT150, TT151, T152, TT165, TT239, TT376 and TT393). Five of these tombs formed a cluster at the eastern end of Dra Abu el-Naga (TT150, TT151, TT152, TT376 and TT393), together with three Ramesside tombs (TT153, TT375 and TT394). TT402 also forms part of this cluster, suggesting a possible date of Tuthmosis IV for its construction (PM I: 444), purely on the grounds of this grouping. The

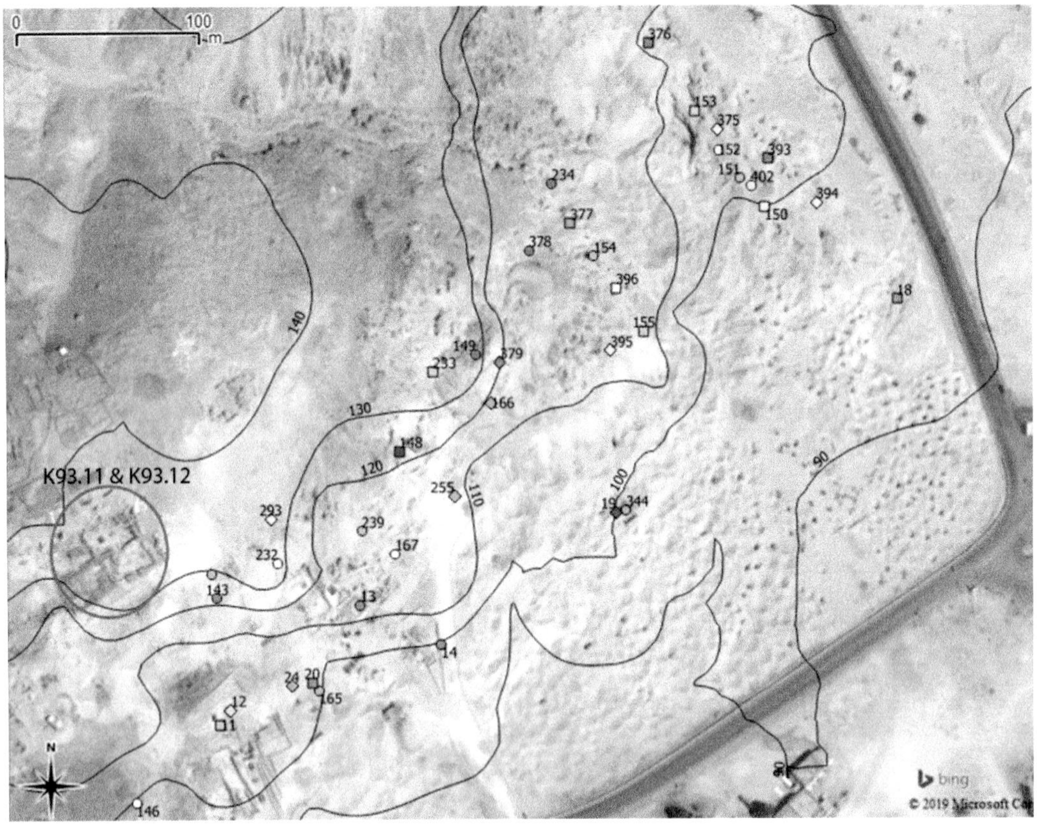

Figure 80: Landscape of Dra Abu el-Naga East (indicating location of K93.11 and K93.12) (Author's own using QGIS)

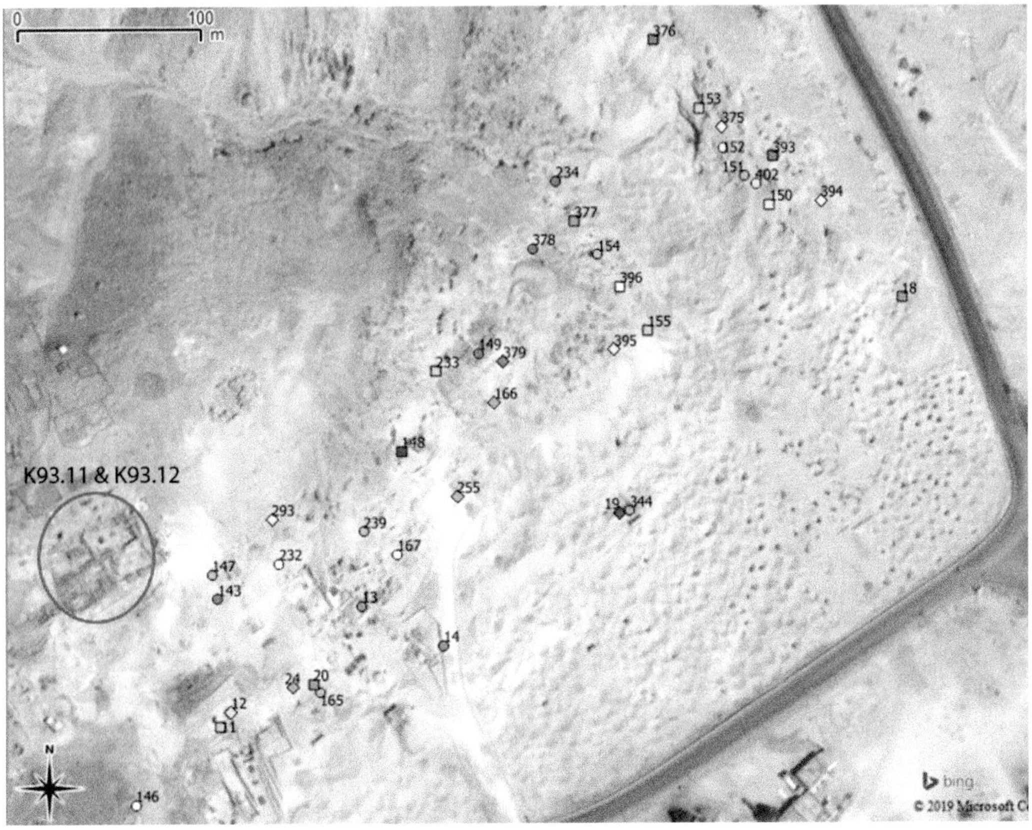

Figure 81: TTs of Dra Abu el-Naga East (indicating location of K93.11 and K93.12) (Author's own using QGIS)

Table 5: Dra Abu el-Naga East TTs distributed by most likely date

Date	No. of Tombs	Tombs
Late Dyn 17 /early 18	*****	TT12, TT146, TT167, TT232, TT396
Dynasty 18	*	TT149
TII /(Hat)/ TIII	*	TT24
Dyn 18 – Hat	*	TT234
Hat / TIII	**	TT11, TT155
Dyn 18 - TIII	*	TT154
Dyn 18 (– TIII / AII)	*	TT378
Dyn 18 – TIII/ AIII	*	TT393
TIII	*	TT18
TIII / AII	**	TT20, TT143
TIV	*	TT376
TIV / AIII	****	TT147, TT151, TT165, TT239, TT393
AIII - Amarna	**	TT150, TT152
Late Dyn 18 - Tut	*	TT402
Hor - SI	**	TT166, TT255
Dyn 19	*	TT379
SI / RII	*	TT19
Late Dyn 19	**	TT13, TT14
Late Dyn 19 / early 20	***	TT153, TT233, TT377
RII	*	TT344
RIII - RV	*	TT148
Ram	*	TT293, TT375, TT394, TT395

other three tombs dating between Tuthmosis IV and Amenhotep III lie a short distance to the west, within 100m of each other (TT147, TT165 and TT239).

There is another cluster of seven tombs located a short distance to the west of the eastern-most group discussed above, at the same altitude of 110m above sea level. Five of the tombs in this cluster date to the early and mid-Eighteenth Dynasty, up to the reign of Tuthmosis III (TT154, TT155, TT234, TT378 and TT396), while the other two date to the Ramesside Period (TT377 and TT395). Of the other Eighteenth Dynasty tombs, TT11 and TT12 are located in particularly close proximity in the west of the area, and both date to the early to mid-Eighteenth Dynasty up to the reign of Tuthmosis III. TT143 and TT147 are located adjacent to each other, 50m to the north, and both date to the mid-Eighteenth Dynasty, between Tuthmosis III and Amenhotep III. TT20, TT24 and TT165 also form a close group, just 30m to the east of TT11 and TT12, and all date between Tuthmosis II and Amenhotep III, so are relatively close in date. Together with TT11 and TT12, this makes a cluster of five Eighteenth Dynasty tombs in this area. These tombs are orientated to the west, towards the 'Great Forecourt of Amun' a ritual space which lies between them and the easternmost row of tombs in Dra Abu el-Naga West (see below).

The relatively few Nineteenth and Twentieth Dynasty tombs in the area also show some patterning by date. TT166 and TT255 both date to the late Eighteenth or early Nineteenth Dynasty and are located 50m apart, while TT13 and TT14 both date to the late Nineteenth Dynasty and are also 50m apart. TT19 and TT344 both date to the reign of Ramesses II (or possibly his predecessor in the case of TT19) and are located adjacent to each other, suggesting a deliberate attempt to site these tombs together. Three tombs date to the late Nineteenth or early Twentieth Dynasty, TT153,

TT233 and TT377, and are all located on the upper slopes but more than 100m apart.

Occupation of Tomb Owners

(See Table 6)

Many tombs in Dra Abu el-Naga East were built by individuals with an unknown occupation, as 17 of the 39 tombs are too damaged to identify the titles of the tomb owner. This makes any conclusions based on occupational groupings in this area of limited use but may provide clues as to the occupation of these unknown tomb owners.

Priests

Nine tombs in Dra Abu el-Naga East belonged to priests (see Figure 82). Three were High Priests, but of different deities (Amenmose-TT19, Amenemopet-TT148, and Ramessenakht-TT293). Ramessenakht-TT293 (Ram) was a 'High Priest of Amun', the only one to be buried in this eastern part of the necropolis (see Chapter 13). This tomb is located on the upper slopes of the area, commanding the best views over the processional route from the landing stage to Deir el-Bahri. The 'High Priest of Mut', Amenemopet-TT148 (RIII-RV) was buried less than 100m away to the north-east, at a similar altitude (see Figure 83). Both tombs date to the Ramesside Period, and while not in particularly close proximity, they have a spatial connection as a result of their elevated position and orientation. Amenmose-TT19 (SI-RII) was the High Priest of 'Amenhotep of the Forecourt', a manifestation of the deified deceased king, Amenhotep I. This tomb is some distance down the slopes from the other 'High Priests'. This individual was also a 'Lector' and '*ḥm-nṯr*' priest of unspecified deities. This tomb is located adjacent to Piay-TT344 (RII), who was the 'Scribe [of Counting the Cattle and] the Herds of Djeserkare', which was the throne name of Amenhotep I. These tombs are located some distance from any others suggesting a link between two contemporary individuals who served the cult of the deceased king during the reign of Ramesses II. These tombs are located over 200m away from K93.11 and K93.12 but are in the same area of the necropolis.

There were two 'Overseers of Priests', again of different deities. Djehuty-TT11 (Hat-TIII) was the 'Overseer of Priests' of Hathor, while Montuherkhepeshef-TT20 (TIII) was the 'Overseer of Priests' of unspecified deity. These tombs are roughly contemporary, located in the same general area and at the same altitude, and approximately 50m apart. TT20 forms a cluster with TT24 (RII) and TT165 (TIV-AIII), but these tombs were not owned by priests. Nebamun-TT24 was a member of the royal administration, while Nehemaaway-TT165 was a 'Sculptor of Amun', so there is a potential connection here between Nehemaaway and Montuherkhepeshef if they were both connected to the Estate of Amun.

Shuroy-TT13 (late Dyn 19) was the 'Chief of the Brazier Burners of Amun', while Huy-TT14 (late Dyn 19) was a '*wꜥb* priest of Amun' (and the deified Amenhotep I). These tombs are contemporary, and located less than 50m apart, but TT13 is located 10m higher up the slopes than TT14 (see Figure 84). The tomb of HPA Ramessesnkaht-TT293 (Ram) (see above), is at the highest point, with TT13 and TT14 located directly below it in a straight line, but with a graduated decrease in altitude. As none of these tombs are precisely dated, it is impossible to say which was built first, but if TT293 was the earliest, the other tombs of less important priests may have been built lower down as a result, but still achieving the desired spatial connection with their HPA. All three tombs would have had the same view overlooking the processional route of the BFV, which would have been an important consideration for priests of Amun when siting a tomb, thus explaining this formation. Neferennpet-TT147 (TIV-AIII) was the 'Head of the Master of Ceremonies of Amun in Karnak' and is at roughly the same altitude, 50m away from

Table 6: Dra Abu el-Naga East tombs distributed by occupational group (n) denotes subsequent tomb occupation

Occupational Group	No. of Tombs	Tombs
Priesthood	*********	TT11, TT13, TT14, TT19, TT20, TT147, TT148, TT233, TT293
Temple Administration	**************	TT11, TT18, TT146, TT147, TT149(2), TT150, TT151, TT165, TT166, TT232 (1&2), TT233, TT255, TT344
Royal Admin	***********	TT11, TT12, TT20, TT24, TT149(2), TT154, TT155, TT232 (1), TT233, TT255, TT344
General Admin	*******	TT11, TT146, TT155, TT165, TT166, TT293(2), TT344
Local Admin	*****	TT11, TT20, TT155, TT234, TT239
Unknown	***************	TT143, TT149, TT152 (1&2), TT153, TT167, TT375, TT376, TT377, TT378 (1&2), TT379, TT393, TT394, TT395, TT396, TT402

Figure 82: TTs of Priests in Dra Abu el-Naga East (Author's own using QGIS)

Figure 83: Courtyard of TT148 (Author's own)

Figure 84: View of Dra Abu el-Naga East showing TT13, TT14, TT148 and TT255 (Author's own)

TT293, perhaps influencing the position of this later tomb. Saroy-TT233 (late Dyn 19-early Dyn 20) was the 'Festival Leader' of an unspecified deity, and his tomb is located 50m to the north of TT148 at a higher altitude. In addition to being the 'High Priest of Mut' (see above), Amenemopet-TT148 (RIII-RV) was also the '3PA', '*ḥm-nṯr* of Amun', 'Divine Father', 'Chief of Secrets' and the 'Greatest of Seers of Ra', so it is possible that Saroy and Amenemopet were contemporary if both dated to the early Twentieth Dynasty.

Temple Administration

13 TTs belonged to the temple administration of the Estate of Amun (see Figure 85). The 'Overseer of the Cattle of Amun', Djehuty-TT11 (Hat-TIII), was buried in relatively close proximity to the 'Overseer of the Granary of Amun', Nebamun-TT146 (late Dyn 17-early Dyn 18), whose tomb lies approximately 60m to the west, and the 'Scribe and Counter of Cattle of Amun' Neferrenpet-TT147 (TIV-AIII), whose tomb lies 90m to the north. The 'Sculptor of Amun', Nehemaaway-TT165 (TIV-AIII), was buried just over 50m to the east of the earlier TT11.

There are four individuals, in addition to Djehuty-TT11, who have titles connected to the cattle of Amun, including the 'Overseer of the Cattle of Amun', Userhet-TT150 (AIII/after Amarna), the 'Counter of the Cattle of the God's Wife of Amun', Hety-TT151 (TIV-AIII), the 'Counter of the Cattle in the Estate of Amun', Saroy-TT233 (late Dyn 19-early Dyn 20), and the 'Overseer of the Cattle' of '...Amun-Ra in the Southern City', '... Amun in Karnak' and of '...all the Gods', and the 'Scribe of Counting the Cattle of Amun' and '...the Cattle and Herds of Djeserkare', Piay-TT344 (RII). Of these tombs, TT150 and TT151 are located in particularly close proximity, just 20m away from each other, and are roughly contemporary, suggesting a link between the two. TT11, TT233 and TT344 are more than 100m away from the tombs of any other individuals with titles relating to cattle. It is interesting that five individuals with similar titles are buried in Dra Abu el-Naga East, suggesting a possible connection between this occupation and this area – perhaps the temple herds were housed on the cultivated land nearby?

The usurper Amenmose-TT149 (Dyn 20) and Saroy-TT233 (late Dyn 19-early Dyn 20) were both 'Overseers of the Huntsmen of Amun'. They could potentially have been contemporary, or succeeded each other in this role, while their tombs are only located 25m apart at the same altitude, suggesting a possible spatial connection between them. Baki-TT18 (TIII) was the 'Chief Servant who weighs the Silver and Gold of the Estate of Amun'. His tomb lies 80m away from TT150 (AIII/after Amarna), and 100m away from TT151 (TIV-AIII). All three tombs date to the Eighteenth Dynasty, and while their owners' titles were different, they were all affiliated to Amun, so a connection between them is possible.

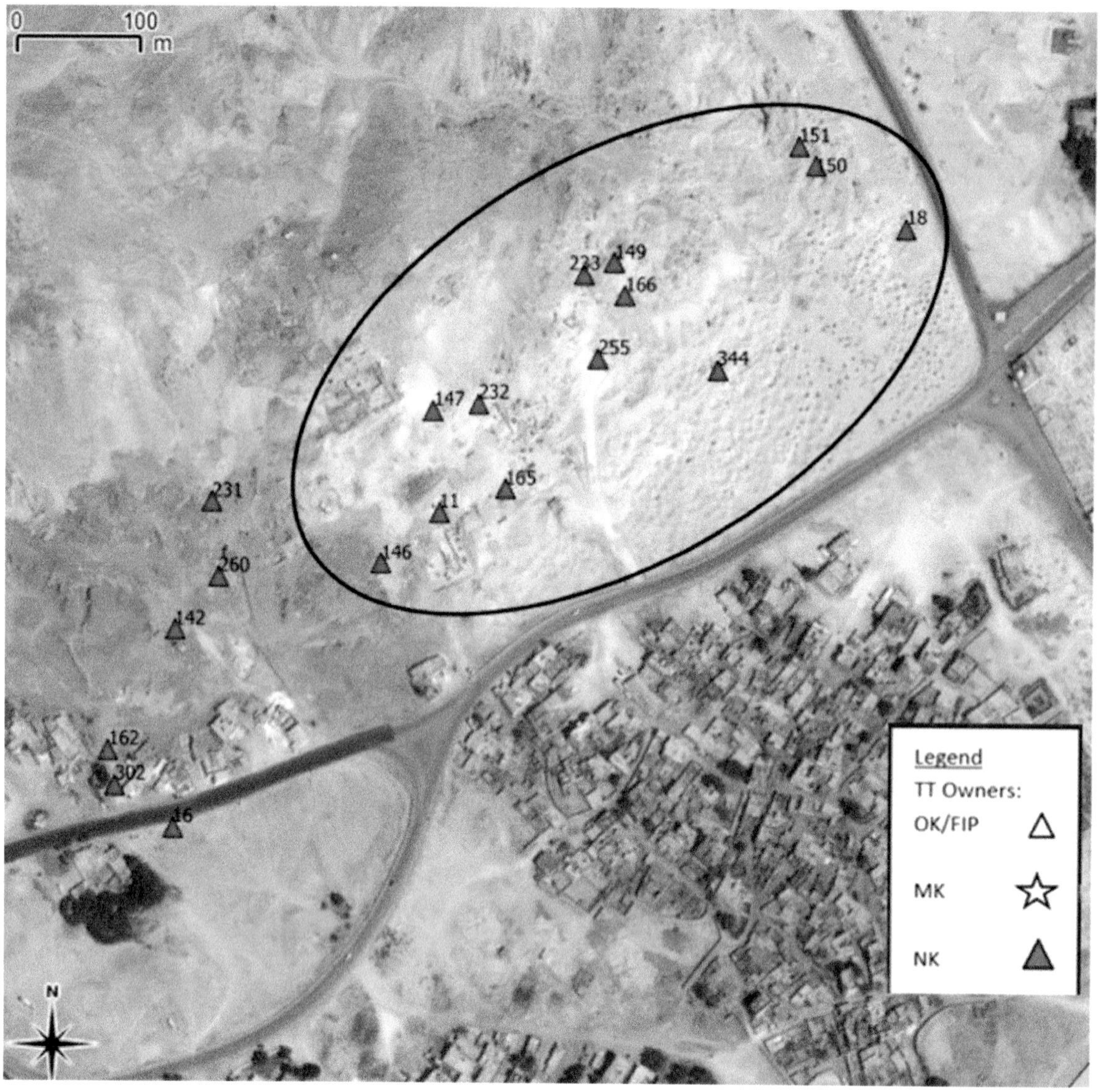

Figure 85: TTs of the Temple Administration in Dra Abu el-Naga East (Author's own using QGIS)

Roy-TT255 (Hor-SI) was the 'Steward in the Estate of Amun' (and was buried near three priests of Amun), while Ramose-TT166 (Hor-SI) was the 'Overseer of Works at Karnak'. These contemporary tombs lie just 50m apart at the same altitude, while both men held important roles in the Estate of Amun so would have been colleagues. Piay-TT344 (RII) lies less than 100m to the east of TT255, and is relatively close in date, so may also be connected. Hety-TT151 (TIV-AIII) was the 'Steward of the God's Wife' (among other titles- see above), but there is no spatial connection with TT255. The 'Secretary of the God's Wife', Amenhotep-TT232 (late Dyn 17-early Dyn 18), was buried 100m to the west of TT255. Both Hety and Amenhotep served the God's Wife of Amun, but they were not contemporary and are located at opposite ends of Dra Abu el-Naga East.

Royal Administration

11 tombs are owned by members of the royal administration (see Figure 86). Djehuty-TT11 (Hat-TIII) was the 'Royal Seal-bearer' and 'Overseer of Works', and his tomb is adjacent to the earlier Hori-TT12 (STII-AI), who was the 'Overseer of the Granary' of Queen Aahhotep. The 'Royal Seal-bearer' and 'Fan-bearer', Montuherkhepeshef-TT20 (TIII), was buried just 50m to the east of TT11 at the same altitude. The contemporary nature of TT20 and TT11 and the shared title 'Royal Seal-bearer' strongly suggests a link between these tombs. Adjacent to TT20 is Nebamun-TT24 (TII-TIII), who was the 'Steward of the Royal Wife', 'Butler of the Palace', 'Chief...' and 'Overseer of Royal Ships', and 'Overseer of the Royal Office'. These tombs are roughly contemporary, which in addition to their spatial connection suggests a link between their owners. TT154 and TT155 lie some distance to the east of this

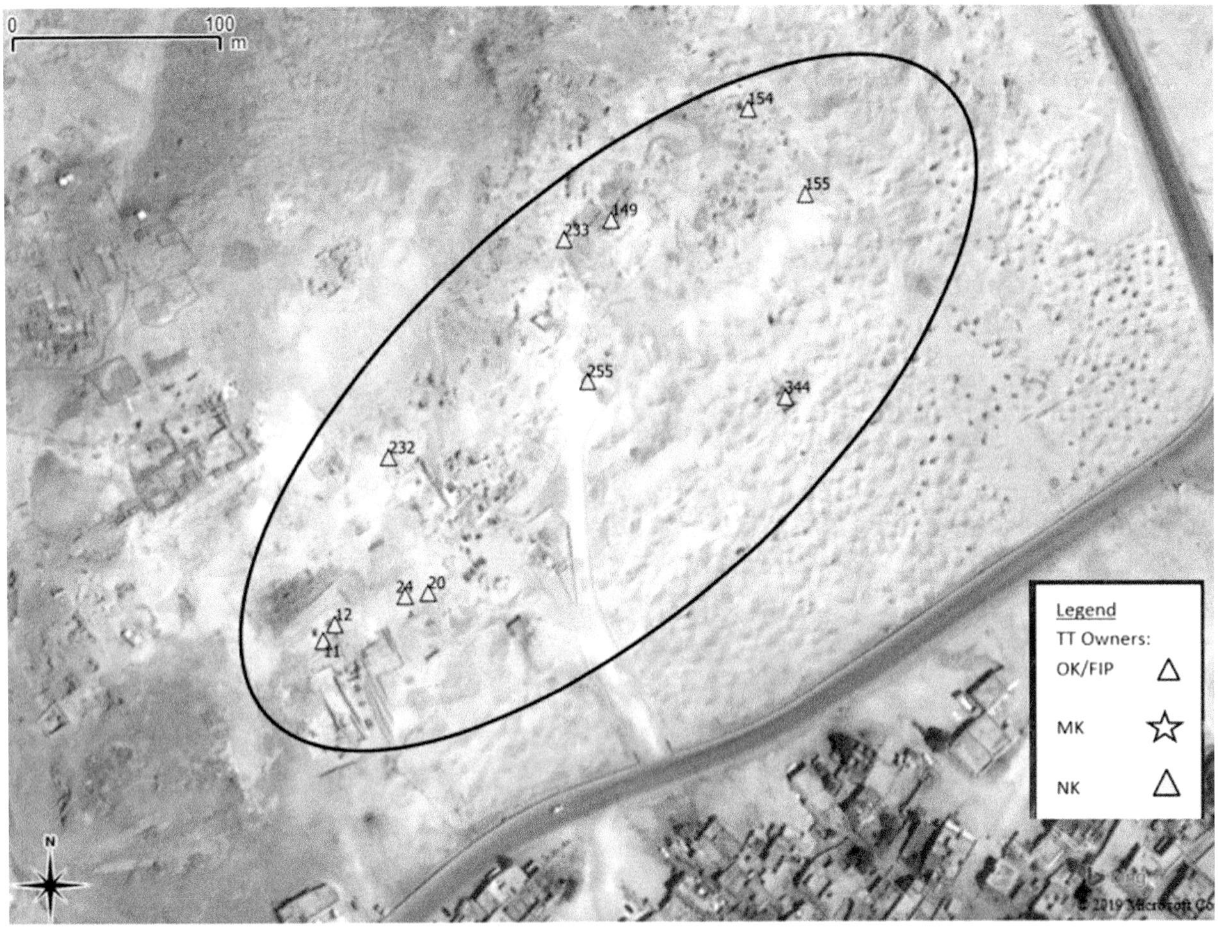

Figure 86: TTs of the Royal Administration in Dra Abu el-Naga East (Author's own using QGIS)

group, less than 50m apart at the same altitude. Teti-TT154 (Dyn 18-TIII) was a 'Butler', while Intef-TT155 (Hat-TIII) was a 'Royal Herald', 'Director of All Works at the Palace', and 'Chief Steward', so these tomb owners were potentially contemporary and both worked at the palace, suggesting a connection.

Saroy-TT233 (late Dyn 19/20) was also a 'Royal Scribe of the Offering Table', 'Keeper of Royal Documents', 'Royal Messenger to Foreign Lands' and 'Royal Scribe', while the tomb's co-owner was Saroy's assistant, Amenhotep-Huy, another 'Royal Scribe of the Offering Table'. TT233 lies 60m north of Roy-TT255 (Hor-SI), another 'Royal Scribe' and 'Steward in the Estate of Horemheb. Piay-TT344 (RII) was another 'Royal Scribe' and his tomb lies 100m to the east of TT255. These royal scribes were buried in the same area but do not form a cluster.

General Administration

There were six members of the general state administration buried in Dra Abu el-Naga East, with a potential seventh as the identification of the second occupant of TT293 is uncertain- see Chapter 13 (see Figure 87). One of the most important was Djehuty-TT11 (Hat-TIII), who was the 'Treasurer' and 'Overseer of Works', amongst other titles. He was buried 60m away from Nebamun-TT146 (late Dyn 17-early Dyn 18), the 'Scribe and Counter of Grain'. The rest of the general administrative tombs are located to the east of the area. Intef-TT155 (Hat-TIII) was the 'Overseer of Granaries', while the later 'Overseer of Cattle', Ramose-TT166 (Hor-SI), was buried 90m to the west. Piay-TT344 (RII) was also a 'Scribe of Counting the Cattle and Herds' (among other titles), and lies 90m to the south of TT155, and 90m to the south-east of TT166. TT344 was only built slightly later than TT166, so there may have been a spatial connection between them. TT293 (Ram) may have been reused by the 'Vizier', Nebmaatrenakht, in the late Twentieth Dynasty, as named on a fragment lying nearby (PM I: 376), but this is unlikely as the identification of the tomb the fragment is from is uncertain (see Chapter 13). TT293 lies more than 100m away from the nearest tomb in this group and does not fit the distributional pattern of other Viziers' tombs. The 'Goldworker' Nehemaaway-TT165 (TIV-AIII) is of unspecified affiliation, therefore classified with the general administration. This tomb is adjacent to

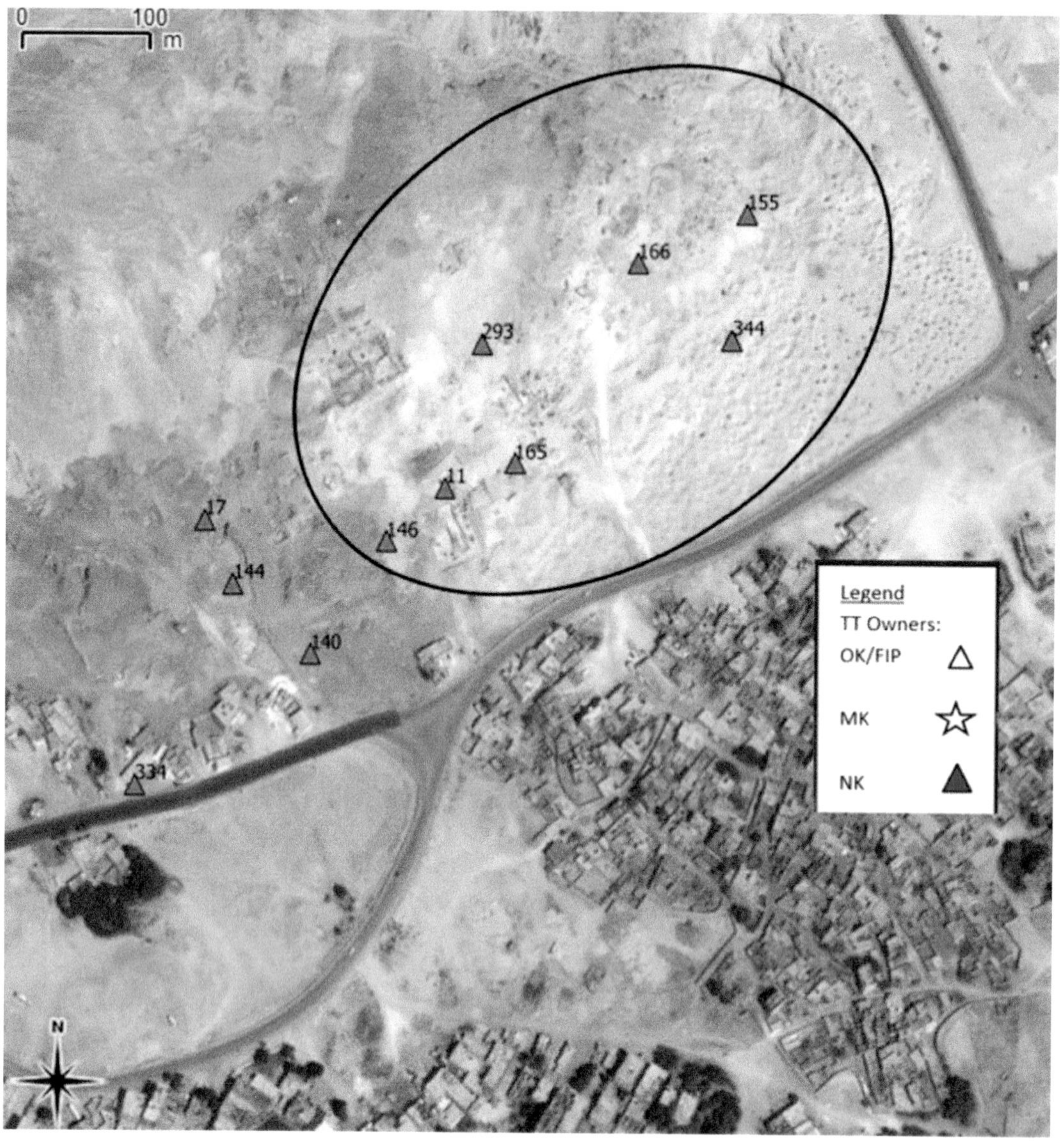

Figure 87: TTs of the General Administration in Dra Abu el-Naga East (Author's own using QGIS)

two of the royal administration (TT20 and TT24), but Djehuty-TT11 (Hat-TIII) lies 60m to the west and is close enough in date to have potentially been the superior of Nehemaaway in his capacity as 'Overseer of Works'.

Local Administration

There were five members of the local administration buried in this area (see Figure 88). Djehuty-TT11 (Hat-TIII) listed 'Great Chief in *Hr-wr*' as one of his many titles, while 50m to the east was his contemporary Montuherkhepeshef-TT20 (TIII), the 'Mayor of Thebu' (the capital of the tenth nome). Penhut-TT239 (TIV-AIII) was 'Governor of all Northern Lands', and his tomb lies 80m to the north of TT20, which only predates it by a couple of reigns. Intef-TT155 (Hat-TIII) was 'Mayor of Thinis' and 'Great Chief of the Thinite nome' in addition to 'Great Chief of the Entire Oasis', but TT155 lies over 200m to the east of these contemporary tombs. Roy-TT234 (Dyn 18-Hat) was the 'Mayor' of an unspecified location, and his tomb lies 90m to the north of TT155.

Military

There are no individuals with military titles buried in Dra Abu el-Naga East.

Unknown

There are 15 tombs with one or more unknown owners, or owners of unknown occupation (TT143, TT149, TT152 – both occupants, TT153, TT167, TT375, TT376, TT377, TT378 – both occupants, TT379, TT393, TT394, TT395, TT396 and TT402), which is more than any other area of the necropolis. This makes the number of conclusions to be drawn about this area limited as

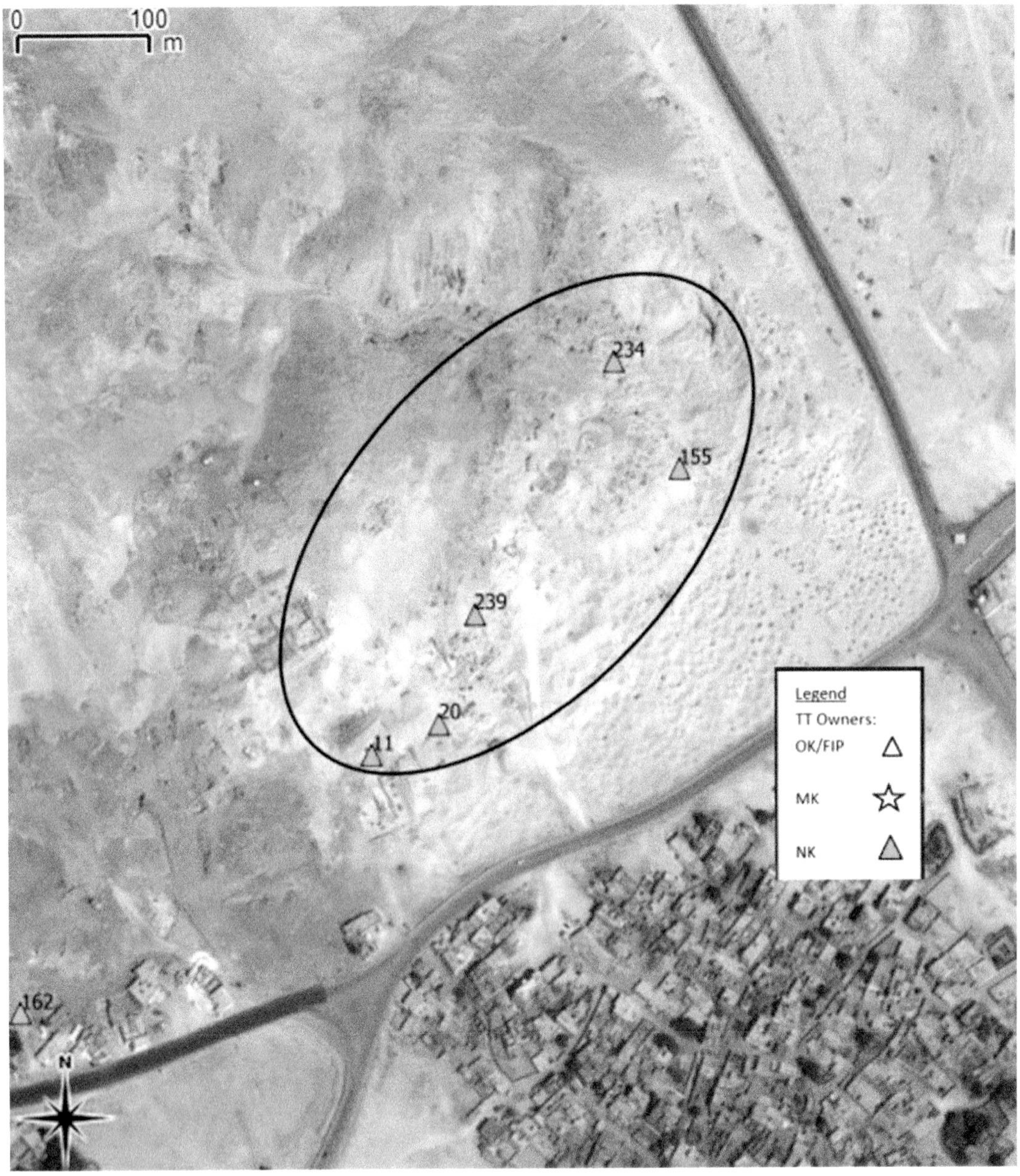

Figure 88: TTs of the Local Administration in Dra Abu el-Naga East (Author's own using QGIS)

there are substantial gaps in the data set in this area in particular, due to the poor state of preservation of the inscriptional evidence.

Relationship between Tomb Owners / Tombs

There is only one known familial relationship from Dra Abu el-Naga East. The 3PA Amenemopet-TT148, was the son of 3PA Tjanefer-TT158, who was buried in Dra Abu el-Naga West, some distance from the tomb of his son. Amenemopet was also the son-in-law of the HPA Ramessesnakht-TT293, who was buried 100m to the west (or even in a family cache in TT148 itself- Ockinga and Binder 2012: 209-19). There must also have been a close relationship between two 'Royal Scribes of the Offering Table', Saroy-TT233 (late Dyn 19-early Dyn 20) and his assistant Amenhotep Huy, as they shared rather than reused TT233 with. This collegial relationship and co-ownership prove a close relationship between these individuals.

Shared Courtyards

There are two examples of shared courtyards in Dra Abu el-Naga East.

TT20 and TT165

TT20 was built first on the northern side of the courtyard, with the later addition of TT165 on the

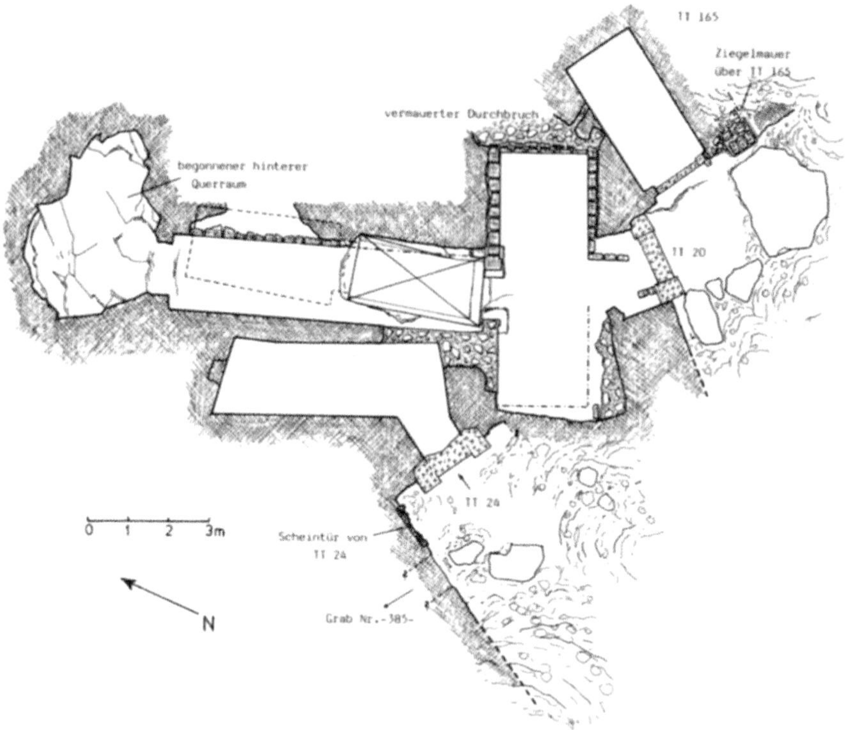

Figure 89: Plan of shared courtyard of TT20 and TT165 (Kampp 1996: Figure 104 – Courtesy of Professor Seyfried)

Table 7: Owners of TT20 and TT165

TT	Dyn	Reign	Name	Title
TT20	18	TIII/ (AII)	Montuherkhepeshef	Fan-bearer; Mayor of Thebu; Overseer of Priests; Royal Seal-bearer; Son of the King; Sole Companion; Hereditary Prince and Mayor;
TT165	18	TIV-AIII	Nehemaaway	Goldsmith; Sculptor of Amun;

eastern side (see Figure 89). These tombs date to a similar period of the Eighteenth Dynasty, but beyond this there is no clear link (see Table 7).

TT19 and TT344

TT19 and TT344 are located opposite each other across a shared courtyard (see Figure 90). These tombs are roughly contemporary, and both tomb owners had a connection to the cult of Amenhotep I so were likely to have known each other and deliberately shared a courtyard in this area associated with Amenhotep I (see Table 8).

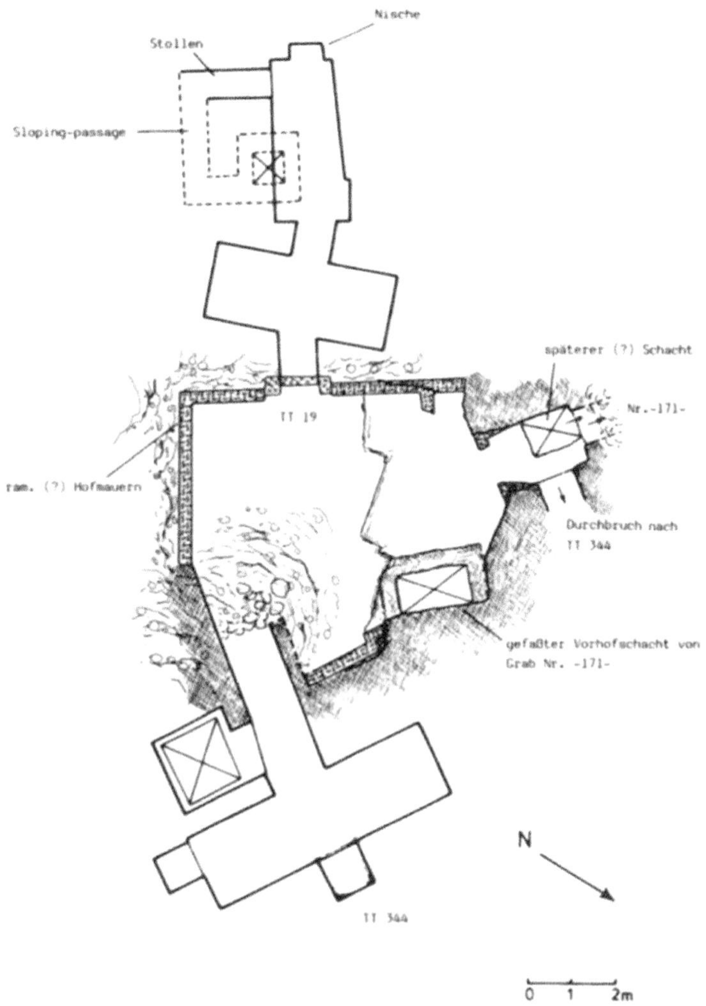

Figure 90: Plan of shared courtyard of TT19 and TT344 (Kampp 1996: Figure 102 – Courtesy of Professor Seyfried)

Table 8: Owners of TT19 and TT344

TT	Dyn	Reign	Name	Title
TT19	19	SI/ RII	Amenmose	**High priest of 'Amenhotep (of the Forecourt,') (=AI);** Lector Priest; Priest;
TT344	19	RII	Piay	Overseer of the Cattle of Amun(-Re) ...; Overseer of the Cattle of All the Gods; (Royal) Scribe (of Counting the Cattle of Amun); Scribe of Counting the Cattle and Herds (of Djeser-ka-re (=AI);

Tomb Reuse

Three tombs in Dra Abu el-Naga East were reused, with two additional possibilities (see Figure 91). These reused tombs do not form a distinct cluster, but some are spatially connected as TT232 and TT293 are adjacent to each other, while TT149 lies along the same contour line, but over 100m to the west. TT149 and TT378 lie within 100m of each other. Four reused tombs were built in the Eighteenth Dynasty, TT149, TT152, TT232 and TT378 (or late Seventeenth in the case of TT232) and one in the Ramesside Period (TT293). Three of these five tombs have a reuse date in the Twentieth Dynasty, a pattern observed throughout the necropolis as new tombs were rarely built at this time, with another reused during the Ramesside Period, potentially also in the Twentieth Dynasty, and one in the Nineteenth Dynasty (see Table 9). There are no examples of Eighteenth Dynasty reuse of

Figure 91: Reused TTs in Dra Abu el-Naga East at the end of the New Kingdom (shown by date of first reuse) (Author's own using QGIS)

TTs in Dra Abu el-Naga, unlike in Qurna and el-Khokha. This is presumably as Qurna and el-Khokha were the most popular burial spots in the Eighteenth Dynasty so were becoming crowded, while space remained for tomb building at Dra Abu el-Naga.

The lack of inscriptional evidence within these tombs makes any link between the occupants difficult to identify. TT149 (Dyn 18) was reused by Amenmose, a 'Royal Scribe' and temple administrator (Dyn 20), but as the original occupant is unknown, no connections can be identified between them. Both Amenhotep-TT232 (late Dyn 17-early Dyn 18) and Tharwasa, who reused his tomb (Dyn 20), worked for the Estate of Amun, and held scribal titles, suggesting a possible occupational connection, but the difference in date and the relatively low status of the occupants makes this unlikely unless they were related. The original owner of TT378 (Dyn 18) and its usurper (Dyn 19) are both unknown, so a connection between them cannot be established.

Two tombs were identified as having potentially been reused by Porter and Moss (1960: 262 and 376), but not by Kampp (1996: 140-143). Porter and Moss believed TT293 (Ram) was possibly reused by the Vizier Nebmarenakht between the reigns of Ramesses IX and Ramesses XI (PM I: 376), on the basis of fragments found within the tomb but the identification of this tomb is problematic (see Chapter 12). The original occupant of TT293, Ramessesnakht, reused K93.11 as a cult chapel, but judging by the lack of burial equipment was not buried there (Rummel 2011: 428). If TT293 was reused, there were no common factors between the two occupants, aside from both holding important positions as HPA and Vizier respectively, so this seems to have been a matter of necessity rather than choice. TT152

(AIII-Amarna) may have been reused in the Ramesside period (PM I: 262), but both occupants are unknown so no link can be identified between them.

Table 9: Reused tombs in Dra Abu el Naga East

TT	Original Date	Date of Reuse
TT149	Dyn 18	Dyn 20
TT152	AIII-Amarna	Ram?
TT232	Late Dyn 17-Early Dyn 18	Dyn 20
TT293	Ram	Dyn 20?
TT378	Dyn 18	Dyn 19

Conclusions

Dra Abu el-Naga is located directly opposite Karnak temple on the east bank and was considered an extension of the sacred space of Amun. In fact, the western end of Dra Abu el-Naga is directly aligned with the central axis of Karnak (see Figures 92 and 93), creating a direct connection between them. Karnak is also visible from the upper slopes of both Dra Abu el-Naga East and West. This area was even termed 'The Great Forecourt of Amun' or '*pꜣ wbꜣ ꜥꜣ n Ỉmn*', as referred to on a lost relief block of the 'God's Wife' Isis from Deir el-Bakhit (Polz *et al.* 2012: 122 n35 and 36; Rummel 2018: 257). The presence of the temple of Menisut to the west, and the double tomb complex of Amenhotep I and Ahmose-Nefertari in the centre, K93.11 and K93.12 (Polz 2007: 172-197) would have influenced tomb placement in this entire area. The presence of three individuals in this area connected to the cult of Amenhotep I (Huy-TT14, Amenmose-TT19, and Piay-TT344) is therefore not surprising. It seems likely that more of these individuals were buried in the tombs with unknown occupants as those affiliated with this cult would have favoured Dra Abu el-Naga over other areas.

To the west lie the tombs of Amenhotep I and Ahmose Nefertari, K93.11 and K93.12. These tombs were spatially connected to the nearby temple of Menisut to the west by means of a substantial causeway and sunken path, which ran southwards from the tomb complex to a wadi which led in a easterly direction down the hill until it met Menisut (see Chapter 13; Polz 2007: 104-111; Rummel 2013: 14-17; Rummel 2018: 259-260). This interconnection between tomb and temple, along with evidence of shrines and cultic activity dating from the early Eighteenth Dynasty onwards in to the Ramesside Period, reveal ritual processional activity in this area (Polz 2007: 172-97). This procession, in addition to that of the BFV and its associated cultic activity, would have influenced tomb placement as tombs were built overlooking the processional routes (see Figures 94 and 95). The distribution of the contemporary tombs, TT19

Figure 92: View from outside TT148 indicating Karnak temple on the East Bank (Author's own)

Figure 93: Zoomed in view of Karnak from Dra Abu el-Naga West (Author's own)

Figure 94: View south indicating the location of Menisut from TT148 (Author's own)

Figure 95: View north-east from outside TT148 over the processional route of the BFV (Author's own)

and TT344, is particularly interesting as they are in such close proximity, lying adjacent to each other.

The earliest New Kingdom tombs in this area were indeed located in the north-east of the area and moved gradually south, however the movement of tombs cannot be generalised as a spread southward (Helck 1962: 225-243). This chapter has shown that this is an over-simplification of the process, with different areas being popular at certain times, linked to occupational groupings and ritual activity in the area. The number of early Eighteenth Dynasty burials here rather than in Qurna may followed tradition from the earlier burials here (Helck 1962: 230-231) or may have chosen this area because of its connections to Amenhotep I and Ahmose Nefertari or the BFV. The processional route of the BFV between its starting point at the Seti I temple and Deir el-Bahri from the Nineteenth Dynasty onwards would have meant it passing in front of Dra Abu el-Naga which would also have influenced tomb distribution. It seems strange that more tombs dating from the early Nineteenth Dynasty onwards are not found in this area, as the closest area of the necropolis to the Seti I temple as a result of the area directly behind the temple being too flat to accommodate rock-cut tombs (see Figure 96).

Figure 96: Seti I Mortuary Temple (Author's own)

Dra Abu el-Naga West

(See Appendix 4)

Location

Dra Abu el-Naga West is bordered by two modern roads, one to the south which leads eastwards towards the village of New Qurna and el-Tarif, and one to the west which follows the causeway towards Deir el-Bahri (see Figure 97). Dra Abu el-Naga West contains 42 TTs, located along the edge of the modern road to the south, between 80m and 140m above sea level, with the flood plain beginning at 80m above sea level in this area (see Figure 98). Three tombs outside the boundary of this area are classed as outlying (TT305, TT306 and TT307) so are discussed at the end of the chapter and are not discussed further here. The majority of tombs here are spread in a narrow band following the contouring of these slopes, with a group of the tombs at a higher altitude clustered more closely together (see Figure 99).

Date of Use

17 TTs in Dra Abu el-Naga West were built in the Eighteenth Dynasty, while 11 of these were built between the reigns of Hatshepsut and Amenhotep II (TT17, TT140, TT142, TT144, TT145, TT164, TT169, TT260, TT261, TT262 and TT401). There were only two tombs in this area prior to the reign of Hatshepsut (TT15 and TT231), and three dating to the reign of Amenhotep III (TT161, TT162 and TT334). One further tomb dates to the end of the Eighteenth Dynasty after the Amarna period (TT333). The remaining 22 TTs are datable to the Nineteenth and Twentieth Dynasties (with two possibly dated to the Twenty First Dynasty), with peaks in usage during the reign of Ramesses II when eight tombs were built in this area (TT16, TT35, TT156, TT157, TT168, TT282, TT288 and TT289), and among tombs datable only to the Ramesside period, when a further five tombs were built (TT236, TT237, TT287, TT302 and TT332) (see Table 10).

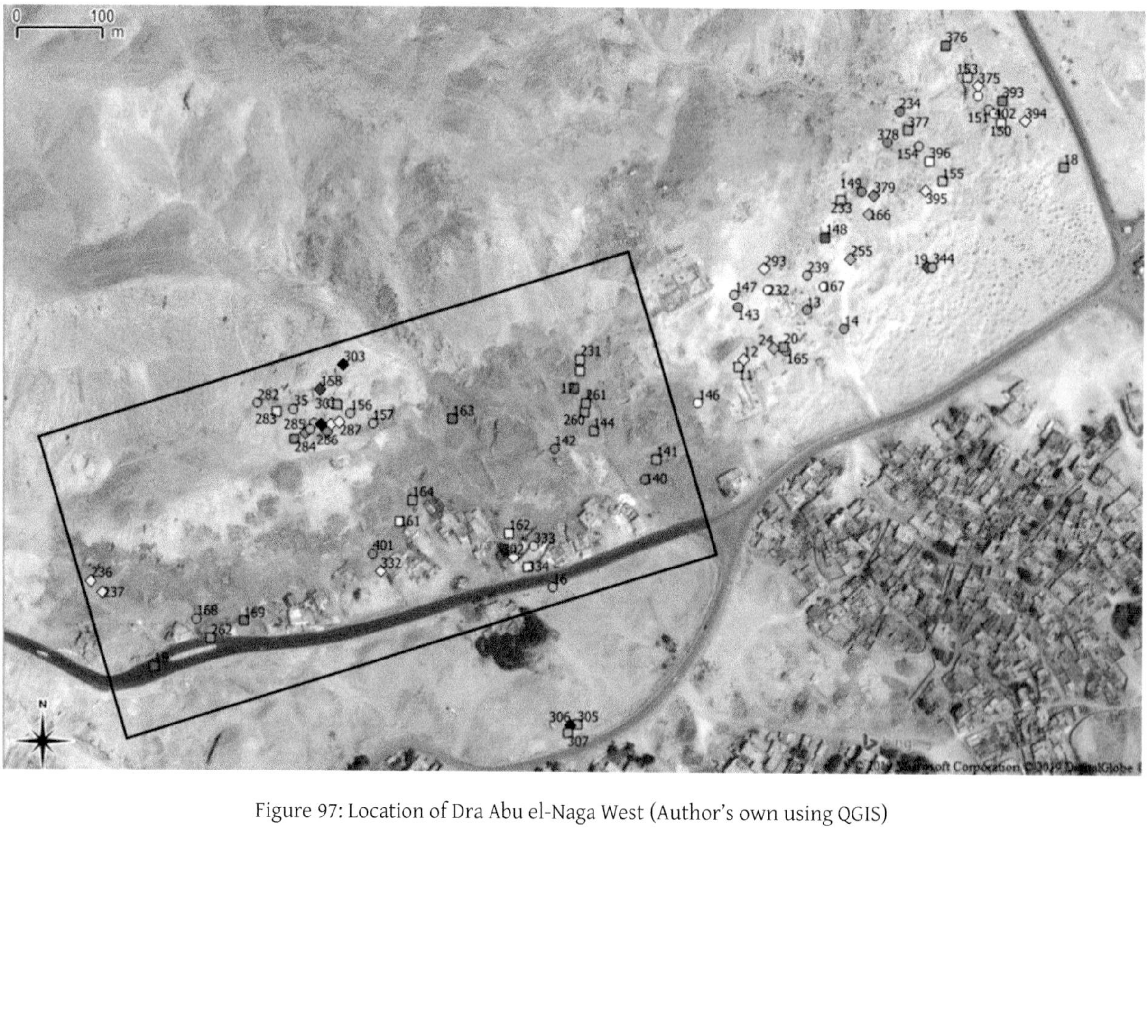

Figure 97: Location of Dra Abu el-Naga West (Author's own using QGIS)

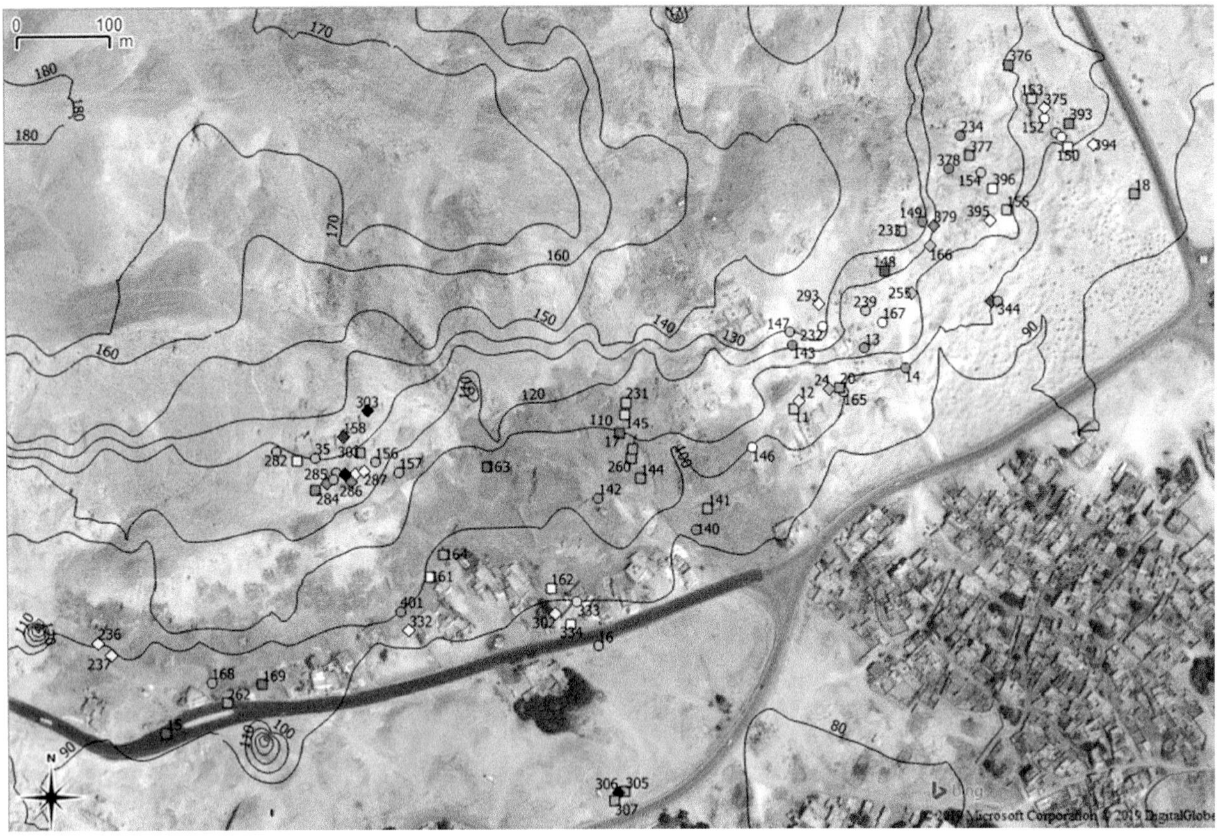

Figure 98: Landscape of Dra Abu el-Naga West (Author's own using QGIS)

Figure 99: TTs in Dra Abu el-Naga West (Author's own using QGIS)

Table 10: Dra Abu el-Naga West TTs distributed by most likely date

Date	No. of Tombs	Tombs
Early Dyn 18	*	TT231
Ah-AI	*	TT15
Hat / TIII	*	TT145
TIII	*****	TT144, TT164, TT260, TT261, TT262
TIII / AII	***	TT140, TT142, TT401
AII	**	TT17, TT169
AIII	***	TT161, TT162, TT334
After Amarna	*	TT333
Dyn 19 - RII	*	TT284
Dyn 19	**	TT285, TT286
Mid/ Late Dyn 19	*	TT163
RII	********	TT16, TT35, TT156, TT157, TT168, TT282, TT288, TT289
RII / Mer	*	TT300
RII - SII	*	TT283
SII/Tau	*	TT158
Ram	*****	TT236, TT237, TT287, TT302, TT332
Late Dyn 19-early 20	*	TT159
Dyn 20	**	TT141, TT301
Dyn 20 / 21	**	TT303, TT304

There is some evidence of clustering by reign. Of the tombs dating between Hatshepsut and Amenhotep II, TT17, TT142, TT144, TT145, TT260 and TT261 are clustered close together, arranged side by side facing roughly south-eastwards, at between 100 and 110m above sea level (although TT142 is located slightly to the west of the rest of the group). TT231, dating to the early Eighteenth Dynasty also forms the northernmost tomb of this group, providing a potential focus for these later burials, or this arrangement may be connected to the direct view across the Nile to Karnak or the position overlooking the processional route towards Deir el-Bahri and K93.11 and K93.12. TT140 is located some distance further down the slope than the rest of the cluster, orientated in the same direction, and close to the only Ramesside tomb in this area, TT141, which is orientated southwards. There are no later tombs in this cluster.

The other Eighteenth Dynasty tombs are all located on the lower slopes but further to the west. TT162 and TT334 (both AIII), and TT333 (Amarna), formed another cluster to the south-west, together with two Ramesside tombs, TT16 and TT302. TT161, TT164 and TT401 were spatially connected, distributed along the same contour line, near Ramesside TT332. TT15, TT169 and TT262 are also located along the same contour line to the west of the other Eighteenth Dynasty tombs, between 90 and 100m above sea level, although they have more distance between them than the other tombs.

Of the TTs dating to the Nineteenth and Twentieth Dynasties, a group of 17 tombs are located in a cluster in the higher slopes of Dra Abu el-Naga West, between 110m and 140m above sea level (TT35, TT156, TT157, TT158, TT159, TT282, TT283, TT284, TT285, TT286, TT287, TT288, TT289, TT300, TT301, TT303 and TT304). As these tombs cannot be dated as precisely as their Eighteenth Dynasty counterparts, this limits the analysis of this cluster. Six of these tombs date to the reign of Ramesses II (TT35, TT156, TT157, TT282, TT288 and TT289), and one further tomb to this or the successive reign of Merenptah (TT300), suggesting that this area was popular during the early Nineteenth

Table 11: Dra Abu el-Naga West TTs distributed by occupational group (n) denotes subsequent tomb occupation

Occupational Group	No. of Tombs	Tombs
Priesthood	***************	TT16, TT35, TT141, TT157, TT158, TT159, TT161, TT168, TT236, TT237, TT261, TT283, TT287, TT303,
Temple Admin	******************	TT16, TT142, TT162, TT169, TT231, TT236, TT260, TT284 (2), TT285, TT289, TT301, TT302, TT303, TT304, TT332, TT401,
Royal Admin	******	TT17, TT163, TT289, TTT300, TT301, TT304,
General Admin	********	TT17, TT140, TT144, TT157, TT262, TT286, TT289, TT334,
Local Admin	*******	TT15, TT156, TT162, TT163, TT288, TT289, TT300,
Military	****	TT145, TT156, TT164, TT282,
Unknown	*****	TT284, TT285 (2), TT288, TT333,

Dynasty. The others are dated only to either the Nineteenth or Twentieth Dynasty, or the Twentieth or Twenty First Dynasty, so cannot be usefully analysed. Another Nineteenth Dynasty tomb, TT163, lies a short distance to the east. The popularity of these higher slopes during the Ramesside Period must be partly due to lack of space in the rest of the necropolis, and the excellent views over the processional route between the Seti I temple to the south-east, and Deir el-Bahri and the Ramesside mortuary temples.

The furthest TTs to the west of the area, TT236 and TT237 (both Ram) are located in close proximity to each other but lie some distance away from any other TTs. There are several tombs positioned at the bottom of the slopes to the west of the area, along the edge of the modern road, TT15, TT169 and TT262 which all date to the first half of the Eighteenth Dynasty, together with TT168 which dates to the reign of Ramesses II.

Occupation of Tomb Owners

(See Table 11)

Priests

There were 14 priests buried here, several with multiple titles (see Figure 100). These included three 'HPA', Nebwenenef-TT157 (RII- who was also a 'High Priest of Hathor'), Bakenkhonsu-TT35 (RII), and Roma (Roy)-TT283 (RII-SII). Bakenkhonsu was also the 'Overseer of Priests' of 'all the Gods of Thebes' and 'Amun-Re', and the 'Chief of Secrets', while Nebwenef was 'Overseer of Priests of all the Gods' and '...of all the Lords of Thebes'. These three HPA are buried on the upper slopes, less than 100m from each other, within the aforementioned Ramesside cluster. TT35 and TT283 lie adjacent to each other in particularly close proximity (see Chapter 13). Other priests of Amun buried in this area include the '2PA', Hornakht-TT236 (Ram), two '3PA', Tjanefer-TT158 (SII-Tau) and Paser-TT303 (late Dyn 20/early Dyn 21), and a '4PA' Raia-TT159 (late Dyn 19/early Dyn 20). None of these tombs can be definitively identified as contemporary to the HPA, but potentially Hornakht-TT236, Tjanefer-TT158 and Raia-TT159, may have served with one or more of them. TT158 and TT303 form part of the Ramesside cluster, lying side by side approximately 40m apart, close to the tombs of the High Priests.

Other priests include the 'Chief Lector Priest' of an unspecified affiliation, Wennefer-TT237 (Ram), and a 'Lector Priest' of the 'Lord of the Gods', Any-TT168 (RII). TT168 is some distance away from any other members of the Amun priesthood. The aforementioned TT236 and TT237 lie adjacent to each other to the west of the area, some distance away from any other tombs. This suggests a possible connection between Hornakht and Wennefer, as they were both Ramesside priests who built their tombs overlooking the eastern end of the causeway leading to Deir el-Bahri, rather than being orientated westwards as lots of other tombs in the area. There were also four 'Divine Fathers', three with no specified affiliation, the two HPA, Bakenkhons-TT35 (RII) and Nebwenenef-TT157 (RII), and Tjanefer-TT158 (SII-Tau), and the 'Divine Father of Amun' Any-TT168 (RII). The first three were buried within the Ramesside cluster, with only TT168 located at the bottom of the slopes.

There were four '*wꜥb* priests', three of whom served Amun, Bakenkhonsu-TT141 (Dyn 20), Tjanefer-TT158 (SII-Tau), and Pendua-TT287 (Ram), and one who served Amenhotep I, Khaemwaset-TT261 (TIII). Another priest of the cult of this deified king was the '*ḥm-nṯr* of Amenhotep of the Forecourt', Panehesi-TT16

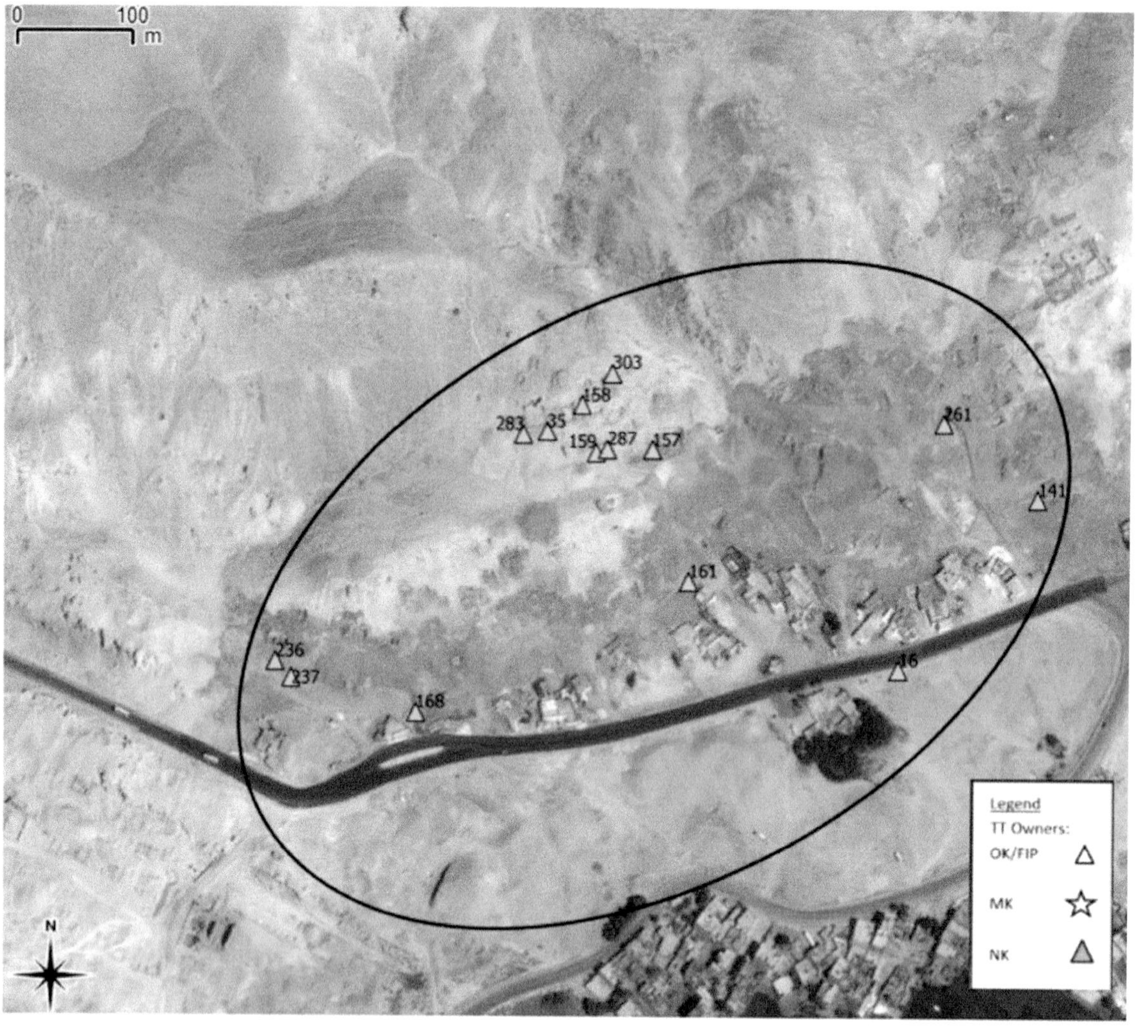

Figure 100: TTs of Priests in Dra Abu el-Naga West (Author's own using QGIS)

(RII). There is no spatial connection between them as they were buried some distance apart and are not in close proximity to any other priests, with the exception of Pendua-TT287 (previously discussed in relation to more senior priestly titles). There were two 'Greatest of Seers', one '...in Thebes', the HPA Nebwenenef-TT157 (RII), and one '...of Ra and Atum', Tjanefer-TT158 (SII-Tau). They were buried within 75m of each other within the Ramesside cluster. There was also Nakht-TT161 (AIII), a 'Bearer of Floral Offerings', who was not buried in close proximity to any priests.

These priests served a range of deities, some unspecified in their tombs. The most common deity is Amun (TT35, TT141, TT157, TT158, TT159, TT161, TT168, TT236, TT283, TT287 and TT303). The tombs of those affiliated to Amun are distributed throughout this area, but six of them make up the Ramesside cluster. Other deities, such as Amun-Re (TT35), Hathor (TT157), Ra and Atum (TT158), and 'All the Gods of Thebes' (TT35 and TT157), are attested within these titles, alongside Amun. There is also a priest of an unknown deity (TT237), whose tomb is located some distance to the south-west.

Two tombs belonged to individuals who served the cult of the deified Amenhotep I (TT16 and TT261), but their tombs lie some 200m apart. However, the area where both tombs are located lies between Menisut, which lies a short distance to the west, and K93.11 to the north-east, so these tombs would have been positioned along the presumed processional route between these structures (Polz 2007: 104-111; Rummel 2013: 14-17). TT261 is also one of the western row of tombs, orientated eastwards towards an apparent clearing, with another row of several tombs to the east, orientated westwards (see Kampp 1996: Plan VI). The space between these rows of tombs could indicate the site of some ritual activity connected to a procession leading to K93.11 and K93.12, which were located to the north east, in addition to that of the BFV, with tombs deliberately positioned here so that the deceased could participate (see below).

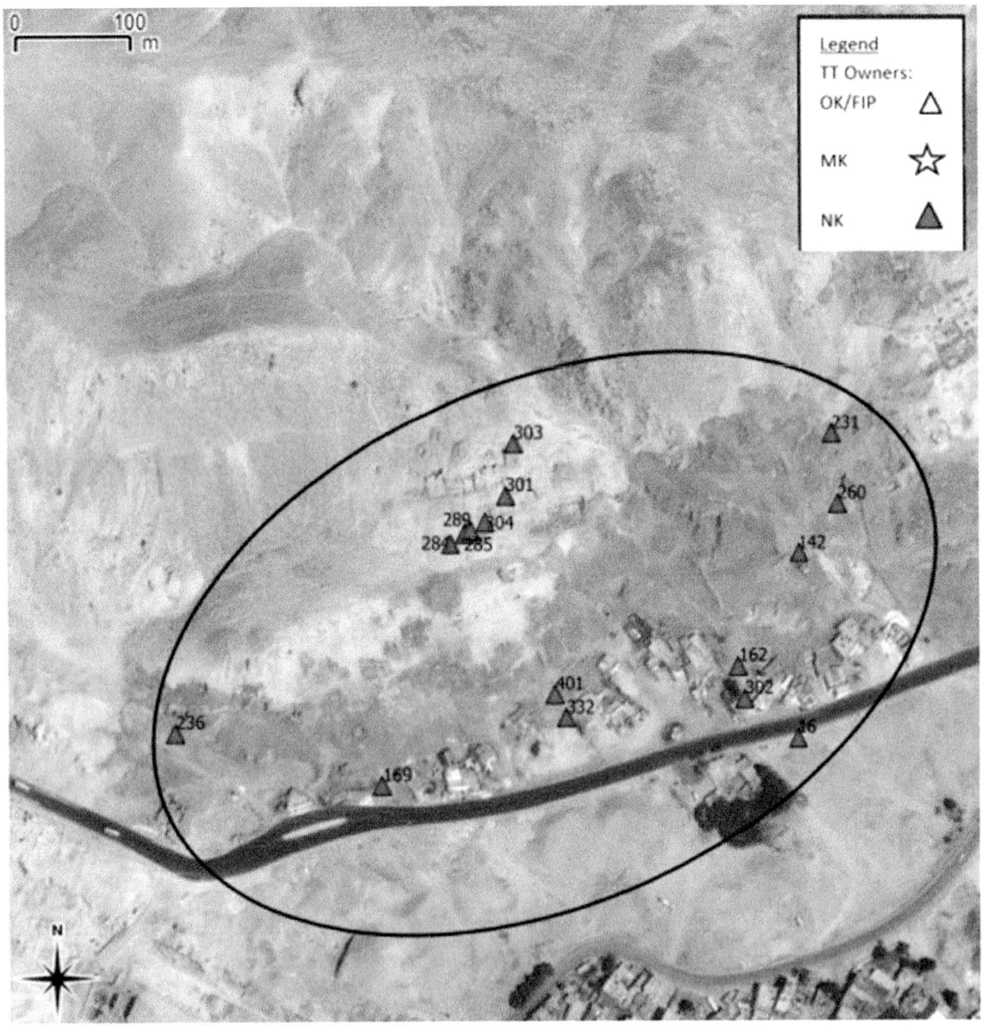

Figure 101: TTs of the Temple Administration in Dra Abu el-Naga West (Author's own using QGIS)

The burial of three 'HPA' in Dra Abu el-Naga West, all dating to the reign of Ramesses II (TT283 may have been later) suggests that there was a deliberate move from Upper Qurna to Dra Abu el-Naga for their burial at this time. Nebwenef-TT157 was the first HPA to be buried here, followed after two intervening HPA by Bakenkhonsu-TT35, who was succeeded by Roma called Roy-TT283 (*LAe* II: 1242–46). The fact that their tombs are clustered together unlike their predecessors in Upper Qurna, suggests that there was a designated area in Dra Abu el-Naga West for the burial of the HPA in the Ramesside Period. These tombs all form part of the aforementioned Ramesside cluster, potentially acting as a focal point for other burials (see Chapter 13). TT35 and TT283 were built some 100m to the west of TT157, despite space being available adjacent to TT157, suggesting a deliberate spacing out of these tombs, within the same general area.

Temple Administration

There were 16 members of the temple administration buried here, most of whom are connected to the Estate of Amun (see Figure 101). Samut-TT142 (TIII-AII) was the 'Overseer of Works' of Amun-Re at Karnak. His tomb occupied a fairly isolated position to the south-east of the main group of tombs, but within 100m of vertical group of six roughly contemporary Eighteenth Dynasty tombs (TT17, TT144, TT145, TT231, TT260 and TT261), two of whom were also members of the temple administration (Nebaum-TT231 and User-TT260 -see below). There were two 'Treasurers of Amun', Hornakht-TT236 (Ram) and Setau-TT289 (RII), whose tombs are not spatially connected as TT289 forms part of the main Ramesside group, while TT236 lies on the lower slopes some distance to the south-west. Senna-TT169 (AII) was the 'Chief of the Goldsmiths of Amun', while Nebseny-TT401 (TIII-AII) held the similar title 'Overseer of the Goldsmiths of Amun'. There was also a 'Goldsmith' and 'Sculptor', Neferrenpet called Kefia-TT140 (TIII-AII), who did not provide an affiliation within his tomb, so is also classified with the general administration. The tombs of these three contemporary individuals are all located on the lower slopes along the same contour line, parallel with the modern road, but more than 100m apart.

Several individuals oversaw elements of food provision in the Estate of Amun, including the 'Overseer of the Granary', Kenamun-TT162 (AIII), the 'Chief Guardian of the Granary', Penrennut-TT332 (Ram), and a 'Counter of the Grain of Amun', Nebamun-TT231 (early Dyn 18). The tombs of these individuals were not spatially connected as TT332 lies adjacent to the earlier TT401, while TT162 is located on the lower slopes in close proximity to TT334 just over 100m to the east at a similar altitude. TT231 lies over 100m to the north of TT162 at a higher altitude, where it forms part of this vertical group of Eighteenth Dynasty tombs, including that of User-TT260 (TIII), who was the 'Overseer of Ploughed Lands', 'Overseer of Field-labourers' and 'Measurer' of Amun, which is less than 100m to the south. TT231 and TT260 also lie within 100m of the aforementioned TT142.

Further titles were connected to religious aspects of temple life, but without esoteric knowledge, such as the two 'Chiefs of the Magazine of Amun', Paraemheb/Userhet-TT302 (Ram) and Paser-TT303 (late Dyn 20/early Dyn 21). Their tombs are not located in close proximity as TT303 forms part of the Ramesside cluster, while TT302 lies some distance to the south on the lower slopes. Panehesi-TT16 (RII), was the 'Chief of the Upper Egyptian Offering Tables of Amun', and there were two 'Scribes of the Offering Table...of the Lord of the Two Lands in the Estate of Amun', Hori-TT301 (Dyn 20- also classified with the royal administration), and '...of Amun' and '...the Lord of the Two Lands', Piay-TT304 (Dyn 20-21). TT301 and TT304 are located within 25m of each other inside the Ramesside cluster, and are discussed further below, but they are hundreds of metres north of TT16. Two members of the temple administration had titles which did not attest Amun, the 'Chief of the Storehouse of Mut', Iny-TT285 (Dyn 19), and the 'Scribe of the Offerings of all the Gods' Pahemneter- the usurper of TT284 (Dyn 20). These tombs are adjacent within the Ramesside cluster.

Royal Administration

There were only six members of the royal administration buried in Dra Abu el-Naga West (see Figure 102). Setau-TT289 (RII) was a 'Steward', Nebamun-TT17 (AII) was a 'Physician of the King' and a 'Royal Scribe', while Amenemhet-TT163 (mid-late Dyn 19) was another a 'Royal Scribe'. There were three 'Scribes of the Offering Table of the Lord of the Two Lands', Anhotep-TT300 (RII-Mer), Hori-TT301 (Dyn 20- also classified with the temple administration as he performed this role within the Estate of Amun), and Piay-TT304 (Dyn 20/21). TT300, TT301 and TT304 form part of the Ramesside cluster, as does TT289, but the potentially contemporary TT300 and TT301 lie in particularly close proximity to each other. TT17 and TT163 lie some distance away from any other members of the royal administration.

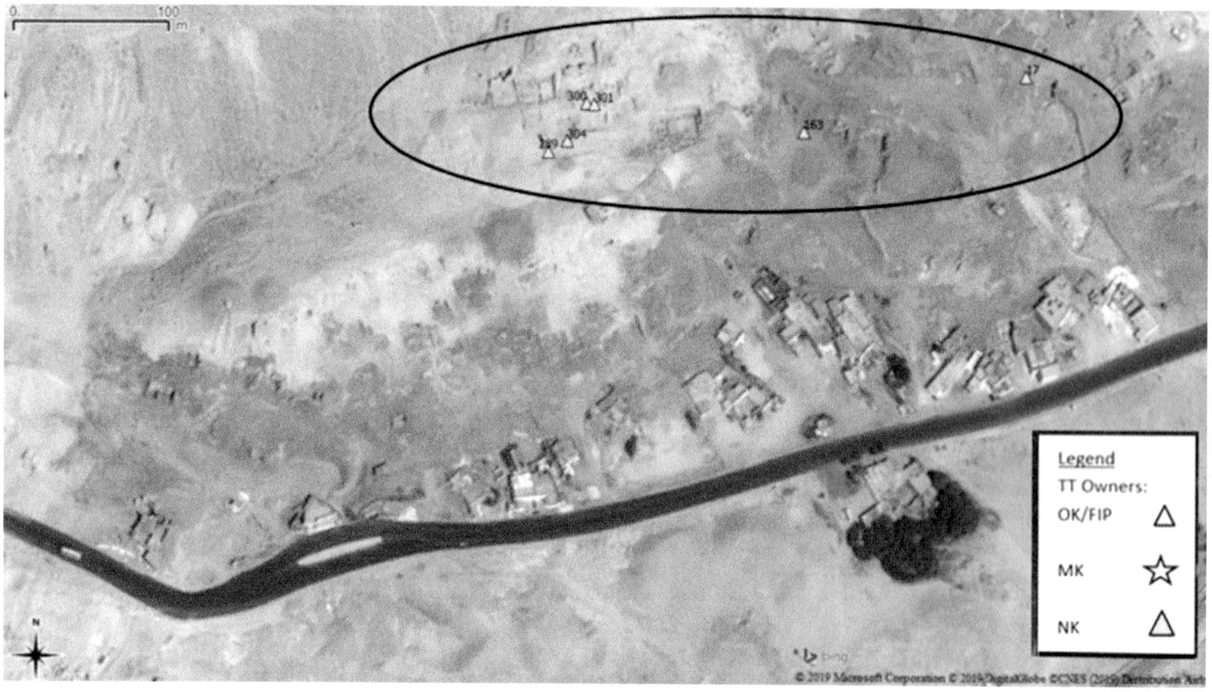

Figure 102: TTs of the Royal Administration in Dra Abu el-Naga West (Author's own using QGIS)

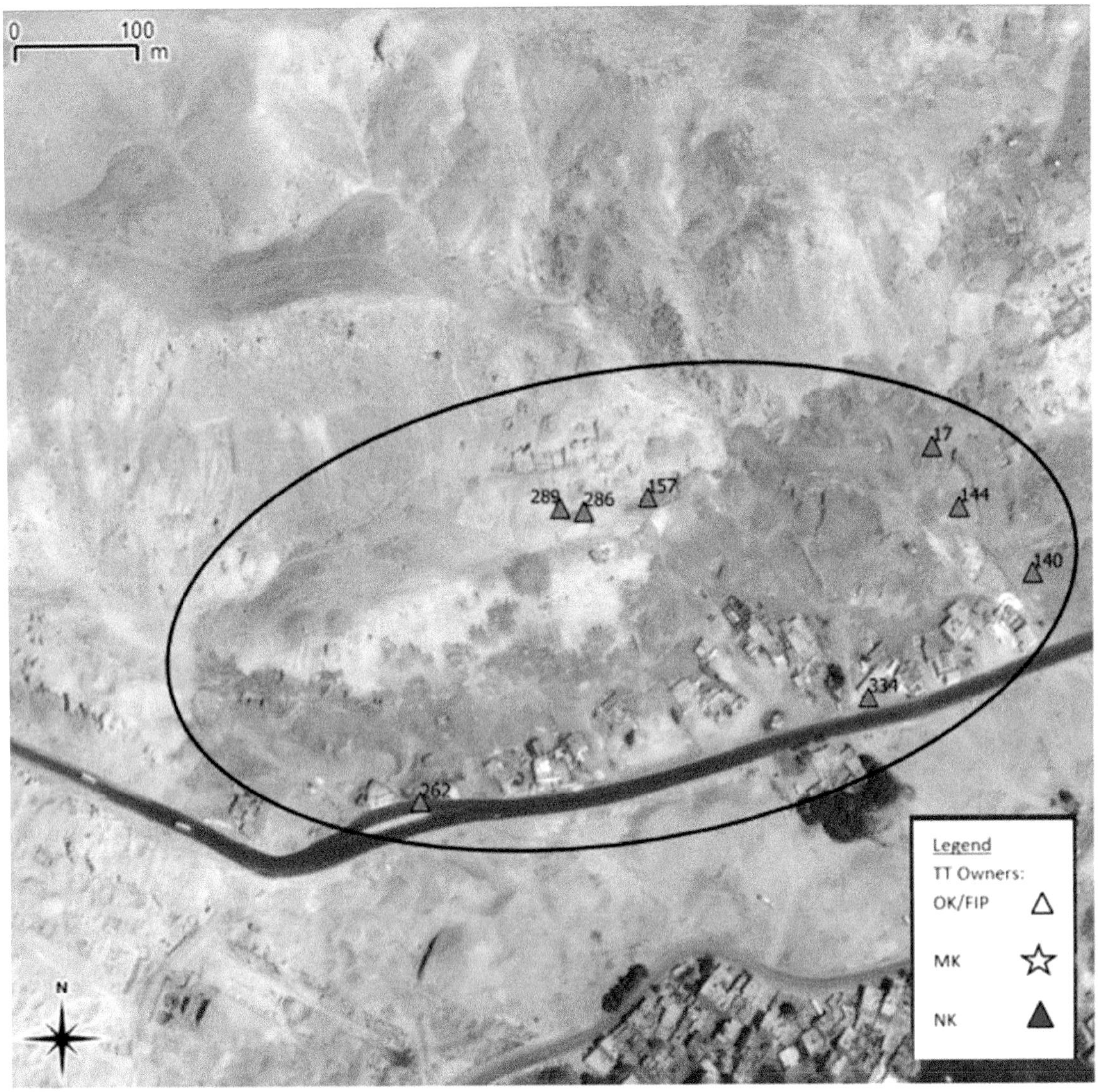

Figure 103: TTs of the General Administration in Dra Abu el-Naga West (Author's own using QGIS)

General Administration

There were eight members of the general administration buried in Dra Abu el-Naga West, whose titles were not explicitly associated with a temple or royal institution (see Figure 103). The most important of these was Nebwennef-TT157 (RII), who was the 'Overseer of Works', 'Overseer of the Treasury', 'Overseer of the Granary', and 'Overseer of all Craftsmen in Thebes' alongside several of the highest priestly titles in the land. His tomb is part of the Ramesside cluster and is not spatially connected to those who held similar administrative titles within the Estate of Amun, as the 'Overseer of Works' of Amun, Samut-TT142 (TIII-AII), the 'Treasurer' of Amun, Hornakht-TT236 (Ram) and the 'Overseer of the Granary of Amun' Kenamun-TT162 (AIII) were all buried some distance away. Only Setau-T289 (RII), the 'Treasurer' of Amun, was also part of this Ramesside group.

Several individuals held titles related to agricultural production, such as the unknown 'Overseer of Arable Land' buried in TT262 (TIII), the 'Head of Field-Labourers', Nu-TT144 (TIII), and the unknown 'Chief of Husbandmen', buried in TT334 (AIII). There is no obvious spatial link between the tombs of these individuals, and none of them are located in the Ramesside cluster. Other general individuals with a title without a specific association include the 'Steward' Setau-TT289 (RII), the 'Chief Physician' Nebamun-TT17 (AII), and a 'Scribe (of the Offering Table)', Niay-TT286 (Dyn 19). Of these tombs, TT286 and TT289 lie adjacent within the Ramesside cluster

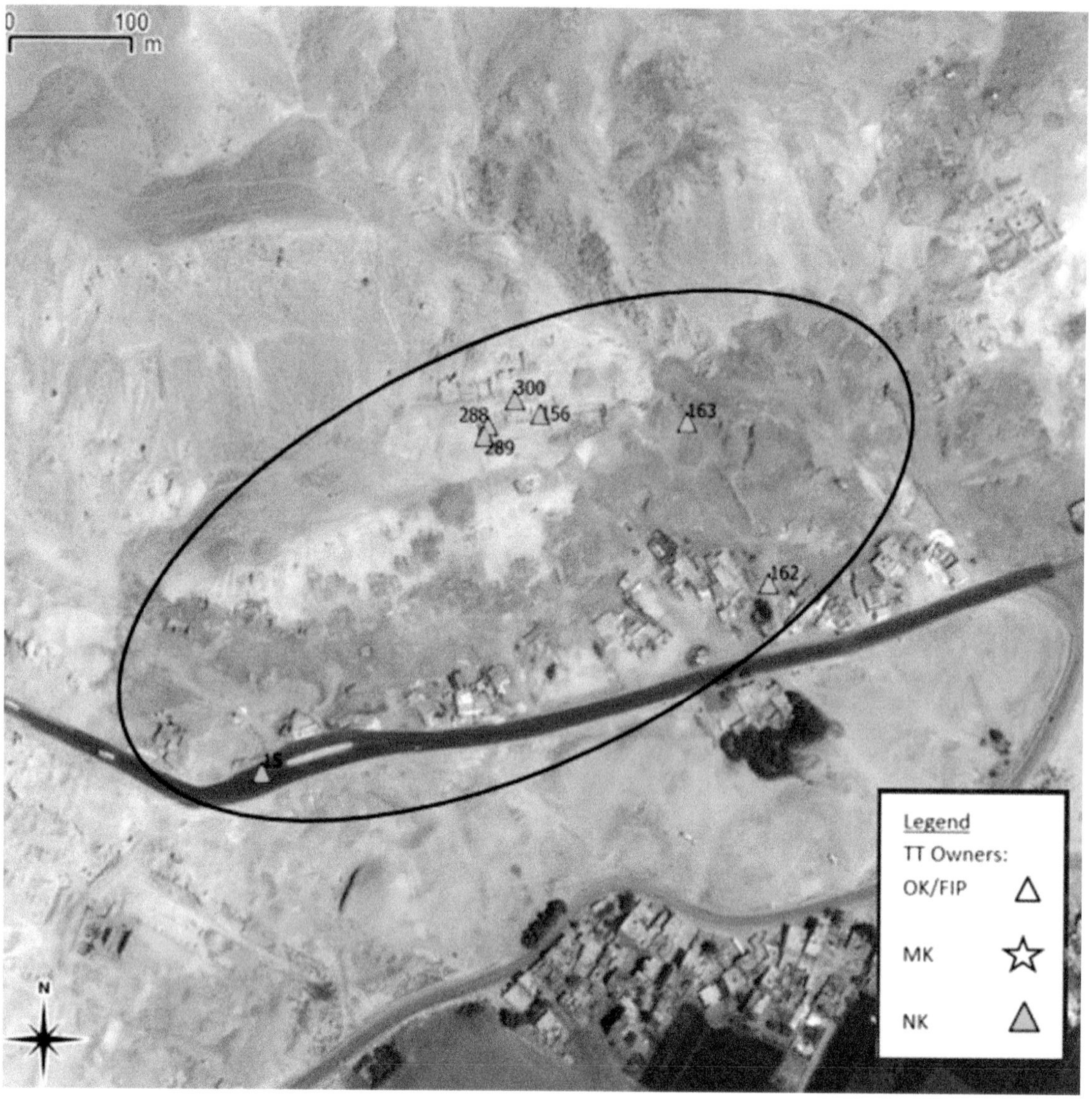

Figure 104: TTs of the Local Administration in Dra Abu el-Naga West (Author's own using QGIS)

The relatively low number of these royal and general officials buried here reflects the general pattern observed throughout the necropolis in the Ramesside Period, as fewer officials are buried in Thebes, and those dating to the Eighteenth Dynasty were buried in Qurna when there was still space available. Generally speaking, those individuals who are buried here are not as important as those officials who were buried in Upper Qurna as there are no 'Viziers' and fewer 'Treasurers' and 'Overseers' of government departments than in other areas of the necropolis.

Local Administration

There were seven tombs in Dra Abu el-Naga West belonging to local administrators, of Thebes or southern lands (see Figure 104). Three contemporary officials held positions in the south as 'Overseers of (Southern) Foreign Lands', Pennesuttawy-TT156 (RII), Setau- who owned T288 (RII-before a Late Period reuse obscured evidence of the original occupant, Kampp 1996: 558-561) and the adjacent TT289 (RII), and Anhotep-TT300 (RII/Mer). Both Setau and Anhotep were also 'King's Son of Kush'. All four tombs belonged to the Ramesside cluster on the upper slopes, so were located in relatively close proximity. There were also three 'Mayors of the Southern City', Tetiky-TT15 (Ah-AI), Kenamun-TT162 (AIII), and Amenemhet-TT163 (mid-late Dyn 19). There is no distributional pattern between the tombs of these three mayors as two are located on the lower slopes some distance apart, while TT163 is located over 100m to the north of TT162, on the outskirts of the Ramesside group.

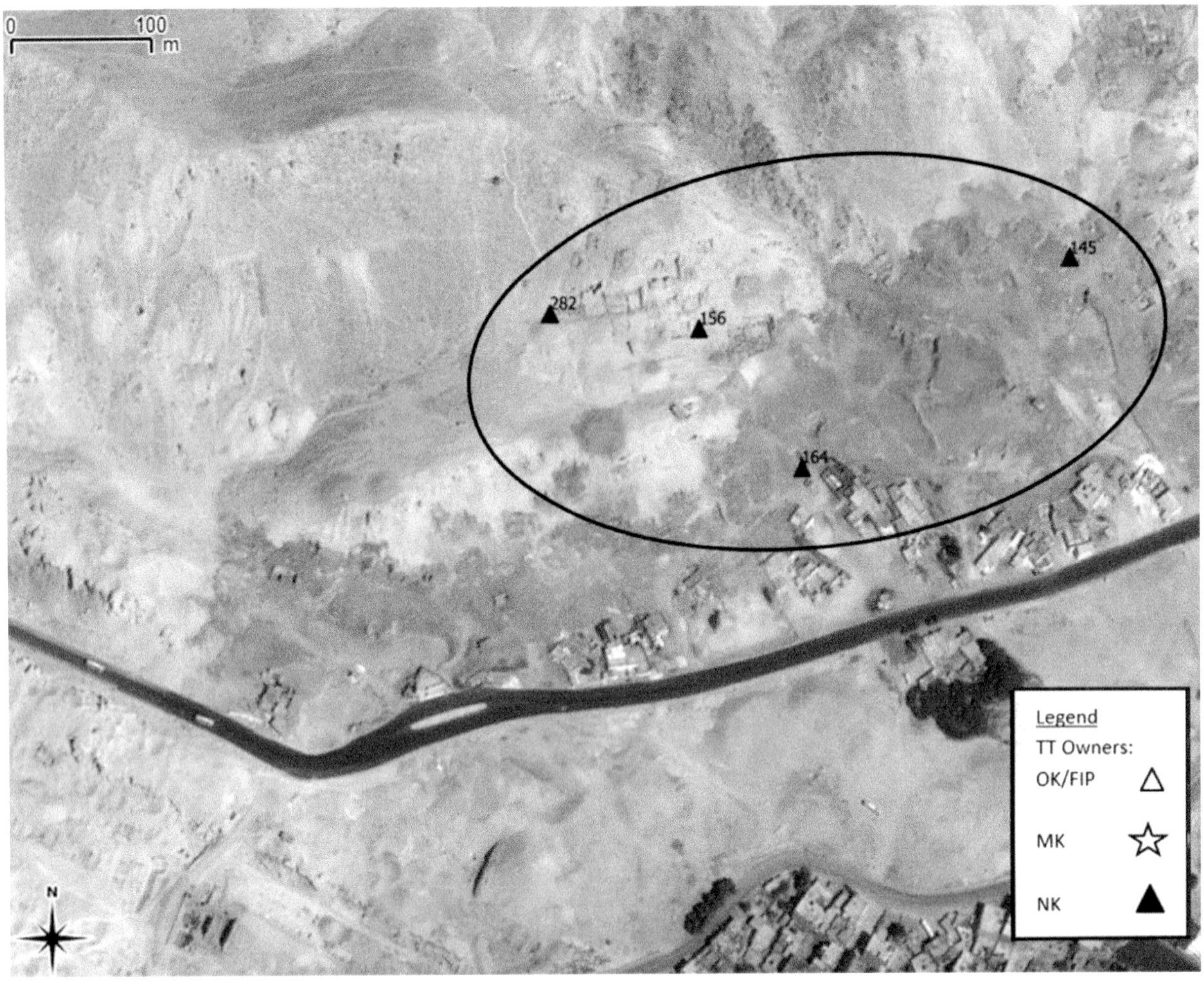

Figure 105: TTs of the Military in Dra Abu el-Naga West (Author's own using QGIS)

Military

Four TTs belonged to members of the military (see Figure 105). Three were 'Captain of Troops', Nebamun-TT145 (Hat-TIII), Pennesuttawy-TT156 (RII) and Nakht/Menunakht-TT282 (RII), while the fourth belonged to a 'Scribe of Recruits', Intef-TT164 (TIII). The contemporary TT156 and TT282 are situated within 100m of each other within the Ramesside cluster on the upper slopes. There is no spatial connection between them and the other military tombs, as TT145 forms part of the Eighteenth Dynasty group to the east, while TT164 lies some distance to the south-east.

Unknown

Three tombs are owned by individuals with unknown titles, TT284 (Dyn 19-RII), TT288 (RII), and TT333 (Amarna). The usurper of TT285 (Dyn 20) is also unknown.

The Ramesside Cluster

This distinct cluster of burials is made up of 17 Ramesside tombs (see Figure 106): TT35 (RII), TT156 (RII), TT157 (RII), TT158 (SII-Tau), TT159 (late Dyn 19-20), TT282 (RII), TT283 (RII-SII), TT284 (Dyn 19-RII), TT285 (Dyn 19), TT286 (Dyn 19), TT287 (Ram), TT288 (RII), TT289 (RII), TT300 (RII/Mer), TT301 (Dyn 20), TT303 (late Dyn 20-21) and TT304 (Dyn 20/21). Nine of these tombs potentially date to Ramesses II, with the majority of others less precisely dated to the Ramesside Period. Two of these tombs were reused during the Twentieth Dynasty (TT284 and TT285). The upper slopes would have afforded a better view than the lower slopes over the procession of the BFV as it moved from the landing stage close to the mortuary temple of Seti I in a south-westerly direction along the processional way past Dra Abu el-Naga West, explaining this choice of location, particularly for those associated with the cult of Amun during the Ramesside Period. It would also have provided views of any procession between Menisut and K93.11 and K93.12, while overlooking Menisut to the west.

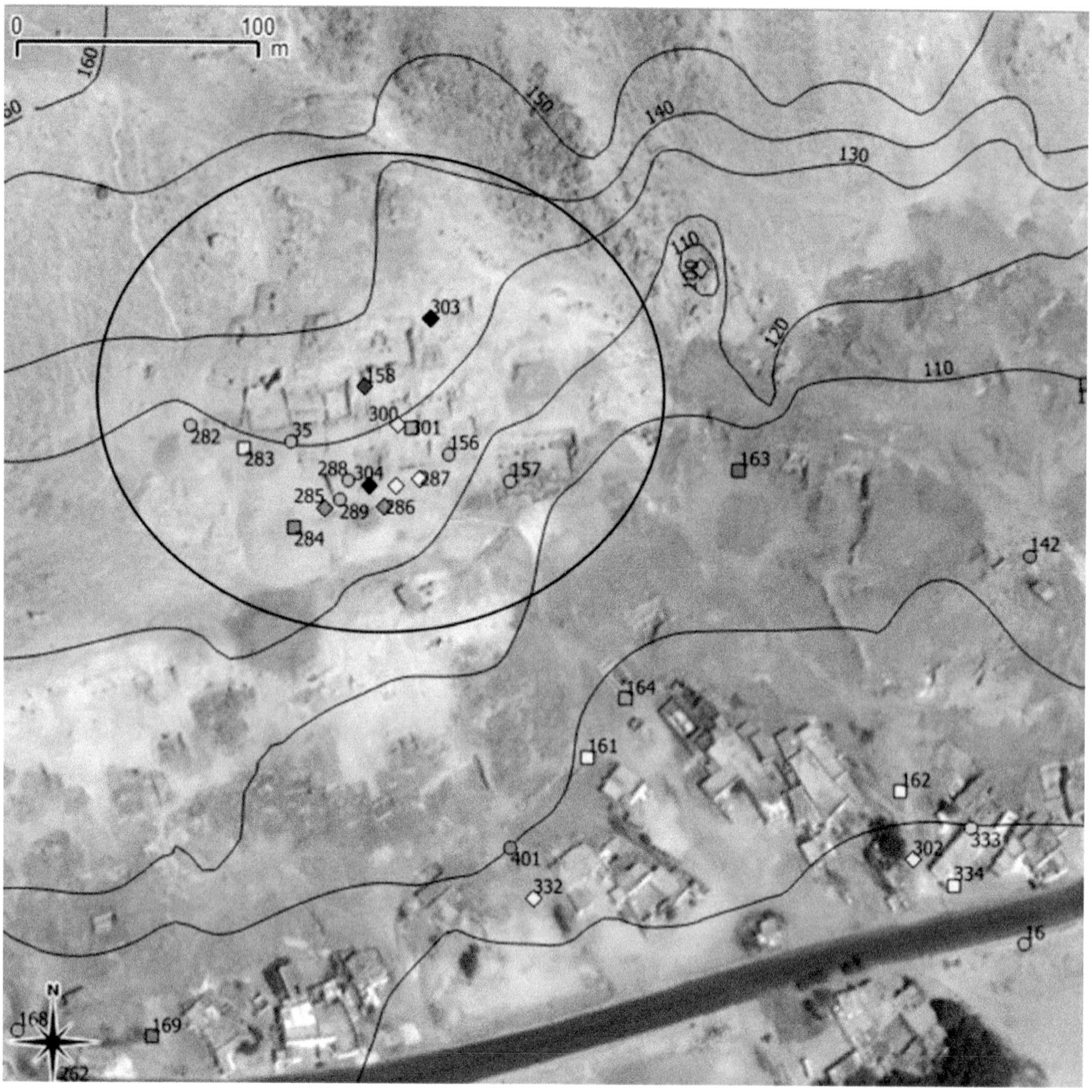

Figure 106: The 'Ramesside Cluster' in Dra Abu el-Naga West (Author's own using QGIS)

The lack of precise dating for the majority of tombs in this group makes the chronological evolution of this cluster problematic, so it is unclear which tomb was built first, thus potentially acting as a focal point for additional burials in this area. Among the earliest tombs situated here were the three consecutive HPA (TT35, TT157 and TT283), whose high status within the cult of Amun, and Thebes as a whole, may have influenced the proximity of other burials, particularly those of priests, within this group. The later burials of two '3PA' (TT158 and TT303), a '4PA' (TT159) and a '*wꜥb* priest' of Amun (TT287) seem likely to have been situated here in an attempt to be buried in close proximity to these HPA. The original owner of TT284 is unknown, but the tomb was reused by a 'Scribe of the Offerings of all the Gods', while TT285 was owned by the 'Head of the Storehouse of Mut', suggesting that even those connected to the cult of Amun in an administrative capacity were interested in spending eternity in the vicinity of these important priests, or this may be coincidental. The fact that seven priests of Amun and two temple administrators were buried in this area is significant.

There were two 'King's Sons of Kush' buried here, Setau-TT288 and TT289, and Anhotep-TT300, who were also 'Overseers of Southern Foreign Lands', as was Pennesuttawy-TT156. Pennesuttawy was also 'Captain of Troops', as was Nakht/Menunakht-TT282, establishing a potential connection between these contemporary individuals. Anhotep-TT300 was also 'Scribe of the Offering Table', as were Niay-TT286, Hori-TT301 and Piay-TT304. The frequency of this title shared by four of these tomb owners suggests another potential connection, although TT301 and TT304 appear to have been later additions to the original group. In addition to King's Son of Kush, Setau-TT289 was also the 'Treasurer of Amun', which may explain why this area was used by multiple HPA and 'King's

Figure 107: The group of TT282, TT283 and TT35, with the mudbrick ramp of TT35 in the centre (Courtesy of the Penn Museum: image no. 34801)

Sons of Kush' as it indicates a possible link between the Estate of Amun and this role. The HPA Nebwenef-TT157 was also a 'Treasurer', although it is not specified in his tomb if this role was in connection to Amun, although this seems likely, thus connecting Setau and Nebwenef who both served under Ramesses II.

Relationship between Tomb Owners / Tombs

There are several known familial relationships between the tomb owners in Dra Abu el-Naga West. One family group is that of the 3PA Tjanefer-TT158 (SII-Tau). The tomb of Tjanefer's son, another 3PA, Amenemopet-TT148 (RIII-RV), is located in Dra Abu el-Naga East, some distance away from the tomb of his father. However, Tjanefer's grandson, another 3PA, Paser-TT303 (late Dyn 20-early 21), was buried next to him (Bierbrier 1975: 6; Ockinga 2006: 142-146). TT158 appears to have served as a model for both TT148 and TT303, showing familial continuity (Bács 2011: 8). Paser is also a descendant of the HPA Bakenkhonsu-TT35 (RII) (Kákosy and Bács 2004: 9-10), whose tomb is located in close proximity to both TT158 and TT303. These three tombs lie adjacent to one another, at the highest level of the Ramesside group, along the same contour line, showing a familial group.

The HPA Bakenkhonsu-TT35 (RII) may also have been the father or brother of his successor, Roma called Roy-TT283 (RII), and their tombs are adjacent to each other (Rummel 2018: 260-262). TT283, the last tomb to be built appears to have been squeezed in between TT282 and TT35, in order for Roma called Roy's tomb to be spatially connected to that of his father, forming a group of three tightly clustered contemporary tombs to the west of the group (see Figures 107 and 108). Nakht/Menunakht-TT282 (RII) does not appear to be related to the other two tomb owners here, but the tomb of his father or grandfather, Pennesuttawy-TT156 (RII), lies 100m away, also within the Ramesside cluster. Roma called Roy-TT283 also had a grandson, Raia-TT159 (late Dyn 19-early 20) (Bierbrier, 1975: 2), whose tomb lies 50m to the east. There may also have been familial connections between Pahemneter-TT284 and Raia-TT159, and Iny-TT285 and Raia-TT159 (Jimenez-Higueras 2016: 62), whose tombs lie within the

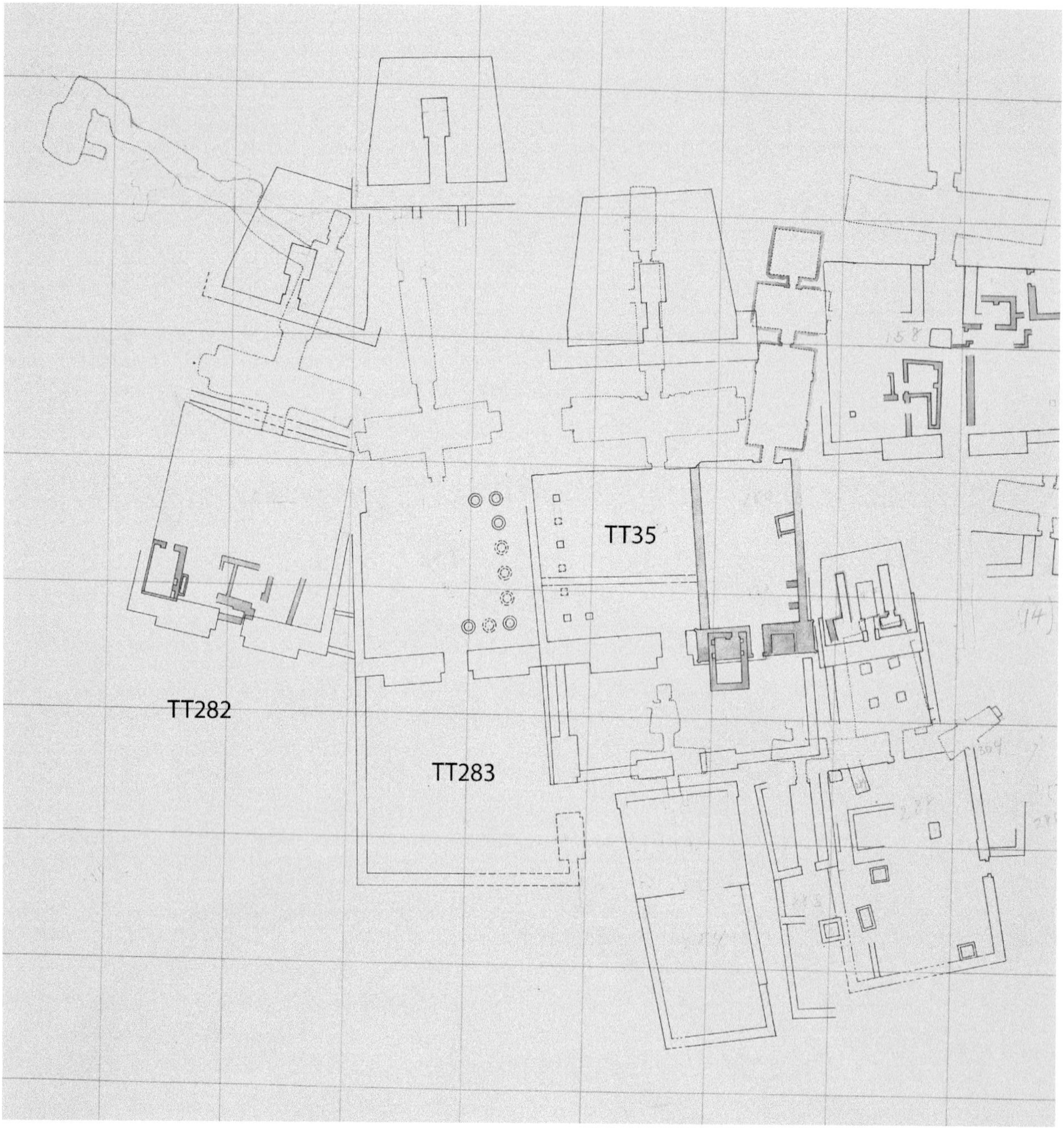

Figure 108: Plan of the tomb group of TT282, TT283 and TT35 (Courtesy of the Penn Museum: image no. 195599)

Table 12: Owners of TT288, TT289 and TT304

TT	Dyn	Reign	Name	Title
TT288	19	RII	(1) Setau	(1) TT 289?
TT289	19	RII	Setau	King's Son of Kush; Overseer of the Southern Foreign Lands; Steward; Overseer of the Treasury of Amun;
TT304	20/21	?	Piay	Scribe of the Offering Table of Amun/the Lord of the Two Lands;

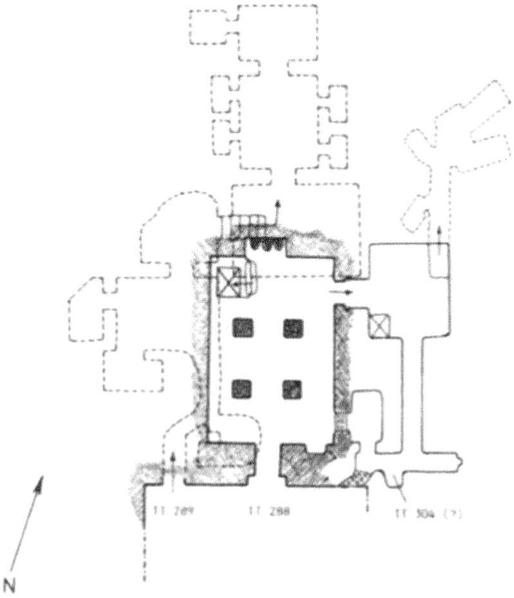

Figure 109: Plan of TT288, TT289 and TT304 (Kampp 1996: Figure 454 – Courtesy of Professor Seyfried)

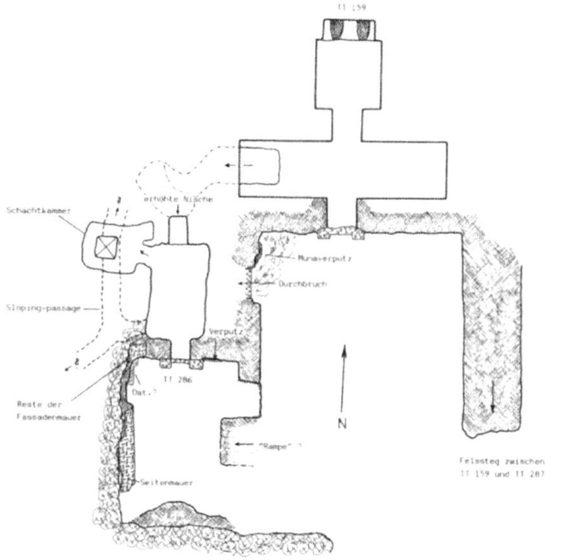

Figure 110: Plan of shared courtyard of TT159 and TT286 (Kampp 1996: Figure 344 -Courtesy of Professor Seyfried)

Table 13: Owners of TT159 and TT286

TT	Dyn	Reign	Name	Title
TT159	Late 19-early 20	?	Rai	4th priest of Amun;
TT286	Late 19	?	Niay	Scribe (of the Offering Table);

aforementioned cluster. Nebamun-TT145 (Hat-TIII) was the father of Paser-TT367 (AII) (Jimenez-Higueras 2016: 82) but this tomb lies some distance away in Qurna.

With the exception of TT145, all tomb owners with familial links in this area were buried within the Ramesside cluster. The relatively large number of familial connections within Dra Abu el-Naga West, and in this cluster in particular, suggests a link between familial grouping and tomb distribution in this area.

Shared Courtyards

There are several tombs with shared courtyards in Dra Abu el-Naga West.

TT288, TT289 and TT304

These three tombs are all located in a row along the northern side of a shared courtyard, with TT288 and TT304 also interconnected with two passages from the transverse hall of TT288 to TT304 (see Figure 109). TT288 occupies the central position so appears to have been built first, followed by TT289. Both tombs were owned by Setau (Kampp 1996: 558-561), and lie adjacent to each other, with TT304 being added as a later addition to the courtyard. TT304 was built much later so as there is no evidence of familial relationship or shared titles between the tomb owners (see Table 12). Piay may have wanted close proximity to an important official who was still remembered, or this location may have been chosen as there was space available on the eastern edge of the courtyard.

TT159 and TT286

TT286 and TT159 share a communal approach, and TT286 is accessed via a ramp which leads from the western side of the courtyard of TT159, where it is located within a small courtyard of its own. These tombs are also connected via an underground passage which leads from the western wall of the transverse hall of TT159 to the niche at the rear of TT286 (see Figure 110). The combination of a shared approach, connecting courtyards and a connecting passage seem to be more than coincidental. This suggests that these tombs were deliberately sited within close proximity, although the reason for this close relationship is unclear. TT159

Table 14: Owners of TT300 and TT301

TT	Dyn	Reign	Name	Title
TT300	19	RII/Mer	Anhotep	**King's son of Kush;** Overseer of the Southern Foreign Lands; Scribe of the Offering Table of the Lord of the Two Lands;
TT301	Late 19/20	?	Hori	Scribe of the Offering Table of the Lord of the Two Lands in the Estate of Amun;

Table 15: Owners of TT17 and TT145

TT	Dyn	Reign	Name	Title
TT17	18	(TIII) AII	Nebamun	Physician (of the King)(in Thebes); Chief Physician; (Royal) Scribe (in Thebes);
TT145	18	Hat/TIII	Nebamun	Captain of Troops;

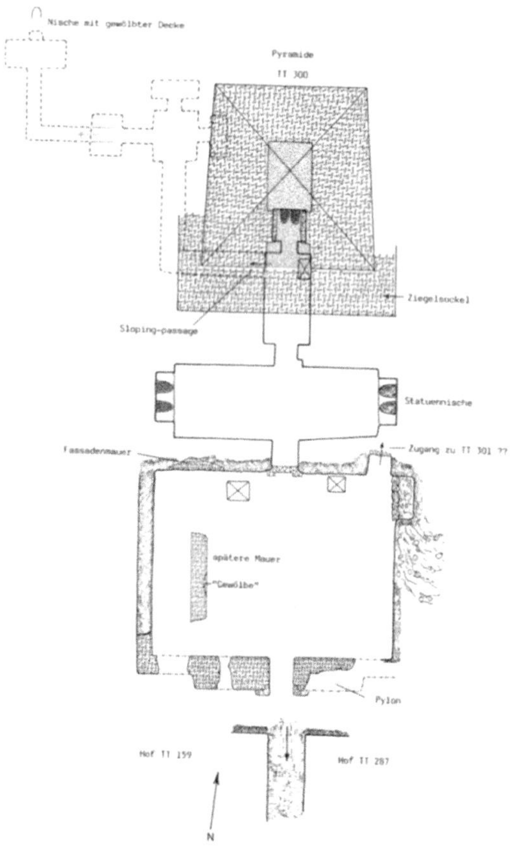

Figure 111: Plan of TT300 showing entrance to TT301 (Kampp 1996: Figure 462 – Courtesy of Professor Seyfried)

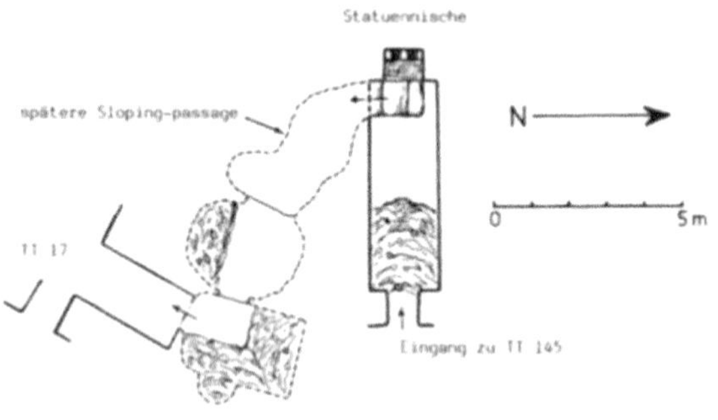

Figure 112: Plan of passage linking TT17 and TT145 (Kampp 1996: Figure 323 – Courtesy of Professor Seyfried)

dates to either the late Nineteenth or early Twentieth Dynasty on stylistic grounds, while TT286 was more securely dated to the late Nineteenth Dynasty so these individuals may have known each other, or even been related. The plan appears to confirm that TT156 was constructed first due to its prominent position facing the entrance to the courtyard, while TT286 was a later addition cut into the side of the courtyard. The tomb owners shared no titles, so a familial link seems most likely (see Table 13).

TT300 and TT301

The entrance to TT301 is in the eastern courtyard of TT300 (see Figure 111). Both tomb owners were 'Scribe of the Offering Table of the Lord of the Two Lands' (see Table 14), which if this role was hereditary suggests a possible family connection between these two tomb owners, with Hori being the son or grandson of Anhotep. It is interesting that both 'King's Sons of Kush' had later burials added onto their courtyards, perhaps indicative of the high esteem they were held in by future generations.

Table 16: Owners of TT260 and TT261

TT	Dyn	Reign	Name	Title
TT260	18	TIII	User	Measurer of [Amun]; Overseer of the Ploughed Lands of Amun; Overseer of the Field-labourers of Amun;
TT261	18	TIII/(AII)	Khaemwaset	*wꜥb* priest of Amenhotep I;

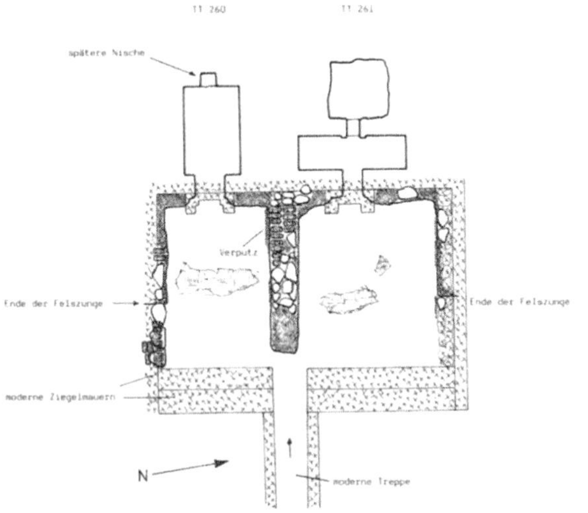

Figure 113: Plan of TT260 and TT261 (Kampp 1996: Figure 433 – Courtesy of Professor Seyfried)

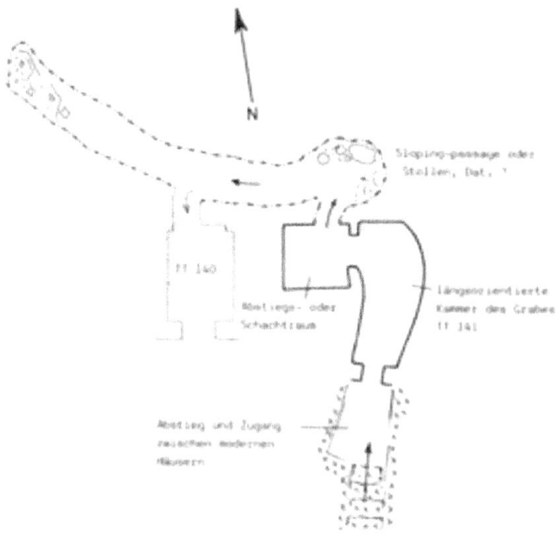

Figure 114: Plan of TT141 and passage to TT140 (Kampp 1996: Figure 319 – Courtesy of Professor Seyfried)

Table 17: Owners of TT140 and TT141

TT	Dyn	Reign	Name	Title
TT140	18	TIII/AII	Neferrenpet called Kefia	Goldworker; Sculptor;
TT141	20	?	Bakenkhonsu	*wꜥb* priest of Amun;

TT17 and TT145

TT145 and TT17 are connected by means of a sloping passage which leads from the rear of TT145 to the northern wall of the transverse hall of TT17 (see Figure 112). The large amount of debris within TT145 makes it impossible to ascertain if the tombs were connected when TT17 was built (Kampp 1996: 430). If this passage was indeed cut when the later tomb was built, the fact that both tomb owners lived in successive reigns and shared the same name, makes a familial link between the two possible. The father of Nebamun-TT17 was named Nebseny from the inscriptions within the tomb, but Nebamun-TT145 could still have been his grandfather. The two tomb owners share no titles (see Table 15).

TT260 and TT261

TT260 and TT261 are both approached by one staircase, and share a courtyard partially divided by a low wall (see Figure 113). As both tombs are contemporary, although there are no common titles (see Table 16), it is possible that the occupants knew each other or were related, and deliberately built their tombs adjacent to each other with shared access.

TT140 and TT141

TT140 can be accessed via a sloping passage which runs from the rear chamber of TT141 into the rear of TT140 and continues past the tomb until it reaches what appears to be a dead end (see Figure 114). It is unclear when this connecting passage was dug (Kampp 1996: 428) so these tombs may have been connected in

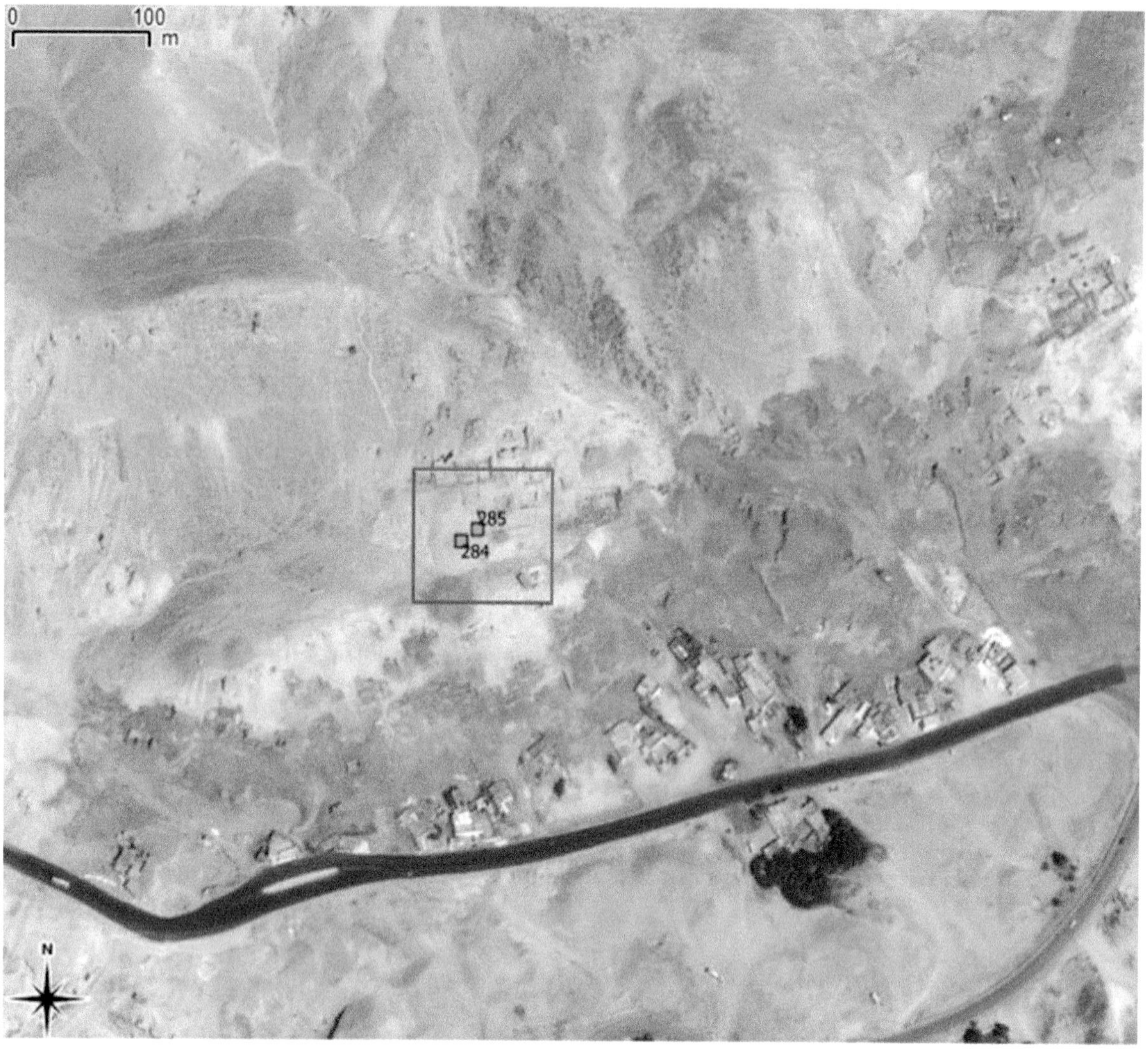

Figure 115: Reused TTs in Dra Abu el-Naga West at the end of the New Kingdom (shown by date of first reuse) (Author's own using QGIS)

Table 18: Reused tombs in Dra Abu el-Naga West

TT	Original Date	Date of Reuse
TT284	Dyn 19-RII	Dyn 20
TT285	Dyn 19	Dyn 20

antiquity, or the more likely alternative is a connecting tunnel was dug by tomb robbers but in the absence of a definitive date all possibilities must be considered. There is no titular link to explain why Bakenkhonsu-TT141 would have connected his tomb to Neferenpet-TT140 in antiquity (see Table 17), except a possible familial relationship but there is no evidence of this.

Tomb Reuse

Only two tombs in Dra Abu el-Naga West were reused during the New Kingdom (TT284 and TT285). They were both built in the Nineteenth Dynasty and reused in the Twentieth Dynasty (see Table 18). They are both located along the southern edge of the 'Ramesside Group', adjacent to each other (see Figure 115). The original occupant of TT284 is unknown, but it was re-used by Pahemneter, a temple scribe, while Iny-TT285 was a temple administrator but the usurper is unknown. Without information about both occupants of each tomb, connections between the tomb owner and usurper cannot be identified.

Figure 116: Outlying tombs to the south of Dra Abu el-Naga West (Author's own using QGIS)

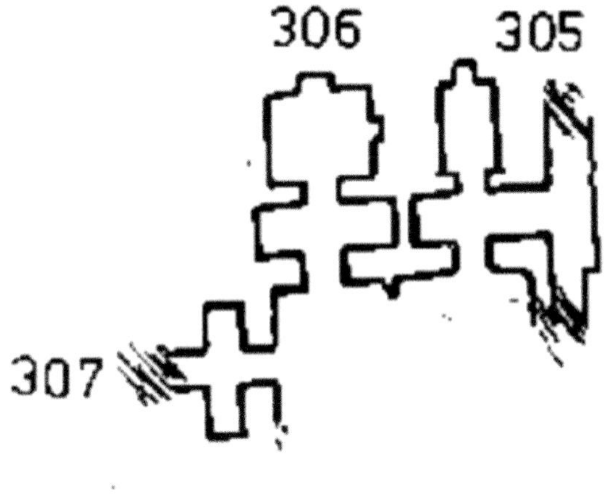

Figure 117: Plan of TT305, TT306 and TT307 (Kampp 1996: Plan VI – Courtesy of Professor Seyfried)

Outlying Tombs

(See Appendix 5)

There is a tight cluster of three tombs located to the south of the main area of Dra Abu el-Naga West, over 150m away from any other tombs (see Figure 116), at the level of the floodplain (TT305, TT306 and TT307). These tombs are included here as they form a distinct cluster and have no tombs between them and the rest of Dra Abu el-Naga, unlike those apparently isolated tombs to the west, which have later Kampp numbered tombs between them and other TTs (Kampp 1996: Plan VI).

TT307 is located on the western side of an open court, while TT306 and TT305 are adjacent to each other on the northern side (see Figure 117). These three tombs date to roughly the same period, and both Paser-TT305 and Irdjanen-TT306 were connected to the Estate of Amun, with the occupation of Tjunefer-TT307 unknown. This could suggest a working relationship between these men within the Estate of Amun. There is no explanation as to why these three tombs occupied such an isolated position, so perhaps these late additions to the necropolis found the best locations taken so found some suitable land further south.

Conclusions

The presence of Menisut just to the west of this area would have influenced tomb placement, particularly of the priests of this temple, such as Khaemwaset-TT261 and Panehesi-TT16, who seem to have desired burial in close proximity to it. The procession between Menisut and the tombs of Amenhotep I and Ahmose-Nefertari in Dra Abu el-Naga East would also have been a factor, as in Dra Abu el-Naga East (see Chapter 5). The processional

Figure 118: Karnak's east-west axis aligned with the southern end of Dra Abu el-Naga West (Author's own)

Figure 119: Zoomed in image of Dra Abu el-Naga West aligned with Karnak's east-west axis (Author's own)

route of the BFV to the south would also have impacted on tomb distribution, as tombs were orientated towards the route in general and the ritual space to the east of the row of tombs between TT231 and TT144, along the route of the *wadi*. As the first stop for the procession in the Nineteenth Dynasty was the temple of Seti I, this would necessitate it passing directly in front of Dra Abu el-Naga on its way to Deir el-Bahri. 'The Great Forecourt of Amun' or '*p3 wb3 ꜥ3 n Imn*' (Polz *et al.* 2012: 122 n35 and 36; Rummel 2018: 257) also influenced tomb distribution, as the semi-circle of eastward-facing tombs to the west of this space clearly demonstrates (Kampp 1996: Plan VI – Appendix 15). Jimenez-Higueras (2016: 180-203) conducted some visibility analysis from each tomb within the Ramesside cluster and has discovered that Menisut and the Seti I temple are visible from the majority of these tombs, thus confirming their influence on tomb distribution within this group. She also attempts to chronologically sequence some of the tombs in this cluster: TT157, TT35, TT283; TT156, TT282; TT159, TT286, TT284; TT300, TT158 (Jimenez-Higueras 2016: 56-57). All four of these short sequences when taken in isolation would suggest a chronological movement in tomb distribution from north to south, as suggested by Helck (1962: 242-43).

The link between the Estate of Amun and this area is demonstrated by the large number of burials of priests and administrators here. As this area lies directly opposite Karnak, in line with the east-west axis of the temple (see Figures 118 and 119) and lies along the processional route of the BFV, it explains why this area was significant to these individuals. Helck (1962: 242-243) suggested that the clustering of these priests within this area during the reign of Ramesses II, was a result of its alignment with Karnak, reflected a change in tomb distribution at this time, as no similar clusters of priests' tombs exist elsewhere in the necropolis. The visibility of Karnak from almost all of the tombs in this cluster has been confirmed (Jimenez-Higueras 2016: 203), thus proving Helck's theory regarding their distribution, although Kampp is rightly sceptical of this connection as a result of the long distance between the two sites and the visibility of Karnak from the majority of the necropolis (Kampp 1996: 120-21). However, the direct spatial link between the two and the frequency of priests' burials within the Ramesside cluster is compelling, and in conjunction with the processional activity in the area provides a satisfactory explanation.

The presence of three 'Overseers of Foreign Lands' within the Ramesside cluster in this area, and only one other in the whole necropolis, TT40 (Tut) in Qurnet Murai, in addition to two 'King's Sons of Kush' and only two others, TT40 (Tut) and TT383 (AIII) in Qurnet Murai, suggests that this area may have been deliberately chosen by holders of these titles in the Ramesside Period.

Chapter 6: Deir el-Bahri

(See Appendices 2 and 6)

Location

Deir el-Bahri lies to the east of the cliffs bordering the Valley of the Kings, at the western end of the causeway leading from the cultivation to the temples of Nebhepetre Montuhotep II, Hatshepsut and Tuthmosis III. The temples are sited within a deep bay flanked by high cliffs to the west and the north. This area includes the northern slopes bordering the causeway leading to the royal mortuary temples, and the area directly within the bay of the cliffs themselves (see Figure 120). The tombs here lie between 130m and 150m above sea level, with the flood plain in this area lying some distance to the east, beginning at 80m above sea level (see Figure 121). Most tombs date to the Middle Kingdom and lie in a row along the steep hills to the north of the causeway, with several more found within the bay of cliffs itself (see Figure 122).

Date of Use

All tombs bordering the northern side of the causeway (see Figure 123) date to the Middle Kingdom, except for TT353, so as such these tombs did not influence New Kingdom tomb distribution. There are no other New Kingdom tombs in this area, although the elevated position, orientation and proximity to both the royal mortuary temples and the processional causeway used throughout the New Kingdom during the BFV (Cabrol 2001: 550), should make this a desirable area to locate tombs, particularly those dating to the reigns of Hatshepsut and Tuthmosis III as their temples are located at Deir el-Bahri (see Figure 124). There are also the remains of a chapel dating to Amenhotep I beneath the temple of Hatshepsut (Winlock 1942: 88). The lack of early New Kingdom tombs in this area suggests that burial in this area was not appropriate at this time and

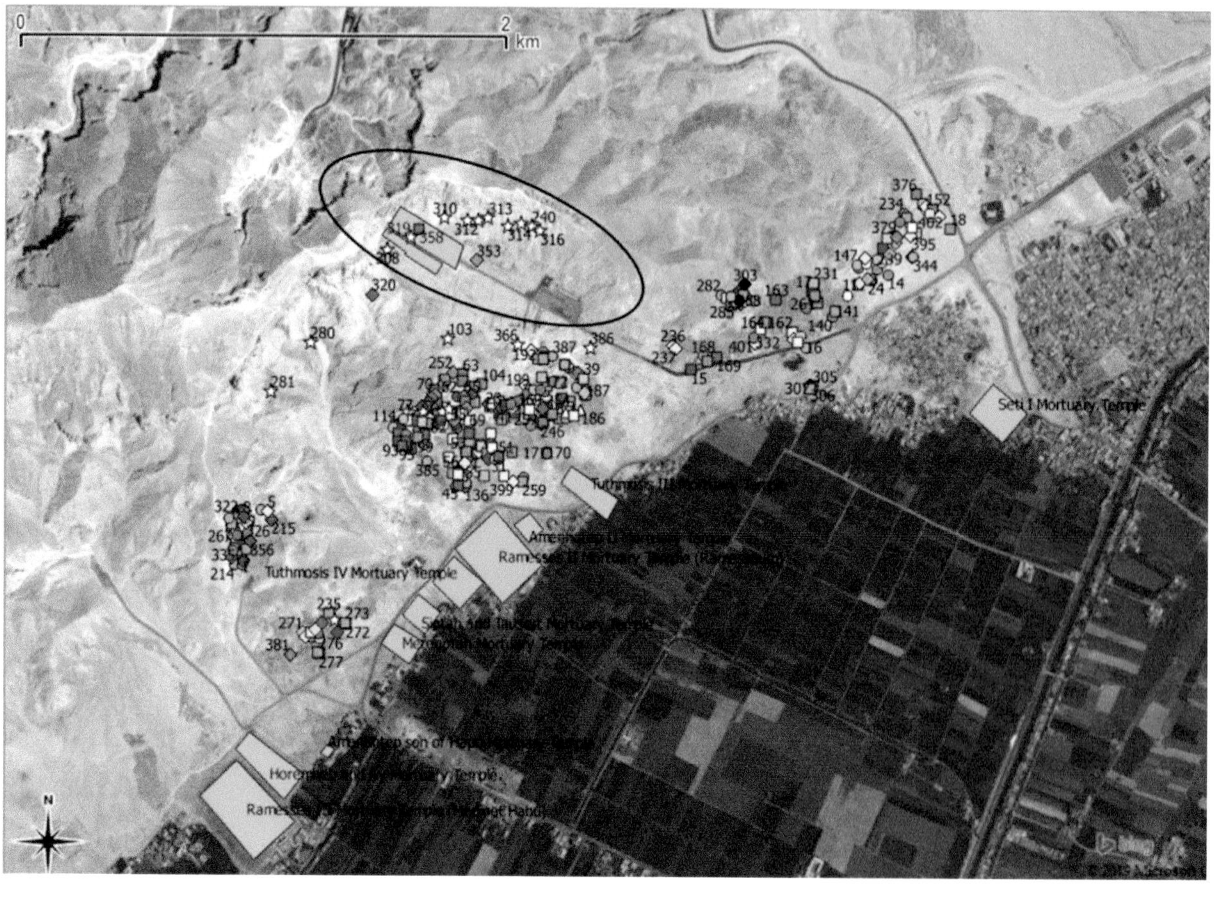

Figure 120: Location of Deir el-Bahri (Author's own using QGIS)

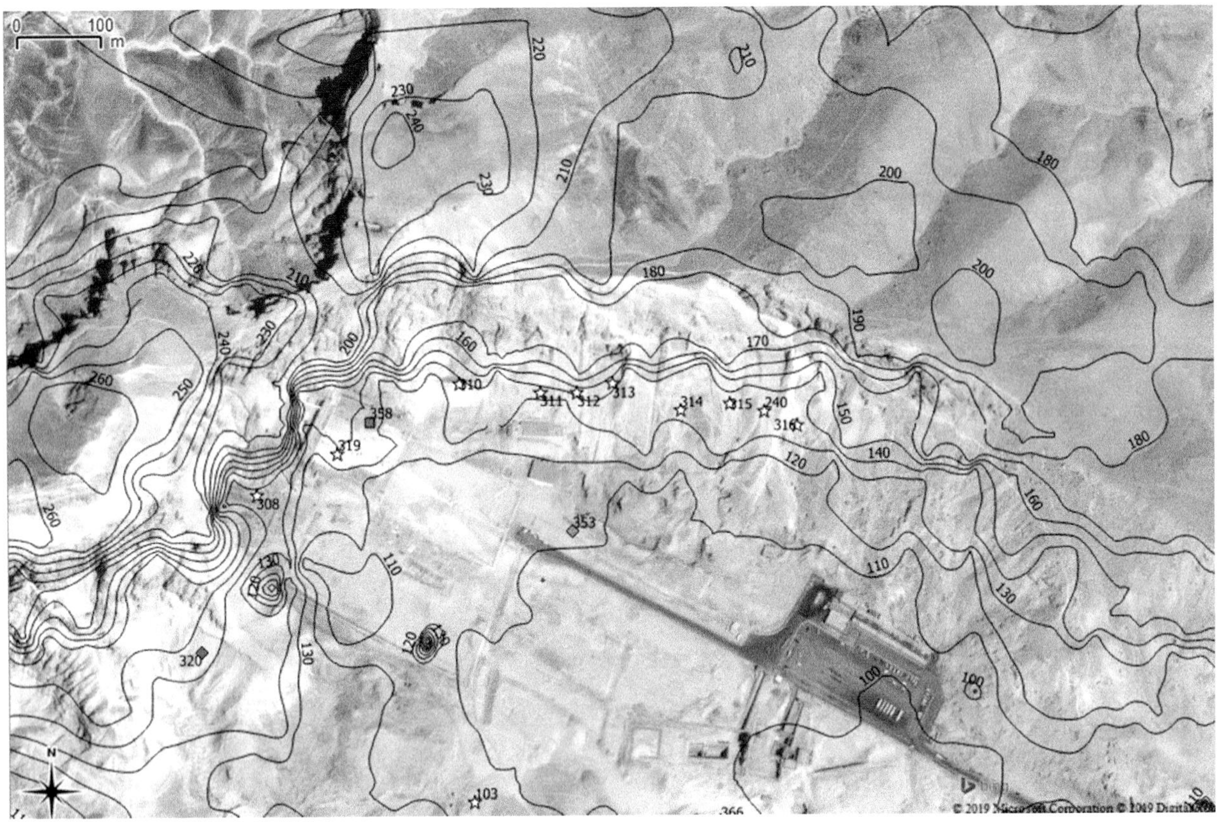

Figure 121: Landscape of Deir el-Bahri (Author's own using QGIS)

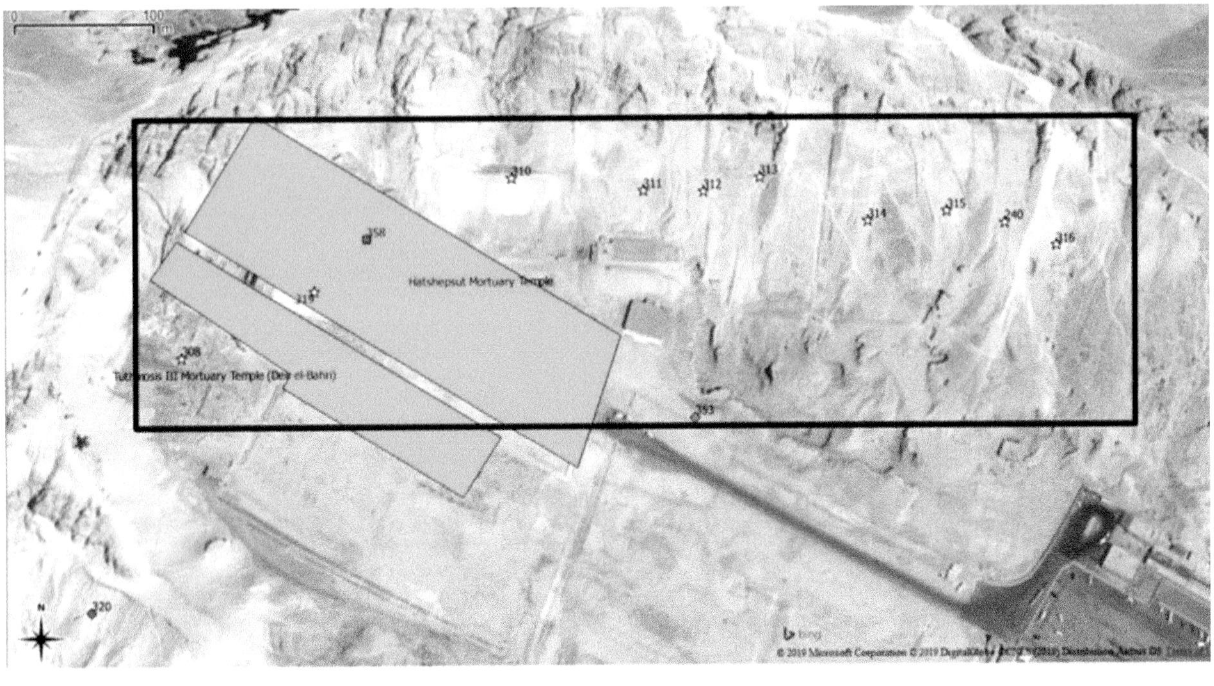

Figure 122: TTs in Deir el-Bahri (Author's own using QGIS)

Figure 123: Middle Kingdom TTs at Deir el-Bahri (Author's own)

Figure 124: Hatshepsut's Deir el-Bahri temple, with Middle Kingdom temple remains to the left (Author's own)

required special permission which was not granted to anyone. The only exception was the tomb of Senenmut (TT353), who received other extraordinary privileges, such as owning two tombs, and having his name and image within the mortuary temple of Hatshepsut (Dorman 1988: 109 and 172; Winlock 1942: 105 and 174). This would also explain why there are no further tombs located at the eastern end of the northern edge of the causeway.

Tomb Reuse

None of the tombs in el-Asasif were reused. These Middle Kingdom Deir el-Bahri tombs were not reused during the New Kingdom, unlike their contemporaries in Qurna, the majority of which were reused during the reigns of Hatshepsut and Tuthmosis III (see Chapter 9). This lack of reuse at a time when Middle Kingdom tombs appear to have influenced later tomb distribution in Qurna also suggesting that this area was restricted by royal prescription.

Another possibility is that the rock in this area although considered suitable by tomb builders in the Middle Kingdom, was not considered as such in the Eighteenth Dynasty. The rock in this area has been described as badly faulted resulting in sinkholes and unstable ground (Winlock 1942: 156-158) and the rock in this area has been identified as consisting of the Tarawan Formation (see Chapter 2), so this seems possible. Indeed, the decoration of these Middle Kingdom tombs had to be executed on a limestone lining as a result of the poor rock quality (Dodson and Ikram 2008: 190-191). The possibility that the Middle Kingdom tombs were no longer visible due to the unstable ground resulting in rock-falls, thus rendering them unable to act as focal point as the Middle Kingdom tombs in Upper Qurna, seems unlikely as there is evidence of them being plundered in the Eighteenth Dynasty (Winlock 1942: 128). There was Eighteenth Dynasty graffiti left in TT319 (Peden 2001: 71-72), and graffiti dating from the Eighteenth to Twentieth Dynasty within an unfinished Middle Kingdom tomb which would have been the westernmost of the row of tombs along the northern edge of the causeway (Marciniak 1981: 299-305; Peden 2001: 72-74; Wente 1984: 47), but none documented in any other Middle Kingdom tombs. This suggests that these tombs were not visited, despite the number of individuals who worked in the area in the Eighteenth Dynasty constructing the temples at Deir el-Bahri, supporting the idea that these tombs were either inaccessible or not visible, rather than a deliberate decision not to build here. It is also possible that orientating tombs to the east, in the direction of Karnak, became more of a concern in the New Kingdom due to the rise in the importance of the god Amun, rather than in the direction of processional routes. The later royal mortuary temples lay between the necropolis and the east bank, so tombs could be orientated in the direction of both, but to choose a location at Deir el-Bahri would have prevented this link with Karnak, rather limiting this interaction with Amun to the period of the annual Beautiful Festival of the Valley.

Occupation of Tomb Owners

Most individuals whose tombs line the northern side of the causeway were connected to the king in some way; either as a family member or a royal official (see Appendix 2). This could also explain why these tombs did not attract New Kingdom neighbours in the same way as TT60, as the tomb owners were either not remembered into the New Kingdom or were not deemed important enough to influence later tomb distribution (see Appendix 6). And yet TT315 belonged to the Vizier Ipi, which begs the question why this Vizier was not remembered or important enough to attract New Kingdom attention, as Antefoker-TT60. This may have simply been a result of poor survival of the tomb decoration and the titles of Ipi, but the prevalence of royal titles in this area could also support a theory that this area was owned by the king, and as such burial here required royal permission, a custom which perhaps continued into the New Kingdom.

TT353 belonging to Senenmut is located further down the hillside than the Middle Kingdom tombs (see Figures 120 and 121), in closer proximity to the mortuary temple of Hatshepsut, and just outside its precinct. This location appears to be due to his close relationship with Hatshepsut, and also the role he played in the design and construction of the mortuary temple. Royal permission may have been granted for these reasons.

Behind the mortuary temple of Hatshepsut, with corridors passing beneath the northern portico of the temple (Winlock 1942: 183) is TT358 (see Figures 120 and 121). This tomb dates to the Eighteenth Dynasty (in addition to TT320 lying some distance to the south – see Outlying Tombs) and belonged to a member of the royal family, Ahmose Meritamun. This would support the idea that royal permission was required to be buried in this area in the New Kingdom. Ahmose Meritamun was the wife of Amenhotep II and her tomb dates to his reign, but she was also the daughter of Tuthmosis III, which may explain its proximity to the temple of her father. The Valley of the Queens was not yet in use for the burials of queens at this time (Winlock 1942: 186), so this area associated with the Middle Kingdom royal female burials, such as the adjacent TT319, and the location of her father's mortuary temple seems like a suitable location for her tomb. Ahmose Meritamun is also depicted in the shrine dedicated to Hathor at Deir el-Bahri (Winlock 1942: 184), connecting her to this area

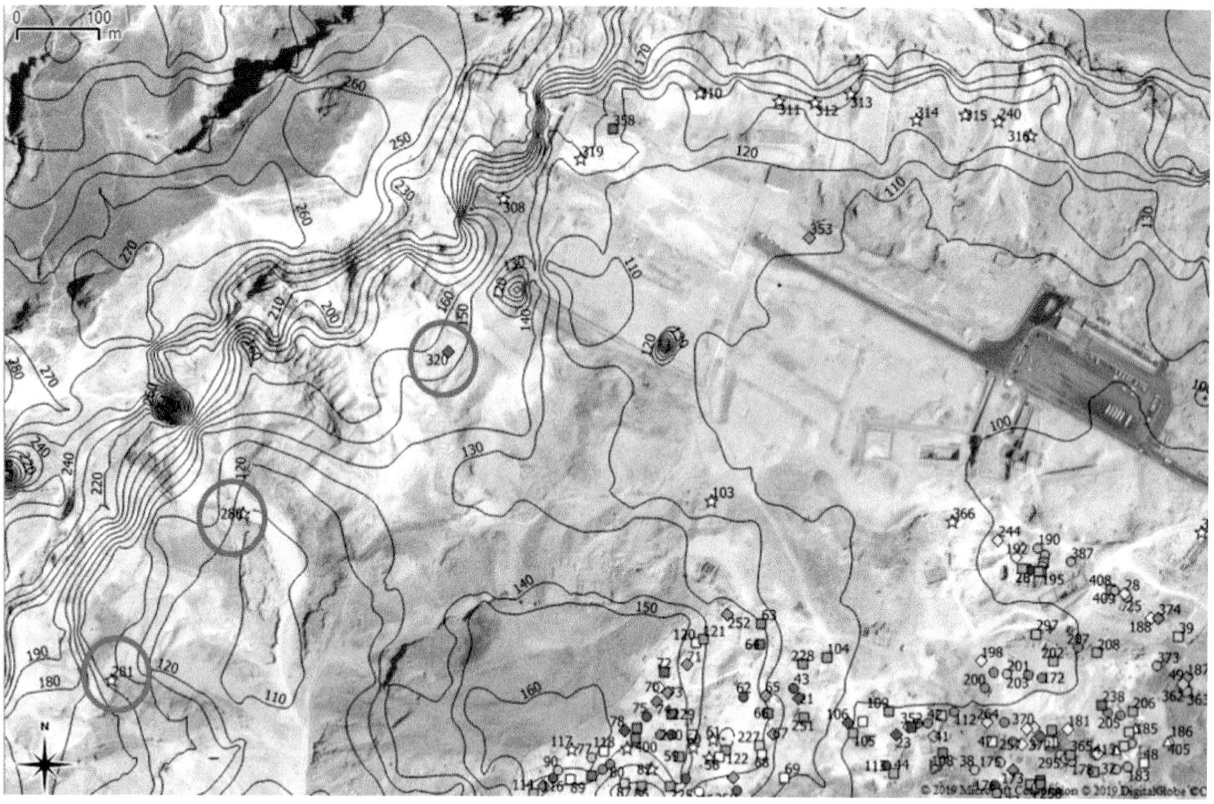

Figure 125: Landscape of outlying TTs (Author's own using QGIS)

and its associated deity. The cult of Hathor was popular during the reign of Montuhotep II, and a number of the women buried around his temple were members of her priesthood, linking Deir el-Bahri to the cult of Hathor during the New Kingdom too (Winlock 1915: 5).

Outlying Tombs

(See Appendix 7)

Three TTs are situated in an isolated position in a valley to the south of Deir el-Bahri, hundreds of metres away from any other tombs (see Figures 125 and 126). TT281 is incorrectly numbered as it is not a private tomb, but rather the remnants of the Middle Kingdom mortuary temple and royal tomb of Amenemhat I (Allen 1996: 2). TT280 belonged to the 'Chief Steward' Meketre, who rather than being buried along the causeway to Deir el-Bahri with the other nobles, instead sited his tomb some distance to the south, close to TT281. The re-dating of TT280 to the reign of Amenemhat I rather than to the previous reign (Arnold 1991: 23 and 38-39) meant that Meketre served both Montuhotep II and his successor, thus explaining the decision to site his tomb in the vicinity of the monument of the last king he served (see Figure 127). TT280 was adjoined by the tomb of Meketre's son Antef, who was also the 'Overseer of Sealers', but no further tombs were dug in this location, presumably as a result of the temple never being completed. TT320 dates to the reign of Ahmose, so before the Valley of the Queens was established as a cemetery for royal burials. The date and the royal occupant could explain the logical choice of this area, close to the area used for members of the royal family in the Middle Kingdom.

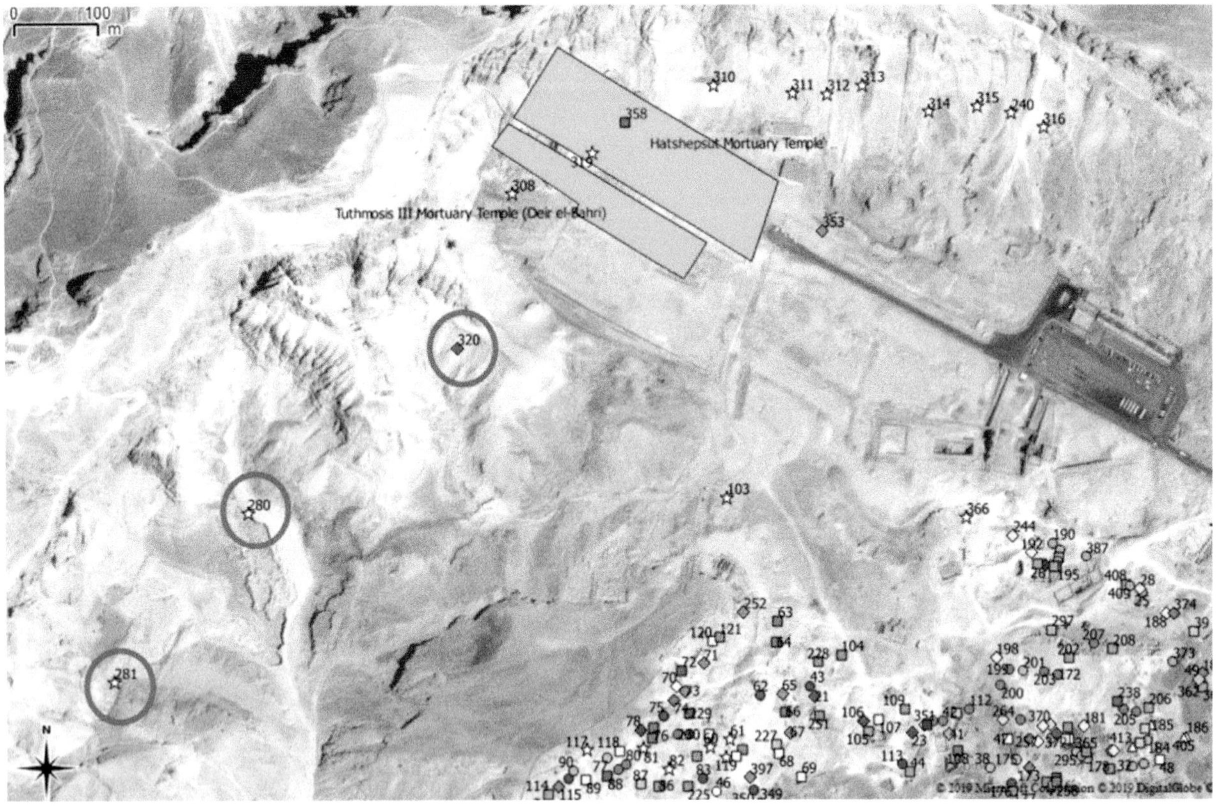

Figure 126: Location of outlying TTs in the valley south of Deir el-Bahri (Author's own using QGIS)

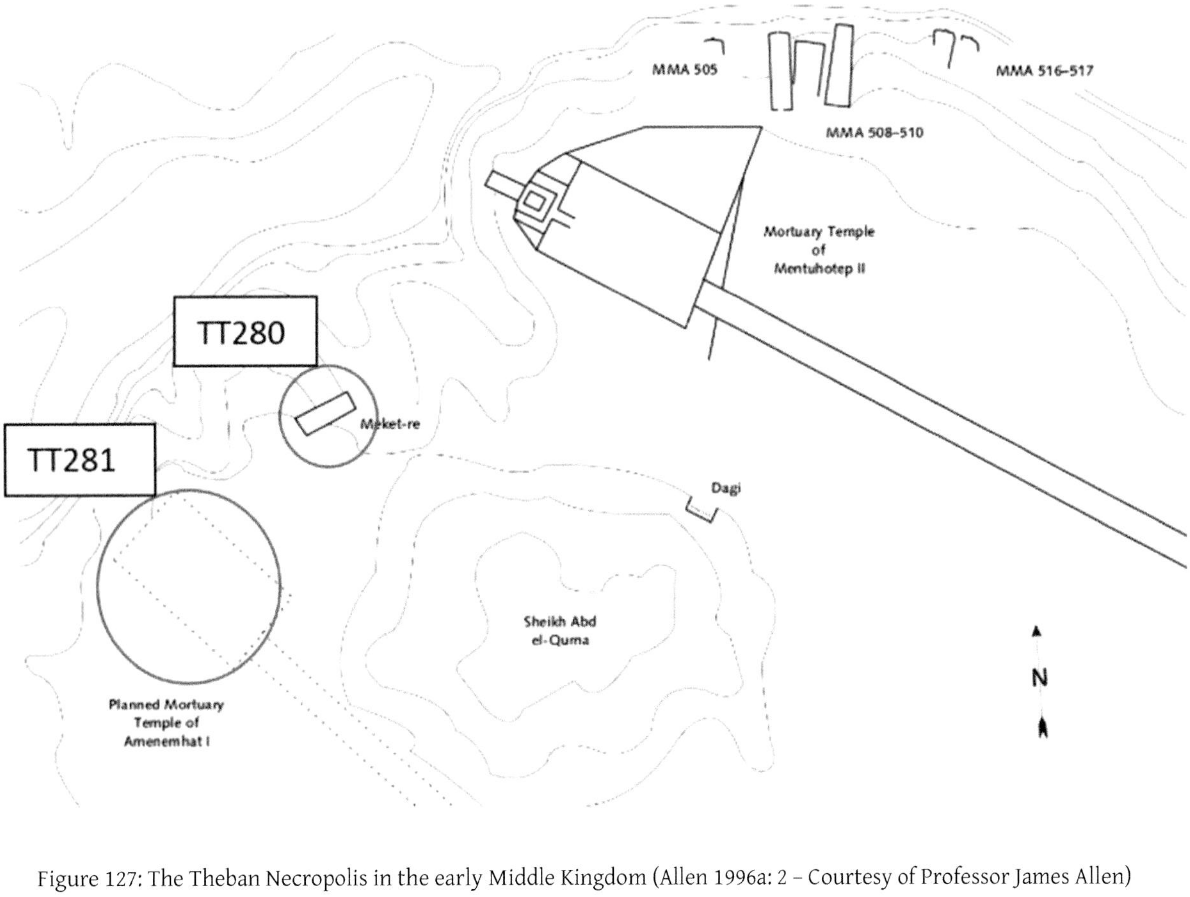

Figure 127: The Theban Necropolis in the early Middle Kingdom (Allen 1996a: 2 – Courtesy of Professor James Allen)

Chapter 7: El-Asasif

(See Appendix 8)

Location

The area of el-Asasif is located to the south of the causeway leading to Deir el-Bahri, with the causeway itself bordering the area to the north, and el-Khokha to the south (see Figure 128). The TTs here are scattered in a narrow band parallel to the Deir el-Bahri causeway, all located between 90m and 100m above sea-level, with the exception of TT366 which lies between 100m and 110m above sea level, with the flood plain in this area beginning some distance to the east at 80m above sea level (see Figure 129). These tombs are located a short distance north of el-Khokha, so appear to be an extension of this area rather than a distinct set of tombs. The southern boundary of el-Asasif used by Kampp (1996) has been shifted slightly to the north to allow TT207, TT208 and TT297 to be included with the el-Khokha tombs rather than el-Asasif tombs (see Chapter 8). This is as a result of the path between these two groups, which is visible from the satellite and naturally divides these two groups of tombs (see Figures 130, 131 and 132). The paths leading through necropolis today hardly differ from the ancient paths, so can be used to help divide the necropolis into areas (Kampp 1996: 121).

Date of use

There were two Middle Kingdom tombs in el-Asasif, TT366 and TT386, but they do not appear to have influenced New Kingdom tomb distribution as the Middle Kingdom tombs did in Qurna (see Figure 133). TT386 is located to the north of the later New Kingdom tombs, under the Middle Kingdom causeway leading to the mortuary temple of Montuhotep II, suggesting that it was built before the causeway. TT366 is located to the west of the New Kingdom el-Asasif tombs, with no other tombs in close proximity.

There are only three Eighteenth Dynasty TTs in el-Asasif. The earliest, Puyemra-TT39, is datable to either the reign of Hatshepsut or Tuthmosis III, both of whom built temples at Deir el-Bahri, thus explaining this choice of tomb location and its orientation towards the causeway. Puyemra was the '2PA' and 'Royal Seal-bearer', whose position as an important priest and

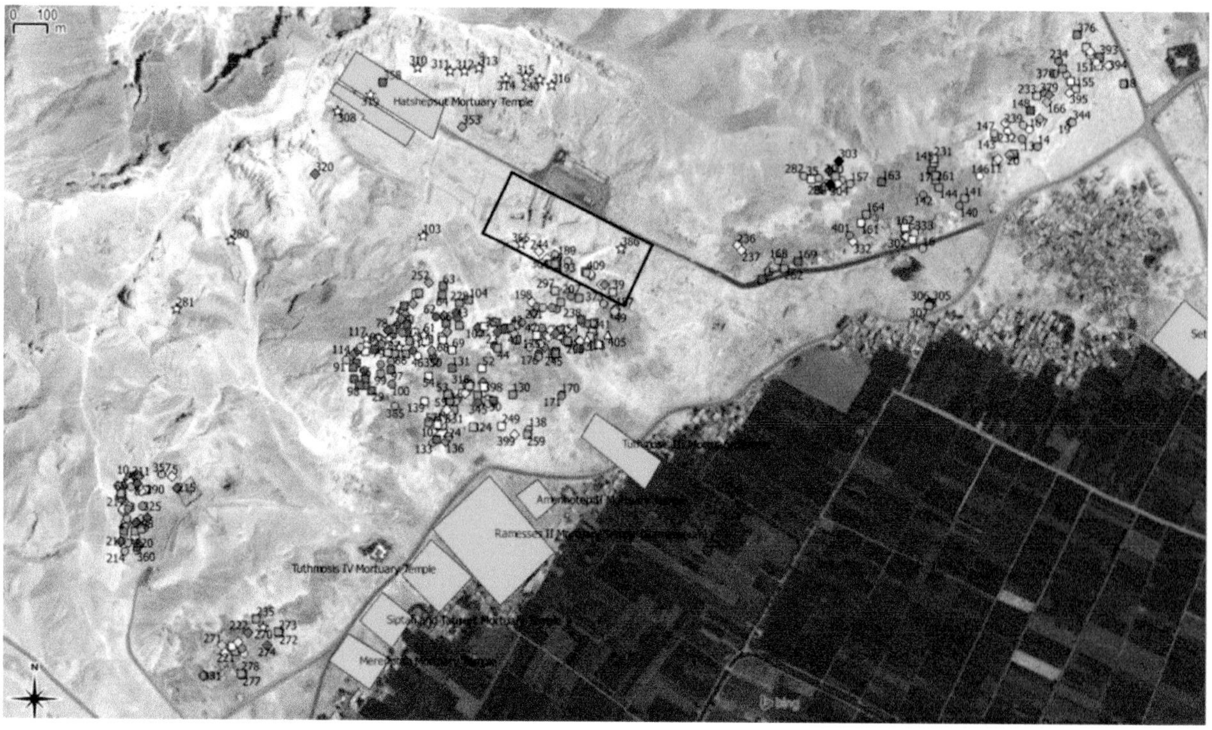

Figure 128: Location of el-Asasif within the Theban Necropolis (Author's own using QGIS)

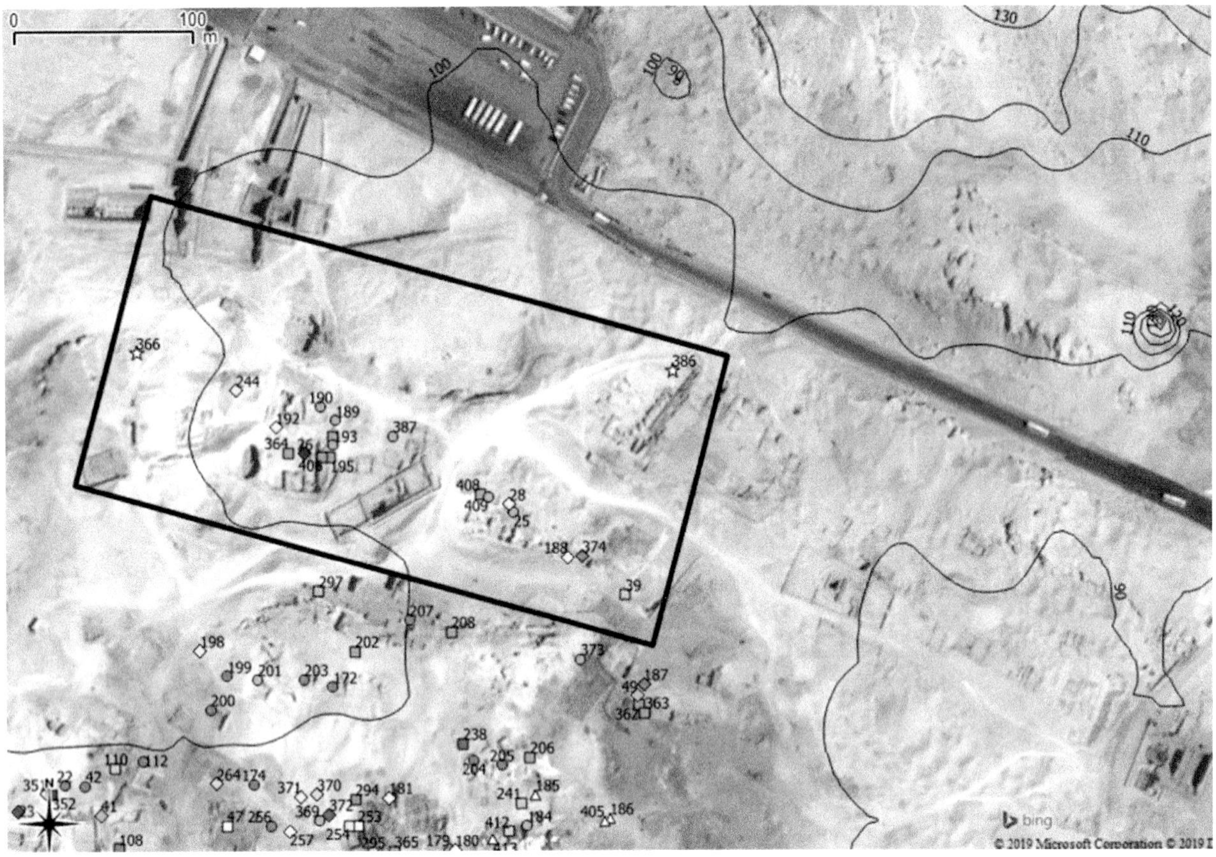

Figure 129: Landscape of el-Asasif (Author's own using QGIS)

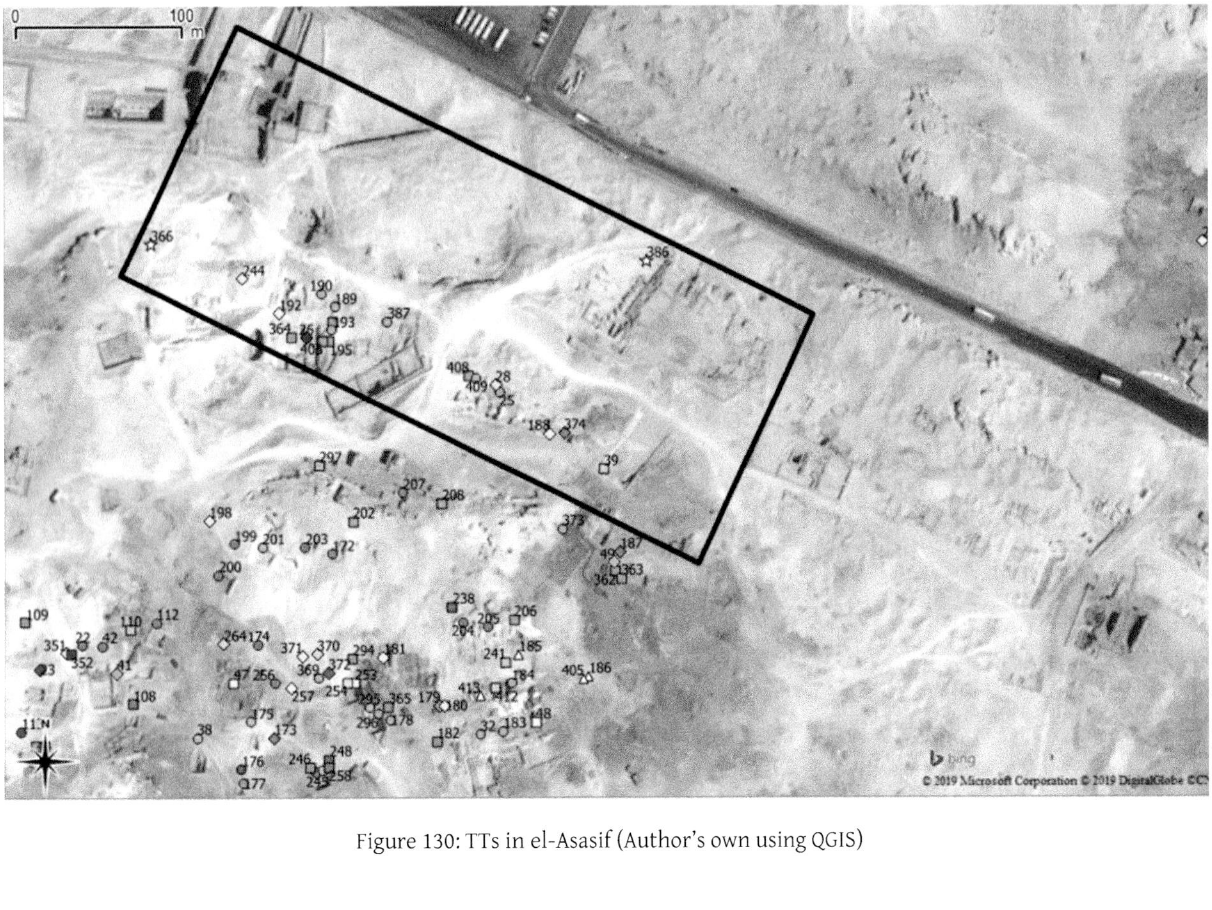

Figure 130: TTs in el-Asasif (Author's own using QGIS)

Figure 131: Path east from el-Asasif to el-Khokha, with el-Asasif on the left and el-Khokha on the right (Author's own)

Figure 132: View from el-Khokha looking west towards el-Asasif (Author's own)

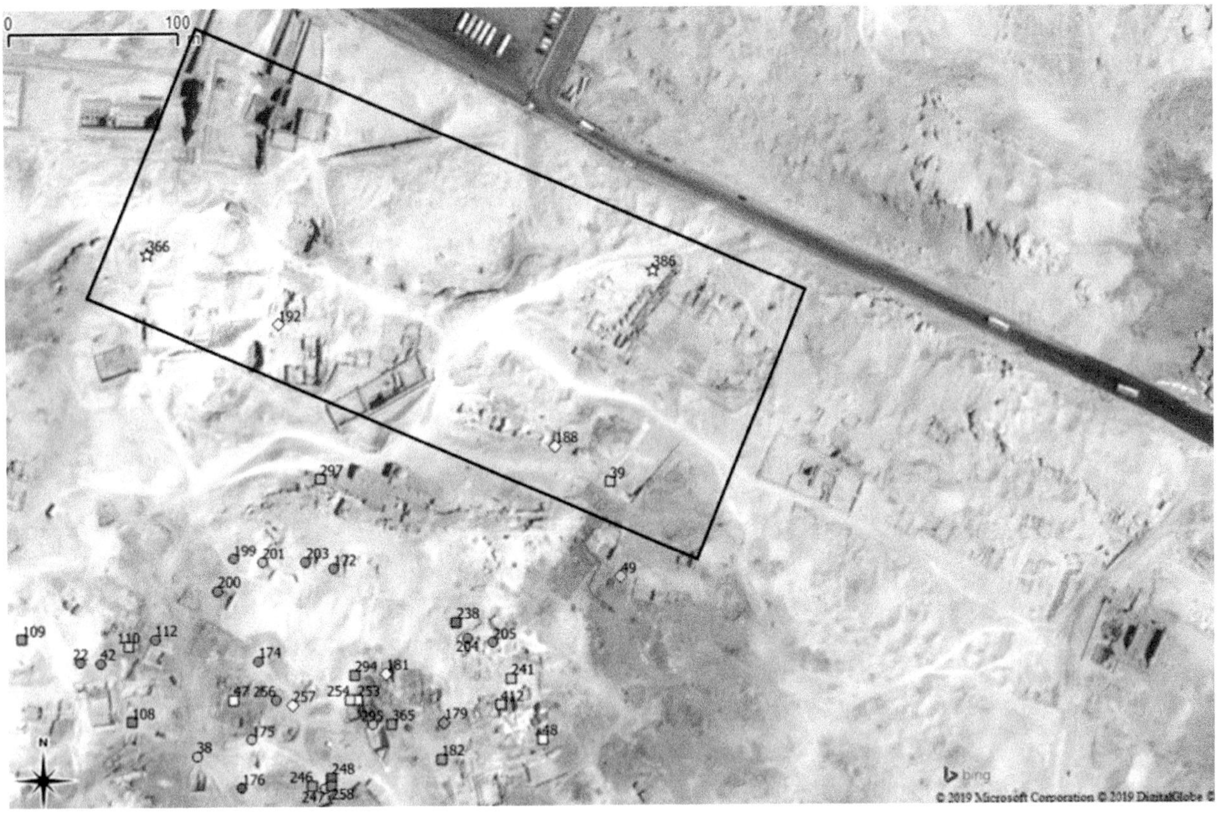

Figure 133: TTs in el-Asasif at the end of the Eighteenth Dynasty (Author's own using QGIS)

royal administration potentially explains his burial in this apparently restricted area. It seems incongruous that no other tombs dating to these reigns were located in this area adjacent to the causeway leading to their temples, suggesting that special permission was required to be buried here in the Eighteenth Dynasty, or perhaps that rock-cut tombs such as those found in Upper Qurna were preferred which could not be accommodated in this area. Both TT188 and TT192 are dated between the reigns of Amenhotep III and Amenhotep IV (Akhenaten), when possibly the rules governing burial in this area may not have been enforced as a result of the Amarna Period. Parennefer-TT188 was a 'Royal Butler' and 'Overseer of Priests of All the Gods', another important priest and member of the palace, while Kheruef-TT192 was the 'Steward' of Queen Tiye, among other important roles within the palace. The royal connections of these Eighteenth Dynasty burials may have explained their inclusion within this area. There does not appear to be any spatial link between them as they are not in close proximity.

Six tombs dated to the Nineteenth Dynasty (TT25, TT189, TT190, TT194, TT387 and TT409) are spread across the central band of this area rather than in a cluster. It is during the reign of Ramesses II that el-Asasif grew in popularity, potentially reflecting a change in permission required to be buried here, possibly connected to the change in emphasis of the BFV from Deir el-Bahri to the Ramesseum. Four of these tombs are clustered around the earlier TT192 (TT189, TT190, TT194 and TT387), while the other two are located together a short distance to the east (TT25 and TT409) (see Figure 134).

By the end of the Nineteenth Dynasty only two further tombs had been built at el-Asasif (see Figure 135). One dates between the reigns of Seti II and Tausert (TT26), and one is datable only to the Nineteenth Dynasty (TT374). TT26 formed part of this cluster around TT192 (see Figure 136), while TT374 was located in the east of the area, in the courtyard of TT188.

Two further tombs in the area are datable only to the Ramesside Period (TT28 and TT244) but they are located at opposite ends of the area (see Figure 137). During the Twentieth Dynasty, five additional tombs were built, although they are not datable to a specific reign. Four of them joined the cluster around TT192 in the west of the area (TT193, TT195, TT364 and TT406), while TT408 is located a short distance to the east, adjacent to TT409 (see Figure 138). It is interesting to note that the majority of Nineteenth and Twentieth Dynasty tombs in el-Asasif are arranged around shared courtyards. TT192 in particular clearly acted as a focal point for later tombs in the New Kingdom, with eight

Figure 134: TTs in el-Asasif at the end of the reign of Ramesses II (Author's own using QGIS)

Figure 135: TTs in el-Asasif at the end of the Nineteenth Dynasty (Author's own using QGIS)

Figure 136: The courtyard of TT26 (Author's own)

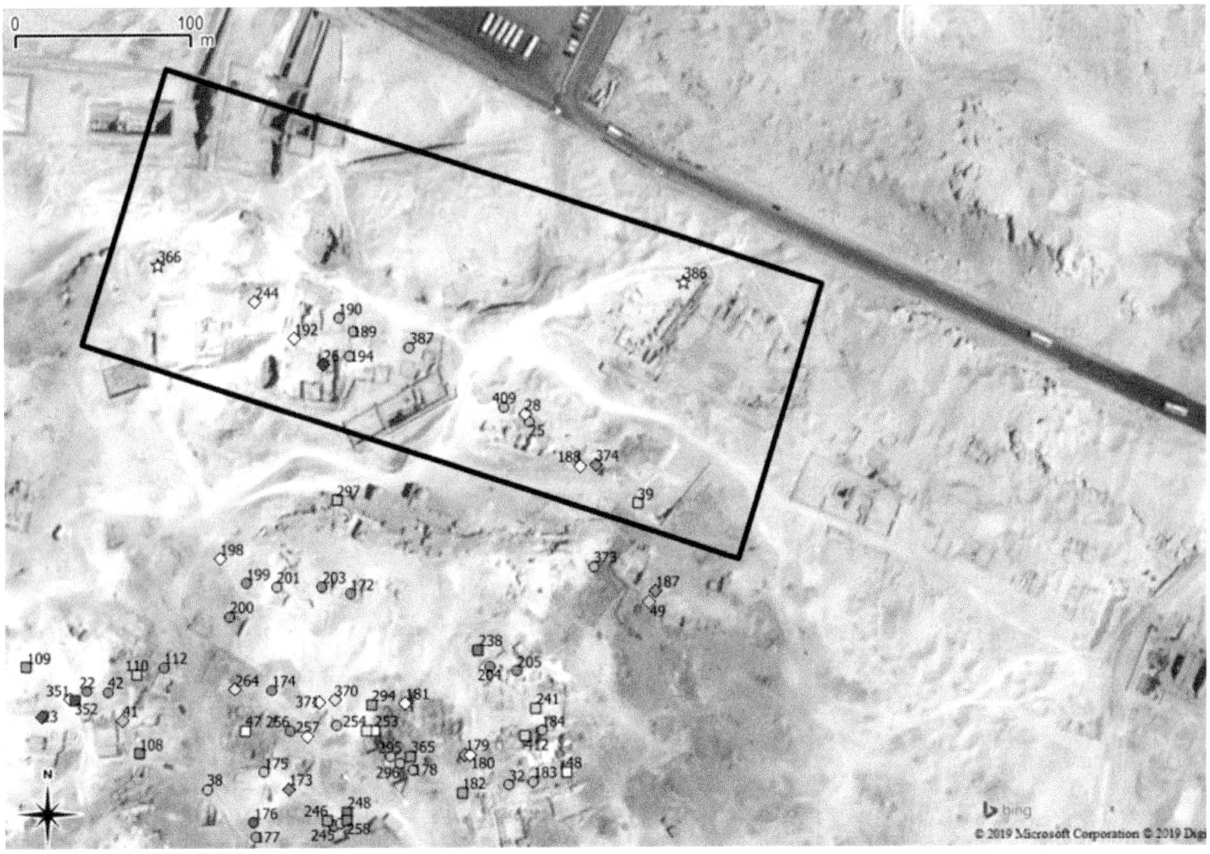

Figure 137: TTs in el-Asasif at the end of the Ramesside Period (Author's own using QGIS)

Figure 138: TTs in el-Asasif at the end of the New Kingdom (Author's own using QGIS)

Table 19: el-Asasif TTs distributed by most likely date

Date	No. of Tombs	Tombs
MK	**	TT366, TT386
Hat / TIII	*	TT39
AIII / AIV	**	TT188, TT192
Dyn 19	*	TT374
RII	******	TT25, TT189, TT190, TT194, TT387, TT409
SII/ Tau	*	TT26
Dyn 19/20 (Ram)	**	TT28, TT244
Dyn 20	*****	TT193, TT195, TT364, TT406, TT408,

later tombs sharing this courtyard (TT26, TT189, TT190, TT193, TT194, TT195, TT364 and TT406), while a further four shared another courtyard to the east of the area (TT25, TT28, TT408 and TT409) (see below).

By the end of the New Kingdom, the area of el-Asasif consisted of a narrow strip of land populated with tombs, perhaps a northern extension of el-Khokha (see Figure 138). The northern extent of the area was demarcated by the remains of the Middle Kingdom causeway, while el-Khokha lay to the south. Space remained to the north east of this area, where no tombs were built. These New Kingdom tombs bordered the southern edge of the Middle Kingdom causeway leading to the mortuary temple of Montuhotep II, suggesting that this causeway was still in use during the New Kingdom.

Occupation of Tomb Owners

(See Table 20)

Priests

There were only three priests buried here (see Figure 139), the 'High Priest' of Khonsu, Amenemhab-TT25 (RII), the '2PA', Puyemra-TT39 (Hat-TIII), and the 'Overseer of the Priests of all the Gods', Parennefer-TT188 (AIII-AIV). These tombs are within 100m of each

Table 20: el-Asasif TTs distributed by occupational group

Occupational Group	No. of Tombs	Tombs
Priesthood	****	TT25, TT39, TT188
Temple Admin	************	TT26, TT28, TT189, TT193, TT194, TT195, TT244, TT364, TT374, TT387, TT408, TT409
Royal Admin	**********	TT26, TT39, TT188, TT192, TT194, TT366, TT386, TT387, TT406, TT409
General Admin	**	TT192, TT409
Local Admin	*	TT387
Military	**	TT26, TT386
Unknown	*	TT190

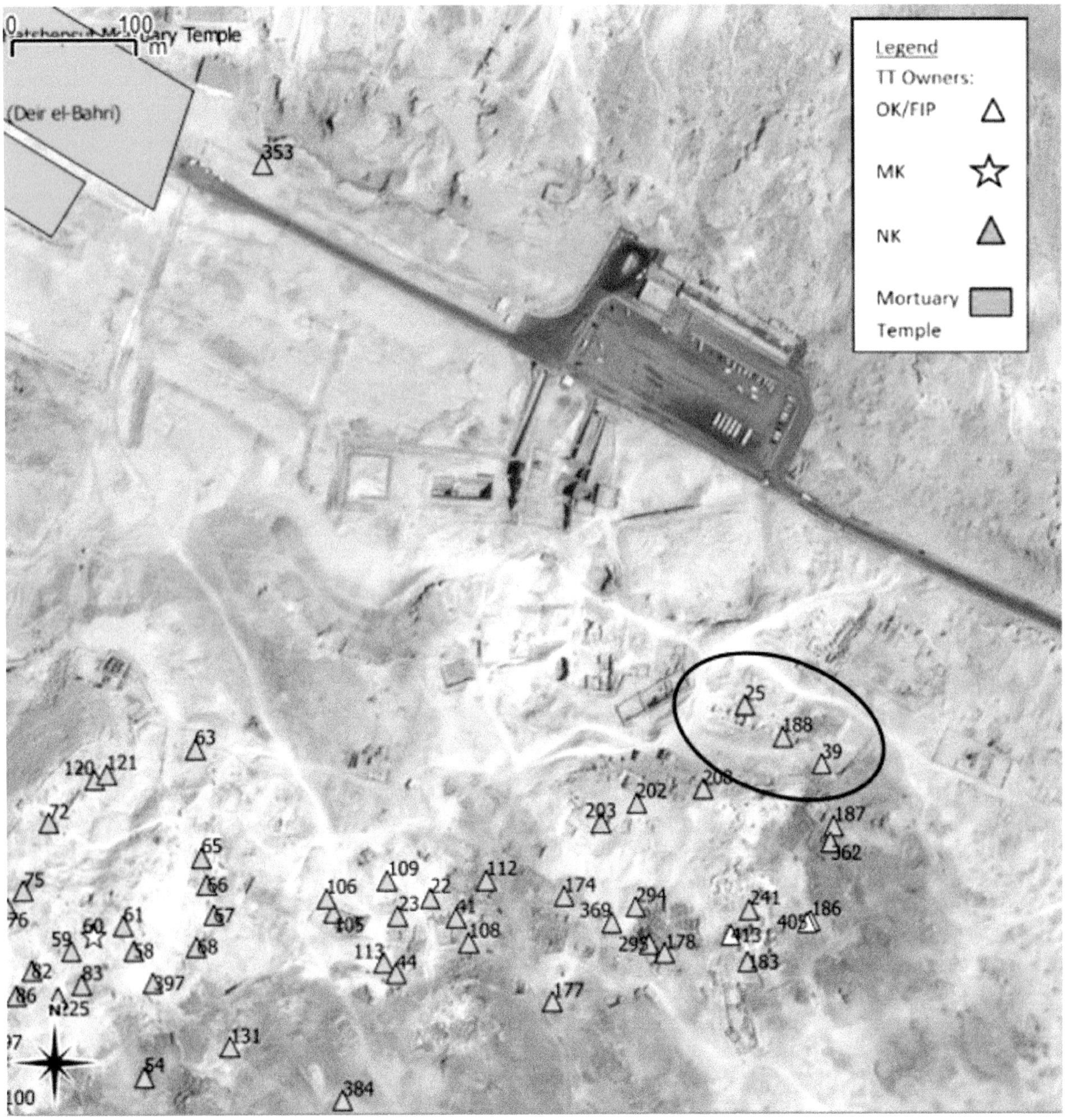

Figure 139: TTs of Priests in el-Asasif (Author's own using QGIS)

Figure 140: TTs of the Temple Administration in el-Asasif (Author's own using QGIS)

other at the eastern end of this area, so in relatively close proximity, but not particularly close in date. There are not enough priests with similar enough titles, or serving the same deity, to prove a spatial connection between them, or with this area of the necropolis.

Temple Administration

12 TTs in el-Asasif were owned by members of the temple administration (see Figure 140). 11 were connected to the Estate of Amun (TT26, TT28, TT189, TT193, TT194, TT195, TT244, TT364, TT374, TT408 and TT409), and they all date to the Ramesside period. These tombs are scattered across this area, but five of them are clustered in the shared courtyard of the earlier tomb of Kheruef called Senaa-TT192 (AIII-AIV). Amenemopet-TT374 (Dyn 19) served an unspecified deity, while Amenemhab-TT364 (Dyn 20) served all the Theban deities. Khnumemhab-TT26 (SII-Tau), and Amenemopet-TT374 (Dyn 19) worked at the Ramesseum, but their tombs are not in particularly close proximity, while the others worked at unspecified locations within the Estate of Amun.

Several of these individuals performed roles within the Treasury of Amun, including the 'Overseer of the Treasury', Khnumemhab-TT26 (SII-Tau), a 'Great One of the Seal in the Treasury', Ptahemheb-TT193 (Dyn 20), and two 'Scribes of the Treasury', Bakenamun-TT195 (Dyn 20) and Amenemopet-TT374 (Dyn 19). Three of these four tombs were located around the shared courtyard of TT192, with the exception of TT374 which was located to the east. There were several other scribes, including two 'Scribes of Divine Offerings', Djehutyemheb-TT194 (RII) and Amenemhab-TT364 (Dyn 20, who was also the 'Scribe of the Granary'). There was also the 'Scribe' and 'Counter of Cattle', Samut called Kyky-TT409 (RII). Of these scribes, Djehutyemheb-TT194 and Amenemhab-TT364 share the courtyard of TT192. Samut called Kyky-TT409 shared a different courtyard to the east, with two other members of the temple administration, a 'Deputy' of the Estate of Amun, Hori-TT28 (Ram) and a 'Head of Servants', Bakenamun-TT408 (Dyn 20), together with the priest, Amenemhab-TT25 (RII). There were also a number of Overseers, including the 'Overseer of Carpenters' and 'Chief of Goldworkers', Nakht-djehuty-TT189 (RII), the 'Overseer of Craftsmen', Pakaru-TT244 (Ram), and the 'Overseer of Marshland

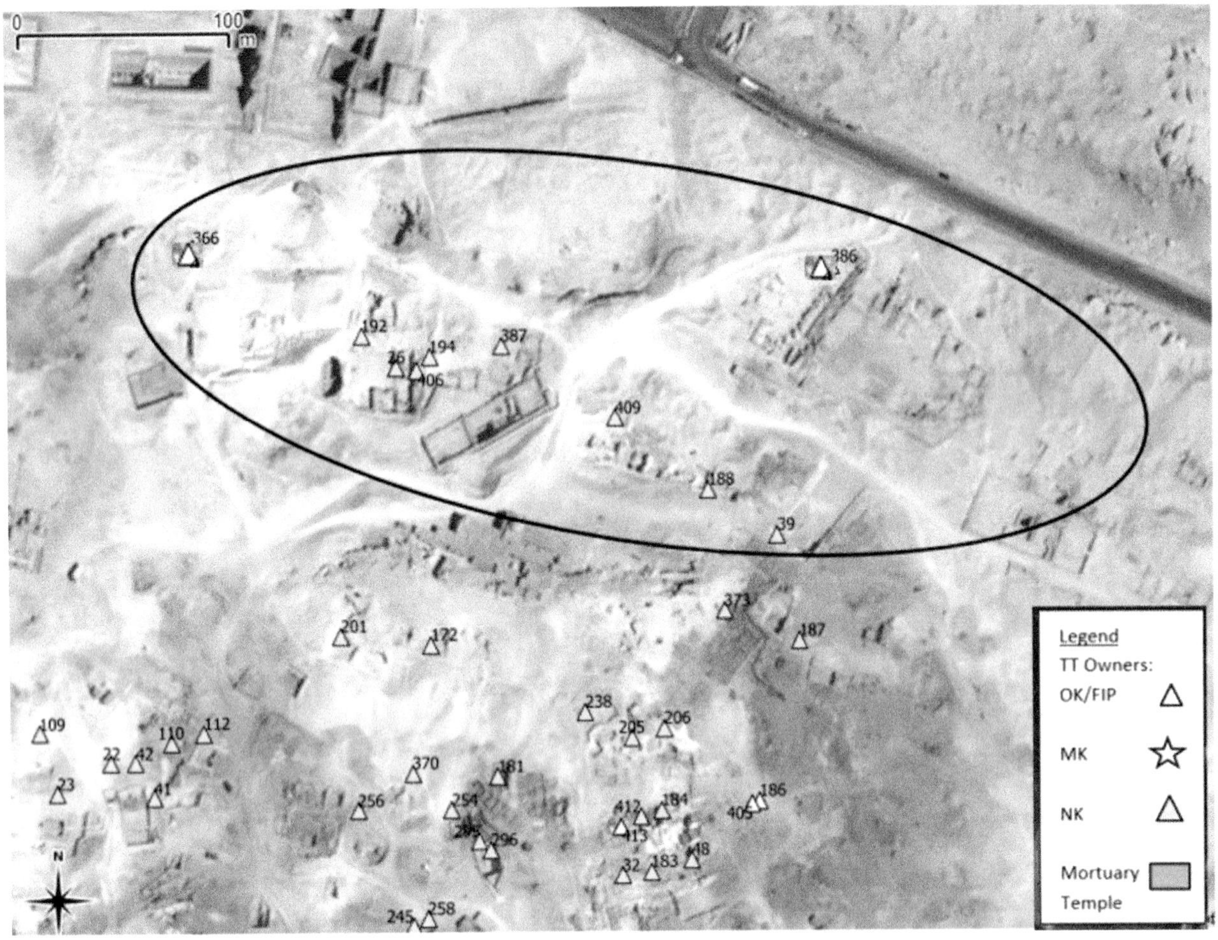

Figure 141: TTs of the Royal Administration in el-Asasif (Author's own using QGIS)

Dwellers', Djehutyemheb-TT194 (RII). TT189 and TT194 are also positioned around this shared courtyard of TT192, while TT244 is located a short distance to the north-west. Six of the eight individuals who shared the courtyard of TT192 were members of the temple administration, while the two other tombs belonged to an unknown individual, TT190 (RII), and a member of the royal administration, Piay-TT406 (Dyn 20).

Royal Administration

There were ten royal officials buried here, including Djar-TT366 and Intef-TT386 (MK) (see Figure 141). The earliest and easternmost New Kingdom TT in this area belonged to the 'Royal Seal-bearer' Puyemre-TT39 (Hat-TIII), which lies within 50m of the 'Royal Butler' Parennefer-TT188 (AIII-AIV), some distance from the other members of the royal administration who were buried to the north-west. Kheruef called Senaa-TT192 (AIII-AIV), the 'Steward' of Queen Tiye, 'Royal Scribe', 'Royal Herald', 'Royal Seal-bearer' and 'Chief of Secrets of the Palace' was buried in the largest tomb in el-Asasif in the north-west of the area, which is also located within 100m of Djar-TT366 (MK), who was the 'Overseer of the Royal Harim' and another 'Royal Seal-bearer'. TT192 appears to have acted as such a focal point during the Ramesside Period with eight later burials being added to its courtyard. There were another five scribes buried here, three 'Royal Scribes', Khnumemhab-TT26 (SII-Tau), Djehutyemheb -TT194 (RII), and Samut called Kyky (TT409- RII), a 'Royal Scribe of the Offering Table of the Lord of the Two Lands', Meryptah-TT387 (RII), and a 'Scribe of the Offering Table of the Lord of the Two Lands' Piay-TT406 (Dyn 20). TT26 and TT406 lie adjacent to each other within the shared courtyard of TT192, while TT194 also shares this courtyard, but TT387 and TT409 are located some distance away to the east. TT386 does not lie within 100m of any other tomb.

General Administration

There were two members of the general administration buried here (see Figure 142), the 'Controller of Monuments', Kheruef called Senaa-TT192 (AIII-AIV),

Figure 142: TTs of the General Administration in el-Asasif (Author's own using QGIS)

in addition to his royal administrative titles), and the 'Overseer of Scribes', Samut called Kyky-TT409 (RII), who held several temple administrative titles.

Local Administration

There was one local administrator (see Figure 143) who held the title 'Overseer of the Foreign Lands', Meryptah-TT387 (RII).

Military

There were two members of the military buried here (see Figure 144), both 'Overseers of the Army', Khnumemhab-TT26 (SII-Tau), and Intef-TT386 (MK), who were buried over 200m apart.

Unknown

There was one further individual with unknown titles (TT190– RII), who has not been classified.

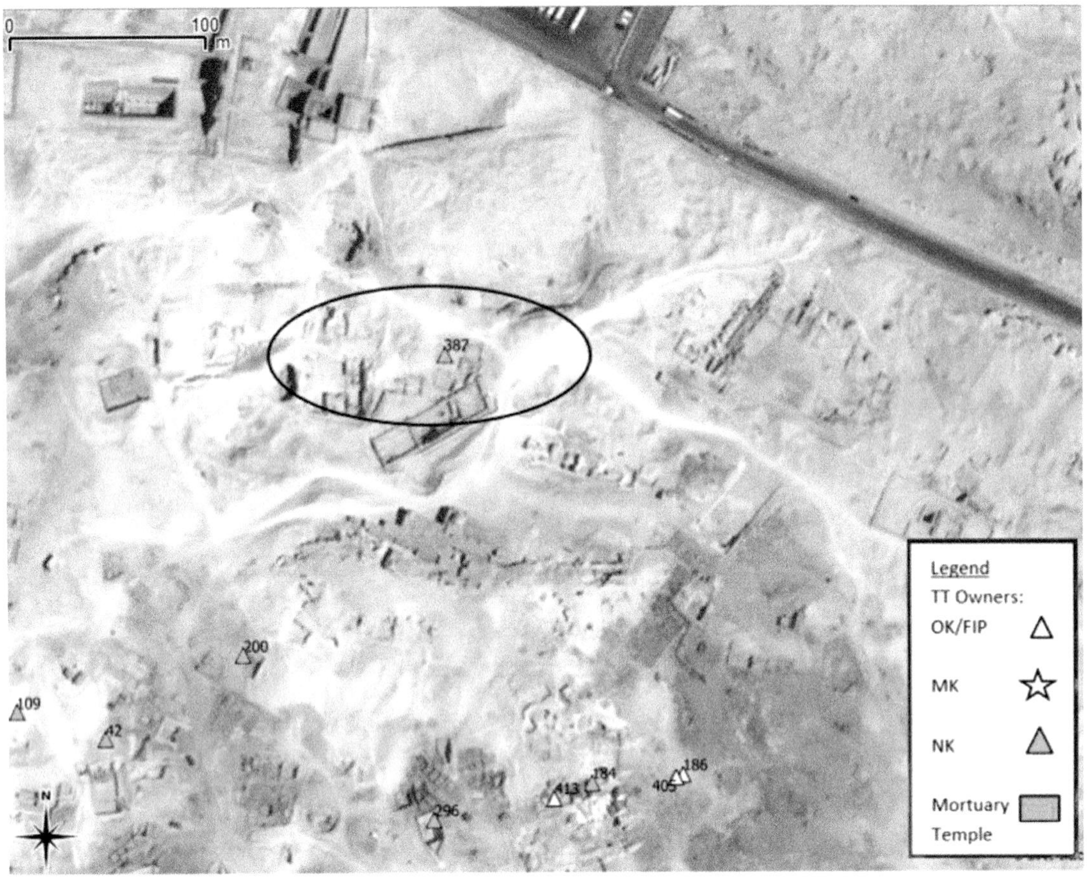

Figure 143: TT of the Local Administration in el-Asasif (Author's own using QGIS)

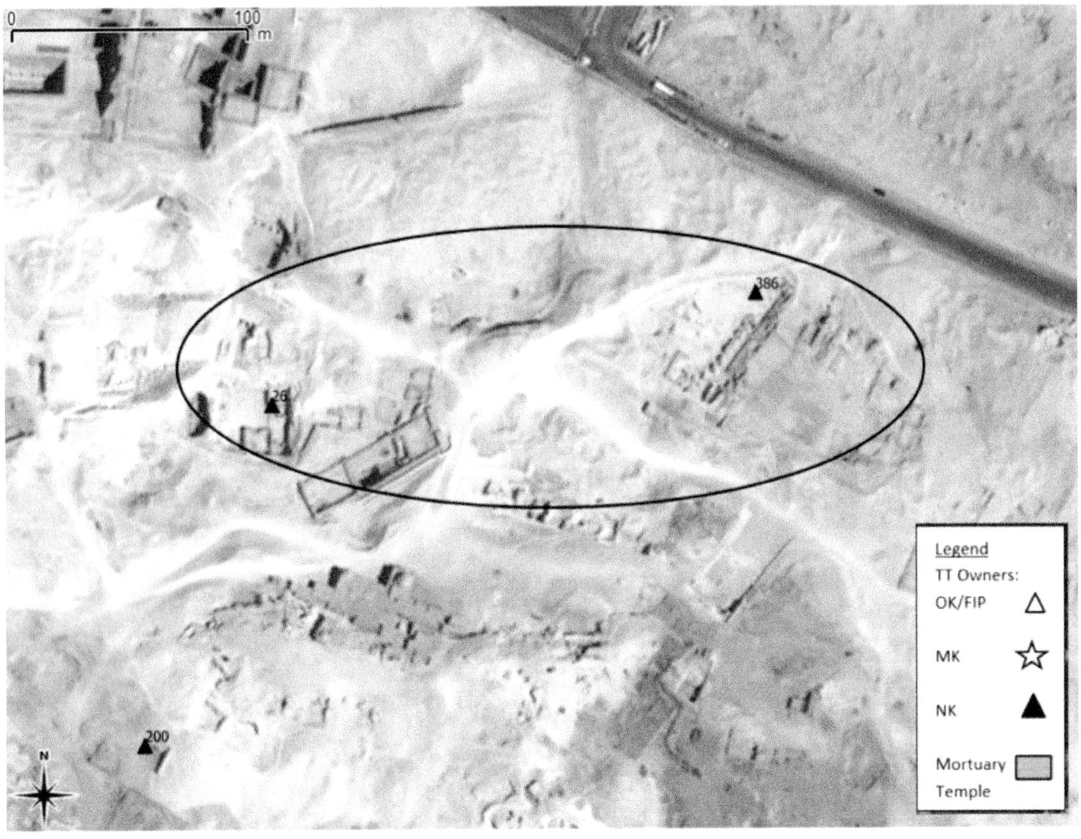

Figure 144: TTs of the Military in el-Asasif (Author's own using QGIS)

Relationships between Tomb Owners / Tombs

There is no evidence of familial relationships between any of the tomb owners in el-Asasif.

Shared Courtyards

A large number of tombs in el-Asasif have shared courtyards, which is particularly striking from such a small data set, in comparison to other areas of the necropolis. This is partly due to the relatively flat nature of the area used for burial here, which lends itself to shared courtyards.

TT26, TT189, TT190, TT192, TT193, TT194, TT195, TT364 and TT406

These tombs lie in a prime position, to the south of the causeways leading to the Deir el-Bahri temples, and in the shadow of the Theban mountain. Kheruef-TT192 was the original tomb, which lies on the western side dominating the courtyard. It is situated directly opposite the staircase which provides access to the shared courtyard. TT192 was the only tomb in this vicinity, a symbol of the power and wealth of its owner, until the other eight tombs were added. These later additions are located around this large courtyard, on the northern, eastern and southern sides, and are much smaller in size, while some have built a wall to partition a section of the courtyard at the entrance to their tomb (see Figure 145). These later tombs date between the Nineteenth and Twentieth Dynasty, but few are securely dated to a specific reign. Seven of the nine tomb owners had administrative rather than religious titles, referring to Amun, which suggests an occupational link (see Table 21). Five of the tomb owners were scribes, but as this was relatively common it is not enough to confirm a link. Four tomb owners had names consisting of the name of a deity, with the ending '*m-ḥb*'. While this was a common format for a name to take, it may suggest a familial connection, although as each name features a different deity, this is less likely. The most likely reasons for this shared courtyard are later individuals wishing to benefit from the large courtyard and monumental staircase so building their tomb in the available space (see Figures 146 and 147). They may also have desired close proximity to an individual who was still remembered, as the amount of graffito left by later scribes within the first and second columned halls of TT192 suggests (PM I: 300).

TT25, TT28, TT408 and TT409

These four tombs opened onto a shared courtyard, with mud-brick walls partitioning this larger space into smaller private courts. TT408 and TT409 lie adjacent to each other, sharing the same partitioned court (see Figures 148 and 149), while across a heap of debris

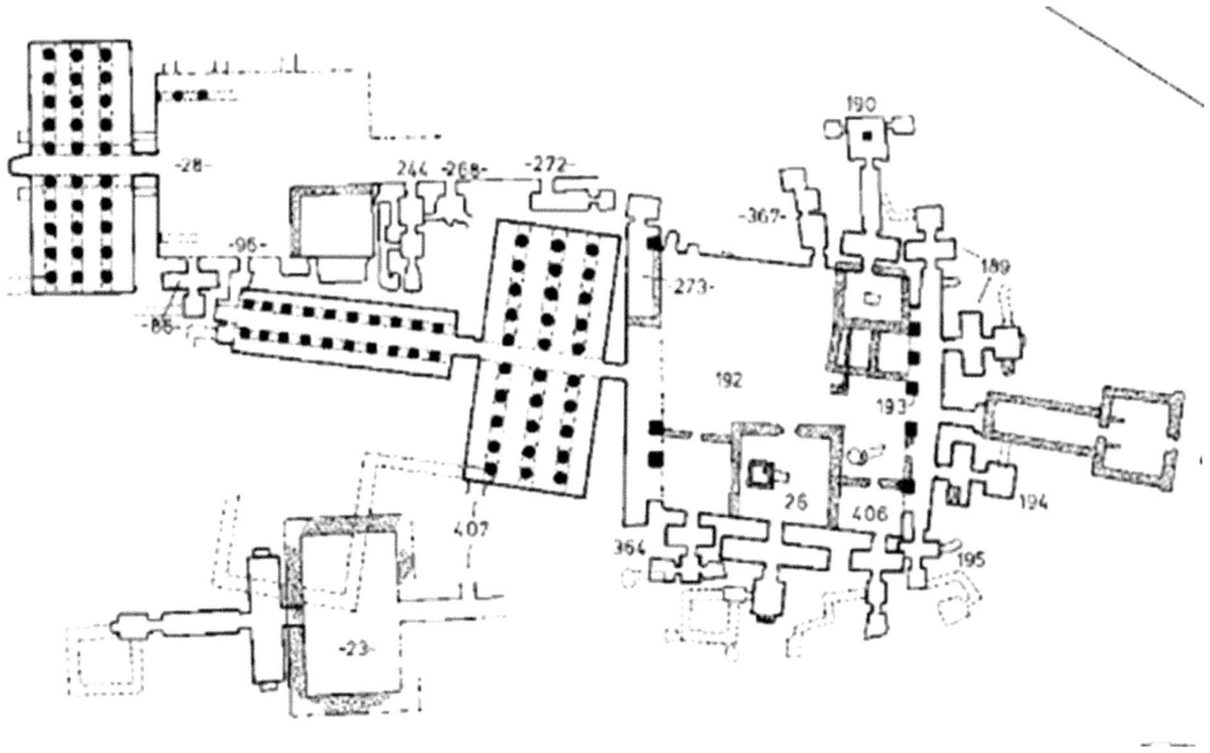

Figure 145: Plan of shared courtyard of TT26, TT189, TT190, TT192, TT193, TT194, TT195, TT364 and TT406 (Kampp 1996: Plan V – Courtesy of Professor Seyfried)

Table 21: Owners of TT26, TT189, TT190, TT192, TT193, TT194, TT195, TT364 and TT406

TT	Dyn	Reign	Name	Title
TT26	19	SII-Tau	Khnumemhab	Overseer of the Treasury of the Ramesseum; Royal Scribe; Overseer of the Army of the Lord of the Two Lands;
TT189	19	end RII-(Mer)	Nakht-djehuty	Overseer of Carpenters (of the northern lake (of Amun)); Chief of Goldworkers in the Estate of Amun;
TT190	19	RII	?	?
TT192	18	AIII-AIV	Kheruef called Senaa	**Steward of the Great Royal Wife Tiye;** Royal Scribe; Controller of Monuments; Chief Royal Herald; Royal Seal-bearer; Overseer of Seal-bearers; Chief of Secrets of the Palace...
TT193	19/20	?	Ptahemheb	Great One of the Seal in the Treasury of the Estate of Amun;
TT194	19	RII	Djehutyemheb	**Overseer of Peasants of the Estate of Amun;** Scribe of the Divine Offerings of the Estate of Amun; Royal Scribe;
TT195	20	?	Bakenamun	Scribe of the Treasury of the Estate of Amun;
TT364	20	?	Amenemhab	Scribe of the Divine Offerings of all the Gods of Thebes; Scribe of the Granary of Amun;
TT406	20	?	Piay	Scribe of the Offering Table of the Lord of the Two Lands;

Figure 146: Entrance to TT192 with the Qurn mountain in the background (Author's own)

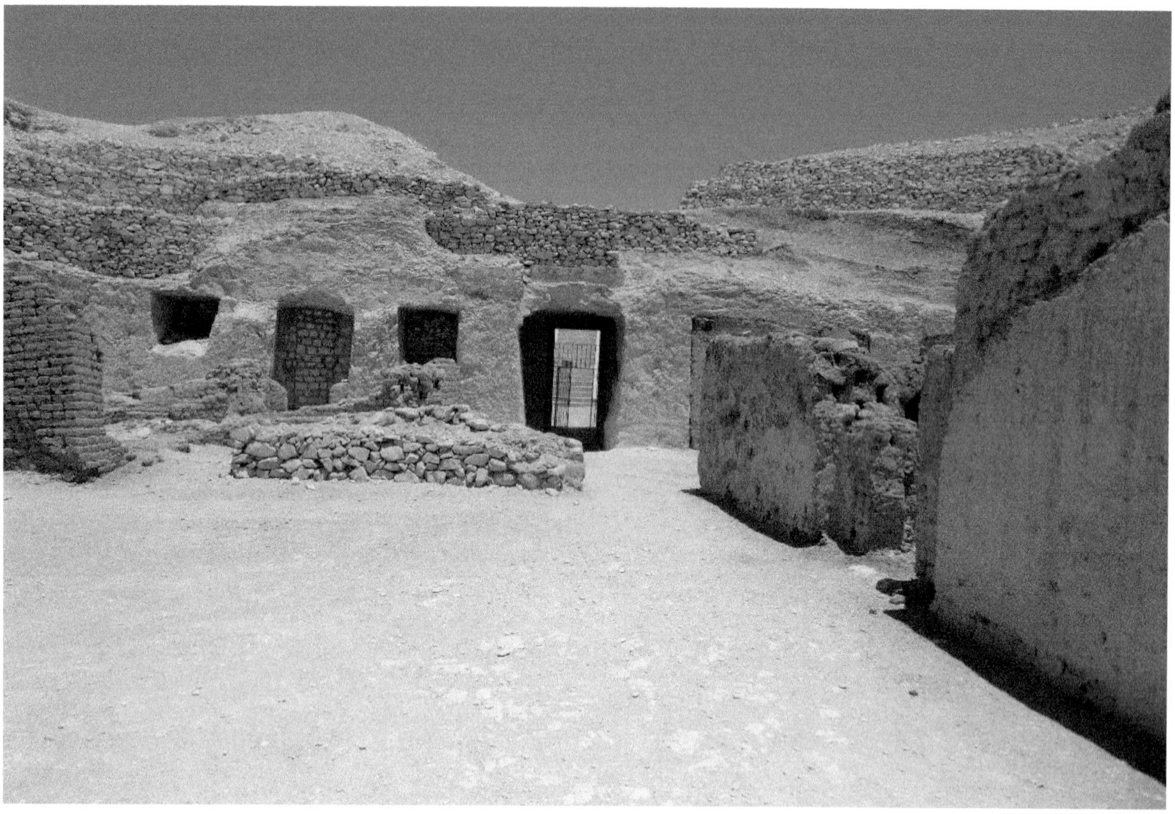

Figure 147: Shared courtyard originally built for TT192 (Author's own)

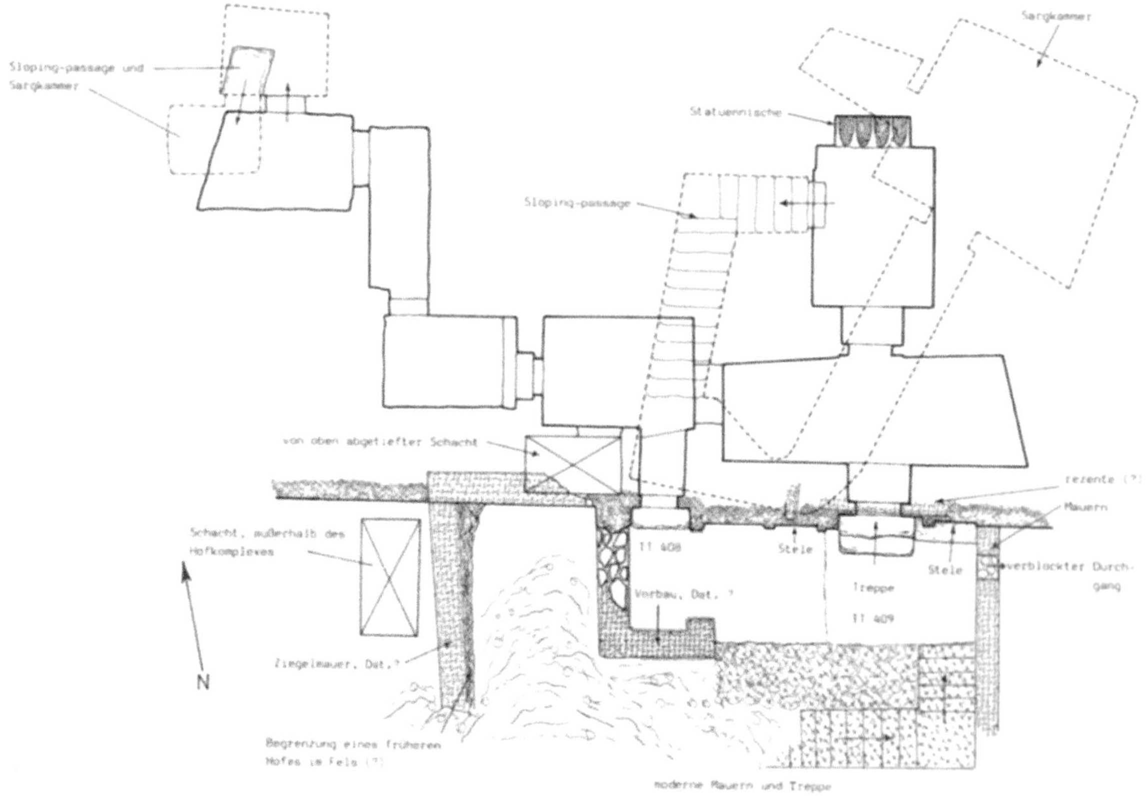

Figure 148: Plan of shared courtyard of TT408 and TT409 (Kampp 1996: Figure 508 – Courtesy of Professor Seyfried)

Figure 149: View over entrance to TT408 and TT409 (Author's own)

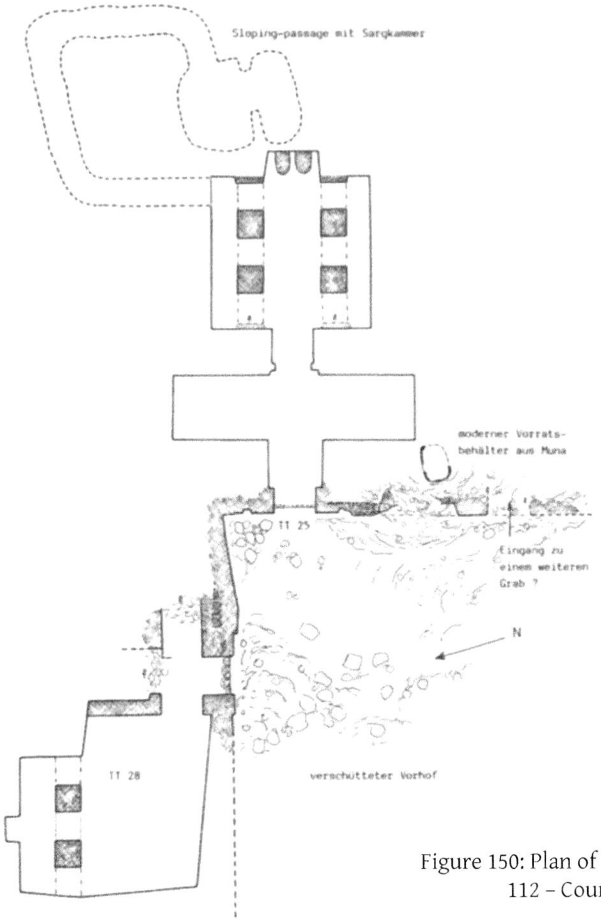

Figure 150: Plan of TT28 and TT25 (Kampp 1996: Figure 112 – Courtesy of Professor Seyfried)

Table 22: Owners of TT28, TT408 and TT409

TT	Dyn	Reign	Name	Title
TT25	19	RII	Amenemhab	High Priest of Khonsu;
TT28	19-21	?	Hori	Deputy of the Estate of Amun;
TT408	19/20	?	Bakenamun	Head of Servants of the Estate of Amun;
TT409	19	RII	Samut called Kyky	(Royal) Scribe ([of] the Estate of Amun), Counter of the Cattle (of Amun/the Lords of Thebes; Overseer of Scribes; Scribe of Counting the Cattle of all the Gods of Thebes; Overseer of Counting the Cattle of all the gods of UE /Thebes /Amun /Montu / Mut / Khonsu;

TT28 and TT25 share a separate court (see Figure 150). These tombs are all of similar date and three of the four individuals had titles connecting them to the Estate of Amun, while the fourth is associated with the Khonsu temple, presumably at Karnak, suggesting a possible occupational link (see Table 22). The owner of TT408 has a son named Amenemhab, who could be the owner of TT25, but without titles this is hard to confirm.

TT188 and TT374

The earlier TT188 holds the predominant position opposite the entrance to the courtyard, while TT374 was built on the eastern side as a later addition (see Figure 151). There are no shared titles (see Table 23) and no evidence of any family connection between the tomb owners, so TT374 was probably located in this

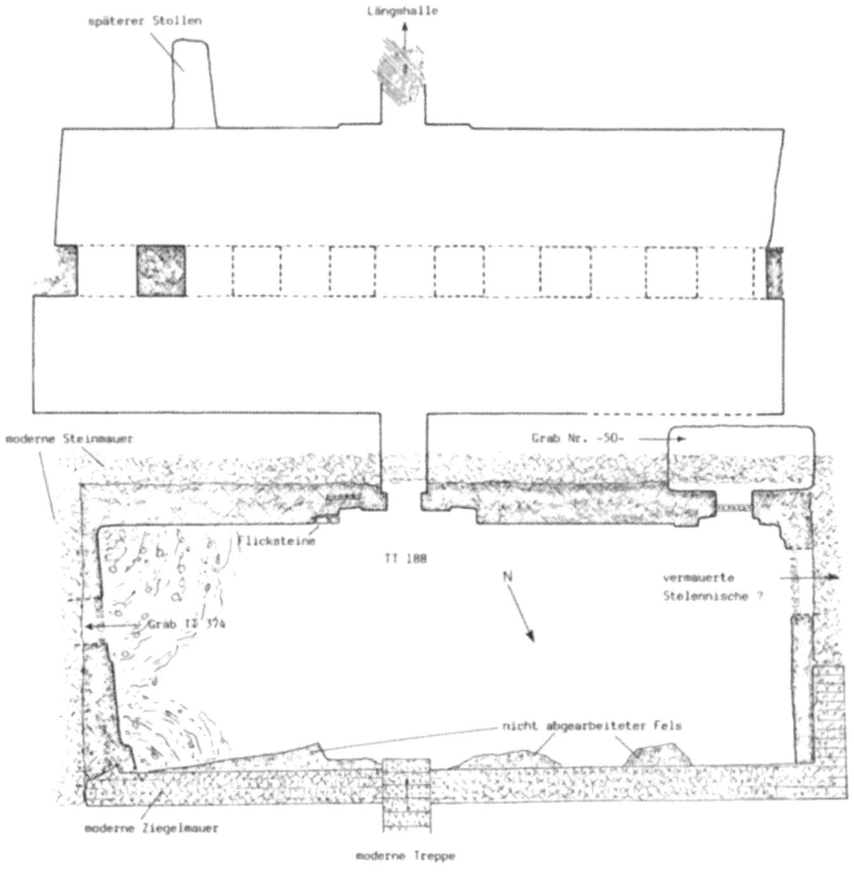

Figure 151: Plan of shared courtyard of TT188 and TT374 (Kampp 1996: Figure 374 – Courtesy of Professor Seyfried)

Table 23: Owners of TT188 and TT374

TT	Dyn	Reign	Name	Title
TT188	18	AIII/ AIV	Parennefer	Royal Butler; Overseer of the Priests of All the Gods;
TT374	19	RII-	Amenemopet	Scribe of the Treasury in the Ramesseum;

position to benefit from the existing courtyard and use the available space.

Tomb Reuse

No TTs in el-Asasif were reused during the New Kingdom.

Conclusions

It is striking how few tombs were located in el-Asasif, particularly as this outwardly appears to have been an extremely desirable location due to its proximity to the Deir el-Bahri temples and the views towards them (see Figure 152) and to a lesser extent the Middle Kingdom tombs (see Figure 153). Aside from the aspiration of the officials who served Montuhotep II, Hatshepsut and Tuthmosis III to be buried within sight of their mortuary temples, these temples remained in use as a destination of the BFV throughout the New Kingdom. Other tombs in the necropolis seem to have been positioned to overlook the processional route of the festival, so this area should be densely populated. Instead the majority of Middle Kingdom tombs are located along the northern edge of the causeway and in Upper Qurna, while tombs dating to Hatshepsut and Tuthmosis III also favour Upper Qurna, possibly as a result of the preference for rock-cut tombs on the upper slopes. This would appear to indicate that tomb construction here was forbidden at this time, presumably as a result of the proximity of the temples and the cultic activity along the causeway, as also noted by Strudwick and Strudwick (1999: 141).

There is only one tomb dating to Hatshepsut or Tuthmosis III located in el-Asasif, suggesting that special permission was required to be buried here. Puyemre-TT39 was only a '2nd Priest of Amun' and 'Royal Seal-bearer', rather than someone of higher status, such as a 'High Priest' or 'Vizier'. The location of Senenmut's tomb, TT353, at Deir el-Bahri seems logical as a result of the special privileges afforded to Senenmut on account of the influence he clearly held as a result of his numerous important titles, but Puyemre does not appear to have enjoyed the same status, so the presence of his burial here, and the absence of others, is unexplained. The presence of Kheruef-TT192 can also be explained as he was Queen Tiye's Steward, and the head of a number of departments associated with the palace. If burial in this area was by royal permission, Kheruef seems to have been influential enough to have been granted a place. He was also important enough in later times to have become the focus of his own cult of high officials as his tomb appears to have acted as a focal point for a number of later burials. The only other Eighteenth Dynasty tomb in el-Asasif was that of the 'Royal Butler' and 'Overseer of Priests', Parrenefer-TT188, another individual with royal connections.

In the Nineteenth and Twentieth Dynasties the area is used a little more frequently, and while some treasurers and other important officials and administrators are still buried here, there are also a number of less important individuals. Does this imply that special permission was no longer required? Or that different criteria now had to be met? Or was this area not as desirable a location to site a tomb as it appears?

Figure 152: View of the Deir el-Bahri temples from el-Asasif (Author's own)

Figure 153: View of Middle Kingdom Deir el-Bahri tombs from el-Asasif (Author's own)

Chapter 8:
El-Khokha

(See Appendix 9)

Location

El-Khokha is bordered by Qurna to the west and south, and el-Asasif to the north (see Figure 154). The northern boundary of el-Khokha used by Kampp (1996) has been shifted slightly northwards, allowing TT207, TT208 and TT297 to be included with el-Khokha rather than el-Asasif. This is due to the proximity of these tombs to the el-Khokha group, as they lie on the southern side of the natural path dividing el-Khokha from el-Asasif. The paths leading through necropolis today hardly differ from the ancient paths, so can be used to help divide the necropolis into areas (Kampp 1996: 121).

The tombs in this area are located between 90m and 100m above sea level, with the flood plain in this area beginning at 90m above sea level (see Figure 155). The highest concentration of tombs is in a band across the middle of the area, particularly in the very centre (see Figure 156). The tombs located in the northern area of el-Khokha are more widely dispersed. To the south there are two tombs in an isolated position, TT170 and TT171, which are too far away to have a spatial connection with the other el-Khokha tombs (see below).

Date of Use

El-Khokha contains 74 TTs, four of which date to the Old Kingdom or First Intermediate Period (TT185, TT186, TT405 and TT413) and the remaining 70 tombs date to the New Kingdom. Of these New Kingdom tombs, 39 date to the Eighteenth Dynasty (TT22, TT38, TT42, TT47, TT48, TT49, TT107, TT108, TT109, TT110, TT112, TT172, TT174, TT175, TT176, TT179, TT181, TT182, TT199, TT200, TT201, TT203, TT204, TT205, TT238, TT241, TT246, TT247, TT248, TT253, TT254, TT256, TT257, TT258, TT293, TT294, TT295, TT365 and TT412), two tombs date to either the late Eighteenth or early Nineteenth Dynasty (TT41 and TT245), and a further 15 date to the Nineteenth Dynasty (TT23, TT32, TT106, TT173, TT177, TT178, TT183, TT184, TT187, TT264, TT296, TT362, TT369, TT370 and TT373). Seven tombs are datable only to the Nineteenth or Twentieth Dynasty (TT180, TT198, TT206, TT208, TT351, TT352

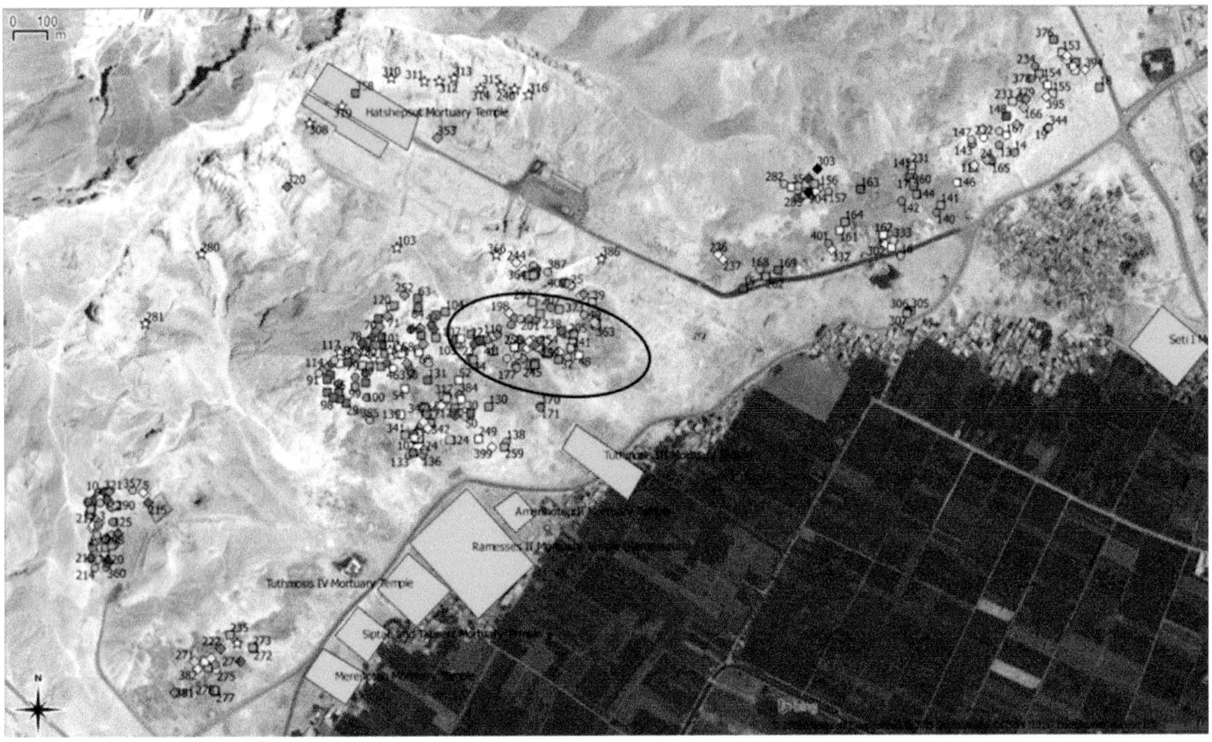

Figure 154: Location of el-Khokha within the Theban Necropolis (Author's own using QGIS)

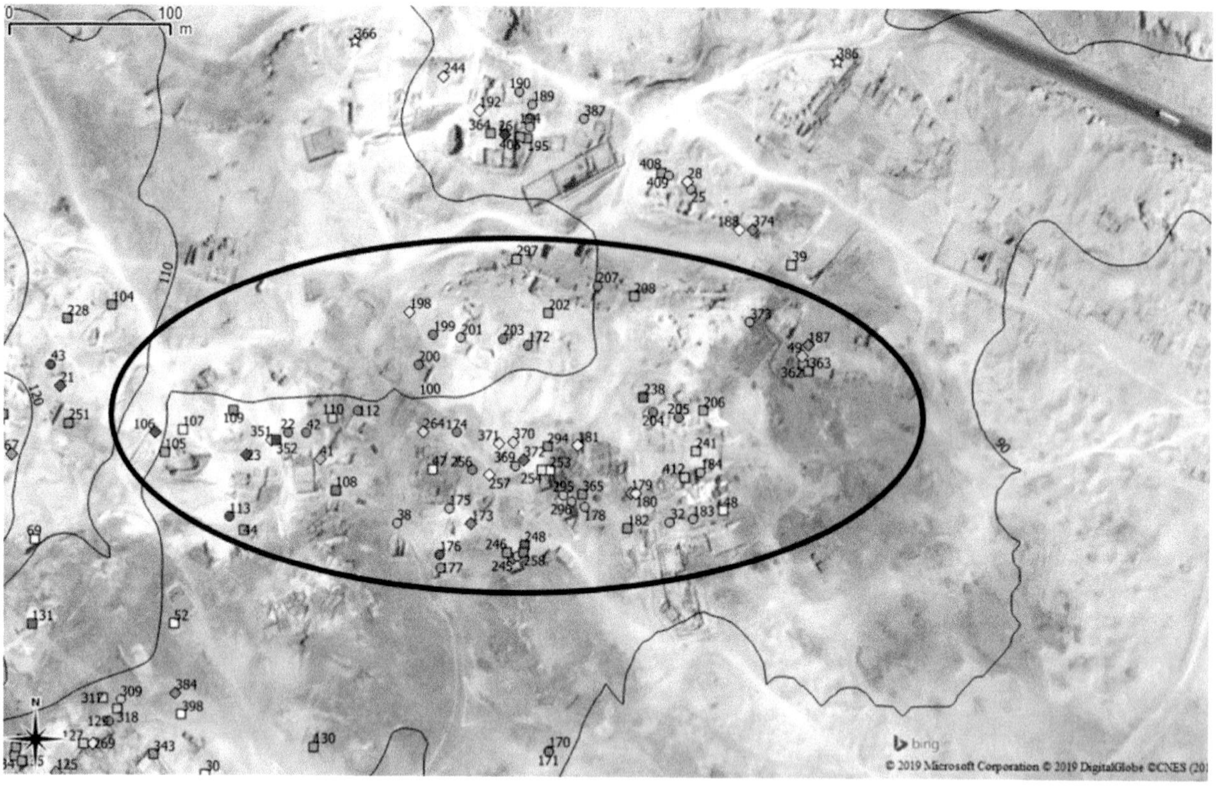

Figure 155: Landscape of el-Khokha (Author's own using QGIS)

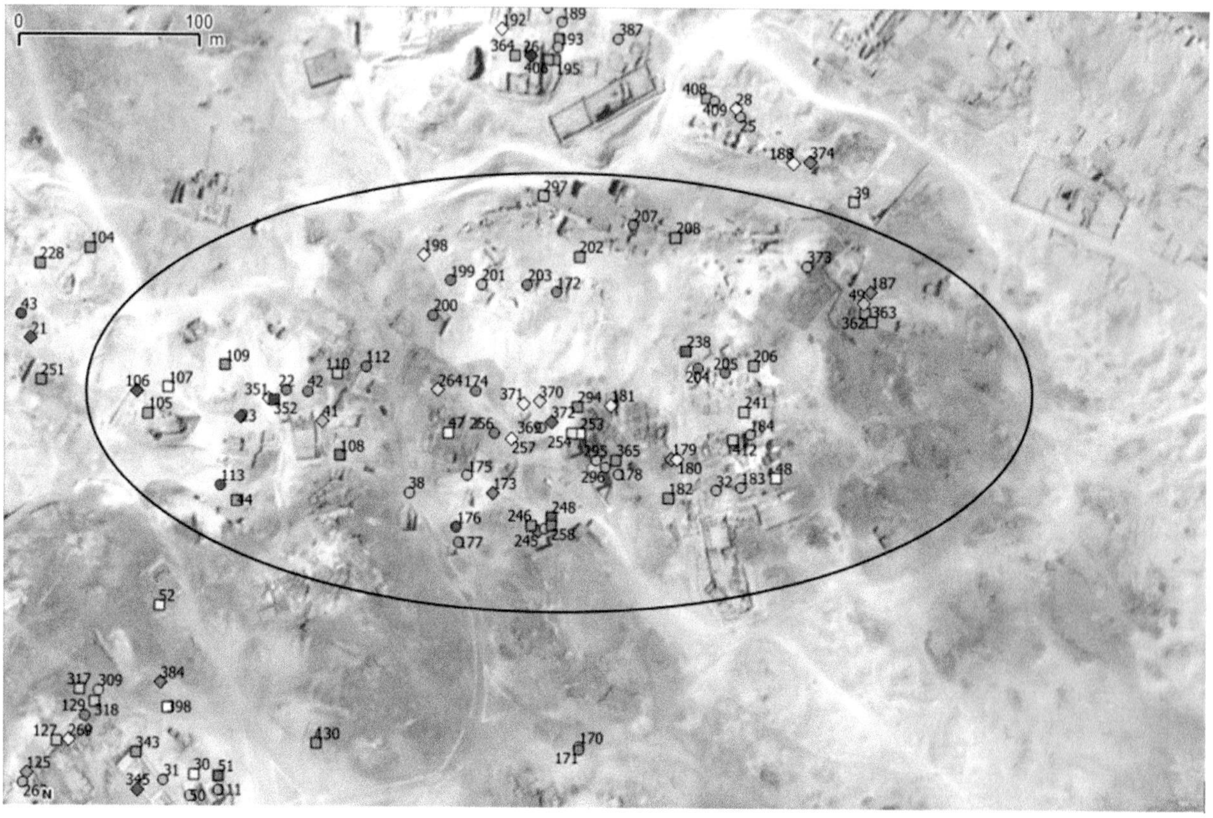

Figure 156: TTs in el-Khokha (Author's own using QGIS)

and TT371) and a further seven tombs date to the Twentieth Dynasty (TT44, TT105, TT202, TT207, TT363, TT372 and TT113). While the Eighteenth Dynasty is the most popular period for burials here, this area was in use throughout the New Kingdom.

The four Old Kingdom/ First Intermediate Period tombs shown here, form a cluster to the east of this area (see Chapter 2). Prior to the reign of Hatshepsut, there was one New Kingdom tomb, datable only to the early Eighteenth Dynasty built in el-Khokha (TT297). This tomb was not located in close proximity to the Old Kingdom/ FIP tombs, but at the northern boundary of the area in an isolated position, with views towards the Deir el-Bahri Middle Kingdom tombs (see Figures 157 and 158). There are relatively few Theban burials datable to the early Eighteenth Dynasty, so this does reflect the pattern in the rest of the necropolis.

During the reigns of Hatshepsut and Tuthmosis III nine tombs were built in el-Khokha (see Figures 159 and 160). The majority of these are clustered around the Old Kingdom/ FIP tombs (TT179, TT182, TT241, TT246, TT294, TT365 and TT412), while two tombs are

Table 24: el-Khokha tombs distributed by most likely date

Date	No. of Tombs	Tombs
OK / FIP	****	TT185, TT186, TT405, TT413
Early Dyn 18	*	TT297
Dyn 18	****	TT174, TT199, TT203, TT204
Hat	*	TT179
Hat / TIII	***	TT110, TT241, TT412
TIII	*****	TT109, TT182, TT246, TT294, TT365
TIII/ AII	*********	TT22, TT42, TT112, TT172, TT200, TT205, TT256
AII	**	TT238, TT248
AII / TIV	*	TT176
TIV	**	TT108, TT258
TIV / AIII	*****	TT38, TT175, TT201, TT247, TT295
AIII	****	TT47, TT48, TT107, TT253
AIII / AIV	**	TT181, TT257
Ay	*	TT49
Post Amarna/ Ay	*	TT254
Hor / SI	*	TT41
Dyn 19	***	TT173, TT187, TT245
SI / RII	*	TT106
RII	*******	TT32, TT178, TT183, TT184, TT296, TT369, TT373
RII / Mer	**	TT264, TT370
RII -	*	TT177
Mer	*	TT23
Dyn 19/20 (Ram)	*****	TT180, TT198, TT351, TT352, TT371
Dyn 20	*******	TT44, TT105, TT202, TT206, TT208, TT362, TT363
RIII	*	TT207
RIII/ RIV	*	TT372
RVIII	*	TT113

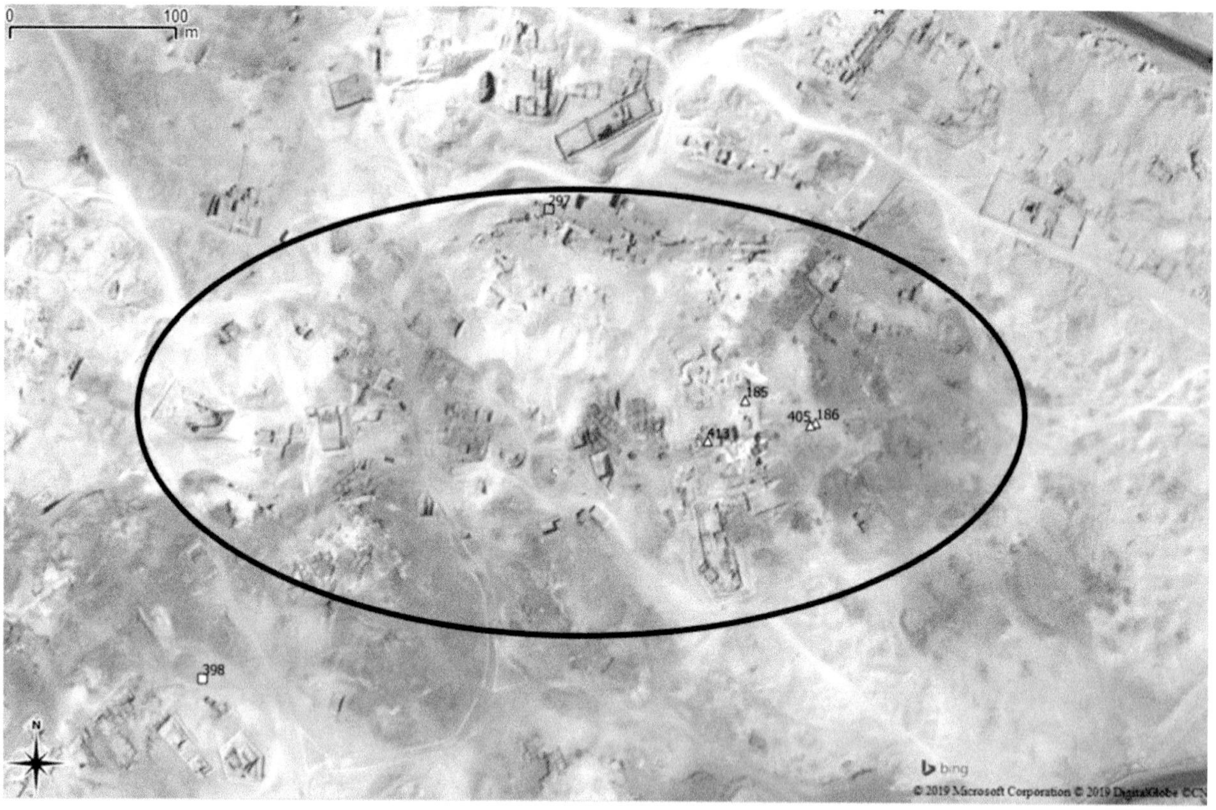

Figure 157: TTs in el-Khokha dated prior to the reign of Hatshepsut (Author's own using QGIS)

located to the west of this group, in close proximity to the tombs of Upper Qurna (TT109 and TT110). It may be significant that tombs built during these reigns were clustered around both the Middle Kingdom tombs in Qurna and the Old Kingdom/FIP tombs here. This appears to be another case of individuals during these reigns associated themselves with the oldest tombs in the necropolis by building their tombs in close proximity. Another potential reason for the choice of this location at this time is its proximity to the Qurna temple of Tuthmosis III, located approximately 200m to the south.

There was a peak in the number of burials in el-Khokha during the reigns of Tuthmosis III and Amenhotep II, with 14 burials dated to these reigns (see Figures 161 and 162). The majority of these are distributed in a line across the west of the area (TT22, TT42, TT109, TT112, TT172 and TT200). This arrangement corresponds with the natural contours of the landscape and provided views towards the Qurna temples of Tuthmosis III and Amenhotep II, so a date to either reign is possible. Based solely on the proximity of this row of tombs to TT110, it seems more likely this tomb dates to the reign of Tuthmosis III. Indeed, TT110 and TT112 lie adjacent to each other making a date for both more likely to be the reign of Tuthmosis III.

There are 14 TTs dated between the reigns of Amenhotep II and Amenhotep III (see Figures 163 and 164). A tight cluster of four tombs around a shared courtyard emerged in the central southern area (TT246, TT247, TT248 and TT258), three of which date between these reigns. Nine tombs now lined the contour line in the west of the area (TT22, TT42, TT107, TT109, TT110, TT112, TT172, TT200 and TT201), two of which date between Amenhotep II and Amenhotep III.

Six tombs date to either Amenhotep III or Amenhotep IV. Four of these tombs are located in the centre, three of them in a row (TT47, TT257 and TT253) with one located slightly to the north (TT181), but all in close proximity to each other (see Figure 165).

By the end of the Eighteenth Dynasty, el-Khokha was well-populated with tombs, with some evidence of clustering by reign (see Figure 166). There was still a line of tombs stretching across the north of the area, with the centre of the southern half of the area being the most popular, and apparent areas of space at the north east and east of the area. There was no gradual spread of distribution as areas fill up as observed in Qurna, but rather certain areas of el-Khokha develop gradually, presumably as result of views towards the mortuary temples of specific kings.

Figure 158: View from northern el-Khokha towards Deir el-Bahri, with Middle Kingdom tombs along the northern causeway visible in the background (Author's own)

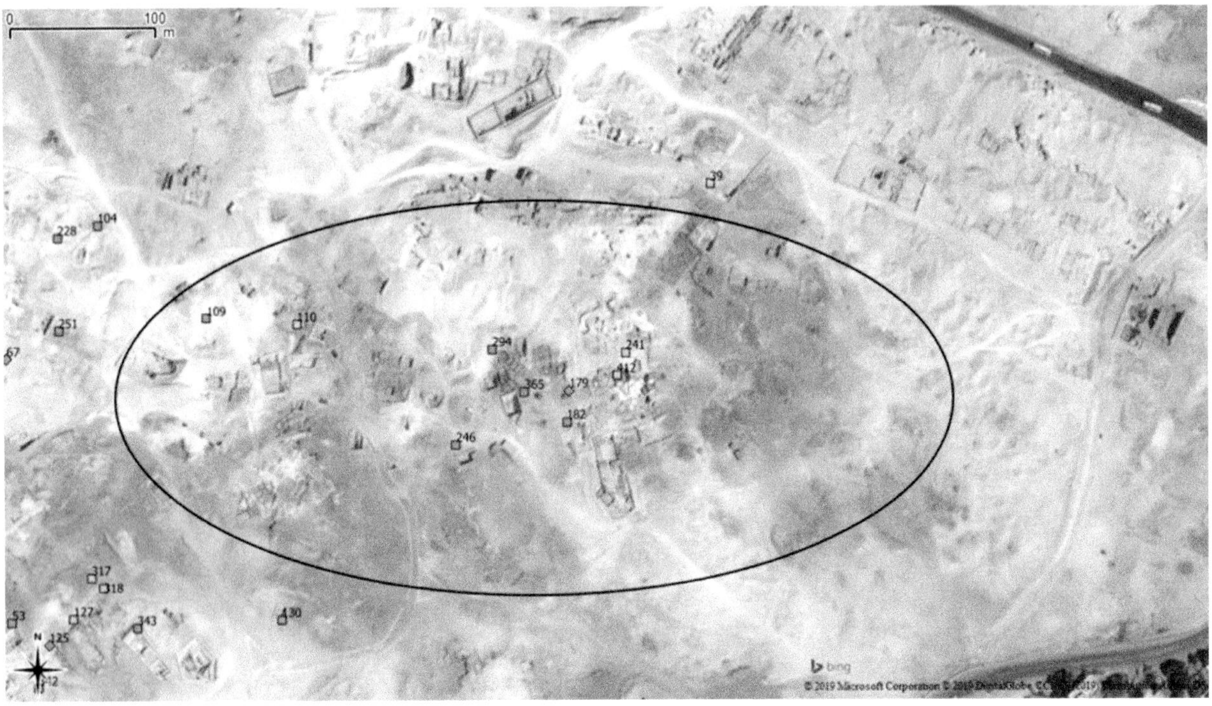

Figure 159: TTs in el-Khokha dated to Hatshepsut/Tuthmosis III (Author's own using QGIS)

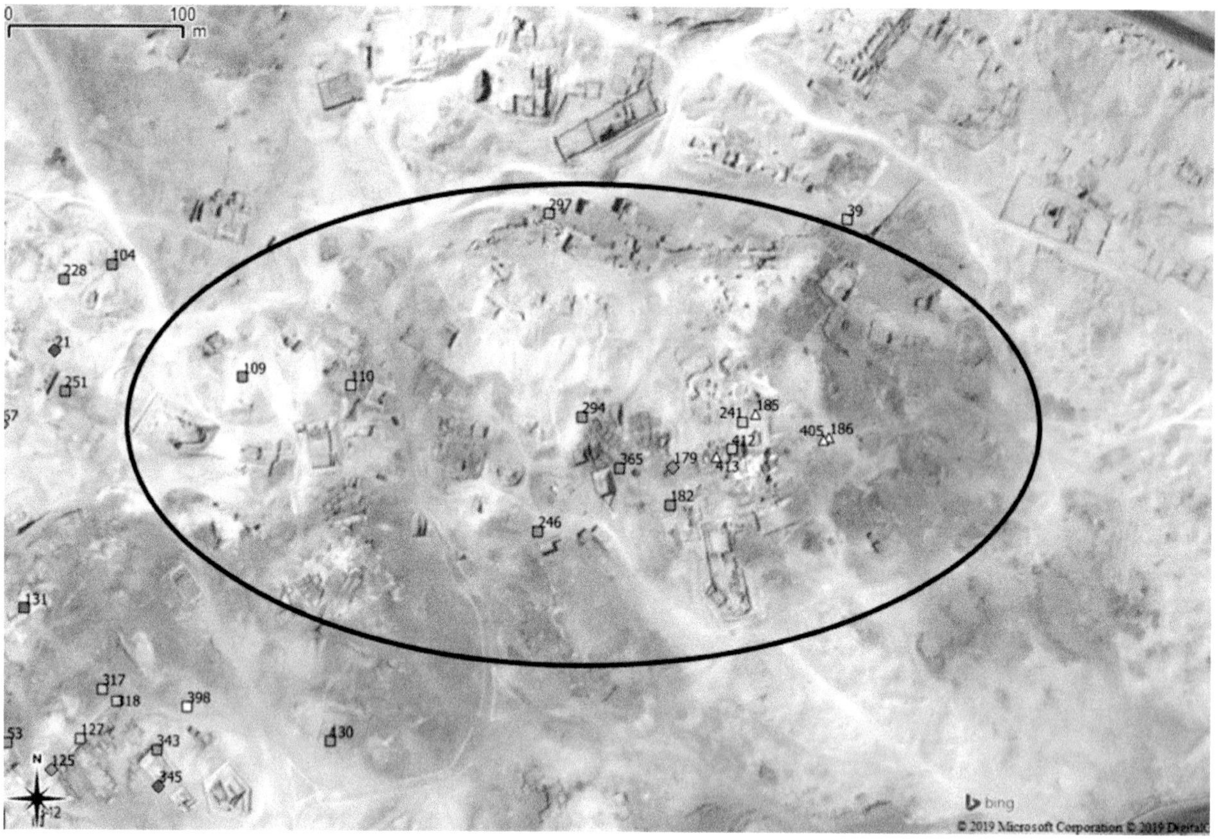

Figure 160: TTs in el-Khokha at the end of the reign of Tuthmosis III (Author's own using QGIS)

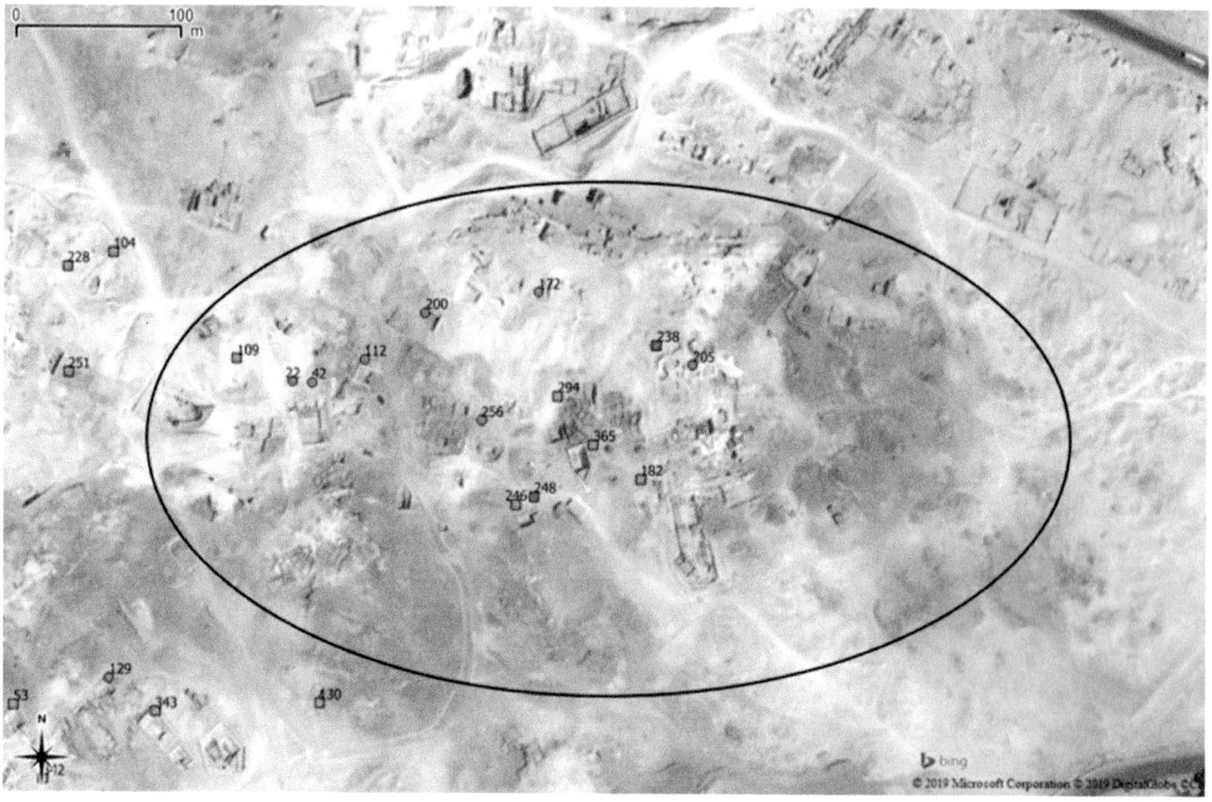

Figure 161: TTs in el-Khokha dated to Tuthmosis III/Amenhotep II (Author's own using QGIS)

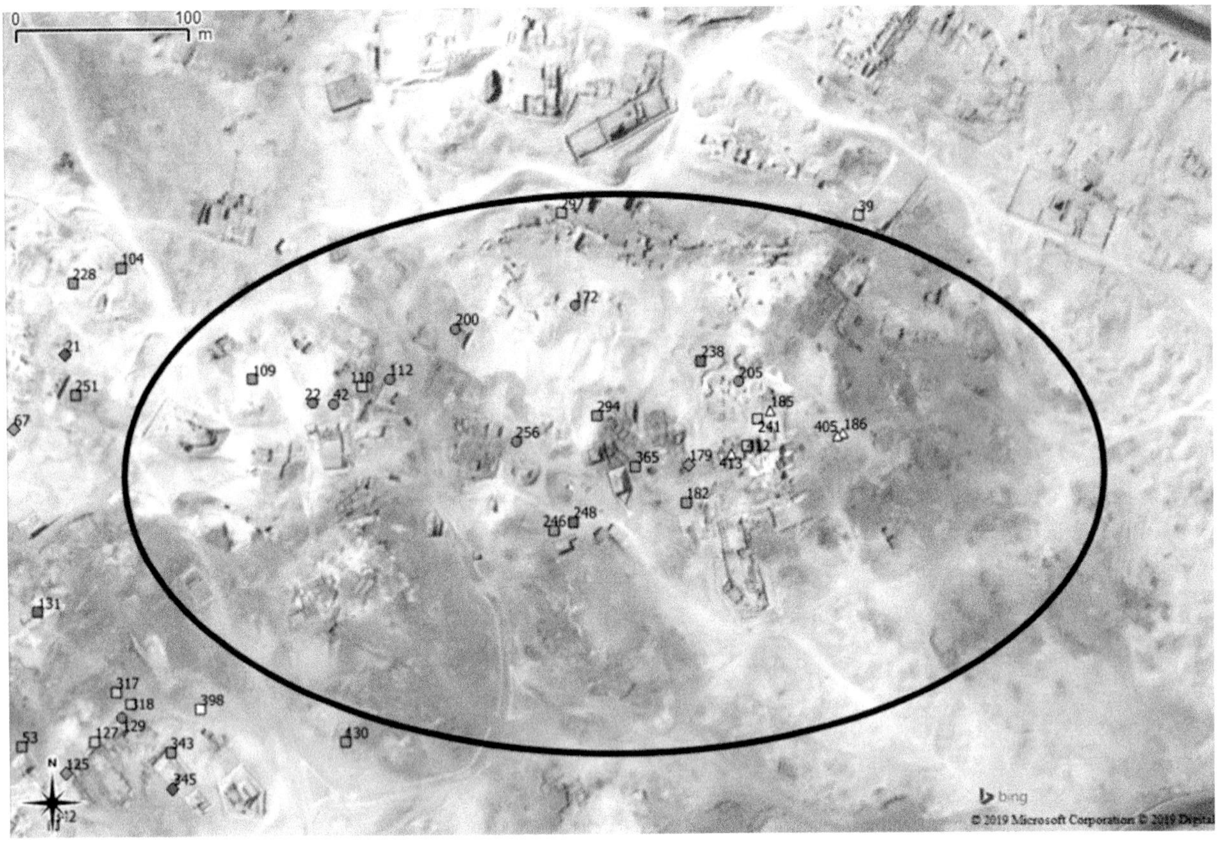

Figure 162: TTs in el-Khokha at the end of the reign of Amenhotep II (Author's own using QGIS)

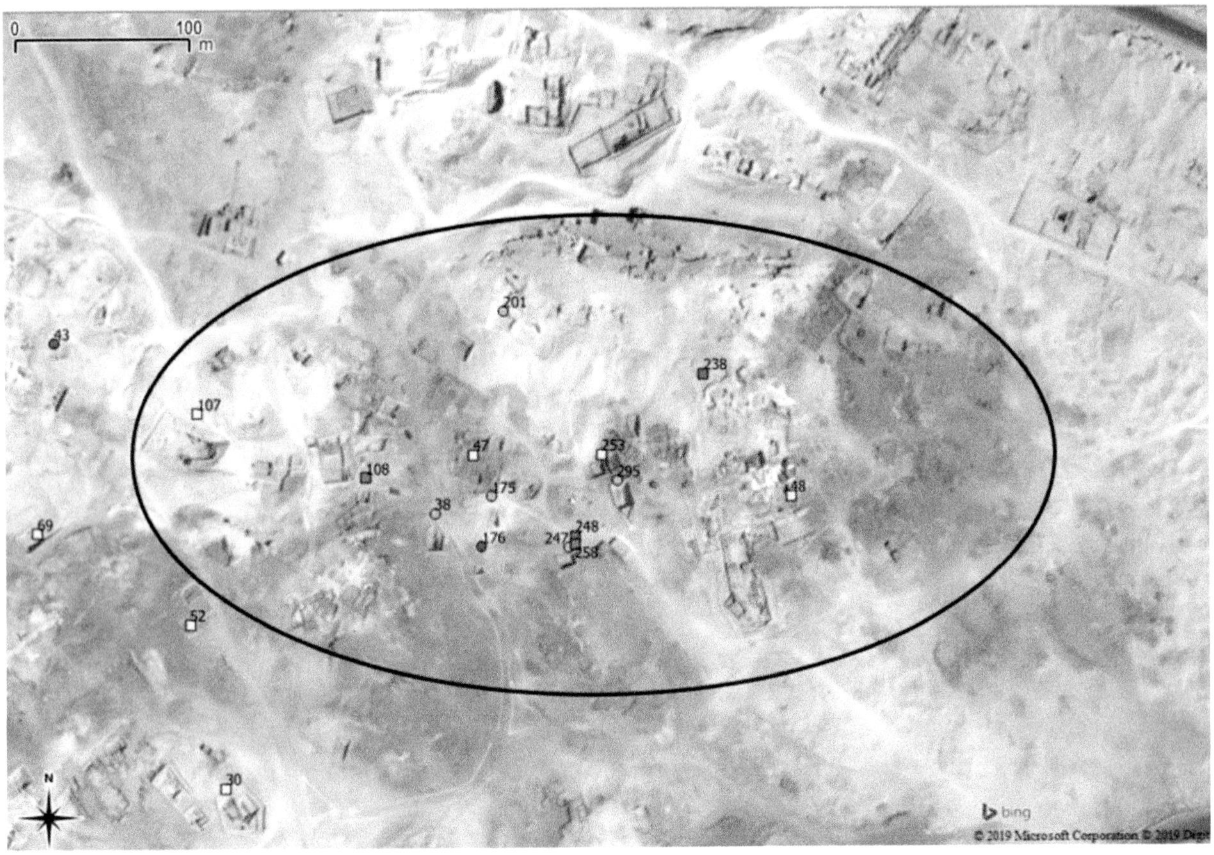

Figure 163: TTs in el-Khokha dated to Amenhotep II, Tuthmosis IV or Amenhotep III (Author's own using QGIS)

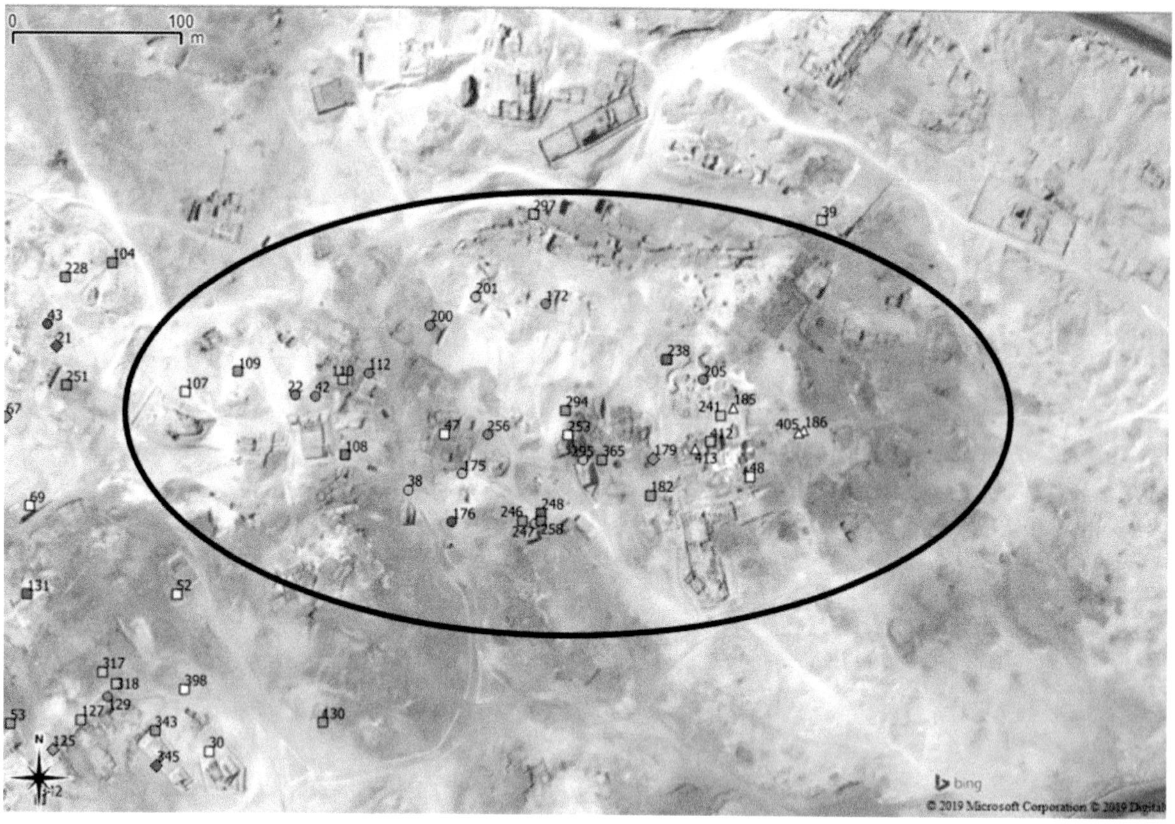

Figure 164: TTs in el-Khokha at the end of the reign of Amenhotep III (Author's own using QGIS)

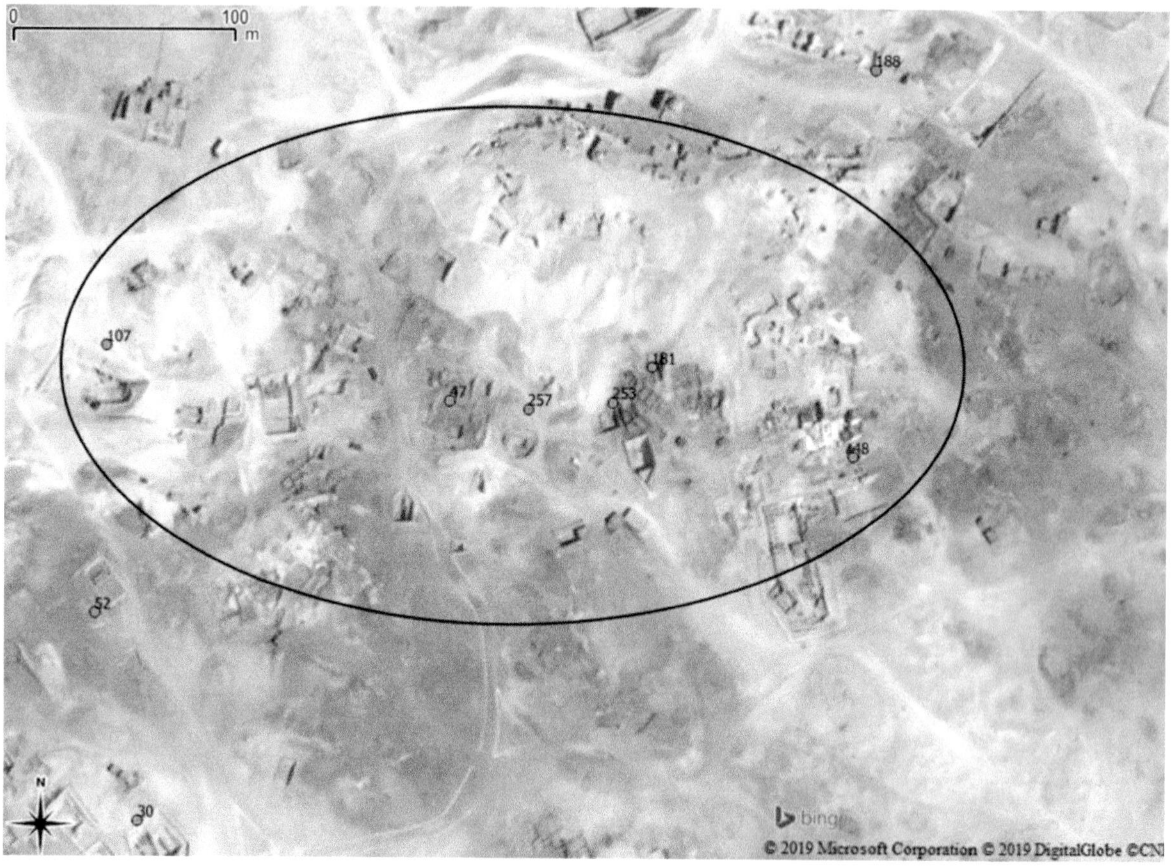

Figure 165: TTs in el-Khokha dated between Amenhotep III and IV (Author's own using QGIS)

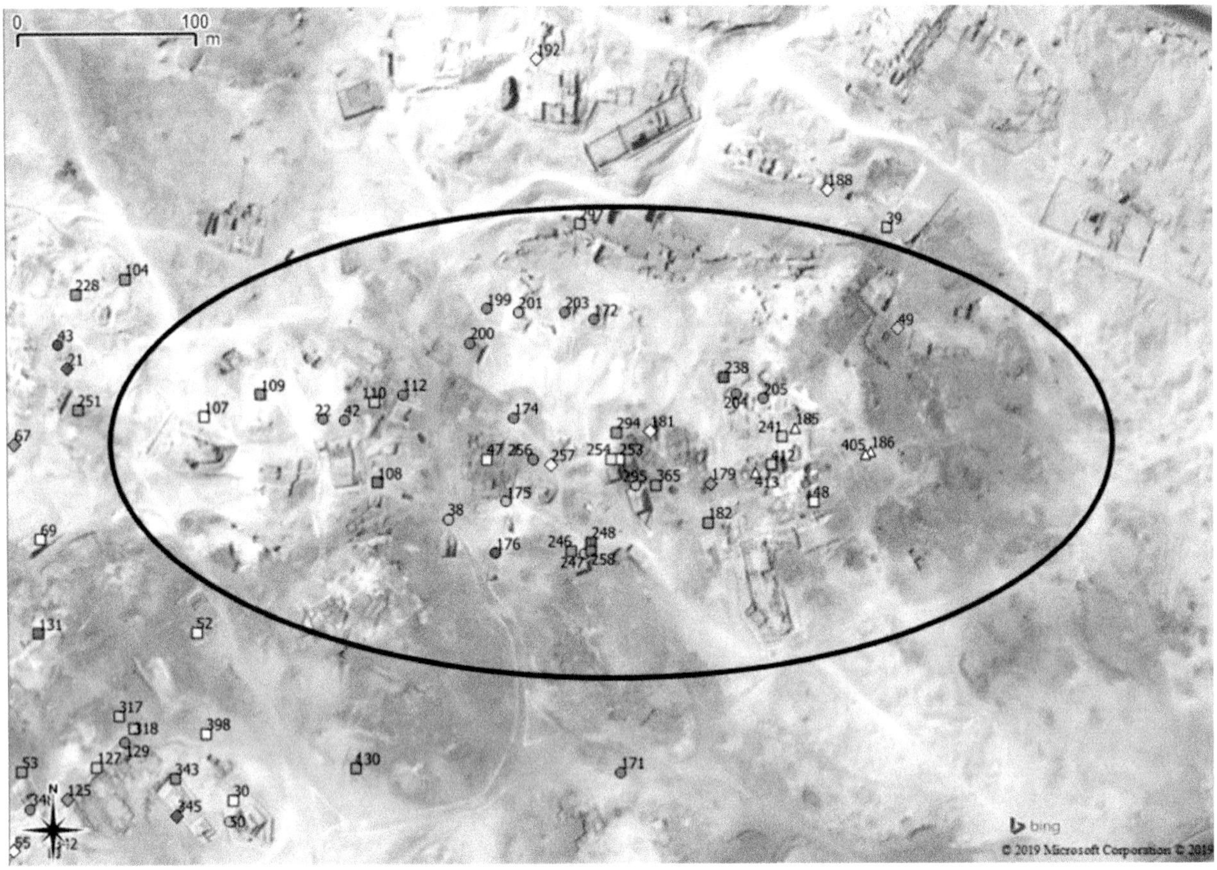

Figure 166: TTs in el-Khokha at the end of the Eighteenth Dynasty (Author's own using QGIS)

There are only two tombs dated to the early Nineteenth Dynasty prior to the reign of Ramesses II (TT41 and TT106). There was another peak in usage during the reign of Ramesses II, when seven tombs were built in the el-Khokha area (see Figures 167 and 168). Six of these are located in close proximity in the centralised southern half of the area (TT32, TT178, TT183, TT184, TT296 and TT369), with one some distance to the north-east (TT373). Both tombs dated to either Ramesses II or Merenptah (TT264 and TT370) are located to the west of the row of the aforementioned Ramesses II group, aligned with each other but not in particularly close proximity (see Figure 169).

By the end of the Nineteenth Dynasty there were a number of tombs located in a band across the centre of el-Khokha. The later Nineteenth Dynasty tombs were located to the north and south of the existing central group (see Figure 169). This area is some distance to the north-east of the Ramesside mortuary temples, so was not chosen as result of its proximity to them, as the lower slopes of Qurna would have been closer. However, this area of el-Khokha was at a higher altitude than Lower Qurna, and would therefore provide views over the processional route of the BFV.

A number of tombs were built in this area during the Ramesside Period and Twentieth Dynasty, but as few are datable to specific reigns, little can be said about patterning. For example, TT351 and TT352 are located adjacent to each other, but as they are only datable to the Nineteenth or Twentieth Dynasty, a specific connection between these tombs by date cannot be established (see Figures 170 and 171).

A distinct cluster of four tombs emerged at this time in the north eastern corner of el-Khokha (TT49, TT187, TT362 and TT363), two of which date to the Twentieth Dynasty (TT362 and TT363). The north, west and centre of the area all received new tombs during this period, so el-Khokha was still a popular location for Theban burials at the end of the New Kingdom, at a time when relatively few tombs were being built in the area (see Figures 171 and 172).

By the end of the New Kingdom, el-Khokha had expanded in three directions, with only the south-east of the area failing to see any building activity during the late New Kingdom (see Figure 172). This was due to the natural expansion of Qurna to the south and east, allowing the cemetery to spread further east towards

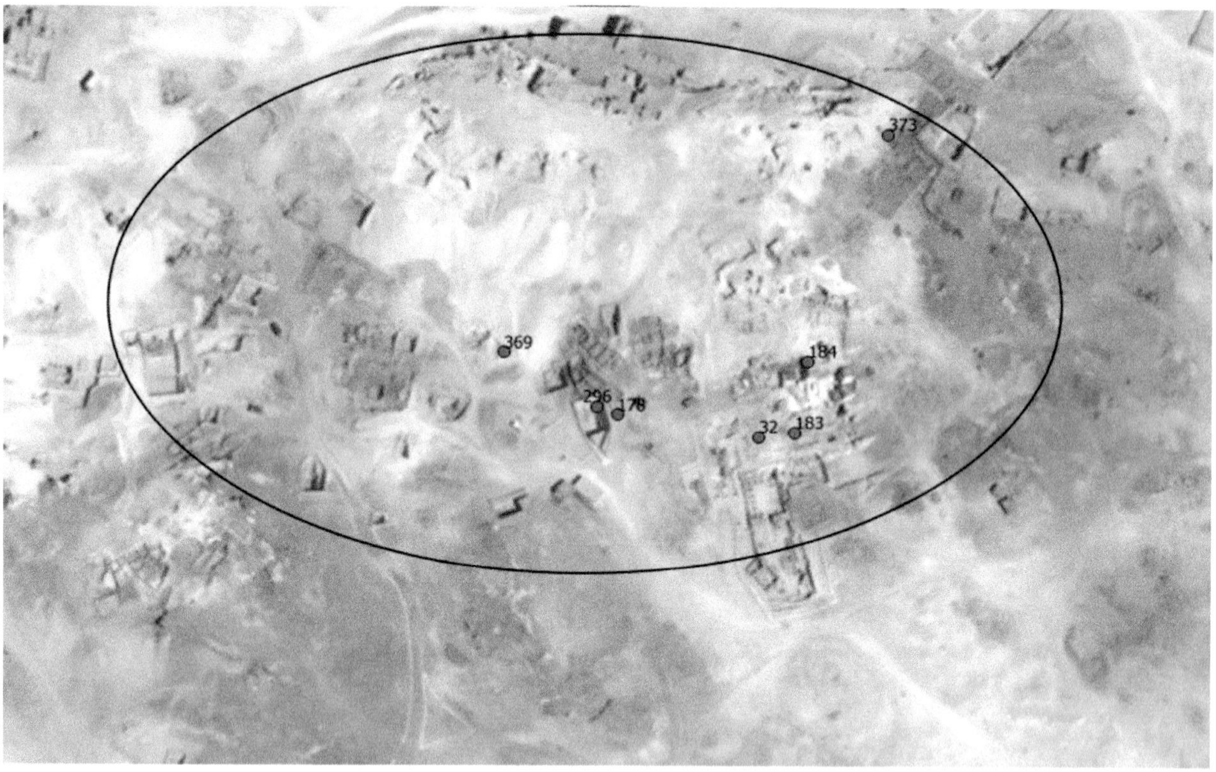

Figure 167: TTs in el-Khokha dated to Ramesses II (Author's own using QGIS)

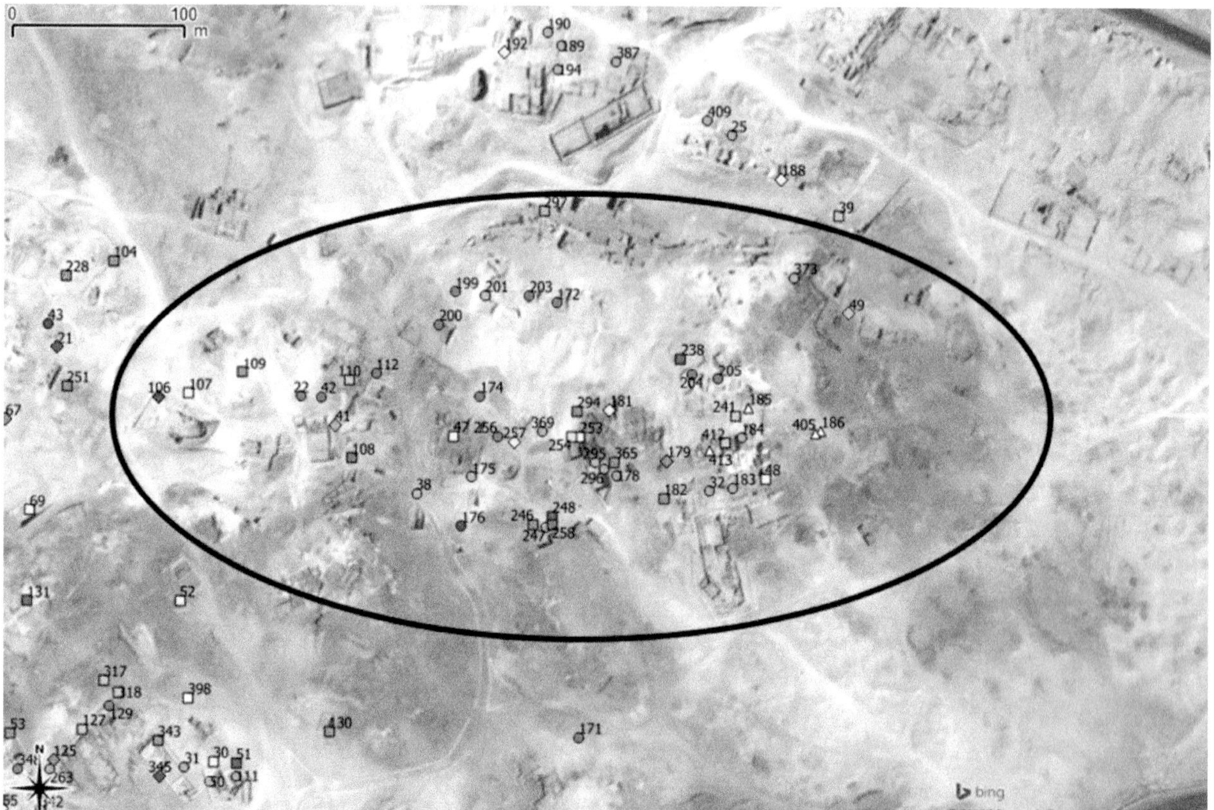

Figure 168: TTs in el-Khokha at the end of the reign of Ramesses II (Author's own using QGIS)

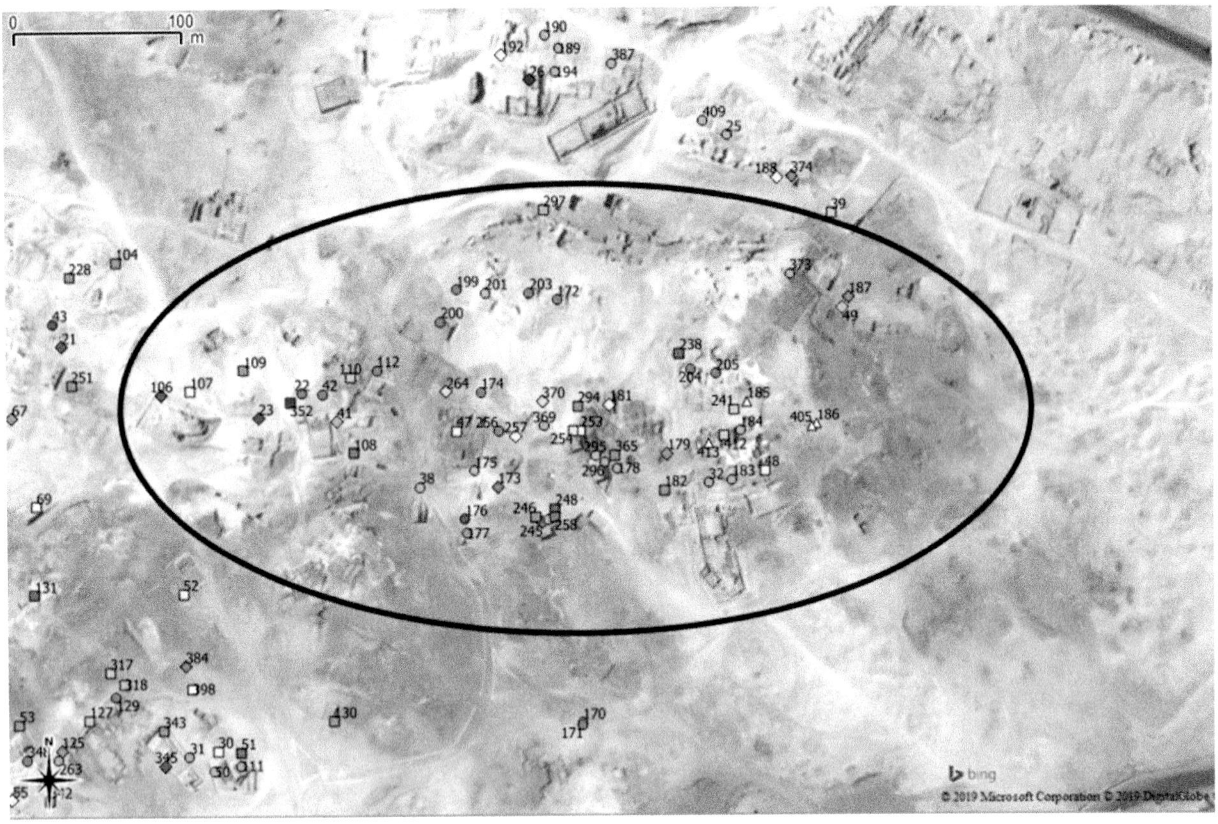

Figure 169: TTs in el-Khokha at the end of the Nineteenth Dynasty (Author's own using QGIS)

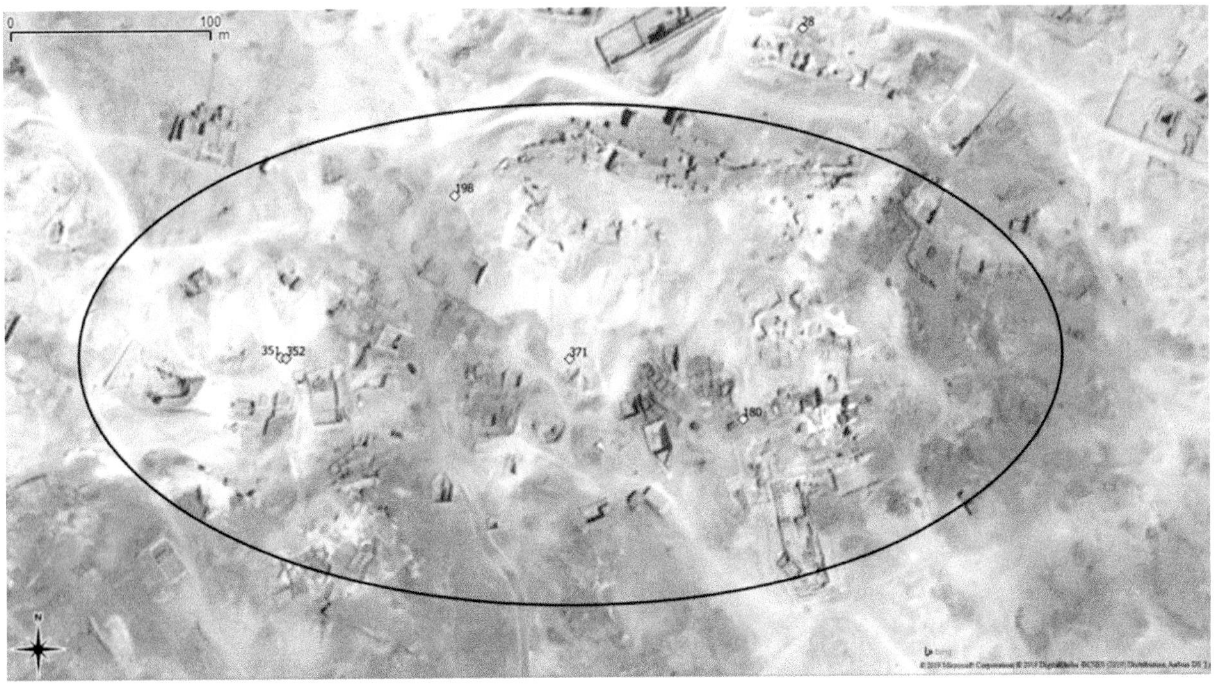

Figure 170: TTs in el-Khokha datable only to the Ramesside Period (Author's own using QGIS)

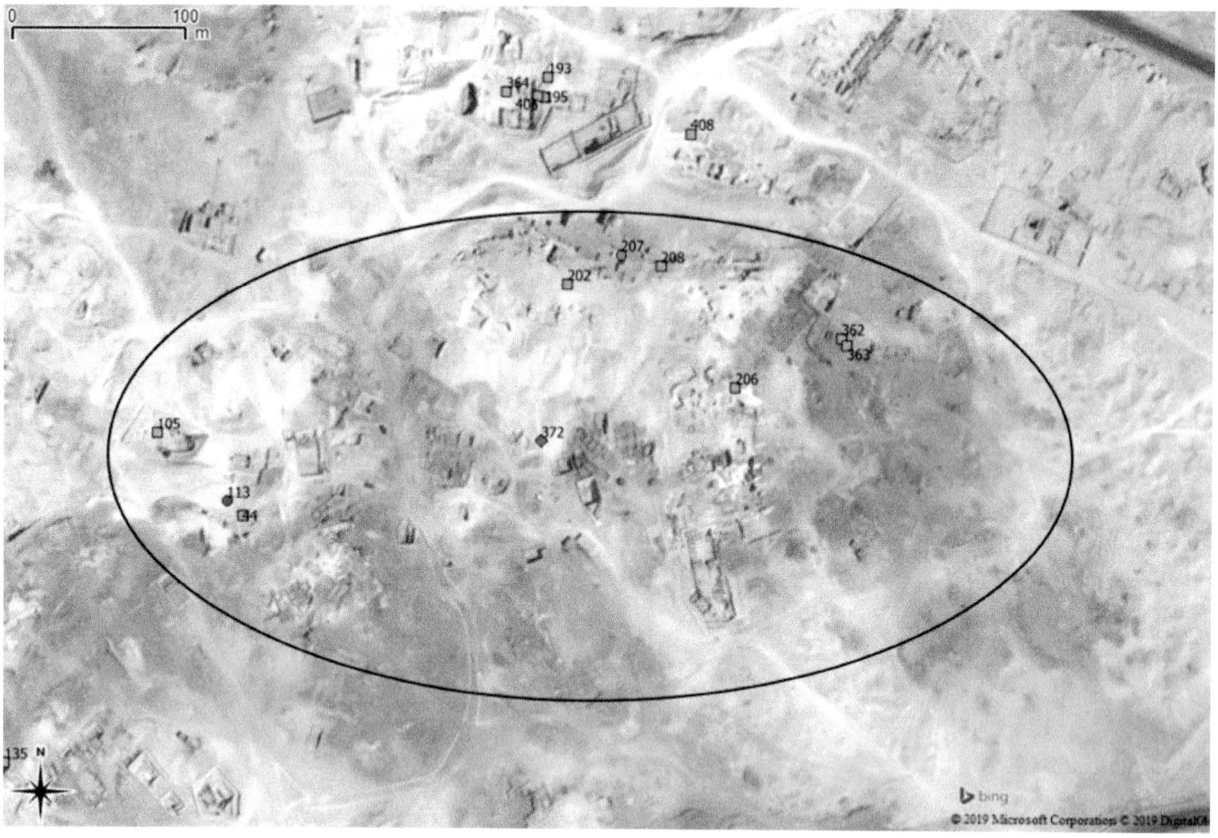

Figure 171: TTs in el-Khokha datable to the Twentieth Dynasty (Author's own using QGIS)

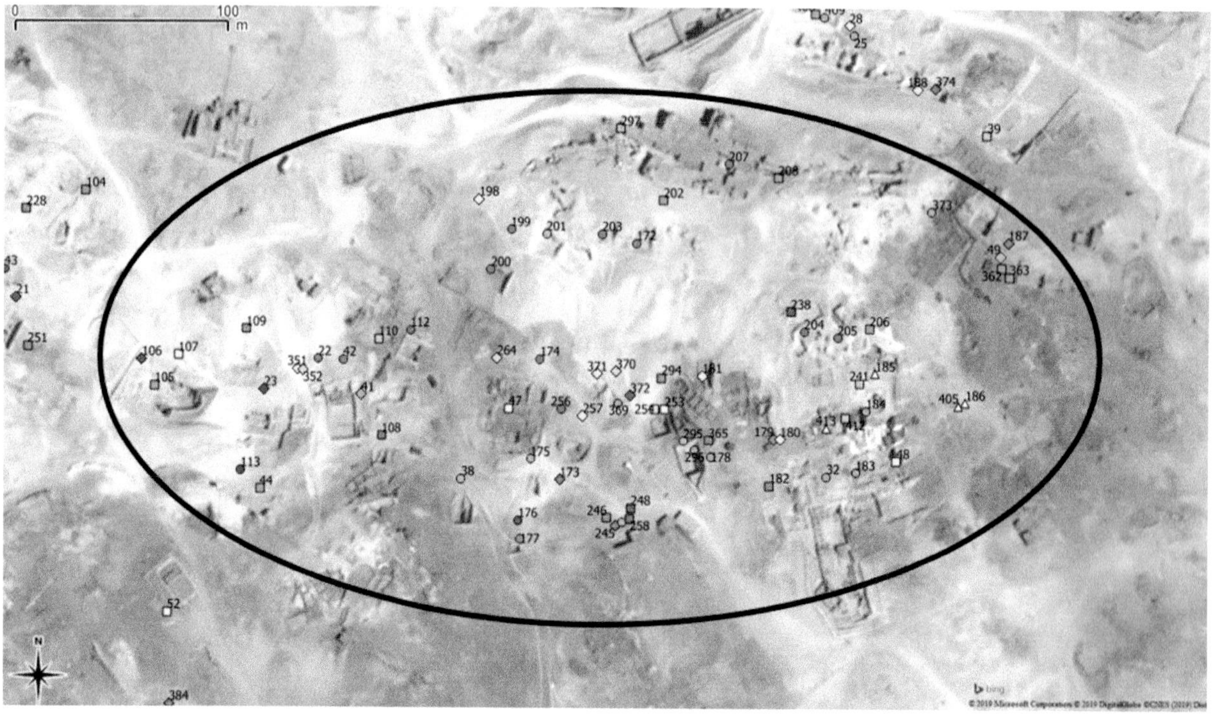

Figure 172: TTs in el-Khokha at the end of the New Kingdom (Author's own using QGIS)

the causeway at Deir el-Bahri. The area to the east of the Old Kingdom/FIP tombs remained empty of tombs, and the necropolis did not expand in this direction.

Occupation of Tomb Owners

(See Table 25)

Priesthood

There are 27 priests buried here, of which five were in reused tombs, and some held multiple priestly titles (see Figure 175). Five 'High Priests' were buried in el-Khokha, a 'High Priest of Amun', Menkheperresoneb-TT112 (TIII-AII), a 'High Priest of Ptah', Khaemwaset-TT369 (RII), a 'High Priest of Inheret' (or Onuris using his Greek name), Nebseny-TT108 (TIV), a 'High Priest of the Moon', Tjay called To-TT23 (Mer), and an unknown individual-TT187 (Dyn 19), who was 'High Priest' of an unspecified deity. Three of these tombs in the westernmost area, all within 100m or less of another High Priest and within 120m of each other (TT23, TT108 and TT112), with TT369 in a more central location, and TT187 to the far east of the area. As the 'High Priests' all served different deities there can be no patterning in terms of their affiliation.

There were five *ḥm-nṯr* priests buried in el-Khokha: Khaemopet-TT105 (Dyn 20), of the 'Noble Ram Sceptre of Amun'; Paser-TT106 (SI-RII), who served Maat; Kynebu-TT113 (RVIII), who worked in the mortuary temple of Amenhotep II; Nakhtamun-TT202 (Dyn 20), who served Ptah; and Khaemwaset-TT369 (RII), who was also the 'High Priest of Ptah' (see above), and second and fourth *ḥm-nṯr* of Amun. TT105 and TT106 are adjacent to each other in the west of the area, with TT113 within 50m of them, but TT202 and TT369 are located some distance away to the east from these tombs, but within 100m of each other. These two priests of Ptah (TT202 and TT369), and two priests of Amun (TT105 and TT369), are not in close enough proximity to each other to suggest a potential link.

There were a large number of '*wꜥb* priests' buried in el-Khokha. There were several '*wꜥb* priests of Amun', specifically the second occupants of TT187-Pakhyhet (Dyn 20) and TT294-Roma (Ram), and the owner of TT362-Paanemwaset (late Dyn 19-early Dyn 20). Of these, TT187 and TT362 were part of a cluster of four tombs in the east of the area, along with two members of the temple administration (TT49 and TT363), all four of whom were affiliated to the god Amun. There were a number of individuals with similar titles affiliated to Amun, including two '*wꜥb* priests in front of Amun', Amenemhab-TT44 (Dyn 20) and Nakhtamun-TT202, (Dyn 20), and a '*wꜥb* priest of Amun 'Great of Majesty'', Aashefytemwaset, who reused TT112 (Ram). There was one '*wꜥb* priest in front of Mut', Aashaket, who reused TT174 (Dyn 20), and a number of '*wꜥb* priests' of unspecified affiliation, Paser-TT106 (SI-RII), Kynebu-TT113 (RVIII), Amenemopet-TT177 (RII-end Dyn 19) and Neferrenopet called Kenro-TT178 (RII). There is no further clustering of '*wꜥb* priests' of a specific affiliation. TT44 and TT113 are adjacent to each other and within

Table 25: el-Khokha tombs distributed by occupational group (n) denotes subsequent tomb occupation [ ] denotes reconstructed titles (Saleh 1977: 12 and 19]

Occupational Group	No. of Tombs	Tombs
Priesthood	************* *************	TT23, TT41, TT44, TT105, TT106, TT108, TT109, TT112 (1 & 2), TT113, TT174 (2), TT177, TT178, TT183, TT186, TT187 (1 & 2), TT202, TT203 (2), TT208, TT241, TT294 (2), TT295, TT362, TT369, TT405, TT413
Temple Administration	************* ************* ********	TT32, TT38, TT41, TT44, TT48, TT49, TT107, TT110, TT173, TT177, TT178, TT179, TT183, TT184, TT185, TT198, TT200, TT204, TT207, TT241, TT247, TT248, TT253, TT254, TT257 (1and2), TT294, TT296, TT297, TT352, TT363, TT365, TT370, TT372
Royal Administration	************* ************* *******	TT22, TT23, TT32, TT41, TT42, TT47, TT48, TT106, TT107, TT109, TT110, TTT112, T172, TT181, TT183, TT184, TT186, TT187, TT201, TT205, TT206, TT238, TT245, TT254, TT256, TT258, TT295, TT296, TT370, TT373, TT405, TT412, TT413
General Administration	***********[*]	TT32, TT41, TT106, TT182, TT186, TT199, TT246, TT254, TT264, TT295, [TT405], TT413
Local Administration	***********	TT42, TT106, TT109, TT184, TT186, TT200, TT296, TT405, TT413
Military	****	TT42, TT200, TT256, TT351
Royal Family	*	TT22 (2)
Unknown	*****	TT175, TT176, TT180, TT246, TT371

Figure 173: Tombs in close proximity in south el-Khokha by the end of the New Kingdom (Author's own)

Figure 174: View from el-Khokha towards Qurna (Author's own)

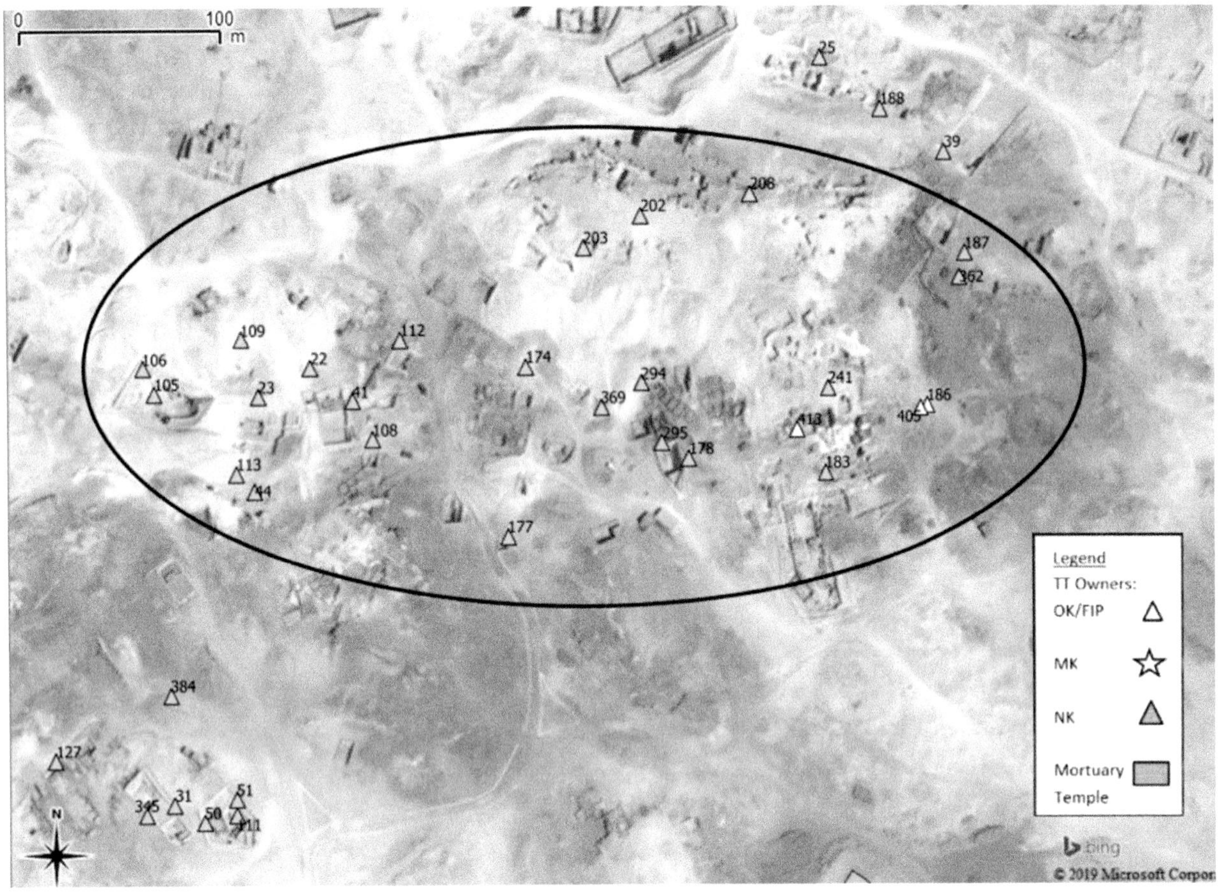

Figure 175: TTs of Priests in el-Khokha (Author's own using QGIS)

100m of this western area where several High Priests are buried. Others are more central (TT112, TT174, TT177, TT178 and TT294) and are loosely arranged within 100m of High Priest Khaemwaset-TT369. TT202 is located in the north of el-Khokha, and while not close to any other '*wʿb* priests', this tomb is within 100m of TT203 and TT208, both of whom are 'Divine Fathers' (see below).

There were also five 'Lector Priests' (TT113- RVIII, TT177- RII-end Dyn 19, TT186- OK-FIP, and TT405 and TT413 - both FIP). Only one had a specified affiliation, Amenemopet-TT177 who was a 'Lector Priest of Amun' in the Ramesseum, so no patterning by affiliation can be determined here. The three earliest tombs were clustered together (see Chapter 4) but there is no spatial connection between the other Lector Priests.

There were two '*sm* priests', Kynebu-TT113 (RVIII), who worked in the temple of Amenhotep II, and Djehutymose called Paroy-TT295 (TIV-AIII), who worked in the 'Place of Embalmment'. These tombs are not in close proximity but are both within 100m of a High Priest. There were also four 'Divine Fathers', two of whom were affiliated to Amun, the 'Head Divine Father of Amun', Menkheperresoneb-TT112 (TIII-AII), and the 'Divine Father of Amun-Re', Roma-TT208 (Ram). Of the others, Nebsumenu-TT183 (RII) served Re-Atum, while Wennefer, who reused TT203 (RII), served both Mut and 'all the lords of Thebes'. TT203 and TT208 are located in the north of el-Khokha, within 100m of each other, but not in close proximity to the other 'Divine Fathers'.

There were also those with esoteric knowledge, including three 'Chiefs of Secrets', Kynebu-TT113 (RVIII), who served Amun, Wennefer-TT203 (reused RII), who served Mut, and Djehutymose called Paroy-TT295 (TIV-AIII), of 'the Chest of Anubis' and 'Place of Embalmment' respectively. There was also the 'Chief of Mysteries' in the 'House of the Morning' or robing room, Ahmose-TT241 (Hat-TIII). These tombs do not appear to be spatially connected. Other priestly titles include three 'Overseers of the Priests', '...of Min and Isis', Amenemopet called Ipy-TT41 (Hor-SI), '... of Inheret' and '...of Osiris' Min-TT109 (TIII), and '...of Upper and Lower Egypt', Menkheperresoneb-TT112 (TIII-AII). All three of these tombs are located in the western area but not in particularly close proximity. There were three 'Festival Leaders', Paser-TT106 (SI-RII) and Nebsumenu-TT183 (RII) served Amun, while

Min-TT109 (TIII-AII) served Osiris. TT106 and TT109 formed part of the western priestly group, within 50m of each other, but TT183 is located some distance to the east. There is no connection by affiliation.

These priests served a range of deities, some serving multiple deities, others not specifying a specific deity in their titles (TT178, TT186, TT187, TT241, TT405 and TT413). The most commonly attested god served by these priests was Amun (TT44, TT105, TT106, TT112 (1 and 2), TT113, TT177, TT183, TT187 (2), TT202, TT294 (2), TT362, TT369). Other deities include: Amun-Re (TT183 and TT208); Ptah (TT202 and TT369); Anubis (TT295); Osiris (TT109); Onuris (TT108 and TT109); Mut (TT174 (2) and TT203); Neith (TT106); Maat (TT106); Min and Isis (TT41); Re-Atum (TT183); the moon-god (TT23); and even 'all the Gods' (TT41, TT173, TT296). Others served the royal mortuary cult of Amenhotep II (TT113 and TT248). Tombs belonging to those serving Amun are found throughout the area, but there are three small clusters: in the western corner, TT106, TT105, TT113 and TT44; in the centre TT294 and TT369; and in the eastern corner, TT187 and TT362. There do not appear to be any spatial connections between the tombs belonging to priests serving other deities.

There seems to be a connection between this western area of el-Khokha and the burial of priests throughout the New Kingdom. There is some evidence of the High Priests acting as a focal point for some burials of less important priests, as there is a loose cluster of priestly tombs in the west where three High Priests are buried (TT23, TT41, TT44, TT105, TT106, TT108, TT109, TT112 and TT113) and also around TT369 in the centre (TT174, TT177, TT178, TT294, TT295 and TT369). There is also a cluster of the earliest priestly tombs in the east of el-Khokha (TT186, TT405 and TT413).

Temple Administration

There were 34 TT owners in el-Khokha, one of whom reused a tomb, who held titles linking them to the temple in an administrative capacity (see Figure 176). The majority were connected to the Estate of Amun (TT32, TT38, TT41, TT44, TT48, TT49, TT107, TT110, TT173, TT177, TT178, TT179, TT183, TT184, TT198, TT200, TT204, TT207, TT247, TT253, TT254, TT257 (1and2), TT294, TT297, TT352, TT363, TT365, TT370 and TT372) while others served multiple (TT173 and TT296) or unspecified deities (TT241). Two of these individuals worked at the Ramesseum (the owner of TT177 and the usurper of TT257), another at Medinet Habu (TT372), and others at the mortuary temples of Tuthmosis III (TT248), and Amenhotep I (TT184), respectively. Those attached to the Estate of Amun are scattered across the area, with a greater density of tombs in the centre.

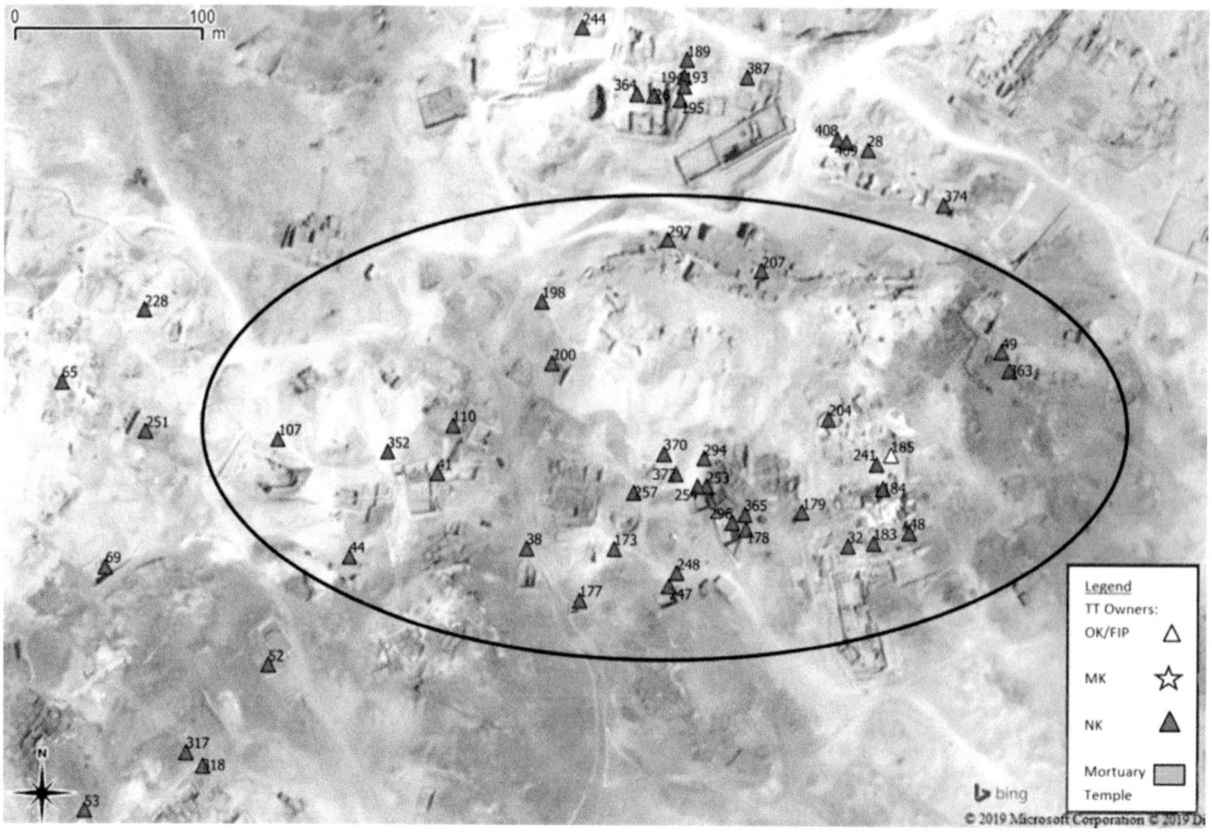

Figure 176: TTs of the Temple Administration in el-Khokha (Author's own using QGIS)

There are no obvious clusters of tombs associated with specific temples.

There were a number of temple scribes buried in el-Khokha, including a 'Scribe of Divine Writings', Ahmose-TT241 (Hat-TIII), and several 'Scribes of Divine Offerings', including Khay-TT173 (Dyn 19) and Nefersekheru-TT296 (RII), who both served 'all the Gods of Thebes', Neferrenopet called Kenro-TT178 (RII) and Horemheb-TT207 (RIII), who both served Amun, and Mahu, who reused TT257 (Dyn 20) and served 'the Lords of Thebes'. The contemporaries Neferrenopet called Kenro-TT178 and Nefersekheru-TT296 shared a courtyard (see below), demonstrating their close connection, while Khay-TT173 was buried just 60m to the west, with no tombs between them, suggesting a deliberate attempt by three potentially contemporary scribes to be buried in close proximity. There are no other spatial connections between the tombs of these temple scribes.

Other temple scribes included the 'Chief Scribe of Amun', Neferhotep-TT49 (Ay), the 'True Scribe' in the Ramesseum, Amenemopet-TT177 (RII-end Dyn 19), two 'Scribes of the Treasury of Amun', Neferrenopet called Kenro-TT178 (RII) (who was also 'Scribe of the Mansion of Gold') and Nefermenu-TT365 (TIII), the 'Scribe of Counting the Grain of Amun', Djeserkarasoneb-TT38 (TIV-AIII), and a 'Scribe of the Temple of Amun', Amenemhab-TT44 (Dyn 20). There is no generalised spatial connection between these temple scribes, but one discrete connection can be made, as the two 'Scribes of the Treasury of Amun' (TT178 and TT365) share a courtyard (see below).

There were two 'Chief Stewards of Amun', Djehutymose-TT32 (RII), and Amenemopet called Ipy-TT41 (Hor-SI), a 'Steward of the 2PA', Djeserkarasoneb-TT38 (TIV-AIII), the 'Chief Steward of the Temple of Djoserkare' or Amenhotep I, Nefermenu-TT184 (RII) and a 'Steward of the God's Wife', Amenemopet called Ipy-TT41 (Hor-SI). These stewards were distributed across the area so do not form an obvious cluster. The only evidence of a spatial connection related to affiliation with this title is between TT38 and TT41, which are within 50m of each other in the west of the area. The closest temple stewards are within 30m of each other in the east of the area but did not specifically work at the same temple (TT32 and TT184).

Many titles involve provisioning the temple with grain, including the 'Overseers of the Granary/ies of Amun', Nefersekheru-TT107 (AIII), Nefermenu-TT184 (RII), Amenhotep/Sen-djehuty-TT294 (TIII), and the unknown owner of TT352 (Ram); the 'Counters of Grain of Amun', Djeserkarasoneb-TT38 (TIV–AIII), Nebamun-TT179 (Hat), Khnummose-TT253 (AIII) (who was also 'Counter of Grain in the Granary of Divine Offerings'), Neferhotep-TT257 (AIII-AIV), and Amenemopet called Thanefer-TT297 (early Dyn 18). The greatest concentration of these titles is towards the centre of the area, with TT179, TT253, TT257 and TT294 within 100m of each other, with TT38 and TT184 also within 100m of the centre of this group. There were a number of titles relating to the temple's cattle, including the three 'Overseers of the Cattle of Amun', Amenemopet called Ipy-TT41 (Hor–SI), Amenemhat called Surere-TT48 (AIII), and Nefersekheru-TT107 (AIII), the 'Overseer of the Oxen and Heifers of Amun', Neferhotep-TT49 (Ay), and the 'Counter of Cattle of Amun', Samut-TT247 (TIV-AIII). There were also two 'Overseers of the Fields of Amun' Amenemhat called Surere-TT48 (AIII), and Amenemopet called Thanefer-TT297 (early Dyn 18). There does not appear to be a spatial connection between any of these tombs as they are distributed across el-Khokha.

Other more diverse titles include two 'Divine Seal-bearers', Amenemhat called Surere-TT48 (AIII), and Senyiker-TT185 (FIP) who were buried within 50m of each other, the 'Chief of the Storehouse of Amun', Rayia-TT198 (Ram), a 'Sailor of the High Priest of Amun' Nebanensu-TT204 (Dyn 18), a 'Noble of Amun', Nebneshem-TT370 (RII-Mer), two 'Makers of Offerings', '...of Amun', Djehuty-TT110 (Hat-TIII), and '...of Tuthmosis III', Djehutymose -TT248 (AII), a 'Captain of the neshmet bark, 'Beloved of Amun'' Dedi-TT200 (TIII-AII), a 'Custodian of the Estate of Tiye' Mose-TT254 (post Amarna/Ay) and a 'Deputy' in the Ramesseum, Mahu-TT257 (reused Dyn 20). These diverse individuals are scattered across the area with no obvious patterning, and no links to others from the same institution. TT100 is in close proximity to TT112, a potentially contemporary HPA, suggesting a possible link.

There were several temple overseers buried here, including the 'Overseer' '...of Singers', Paraemhab-TT363 (Dyn 20), '...Craftsmen', Amenkhau-TT372 (RIII-RIV), '...Recruits', Amenemhat called Surere-TT48 (AIII), '...Hairdressers?', Nefermenu-TT365 (TIII), and an unknown 'Overseer' of incomplete title, Nebneshem-TT370 (RII-Mer). There is no obvious spatial connection between the tombs of these individuals or with those of other temple officials.

Royal Administration

There were 32 royal officials buried here (see Figure 177). They included five 'Royal Butlers': Wah-TT22 (TIII-AII), Djehuty-TT110 (Hat-TIII), Montuywy-TT172 (TIII-AII), Djehutymose-TT205 (TIII-AII), and Neferweben-TT238 (AII). Two of these tombs, TT22 and TT110 are located in close proximity in the western end of this central band of tombs, and another pair,

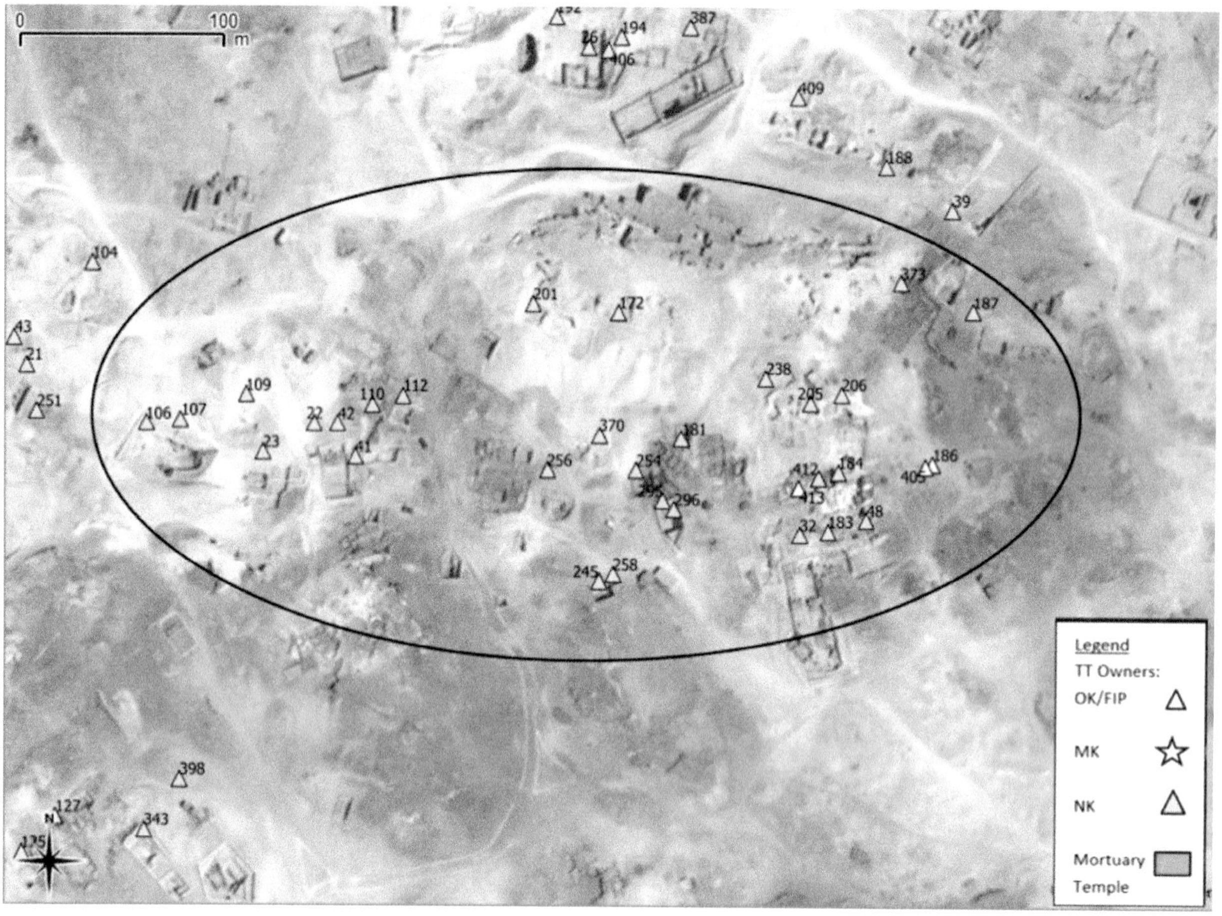

Figure 177: TTs of the Royal Administration in el-Khokha (Author's own using QGIS)

TT205 and TT238 are also in close proximity to the east of the central band of tombs. There are a number of 'Royal Scribes': Tjay called To-TT23 (Mer), who was 'Chief Royal Scribe', 'King's 'Secretary' and 'Scribe of Records'; Djehutymose-TT32 (RII); Amenemopet called Ipy-TT41 (Hor-SI); Amenemhat called Surere-TT48 (AIII); Nefersekheru-TT107 (AIII); Nebsumenu-TT183 (RII); Nefermenu-TT184 (RII); Unknown-TT187 (Dyn 19); Menkheper-TT258 (TIV); Djehutymose called Paroy-TT295 (TIV-AIII); Nebneshem-TT370 (RII- Mer); Amenmessu-TT373 (RII), who was 'Royal Scribe of the Offering Table'; and Kenamun-TT412 (Hat-TIII). Of these Royal Scribes, several spatial connections can be observed. TT23, TT41 and TT107 are located within 100m of each other, TT32, TT48 and TT183 are located side by side within 50m of each, TT184 and TT412 are adjacent to each other towards the east of the central band of tombs, TT187 and TT373 are within 50m of each other to the far east, while in the centre is a loose cluster consisting of TT258, TT295, TT370, and the 'Scribe of the Treasury', Mose-TT254.

Other officials included the 'Royal Seal-bearers': Amenemopet called Ipy-TT41 (Hor-SI), Amenmose-TT42 (TIII-AII), Nefersekheru-TT107 (AIII), Min-TT109 (TIII-AII), Menkheperresoneb-TT112 (TIII-AII), Montuywy-TT172 (TIII-AII), Djehutymose called Paroy-TT295 (TIV-AIII) and Khenti-TT405 (FIP). Of these, TT41, TT42, TT107, TT109 and TT112 are all located within 100m of each other in the west of el-Khokha, suggesting a possible cluster. TT12 also lies adjacent to the 'Royal Butler' Djehuty-TT110 (see Figure 178). There were a number of 'Fan-bearers (on the Right of the King)': Tjay called To-TT23 (Mer), Amenemhat called Surere-TT48 (AIII), Paser-TT106 (SI-RII), and Nebenkemet-TT256 (TIII-AII). Of these, TT23 and TT106 are located 50m apart, in the west close to the Seal-bearers. There were also a number of 'Stewards', including the 'Steward of the Estate' of Amenhotep III, Nefersekheru-TT107 (AIII); two 'Chief Stewards', Amenemhat called Surere-TT48 (AIII) and Nebsumenu-TT183 (RII); and the 'Steward of the Royal Wife', Hor-TT245 (Dyn 19). There was also the 'Custodian of the Estate of Tiye', Mose-TT254 (post Amarna/Ay), who is also included with temple administrators). There is no generalised pattern between these tombs but the two 'Chief Stewards', TT48 and TT183 were buried adjacent to each other towards the east of the central band, suggesting a connection between them. Other titles included an 'Overseer of the Royal Harem', Userhet-TT47 (AIII) and a 'Chief Herald',

Figure 178: TT110 adjacent to TT112 (Author's own)

Re-TT201 (TIV-AIII), whose tombs were not spatially connected to other royal officials.

There were four 'Followers of the King': Amenmose-TT42 (TIII-AII), Nefersekheru-TT107 (AIII), Nebenkemet-TT256 (TIII-AII), and Djehutymose called Paroy-TT295 (TIV-AIII). These tombs do not form a cluster but TT42 and TT107 are within 60m of each other, and TT256 and TT295 are within 50m of each other. Other royal officials included an 'Overseer of Overseers' of the King, Paser-TT106 (SI-RII), a 'Great One of the Lord of the Two Lands' Ipy-TT264 (RII-Mer), and the 'Chief of the Stable of the Lord of the Two Lands' Amenmose-TT42 (TIII-AII) (which is also classed as a military title), but they do not seem to be connected spatially to the tombs of other royal officials. Rarer titles include the 'Nurse' of Amenhotep II, Min-TT109 (TIII), and the 'Attendant of the Sovereign', Nefersekheru-TT107 (AIII), which are within 50m of each other in the west. One of the earliest occupants of the area, Unasankh-TT413 (FIP), was the 'Chancellor of the King of Lower Egypt' (although this title is damaged so not certain- see Saleh 1977: 18), who is located in the same area of the necropolis as the 'Royal Chamberlain of the Great House' Iky-TT186 (OK) (see Chapter 4). These tombs along with TT405 have been included as members of the royal administration on the basis of the late Old Kingdom date given by Saleh (1977: 17, 22 and 27) but if TT405 dates to the First Intermediate Period as Kampp suggests, this grouping would not be accurate.

Khokha was also associated with several royal craftsmen, including the 'Overseer of all the Craftsmen of the King', Amenemhat called Surere-TT48 (AIII), and the 'Sculptors' of the King, Nebamun and Ipuky-TT181 (AIII-AIV). These tombs are within 100m of each other and of similar date. There is also a tomb belonging to the 'Scribe in the Place of Truth', Inpuemheb-TT206 (Dyn 20), who has been classified with the royal administration, as the members of the community at Deir el-Medina were responsible for building the royal tomb so were employed by the king. This was the only tomb outside Deir el-Medina, belonging to a member of the village community. It is possible that he chose to be buried at el-Khokha as he lived in the vicinity rather than within the village itself (Davies 1999: 90). While he definitely held the title of 'Scribe in the Place of Truth', it has been suggested that he was in fact the 'Scribe of the Vizier' (McDowell 1990: 78) or a scribe of the village's support staff or smdt (Davies 1999: 90), rather than a member of the village workforce, so was not of the same importance as the 'Scribes of the Tomb' found within the cemetery at Deir el-Medina. His tomb is located 100m away from the craftsmen in TT48 and

TT181 but is significantly later in date. TT206 is located adjacent to TT204, TT205 and TT238, and both TT205 (TIII-AII) and TT238 (AII) were owned by 'Royal Butlers'. The eldest son of the king, Meryamun, reused TT22 (AIII-AIV), located on the western edge of the area. There could potentially be a connection with the royal official Amenmose in the adjacent TT42 (TIII-AII).

General Administration

12 tombs belonged to the general centralised administration, not affiliated to any specific institution (see Figure 179). There was one 'Overseer of the Town' and 'Vizier', among other titles, Paser-TT106 (SI-RII) who was buried in the western corner of the area, not in close proximity to any other members of the general administration. There were five 'Overseers of the Granaries', Djehutymose-TT32 (RII), Amenemopet called Ipy-TT41 (Hor-SI), Iky-TT186 (OK), Khenti-TT405 (FIP) and Unasankh-TT413 (FIP), four of whom were buried in close proximity in the eastern part of el-Khokha, with the exception of TT41 which is located some distance to the west. Three of these spatially connected tombs were the earliest tombs in the area, with Djehutymose-TT32 locating his later tomb in this area relatively close to his predecessors. There was also an 'Overseer of the Storehouse', Amenirnefer-TT199 (Dyn 18), an 'Overseer of Cattle', Ipy-TT264 (RII-Mer) and a 'Chief of the Library', Djehutymose called Paroy-TT295 (TIV-AIII). These tombs are all located in the centre with the exception of TT199. There are a number of general administrative scribal titles, including 'Scribe of the Treasury' Mose-TT254 (post Amarna/Ay), 'Scribe of the Mat', Amenemhet-TT182 (TIII) and 'Scribe', Senenre-TT246 (TIII)- a common title, excluded from this analysis when occurring alongside more specific titles, but included here as the only title attested to this individual. These scribes are all located within 100m of each other in the centre of the area.

Local Administration

There were nine members of the local administration buried at el-Khokha (see Figure 180). This group includes those associated specifically with the 'Southern City' or 'Town' meaning Thebes, and others who had responsibility for the lands beyond Egypt's borders. They included two 'Mayors', of Thinis and the Oasis, Min-TT109 (TIII), and of 'the Southern City', Nefermenu-TT184 (RII), who were not spatially connected. TT109 is located within 50m of the 'Governor of the Town', Paser-TT106 (SI-RII), in the

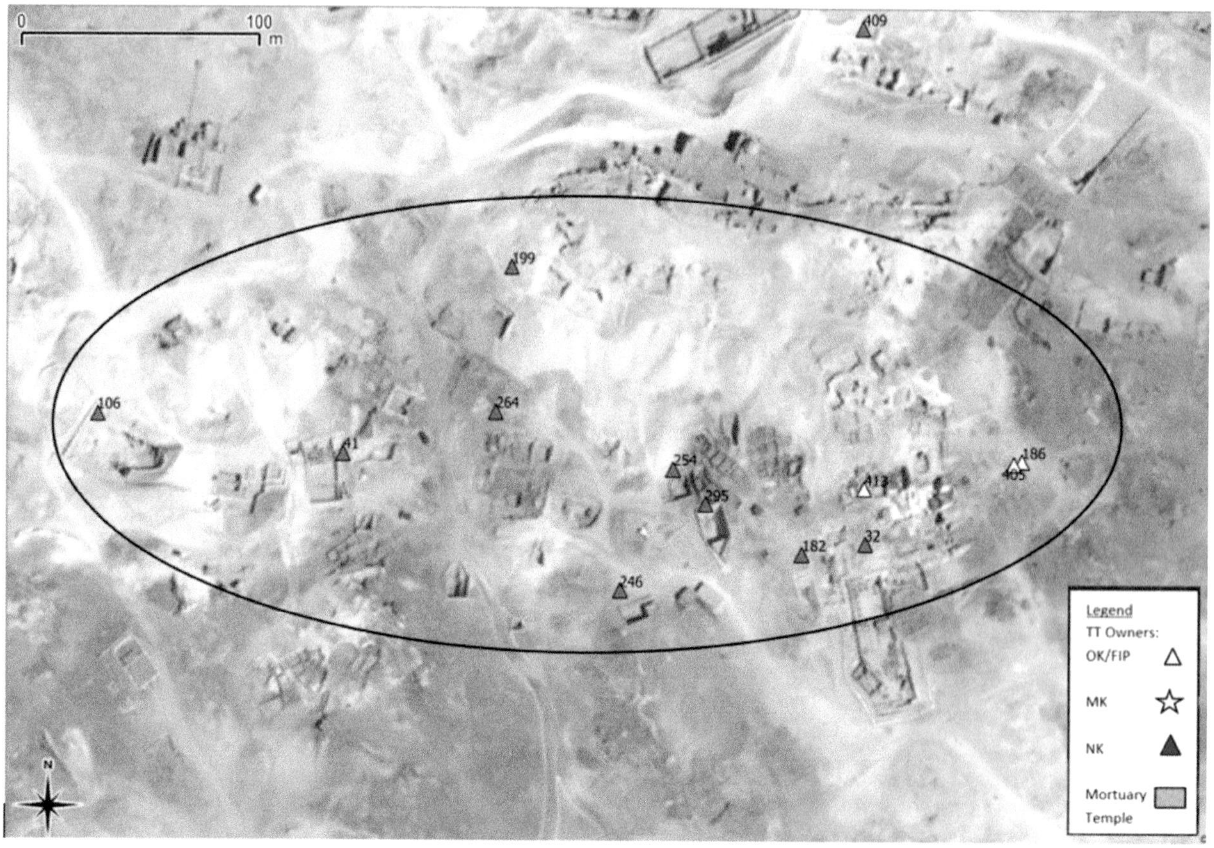

Figure 179: TTs of the General Administration in el-Khokha (Author's own using QGIS)

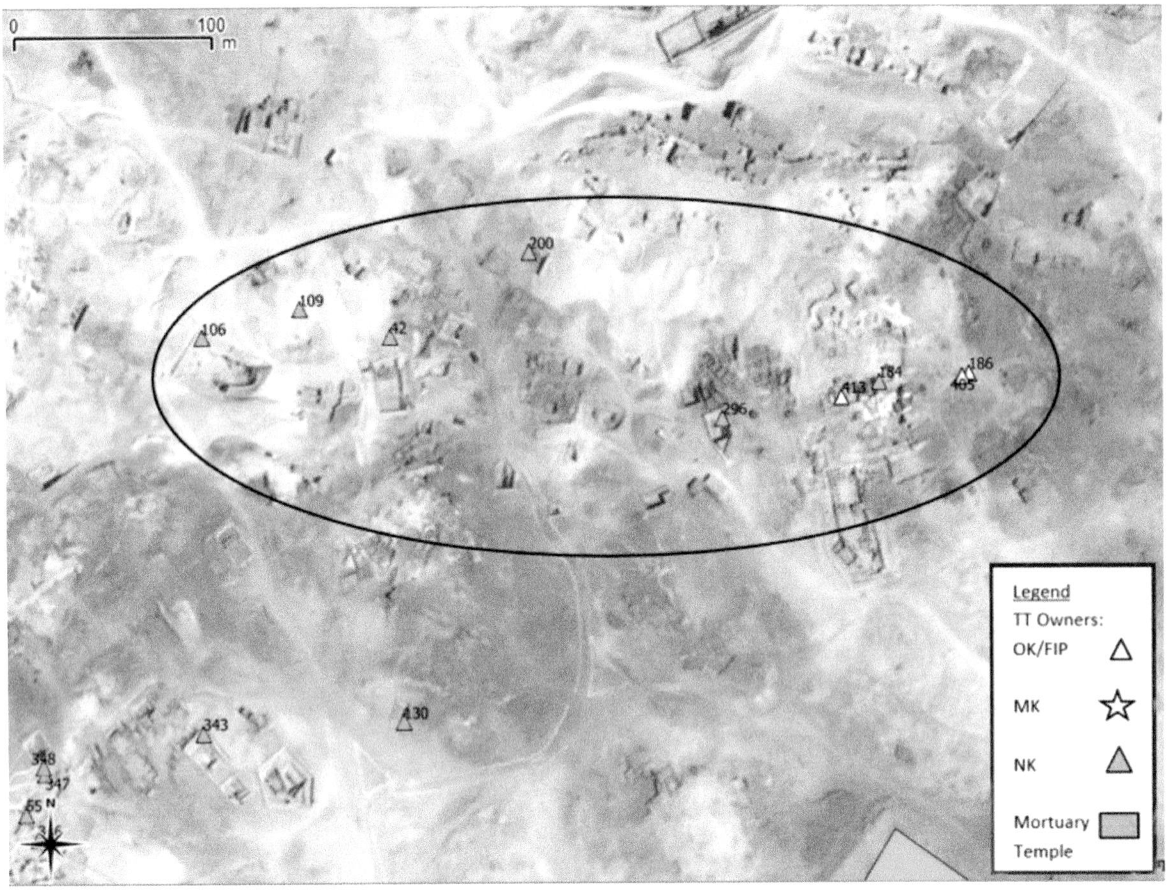

Figure 180: TTs of the Local Administration in el-Khokha (Author's own using QGIS)

far north-west of the area. Also in this area, within 100m of each other, lie the tombs of the 'Overseer of the Northern Foreign Lands', and 'Eyes and Ears of the King', Amenmose-TT42 (TIII-AII), and the 'Overseer of the Deserts on the West of Thebes', Dedi-TT200 (TIII-AII). TT42 is also within 100m of TT109 and TT106. The tomb of 'Deputy of the Treasury...in the Southern City', Nefersekheru-TT296 (RII), lies in the very centre. Three of the earliest tombs in the area belonged to provincial administrators, including the 'Great Chieftains of the Nome', Iky-TT186 (Late OK/FIP), Khenti-TT405 (FIP) and Unasankh-TT413 (FIP), the 'Overseer of the Phyles of the Nome', Iky-TT186, and the 'Chief of Secrets of Every Word that is Brought to the Nome', Khenti-TT405 and Unasankh-TT413. The spatial connection between these early tombs is discussed further in Chapter 4.

Military

There were four individuals with military titles in el-Khokha (see Figure 181). They were the 'Captain of Troops', Amenmose-TT42 (TIII-AII), the 'Chief of the Regiment of Pharaoh', 'Chief of the Medjay' and 'Standard-bearer', Dedi-TT200 (TIII-AII), the 'Chief of the Stable', Nebenkemet-TT256 (TIII-AII), and the 'Scribe of Horses', Aabau-TT351 (Ram). These tombs seem to have a spatial connection as TT351 is located in the western area of el-Khokha in close proximity to TT42, while TT200 and TT256 are only 100m to the east, 60m apart.

Unknown

There are three tombs belonging to unknown individuals, TT175 (TIV-AIII), TT180 (Ram) and TT371 (Ram), and a 'Servant, Clean of Hands', Amenuserhet-TT176 (AII-TIV) who has not been classified.

Relationships between Tomb Owners / Tombs

TT181 was not reused but rather shared by Ipuky and Nebamun, who were both 'Sculptors' of the King', during the reign of Amenhotep III or IV. They were not directly related as their respective parents are depicted on the tomb wall but may have shared a tomb because of their mutual profession and presumed friendship. There was also a familial connection between the two men and the same woman, who may have been the wife of both men (Davies 1925: 9-10), or the wife of Ipuky and sister of Nebamun (Polz 1990: 301-36).

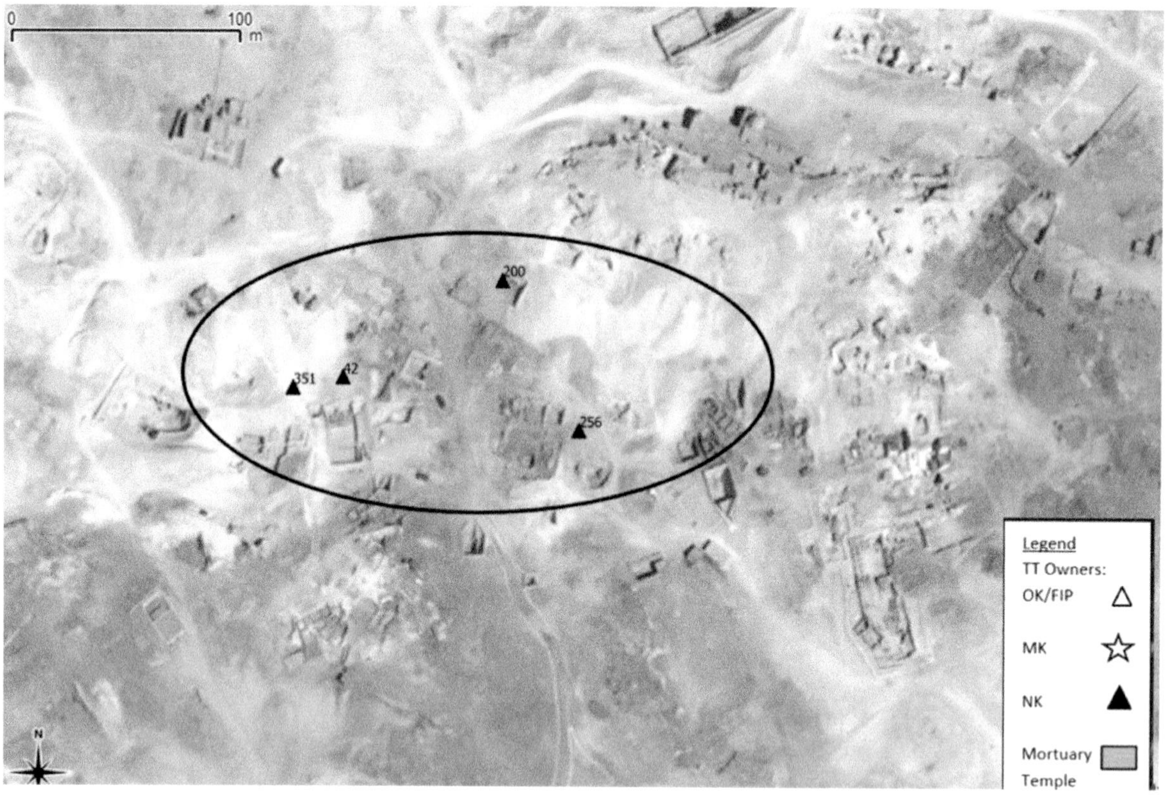

Figure 181: TTs of the Military in el-Khokha (Author's own using QGIS)

There were a number of familial relationships between tomb owners in el-Khokha. TT174 was reused in the Twentieth Dynasty by the '*wꜥb* priest' Aashaket, who was the father of another '*wꜥb* priest', Pakhyhet, who reused TT187. These tombs are both in el-Khokha but not in particularly close proximity. Nebsumenu-TT183 (RII) and Hunefer-TT385 (RII) were brothers with no common titles, but only TT183 is located in el-Khokha, with TT385 located some distance away in the north-west of Lower Qurna. Iky-TT186 (FIP) was the father of Khenti-TT405 (FIP), and these tombs are adjacent to each other and share a courtyard and access (see below).

Shared Courtyards

A number of tombs in el-Khokha have shared courtyards. It is interesting to note the frequency with which shared courtyards are used in el-Khokha, in comparison to other areas of the necropolis where they are less common. This is probably because of the flatter ground which made building courtyards possible, whilst sharing them allowed more tombs to fit into a popular area.

TT105, TT106 and TT107

TT106 is located on the western side of the courtyard opposite the entrance; while TT105 and TT107 are located on the southern and northern sides respectively (see Figure 182). The owners of all three tombs had a connection to Amun, and the owners of TT105 and TT106 were both priests. As the dating of TT105 is uncertain, it is possible that these individuals knew each other. Paser-TT106 was primarily the 'Vizier' and as such held the most important title, but as he was also 'Festival Leader of Amun' he may have encountered the priest Khaemopet-TT105 if they were in office at the same time. Nefersekheru-TT107 (AIII) was an important royal official, and Paser was also closely connected to the king and held some of the same honorary titles (see Table 26). It is possible that TT106 was located here to be close to TT107, whose owner may well have still had influence in the succeeding dynasties or may have been a relative of Paser. TT105 was most likely merely taking advantage of an existing courtyard.

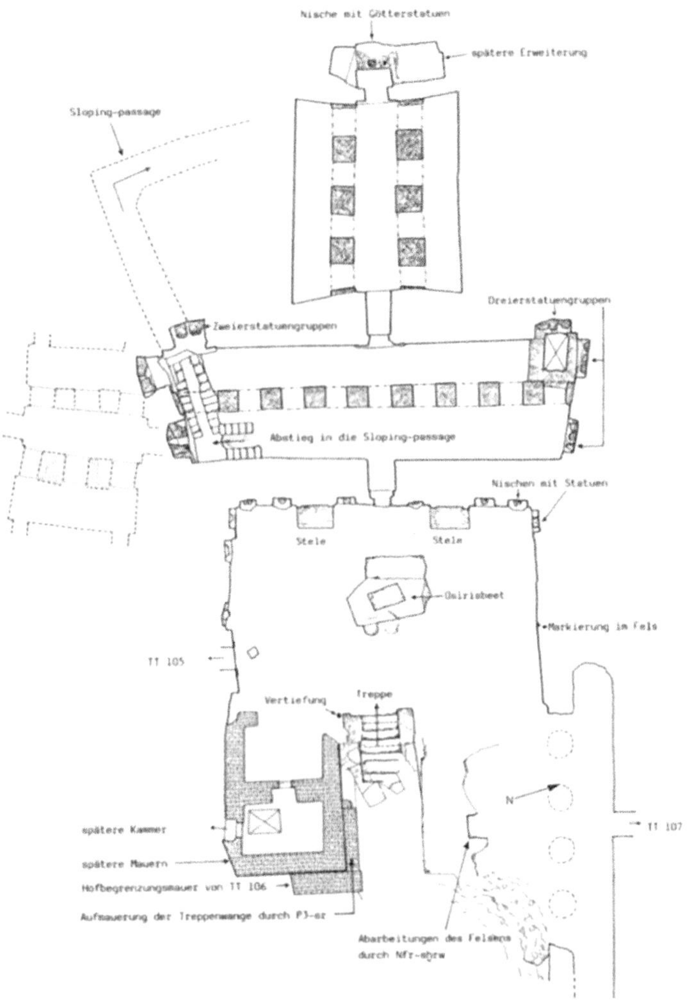

Figure 182: Plan of shared courtyard of TT105, TT106 and TT107 (Kampp 1996: Figure 266 – Courtesy of Professor Seyfried)

Table 26: Owners of TT105, TT106 and TT107

TT	Dyn	Reign	Name	Title
TT105	19/20	?	Khaemopet	Priest of the Noble Ram-sceptre of Amun;
TT106	19	SI/ RII	Paser	**Governor of the Town and Vizier** (of the town); Fan-bearer on the Right of the King; Festival leader of Amun; High Priest of the Great of Magic; Priest of Maat; *wꜥb* priest; Overseer of Chamberlains; Hereditary Prince and Mayor;
TT107	18	AIII	Nefersekheru	Royal Scribe; Steward of the Estate of Amenhotep III; Scribe of the Offering table; Royal Seal-bearer; Steward of the Estate of 'The Sun-disc Gleams'; Overseer of the Granaries of Amun; Overseer of the Cattle of Amun; Overseer of the Works of the Great Nile Flood; Attendant of the Sovereign ...; Mayor in the Great House; Hereditary Prince and Mayor; King's Follower on all Foreign Lands;

TT176 and TT177

TT176 and TT177 are located adjacent to each other, with connecting transverse halls (see Figure 183) although this connection appears to have taken place in modern times. They are currently accessed via the courtyard outside TT177 as the entrance to TT176 is unexcavated. Presuming the tombs have been dated accurately, it is impossible that the occupants knew each other, and they shared no common titles (see Table 27). It is possible that the tomb owners were related, and the similarities between their names might support this, but there is no inscriptional evidence so this may be coincidental. The most likely scenario is a modern breakthrough during tomb robbery.

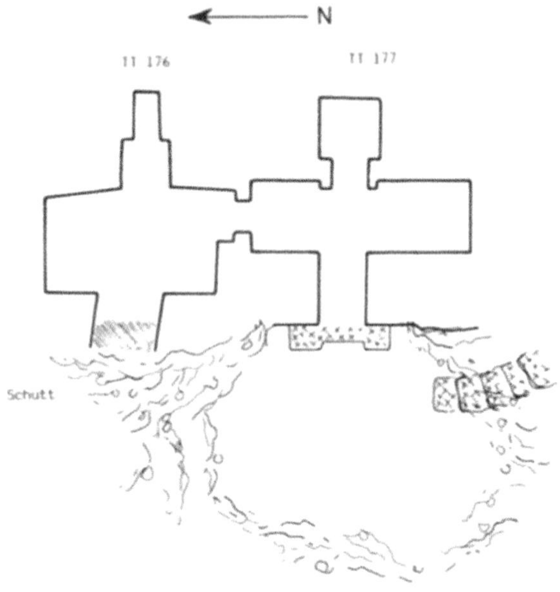

Figure 183: Plan of TT176 and TT177(Kampp 1996: Figure 360 – Courtesy of Professor Seyfried)

Table 27: Owners of TT176 and TT177

TT	Dyn	Reign	Name	Title
TT176	18	AII/TIV	Amenuserhet	Servant, Clean of Hands;
TT177	19	RII-end Dyn 19	Amenemopet	True scribe in the Ramesseum; *wꜥb* priest; Lector priest of Amun In the Ramesseum;

TT256 and TT257

TT256 and TT257 are connected in two places, as both the transverse and long halls are connected (see Figure 184). These breakthroughs probably occurred accidentally during the construction of the later tomb, which would match the unusual shape of TT257 as it would have had to adapt when the breakthroughs occur. This tomb has been included here as two connections exist, but as there are no common titles (see Table 28), accidental breakthroughs seem the most likely explanation.

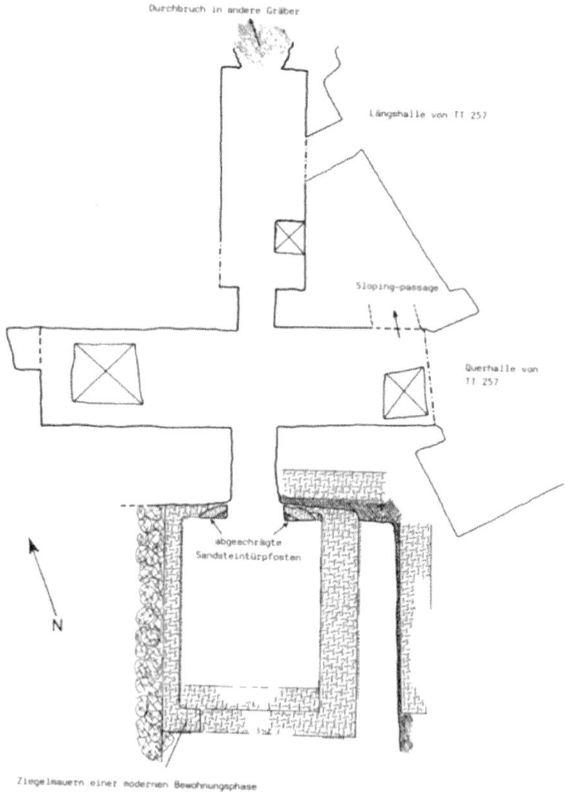

Figure 184: Plan of TT256 and TT257 (Kampp 1996: Figure 430 – Courtesy of Professor Seyfried)

Table 28: Owners of TT256 and TT257

TT	Dyn	Reign	Name	Title
TT256	18	TIII/AII	Nebenkemet	Chief of the Stable; Fan-bearer; Follower of his Lord...;
TT257	18 and 20	AIII/ AIV and Dyn 20	(1) Neferhotep (2)Mahu	(1) Scribe; Counter of the Grain of Amun; (2) Deputy in the Ramesseum; Scribe of Divine Offerings of the Lords of Thebes;

TT245, TT246, TT247, TT248 and TT258

TT246 is located opposite the entrance on the western side of the courtyard, while TT248 lies opposite on the eastern side, and TT258, TT247 and TT245 lie adjacent to each other on the southern side (see Figure 185). These tombs were all roughly contemporary, so it is possible that the tomb owners knew each other or had a familial connection. Four tomb owners had a scribal title, Hor-TT245, Senenre-TT246, Samut-TT247 and Menkheper-TT258, while Menkheper-TT258 and Hor-TT245 had a royal connection (see Table 29).

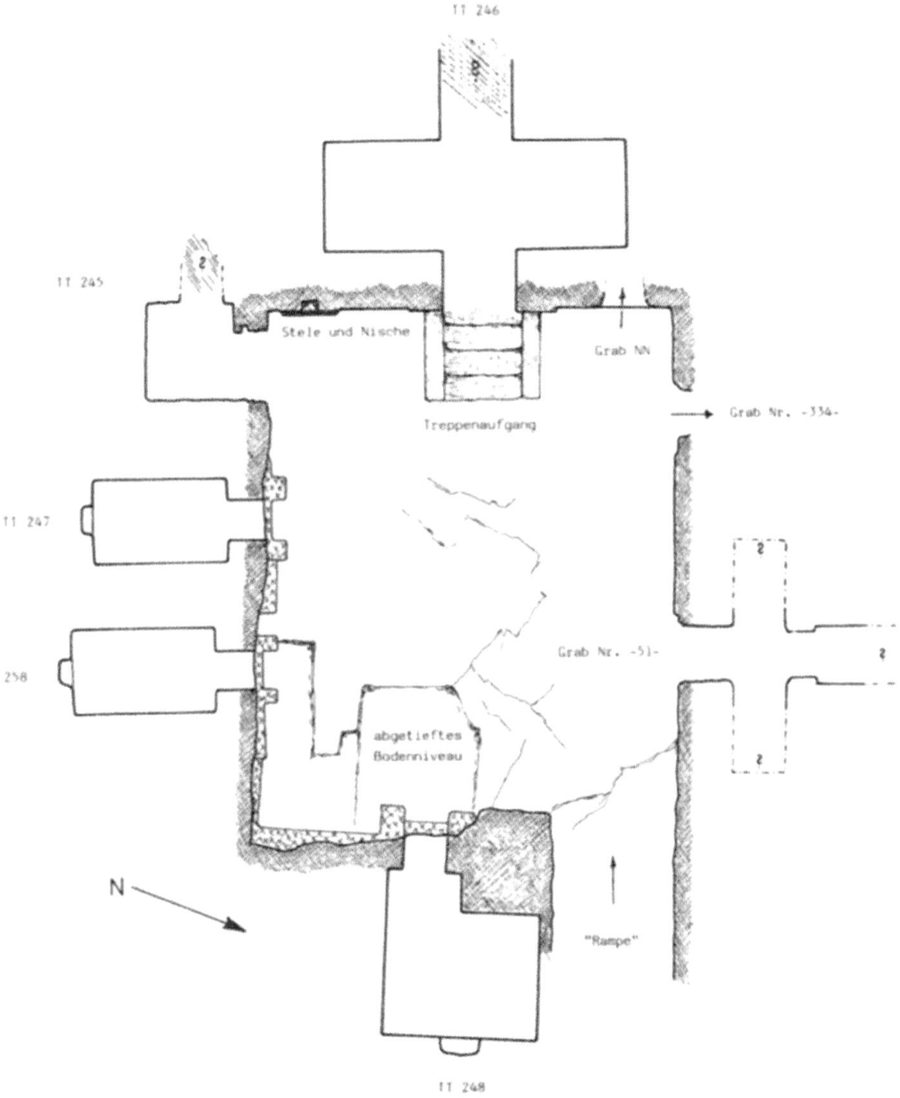

Figure 185: Plan of shared courtyard of TT245, TT246, TT247, TT248 and TT258 (Kampp 1996: Figure 419 – Courtesy of Professor Seyfried)

Table 29: Owners of TT245, TT246, TT247, TT248 and TT258

TT	Dyn	Reign	Name	Title
TT245	18/19	?	Hor	Scribe; Steward of the Royal Wife;
TT246	18	TIII?	Senenre	Scribe;
TT247	18	TIV/ AIII	Samut	Scribe; Counter of the Cattle of Amun;
TT248	18	AII?	Djehutymose	Offerer (Maker of Offerings?) of Menkheperre (=TIII);
TT258	18	TIV	Menkheper	Royal Scribe of the House of the Royal Children; Child of the Nursery;

TT253, TT254 and TT294

TT254 is located on the west of the courtyard, with the shaft leading to TT294 located directly to the right of the entrance. TT253 is situated on the southern side of the courtyard (see Figure 186). There is a clear link between the occupants of this courtyard. All three tombs were roughly contemporary, built during the late Eighteenth Dynasty, and all held administrative titles within the Estate of Amun. The usurper of TT294 was also connected to the Estate of Amun. Amenhotep-TT294 and Khnummose-TT253 both held positions within the Granary of Amun so would have been colleagues, while Khnummose-TT253 and Mose-TT254 both also held scribal titles and had similar names (see Table 30).

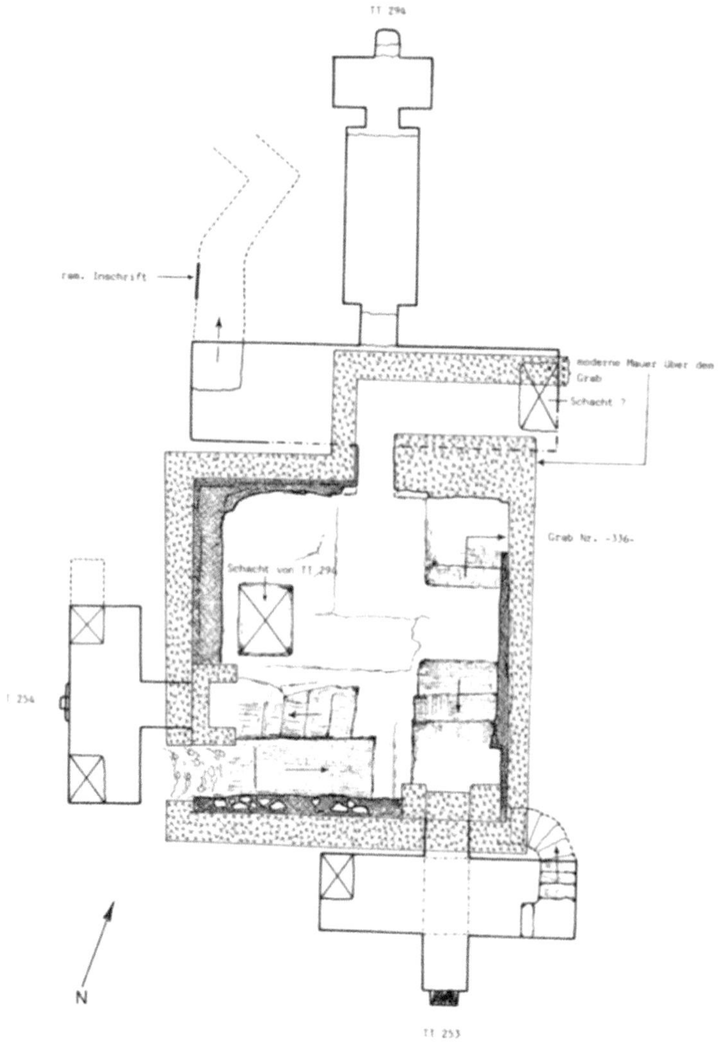

Figure 186: TT253, TT254 and TT294 (Kampp 1996: Figure 427 – Courtesy of Professor Seyfried)

Table 30: Owners of TT253, TT254 and TT294

TT	Dyn	Reign	Name	Title
TT253	18	AIII	Khnummose	Scribe; Counter of Grain in the Granary of Amun; Counter of Grain in the Granary of Divine Offerings;
TT254	18	After Amarna	Mose	Scribe of Treasury; Keeper/Custodian of the Estate of Tiye in the Estate of Amun;
TT294	18 and 19/20	TIII and Ram	(1) Amenhotep / Sen-djehuty (2) Roma	(1) Overseer of the Granaries of Amun; (2) *wꜥb* priest of Amun;

TT178, TT295, TT296 and TT365

All four tombs are located on three sides of a shared courtyard (see Figures 187 and 188). Nefermenu-TT365 (TIII) was the original occupant, followed closely by Djehutymose called Paroy-TT295 (TIV), while Nefersekheru-TT296 and Neferrenopet called Kenro-TT178 were added later (both RII). Nefermenu-TT365 and Djehutymose called Paroy-TT295 have no shared title or workplace so do not appear to have been colleagues but could potentially have been related. Nefermenu-TT365 and Neferrenopet called Kenro-TT178 were affiliated with Amun, thus making a connection possible. The owners of TT178, TT296 and TT365 were all 'Scribes of the Treasury', albeit different treasuries, hinting at a possible connection between tomb allocation and occupation in this area, or a reason why the later tombs of TT296 and TT178 were built in this location to be close to an illustrious predecessor in TT365. In addition to this shared title, both later additions, Nefersekheru-TT296 and Neferrenopet called Kenro-TT178 were 'Scribes of Divine Offerings' during the same reign, establishing a connection between them. It is possible that Nefersekheru-TT296 was the successor of Neferrenopet-TT178,

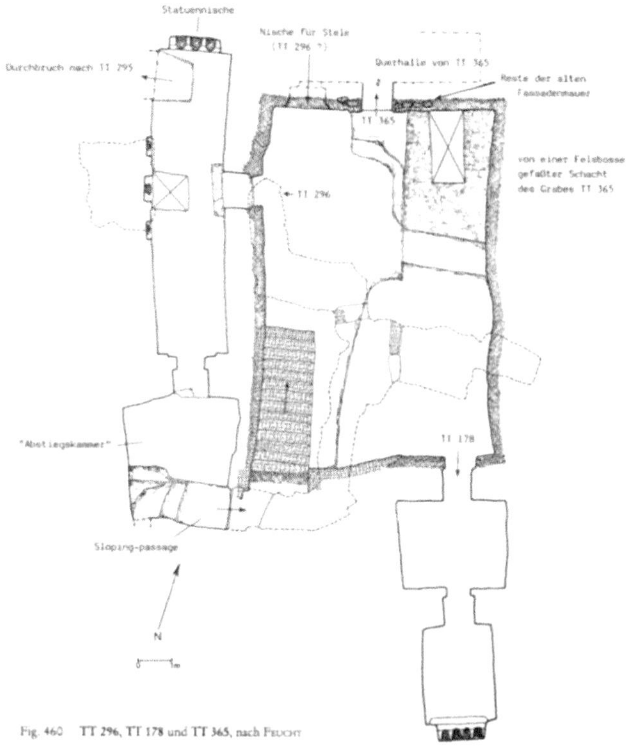

Figure 187: Plan of shared courtyard of TT178, TT295, TT296 and TT365 (Kampp 1996: Figure 460 – Courtesy of Professor Seyfried)

Figure 188: View from above of shared courtyard of TT178, TT295, TT296 and TT365 (Author's own)

or they may have been colleagues. The western end of the southern wall of TT178 depicts the deceased and his wife in mummified form standing before the tomb entrance, with a stela between them and the entrance (see Figure 189). On the stela the bottom row of text says, "The Osiris, Scribe of the Divine Offerings of the house of Amun, Kenro, justified, and his wife, the mistress of the house, Mutemwia, justified. Performed by the *wꜥb* priest of Amun, Nefersekheru, justified" (Hofmann, 1995: 47). This *wꜥb* priest could be the same Nefersekheru as TT296, thus fulfilling his role as *sem* priest in his capacity as his successor, and potentially his son. The names of the owners of TT178, TT296 and TT365 all have the prefix Nefer-, indicating a possible familial connection (see Table 31).

Figure 189: Scene from TT178 (Hofmann 1995: Farbtaf. VI a, Sz. 25 – Courtesy of Dr Eva Hofmann: Ägyptologisches Institut Heidelberg)

TT295 (TIV) is only accessible through TT296 (RII), where an opening was cut into TT295 (see Figure 190) to reuse the burial chamber during the construction of the later TT296 (Hegazy and Tosi, 1983: 9). This architectural evidence seems to confirm that this was a case of utilising available space rather than a deliberately building these tombs in close proximity. The only shared title between the tomb owners was 'Royal Scribe', which is not enough evidence of a connection between the two.

TT179 and TT180

TT179 and TT180 are connected, with TT180 only accessible through TT179 with no separate entrance (see Figure 191). TT180 was an expansion of TT179 for a later burial rather than a separate tomb, but with no information about the occupant of TT180 a connection cannot be established (see Table 32).

Table 31: Owners of TT178, TT295, TT296 and TT365

TT	Dyn	Reign	Name	Title
TT178	19	RII	Neferrenopet called Kenro	Scribe (of the Treasury) of the Estate of Amun-Re; Scribe of Divine Offerings (of the Estate of Amun); Scribe of the Mansion of Gold of Amun; *wꜥb* priest;
TT295	18	TIV	Djehutymose called Paroy	Chief of Secrets in the Chest of Anubis; Chief of Secrets in the Place of Embalmment; *sm* priest (in the Place of Embalmment); Scribe; Embalmer; Hereditary prince, mayor; Seal-bearer of the king of LE; Royal Scribe...
TT296	19	RII	Nefersekheru	Scribe of Divine Offerings of All the Gods of Thebes; Deputy of the Treasury (of the Lord of the Two Lands in the (Southern) city); Scribe of the Treasury of the Lord of the Two Lands; Royal Scribe (of the Lord of the Two Lands)
TT365	18	TIII	Nefermenu	Chief of the Hairdressers? of Amun in Karnak; Scribe of the Treasury of Amun

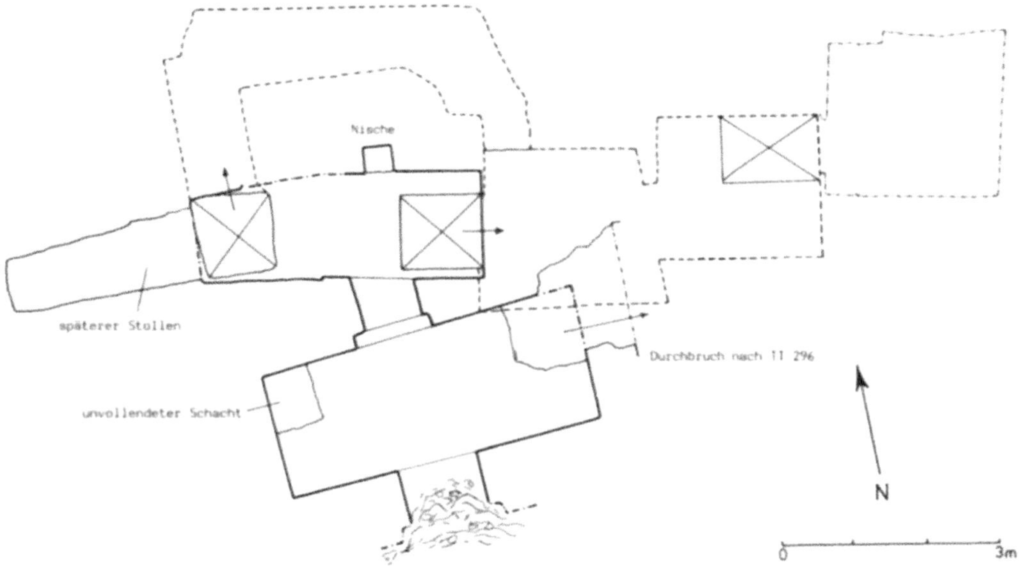

Figure 190: Plan of TT295 and TT296 (Kampp 1996: Figure 459 – Courtesy of Professor Seyfried)

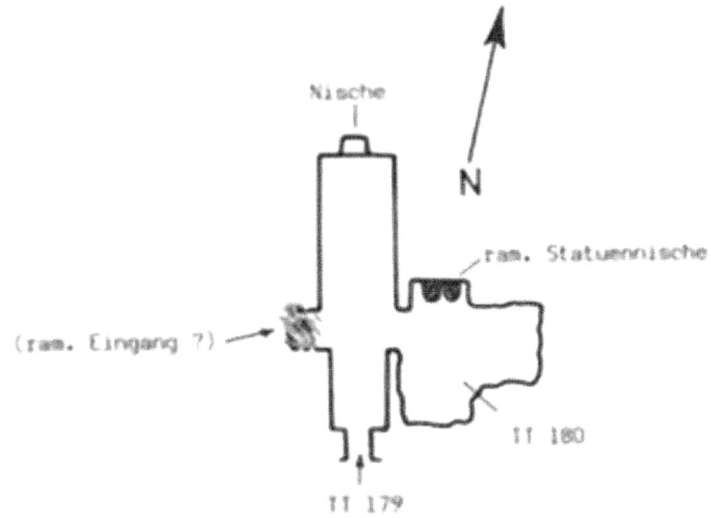

Figure 191: Plan of TT179 and TT180 (Kampp 1996: Figure 363 – Courtesy of Professor Seyfried)

Table 32: Owners of TT179 and TT180

TT	Dyn	Reign	Name	Title
TT179	18	Hat	Nebamun	Scribe; Counter of Grain in the Granary of the Divine Offerings of Amun
TT180	19/20	?	Unknown	Unknown

TT184 and TT412

The western wall of the transverse hall of TT184 provides access to the pillared forecourt of TT412 (see Figures 192 and 193). This breach was probably made accidentally during the construction of the later TT184, but the possibility of a deliberate entrance must be considered. Both tombs were occupied by 'Royal Scribes', but they were built too long apart for the occupants to have known each other (see Table 33). This title may have been hereditary so a familial link is possible, or Nefermenu may have wanted a connection with an illustrious predecessor.

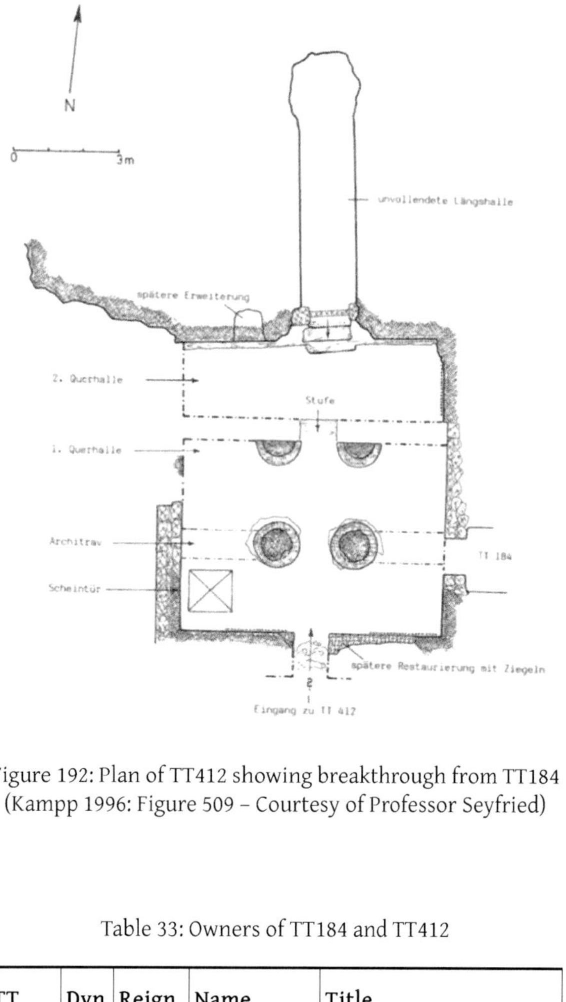

Figure 192: Plan of TT412 showing breakthrough from TT184 (Kampp 1996: Figure 509 – Courtesy of Professor Seyfried)

Table 33: Owners of TT184 and TT412

TT	Dyn	Reign	Name	Title
TT184	19	RII	Nefermenu	**Mayor in/of the Southern city;** Royal Scribe; Chief Steward of the Temple of Djoserkare (AI); Overseer of the Granar(y/ies) of Amun;
TT412	18	Hat/ TIII	Kenamun	Royal scribe;

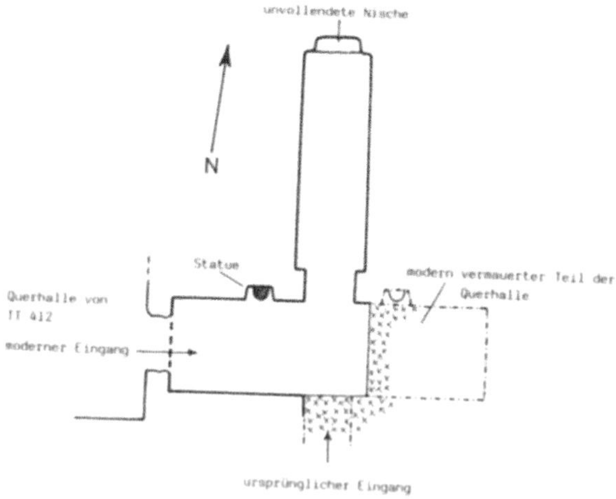

Figure 193: Plan of TT184 showing breakthrough into TT412 (Kampp 1996: Figure 370 – Courtesy of Professor Seyfried)

TT49, TT187, TT362 and TT363

TT49 is the largest and original tomb in the courtyard, located opposite the entrance to the courtyard on the western side. TT187 is on the northern side, with TT363 and TT362 located adjacent to each other on the southern side (see Figure 194). Although the three later tombs cannot be securely dated to a specific reign, there is a clear link as three tomb owners and the usurper of TT187 held titles connected to the cult of the Amun. The original owner of TT187 was a 'High Priest' of an unspecified deity, so could potentially be connected to Amun. The original tomb, TT49, belonged to the 'Chief Scribe of Amun', and its size and prominence suggest that this was an important position. The owners of the later tombs may have built their tombs nearby in order to be in close proximity to an illustrious predecessor in the afterlife. The owners of TT187 and TT362 were both *wꜥb* priests of Amun and may have been contemporaries, so it is possible that they were colleagues (see Table 34). The format of the names of the owners of the latter three tombs all begin with the prefix *pꜣ*, which may be coincidental or may suggest a familial relationship.

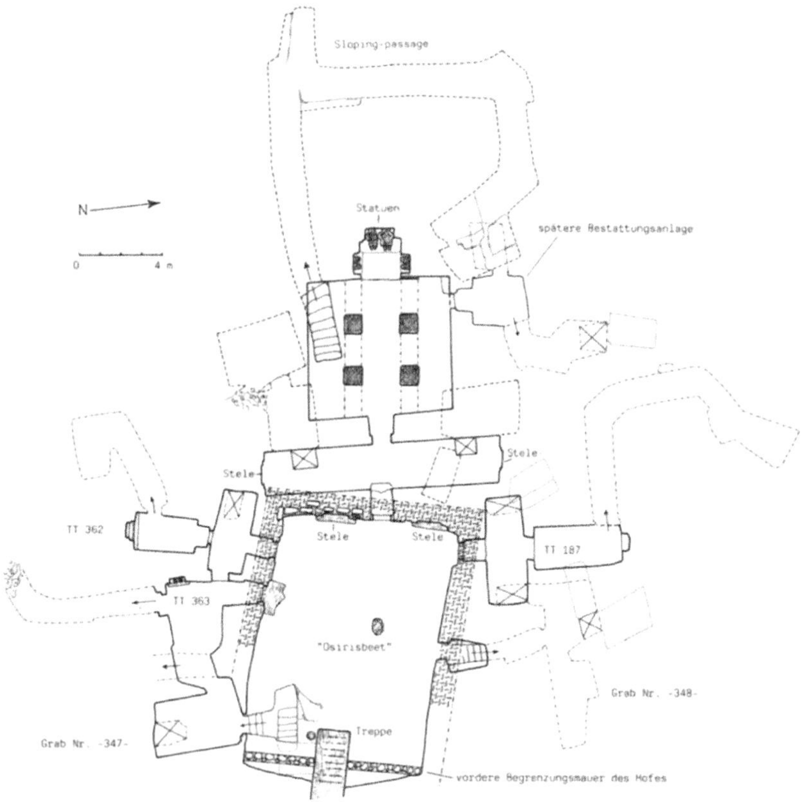

Figure 194: Shared courtyard of TT49, TT187, TT362 and TT363 (Kampp 1996: Figure 149 – Courtesy of Professor Seyfried)

Table 34: Owners of TT49, TT187, TT362 and TT363

TT	Dyn	Reign	Name	Title
TT49	18	Ay	Neferhotep	Chief Scribe of Amun; Overseer of the Oxen and Heifers of Amun
TT187	19 and 20	Dyn 19 and 20	(1) ? (2) Pakhyhet	(1) High priest; Royal scribe; (2) *wʿb* priest of Amun
TT362	late 19	?	Paanemwaset	*wʿb* priest of Amun
TT363	20	?	Paraemhab	Chief of the Singers of Amun

Tomb Reuse

Seven TTs were reused in el-Khokha during the New Kingdom (see Figure 195 and Table 35). Six of these were built during the Eighteenth Dynasty, one dating to Tuthmosis III (TT294), two datable to either Tuthmosis III or Amenhotep II (TT22 and TT174), one to either Amenhotep III or IV (TT257), and the other two cannot be dated to a specific reign (TT174 and TT203). Only one reused tomb was built in the Nineteenth Dynasty but cannot be more precisely dated. The majority of reuse took place during the late New Kingdom, with only one tomb reused during the Eighteenth Dynasty (TT22). This reuse took place in either the reign of Amenhotep II or III, so in the same or following reign after it was built. This was a surprisingly quick usurpation, within living memory of the original occupant, thus indicating a potential personal link between these tomb owners (see below). Another Eighteenth Dynasty tomb was reused during the reign of Ramesses II (TT203). Two tombs were reused during the Ramesside Period (TT112 and TT294) and three more during the Twentieth Dynasty (TT174, TT187 and TT257), but none of these can be dated to a specific reign. This pattern is repeated

Figure 195: Reused TTs in el-Khokha at the end of the New Kingdom, shown by date of reuse (Author's own using QGIS)

Table 35: Reused tombs in el-Khokha

TT	Original Date	Date of Reuse
TT22	TIII/AII	AII/AIII
TT112	TIII/AII	Ram
TT174	Dyn 18	Dyn 20
TT187	Dyn 19	Dyn 20
TT203	Dyn 18	RII
TT257	AIII/AIV	Dyn 20
TT294	TIII	Ram

throughout the necropolis, as money was no longer available to build new tombs at the end of the New Kingdom.

TT22 (TIII-AII) was built by a 'Royal Butler' and reused soon after by the 'King's Eldest Son' (AII-AIII). This could possibly be as a result of a close personal connection between the two men, or the unexpected death of a young crown prince resulting in a lack of suitable tomb, resulting in his sharing this tomb. TT112 (TIII-AII) was built by a 'High Priest of Amun' and reused by a 'Priest of Amun' (Ram). Similarly, TT187 (Dyn 19) was built by a 'High Priest' of an unknown deity (Davies 1993: 7), and reused by a '*wꜥb* priest of Amun' (Dyn 20). If the original owner was a HPA, it is possible that the later '*wꜥb* priest' chose this tomb to associate himself with the earlier HPA. This may suggest a deliberate choice to reuse the tomb of an illustrious predecessor. TT174 (Dyn 18) had an unknown owner and was reused by a '*wꜥb* priest' of Mut (Dyn 20), while TT203 (Dyn 18) also

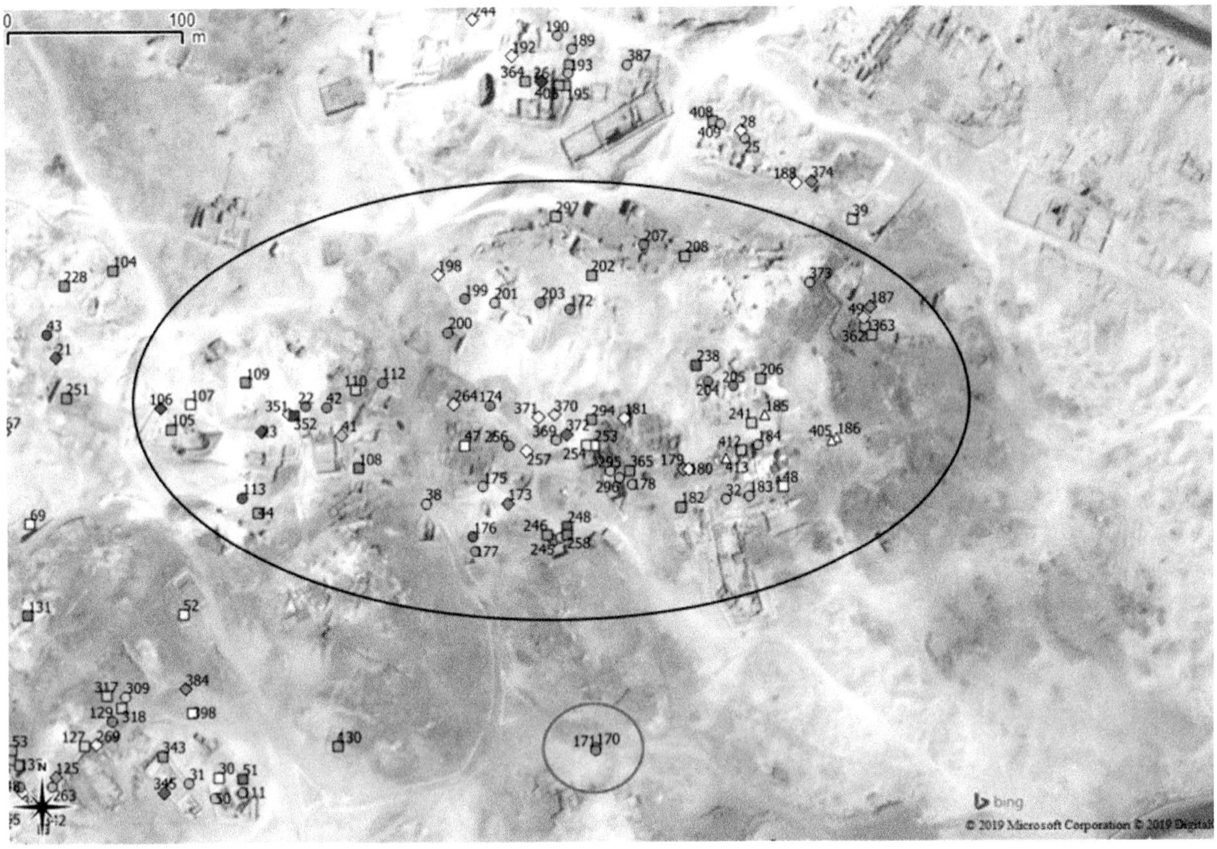

Figure 196: el-Khokha showing the location of TT170 and TT171 (Author's own using QGIS)

had an unknown owner and was reused by a priest of Mut (RII). However, without knowing the titles of the original occupants, a link cannot be established. Both the original owner of TT257 (AIII-AIV) and usurper (Dyn 20), were members of the temple administration, affiliated to Amun. Both occupants of TT294 (TIII and Ram, respectively) were affiliated to Amun but as a member of the temple administration and a priest respectively.

Outlying Tombs

(See Appendix 10)

TT170 and TT171 lie to the south of el-Khokha, in close proximity but at a distance of 100m from the nearest tombs in the area (see Figure 196). There is no obvious link between these tomb owners which would explain why they are located in close proximity in an isolated position. The tombs date to different dynasties, and as the titles of the owner of TT171 are unknown, no further link can be made between them. There is no apparent explanation as to why these tombs were located to the south of the rest of el-Khokha.

Conclusions

During the Eighteenth Dynasty el-Khokha was used steadily, but it was not until the Ramesside Period when it became much more popular. In antiquity el-Khokha was not viewed as a distinct area of the necropolis, but rather as a continuation of Upper Qurna. With less impressive contouring el-Khokha did not provide such good views of the royal mortuary temples and processional routes as Upper Qurna, and was not as visible from the cultivation, so as a result it did not attract as prestigious occupants until this area was full and it naturally expanded eastwards into northern el-Khokha. The presence of the Old Kingdom / First Intermediate Period tombs here seemed to have little effect on Eighteenth Dynasty tomb distribution (see Chapter 4), unlike the Middle Kingdom tombs in Upper Qurna.

The combination of this natural expansion, in conjunction with the construction of TT41 and TT106 in the early Nineteenth Dynasty, blocking the path which connected the two areas (see Chapter 3), led to the increase in use of el-Khokha and the decline of Upper Qurna during the Ramesside Period (see Figures 197 and 198). The tomb owners of el-Khokha were instead mostly priests, including several High Priests although

Figure 197: View of eastern Upper Qurna from el-Khokha (Author's own)

Figure 198: Path leading north-west from el-Khokha to Upper Qurna (Author's own)

not as many as Upper Qurna, members of the temple administration and royal administration. There were relatively few members of the general administration buried here. This suggests that the el-Khokha began to attract more important officials in the Ramesside Period, but by this time there were fewer elite burials in the Theban Necropolis in general.

Chapter 9: Sheikh Abd el-Qurna

Location

Sheikh Abd el-Qurna (referred to hereafter as Qurna) lies to the north of the row of royal mortuary temples, bordered by the cliffs leading to the Valley of the Kings to the north (see Figure 199). The tombs are located between 170m and 80m above sea level, with the flood plain beginning at 80m above sea level in this area (see Figure 200). The area consists of steep upper slopes, commanding an elevated position with views over the cultivation towards the Nile, while tombs located here also had the benefit of increased visibility from the Nile valley. Further down the slopes become less steeply inclined and flatten out closer to the cultivation. It is the most densely populated area of the necropolis, with 125 tombs dating to the New Kingdom or earlier.

The Division between Upper and Lower Qurna

For the purpose of this study this area has been divided into two areas, the upper and lower slopes (see Figure 201). This roughly equates to the division made by Kampp (1996), with a few exceptions (TT52, TT384, TT398 grouped with Lower Qurna rather than Upper Qurna, and TT170 and TT171 grouped with el-Khokha) based on the Digital Elevation Model's contouring data, proximity to other tombs, and also utilising natural divisions between areas of the necropolis made by paths and topography, as these are believed to have remained relatively unchanged since ancient times (Kampp 1996: 121). There is a natural separation between the tombs in Upper Qurna and Lower Qurna, as noted previously, with a few isolated exceptions.

The Evolution of Qurna

The earliest burials date to the Middle Kingdom, located on the upper slopes of Qurna (see Chapter 3). Of the six Middle Kingdom TTs, TT60, TT61 and TT119 were clustered close together in a flat area at 130m above sea level, with TT81, TT80 and TT117 located to the west, more spread out and at a slightly higher altitude. This

Figure 199: Location of Sheikh Abd el-Qurna within the Theban Necropolis (Author's own using QGIS)

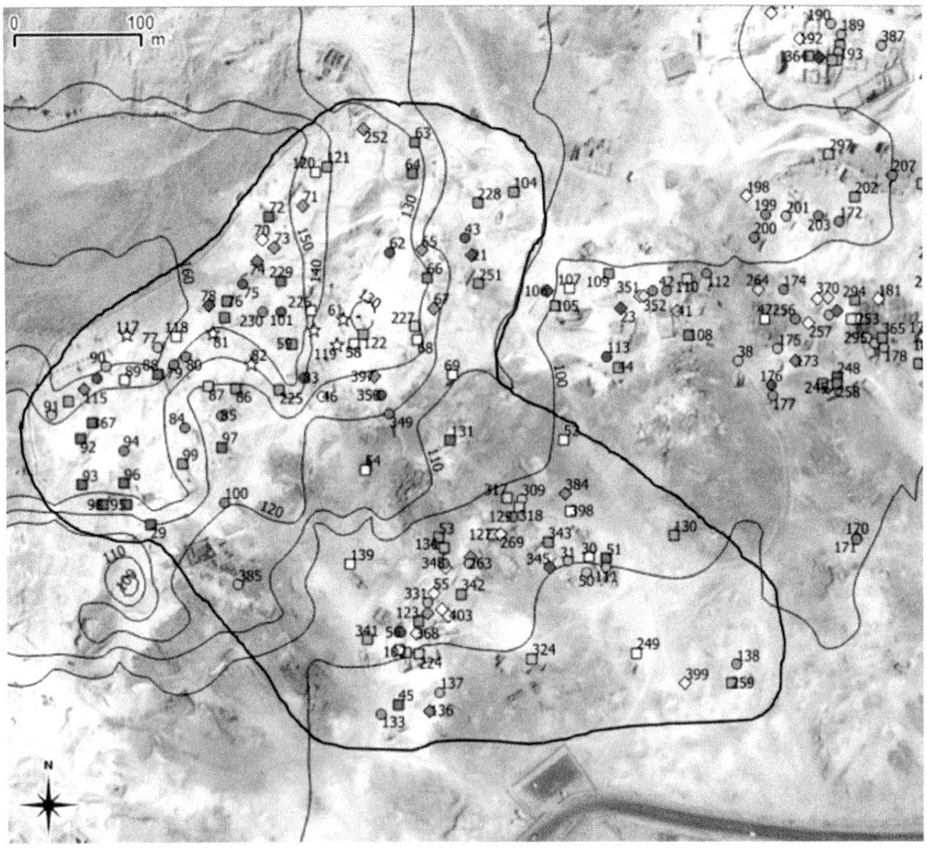

Figure 200: Landscape of Qurna (Author's own using QGIS)

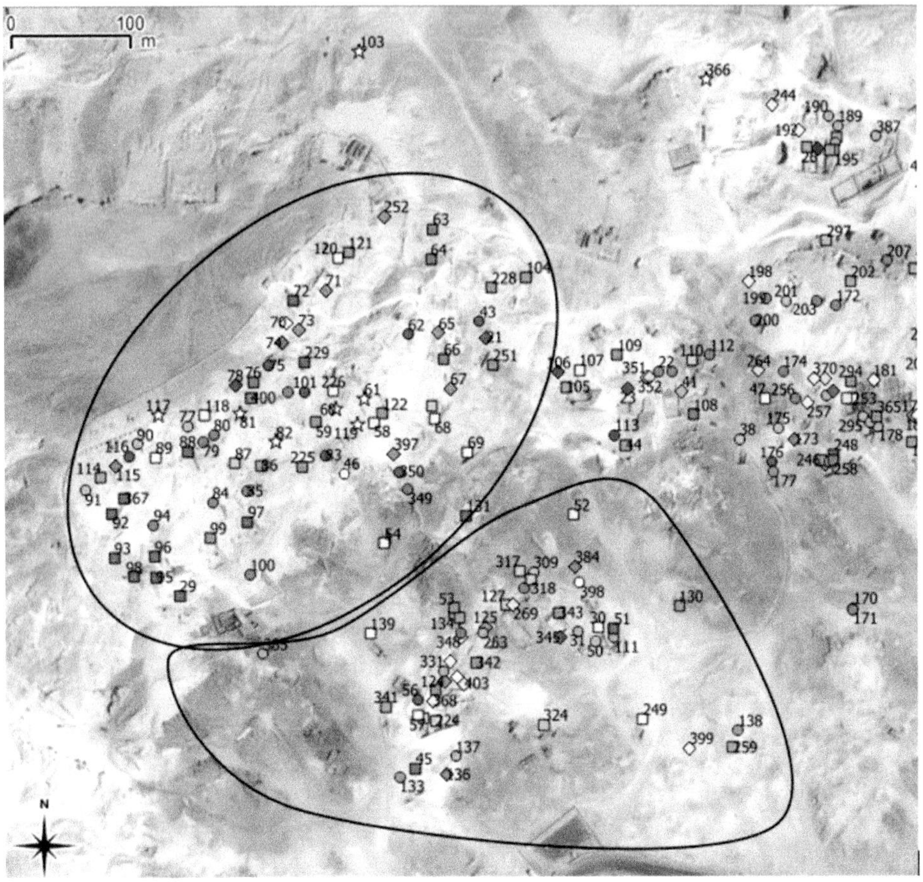

Figure 201: Boundaries of Upper and Lower Qurna (Author's own using QGIS)

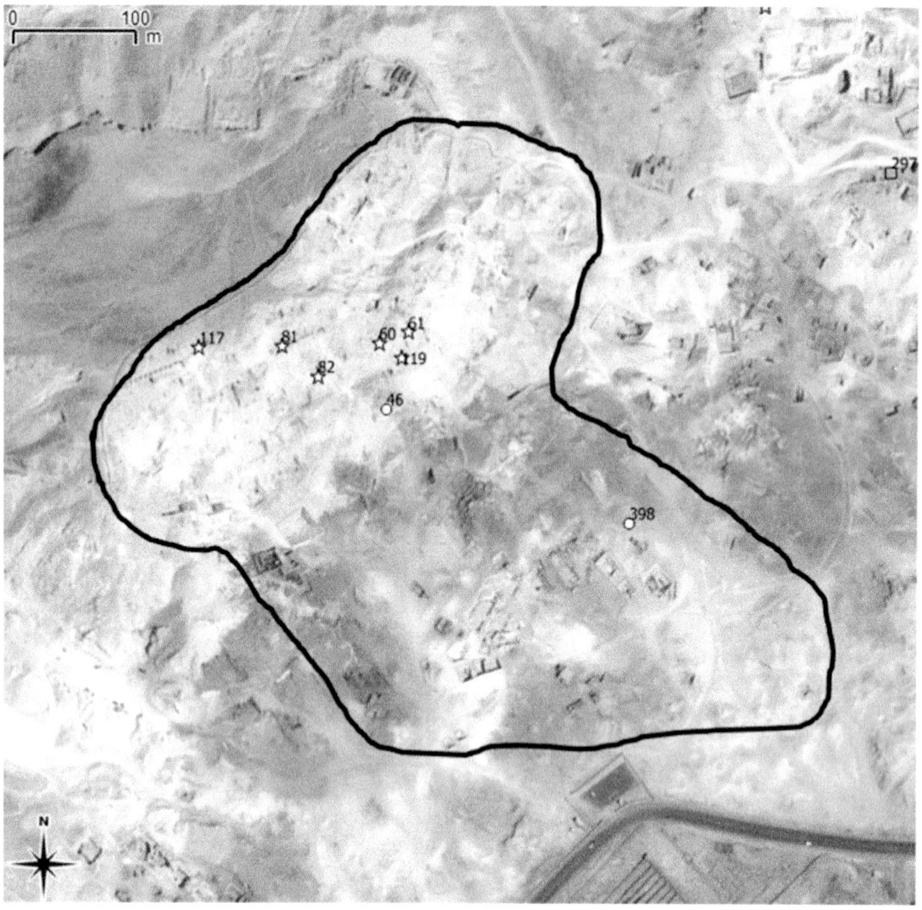

Figure 202: TTs in Qurna prior to the reign of Hatshepsut (Author's own using QGIS)

cluster of Middle Kingdom tombs appears to have acted as a focal point for later tombs, as the potential sites for tomb location close to these earliest tombs were filled first.

At the beginning of the Eighteenth Dynasty, there were relatively few tombs built in Qurna in comparison to Dra Abu el-Naga (see Chapter 5), with only two tombs clearly datable to the late Seventeenth or early Eighteenth Dynasty (TT46 and TT398) (see Figure 202), and several other tombs dating prior to or during the reign of Hatshepsut (see Figure 203).

During the reigns of Hatshepsut and Tuthmosis III there was an influx of tombs on both the upper and lower slopes of Qurna (see Figures 203 and 204). There was a high concentration of tombs clearly dating to Hatshepsut located on the upper slopes, where six tombs dated solely to her reign were distributed. Four of these were built further north than any earlier tombs (TT65, TT67, TT71, TT73 and TT252). This includes a row of four tombs located side by side at the northern end of the upper slopes, three of which are dated to Hatshepsut (TT71, TT73 and TT252), while TT121 dates to the following reign of Tuthmosis III. These tombs were evenly spaced out, with views towards Deir el-Bahri. This area was the closest area to Deir el-Bahri that was in use as a cemetery at this time, suggesting a link between the choice of this location and the temples. Only two tombs solely dated to Hatshepsut's reign were built on the lower slopes, TT124 and TT125.

A group of five tombs dating solely to the succeeding reign of Tuthmosis III are located centrally, in the vicinity of the Middle Kingdom tombs (TT59, TT86, TT99, TT122 and TT225), and a further four tombs are located to the north (TT104, TT121, TT228 and TT251), thus following the pattern of tombs built during Hatshepsut's reign (see Figure 204). This could also be an attempt to locate tombs close to Deir el-Bahri, where Tuthmosis III also built a temple. There is a group of five tombs on the lower slopes dated to Tuthmosis III (TT53, TT123, TT130, TT342 and TT343), in close proximity to those datable to Hatshepsut's reign. This distinct group of tombs (TT53, TT102, TT123, TT124, TT125, TT127, TT224, TT317, TT318, TT342, TT343 and TT345), dated to Hatshepsut or Tuthmosis III (with the exception of the earlier TT398), was located to the west of the Qurna mortuary temple of Tuthmosis III, although there are no tombs directly behind the temple. The location of this

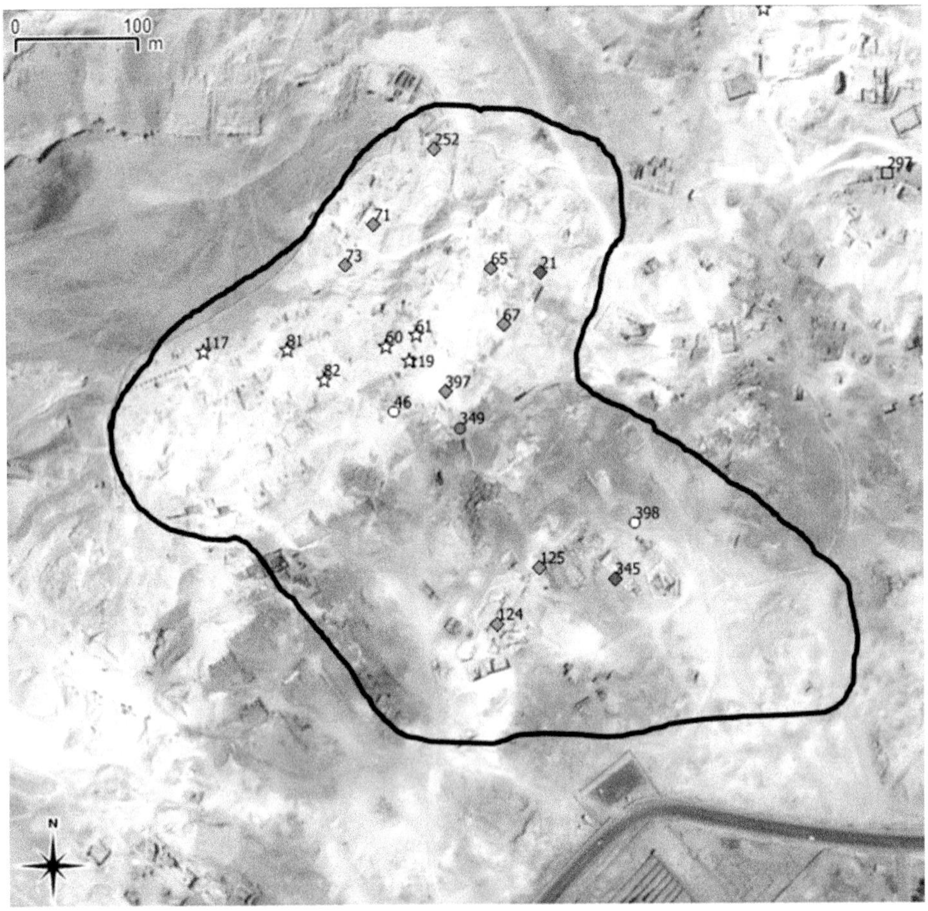

Figure 203: TTs in Qurna conclusively dated prior to the reign of Tuthmosis III (Author's own using QGIS)

group of tombs of this date suggests a link with the site of the royal mortuary temple, so implies a date during the reign of Tuthmosis III rather than Hatshepsut.

There are two tombs on the upper slopes (TT87 and TT227) and five tombs on the lower slopes (TT102, TT127, TT224, TT317 and TT318) that are datable only to either Hatshepsut or Tuthmosis III. These tombs lie close to others dated to both rulers, so their distribution does not help to date them more accurately (see Figure 205). TT21 and TT345 are dated between the reigns of Tuthmosis I and Hatshepsut. As they are both located close to other tombs dating to Hatshepsut or Tuthmosis III, based solely on tomb location, they are more likely to date to the reign of Hatshepsut than earlier as they fit the distributional pattern of her reign. Three of the tombs dating to either Hatshepsut or Tuthmosis III are clustered together to the north of Lower Qurna. TT317 and TT318 are located next to each other, while TT127 is located just to the south. T102 and TT224 also date to this period and lie close to each other in the south of the area.

The popularity of these upper slopes, adjacent to the Middle Kingdom tombs, during the reigns of Hatshepsut and Tuthmosis III, occurred in conjunction with the reuse of the only four Middle Kingdom tombs to be reused in the New Kingdom (TT61, TT82, TT82 and TT119). This suggests a deliberate attempt by individuals during these two reigns to associate themselves with their Middle Kingdom predecessors (see Chapter 3), explaining this choice of burial location. There is still a clear divide between the tombs built on the upper and lower slopes, suggesting differentiation between these areas when siting tombs.

At the end of the reign of Tuthmosis III there was a distinct shift to the western corner of Upper Qurna, to an area where there were no previous tombs (see Figure 206). The earliest datable tomb in this area is from the second half of the reign of Tuthmosis III (TT99), so this shift potentially began towards the end of his reign and continued into the reign of Amenhotep II (see Figure 207). Six tombs on the upper slopes in this area are datable only to either the reign of Tuthmosis III or Amenhotep II (TT79, TT80, TT84, TT85, TT94 and TT100), which may also indicate that the shift in this direction began during the previous reign of Tuthmosis III. Nine of the eleven tombs on the upper slopes are dated to Amenhotep II (TT29, TT88, TT92, TT93, TT95,

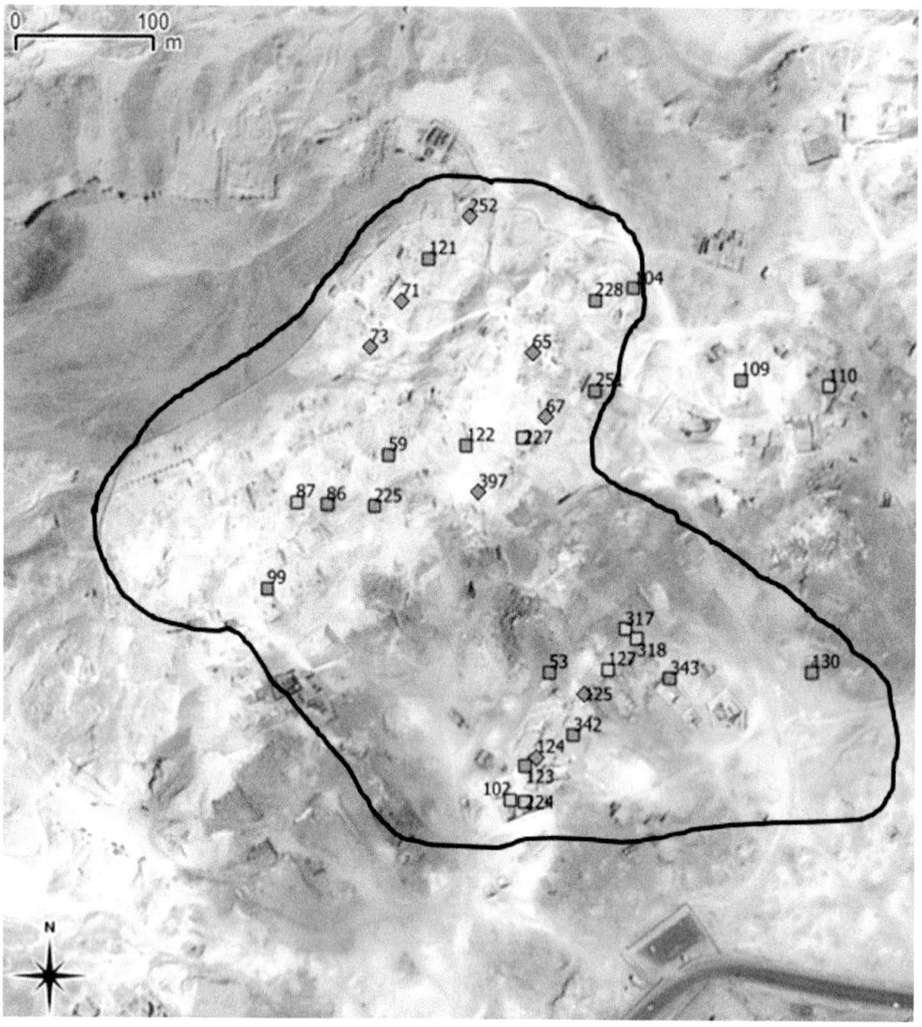

Figure 204: TTs in Qurna datable to Hatshepsut/Tuthmosis III (Author's own using QGIS)

TT96, TT97, TT98 and TT367), and are located in close proximity to each other in this western corner, which is closest to the mortuary temple of Amenhotep II. The extent of this shift was limited by the contours of the Theban hills in this area. The westerly shift is demonstrated by a defined cluster of tombs (TT29, TT92, TT93, TT94, TT95, TT96, TT98 and TT367), with another group in close proximity just across the path (TT79, TT80, TT84, TT85, TT88, TT97 and TT100). This move is probably as a result of a combination of the natural evolution of Upper Qurna, as less space is available in the central area close to the Middle Kingdom tombs, and an attempt to ensure a funerary view towards the mortuary temple of Amenhotep II (and Tuthmosis III for those dating to the previous reign). All of these tombs were located high up the slope, while those in the defined cluster (in addition to some other contemporary tombs) were orientated in the direction of these mortuary temples, suggesting that a line of sight to the mortuary temple of the king they served was a prime concern when siting the tomb.

The two exceptions dating to Amenhotep II, TT72 and TT229, are located to the north, close to those dated to Hatshepsut and Tuthmosis III, suggesting that their construction may have begun during the preceding reign. The owner of TT229 is unknown, but TT72 belonged to Re, who among his many titles was the High Priest of both Amun and the goddess Hathor in the Qurna mortuary temple of Tuthmosis III (Henket-ankh), and High Priest of Amun in Tuthmosis III's temple at Deir el-Bahri. These links to the cult and temples of Tuthmosis III may also explain why Re was buried closer to the Deir el-Bahri temple of Tuthmosis III than that of Amenhotep II, as he had no links there. The façade of Re's tomb is reminiscent of Hatshepsut's Deir el-Bahri temple, with its ramp and upper and lower terraces, also linking this tomb to Deir el-Bahri (see Figure 208). The other exception is TT74 which is datable only between Tuthmosis III and Tuthmosis IV, so its location in the northern area close to Deir el-Bahri would suggest a date to the reign of Tuthmosis III.

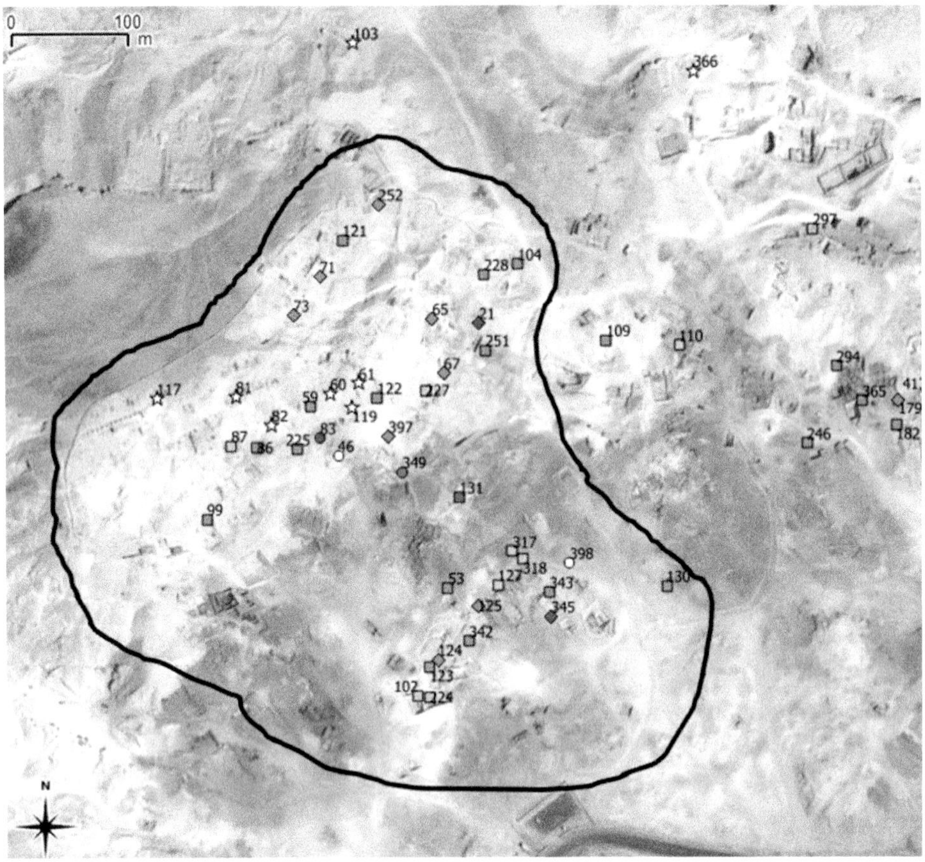

Figure 205: TTs in Qurna at the end of the reign of Tuthmosis III (Author's own using QGIS)

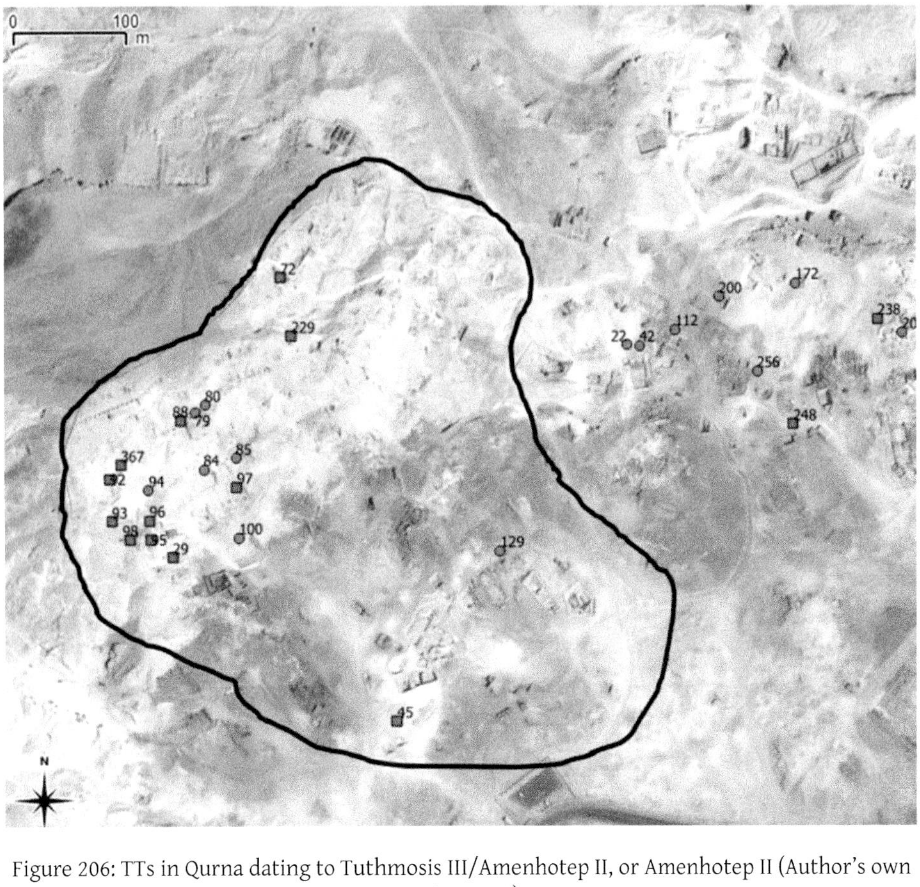

Figure 206: TTs in Qurna dating to Tuthmosis III/Amenhotep II, or Amenhotep II (Author's own using QGIS)

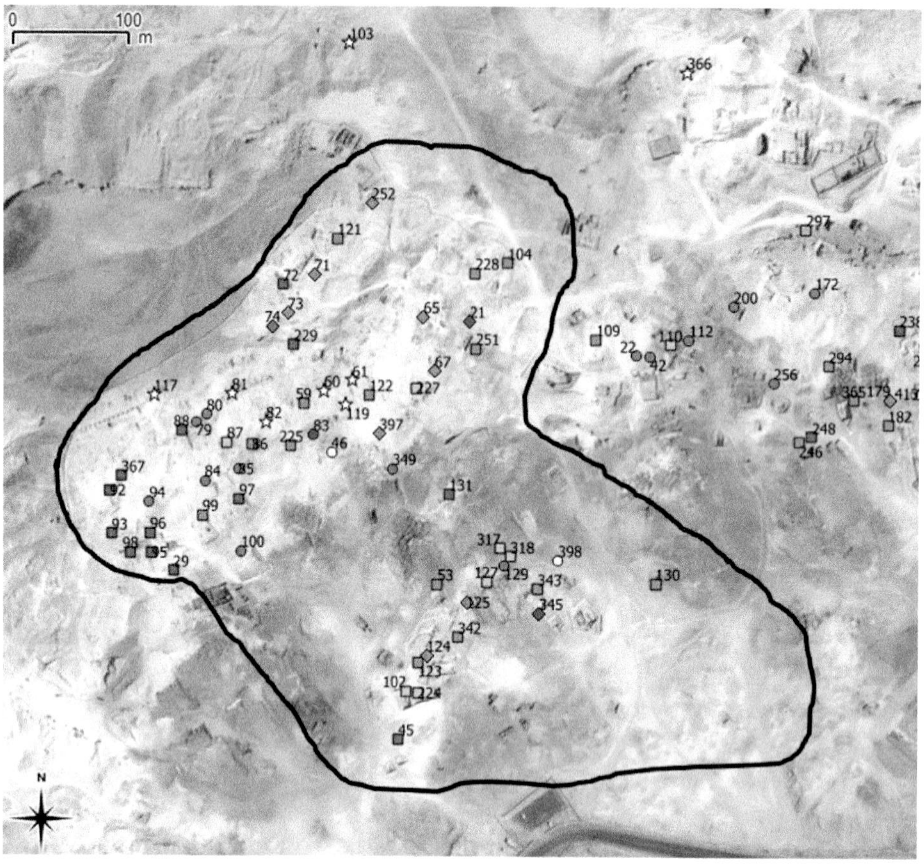

Figure 207: TTs in Qurna at the end of the reign of Amenhotep II (Author's own using QGIS)

After the reign of Amenhotep II, the distributional patterns are less obviously distinguishable by reign. Only one tomb in this western corner is dated after the reign of Amenhotep II (TT91– dated to Tuthmosis IV or Amenhotep III). All other tombs dated from Tuthmosis IV onwards gradually returned to the centralised area of the upper slopes, to the north-east in particular along the top of the cliffs (TT89 and TT90) (see Figure 209). This move was probably as a result of lack of space in the western corner, now densely populated with tombs of Amenhotep II's reign. The lower slopes are also in use at this time (TT56), but the upper slopes are clearly preferred. Three of the tombs dating solely to Tuthmosis IV are located to the east of the area (TT63, TT64 and TT66), while the other two are in close proximity to each other in the centre of the upper slopes (TT76 and TT400). TT78, dated between Amenhotep II and Amenhotep III, is also located in close proximity to TT76 and TT400, suggesting a connection between these three tombs, and a possible date to the same reign of Tuthmosis IV.

Tombs built during the reigns of Tuthmosis IV and Amenhotep III demonstrated this movement northwards and eastwards to fill the gaps in the central area of Qurna (see Figure 210). There was no shift in tomb distribution in Qurna corresponding to the location of the mortuary temple of Tuthmosis IV (to the south-west of that of Amenhotep II), or to that of Amenhotep III, situated to the south-east of the row of mortuary temples. This suggests that in this area at least, proximity to the royal mortuary temple was no longer the primary factor when siting a tomb. The three tombs datable only to either the reign of Tuthmosis IV or Amenhotep III continued this movement north-west and are each within 100m of another tomb from this group (TT77, TT90 and TT91).

The thirteen tombs dated solely to the reign of Amenhotep III (see Figure 211), were distributed evenly throughout Qurna with no obvious clusters, perhaps filling in gaps between existing tombs. Eight of these tombs were located on the upper slopes, more centrally than in the previous reign, while five tombs were located on the lower slopes, showing its increase in popularity as the upper slopes become fuller.

By the end of the reign of Amenhotep III there was still a gap between the occupied areas of the upper and lower slopes of Qurna, so they do seem to have been considered as two separate areas of the necropolis rather than a gradual expansion. The highest concentration of

Figure 208: The façade of TT72 (Author's own)

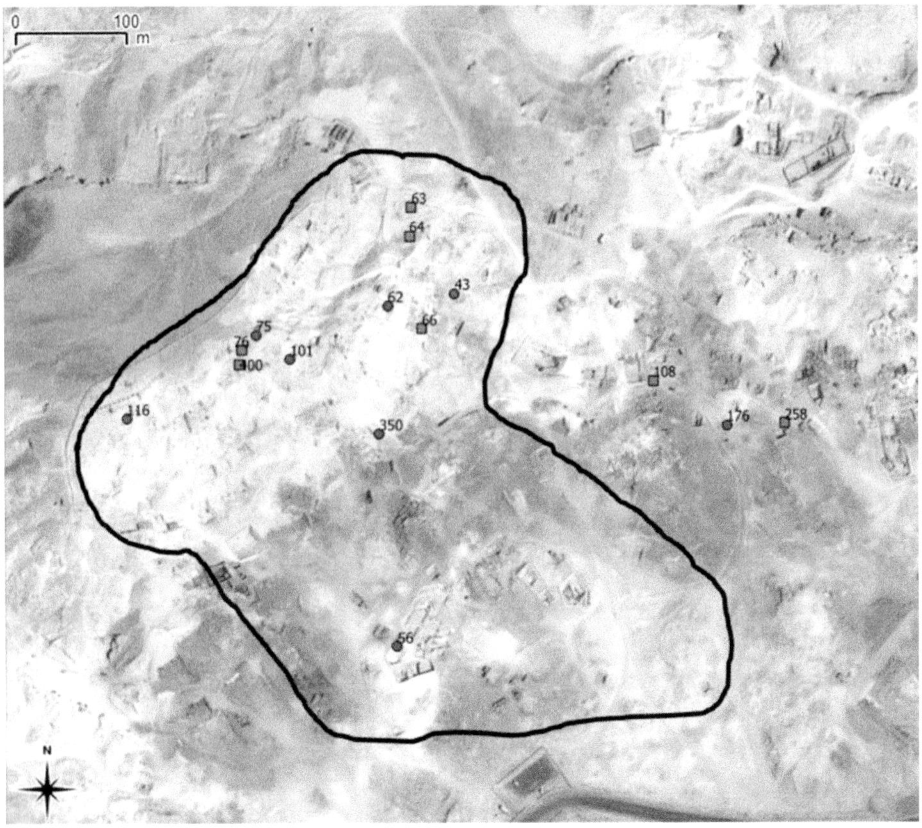

Figure 209: TTs in Qurna dating to Amenhotep II/Tuthmosis IV, and Tuthmosis IV (Author's own using QGIS)

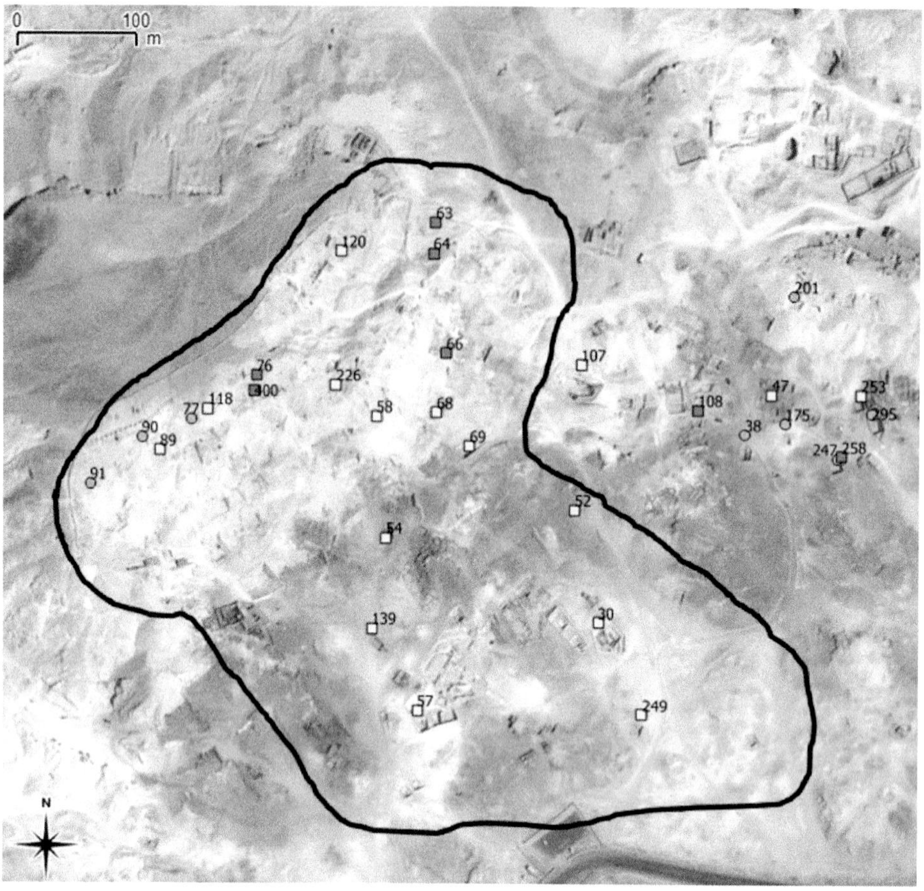

Figure 210: TTs in Qurna dating between Tuthmosis IV and Amenhotep III (Author's own using QGIS)

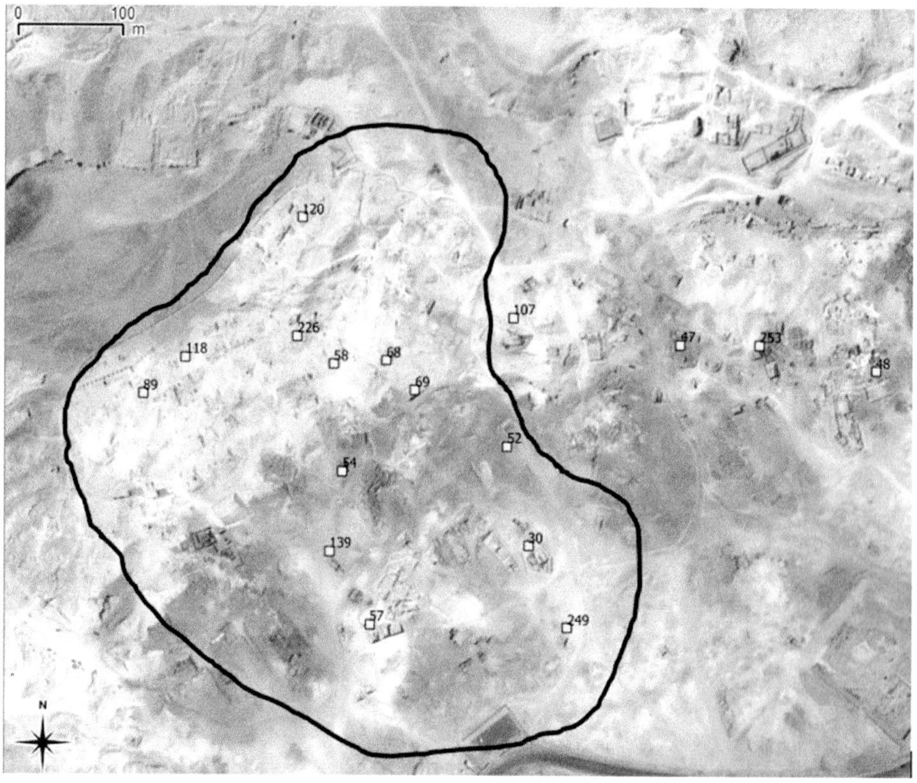

Figure 211: TTs in Qurna dating to Amenhotep III (Author's own using QGIS)

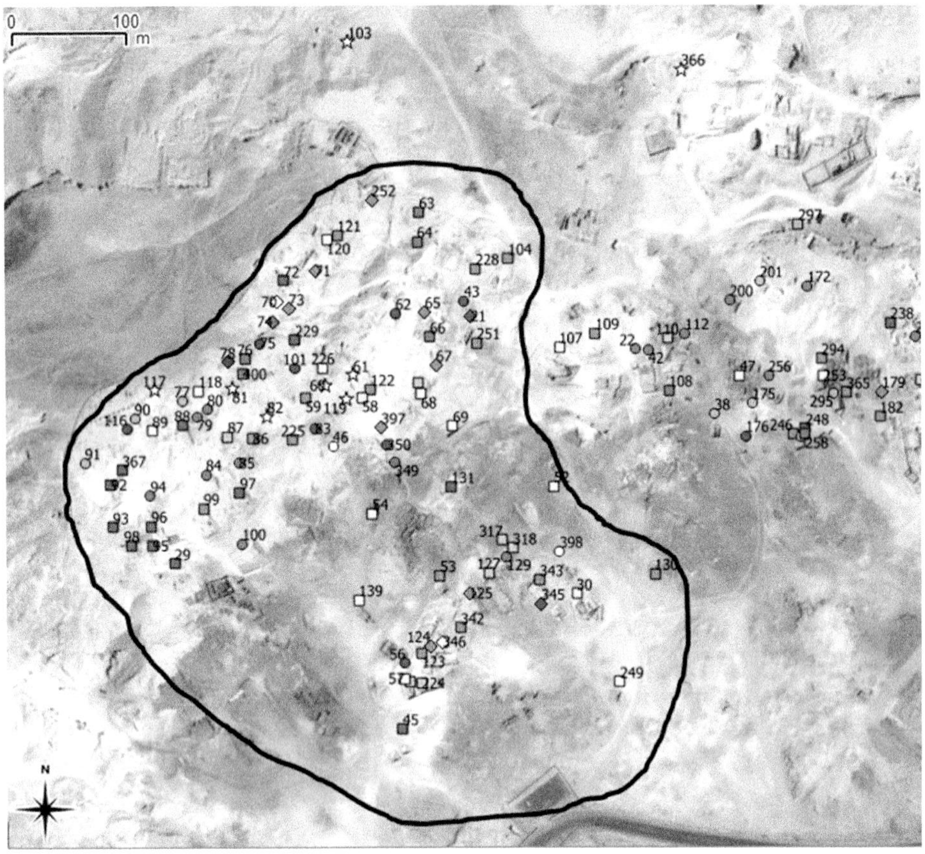

Figure 212: TTs in Qurna at the end of the reign of Amenhotep III (Author's own using QGIS)

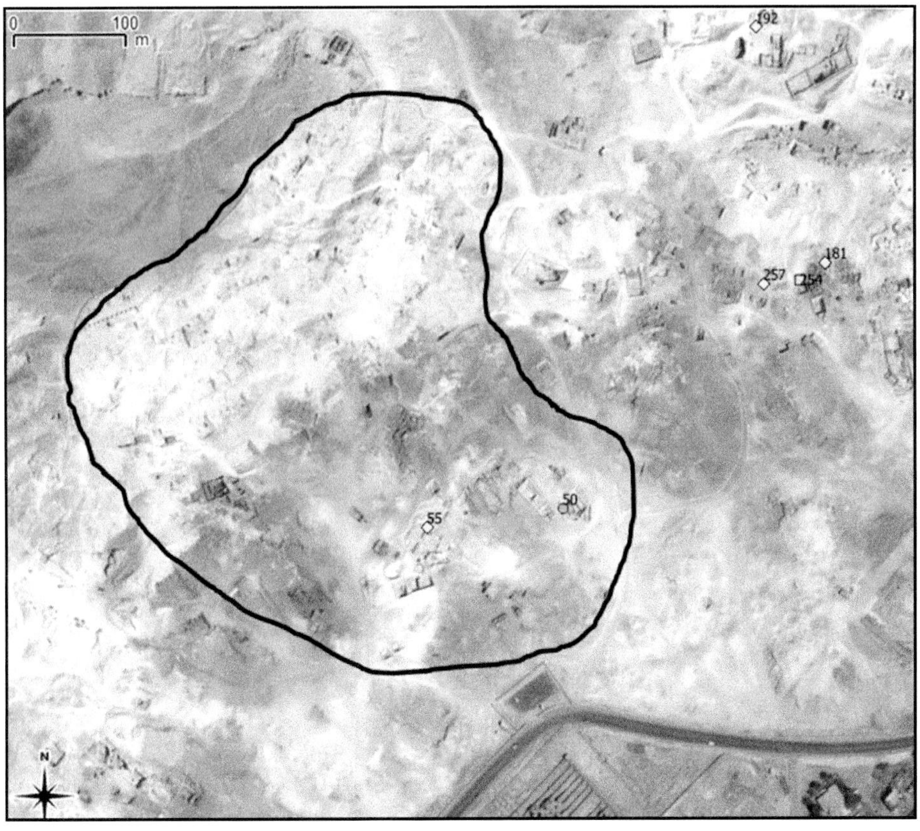

Figure 213: TTs in Qurna dating between Amenhotep III and the end of the Eighteenth Dynasty (Author's own using QGIS)

tombs was still on the upper slopes, but a band of tombs in close proximity to each other stretched across the lower slopes (see Figure 212).

One tomb dated between Amenhotep III and Amenhotep IV was located on the lower slopes of Qurna (TT55). Its elaborate causeway and large courtyard required the space available now only on the emptier lower slopes. At the end of the Eighteenth Dynasty, after the Amarna Period, there was only one clearly datable burial located in this area (TT50). There were no new tombs located on the upper slopes after the reign of Amenhotep III until the Nineteenth Dynasty (see Figure 213).

By the end of the Eighteenth Dynasty the upper slopes of Qurna had the highest concentration of tombs, the majority of which were located close to the Middle Kingdom burials. The cemetery in this area expanded dramatically throughout the dynasty in all directions. There still appears to have been a distinct gap between the burials on the upper and lower slopes, with a few isolated tombs lying within this empty area between the two (TT52, TT54, TT131 and TT139). The tombs on the lower slopes are located in a relatively narrow band across the centre of the area, with plenty of space to the north and south (see Figure 214).

During the early Nineteenth Dynasty, prior to the reign of Ramesses II, there was only one burial, on the lower slopes of Qurna (TT51) (see Figure 215). During the reign of Ramesses II, there were six burials on the lower slopes (TT31, TT111, TT137, TT263, TT331 and TT385) and none on the upper slopes (see Figure 216). This move to the lower slopes may have been as a result of more available space and proximity to the mortuary temple of Ramesses II. There were no tombs located immediately to the north or west of the Ramesseum, when this area would surely have been a popular choice, especially during the reign of Ramesses II.

There were no Nineteenth Dynasty tombs datable to a specific reign built in Qurna after that of Ramesses II. There were three tombs datable only to the Nineteenth Dynasty, one of which was built on the upper slopes of Qurna (TT115), and two more were built on the lower slopes (TT136 and TT384). There was no shift south-westwards to correspond with the construction of the later Nineteenth Dynasty rulers' mortuary temples, suggesting that this was no longer a concern (see Figure 221). The relatively few new tombs built in Qurna during the Nineteenth Dynasty, in comparison to number built during the Eighteenth Dynasty, reflected the situation in the rest of the Theban necropolis.

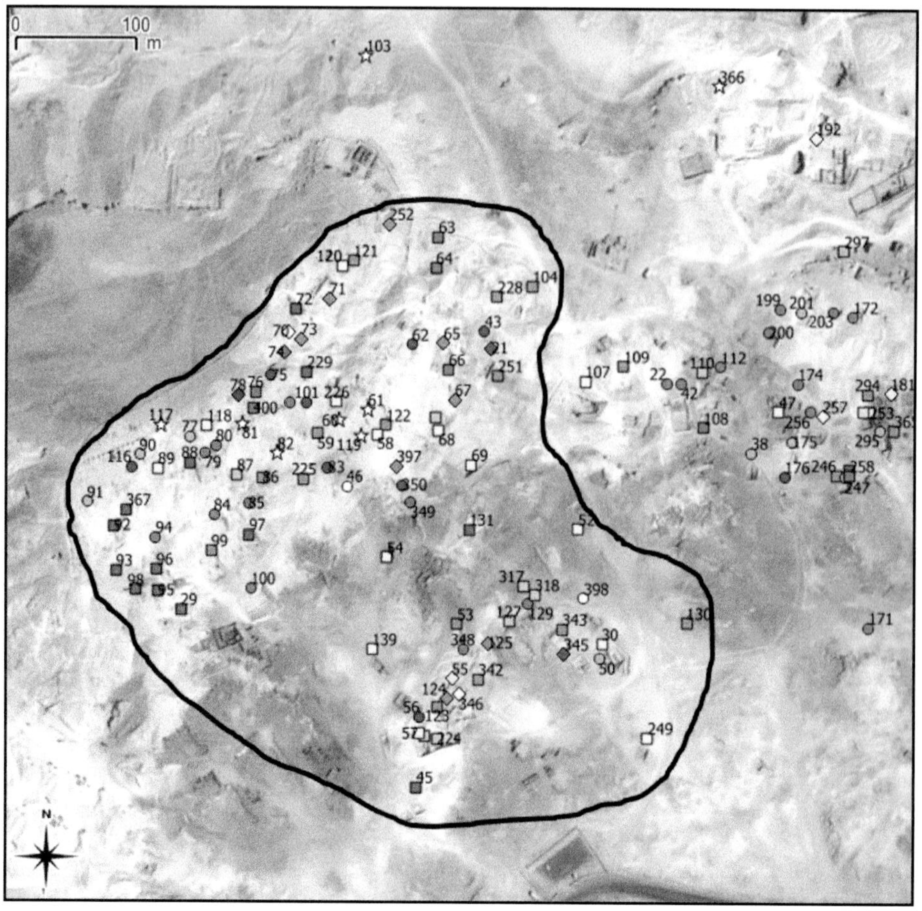

Figure 214: TTs in Qurna at the end of the Eighteenth Dynasty (Author's own using QGIS)

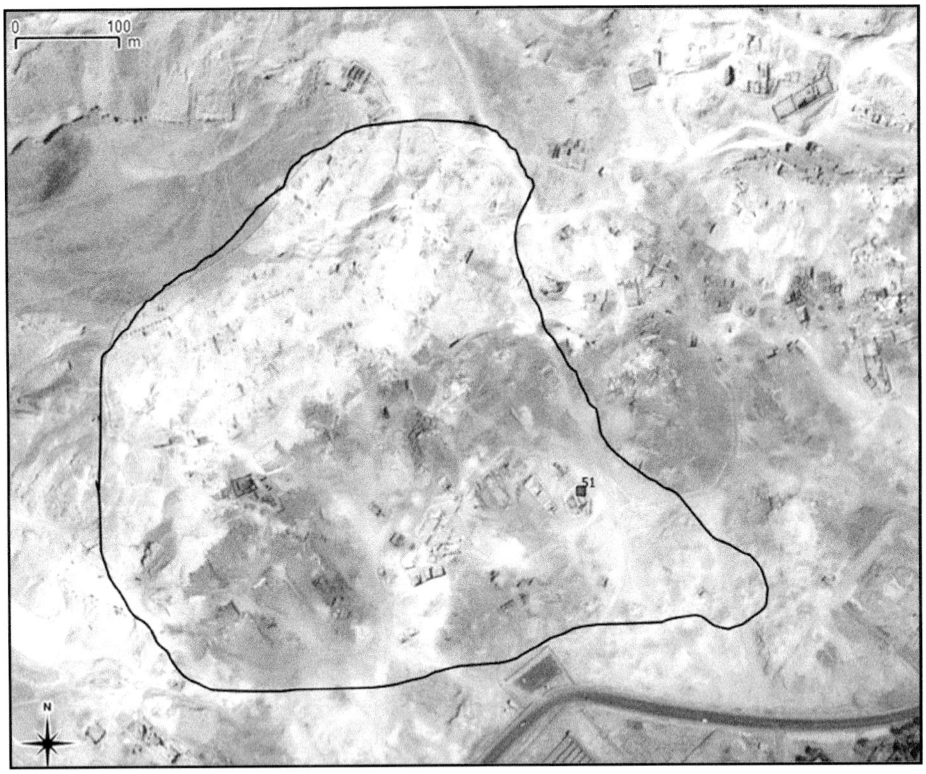

Figure 215: TTs in Qurna dating to the Nineteenth Dynasty prior to Ramesses II (Author's own using QGIS)

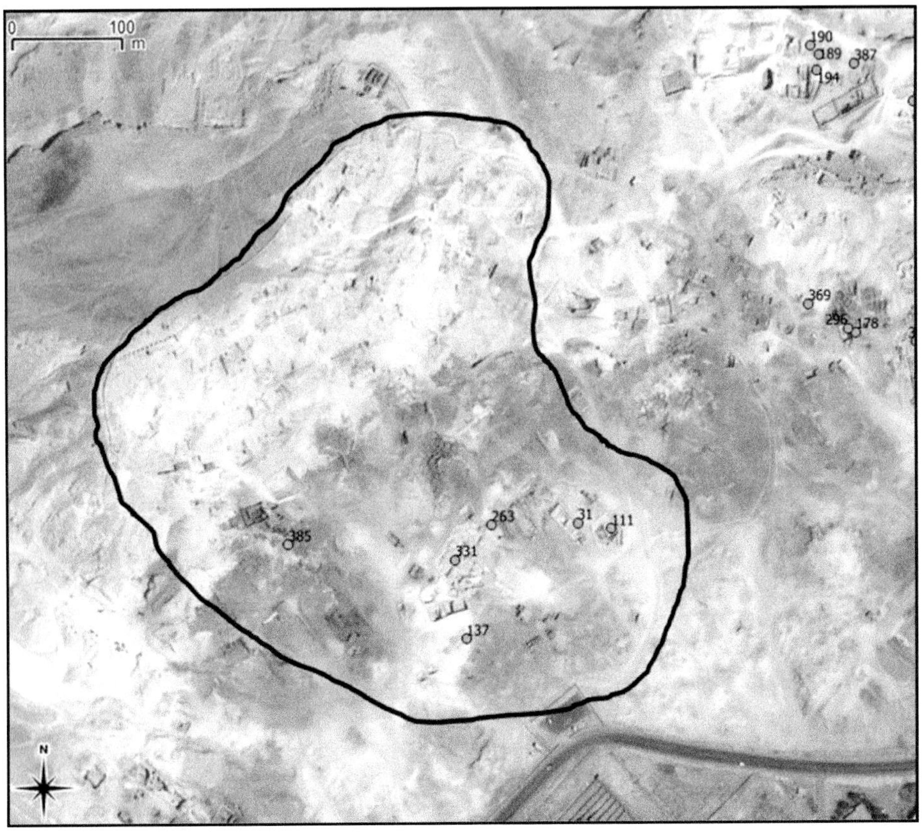

Figure 216: TTs in Qurna dating to the reign of Ramesses II (Author's own using QGIS)

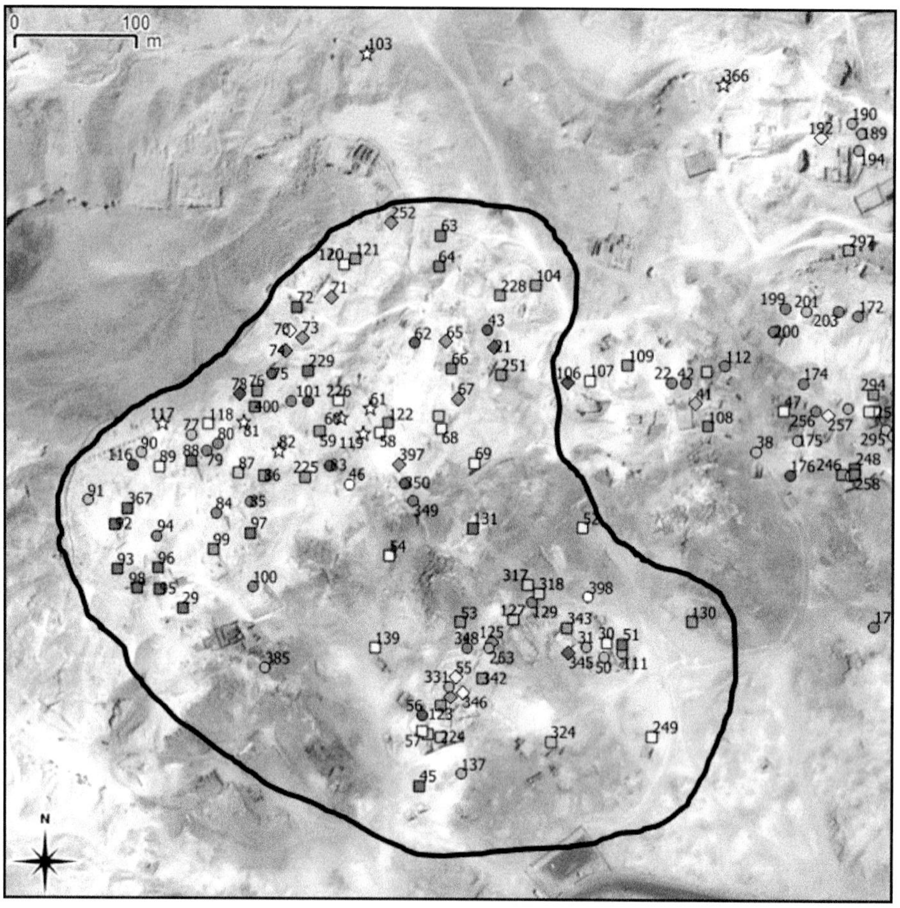

Figure 217: TTs in Qurna at the end of the reign of Ramesses II (Author's own using QGIS)

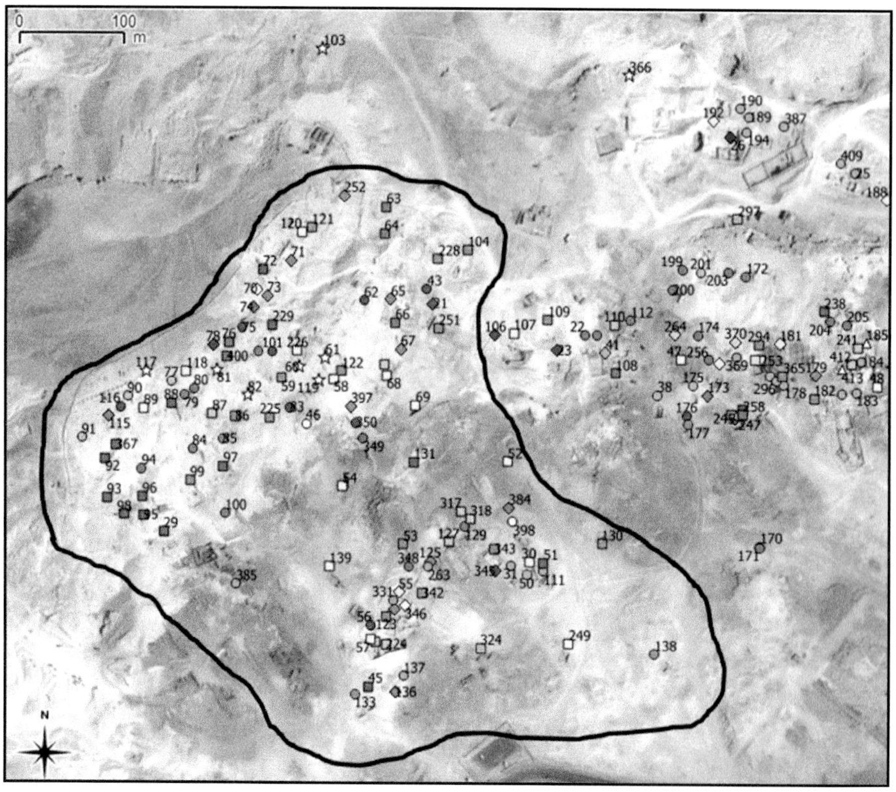

Figure 218: TTs in Qurna at the end of the Nineteenth Dynasty (Author's own using QGIS)

Five tombs are datable only to the Ramesside Period and were all built on the lower slopes (TT269, TT347, TT368, TT399 and TT403), within 100m of at least another of this group. No further tombs were built on the upper slopes at this time (see Figure 219).

Four more tombs were built on the lower slopes (TT134, TT135, TT259 and TT341), while one further tomb was built on the upper slopes (TT114), all datable only to the Twentieth Dynasty (see Figure 220). Without more accurate dating, a link with royal mortuary temples cannot be investigated. The presence of these late New Kingdom tombs confirms that Qurna remained in use as a cemetery throughout the New Kingdom, but not to the same extent as during the Eighteenth Dynasty. The lack of later new burials on the upper slopes was a result of a number of factors. These upper slopes had become saturated with tombs, so the lower slopes were used, probably as a combination of more available space, better rock quality, and from the mid Eighteenth Dynasty onwards, the proximity to the royal mortuary temples and processional way of the BFV. The declining trend for tomb building throughout the necropolis reflected the lack of resources necessary to build new tombs, leading to an increase in tomb-reuse.

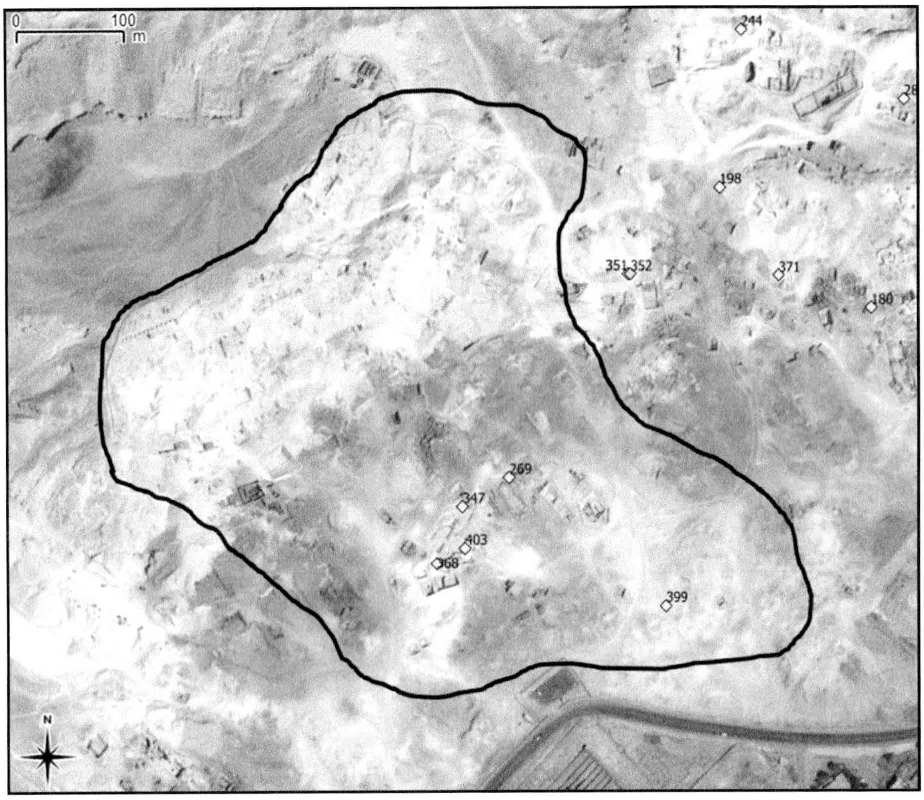

Figure 219: Qurna TTs datable only to the Ramesside Period (Author's own using QGIS)

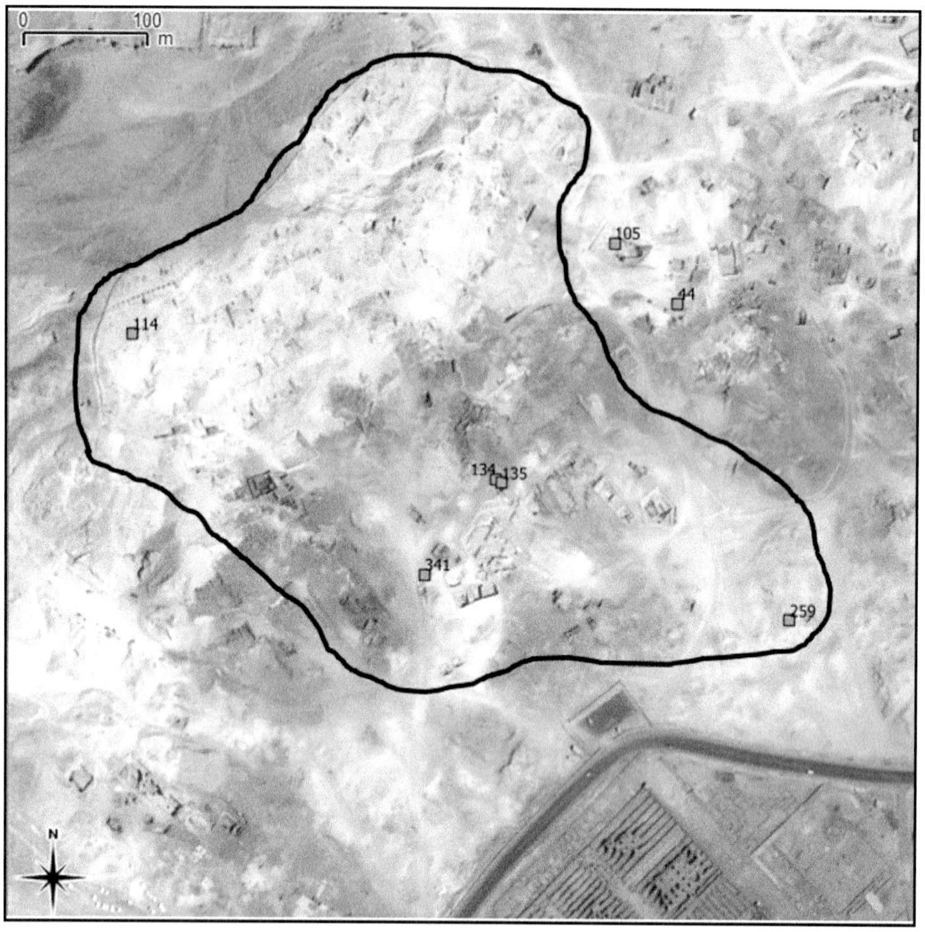

Figure 220: TTs in Qurna datable to the Twentieth Dynasty (Author's own using QGIS)

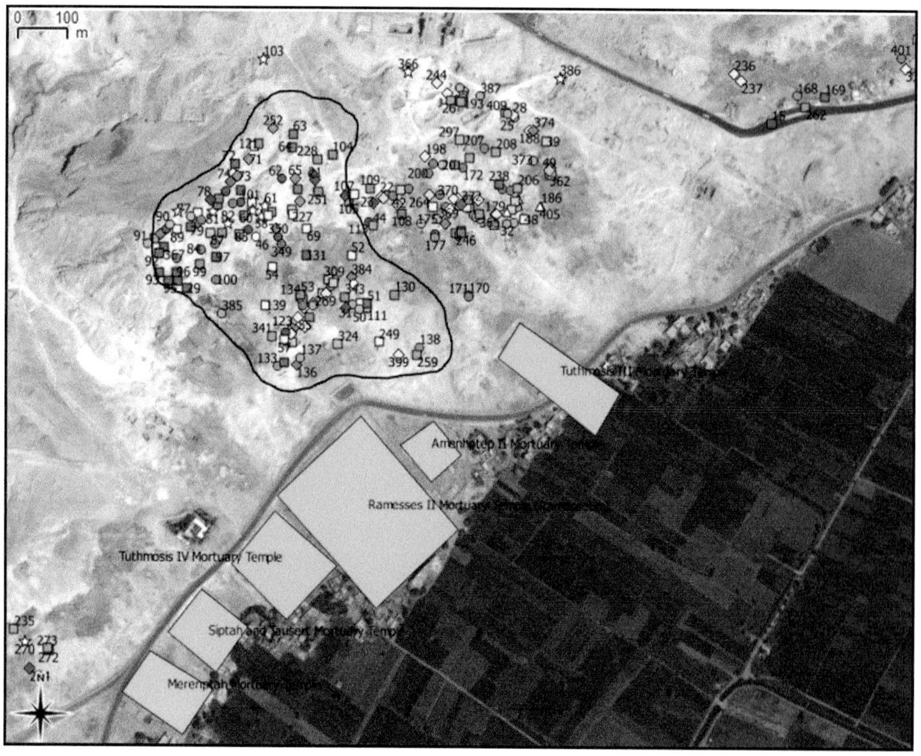

Figure 221: TTs in Qurna at the end of the New Kingdom in relation to royal mortuary temples (Author's own using QGIS)

Upper Qurna

(See Appendix 11)

Location

Upper Qurna is demarcated by the cliffs to the north-west and bordered by Lower Qurna to the south-east and el-Khokha and el-Asasif to the east (see Figure 222). These undulating upper slopes have a steeper incline than the lower slopes, with tombs here located between 100m and 160m above sea level, with the floodplain in this area beginning at 80m above sea level (see Figure 223).

Date of Use

The upper slopes of Qurna contain 77 tombs dating to the New Kingdom or earlier (see Figure 224). Six of these tombs date to the Middle Kingdom (see Chapter 2), but four of these were reused during the New Kingdom. Two date to the Twelfth Dynasty (TT60 and TT61), while the other four date to either the Twelfth or Thirteenth Dynasty (TT81, TT82, TT117 and TT119). One further tomb dates to the late Seventeenth or early Eighteenth Dynasty (TT46). 64 tombs date to the Eighteenth Dynasty (TT21, TT29, TT43, TT54, TT58, TT59, TT62, TT63, TT64, TT65, TT66, TT67, TT68, TT69, TT70, TT71, TT72, TT73, TT74, TT75, TT76, TT77, TT78, TT79, TT80, TT83, TT84, TT85, TT86, TT87, TT88, TT89, TT90, TT91, TT92, TT93, TT94, TT95, TT96, TT97, TT98, TT99, TT100, TT101, TT104, TT116, TT118, TT120, TT121, TT122, TT131, TT225, TT226, TT227, TT228, TT229, TT230, TT251, TT252, TT349, TT350, TT367, TT397, TT400). There is only one tomb dating to the Nineteenth Dynasty (TT115), and one to the Twentieth Dynasty (TT114). These upper slopes were clearly a desirable position, with the space available used initially in the Middle Kingdom, then densely populated with Eighteenth Dynasty tombs, leaving little space for later tombs, forcing them to utilise the lower slopes and other areas for tomb building.

The overwhelming majority of the tombs in Upper Qurna were built in the Eighteenth Dynasty, specifically between the reigns of Hatshepsut and Amenhotep III (see Table 36). Only the six Middle Kingdom tombs and one further tomb, built in the late Seventeenth or early Eighteenth Dynasty, pre-date those attributed to the reign of Hatshepsut. There were only two New Kingdom tombs built in this area after the reign of Amenhotep III, TT115 and TT114, located at the western edge of Upper

Figure 222: Location of Upper Qurna within the Theban Necropolis (Author's own using QGIS)

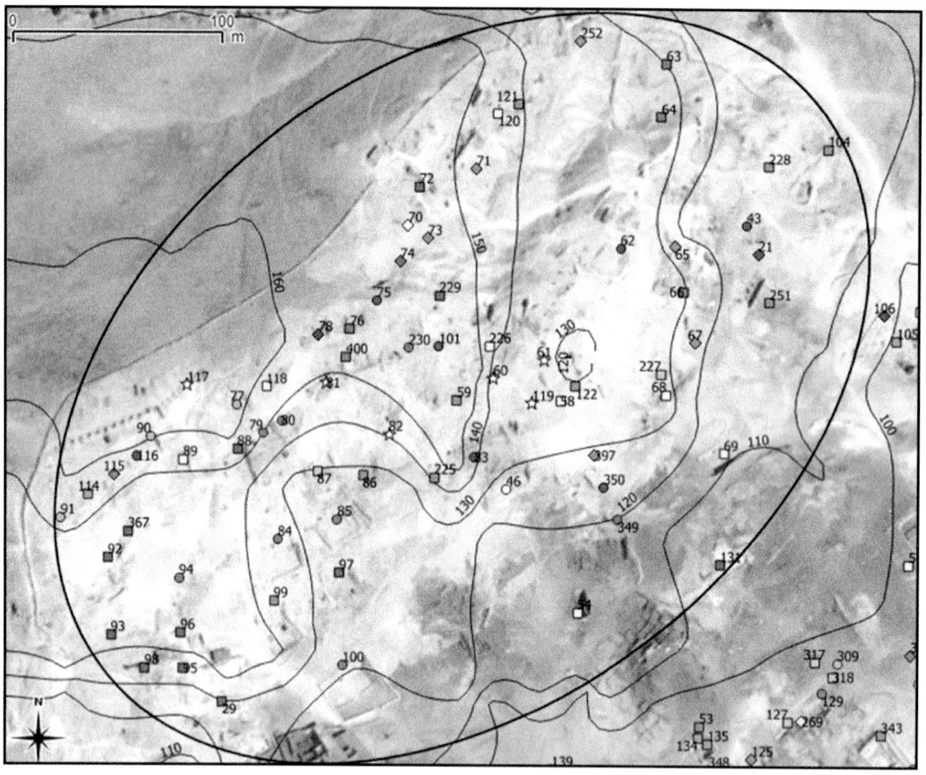

Figure 223: Landscape of Upper Qurna (Author's own using QGIS)

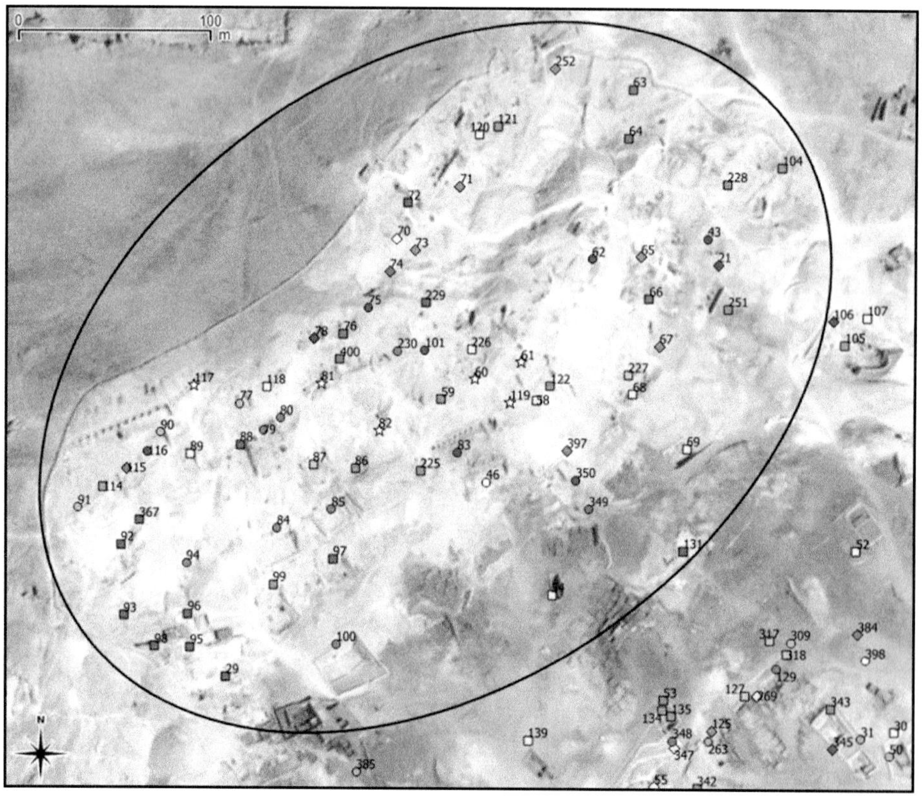

Figure 224: TTs of Upper Qurna (Author's own using QGIS)

Table 36: Upper Qurna tombs distributed by most likely date

Date	No. of Tombs	Tombs
MK	******	TT60, TT61, TT81, TT82, TT117, TT119
Late Dyn 17 /early 18	*	TT46
Dynasty 18	*	T230
Early Dyn 18 – Hat	*	TT349
Ah / TIII	*	TT83
TI / Hat	*	TT21
TI / TIII	*	TT131
Hat	******	TT65, TT67, TT71, TT73, TT252, TT397
Hat / TIII	**	TT87, TT227
TIII	**********	TT59, TT86, TT99, TT104, TT121, TT122, TT225, TT228, TT251
TIII / AII	******	TT79, TT80, TT84, TT85, TT94, TT100
TIII / AII / TIV	*	TT74
AII	***********	TT29, TT72, TT88, TT92, TT93, TT95, TT96, TT97, TT98, TT229, TT367
AII / TIV	******	TT43, TT62, TT75, TT101, TT116, TT350,
AII / TIV / AIII	*	TT78
TIV	*****	TT63, TT64, TT66, TT76, TT400
TIV / AIII	***	TT77, TT90, TT91
Before AIII	*	TT70
AIII	********	TT54, TT58, TT68, TT69, TT89, TT118, TT120, TT226
Dynasty 19	*	TT115
Dynasty 20	*	TT114

Qurna. The limited date range of usage of these upper slopes shows that this area was popular until towards the end of Eighteenth Dynasty, after which time either space ran out, which seems most likely, or the factors influencing tomb distribution changed from proximity to ancestors, to proximity to the mortuary temple of the ruling king, resulted in the focus of tomb building moving to other areas of the necropolis.

The Middle Kingdom tombs appear to have acted as a clear focal point for tomb building at the beginning of the Eighteenth Dynasty, or these upper slopes were the prime location for tomb building on account of their elevated position and views towards the east. During the reign of Hatshepsut and into the reign Tuthmosis III the northern area of Upper Qurna became popular, with some tombs orientated towards Deir el-Bahri (see Figure 225), and then the focus shifted to the south-western area during the reign of Amenhotep II. There are no later identifiable clusters by reign, perhaps due to a lack of space necessitating tomb location where there was sufficient space and decent rock quality. After the Eighteenth Dynasty the upper slopes were saturated with tombs, so the lower slopes and other areas of the necropolis became more popular. The relatively small number of new Ramesside burials throughout the Theban necropolis is a result of the combination of an increase in tomb reuse, and the movement of the burial of officials to the Memphite necropolis, and the area close to the capital at Pi-Ramesses (see Chapter 3).

Figure 225: Upper Qurna tombs cut into the cliffs, with Deir el-Bahri in the distance (Author's own)

Occupation of Tomb Owners

(See Table 37)

Priesthood

There were 34 priests buried in Upper Qurna (including both New Kingdom occupants of TT68 and several individuals who reused existing tombs), several with multiple titles (see Figure 226). Some of the most important individuals in this group were the ten 'High Priests'. There were seven 'High Priests of Amun', who were responsible for eight tombs, Hapusoneb-TT67 (Hat), Meryptah-TT68 (AIII), Re-TT72 (AII), Mery-TT95 and reused TT84 (both AII), Menkheperesoneb-TT86 (TIII), Sennefer-TT96 (AII) and Amenemhet-TT97 (AII). These tombs do not form a distinct cluster, but some spatial connections can be made. TT67 and TT68 are located within 25m of each other, between 120m and 130m above sea level, towards the east of the area. TT72 is located in the north of the area at the highest altitude, close to TT71 of Senenmut. TT84 is located in the west of the area, within 25m of TT97, to the south-east from the same reign, and within 50m of TT85 which lies to the east, while TT95 lies 75m to the south-west.

Only five of these individuals are recognised as 'HPA' from Karnak, four of whom held this office consecutively. The earliest was Hapusoneb-TT67, who was succeeded by Menkheperesoneb-TT86. His successor was Mery-TT84 and TT95, who was in turn succeeded by Amenemhet-TT97 (see Figure 227). The last HPA of Karnak to be buried in this area was Meryptah-TT68 (LAe II: 1242–46). He succeeded Ptahmose (O'Connor and Cline 1998: 194 and 202) whose Theban burial is suggested by the discovery of his funerary cone here, but his tomb has not yet been identified (Hayes 1990: 276). These tombs are not clustered together, although TT86, TT84 and TT97 are in relatively close proximity. After the reign of Amenhotep III, the burials of the HPA from Karnak moved away from Upper Qurna (see Chapter 13).

There were also two 'High Priests' from the mortuary temple of Tuthmosis III, Henketankh, Aahmose-TT121 (TIII), and Re-TT72 (AII). Re was also HPA of three other temples, including Tuthmosis III's Deir el-Bahri temple, the Amun temple, Djeser-set at Medinet Habu, and Menisut at the northern end of the necropolis, as was Sennefer-TT96 (AII). TT121 and TT72 are in relatively close proximity, lying 50m apart in the north of Upper Qurna, with a later tomb, TT120, between them. TT96 lies some distance to the south-west. There was also one 'High Priest of Mut', Ken-TT59 (TIII), and two 'High Priests of Hathor', Re-TT72 (AII), who also held this title at Henketankh, and Amenmehat-TT225 (TIII). TT59 is located within 50m of TT225, while TT225 and TT72 were

Table 37: Upper Qurna tombs distributed by occupational group

Occupational Group	No. of Tombs	Tombs
Priesthood	****************** *****************	TT29, TT54 (2), TT58 (3), TT59, TT60 (MK), TT61 (2), TT63, TT65 (2), TT66, TT67, TT68 (1 and 2), TT72, TT75, TT76, TT78, TT79, TT82, TT83, TT84 (2), TT86, TT92, TT93, TT95, TT96, TT97, TT98, TT99, TT100, TT120, TT121, TT131, TT225, TT397
Temple Administration	******************	TT46 (2), TT54 (1 & 2), TT58 (3), TT65 (2), TT69, TT70 (2), TT71, TT73, TT76, TT78, TT81 (2), TT82 (2), TT86, TT87 (1), TT93, TT95, TT96, TT97, TT99, TT100, TT114, TT122(1 and 2), TT226, TT228, TT251, TT397
Royal Admin	******************* ******************* *******	TT21, TT29, TT43, TT46, TT60 (MK), TT62, TT63, TT64, TT65, TT66, TT67, TT69, TT71, TT73, TT74, TT75, TT76, TT77 (2), TT78, TT80, TT81, TT84, TT85, TT86, TT87, TT88, TT89, TT90, TT91, TT92, TT93, TT94, TT95, TT96, TT98, TT99, TT100, TT101, TT104, TT118, TT131, TT226, TT251, TT252, TT367
General Admin	******************** *******	TT21, TT29, TT46 (2), TT60 (MK), TT61 (2), TT63, TT65, TT66, TT69, TT77, TT79, TT80, TT82 (2), TT83, TT84, TT86, TT87, TT93, TT94, TT95, TT96, TT97, TT99, TT100, TT131, TT349, TT350,
Local Admin	****	TT63, TT81, TT87, TT96
Military	***********	TT74, TT78, TT85, TT87, TT88, TT90, TT91, TT92, TT93, TT230, TT367
Unknown	************	TT58 (1 & 2), TT70, TT81, TT82, TT87 (2), TT115, TT119 (1 & 2), TT227, TT229, TT400

(n) denotes subsequent tomb occupation

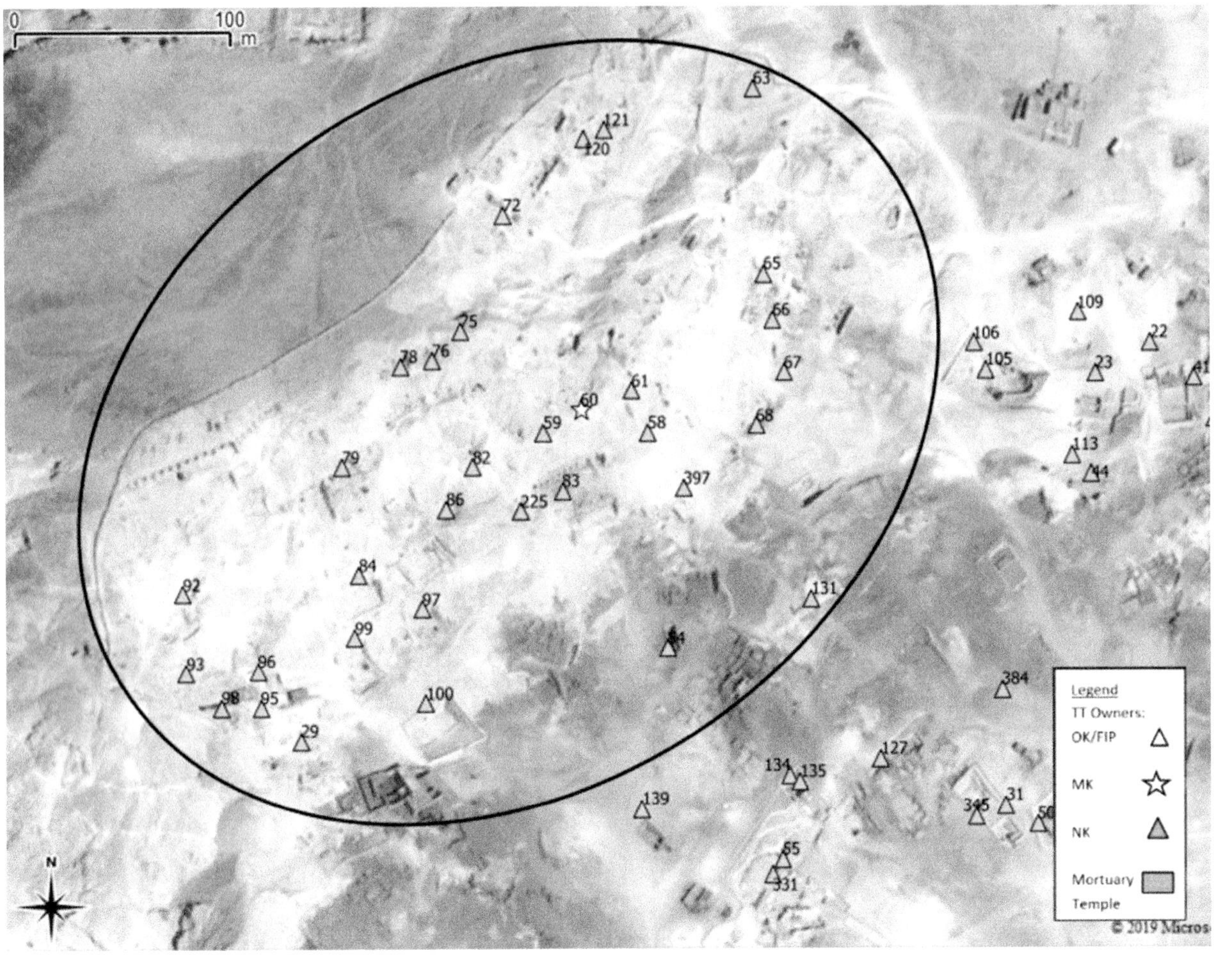

Figure 226: TTs of Priests in Upper Qurna (Author's own using QGIS)

Figure 227: The courtyard of TT97 (Author's own)

located some distance apart. Looking at the general distribution of the tombs of all of these 'High Priests' regardless of affiliation, TT95 and TT96 lie adjacent to each other in the south-west of Upper Qurna, dating to consecutive reigns, suggesting a link between the two, with TT84 and TT97 lying within 100m to the east. This may be suggestive of a potential cluster of 'High Priests' dating to the same period. The burial of eight 'High Priests' of various temples in Upper Qurna supports the idea that was the most desirable religious location for burial, as those holding the highest religious office were buried here.

There were two '2nd Priests of Amun', Amenhotep-saes-TT75 (AII-TIV), and Aanen-TT120 (AIII), one '2nd Priest of 'Amun-Re', Aahmose-TT121 (TIII), and a '3rd Priest of Amun', Kaemheribsen-TT98 (AII). TT120 lies adjacent to TT121 who was also a 'High Priest', possibly suggesting a deliberate attempt by Aanen-TT120 to build his tomb in close proximity. There were only two 'Lector Priests' buried in Upper Qurna, Aahmose-TT121 (TIII) who was the 'Chief Lector Priest of Amun', and the '3rd Lector Priest of Amun' Hapusoneb-TT67 (Hat). These tombs are located some distance apart showing no spatial connection.

Other high-ranking priests included 11 'Overseers of Priests' (OP). Of these, five were 'OP of Upper and Lower Egypt': Hapusoneb-TT67 (Hat); Horemheb-TT78 (AII-AIII); Menkheperesoneb-TT86 (TIII); Mery-TT95 (AII); and Amenemhet-TT97 (AII). Another two were 'OP of all the Gods': Suenmut-TT92 (AII) and Sennefer-TT99 (TIII). Other variations of this title included: 'OP of Amun' Amenemonet, who was the third occupant of TT58 (RII); 'OP of Ahmose Nefertari, the God's Wife and Horus the elder' Sennefer-TT96 (AII); 'OP of Atum, Min at Koptos, Sobek and Anubis' Sennefer-TT99 (TIII); and 'OP of Sobek of Shedet' Sobekhotep-TT63 (TIV). These individuals do not form a distinct group as their tombs were scattered across this area, but there was a higher incidence of their burials within the western group of tombs, as TT92, TT96, TT97, TT99 and TT86 are all located in the same quadrant, within 100m of at least two fellow OP. Senenfer-TT96 and Amenemhet-TT97 were also 'High Priests' (see above), as was Mery-TT95, suggesting a link between this area and the burial of high-ranking priests. TT78 and TT86 are also located within 100m of each other.

There were five tombs belonging to '*ḥm-nṯr*' priests of Maat, who all also held the title 'Vizier', namely Amenemopet called Pairy-TT29 (AII), Antefoker-TT60

(MK), User- TT131 (TI-TIII) and reused TT61 (TI-TIII), Amethu called Ahmose-TT83 (Ah-TIII), and Rekhmire-TT100 (TIII-AII). TT60 and TT61 were built adjacent to each other, while TT83 was located less than 50m to the south, thus forming a group of three of these priests. The other two, TT29 and TT100, were located some distance to the south-west, 75m apart. There were three '*wꜥb* priests' with no specified affiliation, Kenro-who reused TT54 (RII), Imiseba-who reused TT65 (RIX), and Amenemhet-TT97 (AII). There were also three '*wꜥb* priests of Amun', Nakht-TT397 (Hat), Perenkhnum-who reused TT68 (Dyn 20), who was also a '*wꜥb* priest of Mut', and Menkheper(soneb)-TT79 (AII-AIII), who had this role in Henketankh. There is no connection between the affiliation of these *wꜥb* priests and tomb distribution. Of these tombs, TT54, TT68 and TT397 lie within 100m of each other, but this arrangement appears to be by chance rather than deliberate, as a result of the diversity in date and the distance between them.

There was a 'Chief Divine Father of Amun', Amenemhet-TT97 (AII) and eight 'Divine Fathers', Amenemopet called Pairy-TT29 (AII), Sobekhotep-TT63 (TIV), Hepu-TT66 (TIV), Thenuna-TT76 (TIV), Suemnut-TT92 (AII), Kenamun-TT93 (AII), Rekhmire-TT100 (TIII-AII) and Aahmose-TT121 (TIII). TT29, TT92, TT93, TT97 and TT100 were all contemporary and located within 100m of each other in the western area, indicating a potential cluster. TT63 and TT121 are also located within 100m in the north-east. There were also two 'Festival Leaders of Amun', Suemnut-TT92 and Sennefer-TT96 (both AII), and a 'Festival Leader of Atum', and '...all the Gods of Heliopolis', Sennefer-TT99 (TIII). All three of these individuals were buried within 100m of each other within the aforementioned cluster, and date and were roughly contemporary. There were three '*sm* priests', of non-specific deities, Amenemopet called Pairy-TT29 (AII), Kenamun-TT93 (AII), and Rekhmire-TT100 (TIII-AII) who worked in 'the House of Flame'. Again, these three tombs are within 100m of each other, contemporary, and part of the same cluster.

There were three 'Chief of Secrets of the two Cobra Goddesses', Thenuna-TT76 (TIV), Menkheperesoneb-TT86 (TIII), and Kenamun-TT93 (AII), in addition to a 'Chief of Secrets in Karnak', Amenemhet-TT97 (AII). TT76 and TT86 are within 100m of each other, while TT93 and TT97 are again contemporary, and formed part of this western cluster, although they are slightly further than 100m apart, suggesting that this title was not the reason for their inclusion. Other titles include a 'Chief of the Altar', Imiseba-who reused TT65 (RIX), and three 'Master of Ceremonies' of Amun, which literally means the 'Elder of the Forecourt' (Davies and Gardiner 1973: 7), Amenemhet-who reused TT82 (Hat-TIII), and Sennefer-TT96 (AII), who also held this role within the mortuary temple of Tuthmosis I. There is no spatial link between the tombs of the holders of this title.

These priests served a range of deities. The vast majority served Amun: those buried in TT58- RII, TT67- Hat, TT68- AIII and Dyn 20, TT72- AII, TT75- AII-TIV, TT79-TIII-AII, TT82- Hat-TIII, TT84- AII, TT86- TIII, TT92- AII, TT95- AII, TT96- AII, TT97- AII, TT98- AII, TT120- AIII, TT121- TIII and TT397- Hat. Those affiliated to Amun were spread across the area, again with the highest concentration within the western group of tombs. Less commonly attested deities include Amen-Re (TT121-TIII), Mut (TT59- TIII and the usurper of TT68- Dyn 20 - located within 100m), Hathor (TT60- MK, TT72- AII, TT225- TIII), Maat (TT29- AII, TT60- MK, TT61- TI-TIII, TT83- Ah-TIII, TT100- TIII-AII, TT131- TI-TIII), Sobek (TT63- TIV, and TT99- TIII), Atum (TT99 - TIII), Anubis, Min of Koptos, and all the gods of Heliopolis (TT99 - TIII), Horus the elder (TT96- AII), the two cobra goddesses (TT76- TIV, TT86- TIII and TT93- AII), and the cults of Tuthmosis III (TT72- AII, TT79- TIII-AII and TT121- TIII), and Ahmose Nefertari (TT96- AII).

The tombs belonging to priests do not form a single cluster but are spread throughout the area. There are instead smaller groups of tombs in close proximity. TT120 (AIII) and TT121 (TIII) lie adjacent to each other in the north of Upper Qurna. While TT120 is later in date, both tomb owners held the title '2nd Priest of Amun(-Re)', while the similarity of their names, Aanen and Aahmose may suggest a familial link. TT72 (AII) and TT75 (AII) lie along the same contour line as TT120 and TT121, a short distance to the south-west. They were contemporary to each other and were both priests of Amun, with TT72 owned by the 'HPA' and TT75 by a '2PA', possibly the deputy of Re-TT72. A short distance to the south-west lies TT225 (TIII) which is adjacent to TT86 (TIII), with TT84 (TIII-AII) and TT97 (AII) to the south. All four tombs are close in date and belong to 'High Priests', with the latter three affiliated to Amun, and TT225 to Hathor. In the south-western corner, TT95 (AII), belonging to the 'HPA' lies directly in front of the contemporary TT98 (AII), belonging to the '3PA'.

Temple Administration

There were 28 members of the temple administration buried in Upper Qurna (including both occupants of TT54 and TT122), most of whom were connected to the Estate of Amun (see Figure 228). There was a 'Chief Steward' of both Amun and the God's Wife, Senenmut-TT71 (Hat), and four 'Stewards of Amun', Mery-TT95, Sennefer-TT96 and Amenemhet-TT97 (all AII), and Rekhmire-TT100 (TIII-AII). There were six 'Overseers of Works...of Amun' (and other related titles), Senenemut-TT71 (Hat), Amenhotep-TT73 (Hat), Horemheb-TT78 (AII-AIII), Ineni-who reused TT81 (AI-Hat) who was also

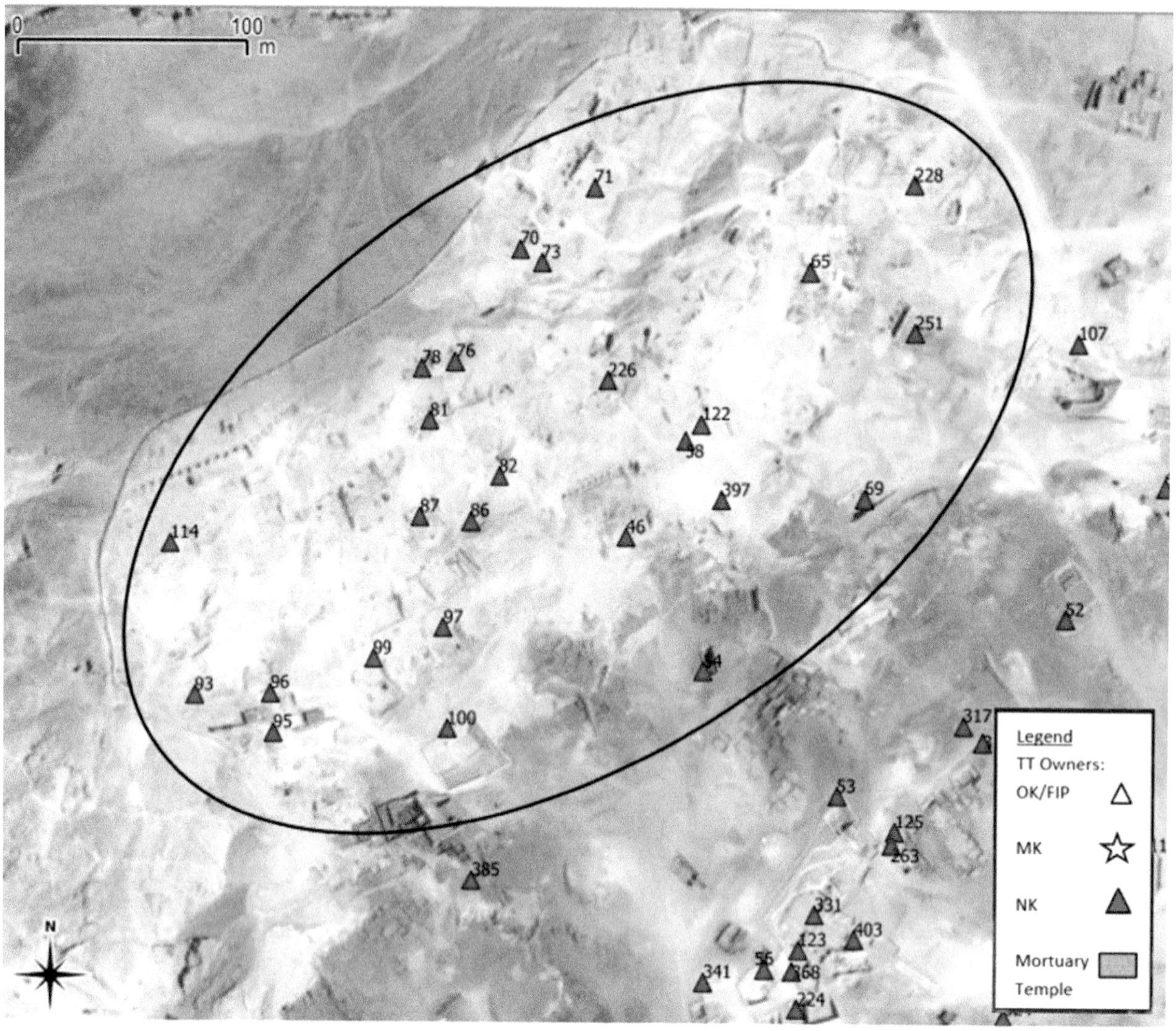

Figure 228: TTs of the Temple Administration in Upper Qurna (Author's own using QGIS)

'Overseer of Every Office in Karnak', Menkheperesoneb-TT86 (TIII), Rekhmire-TT100 (TIII-AII). There were also six 'Overseers of the Storehouse of Amun' (TT87– Hat-TIII, TT93– AII, both occupants of TT122- TIII, TT251-TIII, TT397- Hat) and an 'Overseer of the Servants of Amun' (TT87– Hat-TIII). Titles that do not refer directly to Amun include the 'Chief of the Storehouse of Khonsu', who -was most likely based at the Khonsu temple at Karnak (usurper of TT54– RII).

Several individuals oversaw food provision, including six 'Overseers of the Granary/ies of Amun': Senenmut-TT71 (Hat), Ineni-TT81 (AI-Hat), Menkheperesoneb-TT86 (TIII), Minnakht-TT87 (Hat-TIII), Mery-TT95 and Sennefer-TT96 (both AII). These tombs do not form a distinct cluster, but pairs of spatially connected tombs can be identified, and a higher concentration of these tombs are found in the south-west of Upper Qurna. TT86 and TT87 were contemporary and built adjacent to each other, along the same contour line. This suggests that Menkheperesoneb-TT86 chose to be buried next to his predecessor, and potentially suggesting a family relationship. A predecessor of Minnakht-TT87, Ineni-TT81 lies less than 50m to the north of this pair on the higher slopes, with a line-of-sight connection between these tombs. TT71 lies over 100m to the north east. TT95 and TT96 are also adjacent to each other and date to the same reign, again suggesting a close link between the two owners in life. This pair of tombs lies 100m to the south-west of TT86 and TT87, so in relatively close proximity.

There were five 'Overseers of the Fields of Amun' (and similar titles): Menna-TT69 (AIII), Horemheb-TT78 (AII-AIII), Mery-TT95 (AII), Sennefer-TT96 (AII), who was also 'Overseer of Gardens and the Orchard', and Sennefer-TT99 (TIII). Of these, the roughly contemporary Mery-TT95, Sennefer-TT96 (which is adjacent to TT95) and Sennefer-TT99, who presumably succeeded each other in this role, are also located within this south-western group, within 50m of each other, while TT69 and TT78 are located some distance away. There were seven 'Overseers of the Cattle of Amun': Amenhotep-TT73 (Hat), Thenuna-TT76 (TIV), Horemheb-TT78 (AII-AIII), Kenamun-TT93 (AII), Mery-TT95 (AII), Sennefer-TT96 (AII), and Amenmose-TT251 (TIII). TT73 and TT76 are located 50m apart along the northern edge of the occupied slopes, with TT74 and TT75 between them, both of which were built in the intervening period between TT73 and TT76 being built. This would seem to have been a chronological development of the necropolis rather than an occupational pattern, but TT78 lies adjacent to TT76, making three holders of this title who were buried along this ridge. The three contemporary tombs TT93, TT95 and TT96 are all located within the south-western area of Upper Qurna, again suggesting a link between this group of tombs and the temple administration. TT251 lies some distance away to the east. The final group of overseers were responsible for the personnel provisioning the temple, such as 'Chief of Weavers', Amenemhet-who reused TT82 (Hat-TIII), and 'Overseer of Craftsmen', Amenmose-TT70 (Dyn 20/21). One such craftsman was a 'Sculptor of Amun' Huy-TT54 (AIII). There is no spatial connection between these tombs.

There were several temple scribes buried here. They included a 'Scribe in the Temple of Ramesses 'Beloved like Amun'' (Abu Simbel), 'Scribe of the Temple of Mut' and 'Scribe of the Divine Offerings of Amun', Amenemonet-the third occupant of TT58 (Dyn 20), the 'Chief Temple Scribe of the Estate of Amun' and 'Temple Scribe in the Estate of Amun-Re', Imiseba-who reused TT65 (RIX), a 'Chief Scribe of Divine Offerings', Rekhmire-TT100 (TIII-AII), a 'Scribe of Counting Grain' and 'Counter of Grain', Amenemhet-who reused TT82 (Hat-TIII), and a 'Scribe of the Treasury of Amun', Amenmose-TT228 (TIII). These tombs do not form a distinct cluster, nor is there a strong spatial connection between them. TT228 lies 50m to the north-east of TT65, which is located 100m to the north-east of TT58, while TT82 lies 100m to the west. TT100 lies some distance to the south-west of all these tombs.

In addition to this 'Scribe of the Treasury' (TT228), other roles were connected to the Treasury of Amun, including two 'Overseers of Sealed Things', Ineni-who reused TT81 (AI-Hat), and Sennefer-TT99 (TIII), two 'Overseers of the Treasury', Ineni-TT81 (AI-Hat) again, who was also a 'Seal-bearer', and Mery-TT95 (AII), and a 'Deputy of the Treasury', Imiseba-who reused TT65 (RIX). Other titles were connected to the provision of gold for the treasury included an 'Overseer of the Gold Lands', Sennefer-TT99 (TIII), and a 'Head of Goldworkers' Unknown-TT114 (Dyn 20). There is no clear spatial connection between these individuals. TT95 and TT99 were located within 50m of each other in the south-western area of Upper Qurna, while the much later TT114 was 100m to the north of these tombs. TT81 was just over 100m to the east of TT114, some distance away from TT95 and TT99. TT228 lies some distance to the east of all of them. The addition of TT114 as one of only two Ramesside tombs in Upper Qurna (the other being TT115 with an unknown owner) is unusual, as this title does not seem important enough to warrant inclusion among the influential tomb owners of this area.

Some titles were connected to religious aspects of temple life, but without esoteric knowledge, such as the 'Standard Bearer' of the sacred bark, Nebamun-TT90 (TIV-AIII), who was not buried close to any other temple staff, but the adjacent tombs, Amenmose-TT89 (AIII) and Unknown-TT116 (AII-TIV) were roughly contemporary. There was one 'Door-keeper of Amun', Hekareshu-TT226 (AIII), but this tomb was not in close proximity to other temple staff.

Individuals who referenced other temples within their tomb include the 'Steward of the Temple of the Aten', Ramose-TT46 (AIII/AIV), who by his choice of this cemetery seems likely to have been based at the Aten temple at Karnak rather than Amarna; a 'Scribe in the Temple of Ramesses 'Beloved like Amun'' (Abu Simbel) and 'Scribe of the Temple of Mut', again most likely at Karnak, Amenemonet-the third occupant of TT58 (Dyn 20); the 'High Priest of Mut', Ken-TT59 (TIII); and the 'Steward of the Temple of Tuthmosis III' in the Estate of Amun, Hekareshu-TT226 (AII). TT226 is located within 100m of Aahmose-TT121 (TIII), and not much further from Re-TT72 (AII), who were both 'High Priests' in Henketankh, suggesting a link between the tombs of those who served the cult of Tuthmosis III.

The members of the temple administration were not buried in a single area but scattered throughout Upper Qurna. Some notable clusters include TT70, TT71, TT72 and TT73 in the north of the area. The original occupant of TT70 is unknown, with an 'Overseer of Craftsmen', Amenmose reusing the tomb (Dyn 20/21), but the earlier TT72 and TT73 were owned by important individuals, as Re-TT72 (AII) was the 'High Priest' of several temples, while Amenhotep-TT73 (Hat) was an 'Overseer of Works', 'Chief Steward' and 'Overseer of Cattle'. These tombs were also located close to another 'Overseer of Works', Senenmut-TT71 (Hat), who was also 'Steward of Amun' and was contemporary to Amenhotep-TT73.

TT122 (TIII), TT58 (AIII) and TT397 (Hat) formed a cluster near the centre of the area. Both occupants of TT122-Amenhotep and Amenemhet, and Nakht-TT397 were 'Overseers of the Storehouse of Amun' and are close in date, while TT58 had an unknown original owner.

To the west on the upper slopes lie three tombs of temple administrators within 80m of each other, Roy-TT77, reused by an 'Overseer of Sculptors', not explicitly

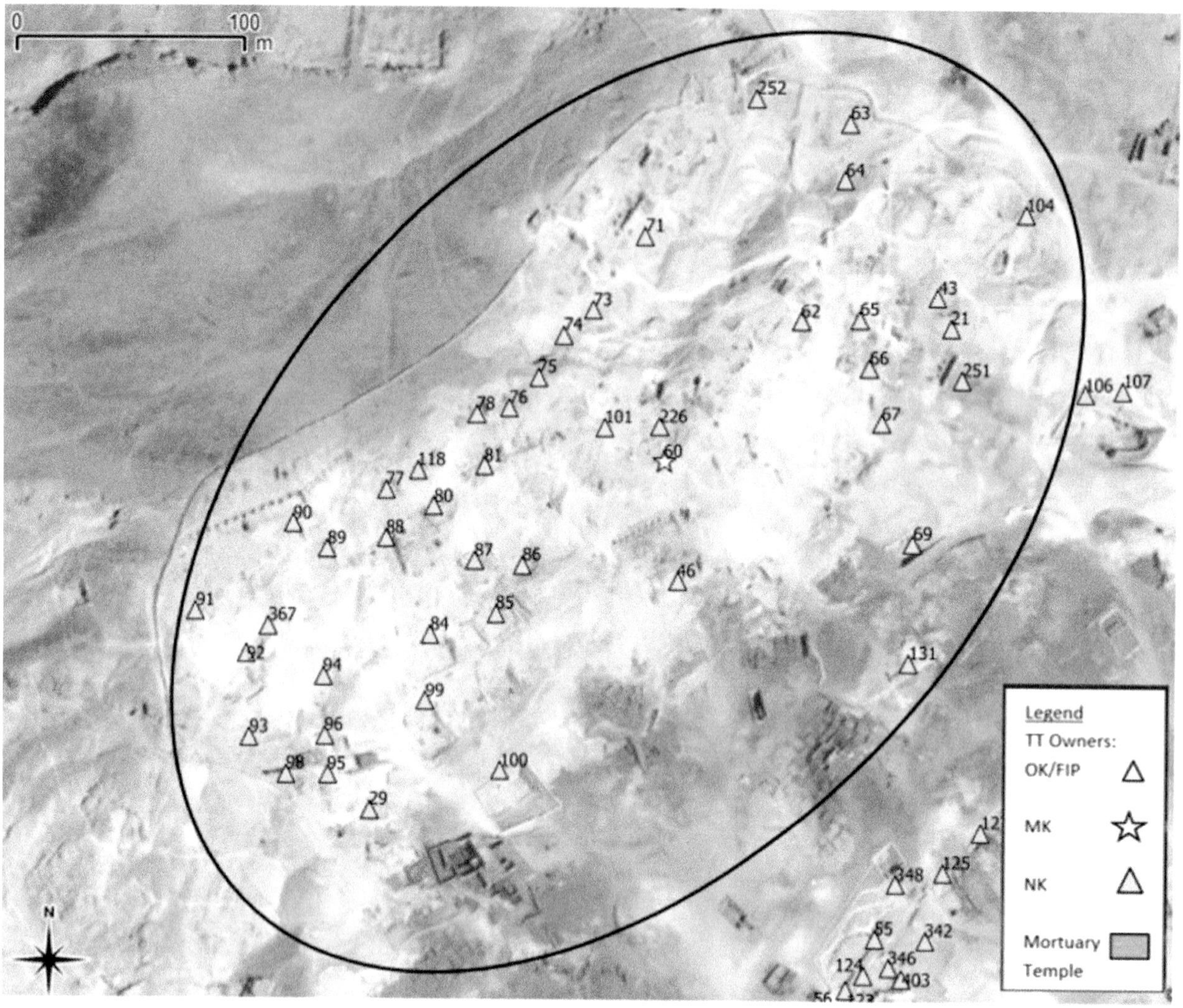

Figure 229: TTs of the Royal Administration in Upper Qurna (Author's own using QGIS)

affiliated to the Amun estate (AIII), Nebamun-TT90 (TIV-AIII), a 'Standard-bearer', and Unknown-TT114 (Dyn 20), the 'Head of Goldworkers'. The tombs of Ineni-TT81 (AI-Hat) and Amenmehet-TT82 (Hat-TIII) are centrally located and adjacent to each other, both built in the Middle Kingdom but reused by contemporary members of the temple administration, albeit with differing roles as Ineni held superior titles to Amenemhet. Sennefer-TT96 (AII) and Sennefer-TT99 (TIII) are roughly contemporary and located in close proximity in the south-west of Upper Qurna. They share no common titles but were both important individuals who shared a name. Amenmose-TT228 (TIII) and Imiseba-who reused TT65 (RIX) were both temple scribes and were buried in close proximity to the east.

Royal Administration

There were 45 members of the royal administration buried in Upper Qurna (see Figure 229). There is less usurpation by these individuals than the priesthood or temple administration, with only two reusing existing tombs (TT46 and TT77 – both around the reign of AIII), while the others all built their own. There were five 'Chief Stewards' of the king buried here: User-TT21 (TI-Hat), Senenmut-TT71 and Amenhotep-TT73 (both Hat), Thenuna-TT76 (TIV) and Kenamun-TT93 (AII). TT71, TT73, and TT76 are all located in the centre of the northern area of Upper Qurna, within 100m of each other, located in a line along the upper ridge, with two other members of the royal administration between them, Thanuny-TT74 (TIII-TIV) and Amenhotep-saes-TT75 (AII-TIV). This line of tombs seems to be developing chronologically, with later tombs being built to the west. TT93 is situated some distance to the south-west and is not spatially connected to the other 'Chief Stewards'. Five further individuals were 'Stewards', Amenmose-TT89 (AIII), Sennefer-TT96 (AII), Sennefer-TT99 (TIII), Hekareshu-TT226 (AIII), and Senamun-TT252 (Hat). TT96 and TT99 are located 50m apart, close to TT93 which is located behind TT96 in the south-western area of Upper Qurna, and these tombs are roughly contemporary. TT89 is located 100m to the north of this group, and TT226 some distance to the east, a short distance to the east of the 'Chief Stewards' group, but TT252 is the northern-most tomb in Upper Qurna, located some distance from any other 'Stewards'. Three individuals were 'Overseer of Royal Works': Hapusoneb-TT67 (Hat) Senenmut-TT71 (Hat), and Hekareshu-TT226 (AIII); while another was 'Director of Royal Works', Iamunedjem-TT84 (TIII-AII). TT226 is located less than 100m to the south of TT71, but TT67 and TT84 are over 100m away from the other tombs.

Scribal titles were also popular here, with 11 'Royal Scribes': Ramose-who reused TT46 (AIII-IV); Thanuny-TT74 (TIII-TIV); Horemheb-TT78 (AII-AIII), who was also the 'Overseer of Royal Scribes of the Army'; Menkheper(soneb)-TT79 (TIII-AII); Djehutynefer-TT80 (TIII-AII) and TT104? (TIII); Iamunedjem-TT84 (TIII-AII); Minnakht-TT87 (Hat-TIII); Kenamun-TT93 (AII); Hekareshu-TT226 (AIII); and Amenmose-TT251 (TIII). There is also a 'Scribe of Royal Accounts (?)' Nebamun-TT65 (Hat). TT74 and TT78 are located 50m apart, while TT79 and TT80 are situated adjacent to each other, just 50m to the south-west, with TT84 and TT87 located within 50m to the south, and TT93 100m further to the south-west. TT226 lies 50m to the south of TT74. TT251 and TT65 lie within 50m of each other to the east, but they and TT46 have no spatial connection to the tombs of the other 'Royal Scribes'.

Other titles include: 'Royal Butler', Suemnut-TT92 (AII); two '1st Royal Heralds', Iamunedjem-TT84 and Ramose called Amay-TT94 (both TIII-AII); and a 'Royal Herald', Sennefer-TT99 (TIII). All four of these tombs were contemporary and located within 50m of each other in the south-western area, suggesting a spatial connection between them. There are also two Royal 'Nurses', Hekerneheh-TT64 (TIV), and Senamun-TT252 (Hat), who were buried within 50m of each other in the north-eastern area, and an 'Overseer of Royal Nurses', Hekareshu-TT226 (AIII), who is not spatially connected to the other 'Royal Nurses'. Senamun-TT252 was Hatshepsut's nurse, so it seems deliberate that this tomb was built in the area of Upper Qurna closest to Deir el-Bahri. There were two 'Overseers of the Storehouse' of the king, Neferrenpet-TT43 (AII-TIV) and Minnakht-TT87 (Hat-TIII), whose tombs are not spatially connected. There was also an 'Overseer of Sculptors of the Lord of the Two Lands', Roy-reused TT77 (AIII), who was buried adjacent to three other members of the royal administration, Menkheper(soneb)-TT79 (TIII-AII), Djehutynefer-TT80 (TIII-AII), and Pehsukher called Thenunu-TT88 (AII). The 'Royal Dignitary', Amenemopet called Pairy-TT29 (AII), was buried adjacent to two 'Royal Seal-bearers', Mery-TT95 and Kaemheribsen-TT98 (both AII).

The largest group of individuals with the same title buried here were the 'Royal Seal-bearers': Antefoker-TT60 (MK), Amenemwaskhet-TT62 (AII-TIV), who was also 'Chamberlain', Sobekhotep-TT63 (TIV), Hekerneheh-TT64 (TIV), Hapusoneb-TT67 (Hat), Senenmut-TT71 (Hat), who was also 'Great Chief of the Palace', Amenhotep-TT73 (Hat), who was also 'Veteran of the King', Thanuny-TT74 (TIII-TIV), Amenhotep-saes-TT75 (AII-TIV), Thenuna-TT76 (TIV), Amenemhab called Mahu-TT85 (TIII-AII), Menkheperesoneb-TT86 (TIII), Pehsukher called Thenunu-TT88 (AII), Amenmose-TT89 (AIII), Suemnut-TT92 (AII), Kenamun-TT93 (AII), Ramose called Amay-TT94 (TIII-AII), Mery-TT95 (AII), Sennefer-TT96 (AII), Amenemhet-TT97 (AII), Kaemheribsen-TT98 (AII), Sennefer-TT99 (TIII), Rekhmire-TT100 (TIII-AII) and User-TT131 (TI-TIII). Spatial connections can be made between TT63 and TT64, contemporary and adjacent to each other, with TT62 50m to the south, and TT67 a further 50m to the south. TT71, TT73, TT74, TT75, TT76 are all located in a line across the central upper slopes, while TT85 and TT86 lie adjacent to each other 100m to the south, with TT88 and TT89 adjacent to each other 50m to the north-west. TT92, TT93, TT94, TT95, TT96, TT97, TT98, TT99 and TT100 are all situated within 100m of each other in this south-western area of the necropolis. All of these tombs lie along the upper slope and into the south-west area, suggesting a possible connection between this title and tomb distribution. TT131 is the only tomb which is not spatially connected to those of any other 'Royal Seal-bearers'.

There were 11 'Fan-bearers': Ramose-who reused TT46 (AIII/IV); Sobekhotep-TT63 (TIV); Thenuna-TT76 (TIV); Ptahemhet-TT77 (TIV-AIII); Horemheb-TT78 (AII-AIII); Pehsukher called Thenunu-TT88 (AII); Suemnut-TT92 (AII); Kenamun-TT93 (AII); Ramose called Amay-TT94 (TIII-AII); Amenmose-TT118 (AIII); and Hekareshu-TT226 (AIII). These individuals were all buried within close proximity. Of their tombs, only TT76 and TT78 lie adjacent to each other at the centre of the upper slopes, with TT118 lying 40m away to the west, adjacent to TT77, which lay a short distance behind TT88. TT92 lies 100m to the south-west, while TT93 and TT94 lie a short distance to the south and east respectively. All of the aforementioned tombs lie along the northern and western perimeters of the populated area of Upper Qurna, with the exception of TT226, which was situated in a more central location, but still only 75m to the east of TT76. Only TT63 and TT46 are not located within 100m of another 'Royal Fan-bearer'.

There were 12 'Eyes...and Ears of the King' (or similar): Hepu-TT66 (TIV); Thanuny-TT74 (TIII-TIV); Ptahemhet-TT77 (TIV-AIII); Horemheb-TT78 (AII-AIII); Djehutynefer-TT80 (TIII-AII); Iamunedjem-TT84 (TIII-AII); Amenemhab called Mahu-TT85 (TIII-AII); Kenamun-TT93 (AII); Sennefer-TT96 (AII); Amenemhet-

TT97 (AII); Sennefer-TT99 (TIII); and Hekareshu-TT226 (AIII). All of these tombs lie within 100m (and in many cases much less) of one or more fellow holders of this title. Again, the central upper slopes and the south-western area hold the highest concentration of these tombs. There were ten 'Attendants' of the king: Thenuna-TT76 (TIV); Horemheb-TT78 (AII-AIII); Amenemhab called Mahu-TT85 (TIII-AII); Pehsukher called Thenunu-TT88 (AII); Nebamun-TT90 (TIV-AIII); Unknown-TT91 (TIV-AII); Suemnut-TT92 (AII); Kenamun-TT93 (AII); Rekhmire-TT100 (TIII-AII); and Djehutynefer-TT104 (TIIII). Their tombs, with the exception of TT104 which was located some distance to the east, are spread along the upper slopes and down into the south-western quadrant of this area, all within 100m of at least one other 'Royal Attendant'. There are also a number of 'King's Followers': Djehutynefer-TT80 (TIII-AII), Iamunedjem-TT84 (TIII-AII), among other royal titles, Pehsukher called Thenunu-TT85 (TIII-AII), among other royal titles, Suemnut-TT92 (AII), Rekhmire-TT100 (TIII-AII), Thanuro-TT101 (AII-TIV) and Paser-TT367 (AII). These individuals were all buried in this south-western quadrant, as with so many members of the royal administration, within 100m of at least one other 'King's Follower', except for TT101 which occupies a more central location.

There are some unique titles here too. There is only one: 'Overseer and Director of the Royal Tomb', Ineni-who reused TT81 (AI-Hat); 'Deputy of the King', Pehsukher called Thenunu-TT88 (AII); 'Standard Bearer of the Royal Ship', Nebamun-TT90 (TIV-AIII); and 'Overseer of Royal Ships' and 'Chief of the Stable' of the King, Suemnut-TT92 (AII). Other rarer titles included: 'Chief of the Courtiers of the Palace', Amenemhet-TT97 (AII) and Sennefer-TT99 (TIII); 'Royal Messenger', Sennefer-TT99 (TIII); 'Great Chief of the Palace', Senenmut-TT71 (Hat) and Menkheperesoneb-TT86 (TIII); and 'Overseer' and 'Scribe of the Fields of the Lord of the Two Lands', Menna-TT69 (AIII).

A significant number of the tombs belonging to the royal administration are located side by side along the highest slopes of Upper Qurna, and several more just slightly in front of this row of tombs, all orientated eastwards towards the cultivation and the river beyond. The dominance of this desirable location by members of the royal administration suggests that they had a certain degree of influence over obtaining the best sites to build their tomb. There is a significant cluster of roughly contemporary members of the royal administration located in the south-western corner (TT29, TT84, TT85, TT86, TT87, TT88, TT89, TT90, TT92, TT93, TT94 TT95, TT96, TT97, TT98, TT99, TT100 and TT367). While their titles are varied, the majority of them held office during the reign of Amenhotep II, reinforcing the idea that these men were colleagues who were also buried in the vicinity of each other. Another cluster lies towards the eastern edge of the area (TT21, TT43, TT62, TT65 and TT251). TT21 and TT65 are roughly contemporary, and these tombs and TT251 belonged to scribes. Two of this cluster date to Amenhotep II or Tuthmosis IV (TT21 and TT62), but there are no other clear links between them.

General Administration

There were 27 members of the general administration buried in Upper Qurna (see Figure 230). These individuals were some of the most important officials in the land. Seven tombs belong to 'Governors of the Town' and 'Viziers': Amenemopet called Pairy-TT29 (AII); Antefoker-TT60 (MK); User-who reused TT61, and built TT131 (TI-TIII); Hepu-TT66 (TIV); Amethu called Ahmose-TT83 (Ah-TIII); and Rekhmire-TT100 (TIII-AII). These Viziers were all buried within 100m of another Vizier, with the exception of TT131, which was the second tomb of User-TT61. The links between these tombs is explored further in Chapter 12. TT82 was reused by Amenemhet (Hat-TIII), who was the 'Steward' and 'Scribe of the Vizier', and also the 'Steward of Counting...' a number of things, and 'Overseer of Ploughed Lands'. He was buried within 100m of both User-TT61 and Amethu called Ahmose-TT83, both of whom he served.

A number of titles relate to the judiciary system, several of which occurred in conjunction with the title of 'Vizier'. These include three 'Overseers of the Law-Courts': Antefoker-TT60 (MK), User-who reused TT61 (TI-TIII), and Hepu-TT66 (TIV); the 'Chief Justice', Amethu called Ahmose-TT83 (Ah-TIII); a 'Judge', Ramose called Amay-TT94 (TIII/AII); 'Supreme Judge', Rekhmire-TT100 (TIII-AII), and User-TT131 (TI-TIII). TT60 and TT61 are adjacent to each other, with TT66 situated 100m to the east, and TT83 just 50m to the south. TT94 and TT100 are within 100m of each other, but neither they nor TT131 are within 100m of any other connected title holders.

There were six 'Overseers of the Granary/ies' buried here: Ramose-who reused TT46 (AIII-IV), Nebamun-TT65 (Hat), Menkheper(soneb)-TT79 (TIII-AII), Iamunedjem-TT84 (TIII-AII), Minnakht-TT87 (Hat-TIII), and Sennefer-TT99 (TIII). A cluster of four of these individuals can be seen in the south-western quadrant, where TT79, TT84, TT87 and TT99 are all located within 100m of each other. Only TT46 and TT65 do not fit this pattern. There were also seven 'Overseers of the Treasury' buried here: Sobekhotep-TT63 (TIV), Djehutynefer-TT80 (TIII-AII), Menkheperesoneb-TT86 (TIII), Kenamun-TT93 (AII), Amenemhet-TT97 (AII), Rekhmire-TT100 (TIII-AII) and User-TT131 (TI-TIII). All these tombs are located in the south-western quadrant,

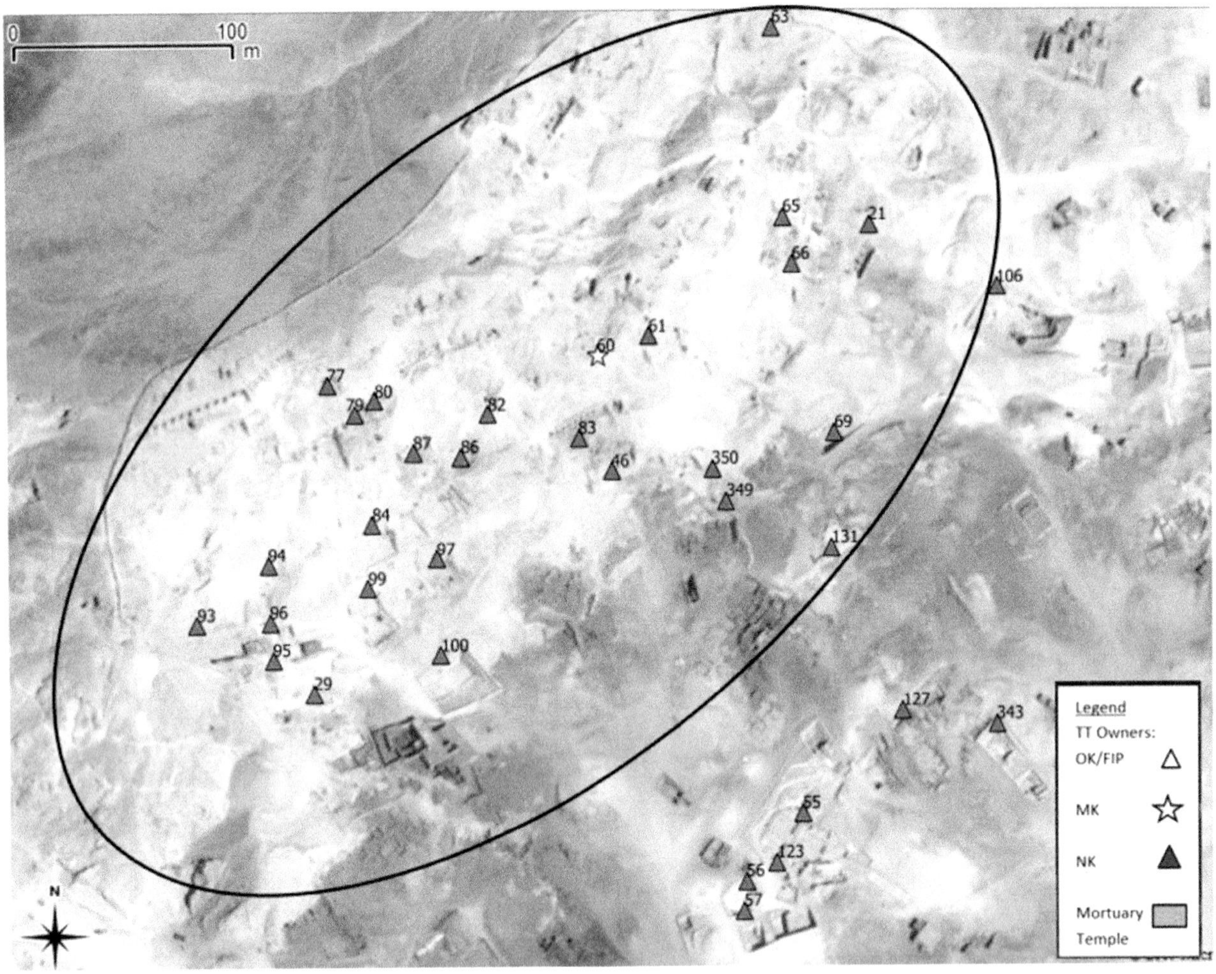

Figure 230: TTs of the General Administration in Upper Qurna (Author's own using QGIS)

with the exception of TT63 in the east, within at least 100m of the tomb of another 'Treasurer', except TT93 which is slightly further away.

There were a number of 'Overseers', 'Directors' and 'Chiefs' buried in Upper Qurna. The most important of these included: 'Overseer of the Overseers' (among other similar managerial titles), Kenamun-TT93 (AII); the 'Chief Overseer of Upper Egypt' and also 'Chief and Overseer of Singers', Mery-TT95 (AII); the 'Chief of the Whole Land' and also 'Overseer of the Storehouse', Amenemhet-TT97 (AII); and another 'Chief of the Whole Land' who was also the 'Chief of Craftsmen' and 'Director of Ceremonial Aprons', Rekhmire-TT100 (TIII-AII). All four of these roughly contemporary individuals were buried in the south-western corner, within 100m of each other. The 'Chief of the Overseers of Craftsmen', Menkheperesoneb-TT86 (TIII) was buried 100m to the north of the 'Chief of Craftsmen' Rekhmire-TT100. The 'Director of the Directors of Work', Ptahemhet-TT77 (TIV-AIII) was buried slightly to the north of this group. There were also a number of overseers of specific areas, some of which may have been connected to the Estate of Amun, but as this is not specified within the tomb they are included with the general administrative overseers. These included: 'Overseer of Calves' and 'Overseer of the Arable Land in the Record Department', Sennefer-TT96 (AII); 'Overseer of Fowlhouses', Tjay-TT349 (Hat); the 'Overseer of the Department of the Wine Cellar', Minnakht-TT87 (Hat-TIII); and the 'Overseer of... Livestock' and a number of additional managerial roles, not replicated elsewhere in this area, of which there are too many to list here, Sennefer-TT99 (TIII). There was also a 'Controller of Kilts', Amenemopet called Pairy-TT29 (AII).

There were three scribes, the 'Scribe of the Fields of the Lord of the Two Lands of Upper and Lower Egypt', Menna-TT69 (AIII), and the 'Scribe of Counting Bread', Unknown-TT350 (AII-TIV), and a 'Scribe' of unspecified affiliation, User-TT21 (TI-Hat). There was also an 'Overseer of Scribes', Rekhmire-TT100 (TIII-AII). Of these tombs, TT69 and TT350 are located 50m apart in the south-east of this area, while TT21 is 100m to the north of TT69. TT100 is not spatially connected to these other scribal tombs.

The majority of individuals with general administrative titles were buried in the central area of Upper Qurna, and in the south-western quadrant. They did not occupy the very highest positions on the slopes, as these seem to have been reserved for members of the royal administration in particular, but also some members of the priesthood and temple administration. There are some identifiable clusters of tombs within this group. All tombs securely attributed to Viziers in the Theban necropolis are located in Upper Qurna, with a defined cluster in the centre of the area, consisting of TT60, TT61 and TT83, and the pairing of TT100 and TT29. TT82, belonging to the 'Steward of the Vizier' is also located close to both TT83 and TT61, belonging to the Viziers he served. There is no cluster of tombs belonging to 'Overseers of the Granaries' but a father (Nakhtmin-TT87) and son (Menkheperresoneb-TT79) who held this title were buried in close proximity to each other, with the son buried just behind the father (Dornan 2003: 39-40). There is a small cluster of tombs (TT77, TT79 and TT80) in particularly close proximity. Of this cluster, TT80 and TT79 were contemporary, serving as 'Overseer of the Treasury' and Overseer of the Granaries' respectively. To the south of them, TT86 and TT87 were also adjacent to each other and contemporary, again serving as 'Overseer of the Treasury' and 'Overseer of Granaries' respectively. These two pairings suggest a desire for contemporary 'Treasurers' and 'Overseers of Granaries' to be buried close together at this time in the Eighteenth Dynasty. The contemporary TT84 and TT99, who were both 'Overseer of Granaries' are also located close to each other. There are other pairs of tombs situated in close proximity, TT83 and TT46, TT349 and TT350, and TT65 and TT66. There are no obvious links between these pairs of tombs. The high concentration of general administrators in the south-western quadrant is also interesting, as TT29, TT84, TT86, TT87, TT93, TT94, TT95, TT96, TT97, TT99 and TT100 are all situated in this area.

Local Administration

There were four members of the local administration buried here, of either Thebes or another region (see Figure 231). There were three 'Mayors', two were 'Mayor

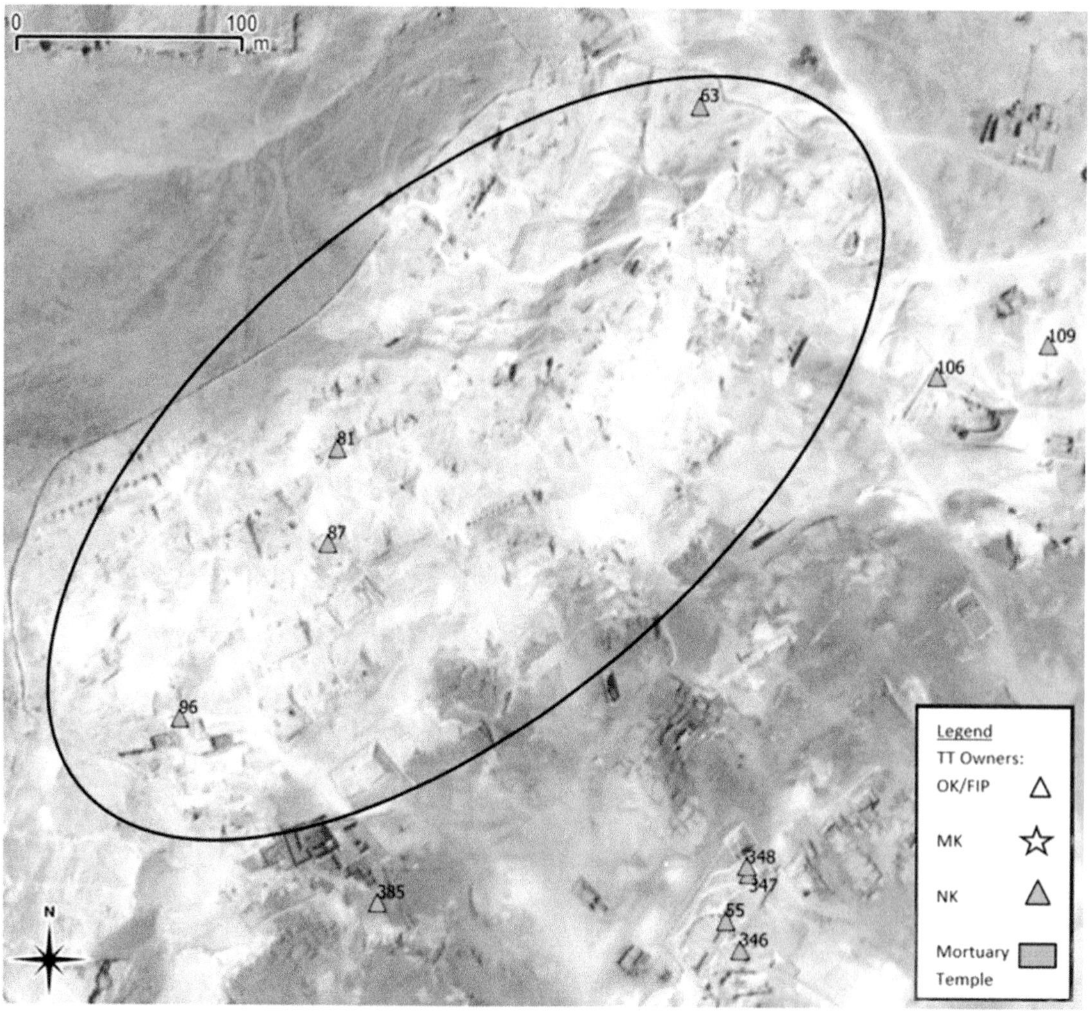

Figure 231: TTs of the Local Administration in Upper Qurna (Author's own using QGIS)

of the (Southern) City' – Thebes, Ineni-who reused TT81 (AI-Hat), and Sennefer-TT96 (AII), and another was 'Mayor' and 'Great One' of 'the Southern Lake' and of the 'Lake of Sobek', in the Fayum, Sobekhotep-TT63 (TIV). There was also an 'Overseer of Foreign Lands', Minnakht-TT87 (Hat-TIII). TT87 lies 30m south of the roughly contemporary TT81, but there are no further spatial connections between these tombs.

Military

There were 11 members of the military buried here, many of whom were also members of the royal administration (see Figure 232). There was an 'Overseer of the Army', who was also the 'Overseer of Army Scribes', 'Scribe of the Army' and 'Scribe of Recruits', Thanuny-TT74 (TIII-TIV). Others military scribes were the 'Scribe of the Army', Men-TT230 (Dyn 18), and the 'Overseer of all Royal Scribes in the Army' and 'Scribe of Recruits', Horemheb-TT78 (AII-AIII). All three military scribes were buried within 50m of each other in the central area of the upper slopes.

Horemheb-TT78 was also the 'Overseer of Horses', as were Minnakht-TT87 (Hat-TIII) and Unknown-TT91 (TIV-AIII). TT87 is located 100m to the south of TT78, but TT91 is located some distance to the west. There were two tombs belonging to 'Chief of the Stable', Suemnut-TT92 (AII) and Kenamun-TT93 (AII), while Suemnut-TT92 was also 'Overseer of Royal Ships', and Nebamun-TT90 (TIV-AIII) was the 'Commander of Royal Ships'. All three of these tombs are located along the western boundary of the area, within 100m of each other. There were two 'Deputies of the Army', Amenemhab called Mahu-TT85 (TIII-AII) and Pehsukher called Thenunu-TT88 (AII), who was also a 'Bowman', whose tombs were situated 50m apart. Four tombs were owned by 'Captains of Troops', Amenemhab called Mahu-TT85 (TIII-AII), Nebamun-TT90 (TIV-AIII), Unknown-TT91 (TIV-AIII), and Paser-TT367 (AII). All four of these tombs are located in the western area of Upper Qurna, with TT90, TT91 and TT367 within 50m of each other in the far west. Nebamun-TT90 and Unknown-TT91 were both also 'Chief of Medjay', and are located within 50m of each other on the upper western slopes.

All of these tombs are located in the western half of Upper Qurna. They are not in a definitive cluster but scattered fairly evenly throughout this area, with several identifiable clusters and pairings, often dating

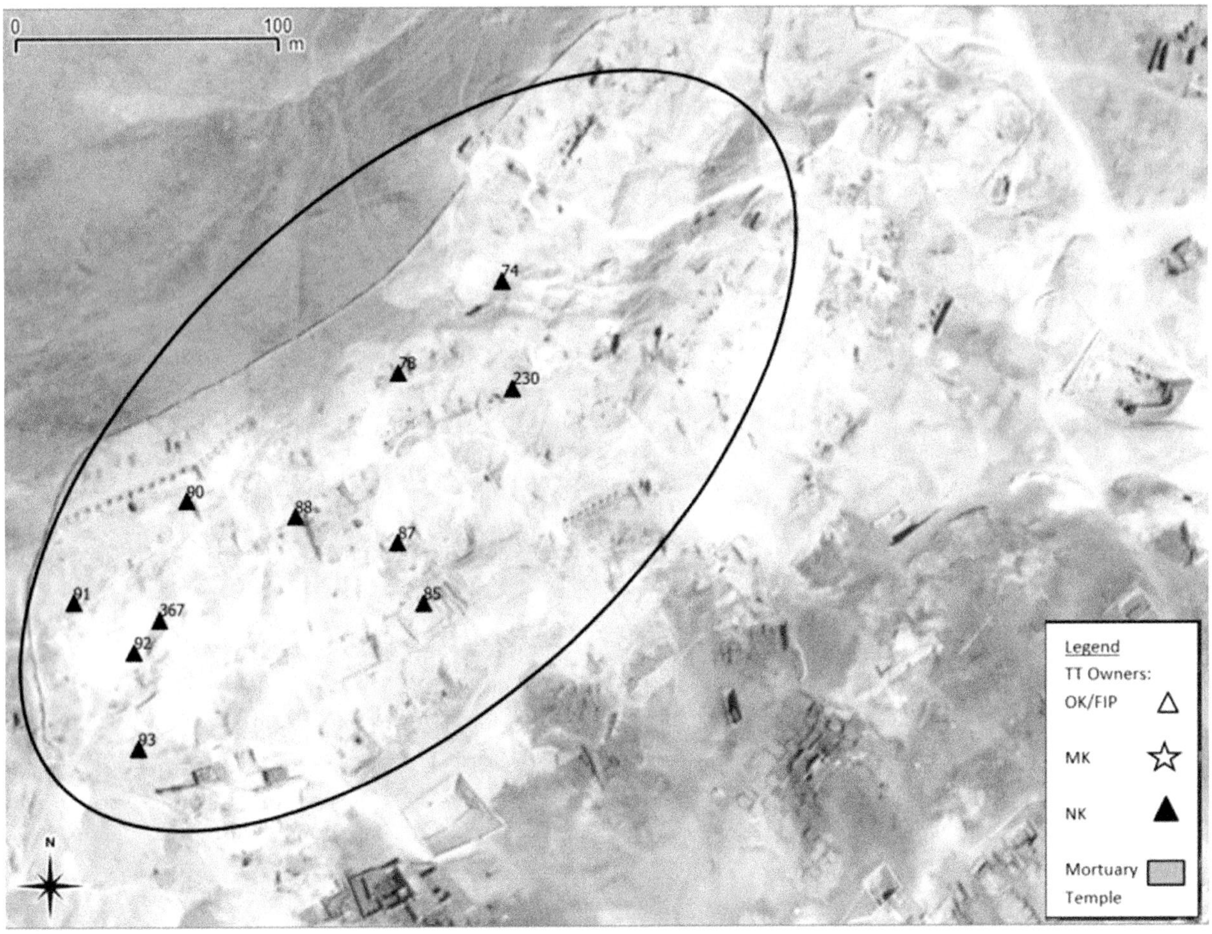

Figure 232: TTs of the Military in Upper Qurna (Author's own using QGIS)

to successive reigns so possibly represented individuals siting their tomb close to a predecessor and potential ancestor.

Unknown

Nine tombs were owned by individuals with unknown titles (TT58, TT70, TT81, TT82, TT115, TT119, TT227, TT229, and TT400), and one additional tomb was reused by an unknown individual TT87. TT58 and TT119 were also reused by unknown individuals (although TT58 was reused a third time by a known usurper).

Relationship between Tomb Owners / Tombs

Some of the familial relationships between tomb owners in Upper Qurna have already been discussed, such as the 'Overseers of the Granary', Nakhtmin-TT87, and Menkheperresoneb-TT79, his son and successor. It is worth noting that TT87 and TT79 are located adjacent to each other, and that Menkheperresoneb located a burial shaft in his courtyard that runs under his father's tomb, thus providing access to his burial chamber (Kampp 1996: 342). Two other family groups involve Viziers and are discussed further in Chapter 12. The largest of these groups was Amethu called Ahmose-TT83, his son and successor User-TT61 and TT131, another son Amenmose-TT228 (located in Lower Qurna), his grandson Rekhmire-TT100, who succeeded User, and his brother-in-law, Ineni-TT81 (Dornan 2003: 37-39). The other was the family of Amenemopet called Pairy-TT29, his brother (or cousin– Shirley 2014: 182) Sennefer-TT96, and their father Ahmose called Humay-TT224 (buried in Lower Qurna). There is also the case of Senenmut-TT71, and Senamun-TT252, who were believed to be brothers on the basis of Senamun and his mother Senemiah depicted receiving offerings in TT71. This has now been disproved, but it is still possible that they were related in some way (Dorman 1988: 165-166; Shirley 2014: 182). TT71 and TT252 are located 80m apart at the northern tip of Upper Qurna.

Shared Courtyards

There are no tombs with shared courtyards in Upper Qurna. This could be as a result of the contoured nature of the landscape, making it unsuitable for constructing large flat courtyards. Shared courtyards were particularly utilised by Ramesside burials, often added onto an earlier courtyard. The lack of space in Upper Qurna meant there was no room left for later burials to exploit a pre-existing courtyard, so may be a reason why there are fewer Ramesside burials.

Tomb Reuse

13 tombs were reused in Upper Qurna during the New Kingdom (see Figure 233 and Table 38). Only one of these tombs was reused more than once (TT58). Four of the reused tombs were built in the Middle Kingdom (TT61, TT81, TT82 and TT119), and nine were built in the Eighteenth Dynasty (one of these possibly built as early as the late Seventeenth Dynasty– TT46). The dates of reuse range from the early Eighteenth Dynasty, right through until the end of the Twentieth Dynasty. Seven tombs were reused in the Eighteenth Dynasty, with incidences of reuse most common during the reigns of Hatshepsut and Tuthmosis III (some less clearly dated but most likely to fit this pattern), when four Middle Kingdom tombs on the upper slopes were reused (TT61, TT81, TT82 and TT119), and during the reign of Amenhotep III when two tombs were reused (TT46 and TT77). TT87 could also potentially fit this pattern. The only exception was TT84 on the upper slopes, built in either the reign of Tuthmosis III or Amenhotep II, and reused soon after its construction in the reign of Amenhotep II.

The other five reused tombs were built during the Eighteenth Dynasty and reused (one twice) after the Dynasty ended. Only two cases of reuse can be securely dated to a specific reign, one to Ramesses II (TT54) and one to Ramesses IX (TT65). The reuse of the remaining tombs cannot be clearly dated to a specific reign, with one datable only to the Nineteenth Dynasty (TT58) and three to the Twentieth Dynasty (TT58 –second reuse, TT68 and TT70 – which could even date to the Twenty-First Dynasty).

The pattern of frequency of reuse during the Eighteenth Dynasty compared to other areas of the necropolis is interesting as the prevalence of new tombs being constructed in Upper Qurna indicates that this was a prosperous period and plenty of space remained on these upper slopes. Where no familial or occupational connection between the tomb owners can be established it is possible that these reused tombs were either considered to be in a particularly good position with a direct sightline to a royal mortuary temple or processional route, or that the tomb itself was coveted by the individual who reused it. The two reused during the Nineteenth Dynasty, particularly TT54 reused during the reign of Ramesses II when a number of new tombs were still being built, seem likely to have been as a result of lack of space for new tomb-building on these desirable upper slopes. The four cases of reuse during the Twentieth Dynasty are to be expected due to the decline in the number of new tombs being built, and a general lack of capability to build new tombs. These individual cases will be analysed further below.

Most of these reused tombs form a loose cluster in the central area of the highest slopes, within 100m of at least one of these Middle Kingdom tombs, with only TT54 found lower down, just over 100m away from the closest Middle Kingdom tomb.

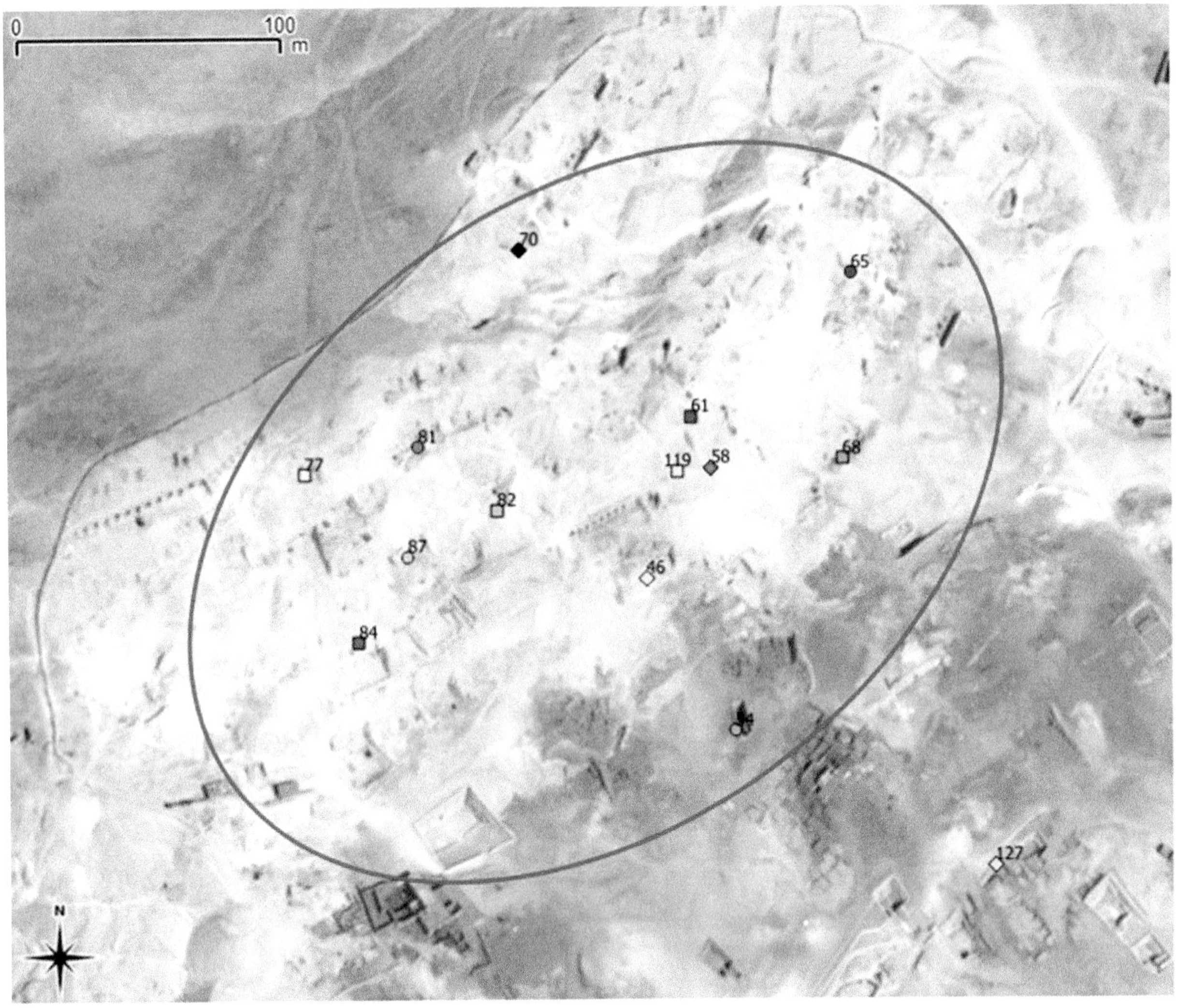

Figure 233: Reused TTs in Upper Qurna at the end of the New Kingdom (shown by date of first reuse) (Author's own using QGIS)

Table 38: Reused tombs in Upper Qurna

TT	Original Date	Date of Reuse
TT46	End Dyn 17-early Dyn 18	AIII-AIV
TT54	AIII	RII
TT58	AIII	Dyn 19 & Dyn 20
TT61	MK	TI-TIII
TT65	Hat	RIX
TT68	AIII	Dyn 20
TT70	Dyn 18 - AIII	Dyn 20/21
TT77	TIV-AIII	AIII
TT81	MK	Ah-Hat
TT82	MK	Hat-TIII
TT84	TIII-AII	AII
TT87	Hat-TIII	TIV-end Dyn18
TT119	MK	Hat-TIII

The original occupants of the four reused Middle Kingdom tombs (TT61, TT81, TT82 and TT119) are unknown so any potential link cannot be proven. TT61 was reused by the 'Vizier' User and is located close to another Middle Kingdom 'Vizier', Antefoker-TT60, suggesting a potential occupation for the original tomb owner. TT81 was reused by Ineni, an important member of the Amun administration and the 'Mayor' of Thebes, while TT82 was reused by Amenemhet, another member of this temple administration and the 'Steward of the Vizier' User. The usurper of TT119 is unknown. The pattern of reuse of Middle Kingdom tombs in the early Eighteenth Dynasty, particularly during the reigns of Hatshepsut and Tuthmosis III, is discussed in more detail in Chapter 4. No other tombs in Upper Qurna are reused during this period.

Of the other Eighteenth Dynasty usurpations, the original occupant of TT46 is unknown, but it was reused by Ramose, who held a range of general, temple and royal administrative titles. This reuse might be explained as a result of fewer tombs being built at Thebes during the Amarna Period. Both TT77 and TT84 were reused in the same or following reign as that in which they were built, which makes a connection between the tomb owners more likely as they were still within living memory. Both owners of TT77 were connected to the royal administration but have no common titles. There is no clear link between the two owners of TT84 from the titles within the tomb, as the original owner Iamunedjem was a member of the royal administration, and the usurper was the HPA Mery, who was also the owner of TT95. Within TT95, Mery listed a number of administrative and priestly roles within the Estate of Amun, but also that of 'Royal Seal-bearer', providing a connection with the royal administration. TT95 also shows that Mery held an equivalent role to Iamunedjem as 'Overseer of the Granary', but within the Estate of Amun, suggesting another potential link. TT87 may potentially have been reused soon after its construction. Its original owner, Minnakht, listed a number of general, temple and royal administrative titles, but its second occupant is unknown. While not classed as a reuse, TT122 contains chapels dating to the same reign belonging to an individual with the same title as the tomb owner, 'Overseer of the Storehouse of Amun', so is more likely to have been a consensual sharing of the same tomb.

The other cases of reuse date to the Ramesside Period when there was very little space available in Upper Qurna to build new tombs. Both individuals buried in TT54 belonged to the temple administration but served different deities and held different titles. TT58 was reused twice, in both the Nineteenth and Twentieth Dynasties. The titles of the first two occupants are unknown, but the final owner, Amenemonet, was the

Figure 234: The façade of TT65 (Author's own)

'Overseer of the Priests of Amun' and was buried there with his father. Both occupants of TT65 were scribes but with different affiliations. The reuse and redesigning of TT65 (see Figure 234) may have been an example of the Twentieth Dynasty tradition of converting an abandoned tomb into a sacred space (Bács 2011: 11-18). Both occupants of TT68 were members of the Amun priesthood, and as the original occupant was the HPA, this could be an attempt by the later '*wꜥb* priest' to associate himself with an influential predecessor. The original occupant of TT70 is unknown, and it is reused by Amenmose, an 'Overseer' of temple craftsmen.

There is a definite pattern of the reuse of Middle Kingdom tombs between the reigns of Hatshepsut and Tuthmosis III. There does not seen to be any general pattern between the dates of usurpations, the titles of occupants, or the locations of the usurped tombs, but rather a case of lack of space necessitating the reuse of existing tombs.

Outlying Tomb

(See Appendix 2)

In an area to the north of Upper Qurna lies TT103 (see Figure 235). This tomb is 110m away from its nearest neighbour in Upper Qurna (see Chapter 3).

Conclusions

There was a greater occurrence of important titles among the tomb owners of Upper Qurna than anywhere else in the necropolis, showing that this area was the most prestigious in which to be buried, particularly in the Eighteenth Dynasty from the reign of Hatshepsut onwards. There was a greater proportion of high officials such as 'Viziers', 'High Priests of Amun', 'Overseers of the Granary', 'Treasurers' and 'Chief Stewards' buried here than in any other area of the necropolis. The vast majority of these important officials were buried here

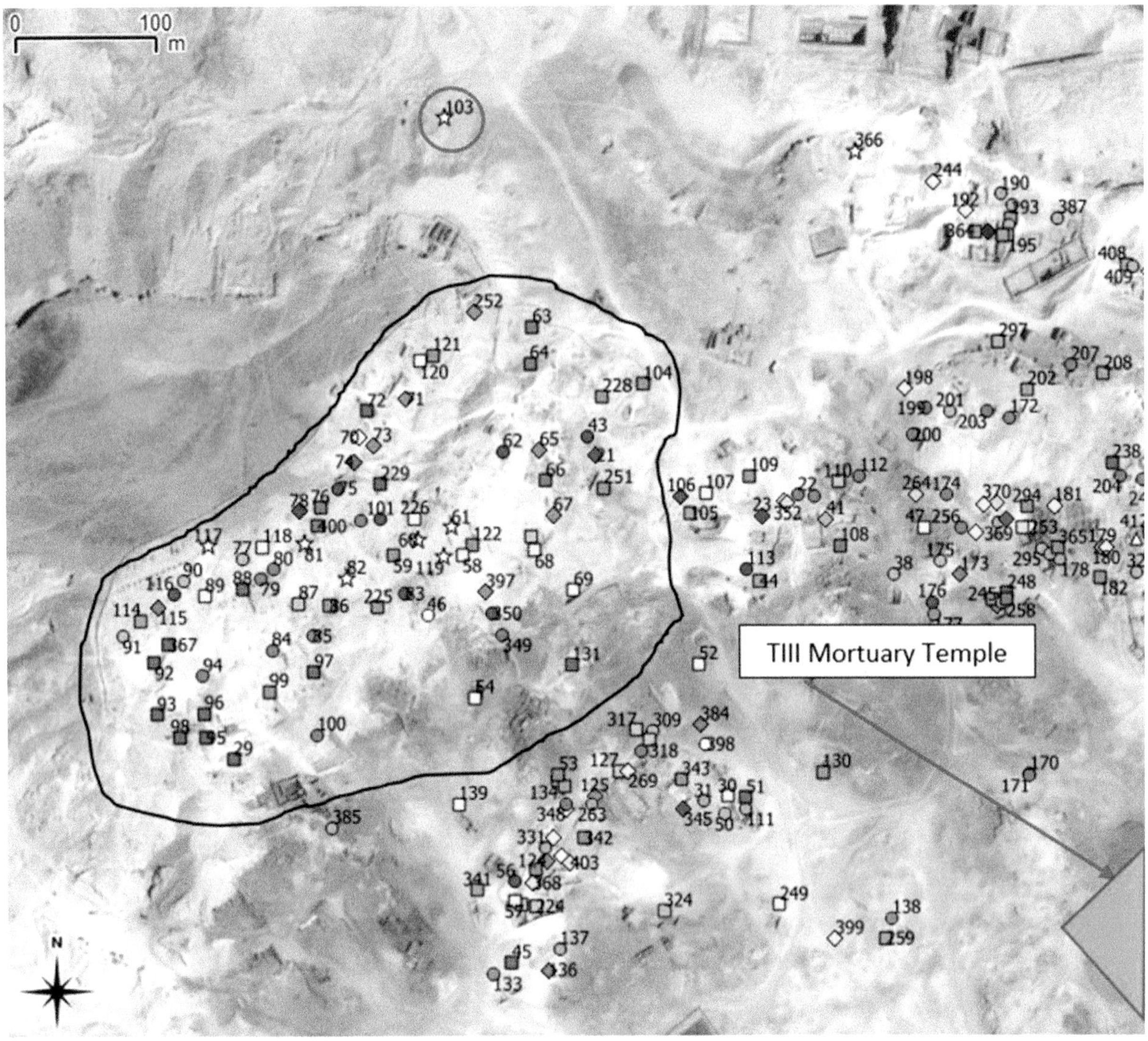

Figure 235: Upper Qurna showing location of outlying TT103 (Author's own using QGIS)

during the Eighteenth Dynasty, after which the upper slopes became too crowded. This area was chosen for a combination of reasons, including the presence of important Middle Kingdom tombs, views towards Deir el-Bahri and the row of royal mortuary temples to the east, and thus the processional route of the BFV. These views towards Deir el-Bahri and the proximity to Middle Kingdom tombs also explain the high proportion of tombs belonging to officials dating to the reigns of Hatshepsut and Tuthmosis III.

All four tombs belonging to the 'High Priests', '*wʿb*' priest and 'Temple Steward' who worked at Henketankh (TT72, TT79, TT121 and TT226) are located high on the upper slopes orientated towards the temple itself (see Figure 235), confirming the idea of a link between tomb distribution and the location of royal mortuary temples. A prime location on the upper slopes overlooking the temple was clearly preferred to a lower site in closer proximity to the temple (see Figure 236).

The most striking clustering of tombs is that of those dating to the reign of Amenhotep II, in the south-western corner of the upper slopes (see Figure 237). The reason for the choice of this area is again linked to the royal mortuary temples, as this area commands views over the temples of Tuthmosis III and most importantly Amenhotep II (see Figures 238 and 239), and the associated processional route. The tombs are also visible from the temples themselves (see Figure 240).

Figure 236: The Qurna mortuary temple of Tuthmosis III (Author's own)

Figure 237: The 'Amenhotep II Quarter' in the south-western corner of Upper Qurna (Author's own)

Figure 238: View from south-western corner of Upper Qurna outside TT96 looking north-east - indicating approximate location of Henketankh (Author's own)

Figure 239: View from the 'Amenhotep II Quarter' overlooking the Amenhotep II temple (Author's own)

Figure 240: View from the Amenhotep II temple of the 'Amenhotep II Quarter' in Upper Qurna (Author's own)

Figure 241: View from south-western corner of Upper Qurna indicating the Amenhotep III temple (Author's own)

Figure 242: The northern cliff-face of Upper Qurna (Author's own)

Lower Qurna

(See Appendix 12)

Location

The slopes of Lower Qurna are bordered by el-Khokha to the north-east, and the row of royal mortuary temples to the south (see Figure 243). The lower slopes have a gentler gradient than the upper slopes. Tombs in this area are located between 80m and 120m above sea level, with the majority located between 90m and 100m above sea level. The flood plain begins at 80m above sea level in this area (see Figures 244 and 245).

Date of Use

Lower Qurna contain 48 New Kingdom tombs and was in use throughout the New Kingdom (see Table 39). The earliest tomb dates to the late Seventeenth or early Eighteenth Dynasty (TT39), while 25 tombs date to the Eighteenth Dynasty (TT30, TT45, TT50, TT52, TT53, TT55, TT56, TT57, TT102, TT123, TT124, TT125, TT127, TT129, TT130, TT139, TT224, TT249, TT317, TT318, TT342, TT343, TT345, TT346 and TT348). TT324 dates to either the late Eighteenth or early Nineteenth Dynasty, while a further 11 tombs date to the Nineteenth Dynasty (TT31, TT51, TT111, TT133, TT136, TT137, TT138, TT263, TT331, TT384 and TT385). Five tombs are datable to the Nineteenth or Twentieth Dynasty (TT269, TT347, TT368, TT399 and TT403), while TT309 can only be dated to between the Nineteenth and Twenty First Dynasty. Four tombs date to the Twentieth Dynasty (TT134, TT135, TT259 and TT341). More than half of the New Kingdom tombs in Lower Qurna were built during the Eighteenth Dynasty, with the fewest built during the Twentieth Dynasty, supporting the idea that this area had had the best locations built upon, forcing later New Kingdom burials to find alternative sites as this area was becoming a less viable option for rock-cut tombs as a result of lack of space.

Only tombs dated to the Eighteenth or Nineteenth Dynasty are dated to a specific reign or reigns. The lower slopes do not show clear periods of popularity as the upper slopes did, but rather steady usage throughout the New Kingdom. From this range of dates it is clear that the lower slopes of Qurna were most popular during the Eighteenth Dynasty, and the reigns of Hatshepsut and Tuthmosis III in particular. The area had a slight resurgence during the reign of Amenhotep III, when three tombs were built in addition to the usurpation of TT102, but as the reigns of these kings were longer than the intervening rulers, this distribution may be as a result of the length of their reigns rather than any other factor.

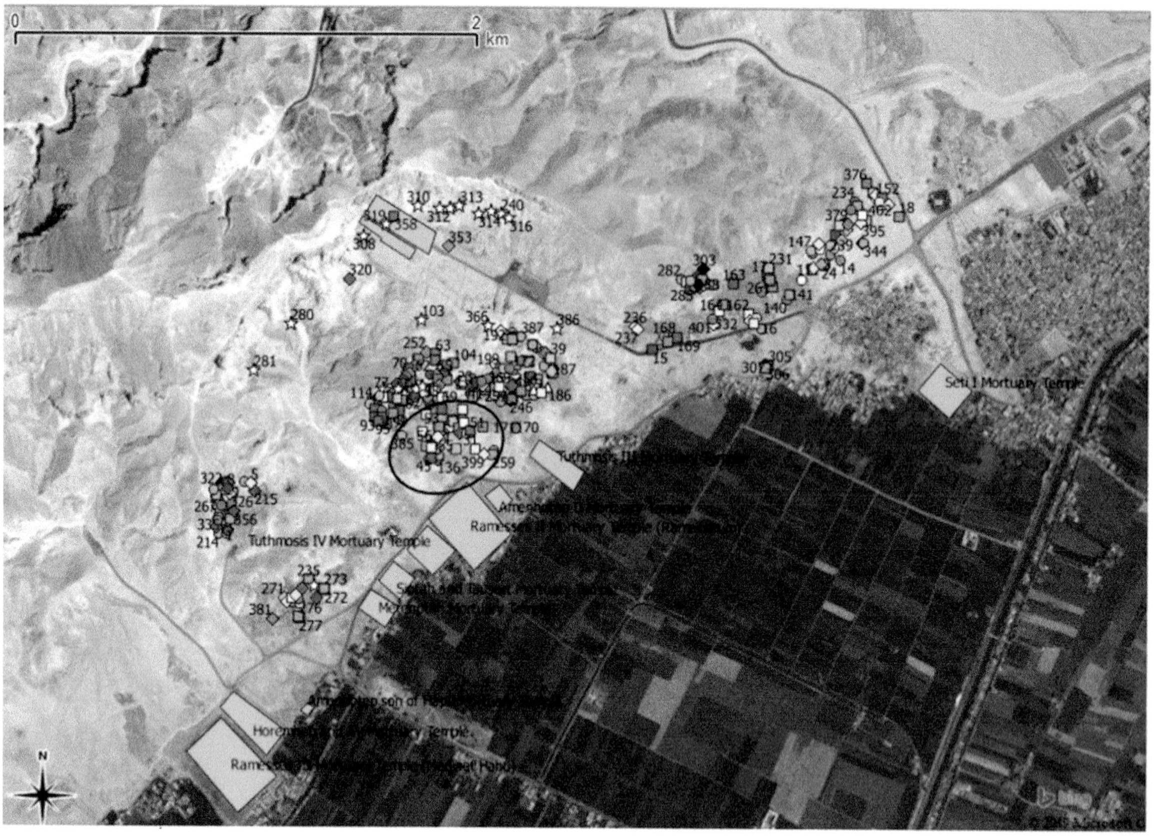

Figure 243: Location of Lower Qurna within the Theban Necropolis (Author's own using QGIS)

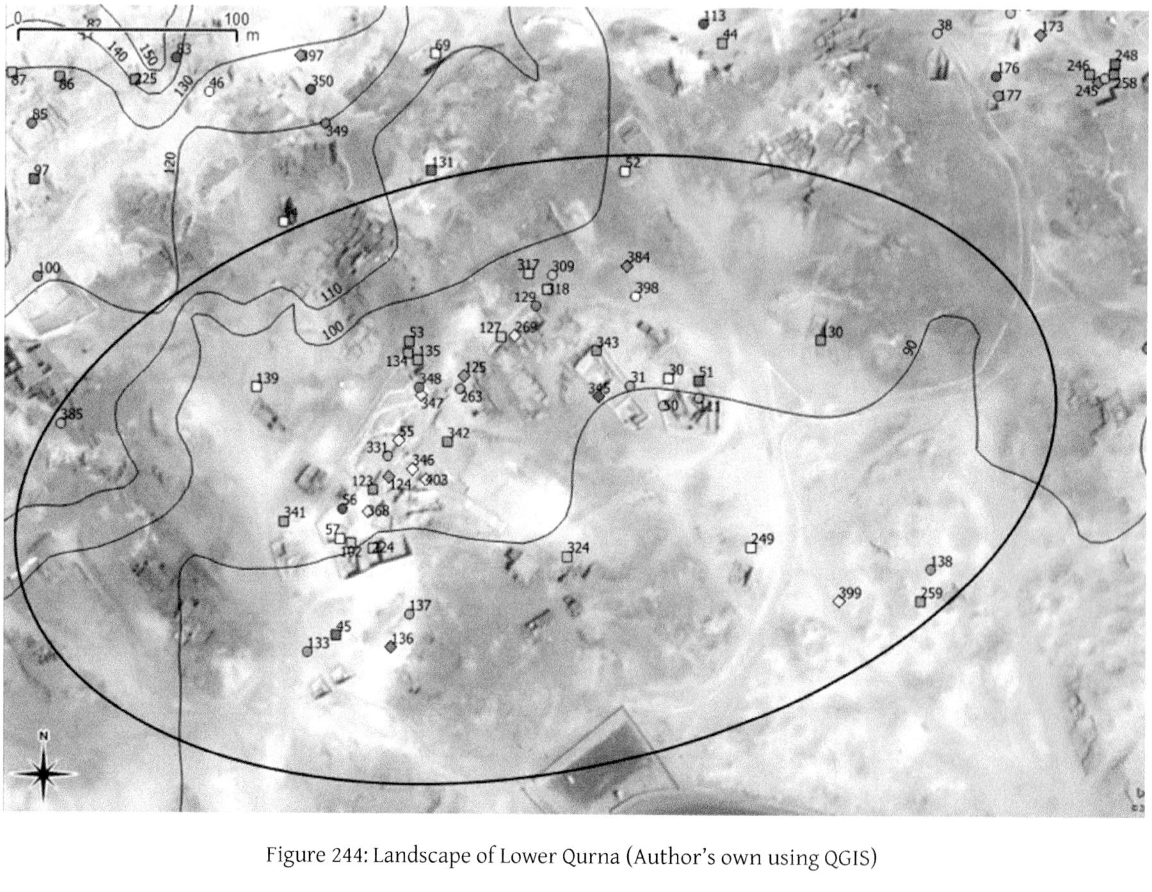

Figure 244: Landscape of Lower Qurna (Author's own using QGIS)

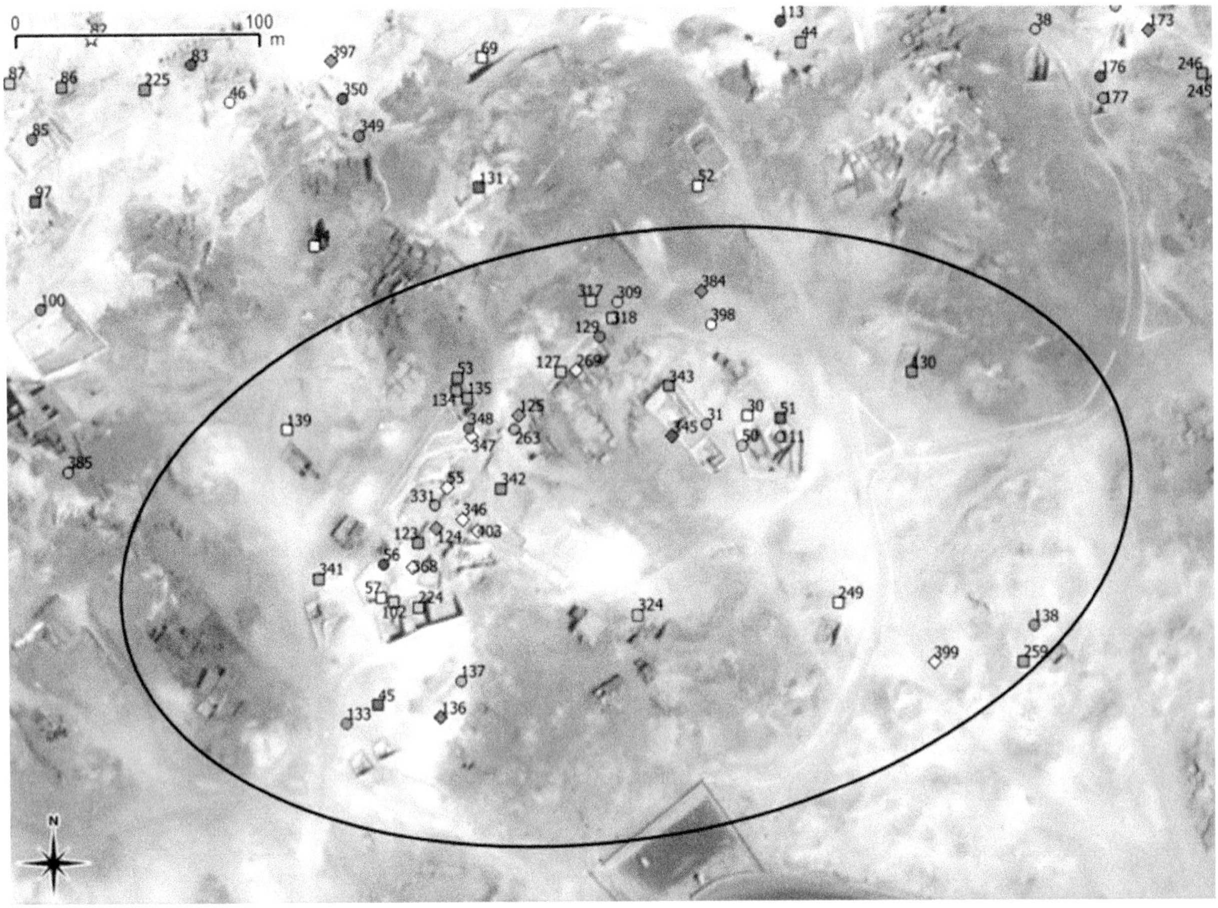

Figure 245: TTs in Lower Qurna (Author's own using QGIS)

Of the 11 Nineteenth Dynasty tombs, eight date to the lengthy reign of Ramesses II (TT31, TT111, TT133, TT137, TT138, TT263, TT331 and TT385). This suggests that this area was particularly popular during this reign, possibly as a result of its proximity to the Ramesseum. The other two Nineteenth Dynasty tombs are not datable to a specific reign (TT136 and TT384). A number of tombs are datable only to the Ramesside Period (TT347, TT368, TT399 and TT403), between the Nineteenth and Twenty First Dynasties (TT309), or to the Twentieth Dynasty (TT134, TT135, TT259 and TT341), and cannot be dated to a specific reign.

It is not possible to accurately analyse any distributional patterns by date for the majority of Nineteenth and Twentieth Dynasty tombs due to the lack of precise dating. From those tombs that can be dated, the evidence suggests that the highest frequency of tombs were built in this area during the longest reign, that of Ramesses II. These tombs are arranged throughout the centre of the area, but do not form an obvious cluster

Occupation of Tomb Owners

(See Table 40)

Priesthood

16 priests were buried here, some holding multiple priestly titles and titles within other occupational groups (see Figure 246). There were four 'High Priests' buried here, none of whom are 'High Priests of Amun'. Three were the 'High Priest of Montu', Khonsu called To-TT31 (RII), Hatiay-TT324 (Ay-SI), who was also 'High Priest of Sobek' and 'Overseer of Priests of all the Gods', and Penne called Sunero-TT331 (RII). Userhet called Neferhebef-TT51 (RI-SI) was 'High Priest of the royal *ka*' of Tuthmosis I, while Khonsu called To-TT31 (RII) held the title 'High Priest' of Tuthmosis III. All four of these High Priests were buried here in the late Eighteenth or early Nineteenth Dynasty, when the upper slopes were becoming overcrowded with tombs. Khonsu called To-TT31 and Userhet called Neferhebef-TT51 were relatively close in date and both held titles associated with royal mortuary temples. They were located in close proximity, with only one earlier tomb, TT30, lying between them, whose original owner is unknown, but

Table 39: Lower Qurna tombs distributed by most likely date

Date	No. of Tombs	Tombs
Late Dyn 17/ early 18	*	TT398
Dyn 18	*	TT348
Dyn 18 - AIII	*	TT346
TI – Hat	*	TT345
Hat	**	TT124, TT125
Hat / TIII	*****	TT102, TT127, TT224, TT317, TT318
TIII	*****	TT53, TT123, TT130, TT342, TT343
TIII/ AII	*	TT129
AII	*	TT45
AII / TIV	*	TT56
TIV / AIII	*	TT52
AIII	****	TT30, TT57, TT139, TT249
AIII / AIV	*	TT55
Ay -SI	*	TT324
Hor	*	TT50
Dyn 19	**	TT136, TT384
RI / SI	*	TT51
RII	********	TT31, TT111, TT133, TT137, TT138, TT263, TT331, TT385
Ram	****	TT347, TT368, TT399, TT403
Dyn 19 - 21	*	TT309
Dyn 20	****	TT134, TT135, TT259, TT341

Table 40: Lower Qurna TTs distributed by occupational group

Occupational Group	No. of Tombs	Tombs
Priesthood	*************	TT31, TT50, TT51, TT55, TT57, TT111 (1), TT127 (2), TT134, TT135, TT139, TT259, TT324, TT331, TT345, TT384
Temple Administration	************* **********	TT30 (2), TT31, TT45 (1 & 2), TT52, TT53, TT56, TT111 (1), TT123, TT125, TT133, TT137, TT138, TT224, TT249, TT259, TT263, TT317, TT318, TT324, TT331, TT341, TT368, TT385, TT403
Royal Admin	************	TT55, TT56, TT57, TT102(2), TT123, TT124, TT125, TT127(1), TT133, TT136, TT137, TT342, TT343, TT346(2), TT348(1), TT398, TT403
General Admin	****	TT55, TT56, TT57, TT123, TT127 (1 & 2), TT343,
Local Admin	*******	TT55, TT130, TT343, TT346(1), TT347, TT348(1), TT385
Military	*	TT346(1)
Unknown	***	TT129, TT269, TT309, TT399

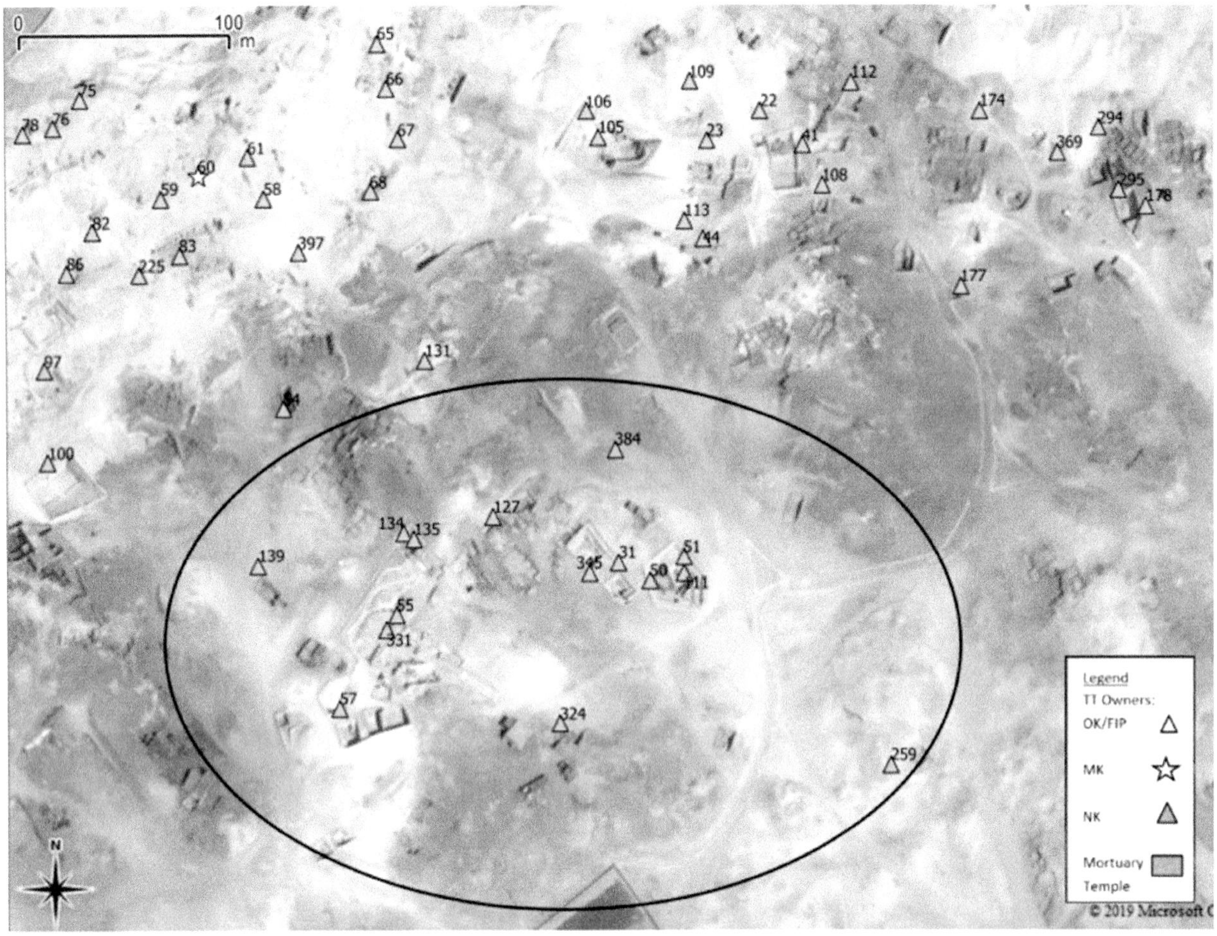

Figure 246: TTs of Priests in Lower Qurna (Author's own using QGIS)

could potentially have also been connected to this royal mortuary cult. These factors suggest a deliberate attempt by the owners of TT31 and TT51 to build these tombs close together. These tombs form part of a cluster, which includes two other tombs owned by priests, Neferhotep-TT50 (Hor) and Amenwahsu-TT111 (RII), who shared a courtyard with TT51. Another tomb in this cluster, Amenhotep-TT345 (TI-Hat) belonged to the eldest son of Tuthmosis I, who was also a '*wꜥb* priest'. It seems significant that Userhet called Neferhebef-TT51, the 'High Priest' of the *ka* of Tuthmosis I, built his tomb close to that of the eldest son of the same king. The three tombs of the three 'High Priests of Montu' are similar in date and lie within 100m of another but do not form a distinct group. TT324 is one of the southernmost tombs in the area, occupying an isolated position at the bottom of the lower slopes. TT31 and TT331 are dated to the same reign and are at the same altitude but are over 100m apart.

There were three '*ḥm-nṯr*' priests buried on these lower slopes. Ramose-TT55 (AIII-AIV) served Maat and was also 'Chief of Secrets of the Two Cobra Goddesses', Khaemhet called Mahu-TT57 (AIII) served Anubis, and also held the title 'Chief of Secrets of the Chest of Anubis', while Thauenany called Any-TT134 (Dyn 20) served 'Amenhotep who Rows on the Water of Amun'. All three of these individuals were buried within 100m of each other, at the western end of the most populated central area of Lower Qurna. TT134 is located adjacent to the tomb of the contemporary Bakenamun-TT135 (Dyn 20), who was a '*wꜥb* priest of Amun'. TT57 is located directly behind TT102 (Hat-TIII) belonging to an unknown occupant, and close to Ahmose called Humay-TT224 (Hat-TIII), who was 'Steward' to the God's Wife.

There were seven '*wꜥb* priests' buried in Lower Qurna, including a '*wꜥb* priest' of Sekhmet, Amenwahsu-TT111 (RII), a '*wꜥb* priest in front of Amun', Bakenamun-TT135 (Dyn 20), and a '*wꜥb* priest' in the Ramesseum, who also appears to have been a priest of the form of Amun of the Ramesseum, 'Amun-United-with Thebes', Nebmehyt-TT384 (Dyn 19). The other four '*wꜥb* priests' were of unspecified deities, including Pairy-who reused TT127 (Ram), Hori-TT259 (Dyn 20), whose other administrative titles related to Amun, Amenhotep-TT345 (TI-Hat), and Pairy-TT139 (AIII), who was '*wꜥb* priest in front'. None

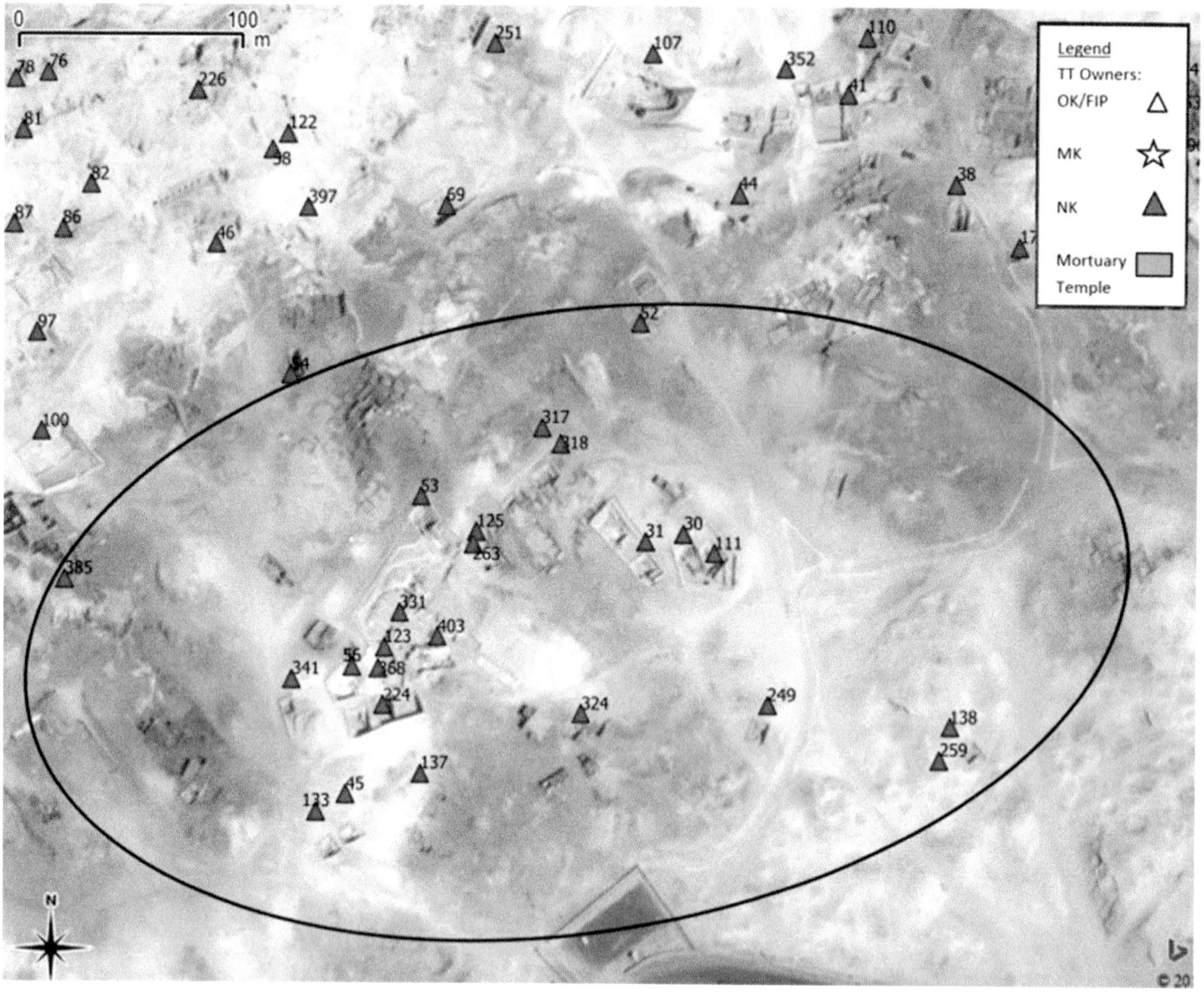

Figure 247: TTs of the Temple Administration in Lower Qurna (Author's own using QGIS)

of these tombs are located in close proximity to any other *wꜥb* priest. They are spread across Lower Qurna with no obvious spatial connection to the tomb of any other priest, with the exception of TT111, TT135 and TT345 (see above).

Other priests included a '*sm* priest' of unspecified deity, Ramose-TT55 (AIII-AIV), but his other titles relate to Maat and the two cobra goddesses; and a 'Divine Father of Amun', Neferhotep-TT50 (Hor) (see above for the spatial connections of these tombs). More unusual priestly titles here included: a 'Festival Leader of all the Gods', Amenwahsu-TT111 (RII); two 'Overseers of the Priests', of 'all the Gods', Hatiay-TT324 (Ay-SI), and of 'Upper and Lower Egypt', Ramose-TT55 (AIII/IV). TT55 is adjacent to Penne called Sunero-TT331 (RII), who was 'High Priest of Montu', thus two high-ranking priests were buried adjacent to each other in a shared courtyard (see below). None of these other tombs are spatially connected to those of any other priests.

These priests served a range of deities, including Amun (TT50, TT135, TT341 and TT384), Montu (TT31, TT324, and TT331), Maat (TT55), Anubis (TT57), Sekhmet (TT111), Sobek (TT324), the two cobra goddesses (TT55), and the royal mortuary cults of Ramesses II (TT384), Tuthmosis I (TT51), Tuthmosis III (TT31), and Amenhotep I (TT134). There is no spatial connection between the tombs of priests serving specific deities.

Temple Administration

There were 25 members of the temple administration buried here (including two who reused existing tombs) (see Figure 247). The majority were connected to the Estate of Amun (the usurper of TT30, TT45– both tomb owners, TT52, TT53, TT56, TT111, TT123, TT125, TT133, TT137, TT138, TT139, TT259, TT263, TT317, TT318, TT341, TT368 and TT385) while others were employed by the Ramesseum in particular whilst still connected to the Estate of Amun (TT133, TT138, TT263 and TT341). TT133 and TT341 are both located within 100m of each other to the west of the main group of tombs in this area, but all these four tombs do not form a distinct group. There are several connections between tombs belonging to employees of the Estate of Amun, but they do not form a distinct group either.

These individuals served the Estate of Amun in a number of capacities. Several individuals were 'Scribes': '...of the Treasury of Amun', Khonsumose-TT30 (Dyn 20); '... of the offering table of the HPA Mery', Djehuty–TT45 (AIII); '...of the Divine Records of Amun', Amenwahsu-TT111 (RII); '...in all the Monuments of Amun', Hori-TT259 (Dyn 20); '...of the Storehouse (of) Amun-united-with Thebes' (the Ramesseum), Piay-TT263 (RII); and '...of Counting the Corn in the Granary of the Divine Offerings of Amun', Djehutynefer-TT317 (Hat-TIII). TT30 and TT111 are located in close proximity (see above), while TT263 and TT317 are also located within 100m of them and each other. There was also a 'Scribe of the Divine Offerings' in the Estate of Montu, Hatiay-TT324 (Ay-SI) and a 'Temple Scribe' at an unidentified temple Merymaat-TT403 (Ram), neither of whose tombs are in close proximity to other temple scribes.

Two further individuals buried here were connected with the temple's granary, as they both held the title 'Overseer of the Granary of Amun', Amenemhet-TT123 (TIII), and Hunefer-TT385 (RII), but their tombs are not located in close proximity to each other or to the Granary Scribe Djehutynefer-TT317 (see above). Amenemhet-TT123 is adjacent to the 'Overseer of the Cattle of Amun', Userhet-TT56 (AII-TIV), which is also relatively close in date, suggesting a potential connection between these individuals. There are two Eighteenth Dynasty stewards of important temple officials, the 'Steward of the High Priest of Amun', Djehuty-TT45 (AII), and the 'Steward of the God's Wife', Ahmose called Humay-TT224 (Hat-TIII). These tombs are both situated in the south-eastern quadrant on the flattest area of the slopes, within 50m of each other. In addition, Djehuty-TT45, there are two other overseers buried here, the 'Chief of the Makers of Linen in the Estate of Amun', Djehutemhab–who reused TT45 (Dyn 20), and the 'Chief of the Weavers' in the Ramesseum, Neferrenopet-TT133 (RII). These tombs are adjacent to each other, which together with the similarity of their titles could perhaps indicate a link, possibly Djehutemhab-TT45 was a descendant of Neferrenopet-TT133.

Less common titles included an 'Astronomer of Amun', Nakht-TT52 (AIII) and an 'Acolyte of Amun', Amenemhat-TT53 (TIII), the 'Overseer of the Administrative District of Amun', Duaerneheh-TT125 (Hat), 'and Chief of Works...in every Monument of Amun', Mose-TT137 (RII). Of these tombs, TT53 is located adjacent to two Twentieth Dynasty priests, Thauenany called Any-TT134 and Bakenamun-TT135, while TT125 is situated adjacent to a later 'Scribe' of the Ramesseum, Piay-TT263 (RII). The difference in date and titles here suggests a coincidental spatial connection rather than deliberate. There was only one 'Overseer of the Treasury of all the Gods' in an unspecified location, Penne called Sunero-TT331 (RII), whose tomb is in close proximity to a number of temple administrative staff including the 'Overseer of the Cattle of Amun', Userhet-TT56 (AII-TIV), and the Overseer of the Granary of Amun', Amenemhet-TT123 (TIII), whose tombs are adjacent.

In addition to Neferrenopet-TT133 and Piay-TT263, two more individuals were employed in the Ramesseum. Nedjemger-T138 (RII) was 'Overseer of the Garden', and Nakhtamun-TT341 (Dyn 20) was 'Chief of the Offering Table', but these tombs are located at opposite ends of Lower Qurna. Other mortuary cults represented in the titles in this area included the 'Keeper of Dates' in the temple of Amenhotep III, Neferennpet-TT249 (AIII), and the 'Overseer of Cattle' of Tuthmosis IV, Khonsu called To-TT31 (RII). Ahmose called Humay-TT224 (Hat-TIII) was the 'Steward' of the deified 'God's Wife' Ahmose Nefertari, so in addition to being classified as a royal official in the service of a queen, he is also grouped with the temple administration as these titles were connected to the queen's mortuary cult (Robins 1993: 44). None of the tomb owners nearby have any connection to Ahmose Nefertari.

Three tombs belonging to temple craftsmen including the 'Chief of the Outline-draughtsmen in the House of Gold', Hori-TT259 (Dyn 20), a 'Stonemason of Amun', Amenmose-TT318 (Hat-TIII), and the 'Overseer of Sculptors of Amun', Amenhotep called Huy-TT368 (Ram). These tombs are not spatially connected to each other but are all located adjacent to one or more members of the temple administration within the Estate of Amun.

Many tombs were owned by individuals affiliated to the Estate of Amun, whether as a priest or administrator. This is to be expected during the New Kingdom when the vast Estate of Amun dominated the Theban area. Across the area there are a number of these individuals buried adjacent to each other or in small clusters, but there does not seem to be a specific area of Lower Qurna reserved for the employees of Amun. A number of individuals are connected to the Ramesseum in their capacity as priests (TT384), or in administrative roles (TT133, TT138, TT263, TT341). These tombs are some distance away from each other, scattered across the area with no evidence of clustering. The proximity of the Ramesseum to Lower Qurna explains why these individuals were buried in this area of the necropolis, as it is located directly behind the rear enclosure wall of the temple. There are also several titles linked to the god Montu, with three priests of Montu (TT31, TT324, and TT331), one of whom was also a scribe in the Montu temple (TT324). These tombs are not in particularly close proximity to each other.

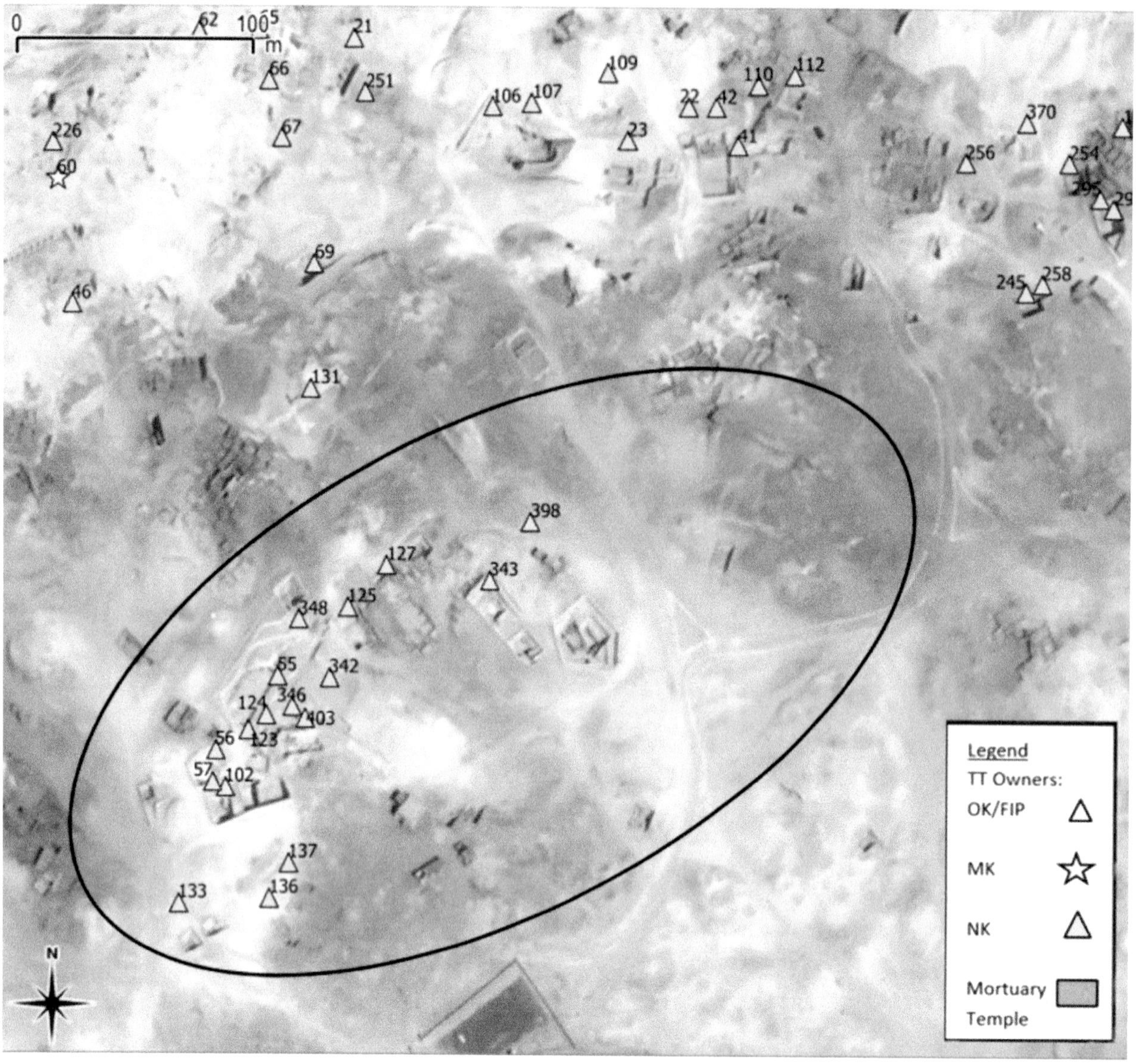

Figure 248: TTs of the Royal Administration of Lower Qurna (Author's own using QGIS)

Royal Administration

There were 17 royal officials buried here (see Figure 248). There were three 'Royal Seal-bearers', Ramose-TT55 (AIII-AIV), who was also 'Chief of Secrets of the Palace', Senemiak-TT127 (Hat-TIII), who was also 'Ears of the King', and Duaerneheh-TT125 (Hat). TT125 and TT127 are contemporary and located adjacent to each other in the centre of the area, suggesting a deliberate spatial connection. TT55 was built several generations later and located at the same height, in a line with these tombs, 30m to the west of TT125, so still in relatively close proximity. Duaerneheh-TT125 also held the titles 'Chief Herald', and 'Trusty Royal Herald, while Djehutymose-TT342 (TIII) was a 'Deputy Chief Royal Herald' and Userhet-TT56 (AII-TIV) was 'Deputy of the Herald'. TT342 is located 25m to the south of TT125, and the closeness in date of these tombs makes a connection between these heralds possible. All three tombs belonging to heralds are relatively close in date and are located within 100m. Khaemhet called Mahu-TT57 (AIII) was also 'Overseer of the Granaries of the Lord of the Two Lands', while Duaerneheh-TT125 was 'Overseer of the Granaries of the Great God'. TT57 and TT125 are located within 100m of each other, across the centre of the area.

There were six 'Royal Scribes' buried in Lower Qurna: Userhet-TT56 (AII-TIV); Khaemhet called Mahu-TT57 (AIII), who was also the 'Eyes of the King...'; Imhotep, who reused TT102 (AIII); Amenemhet-TT123 (TIII), who was also 'Chief Scribe in the Palace'; Senemiak-TT127 (Hat–TIII); and Unknown-TT136 (Dyn 19), who also held a missing title connected to the king. TT56, TT57, TT102 and TT123, are located adjacent to each other to the west of this central band of tombs, making a distinct group. TT136 is located 50m to the south of this cluster, while TT127 lies over 100m to the north-east.

Three 'Stewards' were buried here: the 'Steward' of Tuthmosis I, Ray-TT124 (Hat), who was also 'Overseer of the Storehouse of the Lord of the Two Lands'; the 'Chief Steward', Unknown-TT348 (Dyn 18); and 'Steward', Merymaat-TT403 (Ram). TT124 and TT403 are adjacent to each other, suggesting a deliberate connection between the two, while TT348 is located less than 50m to the north. There were also two individuals responsible for overseeing royal works, the 'Overseer of all Works of the King', Benia called Pahekamun-TT343 (TIII), who was also 'Overseer of the Craftsmen of the Lord of the Two Lands', (as was Duarneheh-TT125 (Hat), whose tomb was located just 60m away), and the 'Overseer of Works of the Lord of the Two Lands in All the Monuments of Amun', Mose-TT137 (RII) whose title fits into this category in addition to that of temple administration. TT343 and TT137 are located some distance apart, with no spatial connection. There are two overseers of the royal household, the 'Chief of Weavers of the Lord of the Two Lands', Neferennopet-TT133 (RII), and the 'Overseer of the Women of the Royal Harem...', Amenhotep-who reused TT346 (RIV). These tombs are located within 100m of each other to the east of the main group of tombs. In addition to these royal officials, there is one further individual who only holds the honorific title 'Child of the Nursery', Kamose called Nentowaref-TT398 (late Dyn 17-early 18), while several others hold this in addition to functional titles, Userhet-TT56 (AII-TIV), Imhotep-who reused TT102 (AIII) and Benia called Pahekamun-TT343 (TIII). TT343 lies within 30m of TT398, while TT56 and TT102 are also in close proximity to each other, but some distance to the west, so the holders of this title do not form a distinct group of tombs.

General Administration

There were seven members of the general centralised administration buried here, including both occupants of TT127 (see Figure 249). The most important of these was the 'Vizier' Ramose-TT55 (AIII-AIV), the only holder of this title to be buried in Lower Qurna. Ramose was also 'Overseer of Works' and 'Overseer of Scribes' (among many other royal administrative and priestly titles). Another 'Overseer of Works' was

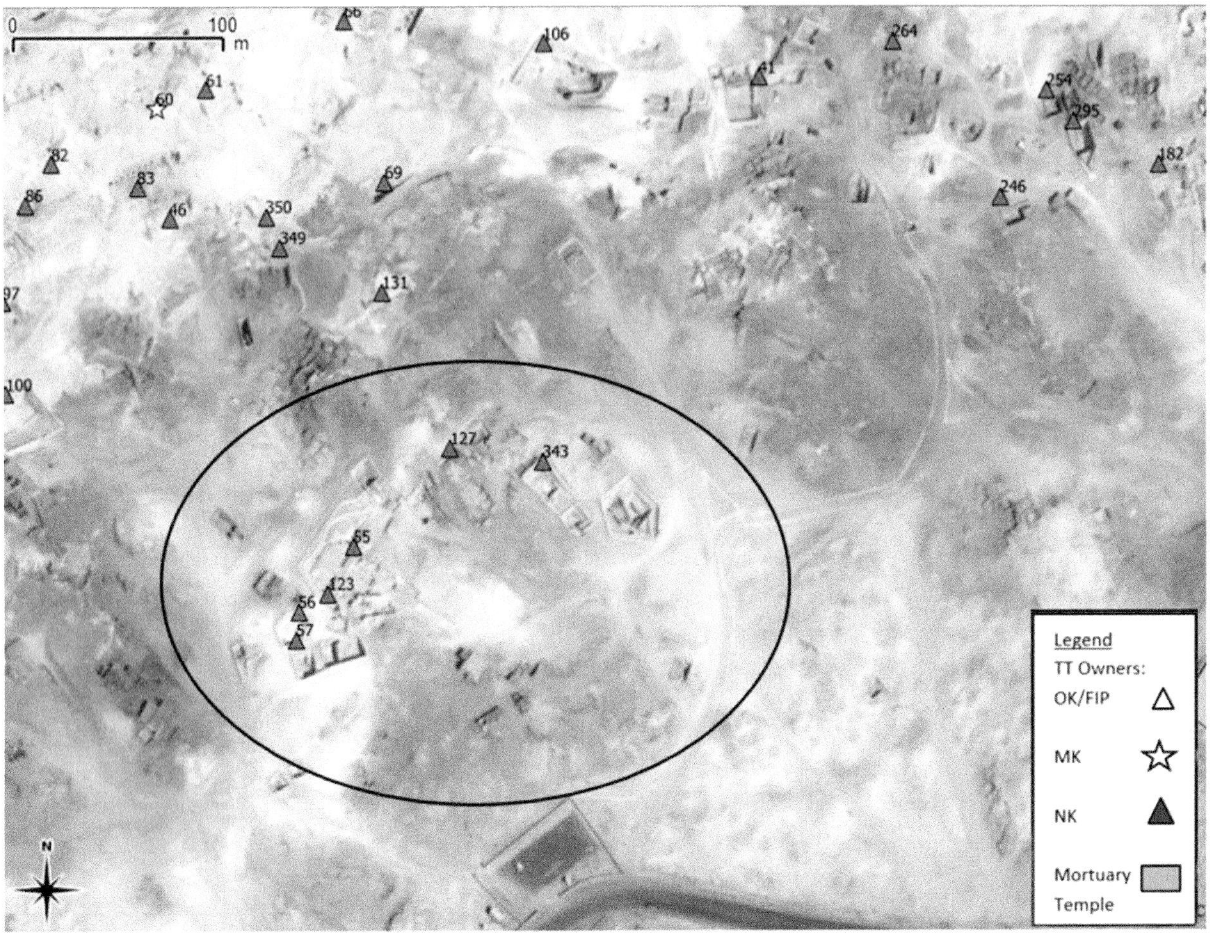

Figure 249: TTs of the General Administration of Lower Qurna (Author's own using QGIS)

Benia called Pahekamu- TT343 (TIII). TT55 and TT343 are located 100m apart, at the same altitude, within the central band of tombs, but not otherwise spatially connected. Benia called Pahekamun-TT343 was also the 'Overseer of Seal-bearers', which would have equated to 'Chief Treasurer'. Another two treasurers were buried in TT127, and both held the title 'Overseer of the Treasury', Senemiak (Hat-TIII) and Pairy (Ram). TT343 and TT127 are in relatively close proximity, less than 50m apart, with TT127 located just behind TT343. These tombs were potentially built during the same reign, so a connection between these tombs is likely. The 'Overseer of the Treasury of all the Gods', Penne called Sunero-TT331 (RII), was buried 100m to the west.

Several individuals were responsible for the provision of food, including: the 'Overseer' and 'Chief of Secrets' of the Granaries, Khaemhet called Mahu-TT57 (AIII); three 'Counters of Bread...', Userhet-TT56 (AII-TIV), Amenemhet-TT123 (TIII) who was also 'Overseer of Bread', and Senemiak-TT127 (Hat-TIII), who was also 'Overseer of all Herbs/Vegetables' and 'Scribe of the Offering Table'. Two of these individuals also had titles connected to the funerary workshop, the 'Chief in the Funerary Workshop' and 'Chief of the Coffin', Khaemhet called Mahu-TT57 (AIII), and the 'Senior of the Funerary Workshop', Senemiak-TT127 (Hat-TIII). TT57, TT56 and TT123 are situated adjacent to each other, side by side, and are relatively close in date, suggesting a deliberate attempt to site these tombs together. The Vizier Ramose-TT55 (AIII-AIV), who oversaw all food production in his role as Vizier also forms part of this line of tombs (see Figure 250). TT127 is located within 100m of this cluster, at the same altitude, but not close enough to suggest a connection.

Local Administration

There were seven members of the local administration buried on these lower slopes, holding regional titles (see Figure 251). They include two 'Mayors', Unknown-TT348 (Dyn 18), and Hunefer-TT385 (RII) and a 'Governor of the Town' (and 'Mouth of Nekhen'), Ramose-TT55 (AIII-AIV). TT348 is located 25m to the north of TT55, but TT385 is located some distance to the west in an isolated position. There is also an 'Overseer of Works in Thebes', Benia called Pahekamun-TT343 (TIII), an 'Overseer of the Shore in the Southern City', May-TT130 (TIII) and a 'Scribe of the Nome...', Hori-TT347 (Ram). TT130 and TT343 are within 100m of each other, with TT347 located 100m to the west of TT343, but none of these tombs are in close proximity to any other local administrators.

Military

Only one tomb owner in Lower Qurna held both military and local titles, 'Chief of the Medjay' and 'Overseer of the Foreign land of Retjenu', Penre-TT346 (before AIII) (see Figure 252). TT346 is located directly to the

Figure 250: TT123 and TT55 in close proximity (Author's own)

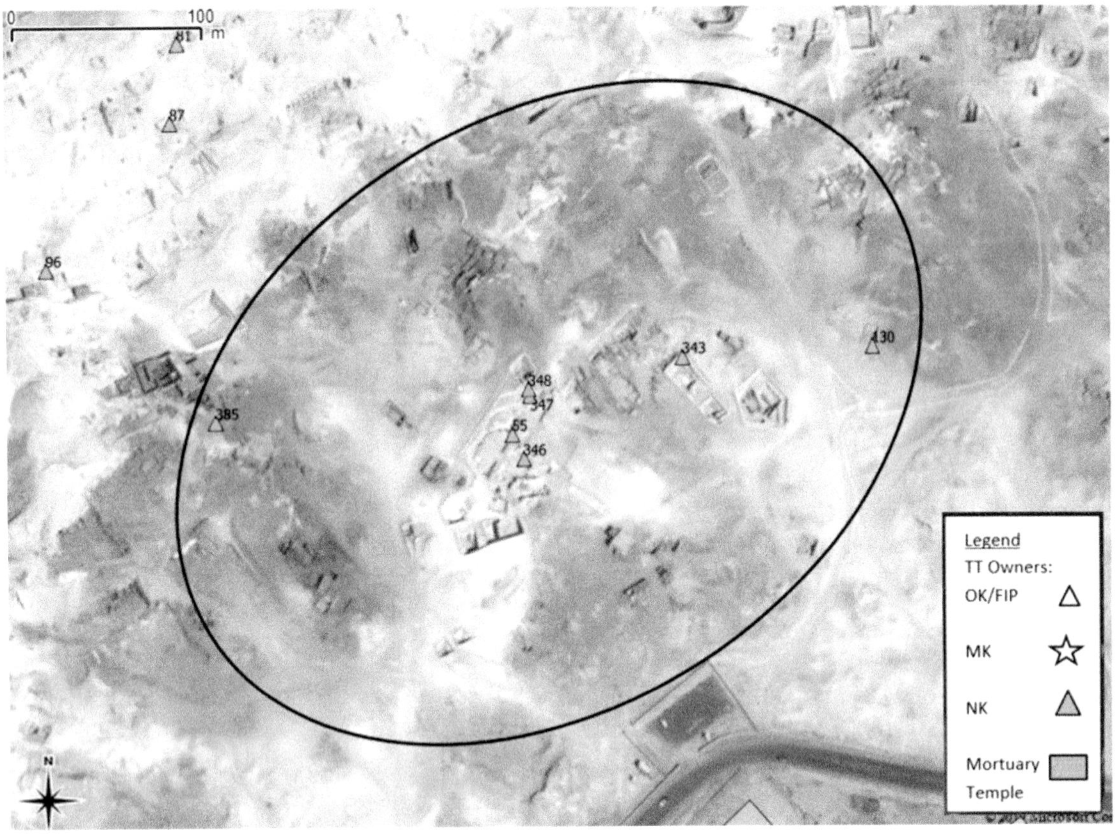

Figure 251: TTs of the Local Administration in Lower Qurna (Author's own using QGIS)

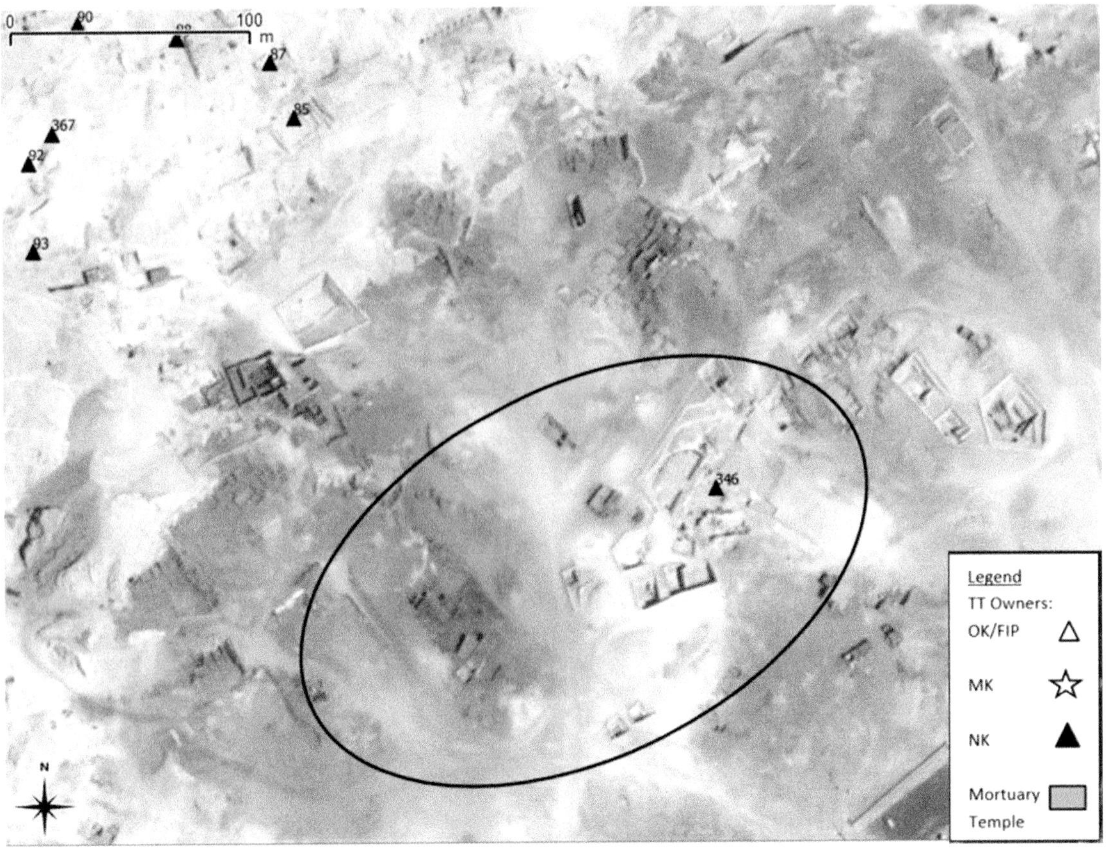

Figure 252: TT of the Military in Lower Qurna (Author's own using QGIS)

south of Ramose-TT55 (AIII-AIV), in close proximity, suggesting a potential link between these two potential contemporaries.

Unknown

The four remaining tombs are owned by individuals with unknown titles (TT129, TT269, TT309 and TT399).

Relationships between Tomb Owners / Tombs

Several familial relationships are known among the tomb owners in Lower Qurna. Khaemhet called Mahu-TT57 (AIII) shared a courtyard with his father, Imhotep-who reused TT102 (AIII). The fact that these tombs are adjacent to each other and have a shared courtyard appears to have been a deliberate choice by father and son to spend eternity in close proximity. Djehuty-TT45 (AII) is the 'Steward of the High Priest of Amun, Mery', while Mery himself was buried in Upper Qurna in TT95. This steward was not buried in close proximity to the individual he served, unlike the 'Steward of the Vizier' in Upper Qurna, Amenmehet-TT82 who was buried close to his masters User-TT61 and Amethu called Ahmose-TT83 (see Chapter 8). Ahmose called Humay-TT224 (Hat-TIII), the 'Steward of the God's Wife', has two sons buried some distance away in Upper Qurna in TT29 (AII) and TT96 (AII) respectively. These sons attained higher positions in society than their father, so they were afforded burial on the more prestigious upper slopes (see Chapter 9).

Shared Courtyards

TT57 and TT102

Both New Kingdom tombs within this shared courtyard (see Figures 253 and 254) date to the Eighteenth Dynasty. Khaemhet called Mahu-TT57 and Imhotep-who reused TT102 both date to the reign of Amenhotep III and shared the title 'Royal Scribe' (see Table 41). Khaemhet (TT57) is in fact the son of Imhotep, who

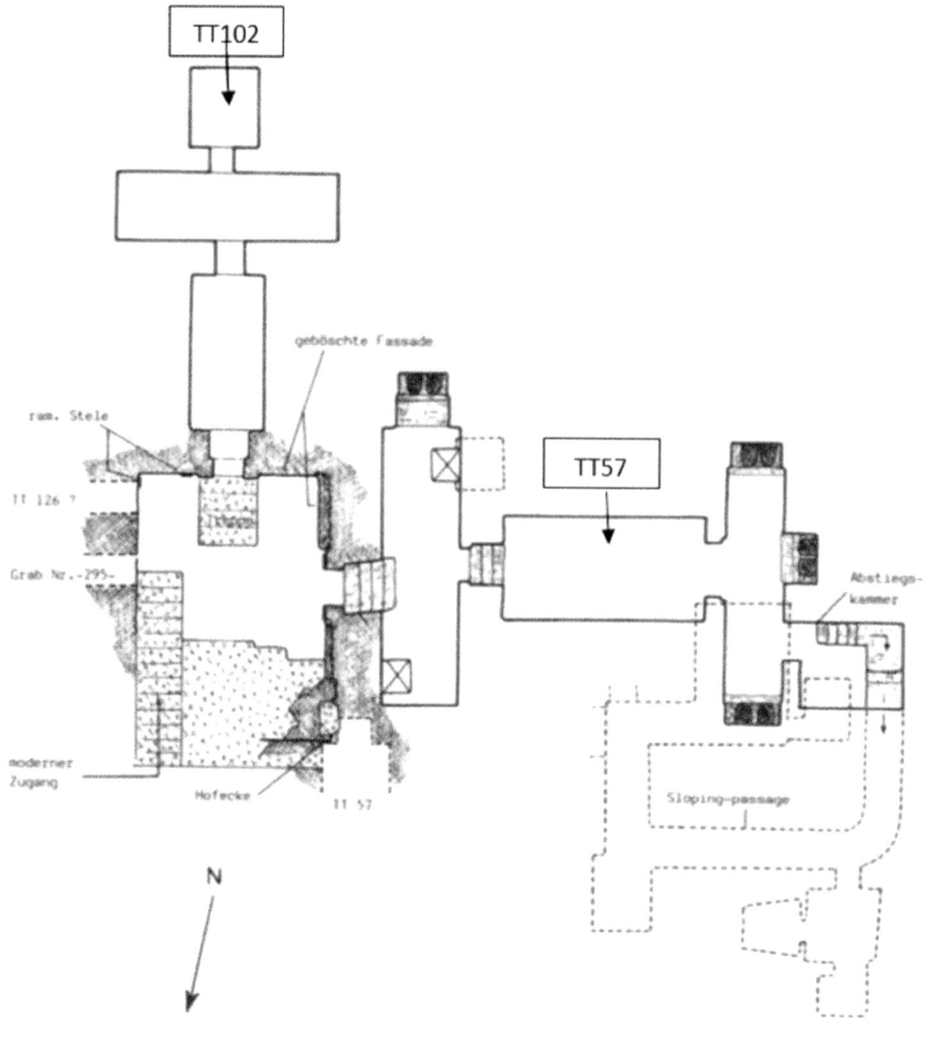

Figure 253: Plan of shared courtyard of TT57 and TT102 (Kampp 1996: Figure 156 – Courtesy of Professor Seyfried)

Table 41: Owners of TT57 and TT102

TT	Dyn	Reign	Name	Title
TT57	18	AIII	Khaemhet called Mahu	**Royal Scribe;** **Overseer of the Granaries (of the Lord of the Two Lands /U and LE);** Eyes of the King in the Cities of UE, His Ears in the Districts of LE; Hereditary Prince and Mayor; Priest of Anubis; Chief of Secrets of the Granaries; Chief of Secrets (of the Chest of Anubis); Chief in the Funerary Workshop; Chief of the Coffin;
TT102	18	(1) Hat/ TIII (2) AIII	(1) ? (2) Imhotep	(1) ? (2) Royal Scribe; Child of the Nursery;

Figure 254: Shared courtyard of TT57 and TT102 (Author's own)

reused TT102. At the rear of TT57 is a niche with statues of the deceased and his father Imhotep, with the wife of Khaemhet between them (PM I: 119; Kampp 1996: 375). This statuary confirms the relationship between the individuals sharing this courtyard. The third tomb sharing this courtyard, TT126, dates to the Late Period so is not relevant to this study.

TT55 and TT331

TT331 was built in the western corner of the original courtyard of the earlier TT55 (see Figures 255 and 256). Although not contemporary, both men were high-ranking priests (see Table 42), thus explaining a potential reason why the later Penne called Sunero would site his tomb next to another important priest. The monumental nature of the causeway leading to TT55, the sizeable courtyard and the status of Ramose-TT55 would all have made this a desirable spot to locate the later TT331.

TT53, TT134 and TT135

TT53 originally occupied this courtyard, located on the northern side directly opposite the entrance ramp, while TT135 and TT134 were adjacent to each other

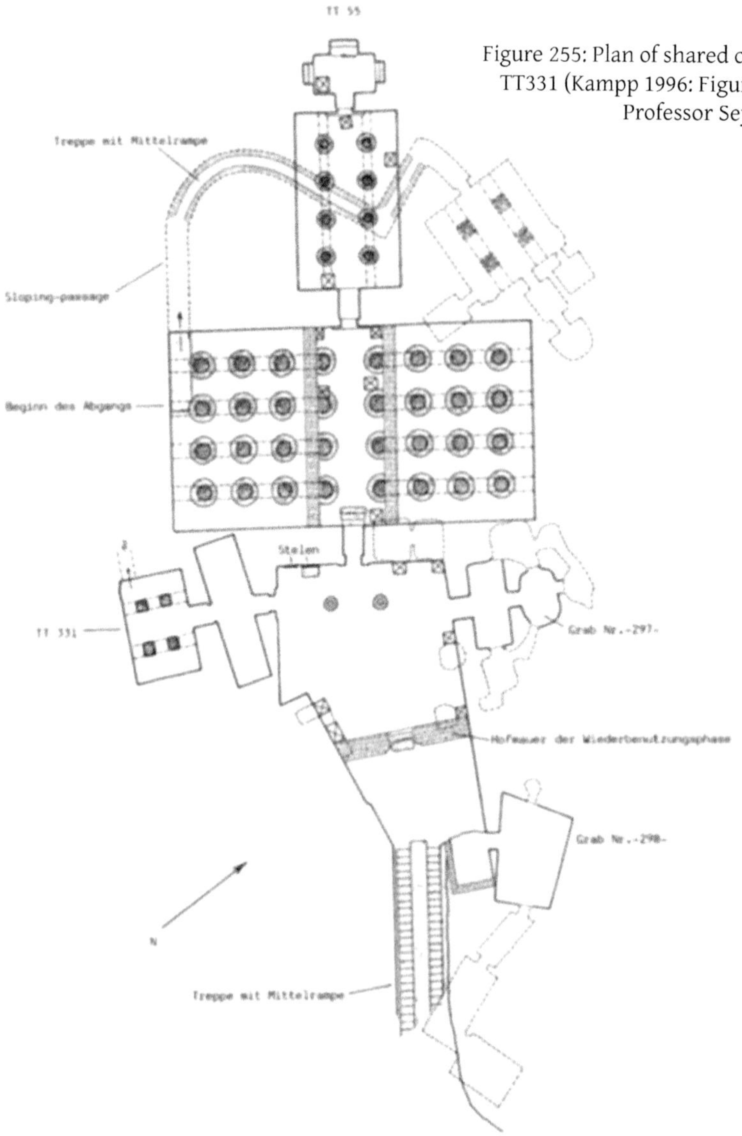

Figure 255: Plan of shared courtyard of TT55 and TT331 (Kampp 1996: Figure 153 – Courtesy of Professor Seyfried)

Table 42: Owners of TT55 and TT331

TT	Dyn	Reign	Name	Titles
TT55	18	AIII/AIV	Ramose	**Governor of the town and Vizier;** Royal Seal-bearer; Overseer of Works in the Great Monuments; Overseer of the Priests of U and LE; Chief of Secrets of the Two Cobra Goddesses; Chief of Secrets of the Palace; Priest of Maat; *sm* priest; Overseer of Scribes; Hereditary Prince and Mayor; Spokesman who Makes Peace in the Entire Land; Chief of the Entire Land; Controller of (all) Kilts; *sab;* Mouth of Nekhen; Great/Sole Companion of the Lord of the Two Lands;
TT331	19	RII	Penne called Sunero	High Priest of Montu; Overseer of the Treasury of all the Gods;

Figure 256: Shared courtyard of TT331 and TT55 (Author's own)

on the western side (see Figure 257). All three tomb owners had titles connecting them to the priesthood of Amun (see Table 43) but as the latter two tombs cannot be securely dated to a specific reign, and no specific titles are shared, there is not enough evidence to make a definite link between this group. The most probable reason for the later additions to the courtyard was the presence of a sizeable courtyard with space for more tombs to be dug, while the connection to Amun may also have been a factor.

TT346 and TT403

TT346 and TT403 occupy the eastern and southern sides of a small, shared courtyard (see Figure 258). There is no obvious link between these tombs as they are not built during the same period (although TT403 was originally dated to the Eighteenth Dynasty (PM I: 445)) and the occupants have no shared titles or workplace (see Table 44).

TT125 and TT263

TT125 is located on the northern side of the courtyard, opposite the entrance, while TT263 was a later addition on the western side (see Figure 259). Both tomb owners held positions within the Estate of Amun, but as they lived several reigns apart, and had different workplaces and no common titles (see Table 45), there is no evidence of a clear link between these individuals.

TT30, TT50, TT51 and TT111

These four tombs shared a courtyard, each occupying its own side (see Figures 260 and 261). The earliest, TT30 (AIII), has a monumental façade and lies directly opposite the entrance to the courtyard. TT50 (Hor) built next on the west of the courtyard, followed by TT51 (RI-SI) on the east. The last to be built on the southern side was TT111 (RII). TT111 was reused in the Ramesside period, and TT30 was reused in the Twentieth Dynasty. The construction of all four tombs took place between the late Eighteenth and early Nineteenth dynasty, so it is possible that some of the occupants were contemporaries. The two usurpers may also be contemporaries.

The occupation of the original occupant of this courtyard (TT30) is unknown, but it seems likely that he was important as he could afford a monumental façade. The three later tombs may have been located here to make use of an existing courtyard or may have been built close to an illustrious predecessor. As the other tomb owners are priests, it seems likely that the owner of TT30 was also a priest, potentially a 'High Priest' to attract these later burials. There is a clear connection

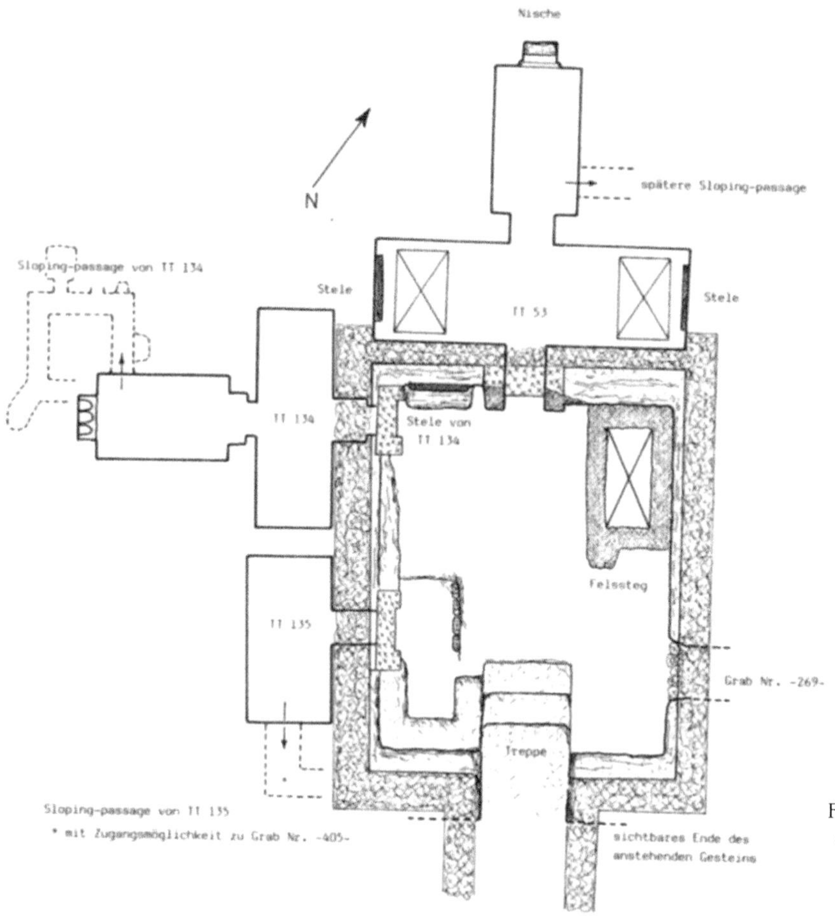

Figure 257: Plan of shared courtyard of TT53, TT134 and TT135 (Kampp 1996: Figure 151 - Courtesy of Professor Seyfried)

Table 43: Owners of TT53, TT134 and TT135

TT	Dyn	Reign	Name	Titles
TT53	18	(Hat)/ TIII	Amenemhat	Acolyte of Amun;
TT134	20	?	Thauenany called Any	Priest of Amenhotep who Rows on the Water of Amun;
TT135	20	?	Bakenamun	*wʿb* priest in Front of Amun;

to the god Amun and his estate among the owners of two of the tombs and the usurper of TT30, while all three known tomb owners, and the usurper of TT30 had a connection to a temple, whether in a religious or administrative capacity (see Table 46).

TT30 was reused in the Twentieth Dynasty by Khonsumose, potentially as an attempt to associate himself with an important individual, or lacking the resources to build his own tomb, chose an existing tomb with this monumental façade. Khonsumose and Amenwahsu-TT111 were both scribes, suggesting a potential connection between them. There is no evidence of a familial relationship between the inhabitants of this courtyard.

TT138 and TT259

TT138 was built on the north side of the courtyard, while the later TT259 was built on the western side (see Figure 262). Both tomb owners held positions within the Estate of Amun (see Table 47), but as they lived several reigns apart and held different titles, there is no other clear link between them.

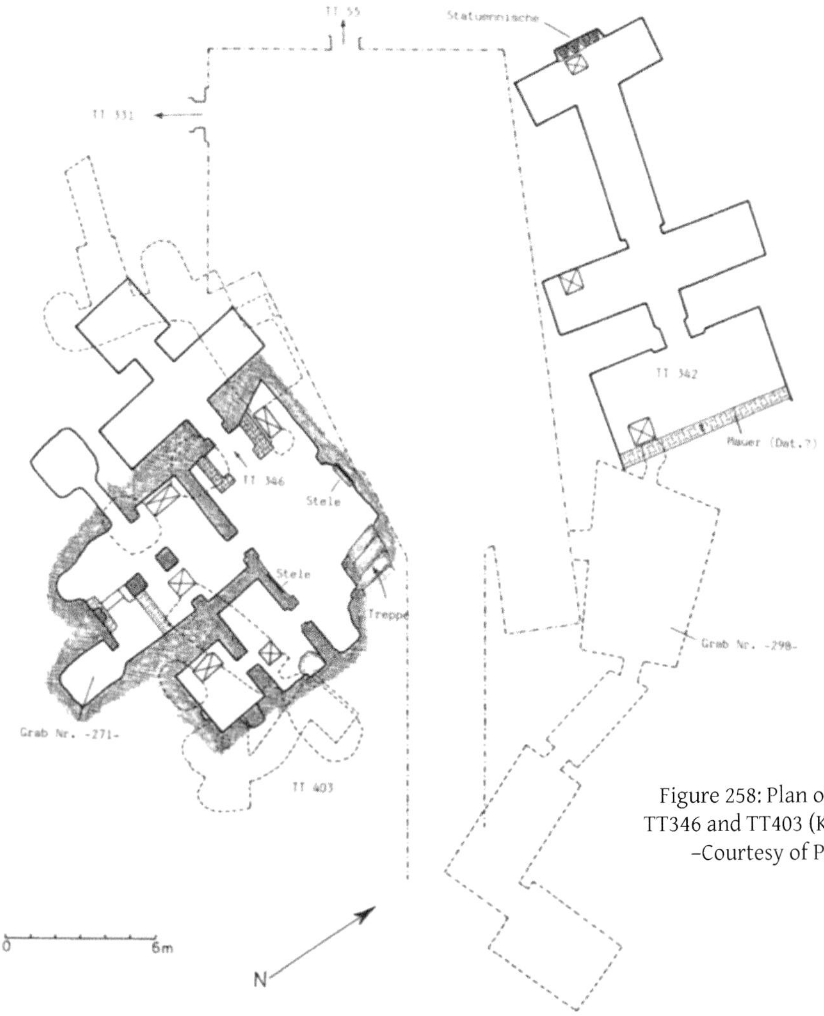

Figure 258: Plan of shared courtyard of TT346 and TT403 (Kampp 1996: Figure 476 –Courtesy of Professor Seyfried)

Table 44: Owners of TT346 and TT403

TT	Dyn	Reign	Name	Title
TT346	18 & 20	Dyn 18-AIII & RIV	(1) Penre (2) Amenhotep	(1) Chief of the Medjay (=police); Overseer of Foreign Land of Retjenu (=Syria); (2) Overseer of the Women of the Royal Harem of the Adoratress Tentopet (=wife of RIV);
TT403	19-20	Ram	Merymaat	Temple Scribe; Steward;

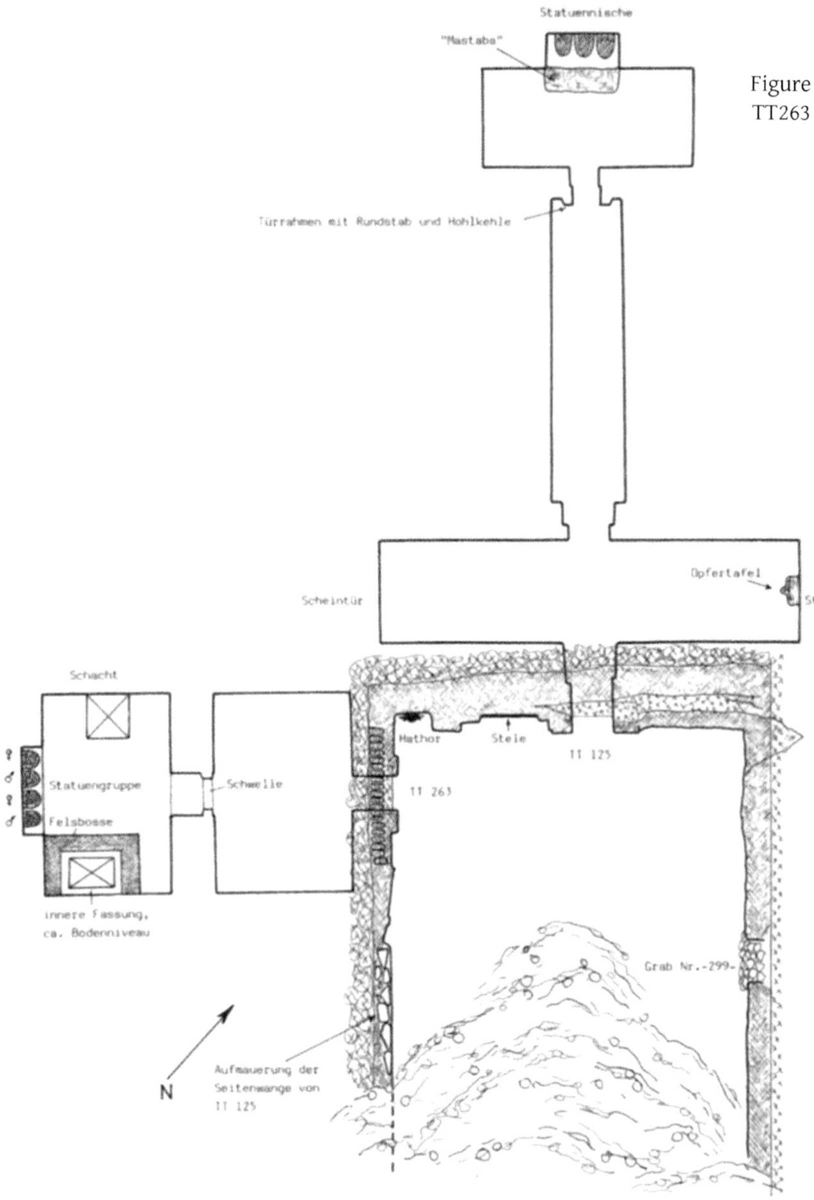

Figure 259: Shared courtyard of TT125 and TT263 (Kampp 1996: Figure 307 - Courtesy of Professor Seyfried)

Table 45: Owners of TT125 and TT263

TT	Dyn	Reign	Name	Title
TT125	18	Hat	Duaerneheh	**Chief Herald of the Lord of the Two Lands;** Royal Seal-bearer; Overseer of the Granaries of the Good God; Overseer of all the Craftsmen of the King; Overseer of all Works of the King; Overseer of the Administrative District (of Amun); Hereditary Prince, Mayor; Sole Companion;
TT263	19	RII	Piay	Scribe of the Storehouse (of) Amun-united-with-Thebes; Scribe of the Storehouse in the Ramesseum; Chief of the Storehouse of Amun-united-with-Thebes in the Ramesseum;

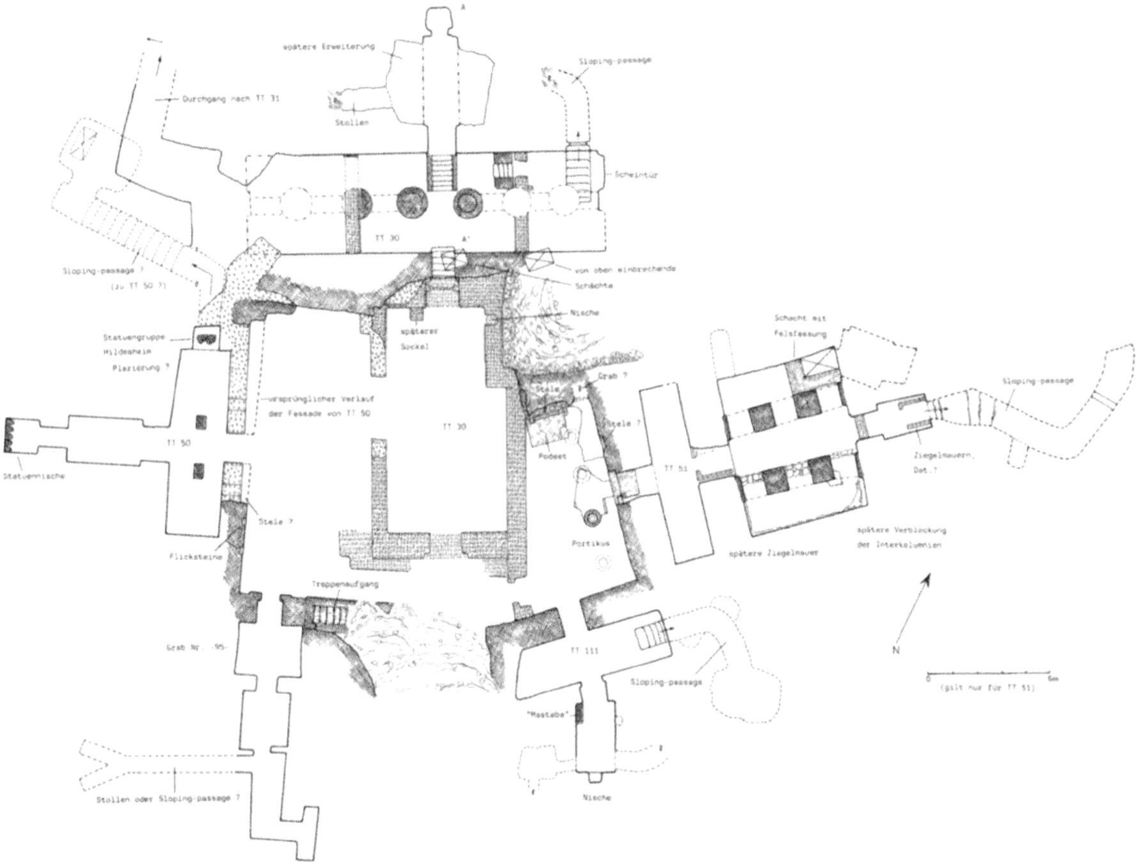

Figure 260: Plan of shared courtyard of TT30, TT50, TT51 and TT111 (Kampp 1996: Figure 121 – Courtesy of Professor Seyfried)

Table 46: Owners of TT30, TT50, TT51 and TT111

TT	Dyn	Reign	Name	Titles
TT30	18 & 20	AIII and Dyn 20(RIII?)	(1) ? (2) Khonsumose	(1) ? (2) Scribe of the Treasury of the Estate of Amun;
TT50	18	Hor	Neferhotep	Divine father (of Amun);
TT51	19	RI/ SI	Userhet called Neferhebef	High Priest of the Royal *ka* of Aa-kheper-ka-Re (TI); High Priest (of Aa-kheper-ka-re) (TI);
TT111	19 &19/20	(1) RII (2) Ram	(1) Amenwahsu (2) ?	**(1) Divine Scribe (in the Estate of Amun);** Scribe of the Divine Records (in the Estate of Amun); Festival leader of all the gods in their festivals; Chief in the Estate of Amun; *wꜥb* priest of Sekhmet;

Figure 261: View from above of shared courtyard of TT30, TT50, TT51 and TT111 (Author's own)

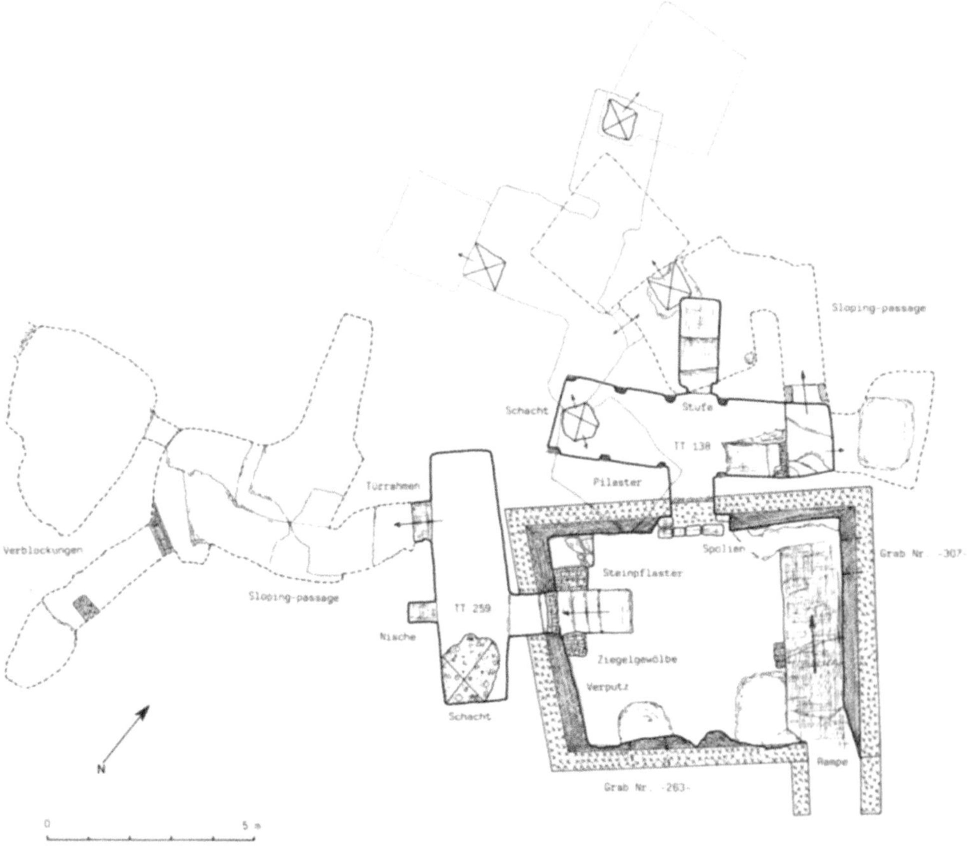

Figure 262: Plan of shared courtyard of TT138 and TT259 (Kampp 1996: Figure 316 – Courtesy of Professor Seyfried)

Table 47: Owners of TT138 and TT259

TT	Dyn	Reign	Name	Title
TT138	19	RII	Nedjemger	Overseer of the Garden (in the Temple of User-maat-re Setep-en-re in the Estate of Amun) (=Ramesseum);
TT259	20	?	Hori	*wꜥb* priest; Scribe in all the Monuments of the Estate of Amun; Chief of the Outline-Draughtsmen in the House of Gold of the Estate of Amun;

Tomb Reuse

Six tombs in Lower Qurna were reused during the New Kingdom (see Figure 263 and Table 48), one during the reign of Amenhotep II (TT102- built Hat-TIII), one during the Ramesside Period (TT127– Hat-TIII), and four during the Twentieth Dynasty (TT30- AIII, TT45- AII, TT111- RII and TT346- AIII). Five of these six reused tombs were built during the Eighteenth Dynasty, when more choice was available when siting tombs, so it seems likely that these tombs were reused due to their desirable location as the necropolis became more crowded, rather than to a connection with the original tomb owner. Only one reused tomb was built in the Nineteenth Dynasty (TT111).

Some links can still be made between the original tomb owners and the later occupants. Both owners of TT127

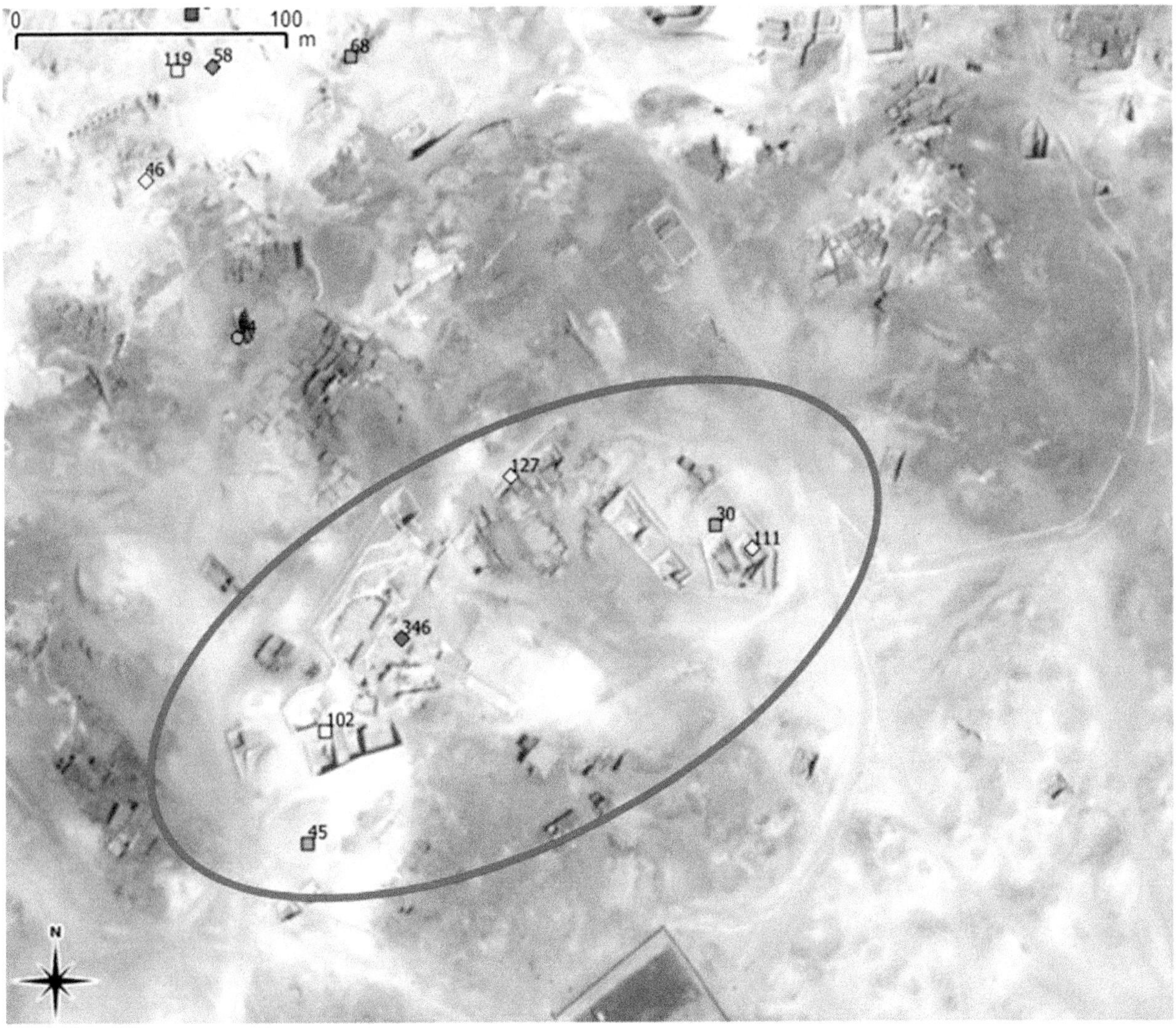

Figure 263: Reused TTs in Lower Qurna at the end of the New Kingdom, shown by date of reuse (Author's own using QGIS)

Table 48: Reused tombs in Lower Qurna

TT	Original Date	Date of Reuse
TT30	AIII	Dyn 20
TT45	AII	Dyn 20
TT102	Hat-TIII	AIII
TT111	RII	Ram
TT127	Hat-TIII	Ram
TT346	Dyn 18-AIII	RIV

hold the title 'Overseer of the Treasury' (although the original owner also held many additional titles), providing a link between them. Both owners of TT45 had similar names, 'Djehuty' and 'Djehutyemhab', and held similar titles as they are both 'Chief' of the workforce responsible for linen production at the Estate of Amun, providing a professional association between the two, as also identified by Bács (2018: 25). The two owners of TT346 have no titles in common. The original owners of TT30 and TT102, and the usurper of TT111 are both unknown, so a link cannot be established between the occupants.

Conclusions

Lower Qurna was popular from the Eighteenth Dynasty onwards, when space was still available in Upper Qurna. However, the occupants of Lower Qurna were less prestigious than those of Upper Qurna, as no Viziers were buried here until the reign of Amenhotep III when the upper slopes were becoming overcrowded. The peak in use observed during the reign of Ramesses II onwards is explained by the proximity of Lower Qurna to the Ramesseum. Although the views were not as good as from the upper slopes, the flat nature of the terrain still allowed good views of the temple and the processional route (see Figures 264 and 265). The space directly behind the Ramesseum area is the closest area of the necropolis to the Ramesseum but this was not used for tomb building (see Figure 266 and Chapter 3). The lack of burials in this area throughout the succeeding reigns suggests that burial in this area was restricted, perhaps in a similar way to the area adjacent to the Deir el-Bahri temples and causeway. This area may also have formed part of the temple's domain or may have been kept clear of tombs for a specific reason connected to the temple itself, to ensure that there was a clear area between the Ramesseum and the cliffs leading to the Valley of the Kings.

Figure 264: View north across Lower Qurna (Author's own)

Figure 265: View north-west from the Ramesseum, towards Qurna (Author's own)

Figure 266: View south-west from the Ramesseum showing space behind (Author's own)

Chapter 10: Qurnet Murai

(See Appendix 13)

Location

Qurnet Murai is located at the southern end of the necropolis, to the south-east of the village of Deir el-Medina. The tombs in this area are located between two modern roads, one leading north to Deir el-Medina and the other running east between the Valley of the Queens and the royal mortuary temples (see Figure 267). The tombs are distributed in a wide band parallel to the modern roads, between 90m and 120m above sea level, with the floodplain in this area beginning at 90m above sea level (see Figure 268). The area itself is the smallest area of the necropolis.

Date of Use

There are 16 TTs in this area (see Table 49). Of these one dates to the Middle Kingdom, reused in the Ramesside period (TT270), and the other fifteen were built during the New Kingdom (see Figure 269). Five tombs date to the Eighteenth Dynasty, and the other ten date to the Ramesside period, with two of these more securely dated to the Nineteenth Dynasty, and a further seven to the Twentieth Dynasty. These dates show that this area of the necropolis was in steady use from the mid-Eighteenth Dynasty until the end of the New Kingdom.

By the end of the Eighteenth Dynasty, in addition to the Middle Kingdom TT270, there were only five tombs in this area of the necropolis. The earliest, TT276, dates between Tuthmosis III and Amenhotep II, the second, TT383, dates to the reign of Amenhotep III, while three more date to the end of the dynasty after Amarna, TT40, TT271 and TT275. These five Eighteenth Dynasty tombs are clustered together and are not near the earlier TT270, so this Middle Kingdom tomb did not seem to be a factor when choosing this area of the necropolis (see Figure 270). The construction of several tombs in this area after the Amarna period is relevant, suggesting that these individuals built tombs in this area to be

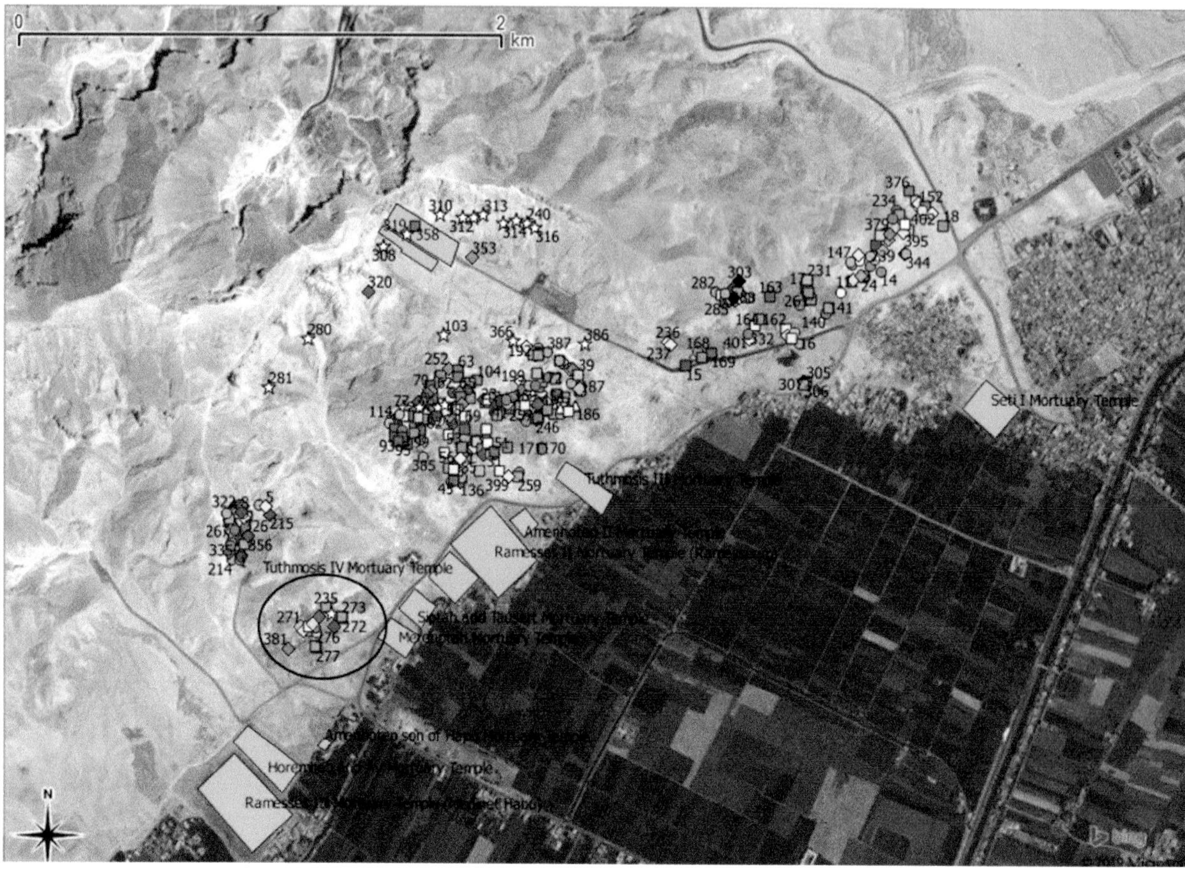

Figure 267: Location of Qurnet Murai within the Theban Necropolis (Author's own using QGIS)

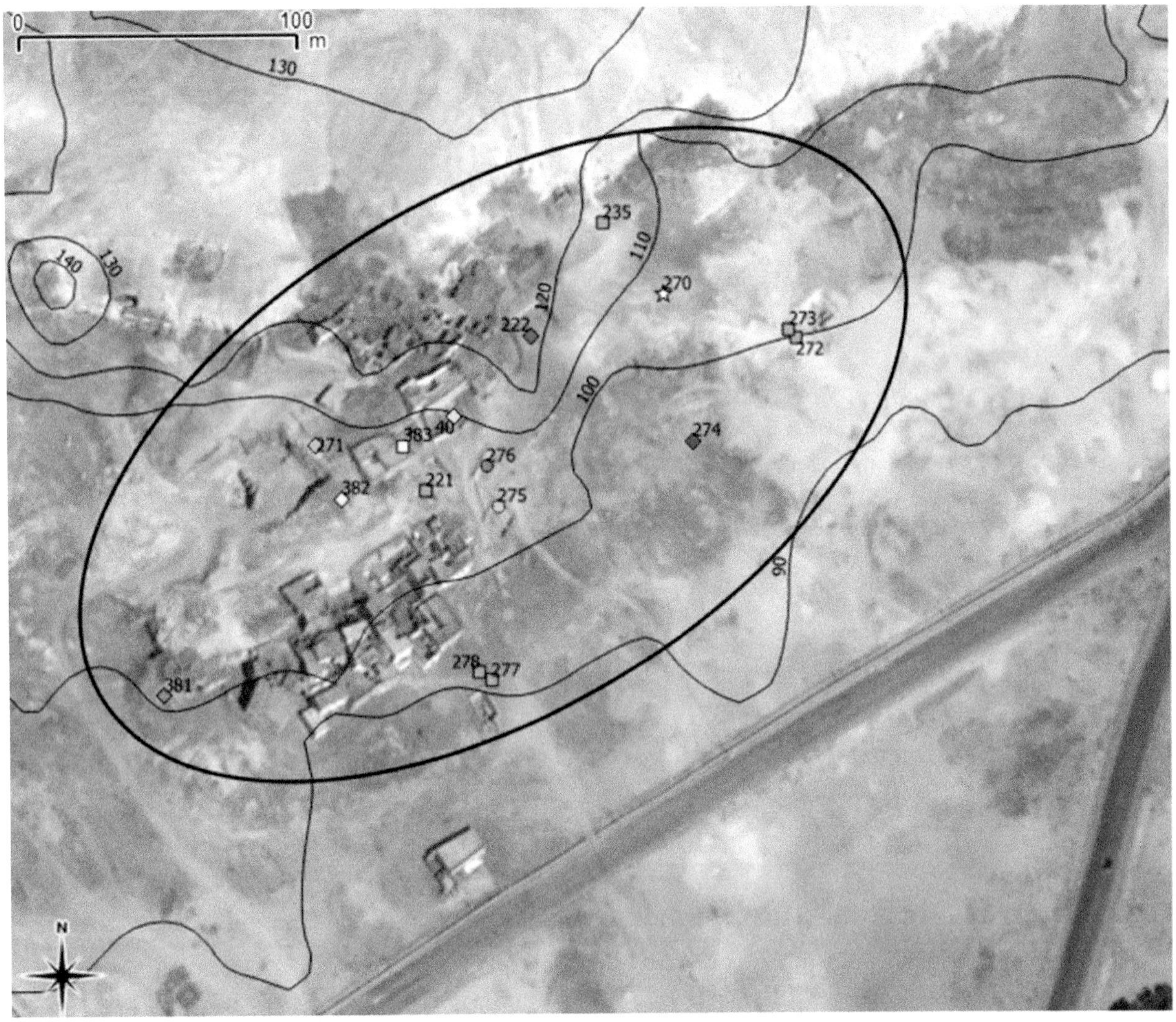

Figure 268: Landscape of Qurnet Murai (Author's own using QGIS)

close to the king they served, as the mortuary temple of these late Eighteenth Dynasty rulers were located at this southern end of the necropolis (see Figure 271). The processional route of the BFV would also have evolved at this time to include this area.

TT274 dates to the Nineteenth Dynasty, specifically to the reign of Merenptah whose mortuary temple lies 200m to the east. TT382 is datable only to the Ramesside Period. The presence of a Ramesside tomb makes sense, as the Ramesseum lies to the north of Merenptah's mortuary temple, and the mortuary temple of Ramesses III is at Medinet Habu to the south, so the BFV would have passed these tombs. Only TT270 was reused, and this also took place during the Ramesside period, thus fitting this pattern. There is one tomb dated between the reigns of Ramesses III and Ramesses IV (TT222), and six tombs datable only to the Twentieth Dynasty (TT221, TT235, TT272, TT273, TT277 and TT278). The presence of a relatively large number of Twentieth Dynasty tombs in this specific area could be explained by the lack of space elsewhere in the necropolis at this time.

The data set here is too limited to enable patterns to be identified according to date as the area is small and there are no sets of multiple tombs dating to the same reign(s) to analyse. However, there are two clearly identifiable pairs of tombs located in particularly close proximity, TT277 and TT278, and TT272 and TT273. These tombs all date to the Twentieth Dynasty but without more accurate dating this is of limited interest by the criteria of date alone.

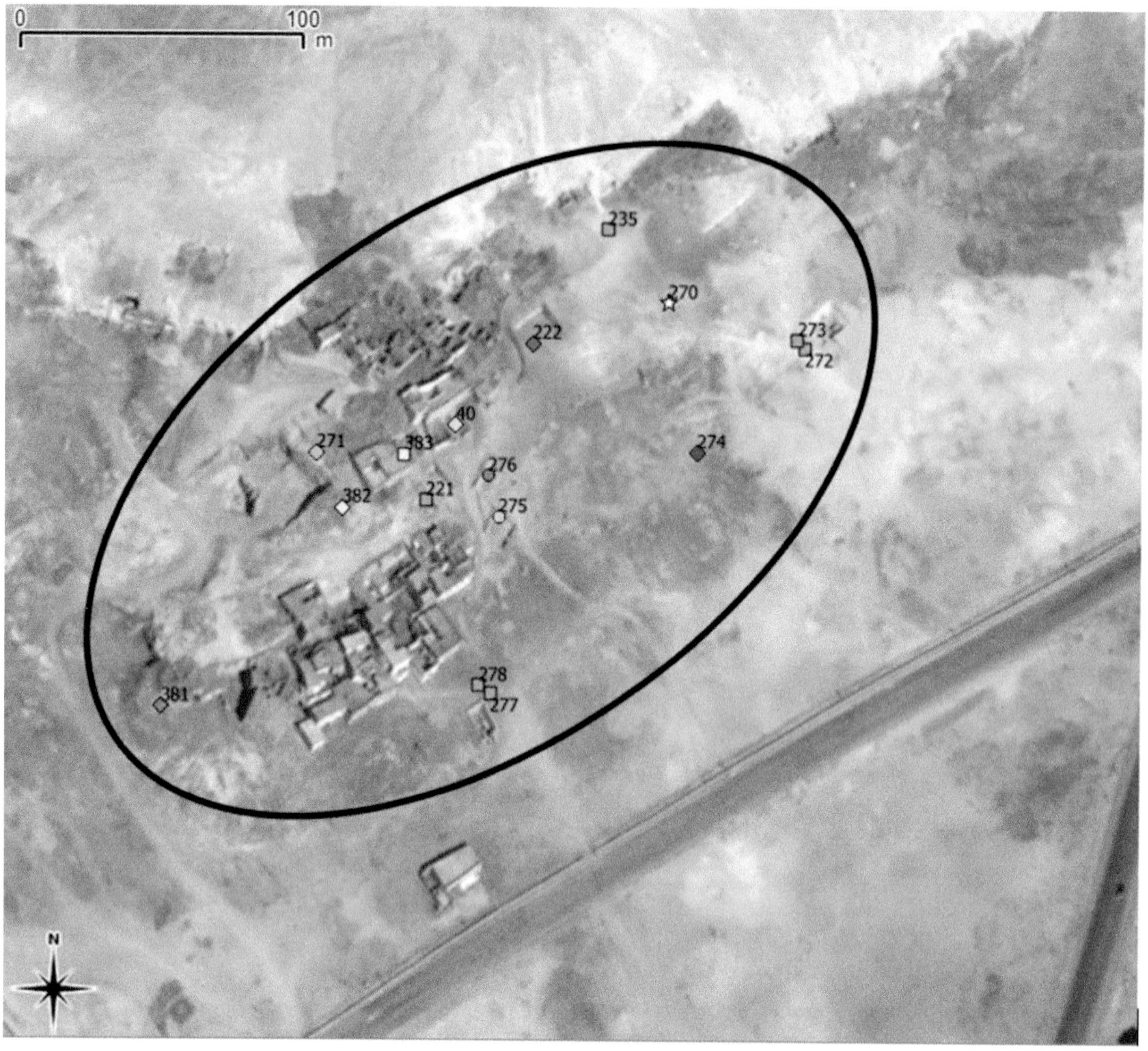

Figure 269: TTs in Qurnet Murai (Author's own using QGIS)

Table 49: Qurnet Murai TTs distributed by most likely date

Date	No. of Tombs	Tombs
MK	*	TT270
TIII / AII	*	TT276
AIII	*	TT383
Tut	*	TT40
Ay	*	TT271
After Amarna	*	TT275
Dyn 19	*	TT381
Mer	*	TT274
RIII/ RIV	*	TT222
Ram	*	TT382
Dyn 20	******	TT221, TT235, TT272, TT273, TT277, TT278

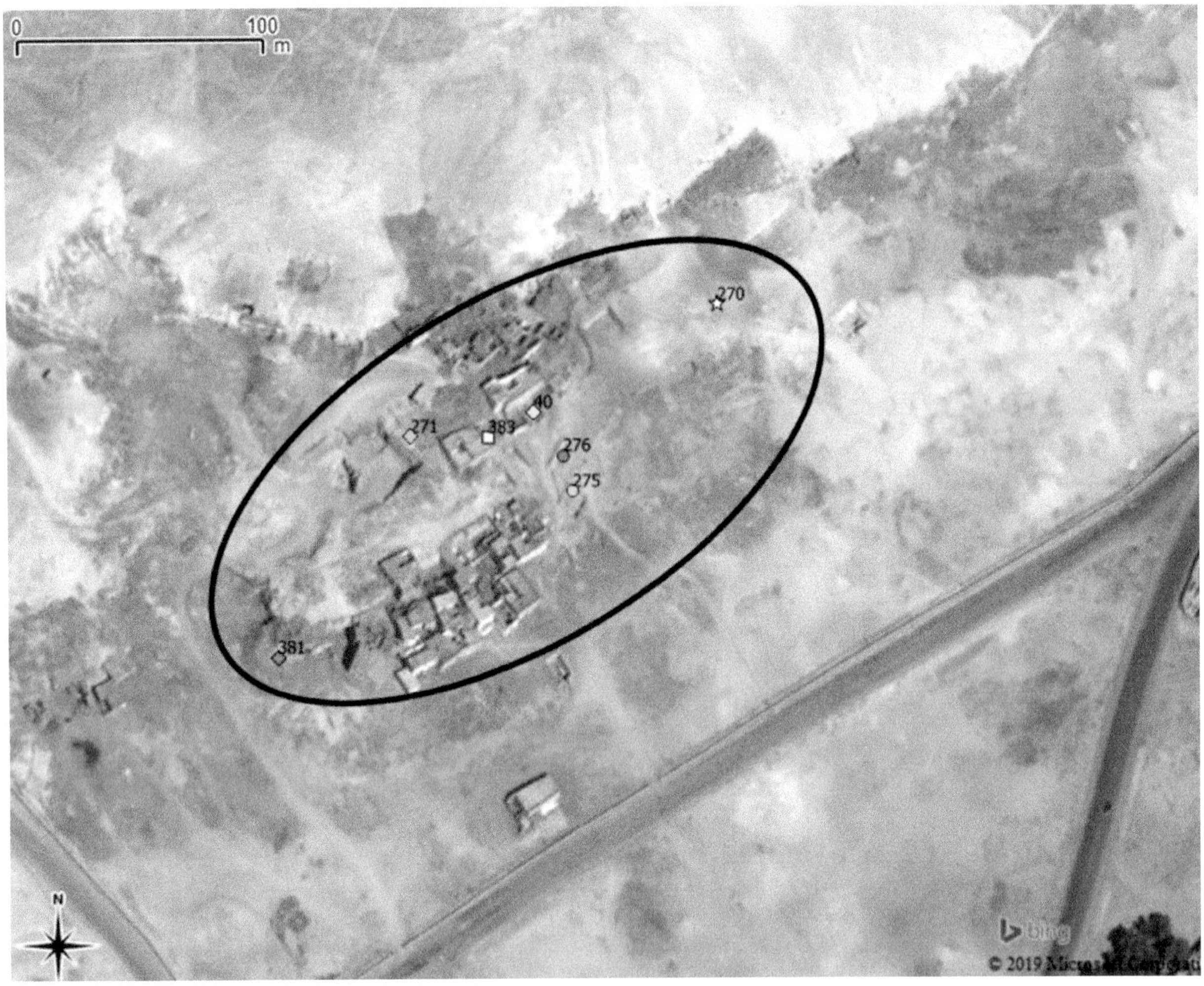

Figure 270: TTs at the end of the Eighteenth Dynasty (Author's own using QGIS)

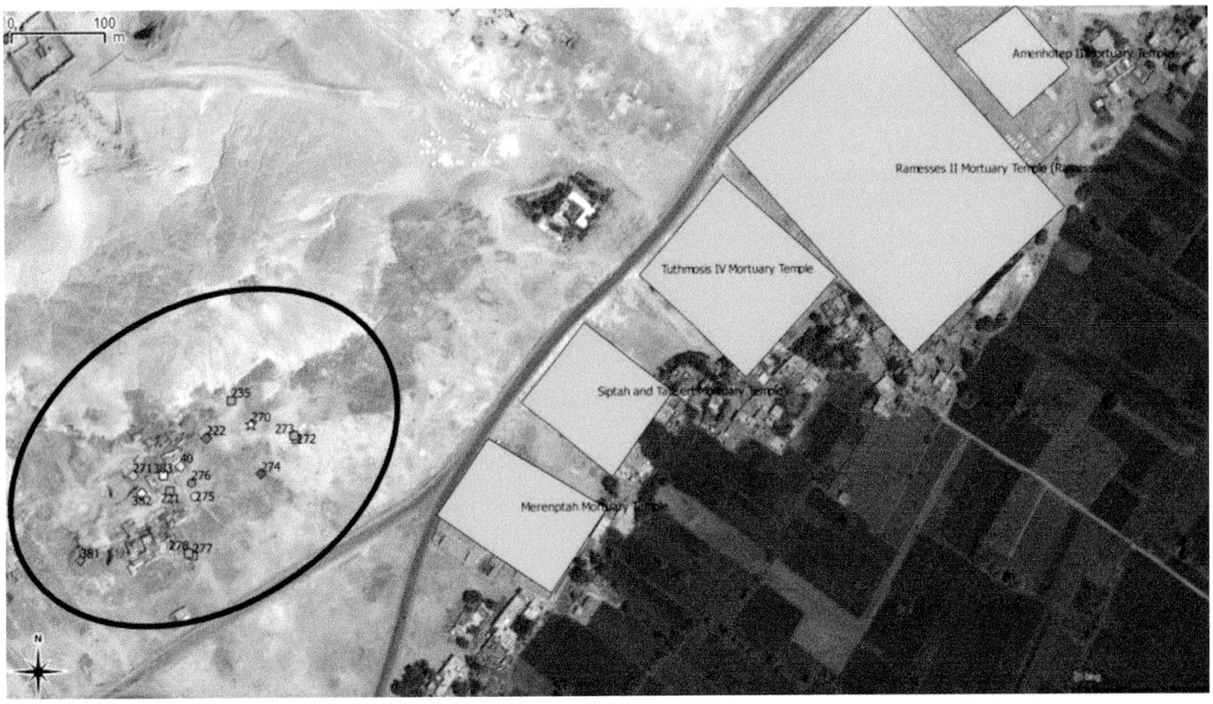

Figure 271: TTs at the end of the New Kingdom (Author's own using QGIS)

Table 50: Qurnet Murai Tombs distributed by occupational group

Occupational Group	Number of Tombs	Tombs
Priesthood	********	TT222, TT235, TT270(2), TT272, TT274, TT275, TT277, TT382
Temple Admin	***	TT40, TT221, TT278
Royal Admin	*****	TT40, TT271, TT273, TT276, TT381
General Admin	**	TT276, TT382
Local Admin	**	TT40, TT383
Military	*	TT221
Royal Family	*	TT383
Unknown	*	TT270

(n) denotes subsequent tomb occupation

Occupation of Tomb Owners

(See Table 50)

This area of the necropolis was used as a place of burial by a range of individuals. The owner of the sole Middle Kingdom burial (TT270) is unknown, as inscriptional evidence of the first occupant does not survive (Kampp, 1996: 543). The first New Kingdom individual to be buried at this southern end of the necropolis was Amenemopet-TT276 (TIII-AII) who held a string of important titles. At the time this tomb was built, the line of royal mortuary temples did not yet extend this far south, with the exception of the mortuary temple of Tuthmosis II which lay just to the south of Qurnet Murai, providing a possible explanation for this tomb's location. Another potential reason is that the Middle Kingdom occupant of TT270 was someone who Amenemopet wanted to be associated with, but without inscriptional evidence this is speculative. This tomb of such an important official is located centrally in this area, so could possibly have served as a focal point for later burials.

Priests

There were eight priests buried in Qurnet Murai, some of whom held multiple priestly titles (see Figure 272). These tombs do not form a distinct group, nor are they in particularly close proximity within this relatively small area, with only two located in the central cluster of tombs (TT275 and TT382). There is however a particularly high incidence of titles associated with the cults of the Theban god of war, Montu, and the Memphite deity, Sokar. There are four 'High Priests of Montu', Hekermaatrenakht called Turo-TT222 (RIII-RIV), Userher-TT235 (Dyn 20), Amenwahsu-TT274 (Mer), and Usermontu-TT382 (Ram). It seems likely that these individuals worked at the Montu temple at Karnak, as this was the closest temple for this deity. Karnak is opposite the northern end of the necropolis, and the Montu temple lay to the north of the Amun precinct, so this does not explain the burial of these priests in this southern area. Hekermaatrenakht called Turo-TT222 was also the 'Overseer of Priests of all the Gods', while Amenwahsu-TT274 was also a '*sm* priest' in the Ramesseum, which is located a short distance from Qurnet Murai, providing a better explanation for his burial here.

Four further individuals were connected to the cult of Sokar, as both Amenemwia- TT270 (Ram) and Khaemopet-TT272 (Dyn 20) were 'Lector Priest in the Temple of (Ptah-Sokar', while both Sobekmose-TT275 (post-Amarna) and Ameneminet-TT277 (Dyn 20) were 'Divine Father' in the temples of both Sokar and Amenhotep III. While these four tombs are not in particularly close proximity, the presence of this number of individuals connected to the Sokar cult is significant. The mortuary temple of Amenhotep III, located a short distance to the east of Qurnet Murai, also served as a temple to Ptah-Sokar-Osiris, whether as separate temples within the same complex, or as two halves of a single temple. The titles of those employed in the cult of Ptah-Sokar-Osiris here are most commonly referred to as priests attached to the '*ḥwt-skr*' (Shafer, 1997: 102), so these individuals would have worked within the temple and were buried close by, thus explaining their presence here. The majority of these priests held multiple titles, as Khaemopet-TT272 was also a 'Divine Father of Amun', Ameneminet-TT277 was also a 'Lector Priest', and both were *wʿb* priests, in addition to Amenemwia-TT270 and Sobekmose-TT275. The relatively high incidence of priestly titles here could be as a result of the royal mortuary temples being

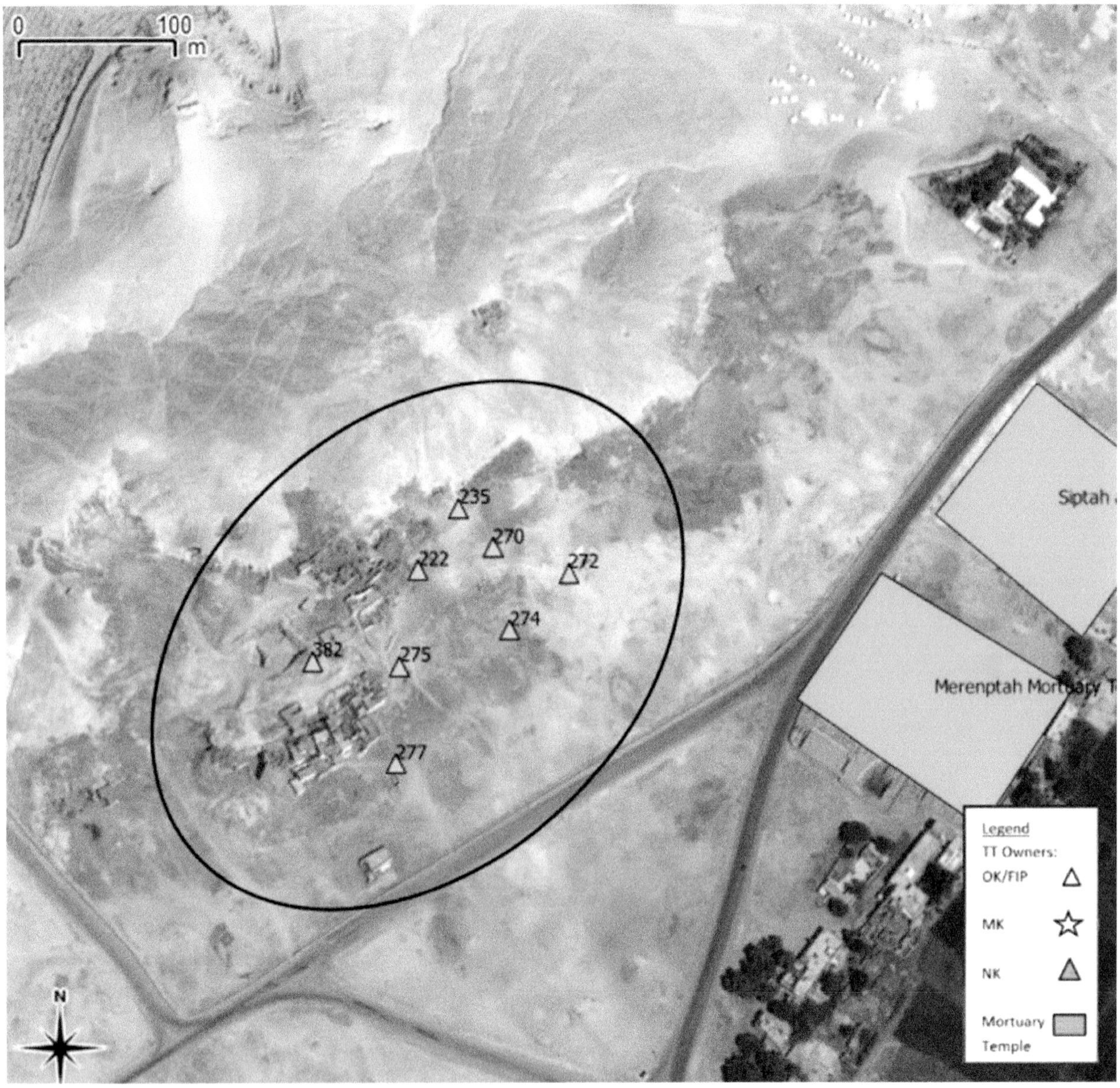

Figure 272: TTs of Priests in Qurnet Murai (Author's own using QGIS)

located further south along the edge of the cultivation from the late Eighteenth Dynasty onwards.

Temple Administration

There were three members of the temple administration buried in this area (see Figure 273). Amenhotep called Huy-TT40 (Tut) was the 'Overseer of the Cattle of Amun', Horimin-TT221 (Dyn 20) was the 'Scribe of the Temple' and 'Scribe of the Army' in the Ramesseum, while Amenemhab-TT278 (Dyn 20) was a 'Herdsman of Amun-Re'. All three of these individuals were connected to the Estate of Amun and are located within a 100m area, with TT40 and TT221 in particularly close proximity, with TT221 located just in front of TT40. However, there are too few tombs of this type in this area for any clear patterns to be drawn.

Royal Administration

Five members of the royal administration were buried here (see Figure 274). Amongst his other titles, Amenhotep called Huy-TT40 (Tut) was a 'Royal Scribe', 'Messenger of the King upon every Foreign Land' and 'Fan-bearer on the Right of the King', while Nay-TT271 (Ay) was another 'Royal Scribe', and Sayemitef-TT273 (Dyn 20) was a 'Scribe'...in the Estate of his Lord'. Amenemopet-TT276 (TIII-AII) was a 'Royal Seal-bearer' and 'Chamberlain', while Ameneminet-TT381 (Dyn 19) was a 'Messenger of the King'. The three scribes were buried within the central cluster of tombs, within 100m of each other (TT40, TT271 and TT276), while the other two were not in close proximity.

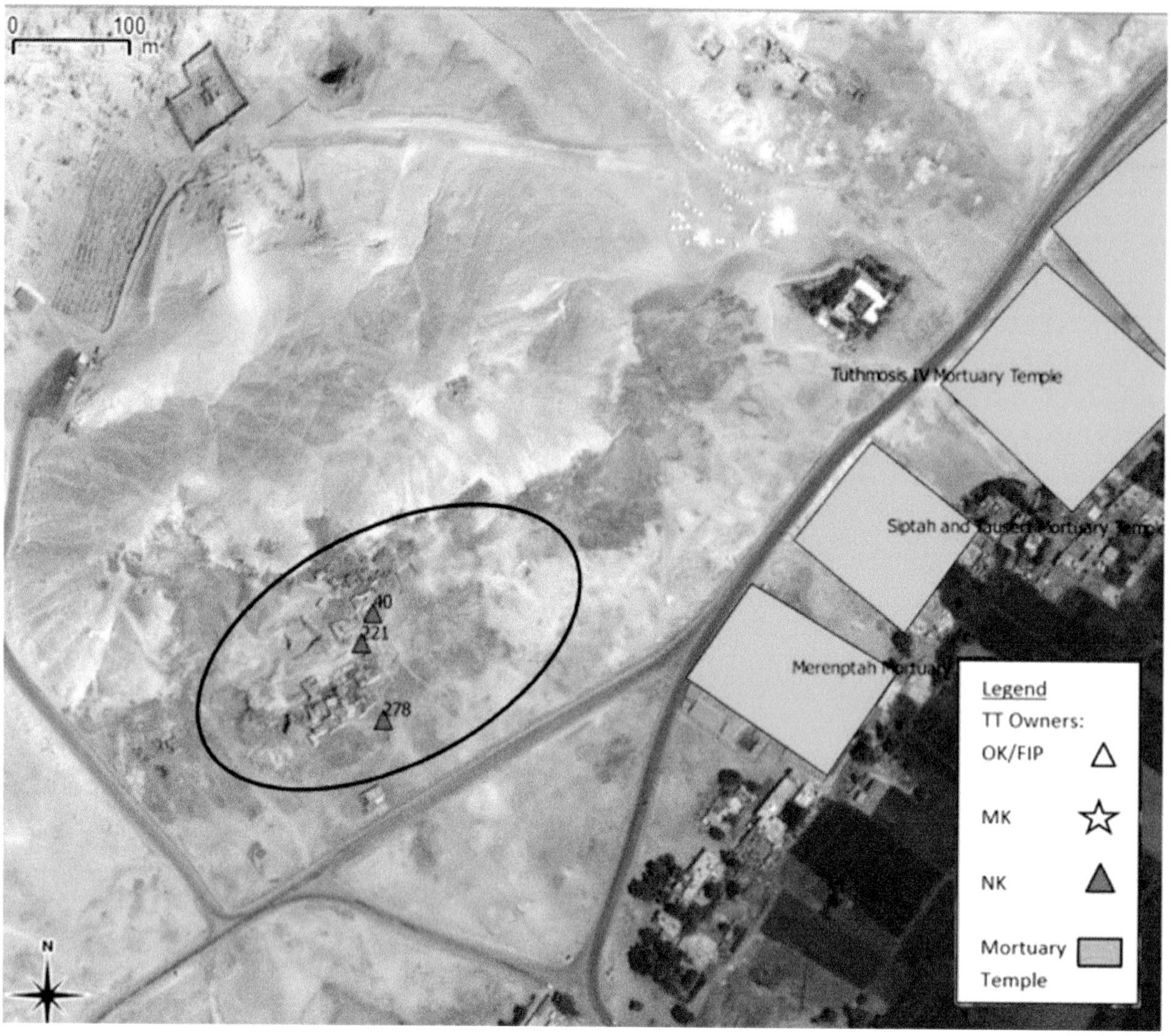

Figure 273: TTs of the Temple Administration in Qurnet Murai (Author's own using QGIS)

General Administration

Only two tombs belonged to members of the general administration (see Figure 275). They were both 'Overseers of the Treasury', Amenemopet-TT276 (TIII-AII) and Usermontu-TT382 (Ram), and their tombs were located in relatively close proximity within this central cluster. There is no further inscriptional evidence to link these two individuals, who lived many years apart. Usermontu-TT382 was also 'Chief Steward' and 'Overseer of Cattle in the Granary'.

Local Administration

There were two local officials buried in this area (see Figure 276). They were both 'King's Son of Kush', suggesting a possible connection between Nubia and those buried in this area. Amenhotep called Huy-TT40 (Tut) (who was also was also 'Overseer of Southern Foreign Lands'), and Merymose-TT383 (AIII) were buried adjacent to each other within the central cluster. TT383 contains a scene of Merymose standing with his 'Scribe of Documents', Huy, while the sandstone jamb originally from TT383 was found in TT40 (PM I: 436). Could this be the same individual as Amenhotep called Huy, who then succeeded Merymose in this office? TT276 (TIII-AII) also contains scenes of Nubian tribute, suggesting a possible link between this tomb owner and Nubia (PM I: 352). The southern end of the necropolis seems a fitting place for those with a Nubian connection to have been buried, as the closest area to Nubia while still benefiting from proximity to Thebes and the associated rituals, but the huge distance between Thebes and Nubia makes this explanation unlikely. Qurnet Murai is the closest area of the necropolis to the mortuary temple of Ay and Horemheb (begun by Tutankhamun), and to that of Amenhotep III. It seems likely therefore that these two important individuals chose this area as a result of

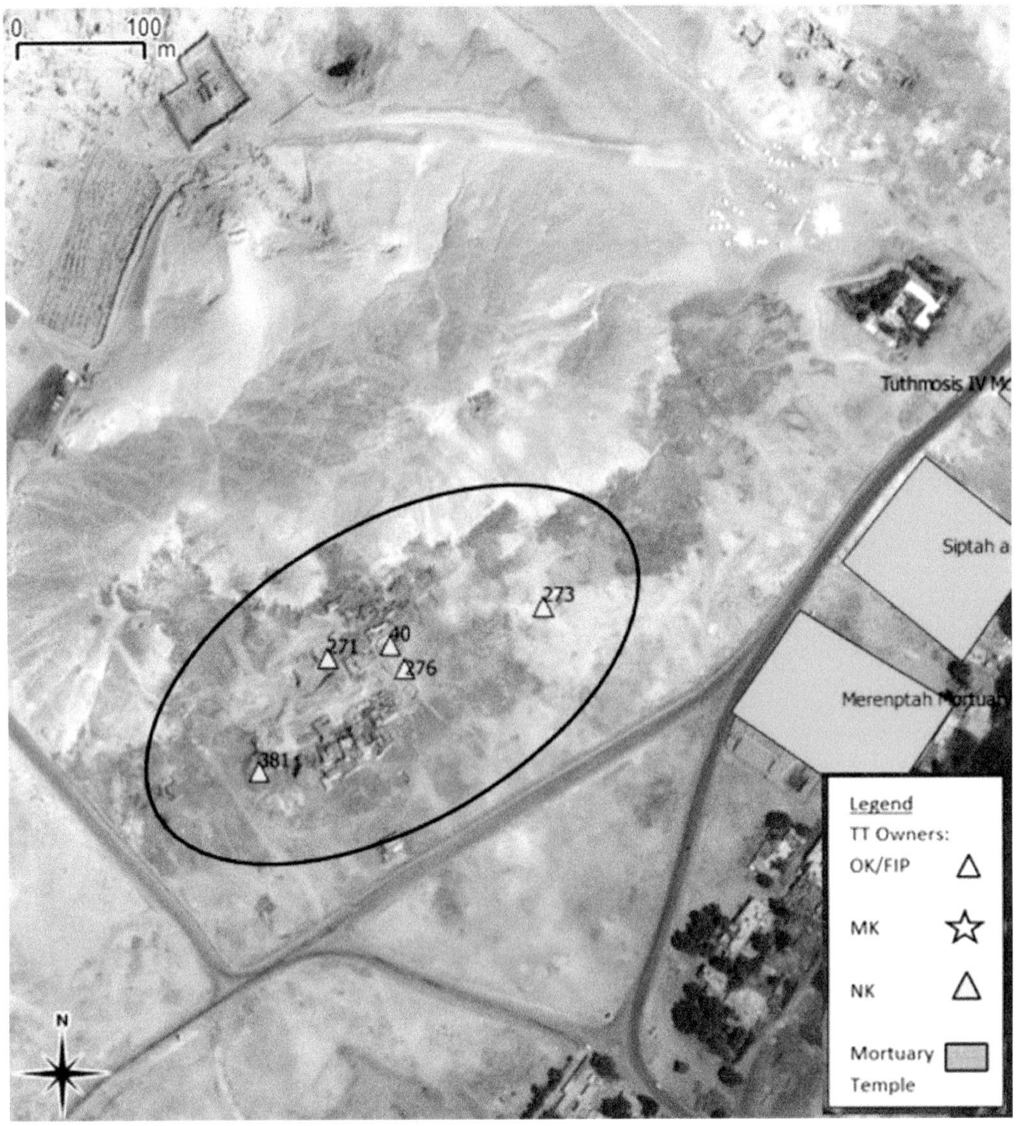

Figure 274: TTs of the Royal Administration in Qurnet Murai (Author's own using QGIS)

its proximity to the mortuary temples of the respective kings they served. The 'Royal Scribe' Nay-TT271 served Ay, so this would explain the location of his tomb too.

Military

One military title is found in Qurnet Murai (see Figure 277). Horimin-TT221 (Dyn 20) was a 'Scribe of the Army' who worked in a temple in Western Thebes (we know from his other titles this was probably the Ramesseum). He was buried within 50m of two other scribes, Amenhotep called Huy-TT40 (Tut), and Nay-TT271 (Ay).

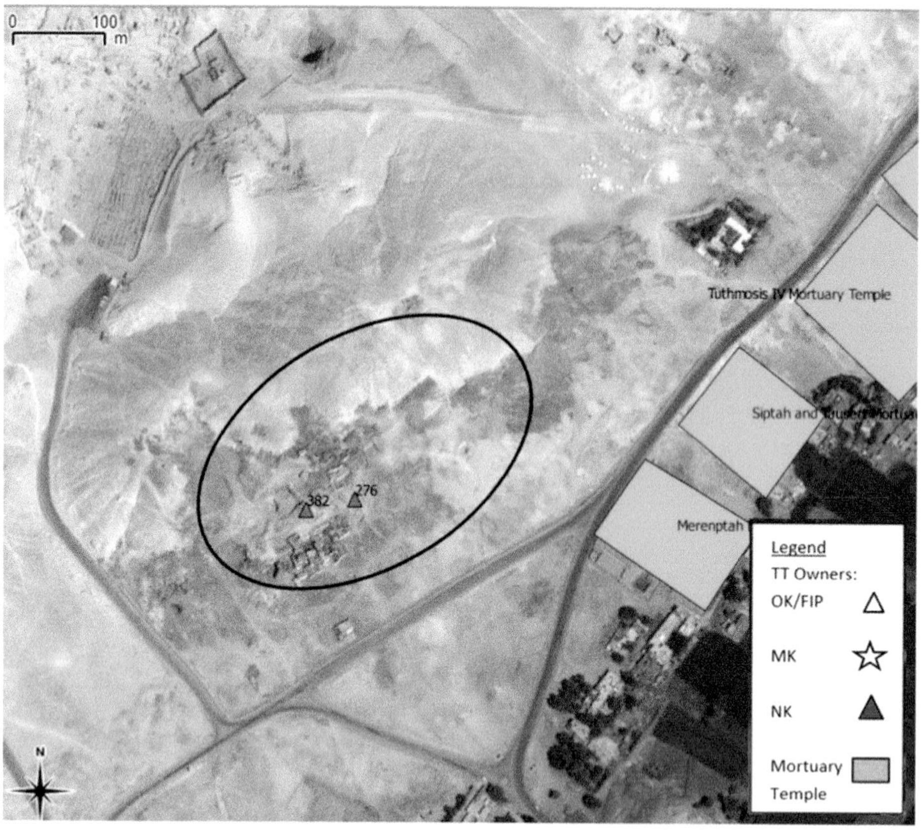

Figure 275: TTs of the General Administration in Qurnet Murai (Author's own using QGIS)

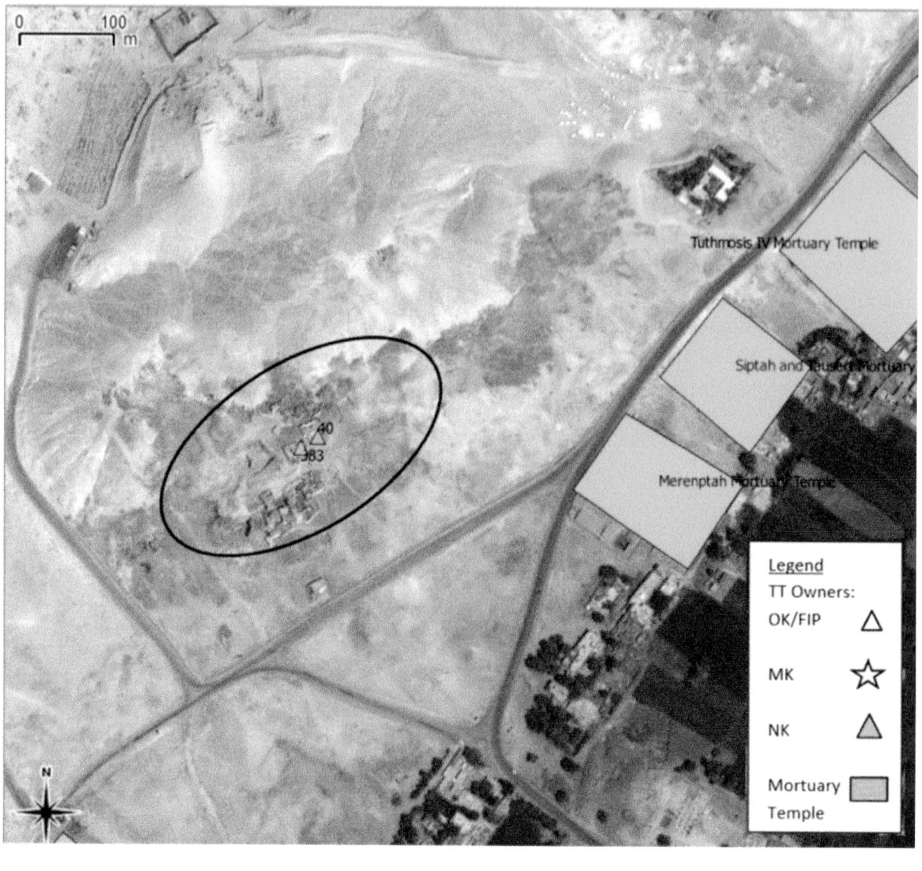

Figure 276: TTs of the Local Administration in Qurnet Murai (Author's own using QGIS)

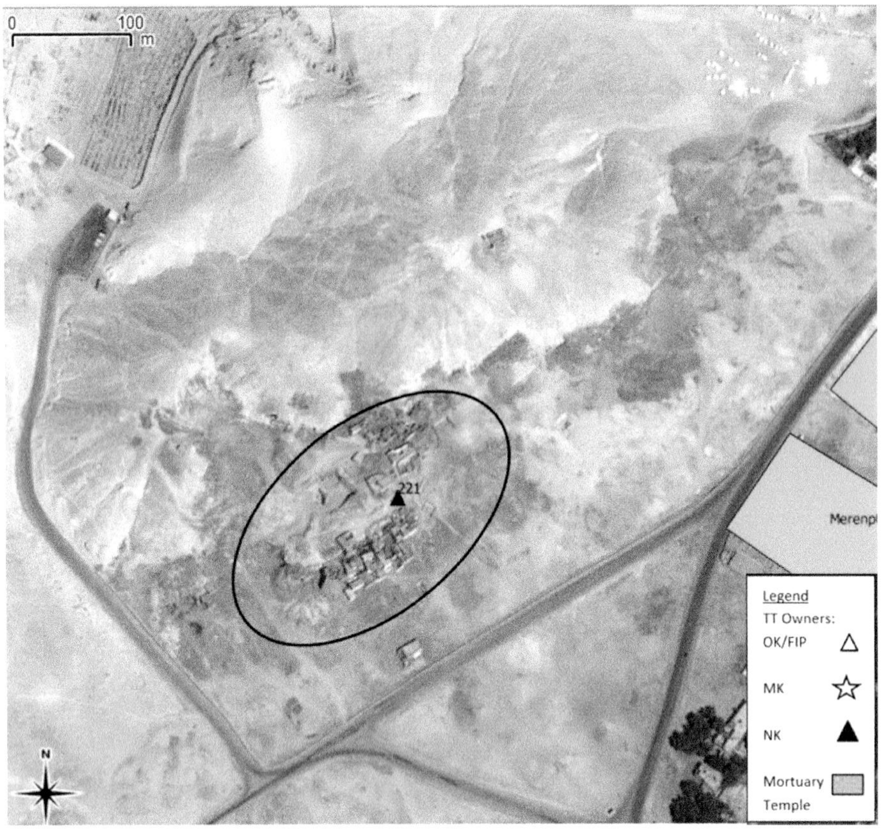

Figure 277: TT of the Military in Qurnet Murai (Author's own using QGIS)

Relationships between Tomb Owners / Tombs

There is no inscriptional evidence of any familial relationships between the tomb owners at Qurnet Murai, as the few surviving names of parents and wives do not reveal any common factors. The similarity between the names of the Amenemopet-TT276 (TIII-AII) and Ameneminet-TT277 (Dyn 20) and the proximity of their tombs might have suggested a potential connection, but the significant difference in date and lack of common titles makes this unlikely. Ameneminet-TT277 shares the same name as the owner of TT381, and both tombs are Ramesside. A headless statue found in the courtyard of TT277 is inscribed as 'Royal Herald Ameneminet' (PM I: 355). Ameneminet-TT381 was similarly titled, the 'Messenger of the King to every Land', based on another headless statue, inscribed with this name and title, found in this uninscribed tomb (PM I: 435). If both statues belonged to the owner of TT381 this would establish a connection between the two men.

Shared Courtyards

TT277 and TT278

TT277 and TT278 occupy a position on the low slopes at Qurnet Murai, opening onto adjacent sides of a shared courtyard (see Figures 278 and 279). Both date to the Twentieth Dynasty, but TT277 was originally thought to have been built first (D'Abbadie, 1954: 1). The tomb owners had no obvious occupational link that may have influenced their decision to be buried in such close proximity (see Table 51). They may have been contemporaries, friends, or even relatives as their names are very similar, who chose to spend eternity together, but with no common titles or explicit familial relationship there is not enough evidence to make a definite link between these individuals.

TT272 and TT273

These tombs are adjacent to each other on the western side of the same courtyard (see Figure 280). They both date to the Twentieth Dynasty but with no definitive reign, relationship or common titles there is not enough evidence to make a link between these individuals (see Table 52).

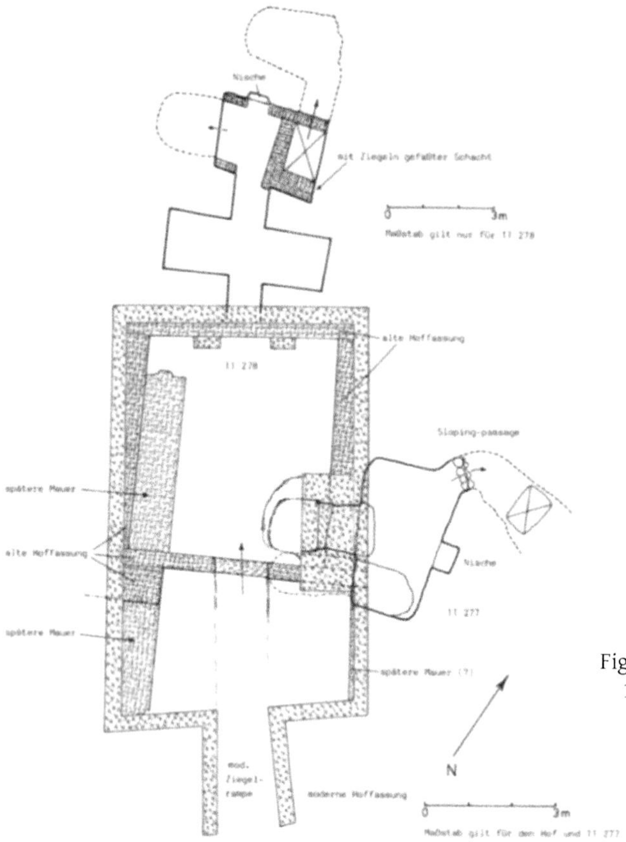

Figure 278: Plan of TT278 and TT277 (Kampp 1996: Figure 444 – Courtesy of Professor Seyfried)

Table 51: Owners of TT277 and TT278

TT	Dyn	Reign	Name	Titles
TT277	20	?	Ameneminet	**Divine father of Ptah(-Sokar);** Divine father of the temple of Neb-Maat-Ra (AIII) and of the temple of Sokar; Divine father in the temple of Sokar; *wꜥb* priest; Lector priest; Chief of secrets in the temple of eternity;
TT278	20	?	Amenemhab	Herdsman of Amun-Re;

Figure 279: Shared courtyard of TT277 and TT278 (Author's own)

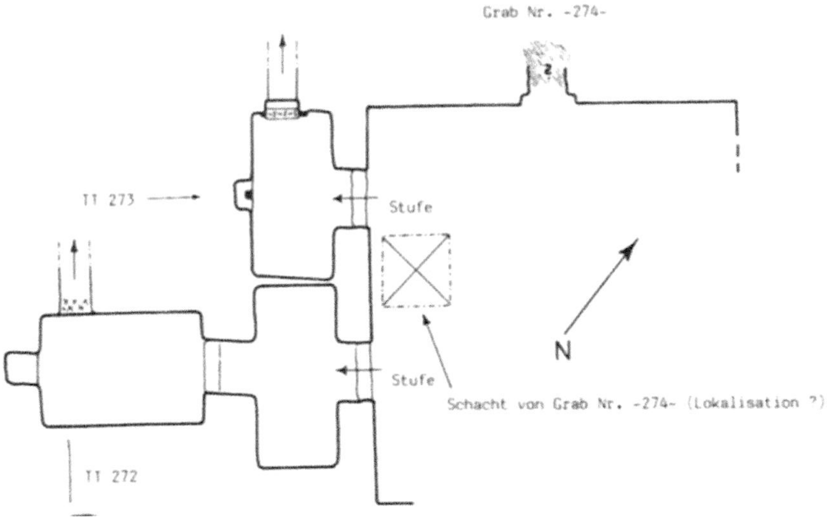

Figure 280: TT272 and TT273 (Kampp 1996: Figure 441 – Courtesy of Professor Seyfried)

Table 52: Owners of TT272 and TT273

TT	Dyn	Reign	Name	Title
TT272	20	?	Khaemopet	Divine father of Amun in Thebes; *wꜥb* priest; Lector priest in the temple of Sokar;
TT273	20	?	Sayemitef	Scribe in the estate of his Lord;

Tomb Reuse

Only one tomb in Qurnet Murai was reused during the New Kingdom, to the east of the area (see Figure 281 and Table 53). TT270 was built in the Middle Kingdom, while its reuse is datable only to the Ramesside Period. TT270 was reused by the priest Amenemwia, but without knowing the occupation of the original occupant, a reason for the reuse of this single tomb is unknown. It is strange that this Middle Kingdom tomb was not reused in the Eighteenth Dynasty, as the Middle Kingdom tombs in Qurna were. As seven Twentieth Dynasty tombs were built in Qurnet Murai, it seems likely that this reuse dated to this period when the rest of the necropolis was full. All of the tombs in closest proximity, within 50m of TT270 date to the Twentieth Dynasty (TT222, TT235, TT272 and TT273), with the exception of TT274 which dated to Merenptah. Khaemopet-TT272 held similar titles to Amenemwia-TT270 as both men were '*wꜥb* priests' and 'Lector Priests in the Temple of Sokar', so could potentially have been colleagues. The tombs of three 'High Priests of Montu' within 50m may also have influenced the reuse of TT270 (TT222, TT235 and TT274), but we would expect TT270 to have been reused by a priest of Montu if this were the case, so perhaps proximity to the 'Overseer of Priests of All the Gods' (TT222) was the important factor here, as he could potentially have been the superior of the usurper of TT270.

Conclusions

This area seems to have been predominantly chosen as a burial site by those who worked in the nearby royal mortuary temples as a result of its proximity to them and the proximity to temples of the kings they had served (particularly TT40, TT271, TT275 and TT383). This shift to the southern end of the necropolis as a result of the connection with the late Eighteenth Dynasty mortuary temples built in this southern

Figure 281: Reused TTs in Qurnet Murai at the end of the New Kingdom, shown by date of reuse (Author's own using QGIS)

Table 53: Reused tombs in Qurnet Murai

TT	Original Date	Date of Reuse
TT270	MK	Ram

Figure 282: The entrance of TT40 (Author's own)

area was proposed by Helck (1962: 241) and has been confirmed here. Another factor in the increase of use of this area during the Ramesside Period was that there was little room elsewhere in the more desirable locations, so Qurnet Murai was chosen as one of the few places a large tomb could still be built, such as TT40 (see Figure 282), TT271 and TT276 (see Figure 283). It seems likely that there are more tombs to be found in this area with more conclusions to be made (Gabolde, 1995: 160; Kampp, 1996: 121).

Three individuals had titles associating them with Amenhotep III. Sobekmose-TT275 and Ameneminet-TT277 were priests in his mortuary temple (discussed above), while Merymose-TT383 was 'King's Son' of Amenhotep III and his tomb dated to this reign, supporting the connection between the use of this southern area of the necropolis and the location of the mortuary temple of Amenhotep III. The mortuary temple of Amenhotep III is also visible to the east from the upper slopes of Qurnet Murai (see Figure 284). TT40 and TT271 date to the reigns of Tutankhamun and Ay respectively, whose collaborative mortuary temple was located adjacent to Medinet Habu (see Chapter 2). As Medinet Habu can be seen from the entrance of TT40, it seems probable that this late Eighteenth Dynasty temple was also visible (see Figure 285).

Two individuals, Horimin-TT221 (Dyn 20) and Amenwahsu-TT274 (Mer) worked at the Ramesseum. Although this area lies some 500m to the south of the Ramesseum, these tombs were built at a time when the slopes to the north and west of the Ramesseum in Qurna were crowded with tombs, and the area directly to east of the Ramesseum was apparently deliberately left clear of tombs (see Chapter 3). This relatively empty area had plenty of space for tomb building, was closer to the Ramesseum than Dra Abu el-Naga to the north and had a good view of the Ramesseum to the north (see Figures 286 and 287).

Figure 283: View looking west towards Qurnet Murai (Author's own)

Figure 284: View east from Qurnet Murai to the mortuary temple of Amenhotep III (Author's own)

Figure 285: View south from TT40 towards Medinet Habu (Author's own)

Figure 286: View north to the Ramesseum from TT221 (Author's own)

Figure 287: Zoomed in view north to the Ramesseum from TT221 (Author's own)

Chapter 11: Deir el-Medina

(See Appendix 14)

Location

Deir el-Medina is located at the southern end of the necropolis, to the east of the modern road leading to the Valley of the Queens, and to the south of the Valley of the Kings, which lies beyond the hill to the north of the village (see Figure 288). The tombs are located between 110m and 150m above sea-level (see Figure 289). The flood plain lies some distance to the east of the village, at 90m above sea-level. The tombs at Deir el-Medina are only of limited use to this study as a result of the restricted space available for burial and the lack of diversity amongst those buried here. The tomb owners were all craftsmen and scribes who lived in the village, so the distribution of their tombs reveals little about the patterns found in other areas of the necropolis. However, patterns can be identified by looking at tombs in terms of reign. The cemetery lies on the slopes to the west of the workmen's village (see Figures 290 and 291).

Date of Use

The settlement of Deir el-Medina was occupied from the reign of Tuthmosis I until the Amarna period, when the site was apparently abandoned and destroyed by fire, before being reorganised and expanded during the reign of Horemheb (Bierbrier 1982: 65). The site was finally abandoned during the reign of Ramesses XI, when the inhabitants sought the relative safety of Medinet Habu (Bierbrier 1982: 119).

There are 54 TTs in the cemetery at Deir el-Medina, all dating to the New Kingdom (see Table 54). Only six tombs date to the Eighteenth Dynasty (TT8, TT291, TT325, TT338, TT340 and TT354), with an additional two tombs dated to either the Eighteenth or Nineteenth Dynasty (TT6 and TT268). 27 tombs date to the Nineteenth Dynasty (TT1, TT2, TT4, TT7, TT10, TT210, TT211, TT212, TT215, TT216, TT217, TT218, TT219, TT220,

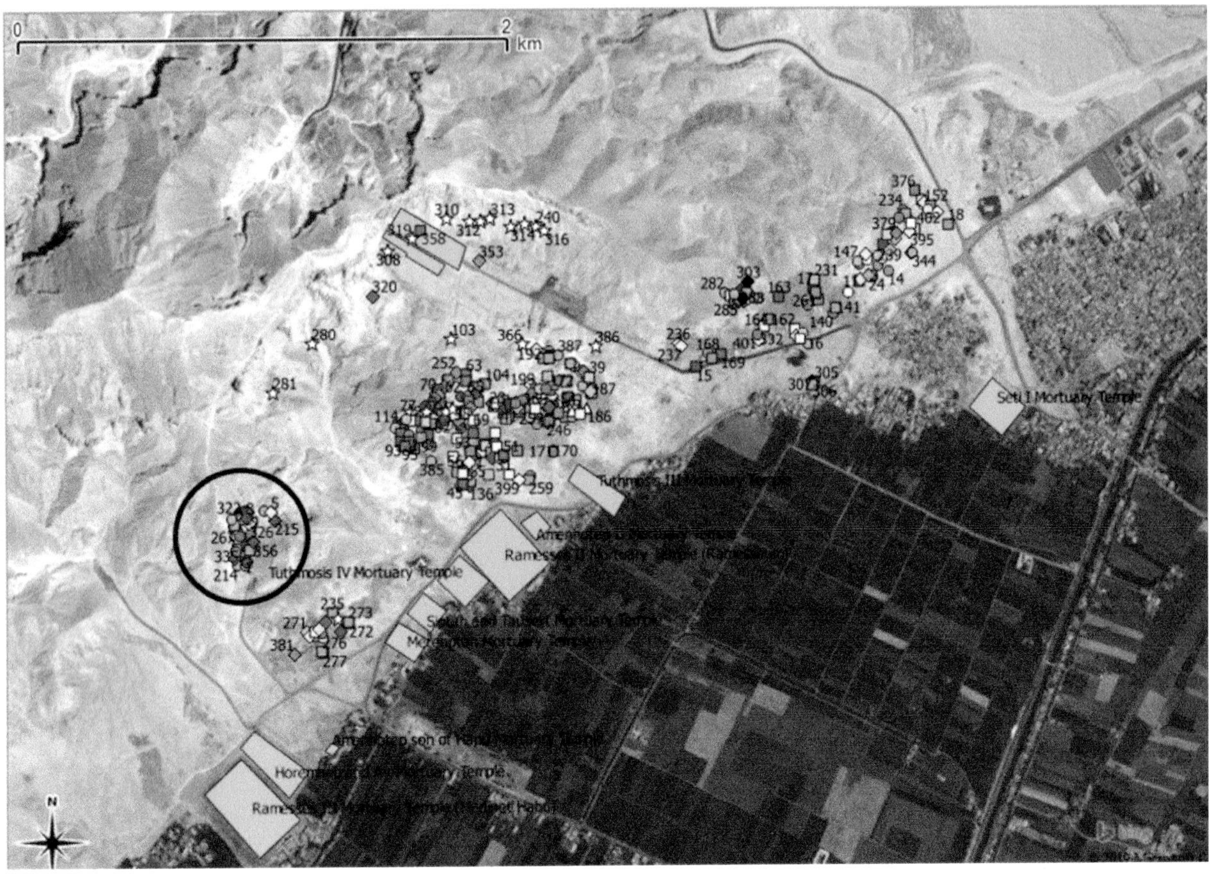

Figure 288: Location of Deir el-Medina within the Theban Necropolis (Author's own)

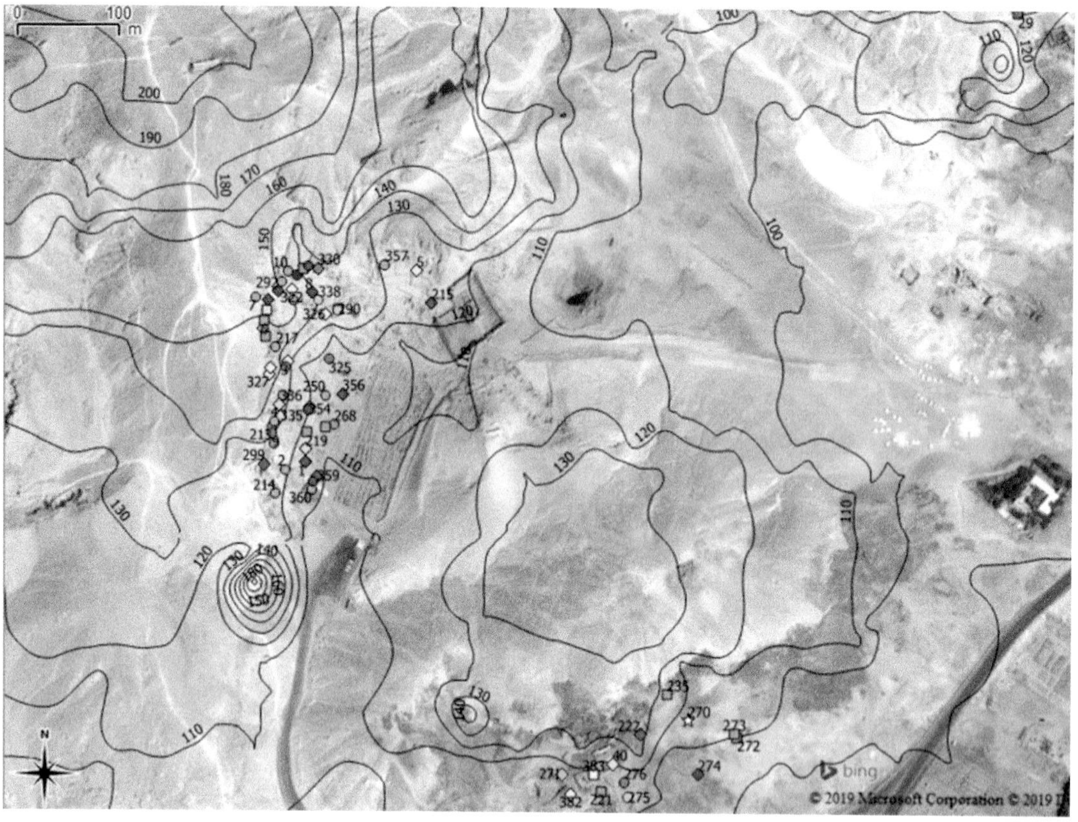

Figure 289: Landscape of Deir el-Medina (Author's own using QGIS)

Figure 290: TTs of Deir el-Medina (Author's own using QGIS)

Figure 291: Plan of Deir el-Medina, showing the cemetery to the west of the village (Dodson and Ikram, 2008: 334 – Courtesy of Professor Aidan Dodson)

TT250, TT265, TT292, TT323, TT330, TT335, TT336, TT337, TT339, TT356, TT357, TT360 and TT361), and only five tombs date to the Twentieth Dynasty (TT213, TT267, TT299, TT355 and TT359). With the exception of TT267 these Twentieth Dynasty tombs are located in the southern half of the cemetery, but again there is no evidence of clustering by date. A further 14 tombs are datable only to either the Nineteenth or Twentieth Dynasty (TT3, TT5, TT9, TT214, TT266, TT269, TT290, TT298, TT321, TT322, TT326, TT327, TT328 and TT329).

Three tombs date to the early to mid-Eighteenth Dynasty (TT8, TT340 and TT354). The earliest TT in Deir el-Medina, TT340, is only datable prior to the reign of Hatshepsut, followed by TT354 dated between the reigns of Amenhotep II and Tuthmosis IV, and TT8, dated between the reigns of Amenhotep II and Amenhotep III. Two tombs date to the late Eighteenth Dynasty after the Amarna period, between the reigns of Tutankhamun and Horemheb (TT291 and TT338). One additional tomb is dateable only to the Eighteenth Dynasty (TT325). Of these Eighteenth Dynasty tombs, TT8 and TT338 are located adjacent to each other, with TT291 nearby. The other Eighteenth Dynasty tombs are located within 100m, but not in particularly close proximity (see Figure 292). This lack of Eighteenth

Table 54: Deir el-Medina TTs distributed by most likely date

Date	No. of Tombs	Tombs
Dyn 18	*	TT325
-Hatshepsut	*	TT340
AII-TIV	*	TT354
AII-AIII	*	TT8
Tut-Hor	**	TT291, TT338
Hor–RII	*	TT6
Dyn 18-19	*	TT268,
SI	**	TT323, TT361,
SI-RII	*****	TT1, TT215, TT265, TT292, TT356,
RII	**************	TT2, TT4, TT7, TT10, TT210, TT212, TT214, TT217, TT218, TT250, TT337, TT339, TT357, TT360
RII-Mer	****	TT219, TT220, TT335, TT336,
RII-SII	*	TT216
SII-Sip	*	TT211
Dyn 19	**	TT329, TT330
RIII	**	TT9, TT213
RIII-RIV	**	TT299, TT359,
Ram	*******	TT3, TT5, TT269, TT322, TT326, TT327, TT328
Dyn 20	******	TT266, TT267, TT290, TT298, TT321, TT355

Figure 292: TTs in Deir el-Medina at the end of the Eighteenth Dynasty (Author's own using QGIS)

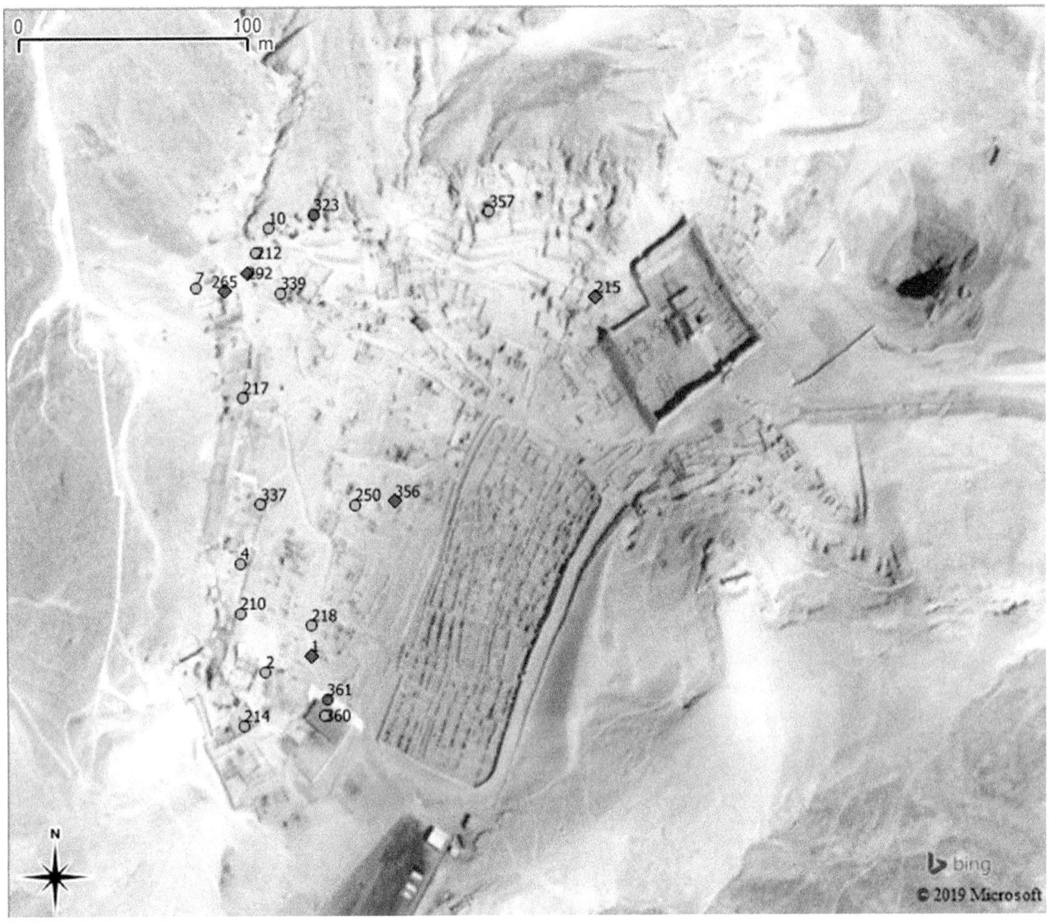

Figure 293: TTs in Deir el-Medina dated to the reign of Seti I/Ramesses II (Author's own using QGIS)

Dynasty tombs is a result of the destruction of the village during the Amarna period, so this is not a reflection of the Eighteenth Dynasty cemetery.

During the Nineteenth Dynasty the Deir el-Medina cemetery really evolved. Two tombs date to the reign of Seti I (TT323 and TT361), while a further five are datable only to either Seti I or Ramesses II (TT1, TT215, TT265, TT292 and TT356). There was a peak in usage during the reign of Ramesses II as 14 tombs are dated specifically to his reign (TT2, TT4, TT7, TT10, TT210, TT212, TT214, TT217, TT218, TT250, TT337, TT339, TT357 and TT360. These tombs were distributed throughout the cemetery, but the northern western corner has the highest frequency of these early Nineteenth Dynasty tombs (see Figures 293 and 294).

Four tombs in the southern end of the cemetery are dated to either Ramesses II or Merenptah (TT219, TT220, TT335 and TT336), while additional tombs are dated between Ramesses II and Seti II (TT216), and Seti II and Siptah (TT211). Two further tombs are datable only to the Nineteenth Dynasty and were located at opposite ends of the cemetery (TT329 and TT330) (see Figure 295).

By the end of the Nineteenth Dynasty, the north-western end of the cemetery was still the most populated, with few TTs in the centre, and an even distribution of tombs to the south. The surviving Eighteenth Dynasty tombs are located on the lower slopes closest to the village, in the northern and central area. In the Nineteenth Dynasty the cemetery expanded to the upper slopes, further away from the village (see Figure 296), presumably as a result of the superior view and the lower slopes becoming more crowded.

There are several tombs datable only to the Ramesside Period (TT3, TT5, TT269, TT322, TT326, TT327 and TT328). Of these, TT3, TT327 and TT328 are in close proximity in the centre of the cemetery (see Figure 297).

Both tombs dated to the reign of Ramesses III (TT9 and TT213) are located adjacent to each other in the south-eastern area of the cemetery, suggesting some clustering by date. Two tombs date between Ramesses III and IV (TT299 and TT359), both located in the south-eastern area of the cemetery within 50m of the Ramesses III tombs. TT299 is also located at the same altitude as TT9 and TT213, just 25m away. Six tombs

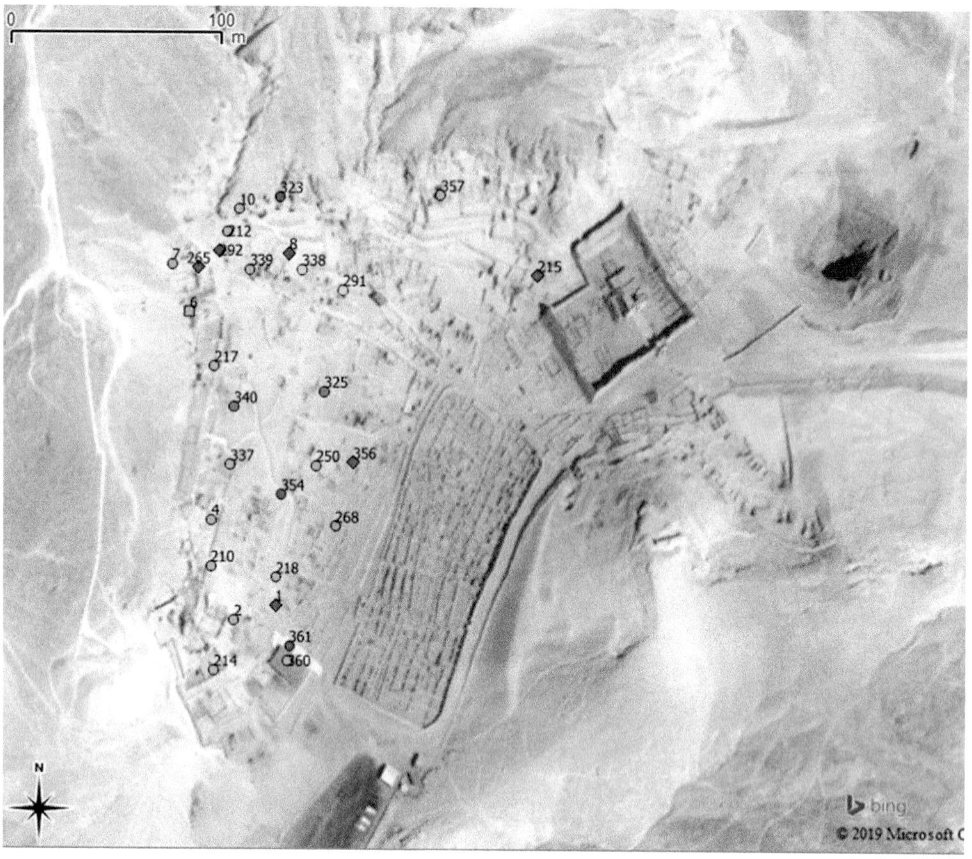

Figure 294: TTs in Deir el-Medina at the end of the reign of Ramesses II (Author's own using QGIS)

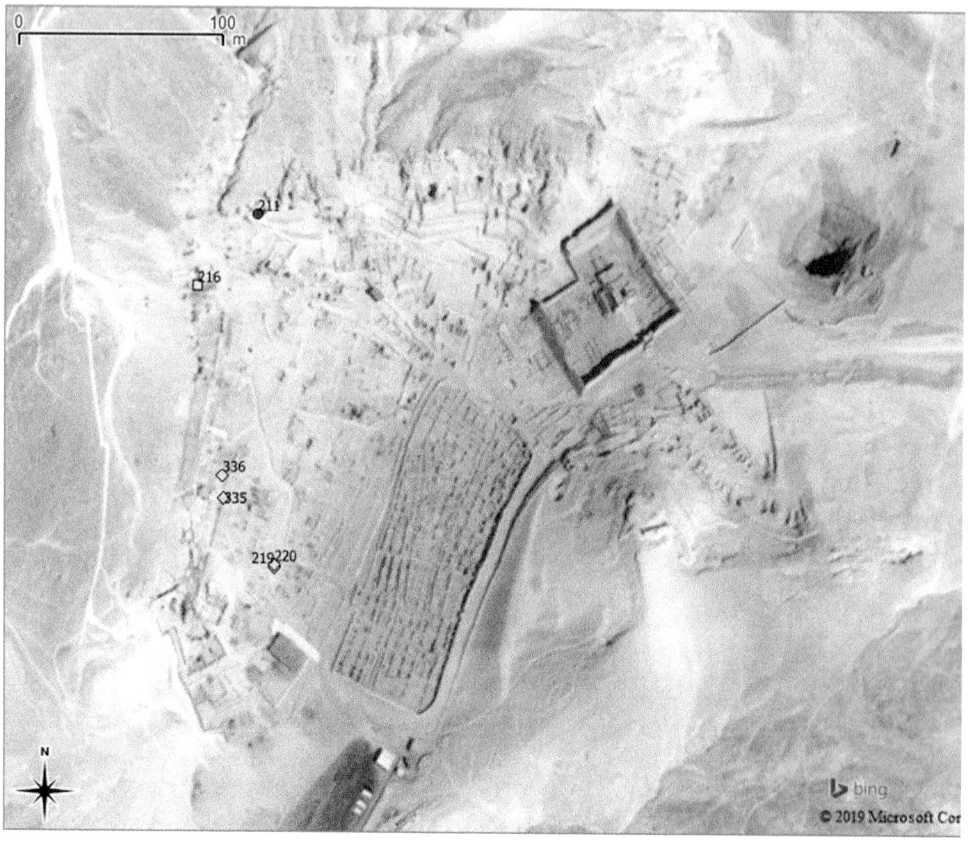

Figure 295: TTs in Deir el-Medina dated between Merenptah and the end of the Nineteenth Dynasty (Author's own using QGIS)

Figure 296: TTs in Deir el-Medina at the end of the Nineteenth Dynasty (Author's own using QGIS)

are dated to the Twentieth Dynasty (TT266, TT267, TT290, TT298, TT321 and TT355). Of these, TT266 and TT267 are located adjacent to each other in the north eastern half of the necropolis, and TT298 and TT355 are also adjacent to each other at the southern end of the necropolis (see Figure 298).

By the end of the New Kingdom, some space remained in the centre of the cemetery, where any view to the east would have been obscured by the hill of Qurnet Murai, presumably explaining why this location was less popular (see Figure 299). Tombs lined the upper slopes of the Deir el-Medina cemetery, and the southern end was well-populated. There are a number of tombs along the northern limits of the cemetery, surrounding some of the oldest tombs in the area, in addition to three isolated tombs to the north-east of the main cemetery, close to the current temple walls (see Figures 300, 301 and 302).

Figure 297: TTs datable only to the Ramesside Period (Author's own using QGIS)

Figure 298: TTs in Deir el-Medina dating to the Twentieth Dynasty (Author's own using QGIS)

Figure 299: TTs in Deir el-Medina at the end of the New Kingdom (Author's own using QGIS)

Figure 300: View from the entrance to the village, looking west towards the cemetery (Author's own)

Figure 301: View across the upper slopes, looking north-west (Author's own)

Figure 302: View across the lower slopes, looking north towards the temple (Author's own)

Occupation of Tomb Owners

(See Table 55)

This cemetery was solely reserved for the use of craftsmen and those who inhabited the village of Deir el-Medina. As a result of the limited range of titles of those buried here, the most common titles of the tomb owners have been analysed rather than general occupational groups as in the rest of the necropolis (see Figure 303).

Servants of the Place of Truth

35 tombs belong to 'Servants in the Place of Truth' (see Figure 304) or variants thereof, a title which often appeared alongside other titles. The tombs of these ordinary workmen were scattered throughout the necropolis but several individuals with this title were buried in particularly close proximity: Ken-TT4 (RII), Amenmose-TT9 (RIII), Raweben-TT210 (RII) and Penamun-TT213 (RIII); Amennakht-TT218 (RII), Nebenmaat-TT219 (RII-Mer) and Khaemteri-TT220 (RII-Mer); Irynefer-TT290 (Dyn 20) and Nu and Nakhtmin-TT291 (late Dyn 18); Turobay-TT327 and Hay-TT328 (both Ram); Nakhtamun-TT335 (RII-Mer) and Neferenpet-TT336 (RII-Mer) whose tomb is also adjacent to Ken-TT337 (RII); Pashedu-TT3 (Ram) and Amenemhat-TT340 (early Dyn 18).

Foremen

The most important individuals buried here were the 'Chief Workmen' or 'Foremen' (see Figure 305) and

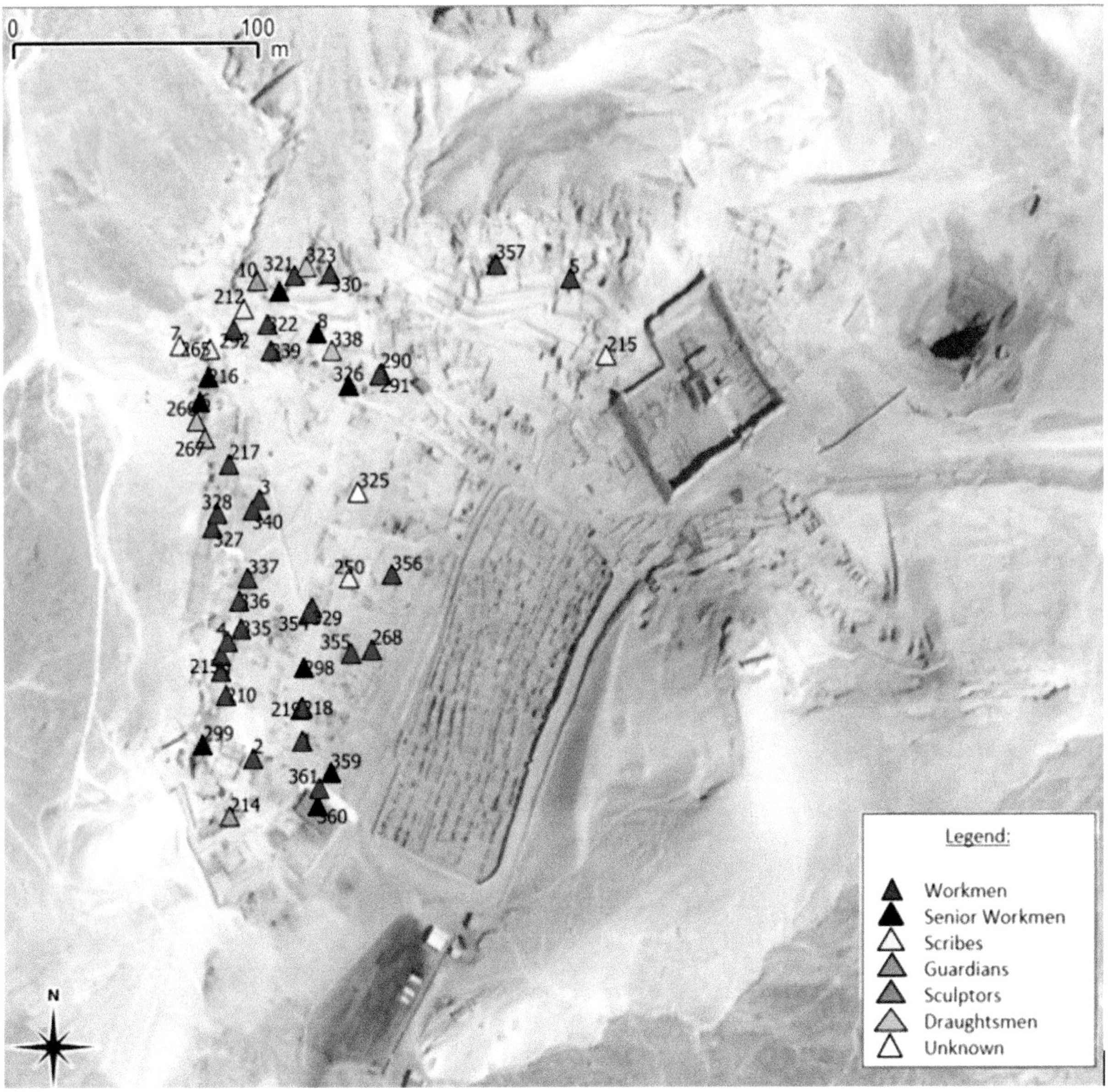

Figure 303: TTs in Deir el-Medina (Author's own using QGIS)

Table 55: Deir el-Medina tombs distributed by common titles

Title	Number of Tombs	Tombs
Servant in the Place of Truth	****************** *****************	TT1, TT2, TT3, TT4, TT5, TT9, TT10 (1 & 2), TT210, TT211, TT213, TT217, TT218, TT219, TT220, TT268, TT290, TT291 (1 & 2), TT292, TT298 (1 & 2), TT299, TT321, TT322, TT327, TT328, TT329 (1 & 2), TT330, TT335, TT336, TT339 (1 & 2), TT340, TT354, TT355, TT356, TT357, TT361
Foreman/ Chief in the Great Place	********	TT6, TT8, TT216, TT298, TT299, TT326, TT359, TT360
Chief Craftsman	**	TT266, TT267
Overseer of Works	****	TT8, TT216, TT299, TT359
Scribe in the Place of Truth	*****	TT7, TT212, TT215, TT250, TT265
Guardian in the Place of Truth	**	TT10, TT214
Sculptor	*****	TT4, TT217, TT335, TT336, TT337
Draughtsman	***	TT267, TT323, TT338
Unknown	**	TT269, TT325

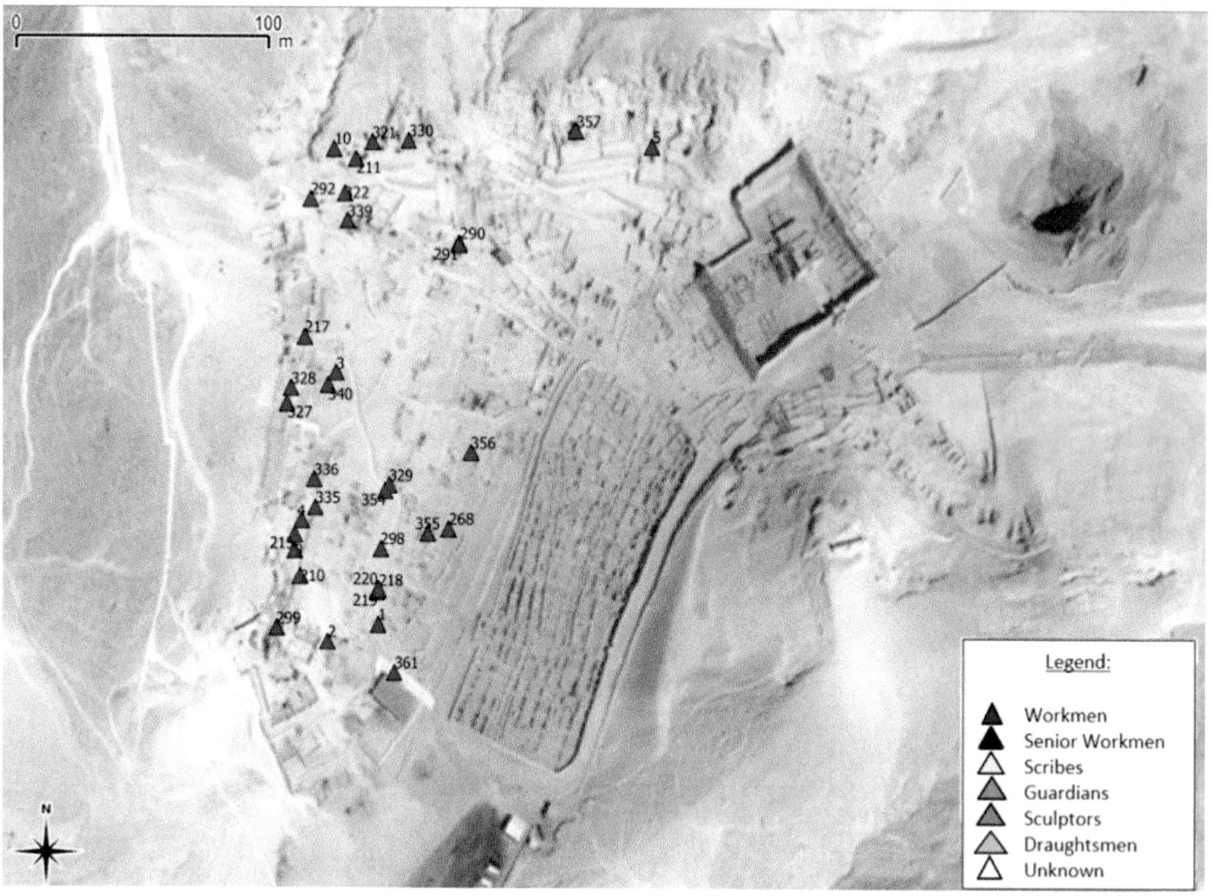

Figure 304: TTs of the 'Servants of the Place of Truth' in Deir el-Medina (Author's own using QGIS)

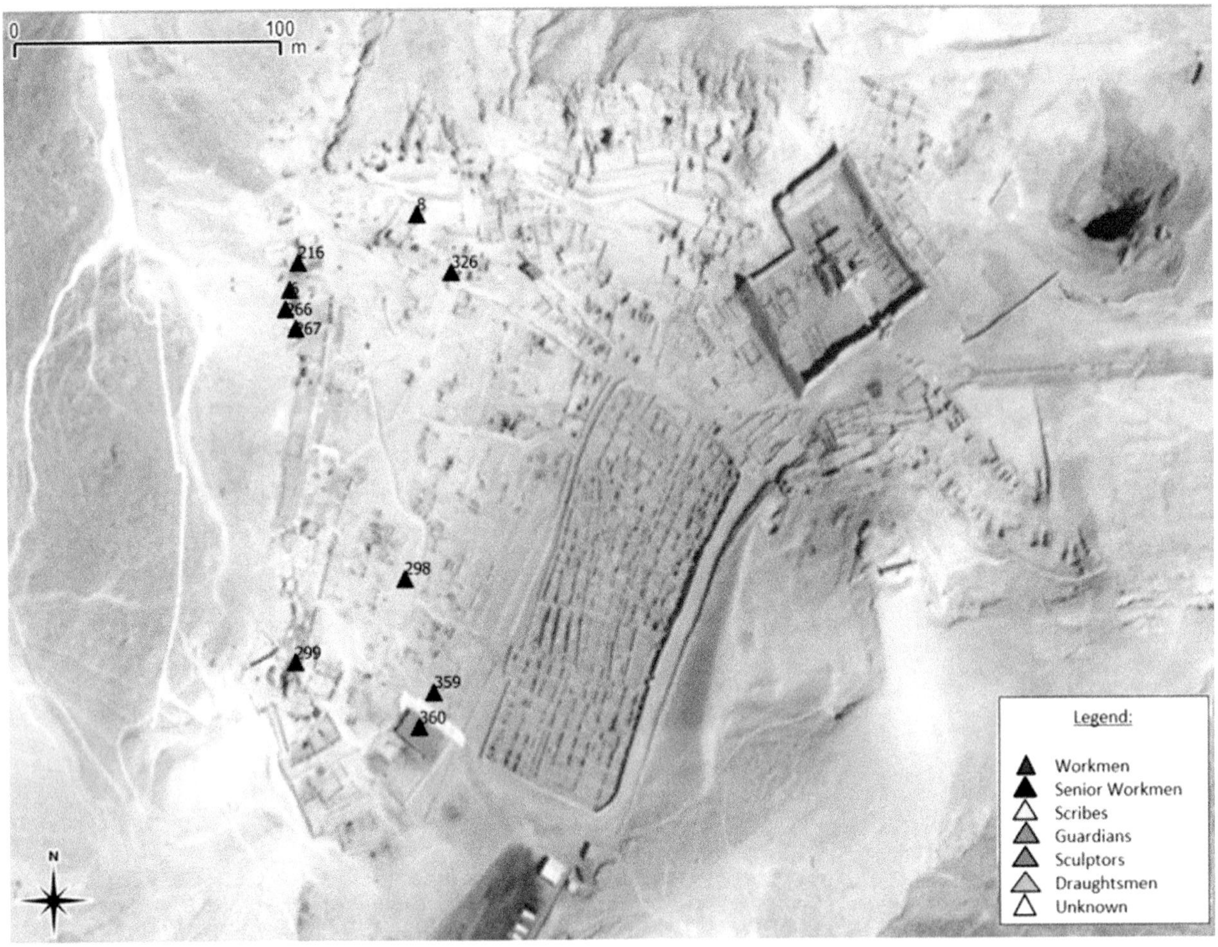

Figure 305: TTs of the 'Senior Workmen' in Deir el-Medina (Author's own using QGIS)

the senior 'Scribes of the Tomb' (Peden 2011: 382-83). Seven Ramesside tombs belonged to 'Foremen in the Place of Truth', Neferhotep and Nebnefer-TT6 (Hor-RII), Neferhotep-TT216 (RII-SII), Baki-TT298 (Dyn 20), Inherkhau-TT299 (RIII-RIV), Pashedu-TT326 (Ram), Inherkhau-TT359 (RIII-RIV) and Kaha-TT360 (RII), with an additional 'Chief in the Great Place' of the Eighteenth Dynasty, Kha-TT8 (AII-AIII). Paneb-TT211 (SII-Sip) was also a 'Foreman' but this title is not attested in his tomb, so he is not included here. There were two further 'Chief Craftsmen of the Lord of the Two Lands', one in the 'Place of Truth', Amennakht-TT266 (early Dyn 20) and the other in the 'House of Eternity', Hay-TT267 (Dyn 20), who was also 'Deputy of the Workmen in the Place of Truth', 'Maker of the Images of All the Gods in the House of Gold' and 'Temple Scribe of the Estate of Amun'. There was also an additional 'Overseer of Workmen' and 'Mayor' in the necropolis, Amenemopet-TT215 (SI-RII).

The foremen, as affluent members of the community, boasted impressive funerary monuments, containing a wealth of inscriptional evidence which enables us to build a more detailed genealogy of these individuals (Davies 1999: 2). The tomb of the 'Foremen of the Right Side', Neferhotep (I) and his son Nebnefer, TT6 (Hor-RII) was located adjacent to the tomb of Neferhotep's grandson, and Nebnefer's son, another foreman named Neferhotep (II), TT216 (RII-SII) (see Figure 305). All three foremen were of successive generations, showing the hereditary nature of the office (Davies 1999: 31). The elevated position of these tombs with views of the Ramesseum and the east bank, in conjunction with the ability to locate these family tombs side by side, demonstrates the influence these foremen must have had when it came to tomb allocation. As all three men were foremen during the reign of Ramesses II (Davies 1999: 31), the Ramesseum would have been under construction when their tombs were built, so this location may have chosen on account of its views over the mortuary temple of the king they all served. The latter Neferhotep (TT216) had no sons and was succeeded as Foreman by Paneb-T211 (SII-Sip), who was not the biological son of Neferhotep, but had been brought up by him (Davies 1999: 35), thus providing a possible explanation for this succession. Paneb was also the grandson of Kasa-TT10 (RII) (Davies, 1999: 34), whose tomb is just behind his own. His predecessor,

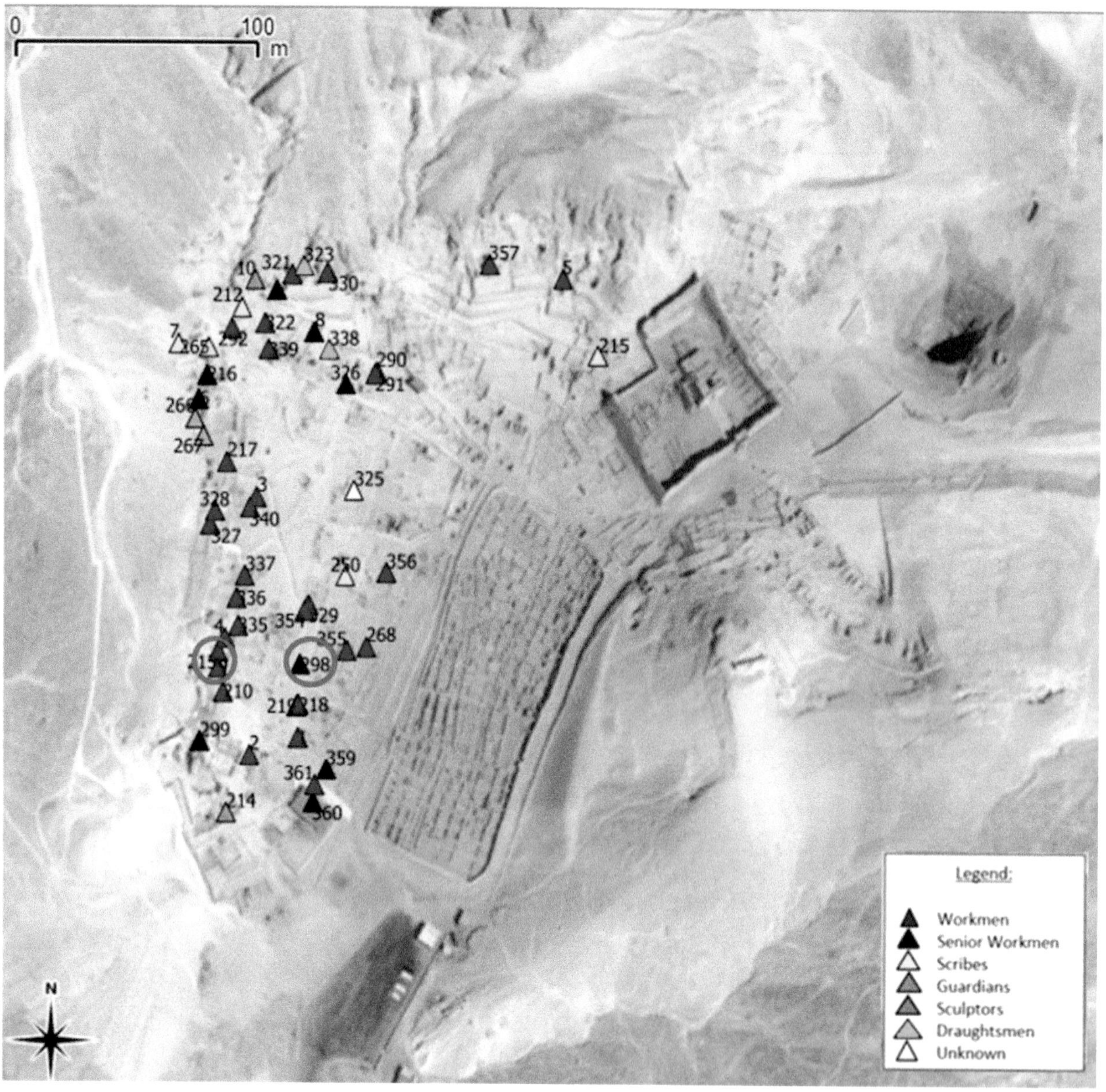

Figure 306: Baki's family group (Author's own using QGIS)

Neferhotep II's tomb (TT216) is also nearby. This burial pattern again demonstrates the importance of being buried close to family members, even those with a paternal role while not related by blood.

Another family cluster of tombs are related to Baki-TT298, who was the 'Foreman of the Left Side' during the reign of Seti I (Davies 1999: 2), who shared TT298 with his father Wennefer. Kampp (1996: 568) dates TT298 to the Twentieth Dynasty, contradicting the date of office given by Davies, while Porter and Moss only date the tomb to the Ramesside Period (PM I: 379). The tomb of Baki's son (or son-in-law), Penamun-TT213 (RIII- which again seems a little late if Baki was 'Foreman' in the reign of Seti I), is adjacent to the tomb of his brother (or brother-in-law) Amenmose-TT9 (RIII) (Davies 1999: 3). Amenmose may also have been the father-in-law of Baki (Davies 1999: 7), but either way a familial relationship has been established. Both tombs are in the court of TT4, a short distance behind their father's tomb (TT298), showing a desire for the family to be buried together (see Figure 306).

Baki was succeeded in office by Pashedu, who owned two tombs, TT3 (Ram), which he built while merely a 'Servant in the Place of Truth'), followed by TT326 (Ram) which he built after attaining the office of 'Foreman' (Davies 1999: 2). His later tomb is located to the north of the cemetery, a distance away from his predecessors, but closest to the 'Chief in the Great Place' Kha-TT8 (AII-AIII), perhaps suggesting a desire to associate himself with a more distant ancestor rather

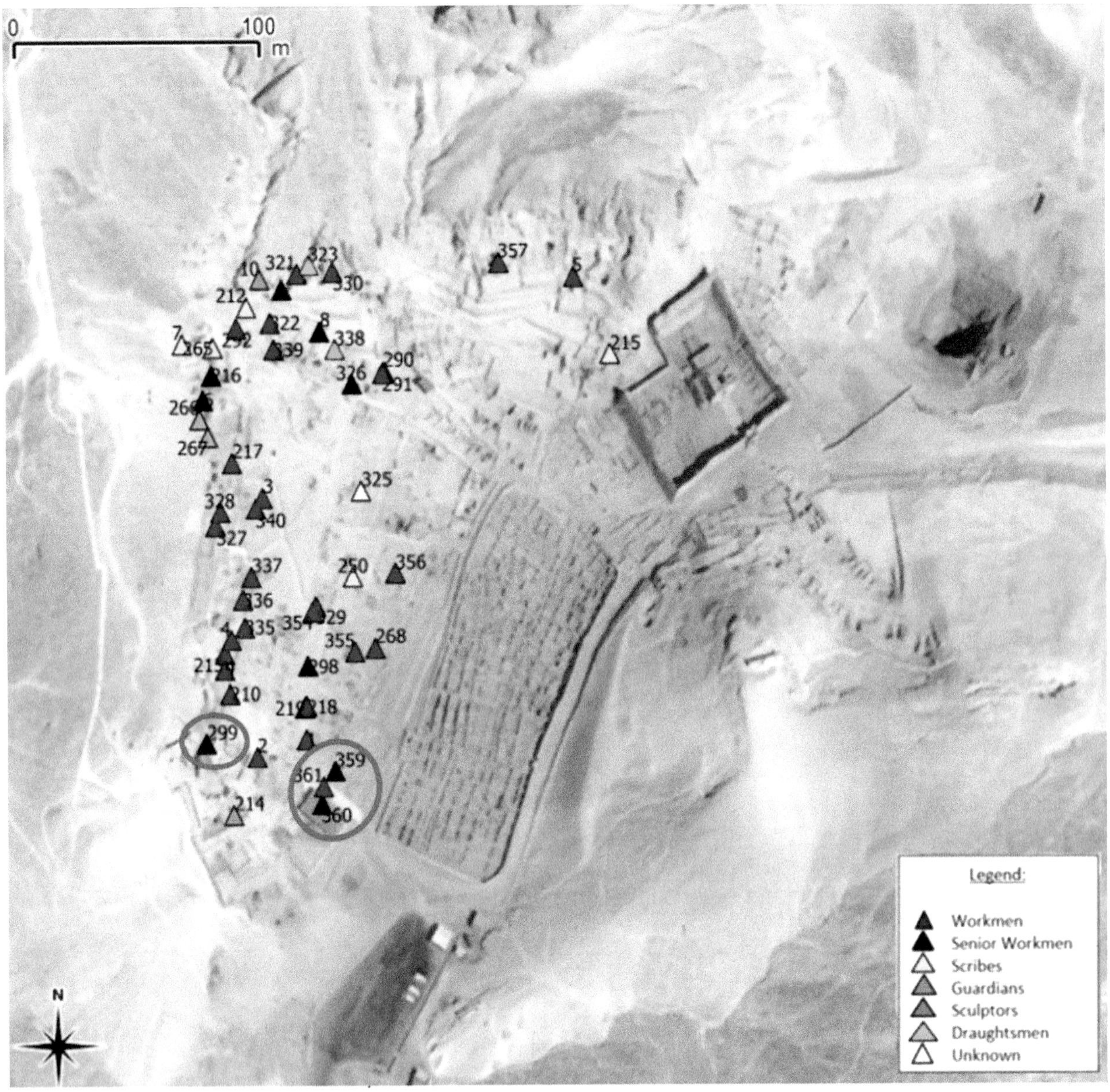

Figure 307: Kaha's family group (Author's own using QGIS)

than his predecessor. The tombs of Pashedu's relatives have not been identified.

Pashedu was succeeded by Kaha-TT360 (RII) as 'Foreman of the Left Side' (Davies 1999: 279). The cluster of tombs belonging to Kaha and his descendants is located some distance away from these earlier foremen, forming a family group of their own at the southern end of the village (see Figure 307). His son was another 'Foreman', Inkherkhau, who often has two tombs accredited to him, TT299 and TT359 (both RIII-RIV). However, Davies (1999: 21) uses genealogical evidence to prove that they actually belonged to two different foremen named Inkherhau. TT299 belonged to Kaha's son and is situated behind the tomb of his father, in relatively close proximity, while TT359 belonging to Kaha's great grandson, and is located to the north of his grandfather, separated only by the tomb of his own ancestor and Kaha's father, the 'Chief Craftsman' Huy-TT361 (SI) (Davies 1999: 13). There is also a statue of Kaha in the courtyard of the tomb of his co-foreman Neferhotep-TT216 (RII-SII) (Davies 1999: 14 and 279), demonstrating the close bond between the foremen of the right and left sides. Four foremen were also 'Overseer of Works', Kha-TT8, Neferhotep-TT216, Inkherkhau-TT299 and Inkherkhau-TT359, but their tombs are not in close proximity.

The tombs of two 'Chief Craftsmen', Amennakht-TT266 (early Dyn 20) and Hay-TT267 (Dyn 20) are also located in close proximity to each other, which in conjunction with the inscriptional evidence (O.

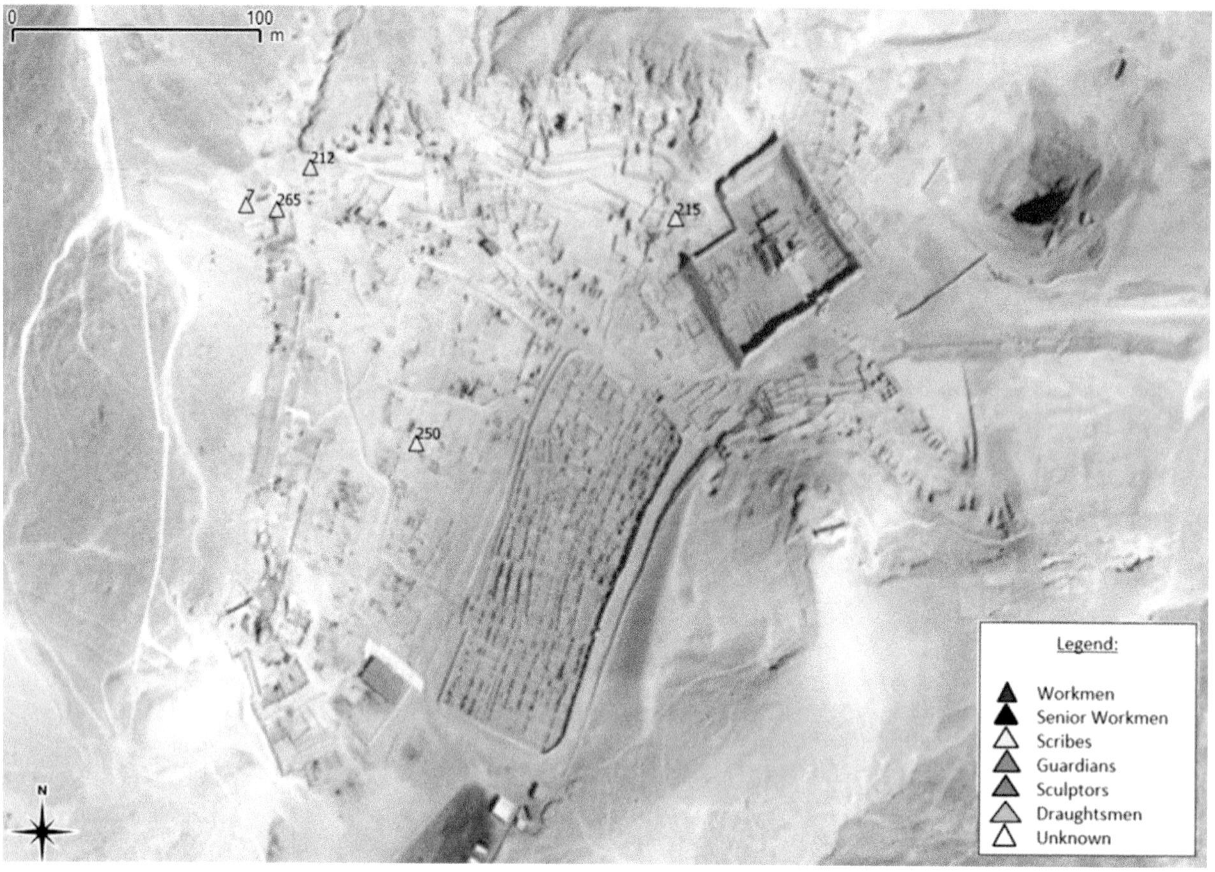

Figure 308: TTs of the 'Scribes' in Deir el-Medina (Author's own using QGIS)

BM 8494) reinforces the idea that Amennakht was the father of Hay (Davies 1999: 63 and 66; Bierbrier 1982: 38). This filial relationship and a shared title (although Hay also rose to the position of 'Deputy') resulted in the spatial connection between their tombs. These tombs are not only adjacent to each other, but also to the earlier tombs of Neferhotep and Nebnefer-TT6 and Neferhotep-TT216, forming a row of tombs owned by those in a position of authority.

Scribes

Five tombs belonged to scribes, TT7, TT212, TT215, TT250 and TT265 (see Figure 308). The earliest are attributed to the 'Royal Scribe' (among other important titles, such as 'Overseer of Workmen' and 'Mayor' of the Necropolis) Amenemopet, who held office during the reign of Seti I and the beginning of the reign of Ramesses II (Davies 1999: 124). TT215 (SI-RII) was his tomb chapel, while TT265 (SI-RII) appears to be his burial chamber rather than a separate tomb (Davies 1999: 76). The well-known 'Royal Scribe' Ramose, who held the title from Year 5 to Year 38 of the reign of Ramesses II (Davies 1999: 125), owned three tombs, TT7, TT212 and TT250 (all RII). Of these three tombs, TT7 is regarded as the final resting place of Ramose, while the other two tombs may have been prepared for his servants (Davies 1999: 83). TT7 is located adjacent to the tombs of the foremen Neferhotep and Nebnefer-TT6 (Hor-RII) and Neferhotep-TT216 (RII-SII), who were also in position during the reign of Ramesses II, suggesting a spatial connection between the tombs of the village hierarchy. The burial chamber of Ramose's predecessor, Amenemopet-TT265 (SI-RII), is located in the court of TT7 (Davies 1999: 76), while TT212 is also located in close proximity. As TT265 predates the other tombs, this appears to have been a deliberate attempt by Ramose to build his own tombs in the vicinity of his predecessor to establish a link, as he was an outsider with no familial connections in the village (Davies 1999: 79).

It is unclear whether Ramose directly succeeded Amenemopet as 'Scribe', or if Amenemopet's son Minmose and grandson Amenemopet acted as scribe in the intervening years (Davies 1999: 77). Even if Ramose was not his direct successor, Amenemopet would have been respected in the village as a result of the considerable amount of time he held this position, thus explaining Ramose's desire to associate himself with him. Ramose is also attested in the tombs of several colleagues, TT4 and TT10 (both RII), and TT219 and

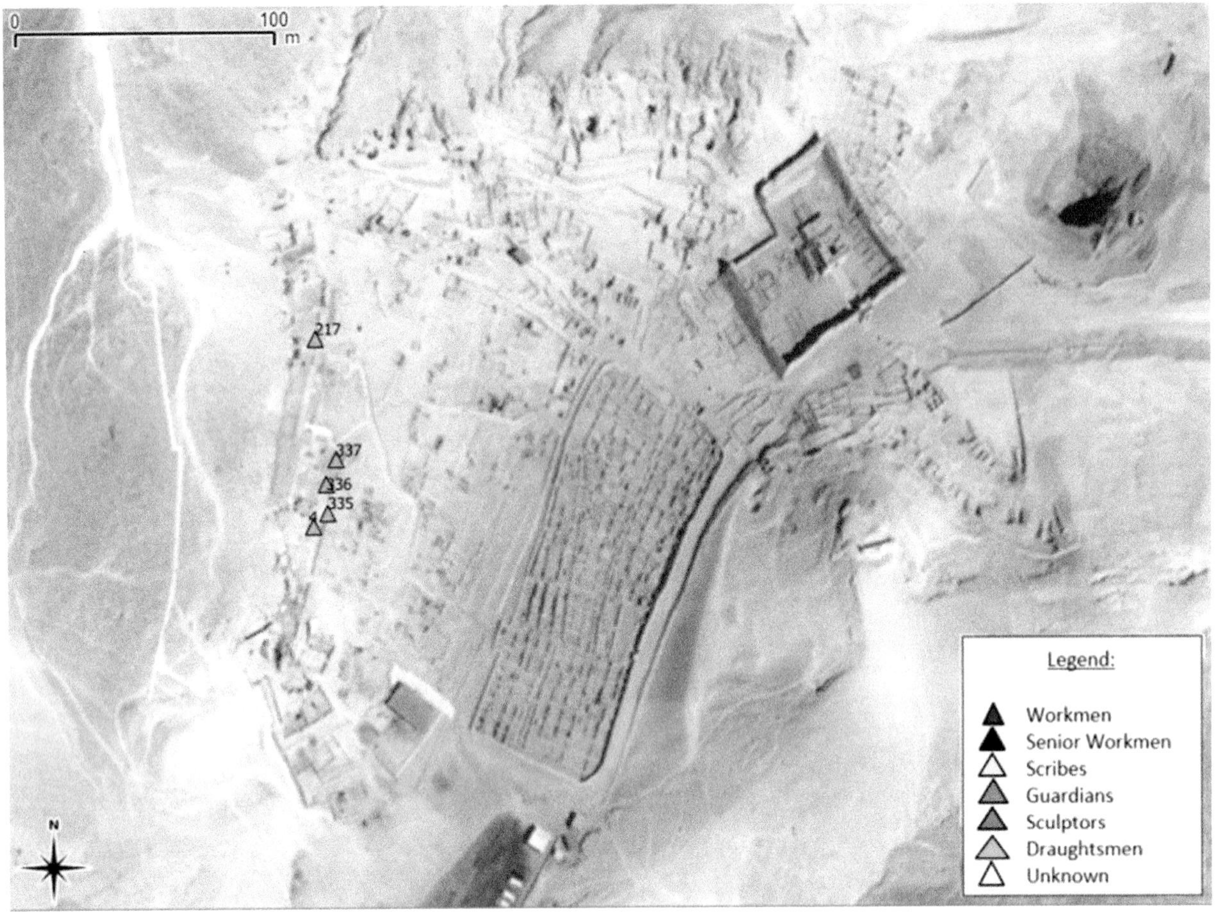

Figure 309: TTs of the 'Sculptors' in Deir el-Medina (Author's own using QGIS)

TT336 (both RII-Mer) (Davies 1999: 81). Of these tombs, TT10 is adjacent to Ramose's TT212, perhaps suggesting a particularly close link between him and Penbuy and Kasa.

Sculptors

There were five TTs belonging to sculptors at Deir el-Medina (see Figure 309). The 'Sculptor of Amun' Ken-TT4 (RII) may also have owned TT337 (RII), as both tomb owners had the same name and titles, or TT337 may have been built by the father-in-law of Ken (Bruyére 1924-25: 80), but there is not enough inscriptional evidence to determine which scenario is most likely. Both tombs are located along the same contour line, separated only by the tombs of another sculptor, Nakhtamun-TT335 (RII-Mer), and his brother Neferenpet-TT336 (RII-Mer). The grouping of the tombs of three sculptors in this area suggests from this limited evidence that they may have been deliberately buried near each other. The other 'Sculptor' Ipuy-TT217 (RII) was buried to the north of this group, a short distance west from the contour line on which the other sculptors' tombs are situated.

Guardians

Two TTs belonged to 'Guardians' (see Figure 310). The tomb of the 'Guardian in the Place of Truth' and 'Servant of Amun in Thebes', Khawyheb-TT214 (RII), lies some distance away from the other tombs on the eastern edge of the cemetery. Khawyheb was depicted in the tomb of Kasa and Penbuy-TT10 (RII) (Davies 1999: 192), while Penbuy also shared the title 'Guardian' so these men would have had a close professional relationship, explaining this depiction, but they are not buried in each other's vicinity as with other professions.

Draughtsmen

Three TTs belonged to the 'Outline-draughtsmen' (see Figure 311). Pashedu-TT323 (SI) and Karo-TT338 (Amarna) were buried in the northern part of the cemetery, roughly contemporary and in relatively close proximity, but they are not aligned with each other so a connection cannot be established (see Figure 297). Hay-TT267 (Dyn 20) also held this title and was also buried in the northern part of the cemetery but some distance to

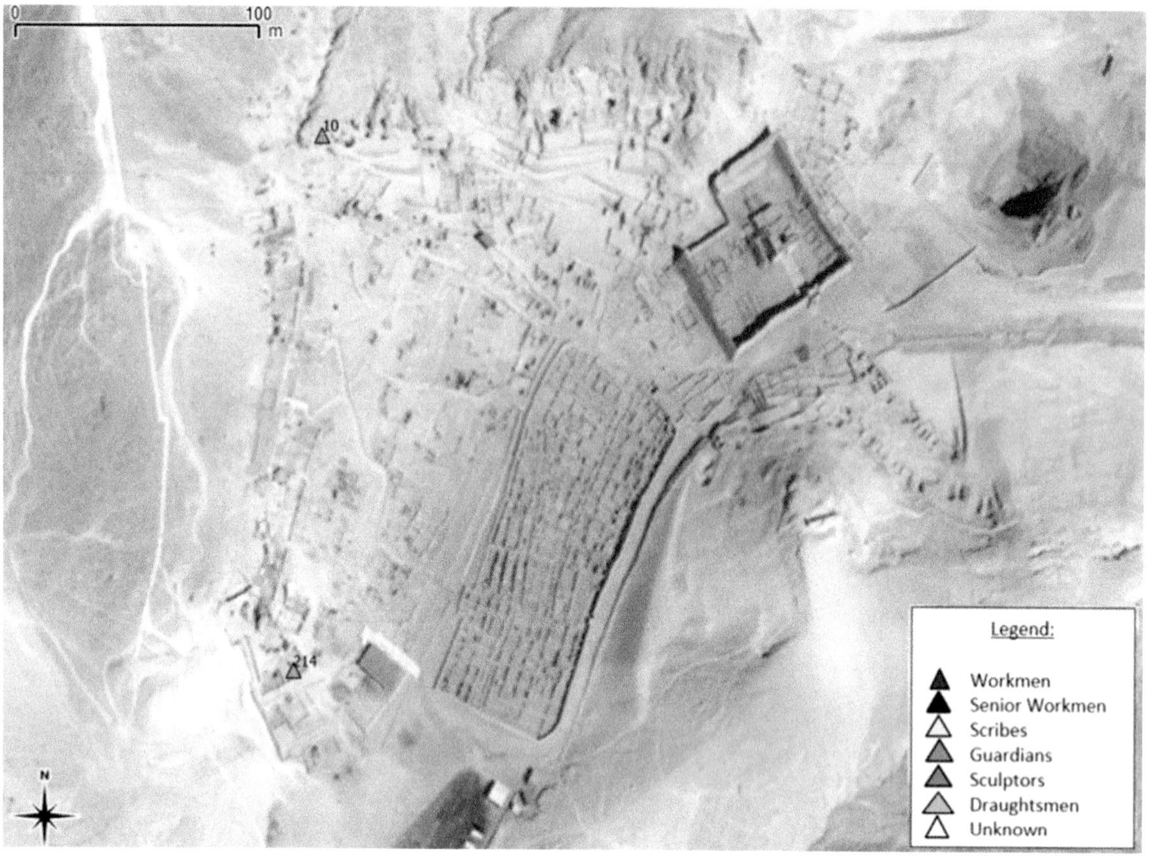

Figure 310: Tombs of the 'Guardians' in Deir el-Medina (Author's own using QGIS)

Figure 311: TTs of the 'Outline-draughtsmen' in Deir el-Medina (Author's own using QGIS)

the west of these tombs. Two further individuals have unknown titles (TT269- Ram, and TT325-Dyn 18).

Relationships between Tomb Owners / Tombs

The confined nature of the village makes familial relationships easier to trace than at other sites, but as with all ancient relationships, there are a number of factors which make this problematic. The reuse of names and the frequency with which they recur, and the lack of differentiation between the words used to designate relationships, makes positive identification of individuals a complex task (Davies 1999: xxiii).

Several Deir el-Medina tombs are located close to family members. There are several tombs belonging to fathers, sons, and in some case three generations of the same family. Sennedjem-TT1 (SI-RII) and Khabekhet-TT2 (RII) were father and son and both 'Servants in the Place of Truth', while their tombs were located adjacent to each other. TT1 is a family tomb, containing the burials of Sennedjem, a brother and a son (Davies 1999: 43), perhaps indicating a particularly close-knit family. TT218, TT219 and TT220 are owned by a family group of 'Servants in the Place of Truth'. TT218 (RII) is owned by the father Amennakht, TT219 (RII-Mer) is owned by his son Nebenmaat, and TT220 (also RII-Mer) belongs to another son Khaemteri (Davies 1999: 326). The tombs are approached by a shared entrance hall, while the tomb chapels themselves are connected and lie side by side. TT10 (RII) was occupied by Kasa (and Penbuy), while Kasa's grandson Paneb's tomb, TT211 (SII-Sip), is located adjacent to it, in what appears to be a deliberate attempt to be buried close to his grandfather. TT213 (RIII) is owned by Penamum, and this tomb is aligned with his father Baki's tomb (TT298- Dyn 20) which lies a short distance to the east. TT6 (Hor-RII) is occupied by Neferhotep and his son Nebnefer, while Nebnefer's son is buried some distance away in TT337 (RII), so there is no obvious decision for Nebnefer's son to be buried close to his father and grandfather.

Four brothers were buried in the village necropolis, the 'Servant in the Place of Truth' Raweben-TT210 (RII) (most likely one of these brothers, although his parentage is problematic – Davies 1999: 180), the 'Sculptor' Ipuy-TT217 (RII), the 'Sculptor of Amun' and 'Servant in the Place of Truth' Nakhtamun-TT335 (RII-Mer), and 'Servant in the Place of Truth' Neferenpet-TT336 (RII-Mer) (Davies 1999: 178-179). All four tombs are situated along the western edge of the cemetery, along the same contour line, but TT217 lies a short distance to the north of TT335 and TT336, which lie adjacent to each other (as mentioned above), while TT210 is slightly further south but still aligned with the other tombs. In addition to appearing in the tombs of his brothers (TT335 and TT336), Ipuy-TT217 also appears in TT2 (RII), which belonged to his sister and her husband, Khabekhnet (Davies 1999: 179), which is located a short distance to the south. Nakhtamun-TT335 was also buried just to the north of his brother-in-law, Ken-TT4 (RII) (Davies 1999: 181), again suggesting a familial link between these tombs.

The 'Guardian' Penbuy shared TT10 (RII) with the 'Servant of the Place of Truth' Kasa. This tomb-sharing appears to be a result of an inter-family marriage, as Penbuy married Amentetwosret, who was either the sister or daughter of Kasa (Davies 1999: 195). The other of Penbuy's wives was Iretnofret, who was either another daughter of Kasa (Bruyere 1952: 63) or a daughter of Sennedjem-TT1 (SI-RII) (Davies 1999: 195). As TT10 and TT1 are located at opposite ends of the necropolis there is no obvious familial link between them, making the paternity of Iretnofret more likely to be Kasa, based solely on tomb location. The 'Servant in the Place of Truth', Penshenabu-TT322 (Ram), was the brother of Penbuy (Davies 1999: 181), and their tombs are located in close proximity, indicating this close fraternal connection.

TT329 (Dyn 19) is owned by the 'Servant in the Place of Truth', Mose, but its southern annexe appears to have belonged jointly to two other 'Servants in the Place of Truth', another Mose and Ipy. The owners of the annexe are tentatively identified as the grandson and son of the tomb owner Mose (PM I: 397), but there is no inscriptional evidence of their relationship so they may have just been close friends as they share several monuments in the village (Davies 1999; 209). Ipy also appears to have been a member of the same family as Amenwia-TT356 (SI-RII) (Davies 1999: 210), who was buried nearby. The foreman Kaha-TT360 (RII) is mentioned in TT2 which is located nearby, suggesting that these contemporary individuals were close.

Shared Courtyards

The unique nature of Deir el-Medina meant that there was limited space available for tombs, resulting in the crowded terraces of the cemetery. This in turn left little space for courtyards, while the close proximity of the tombs makes identifying any shared communal space at their entrance problematic. The existence of shared courtyards of any size seems unlikely as the tombs were orientated towards the village itself, making the presence of tombs occupying adjacent sides of the courtyard as in other areas of the necropolis impossible. There is however an example of a group of tombs with a shared entrance.

TT218-TT220

TT218, TT219 and TT220 are located at the southern end of the village, adjacent to TT1 (see Figure 312). Although three separate tombs are numbered and

Figure 312: Plan of Deir el-Medina showing the location of TT218-TT220 (Dodson and Ikram 2008: 334 - Courtesy of Professor Aidan Dodson)

Table 56: Owners of TT218, TT219 and TT220

TT	Dyn	Reign	Name	Titles
TT218	19	RII	Amennakht	Servant in the Place of Truth (on the West of Thebes);
TT219	19	RII/ Mer	Nebenmaat	Servant (of the Lord of the Two Lands) in the Place of Truth (on the West of Thebes);
TT220	19	RII/ Mer	Khaemteri	Servant in the Place of Truth;

Figure 313: Shared entrance of TT218, TT219 and TT220 (Author's own)

Figure 314: View from the shared entrance of TT218, TT219 and TT220 (Author's own)

three distinct occupants have been identified, there is only one shared entrance and decorated room leading to the three individual decorated chapels (see Figure 313). The tombs are roughly contemporary, dating between Ramesses II and Merenptah. All three tomb owners were 'Servants of the Place of Truth', so were colleagues, living and working together (see Table 56). Inscriptional evidence also reveals a familial link (see above). These close family ties resulted in the occupants pooling resources to build this family tomb, deliberately choosing to remain together for eternity. There is no obvious advantage to the choice of this location as the eastern hill obscures any view of the royal mortuary temples or processional routes (see Figure 314).

Tomb Reuse

There is no evidence of the reuse of any TTs in Deir el-Medina during the New Kingdom. This was presumably as the potential occupants of this cemetery all belonged to the workmen's community, so the reverence paid by the community to their ancestors may have prevented

Figure 315: View of the upper slopes of the Deir el-Medina cemetery looking south-west from behind the Ramesseum (Author's own)

Figure 316: Zoomed-in view of the upper slopes of the Deir el-Medina cemetery looking south-west from behind the Ramesseum (Author's own)

Figure 317: View of the hill to the east of Deir el-Medina (Author's own)

this from occurring, in conjunction with the capability of the workmen to build and decorate their own tombs without relying on an external workforce and resources as in the rest of the necropolis.

There were six shared tombs (TT6, TT10, TT291, TT298, TT329 and TT339), occupied by two or more individuals who were usually related or close colleagues, but they were both represented within the tomb and dated to the same period, rather than the tomb being reused at a later date. The damage done to the cemetery prior to the reign of Horemheb (Bierbrier 1982: 65) may also have destroyed earlier tombs or evidence of original occupation of existing tombs.

Conclusions

The high concentration of Ramesside tombs on the upper slopes is as a result of superior views towards the royal mortuary temple. The north-western corner is the highest area of the cemetery, with tombs located between 130m and 160m above sea level. The secluded nature of the village, enclosed by hills to the east, west and south, meant a view eastward towards the royal mortuary temples was hard to attain in a burial. However, the mound located to the east of the village is only 130m high so the group of Nineteenth Dynasty tombs on the upper slopes were built at a higher altitude than this so there was visibility from these tombs towards the Ramesseum and other Ramesside mortuary temples to the east and vice-versa (see Figures 315 and 316). The central and southern areas of the cemetery are at a lower level; thus, visibility was obstructed by the mound to the east (see Figure 317), making the upper slopes at the northern end of the cemetery the most desirable for this reason.

Chapter 12: Tombs of Viziers and their Colleagues

This case-study of all known TTs belonging to New Kingdom Viziers and the surrounding tombs demonstrates the potential spatial connections between those who held the same title, their family, colleagues and contemporaries. It seems sensible that if patterns can be observed amongst the tombs of the most influential New Kingdom official, then patterns also existed amongst other groups of individuals, although it is beyond the scope of this project to analyse the holders of every title in such detail. The Vizier (and the High Priest of Amun – see Chapter 13) has been chosen as someone important enough to have had a say in his own choice of burial site, and to potentially influence tomb distribution of others.

Patterns between the tombs of Old Kingdom Viziers have been identified at Saqqara (Roth 1988: 206), so it seems likely that such patterns will also be observed at Thebes. During the majority of the New Kingdom two Viziers were appointed by the king, one Northern Vizier and one Southern Vizier. Most Viziers buried at Thebes were Southern Viziers, for whom most evidence survives (Van den Boorn, 1988: 335). Two sources regarding the role of the Vizier and his potential colleagues are first analysed in order to identify relevant individuals who were buried nearby.

The Duties of the Vizier

The 'Duties of the Vizier' text is inscribed in the tombs of several Viziers of the Eighteenth and Nineteenth Dynasties (chronologically: TT131, TT100, TT29, TT66 and TT106) (Van den Boorn 1988: 1; PM I: 474). This text presents the Vizier (*ṯ3ty*) as the head of all branches of central government, with oversight- or at least leadership- of the highest functionaries, and the overseer of the exercise of central authority throughout the country. The fullest version of this text (*Urk.* IV: 1103,14–1117,5) occurs in TT100-Rekhmire, alongside the installation speech made by Tuthmosis III during his appointment as Vizier (PM I: 206–09). The translation of this text (Van den Boorn 1988: 12–290) is referred to here in order to establish the relationship the Vizier had with other officials. The number of the column of the Rekhmire version of 'The Duties' is cited as 'R' followed by the column in which the text can be found (Van den Boorn 1988: 10).

The text begins by describing the arrangements for the formal sittings in the bureau of the Vizier. The 'Chamberlain' (*ỉmy-r ʿẖnwty*) was at the right-hand side of the Vizier during these proceedings, while the 'Keeper of Items, with Right of Entry' (Quirke 2004: 86), or 'Curator of the Access' (*ỉry-ẖt ʿḳ*) was on his left (R2: Van den Boorn 1988: 13). As these individuals were important enough to be seated directly beside the Vizier, the close relationship between these officials is clear. Before him were the 'Great Ones of the Ten of Upper Egypt' (*wrw-mḏ-šmʿw*), while the 'Scribes of the Vizier' (*sšw nw ṯ3ty*) were beside him (R2: Van den Boorn 1988: 13).

The individual who worked most closely with the Vizier was the 'Overseer of the Treasury' (*ỉmy-r ḫtmt*). The two men exchanged daily reports on each other's affairs, particularly concerning the palace and every government department (R5-R7: Van den Boorn 1988: 55). This mutual sharing of information suggests that these individuals did not have a typical superior and sub-ordinate relationship, but were more equals, albeit with the Vizier holding the higher office (Van den Boorn 1988: 72-73). The title '*ỉmy-r ḫtmt*' (literally meaning 'Overseer of Sealed Items') is attested in the 'The Duties of the Vizier' referring to the 'Overseer of the Royal Treasury', while the '*ỉmy-r pr ḥḏ*' is only attested after the reign of Hatshepsut, referring to 'Overseer of the State Treasury' (Van den Boon 1988: 361).

The Vizier summons and gives commands to members of the provincial administration such as the 'Mayors' (*ḥ3tyw-ʿ*) and 'Rulers of a Domain' (Quirke 2004: 148) or 'Settlement Leaders' (*ḥḳ3w-ḥwwt*) (R11: Van den Boorn 1988: 88). He would therefore necessarily have worked particularly closely with the 'Mayor of Thebes' (*ḥ3ty-ʿ m nỉwt rsyt*). The 'Councillors of Rural Districts' (*ḳnbtyw nw w*) were summoned and dispatched by the Vizier, in order for them to report from their districts (R19: Van den Boorn 1988: 172).

The Vizier consulted the 'Overseer of Fields' (*ỉmy-r 3ḥwt*) and 'Council of the Mat' (*ḏ3ḏ3t nt ṯm3*) regarding petitions made to him regarding fields (R18: Van den Boorn 1988: 147) and dispatched the 'Scribes of the Mat' (*sšw nw ṯm3*) to carry out his instructions (R26: Van den Boorn 1988: 265). He was also responsible for endowing state-owned *šd* fields (R20: Van den Boorn 1988: 185) which were assigned as a reward to sub-ordinate officials. He established the land boundaries of every domain (*ḏ3tt nbt*), a term which can also denote a funerary concession (Van den Booorn, 1988: 271), every *sm* field and every divine offering (*ḥtp-nṯr nb*) (R27: Van den Boorn 1988: 265). This demonstrates the ultimate control which the Vizier had over apportioning state land (thus potentially the same may have been true for plots for tomb building?) (Edwards 1965: 25-26). As one of his duties is to make an inventory of all cattle (*k3w nb*) (R31: Van den Boorn 1988: 286), the Vizier would also have been familiar with the 'Overseer of Cattle'.

Other important colleagues included: the 'Steward' (*imy-r pr*) (R31: Van den Boorn 1988: 286); 'Messengers of the Vizier' (*wpwtyw n ṯ3ty*) (R3: Van den Boorn 1988: 13), and 'Messengers of the Palace' (*wpwty nb n pr nsw*) (R21: Van den Boorn 1988: 202); 'Investigators' (*sḏmw*) and 'Scribes' (*sšw*), from the 'Great Prison' (*ḫnrt wr*) who sealed and delivered documents regarding any government department (R16: Van den Boorn 1988: 133). He received reports from the 'Police' (*šnt*), and 'Overseers of the District' (*imyw-r w*) (R3-R4: Van den Boorn 1988: 42-43). He appointed the 'Disputes Overseer' (Quirke 2004: 106) or 'Chief of Police' (*imy-r šntw*), (R25: Van den Boorn 1988: 250), and the leading 'Member(s) of Magistracy' (*nty m srwt*) throughout Egypt, who reported back to him in his capacity as in overall charge of the judiciary (R22: Van den Boorn 1988: 208).

He organised the king's military escort (*mšꜥ*), organised the remainder of the army who remained behind and gave instructions to the 'Head of the Army' (*ḏ3ḏ3t nt mšꜥ*), so worked closely with military commanders (R23: Van den Boorn 1988: 218). In addition to this he received reports from the garrisons of the Upper Egyptian fortresses (*mnnw šmꜥ*) (R25: Van den Boorn 1988: 250). These reports were read to him by the 'Door-Keeper of the *ꜥrryt*' (*iry ꜥ3 n ꜥrryt*) (R36: Van den Boorn 1988: 289).

In addition to the officials referred to explicitly by title, there is a reference to 'every official' (*i3t nbt*) being invited to enter the Bureau of the Vizier (R24: Van den Boorn 1988: 229), reinforcing the idea that every official was permitted access to the Vizier (Van den Boorn 1988: 230-31). Any petitioner, irrespective of rank, could attend his daily audience to take counsel or seek justice, so he would have worked with a range of individuals, acting as an intermediary between the common people, government officials and the king himself.

The 'Duties' is a useful source but is not a comprehensive list of all of the Vizier's colleagues. As the king's deputy, the Vizier would have worked with the 'Royal Butler' (*wb3-nswt*) who is not attested in the 'Duties'. There is also no mention of the 'Steward of the Vizier' (*imy-r pr n ṯ3ty*) although the owner of TT82 held this title. Overseeing royal building works is also absent among the list of responsibilities, although attested as such in the Middle and New Kingdom (Helck 1958: 44). The absence of this duty is probably a result of the lack of monumental building work at the beginning of the Eighteenth Dynasty when this text first appears (Van den Boorn 1988: 361). This role would have necessitated working alongside the 'Overseer of Building Works' (*imy-r k3t*). The 'Overseer of Granaries' (*imy-r šnwty*) is also missing, as local officials seem to have had control over local food supplies (Van den Boorn 1988: 243) but as the Vizier was responsible for overseeing the provision of food to all who should receive it (R28: Van den Boorn 1988: 283), this necessitates a relationship with this official.

The Estate of Amun is not explicitly referred to in the 'Duties', but its vast wealth made it crucial to the Egyptian economy. The relationship between the temple and the palace was interdependent. The king enhanced the temple with royal building projects, and donated offerings (see below) and agricultural *khato* land, which was owned by the king but administered by the temple, as listed in the Twentieth Dynasty in Papyrus Wilbour (Gardiner 1948b). The *sm* fields are described in P. Wilbour as temple domain but come under the jurisdiction of the Vizier as state-owned land in the 'Duties', suggesting that this was state-owned land originally, donated to the temple (Van den Boorn, 1988: 273). The Wilbour Papyrus also contains a list of individuals who cultivated temple land, including the Vizier himself who acted as a landlord, employing labourers to farm the land (Gardiner 1948b: 76 line 13; 90 line 13). This reinforces the idea of a close relationship between the Vizier and the temple.

There is an example of the temple reciprocating in the late Twentieth Dynasty when the craftsmen at Deir el-Medina were paid by the temple when the state could not pay, while the workmen were protesting outside, regarding it as a potential source of payment (Gardiner 1948a: 64 line 12 – 65 line 4). On other occasions they were paid by the temple of Maat at Karnak (Peet 1930: 12 n.1), proving that the temple and the state were closely linked. The Vizier's responsibilities extended into the Estate of Amun as he inspected the divine offerings (*ḥtp-nṯr nb*) (R27: Van den Boorn 1988: 265) and investigated where they ended up (R28: Van den Boorn 1988: 283). He also collects and inspects the deliveries of the workshops (*gsw-prw*) (R29 and R30: Van den Boorn 1988: 284-285). Hatshepsut's 'Chief Steward' Senenmut also held the title 'Chief Steward of Amun' (*imy-r pr n Imn*) proving that an important position at court and an important position within the religious administration were not mutually exclusive, so the temple was not a totally independent institution. The 'High Priest of Amun' was appointed by the king until after the reign of Ramesses (two Viziers even became 'High Priest of Amun', including Paser), so certainly in the Eighteenth Dynasty the Vizier and the priesthood would have been closely associated. It was later in the Nineteenth and

Figure 318: Berlin Trauer Relief (Courtesy of the Staatliche Museen zu Berlin)

Twentieth Dynasties when the relationship between the state and the temple may have been less intimate.

The early date of the 'Duties' also limits its usefulness as a source to identify New Kingdom titles associated with the office of the Vizier. James (1985: 54) dates the text to the late Twelfth or Thirteenth Dynasty, whereas Van den Boorn (1988: 375) more convincingly dates the text to the early Eighteenth Dynasty, specifically the reign of Ahmose, as an amalgamation of a number of Middle Kingdom and early New Kingdom sources. The prevalence of Middle Kingdom titles supports an early date, although Van den Boorn has proved that these titles occurred until the end of the Seventeenth Dynasty, and often well into the Eighteenth Dynasty (Van den Boorn 1988: 352). The use of Middle Kingdom titles also explains why a large number of New Kingdom titles are not attested in the 'Duties', particularly those pertaining to the Estate of Amun, as the temple rose to prominence during the Eighteenth Dynasty. The text reflects royal propaganda regarding the idealised activities of a Vizier at the beginning of the New Kingdom, but the reality of the role may have been somewhat different. The nature of the office and thus the relationship with other officials evolved as the New Kingdom progressed, but the original text still impressed Viziers who followed later in the new Kingdom. This is also a contributory factor when considering later New Kingdom titles and relationships.

Berlin Trauer Relief

The 'Berlin Trauer relief' (see Figure 318), originally from a Saqqara tomb, is currently displayed at the Neues Museum, Berlin (Ident. Nr. ÄM 12411). The bottom register of this relief demonstrates state hierarchy during the reign of Tutankhamun, as it depicts the 'Hereditary Noble' (*iry-pꜥt*) and 'General' (*imy-r mšꜥ*) Horemheb observing the funeral of an official. He is the largest figure, therefore the most important, and he is followed by the core government in order of precedence from right to left. Directly behind Horemheb come the two individuals with the two titles 'Overseer of the Town' (*imy-r niwt*) and 'Vizier' (*ṯꜣty*). They are followed by a procession of nine individuals. The first holds the titles of both 'Royal Scribe' (*sš nsw*) and 'Steward' (*imy-r pr*), and the next holds both the titles of 'Royal Scribe' (*sš nsw*) and 'Treasurer' – literally 'Overseer of Sealed Items' (*imy-r ḫtmt*). Next comes the 'Overseer of the Law Court' (*imy-r rwyt*), followed by another 'General' (*imy-r mšꜥ*). Behind them is the 'Chamberlain' (*imy-r ꜥḫnwty*), and then another 'Treasurer' – literally the 'Overseer of the House of Silver' (*imy-r pr-ḥḏ*). They are followed by two priests, first the 'Greatest of Seers' (*wr mꜣw*), the title of the High Priest of Re of Heliopolis (Quirke 2004: 129), and then a *smt* priest (which also forms part of the title of the High Priest of Ptah (Peterson 1969: 8-10), which would make sense in this context). Last in this procession comes the 'Mayor' (*ḥꜣty-ꜥ*).

The Saqqara provenance of this relief explains the prominence of divine cults in the proximity of Memphis rather than the cult of Amun at Thebes, but the same principles can be applied. The inclusion of these priests reinforces the notion that state and temple worked closely together, so a co-operative relationship with the High Priests was an essential part of a Vizier's role. The non-religious titles show the most important state officials in hierarchical order, behind the Vizier position who leads the procession as the head of government. This evidence confirms the importance of Treasurers – both '*imy-r ḫtmt*' and the later title '*imy-r pr-ḥḏ*', which does not appear in 'The Duties' as it is only attested from the reign of Hatshepsut onwards, after its composition (Van den Boon 1988: 361). The Steward, Chamberlain, Judge and Mayor are all present in this procession, emphasising their importance and links with the Vizier as detailed in 'The Duties' (see Figure 319).

Figure 319: Relevant section of the Berlin Trauer Relief (Courtesy of the Staatliche Museen zu Berlin)

Figure 320: Satellite view of Viziers' tombs (Author's own using Google Earth)

Methodology

TTs of Viziers are considered in chronological order. Their location is analysed in relation to the tombs of earlier Viziers (see Figure 320), and then to the surrounding contemporary tombs within a 100m radius. This specific radius has been chosen as each Vizier's tomb is within at least 100m of another Vizier's tomb, and this provides a large enough area surrounding the tomb to identify potential clusters (see Figure 321). Only neighbouring tombs dated by Kampp to a relevant specific reign(s) are included, excluding those of less certain date due to the limited usefulness of these tombs to the study. The tombs are listed in chronological order, starting with the earliest tombs located closest to the tomb of the Vizier, and using the Vizier's tomb acting as a central focal point, gradually working outwards to an extent of 100m radius from the tomb. In the event of the lack of tombs dating to a specific reign or reigns, less definite dating criteria will be used, such as tombs dating to the same Dynasty. In the event of two or more Viziers with tombs in close proximity, both holding office during the same reign, the neighbouring tombs have been analysed in connection to the earliest Vizier's tomb and highlighted when analysing successive Vizier's tombs to indicate they have been previously discussed.

Connection with Viziers of the Middle Kingdom

TT61 was originally a Middle Kingdom tomb, reused by the Vizier User between the reigns of Tuthmosis I and

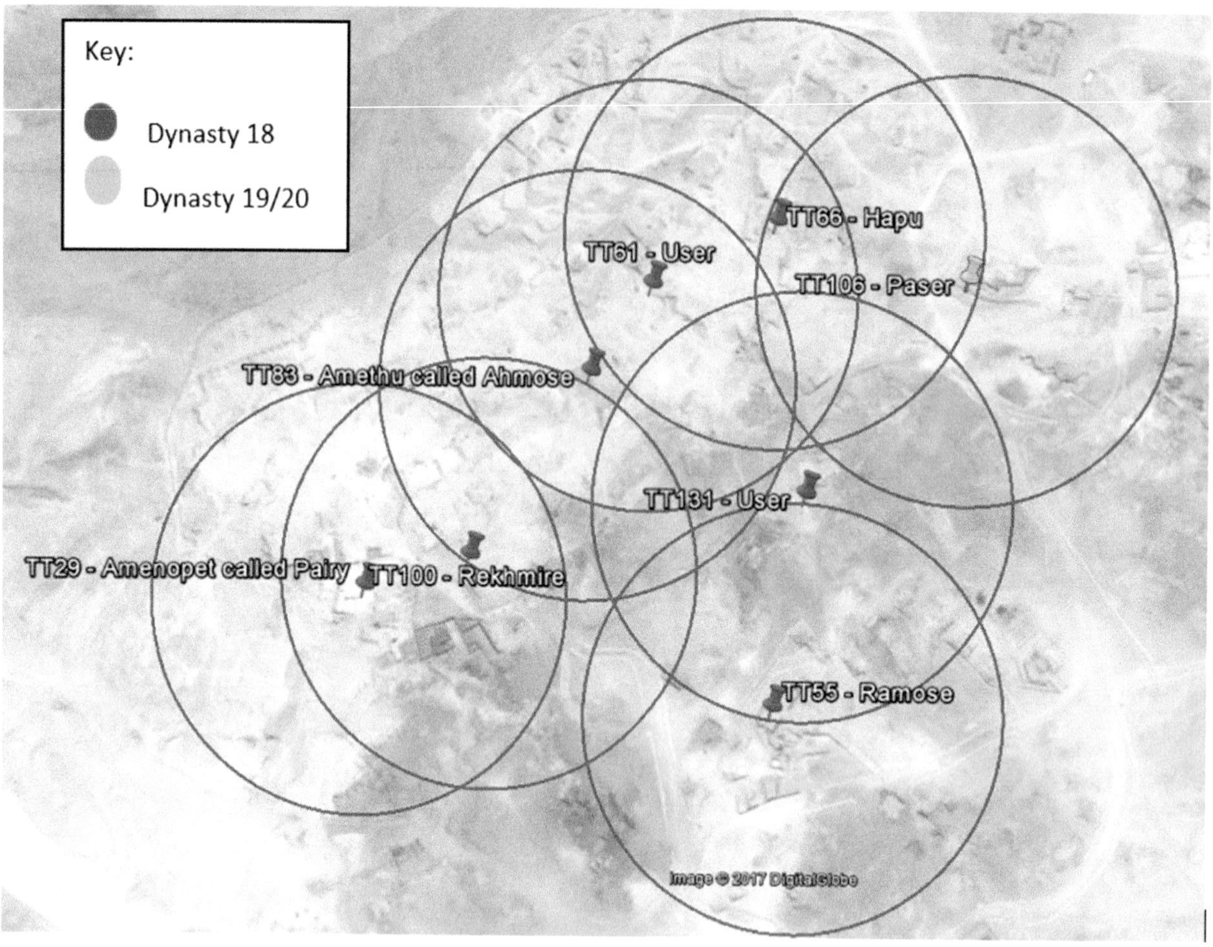

Figure 321: Viziers' TTs in Qurna with a 100m (Author's own using Google Earth)

Tuthmosis III (Kampp 1996: 277). The occupation of the original occupant is unknown as the names and titles do not survive. This tomb is in the vicinity of another better-preserved Middle Kingdom tomb, TT60, which belonged to Vizier Antefoker. It is possible that the original occupant of TT61 was also a Vizier, which would explain why User chose to be buried here. User's father, the Vizier Amethu called Ahmose, was buried in TT83 which is situated below TT60, again suggesting a desire by the Viziers under Tuthmosis III to identify with this Middle Kingdom Vizier (see Figure 322). The thirty-six examples of graffiti left in TT60, particularly during the early Eighteenth Dynasty, show that this tomb was visited in antiquity. One piece of graffiti is from the owner of TT83, the User's steward, Amenemhat. He wrote, 'The scribe Amenemhat, son of the elder of the forecourt [Djehutymes, born of [An]tef, came to see [this] tomb of the Vizier Antefoker. It was pleasant in [his] heart ... profitable for eternity. His name shall exist ... offerings in it, saying: 'An offering which the king gives to Osiris in front of [the westerners] ... Ra, and the gods, lords of the necropolis; invocation offerings of bread and beer, oxen and geese, linen and cloth, incense and oil, all things good and pure which heaven gives and earth creates and Nile brings as his offering to the *ka* of Antefoker, justified" (Davies *et al.* 1920: 121). This shows the high esteem in which this Vizier was still held in the Eighteenth Dynasty.

These Eighteenth Dynasty Viziers were associating themselves with the power exerted by the Middle Kingdom Viziers, serving in a unified Egypt ruled by a powerful king, a situation these later Viziers now found themselves in once more. During the Second Intermediate Period, specifically the Thirteenth Dynasty, the Viziers provided stability in the Theban region (James 1985: 54). The office of Vizier became hereditary in the Middle Kingdom, a tradition that was followed once more in the early Eighteenth Dynasty when these tombs were built, suggesting a tradition continuing from these Middle Kingdom Viziers (Van der Boorn 1988: 346-347). Two other Middle Kingdom Viziers are buried in the Theban necropolis. The tomb of Vizier Dagi, TT103, is also situated in Qurna but in an isolated position to the north of TT60 and TT61, over 100m away from its nearest neighbour. The tomb of Ipi-TT315, is situated in Deir el-Bahri, so this is not in the

Figure 322: View of TT83 in relation to TT60 (Author's own)

vicinity of any known tombs of New Kingdom Viziers (Soliman 2009: 80).

New Kingdom Viziers

TT83 - Amethu called Ahmose

The Viziers who served Ahmose and Amenhotep I have not been securely identified (Van den Boon 1988: 368), while the first known New Kingdom Vizier, Imhotep, who held office during the reign of Tuthmosis I, was buried in the Valley of the Queens (Hornung, 1975: 202). The earliest New Kingdom Vizier to have a TT identified in the private necropolis is Amethu called Ahmose (hereafter referred to as Ahmose), who was the founder of a dynasty of Viziers. He was Vizier during the reign of Hatshepsut and into the early reign of Tuthmosis III and was succeeded by his son User. User was succeeded by Rekhmire, Ahmose's grandson.

Ahmose was buried in TT83, which is situated amongst a number of Middle Kingdom tombs, although Kampp does not believe it to be reused, but rather built in the Eighteenth Dynasty as a result of its T-shaped design (Kampp 1996: 330-332). If this tomb was indeed built in the New Kingdom, it shares some characteristics of the Middle Kingdom *saff* tomb (Soliman 2009: 81), suggesting a desire to imitate the tombs of Ahmose's predecessors (see Figure 323). TT83 is located just below TT60, which belonged to the Twelfth Dynasty Vizier Antefoker, again suggesting Ahmose is identifying himself with Middle Kingdom Viziers (see Figure 324).

Five Middle Kingdom tombs lie within a 100m of TT83 (see Figure 324). Antefoker-TT60, and the tombs of two unknown individuals, TT61 and TT119, are located in a cluster to the east of TT83. Two further unknown individuals owned TT81 and TT82, which lie to the north west of TT83. TT83 is situated centrally and in close proximity to these tombs, suggesting a deliberate decision by Ahmose to site this tomb in an area occupied by important members of the Middle Kingdom government, thus associating himself with this former period of stability and prosperity, in a manner reminiscent of Hatshepsut locating her Deir el-Bahri mortuary temple adjacent to the earlier Middle Kingdom temple of Montuhotep II.

Four of these Middle Kingdom tombs were reused in the early Eighteenth Dynasty, reinforcing the idea that association with the Middle Kingdom was an important concern at this time, or that these specific tombs were chosen for reuse as they wished to be buried close to the Viziers they served. This may also have been an attempt at utilising existing tombs to save money and resources at the beginning of the New Kingdom. The surviving titles demonstrate the connection between this area of the necropolis and the office of Vizier, as TT61 is

Figure 323: Entrance of TT83 (Author's own)

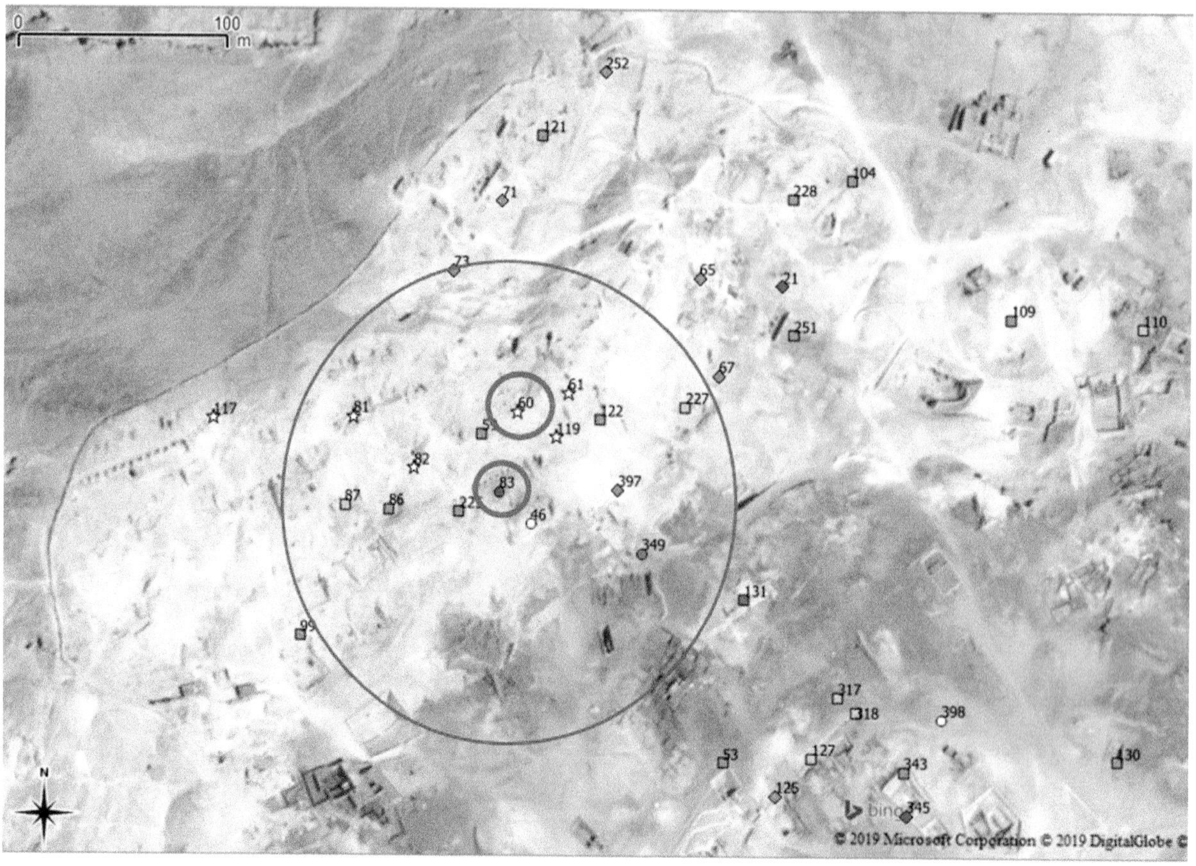

Figure 324: TT83 in relation to TT60, with TTs within a 100m radius (showing TTs dating up to the end of the reign of TIII (Author's own using QGIS)

Figure 325: Façade of TT81 (Author's own)

reused by Ahmose's son, the 'Vizier' User (TI-TIII), and TT82 by the 'Steward of the Vizier User' Amenemhet (Hat-TIII). TT81 is reused by Ahmose's brother-in-law Ineni, who would have known both Ahmose and User in their capacity as Vizier as well as a familial connection (see Figure 325). This suggests that Ahmose's close colleagues and family members deliberately reused tombs in close proximity to the Vizier incumbent at the time when they chose their tombs. The particularly close connections between the usurpers of TT61, TT81 and TT82 with Ahmose are striking, as two tombs were used by family members and close colleagues, and another by a close sub-ordinate.

A number of early Eighteenth Dynasty TTs also form part of this cluster (see Table 57). TT46 (late Dyn 17-early 18) is located directly in front of TT83, and appears to predate TT83. Tjay-TT349 (early Dyn 18-Hat) may either predate or be contemporary to TT83. If it does date to Hatshepsut, then Tjay may have been Ahmose's subordinate, as the Vizier was responsible for overseeing food production, but they would not have been close colleagues.

Amenhotep-TT73 (Hat) was the 'Overseer of Works on the Great Obelisks in the Temple of Amun' and 'Chief Steward', so would have worked closely with the Vizier. The 'Steward' is referred to in 'The Duties', while the omission of the 'Overseer of Works' title is explained by the date of the text (see above). Nakht-TT397 (Hat) was a '*wꜥb* priest of Amun', 'Overseer of the Magazine of Amun' and 'First King's Son of Amun'. His roles within the Estate of Amun, may have brought him into contact with the Vizier, but they would not have had a particularly close working relationship.

Minnakht-TT87 and Siamun-TT227 (both Hat-TIII) are in close proximity to TT83. Minnakht-TT87 was the 'Overseer of the Granaries of Upper and Lower Egypt', 'Overseer of Horses of the Lord of the Two Lands', and 'Royal Scribe'. These titles would have necessitated a close working relationship with the Vizier (Ahmose or User), as the 'Overseer of the Granaries' relationship is discussed above, the military connections are cited in the 'Duties' and the Trauer Relief (see above) and the 'Royal Scribes' are positioned directly behind the Viziers on the Trauer Relief. The titles of Siamun-TT227 are unknown.

Those tombs built during the reign of Tuthmosis III may have deliberately been built close to TT83 to create a spatial connection between their owners and the Vizier they served (see Figure 325). There are four tombs dating to Tuthmosis III within 100m of TT83, of which three belong to High Priests. The 'High Priest of Mut' Ken-TT59 (TIII) lies to the north, forming of a row of tombs along the same contour line as TT61 and TT60 (both MK), while the 'High Priest of Hathor'

Table 57: TTs within a 100m radius of TT83 (Potentially contemporary TTs to the end of the reign of TIII)

Tomb	Reign	Name	Titles
TT59	TIII	Ken	High priest of Mut;
TT61	MK (reused TI-TIII)	Unknown (User)	Unknown (**Governor of the town and Vizier;** Overseer of the 6 Great Temples/Law-courts; Priest of Maat... etc)
TT73	Hat	Amenhotep	Overseer of works on the two great obelisks in the Estate of Amun; Chief steward; Royal Steward; Overseer of the Cattle of Amun; Royal seal-bearer;
TT86	TIII	Menkheperesoneb	**High Priest of Amun**; Overseer of the Priests of U and LE; Overseer of the Granaries of Amun; Treasurer; Overseer of Works of Amun; Royal Seal-bearer; Chief of the overseers of the craftsmen etc;
TT87	Hat-TIII	Minnakht	(1) Overseer of the Granaries of U and LE; Overseer of the Granary (of Amun); Overseer of the Storehouse of Amun (and the king); Overseer of the Servants of Amun; Overseer of Horses of the Lord of the Two Lands; Royal scribe; Overseer of the foreign lands of U and LE; Overseer of the great place; Overseer of the department of the wine cellar;
TT119	MK (reused Hat/TIII)	Unknown (Unknown)	Unknown (Unknown)
TT122	TIII	Amenhotep	(1) & (2) Overseer of the storehouse of Amun;
TT225	TIII	Amenemhat?	High priest of Hathor;
TT227	Hat/TIII	Siamun?	Unknown
TT349	-Hat	Tjay	Overseer of Fowlhouses
TT397	Hat	Nakht	*wꜥb* priest of Amun, Overseer of the Magazine of Amun; First King's Son of Amun.

Amenemhat-TT225 (TIII), was located to the west of TT83. As the Vizier regulated aspects of temple administration, he would have been familiar with these individuals, while the priests depicted on the Trauer Relief also suggest a closer relationship. Ahmose would have worked more closely with 'Menkheperesoneb-TT86 (TIII), located to the west, who was 'High Priest of Amun' 'Overseer of the Granaries of Amun', 'Chief of the Overseers of Craftsmen', and 'Treasurer'. As 'Treasurer' he was the Vizier's closest colleague as attested in both 'The Duties' and the Trauer Relief.

TT61 and TT131 – User / Useramun

User was appointed Vizier during the reign of Tuthmosis III, succeeding his father Amethu called Ahmose in this office, after a period as co-Viziers. This ceremony is detailed in TT131 (PM I: 246). He constructed two tombs, TT61 and TT131, and it is unclear which one he was buried in. TT61 is higher with a superior view of the Nile and the east bank but is smaller than TT131 so was perhaps built earlier in his career, suggesting that he did not expect to attain the office of Vizier. This tomb is unusual as the Amduat and the Litany of Re appear on the walls of the burial shaft, which were previously royal funerary texts (Dziobek 1993: 129). Both TT61 and TT131 were in close proximity to the earlier Viziers buried in TT60 and TT83 (see Figures 326 and 327).

TT131, located further down the slope, is larger and of a more monumental nature (see Figure 328), perhaps built later in his career reflecting an unexpected elevation in status after reaching his highest office of Vizier, as suggested by the presence of the text of installation as co-Vizier in this tomb rather than TT61. It appears to be the first private Theban tomb to be surmounted by a pyramid (see Figure 329), also previously attributed to royalty, which in combination with the royal funerary texts in TT61 reflect the high status of its owner (Dziobek 1993: 131). It is datable

Figure 326: Vizier's tombs: TT60, TT61, TT83 and TT131 (Author's own)

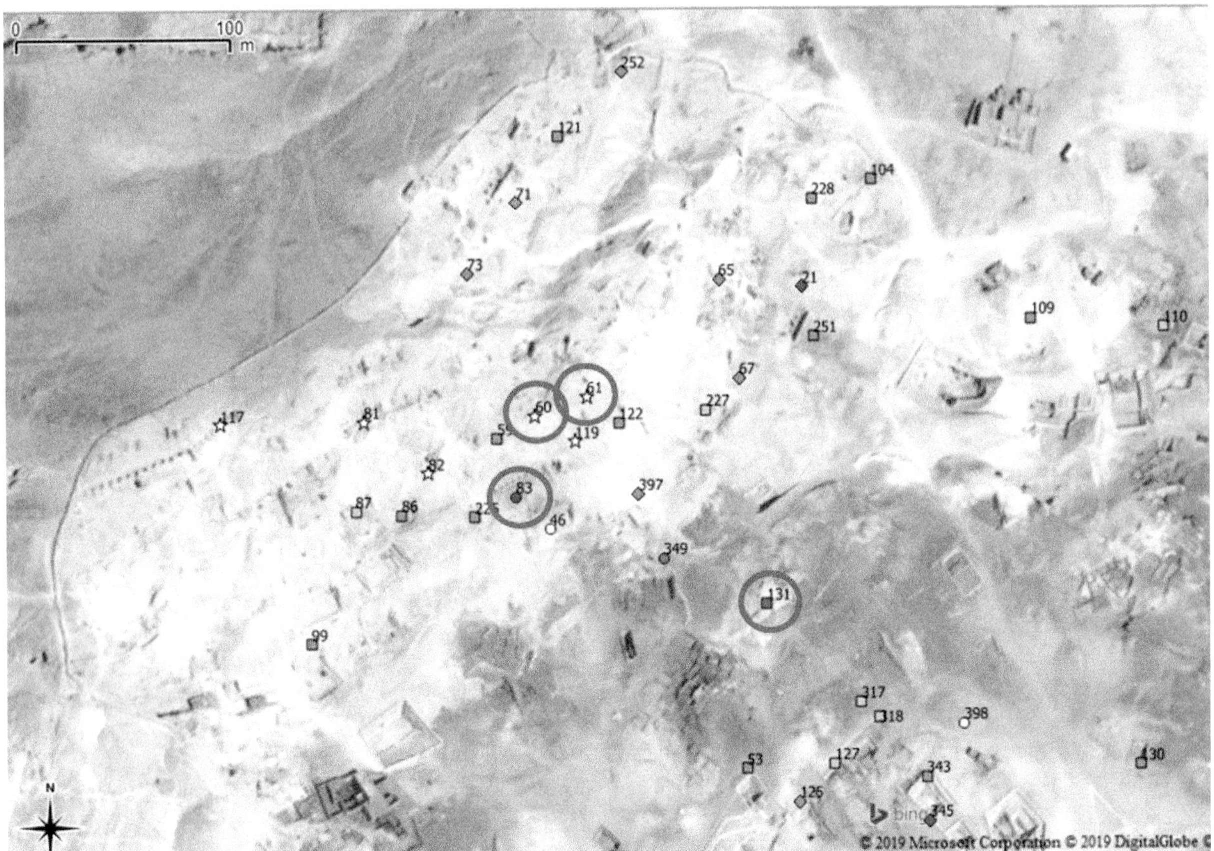

Figure 327: TT61 and TT131 in relation to tombs of earlier Viziers (showing TTs dating up to the end of the reign of TIII)

Figure 328: Façade of TT131 (Author's own)

only between the reigns of Tuthmosis I and Tuthmosis III (Kampp 1996: 277), although it seems more likely to have been constructed in the reign of Tuthmosis III after User was appointed Vizier. TT61 was a reused Middle Kingdom tomb (see above) which may also explain why User chose to build himself a new tomb in addition to his earlier effort to associate himself with Viziers of the Middle Kingdom. TT61 was also closer to the tomb of his father, TT83, who is also depicted in two scenes within TT131, which includes the text of the 'Teaching of Amethu', demonstrating the influence his father had on him (PM I: 246).

TT61 appears to have been decorated prior to the construction of TT131 so is analysed first. Several tombs occur within a 100m diameter of both TT83 and TT61, as they are just over 100m apart (see Figure 330), but only those with a possible construction or reuse during the reign of Tuthmosis III are relevant here (see Table 58). Relevant tombs which were discussed in relation TT83 (see Table 57) are not discussed again here unless they contain specific references to User.

The tomb of User's father and predecessor, Ahmose, TT83 (Ah-TIII), lies within 50m to the west of TT61 (see above), so there is a spatial connection between the tombs of these Viziers. TT82 (MK) has also been discussed above but as this tomb was reused by the 'Steward of the Vizier' (Hat-TIII), its position requires further discussion here. Amenemhet was also the 'Overseer of Ploughed Lands', among other titles, which would have brought him into contact with the Vizier, in addition to a number of administrative titles connecting him to the Estate of Amun. TT82 was reused between the reigns of Hatshepsut and Tuthmosis III, so Amenemhet would have known and served both User and Ahmose in their capacity as Vizier, which may explain his decision to be buried close to both of them. This may also have been a favour bestowed upon him by the Viziers in return for his loyal service. There are two scenes within the tomb where these Viziers are depicted, one showing Amenemhet's relatives at a banquet before User and his wife, and another showing Amenemhet offering to Amethu and his wife thus demonstrating how close Amenemhet's relationship was with both men (PM I: 163-164).

Amenhotep-TT122 (TIII) was User's brother (see above) so is mentioned again here. It is one of the closest tombs to TT61, lying a short distance to the south-east. A banquet scene within the tomb shows Amenhotep and other relatives offering to User and his wife, emphasising the family connection between these individuals, who would also have had a working relationship (PM I: 235). A short distance to the north east of TT61 lies 'Royal Scribe' and 'Commander of

Figure 329: Remains of the pyramid at TT131 (Author's own)

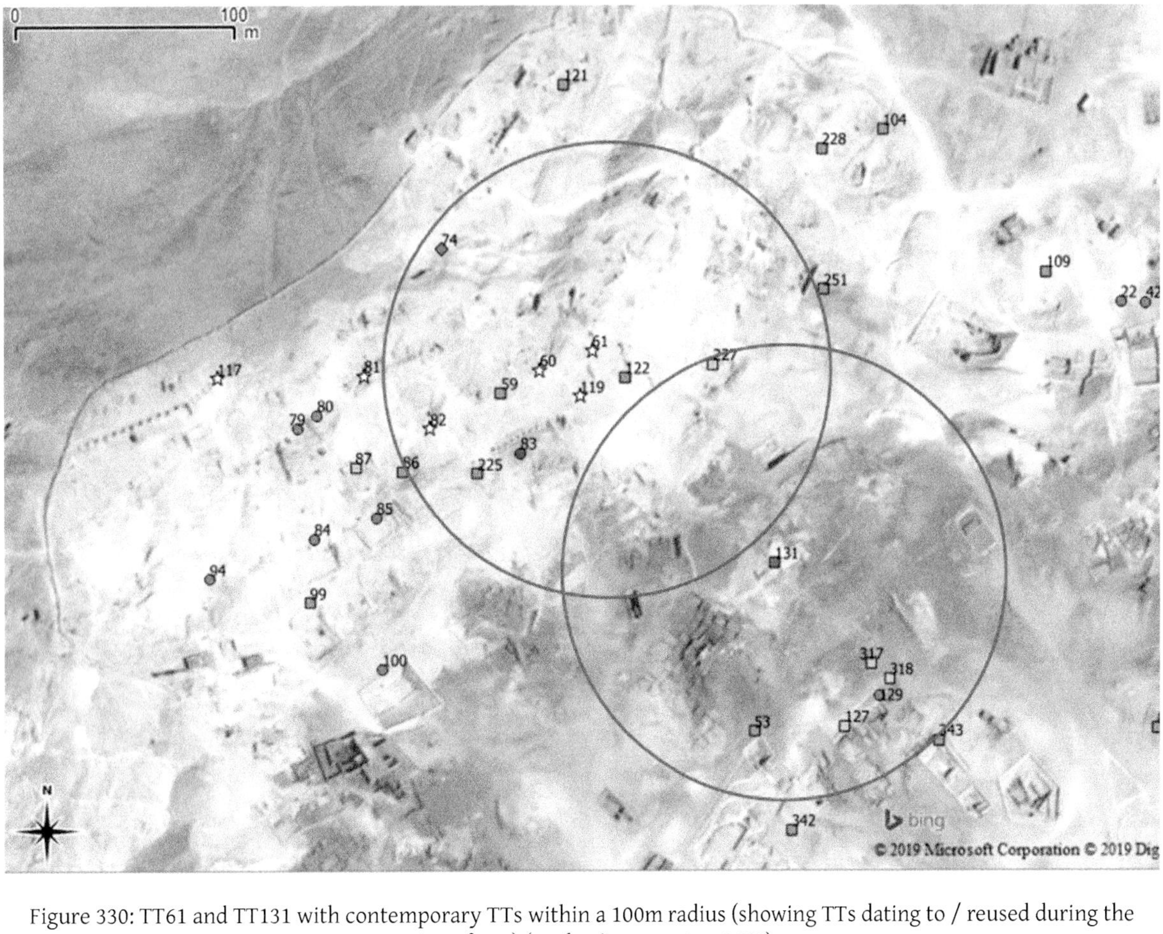

Figure 330: TT61 and TT131 with contemporary TTs within a 100m radius (showing TTs dating to / reused during the reign of TIII) (Author's own using QGIS)

Table 58: Contemporary TTs within a 100m radius of TT61

Tomb	Reign	Name	Title
TT59	TIII	Ken	See Table 57
TT74	TIII-TIV	Thanuny	Royal Scribe; **Overseer of Royal/Army Scribes;** Overseer of the Army; Royal Seal-bearer; Eyes...and Ears of the King...; etc.
TT82	MK (Hat-TIII)	Unknown (Amenemhet)	See Table 57
TT83	Ah-TIII	Amethu called Ahmose	Governor of the Town, Vizier
TT86	TIII	Menkheperesoneb	See Table 57
TT119	MK (Hat/TIII)	Unknown (Unknown)	See Table 57
TT122	TIII	Amenhotep (&Amenemhet)	See Table 57
TT225	TIII	Amenemhat	See Table 57
TT227	Hat/TIII	Siamun?	See Table 57

Table 59: Contemporary TTs within a 100m radius of TT131

Tomb	Reign	Name	Title
TT53	TIII	Amenemhat	Acolyte of Amun
TT123	TIII	Amenemhet	(Royal) Scribe; Overseer of the Granary of Amun; Counter/Overseer of Bread; Chief Scribe in the palace;
TT127	Hat/TIII	Senemiak	(Royal) Scribe; Treasurer; Royal Seal-bearer; Counter of Corn/Bread; Overseer of all Herbs/Vegetables; etc...
TT129	TIII/AII	Unknown	Unknown
TT227	Hat/TIII	Siamun?	See Table 58
TT317	Hat/TIII	Djehutynefer	Scribe of Counting Corn in the Granary of the Divine Offerings of Amun;
TT318	Hat/TIII	Amenmose	Stonemason of Amun
TT343	TIII	Benia called Pahekamun	Overseer of Works; Overseer of the Seal-bearers (=Chief Treasurer); Overseer of the Craftsmen of the Lord of the Two Lands;

Soldiers' Thanuny-TT74 (TIII-TIV), who would have had a close collegial relationship with the Vizier as these titles are attested in both 'The Duties' and the Trauer Relief. The uncertain date of TT74 makes it potentially relevant to several Viziers.

TT131 is located to the south of this cluster, in a relatively isolated position with no earlier or contemporary tombs in close proximity (see Figure 330). The closest tomb to TT131 is Djehutynefer-TT317 (Hat-TIII), some 60m to the south, who was the 'Scribe of Counting Corn in the Granary of the Divine Offerings of Amun'. In close proximity to TT317 is Amnemose-TT318 (Hat-TIII), who was a 'Stonemason of Amun'. These individuals worked for the Estate of Amun, but as the Vizier also oversaw the provision of offerings and the workshops (see above), they would have been acquainted but not close colleages. Senemiak-TT127 (Hat-TIII) was the 'Treasurer', 'Royal Scribe' and 'Overseer of all Herbs/ Vegetables'. As 'Treasurer' this individual occupied the role most closely associated with that of Vizier (see above), and in his capacity as 'Royal Scribe' and an

'Overseer' of food production, the two would certainly have worled together. Amenemhat-TT53 (TIII) was one of the closest burials to TT131, but as an 'Acolyte of Amun' he was not a direct colleague of the Vizier. Amenemhet-TT123 (TIII) was a 'Royal Scribe', 'Overseer of the Granary' and 'Counter of Bread'; while the tomb of the 'Overseer of Works' Benia called Pahekamun-TT343 (TIII) lies 100m to the south of TT131. Both men would have had a collegial relationship with the Vizier, as the titles of 'Royal Scribe', 'Overseer of the Granary of Amun' and 'Overseer of Works' have been discussed above. TT129 (TIII-AII) is of unknown ownership.

TT100 - Rekhmire

Late in the reign of Tuthmosis III, User was succeeded by his nephew Rekhmire, the son of his brother Neferweben, and the grandson of Amethu called Ahmose. Rekhmire has both his predecessors depicted in his tomb along with other relatives, showing their close familial connection (PM I: 210). He was confirmed in his office by Amenhotep II after the death of Tuthmosis III, but some confusion surrounds the end of his Vizierate, as images of Rekhmire in his tomb have been systematically destroyed, perhaps suggesting a controversial end to his career. His tomb is located a short distance to the south from the earlier Viziers (see Figure 331). He may have chosen a spot slightly removed from his predecessors as a result of being less closely related than User and Ahmose were, or the lower slopes may have been popular during this period as a result of better-quality rock and the upper slopes becoming crowded. His tomb is in an elevated position facing east and entered through a private walled courtyard (see Figures 332 and 333).

Tombs within a 100m radius of TT100, potentially dating to the reign of Tuthmosis III or Amenhotep II are relevant as Rekhmire was appointed as Vizier by Tuthmosis III and continued in this role into the reign of Amenhotep II (see Figure 334 and Table 60). Tombs dated to Tuthmosis III and previously discussed in relation to TT83 are not discussed further here but are still relevant to TT100 for the same reasons. Tombs dating to the reign of Amenhotep II are relevant in relation to both TT100 and TT29, as both tomb owners served as Vizier during this reign.

The first group of tombs to be discussed here are arranged in a group to the west of TT100, in an east-

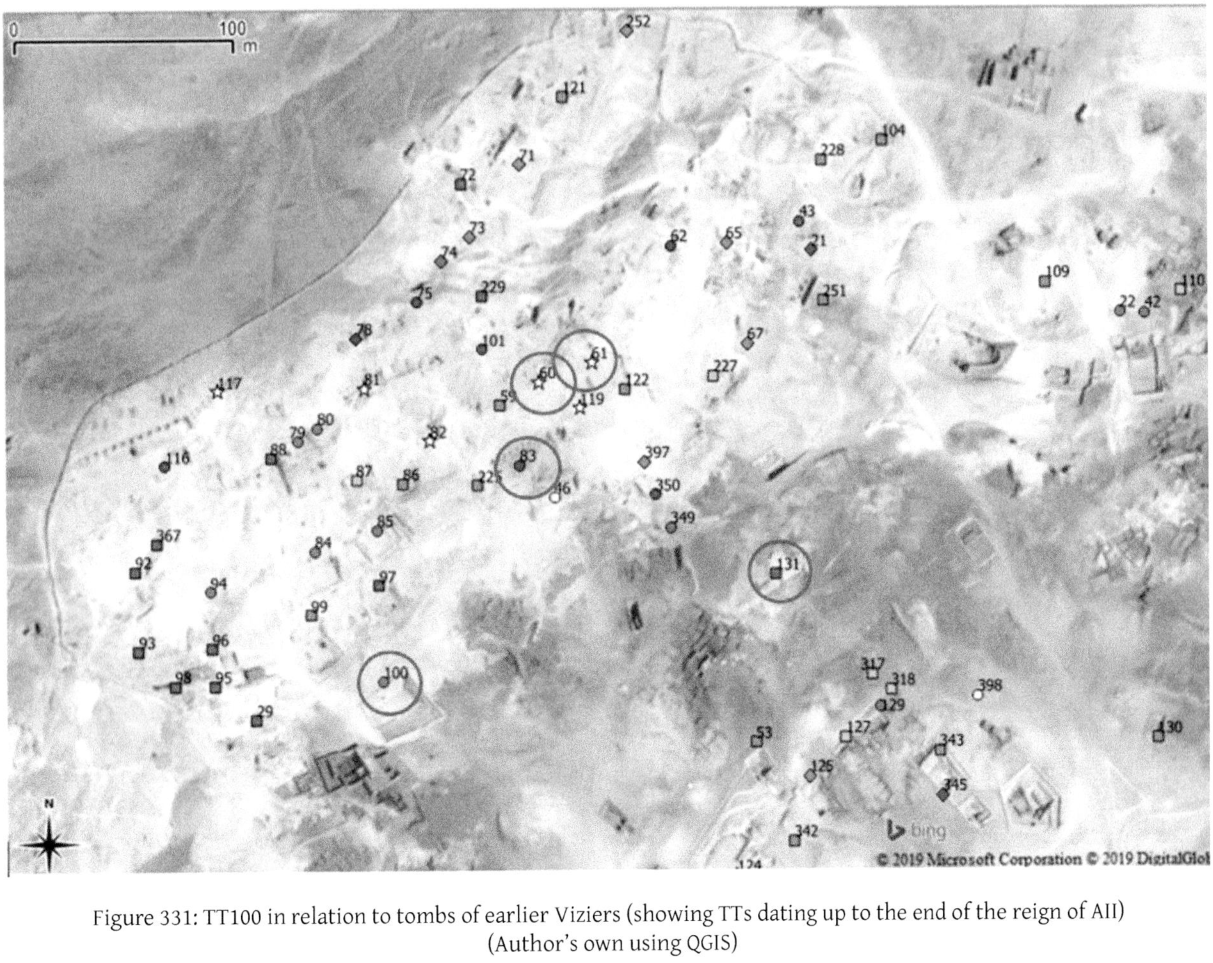

Figure 331: TT100 in relation to tombs of earlier Viziers (showing TTs dating up to the end of the reign of AII) (Author's own using QGIS)

Figure 332: View towards TT100 (Author's own)

Figure 333: Courtyard of TT100 (Author's own)

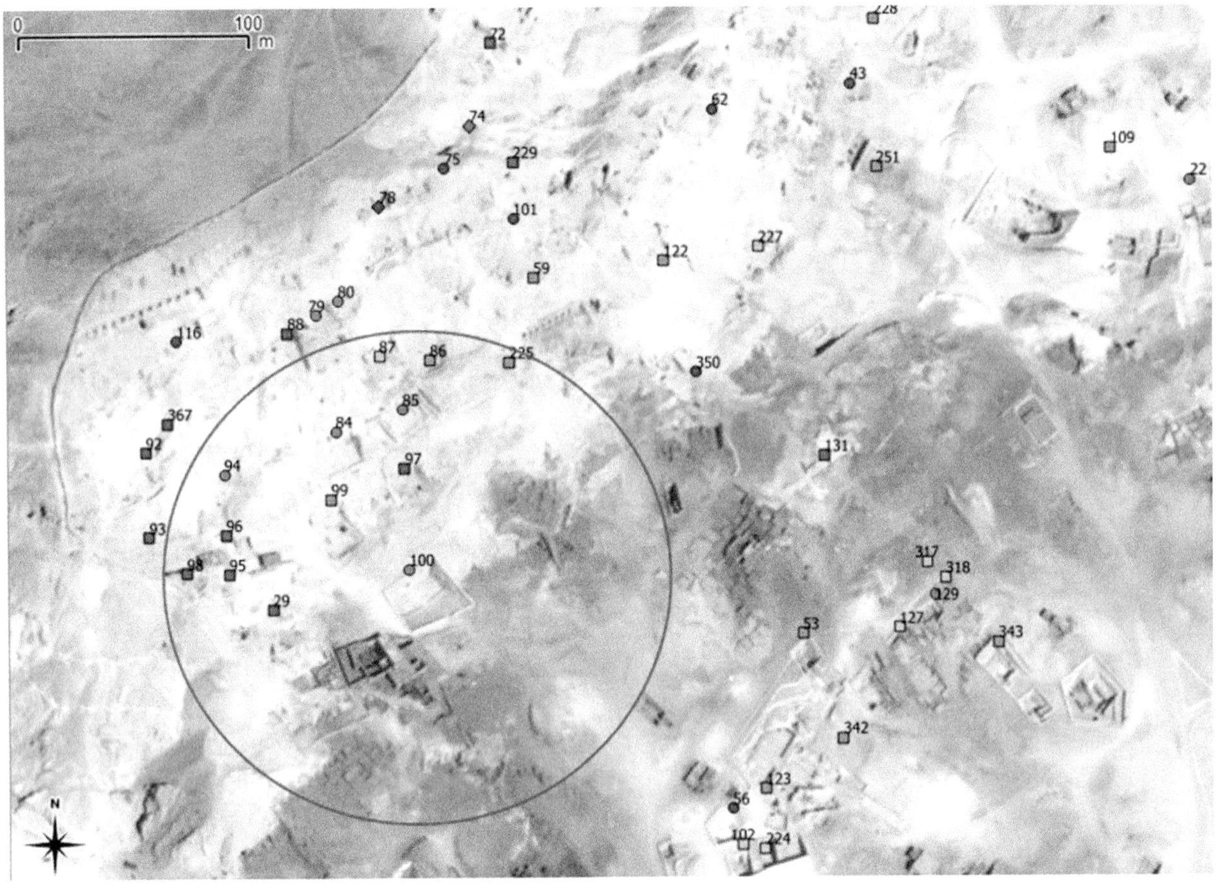

Figure 334: TT100 with contemporary tombs in a 100m radius (showing TTs dating to the reign of TIII/AII)

facing semi-circle. Amenemopet called Pairy-TT29 (AII), Rekhmire's successor, lies adjacent to TT100 so seems to have been intentionally situated near his predecessor, and built after TT100. Although there is no evidence of a familial relationship between Rekhmire and his successor, this does suggest a close relationship, or at least a connection between them as a result of the Vizierate. Adjacent to TT29 is the 'High Priest of Amun' Mery-TT95 (AII) (who also reused TT84-AII), with the 'Third Priest of Amun' Kaemheribsen-TT98 (AII) situated behind it. These two tombs do not fit the pattern of other contemporary tombs in this group, as they belong to priests rather than important members of the administration. In their capacity as priests, and the High Priests in particular, they would have known both Viziers (see above).

Sennefer-TT96 (AII) is located to the north-west of TT100, slightly further up the hill than the previous tombs (see Figures 335 and 336). Sennefer was the brother of Rekhmire's successor, so it seems likely that this tomb would have been adjacent to TT29 had there been space available, rather than them being separated by TT95, which may suggest a familial relationship between these tomb owners, or the prior existence of TT95. In his capacity as the 'Mayor' of Thebes, and 'Overseer of the Arable Land in the Record Department' he would have had very close links to the Vizier – certainly to his brother but also potentially his predecessor. The record department is mentioned in the 'Duties' as being under the authority of the Vizier, and the title 'Mayor' is also referred to as a colleague of the Vizier. He also held a number of important roles within the Estate of Amun, but as 'High Priest of Amun in Menisut', and 'Overseer of Priests...' he would also have worked with the Vizier (see above). A scene within TT96 depicts Sennefer offering a bouquet of Amun to his brother, Amenemopet called Pairy, demonstrating their close relationship (PM I: 198). Ramose called Amay-TT94 (TIII-AII) lies just to the north of TT96 and was owned by 'Royal Seal-bearer' and 'Judge in the Whole Land', so would have been a colleague as Judge was one of the responsibilities of the Vizier as attested in the 'Duties'.

A short distance to the north-west of TT100 lies another Sennefer-TT99 (TIII), who was the 'Treasurer of Amun', 'Overseer of the Priests of all the Gods', and 'Overseer of the Granary' among other titles. In both his religious and administrative roles, Sennefer would have been a close colleague of the Vizier, as reinforced by the 'Duties' and Trauer Relief. Amenemhet-TT97 (AII),

Table 60: Contemporary TTs within a 100m radius of TT100

Tomb	Reign	Name	Title
TT29	AII	Amenemopet called Pairy	Governor of the Town, Vizier; Priest of Maat; Divine Father; *sm* priest; Mouth of Nekhen; Chief of the entire land; etc...
TT84	TIII/AII AII	(1) Iamunedjem (2) Mery	(1) First Royal Herald; Royal Scribe; Overseer of the Granaries of U and LE; Overseer of the Law Court (of the King); Director of all Royal works; etc (2) High Priest of Amun (TT95)
TT85	TIII/AII	Amenemhab called Mahu	**Lieutenant Commander of the Army** (of the Lord of the Two Lands); Captain of the Troops; Royal Seal-bearer; Attendant of the Lord of the Two Lands; etc...
TT86	TIII	Menkheperesoneb	See Table 57
TT87	Hat/TIII	Minnakht	See Table 57
TT94	TIII/AII	Ramose called Amay	**First Royal Herald;** Fan-bearer (of the Lord of the Two Lands); Royal Seal-bearer; Judge in the Whole Land; etc...
TT95	AII	Mery	High Priest of Amun; Overseer of the Priests of U and LE; Steward of Amun; Treasurer of Amun; Divine Father of the Great Place; Overseer of the Granary of Amun; Overseer of the Fields of Amun; Royal Seal-bearer; Overseer of Cattle (of Amun);
TT96	AII	Sennefer	Mayor of the Southern City; Steward of Amun; Overseer of Priests...' Overseer of the Granaries of Amun; Overseer of the Fields of Amun; High Priest of Amun in Menisut; Royal Seal-bearer; Overseer of the Cattle of Amun; Steward (of the Lord of the Two Lands) Djeserkare (=AI); Overseer of the Arable Land in the Record Department; etc...
TT97	AII	Amenemhet	**High priest of Amun;** Overseer of the Priests of U and LE; Steward of the Estate of Amun; Treasurer; Royal Seal-bearer; Overseer of the Storehouse; etc...
TT98	AII	Kaemheribsen	Third Priest of Amun; Royal Seal-bearer;
TT99	TIII	Sennefer	**Treasurer of Amun;** Royal Seal-bearer; Overseer of the Granary; Overseer of the Gold Lands of Amun; Overseer of all the Priests of all the Gods; etc...
TT225	TIII	Menkheperesoneb	See Table 57

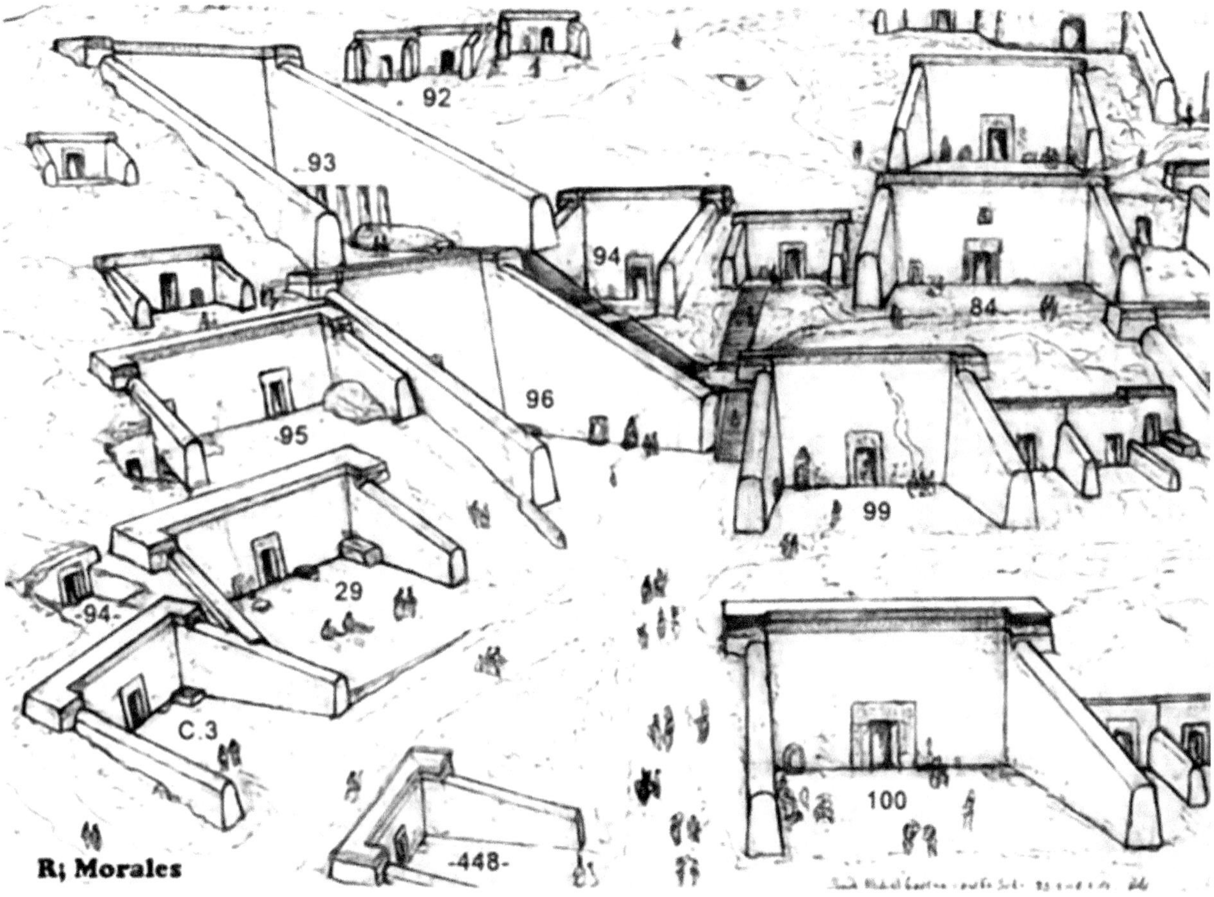

Figure 335: Drawing by R. Morales of the area surrounding TT100 and TT29 (Courtesy of R. Morales)

located to the north of TT100, was another 'High Priest of Amun', thus he was another important individual with a collegial relationship with the Vizier (see above). Further to the north is Amenemhab called Mahu-TT85 (TIII-AII), who was the 'Lieutenant Commander of the Army' and 'Captain of Troops'. These roles would have necessitated a working relationship with the Vizier, as the connection between military commanders and the Vizier is confirmed by the reference in 'The Duties' and the presence of a 'General' behind the Vizier in the procession on the Trauer Relief. Iamunedjem-TT84 (TIII-AII) would also have worked closely with the Vizier in his capacity as 'Royal Scribe', 'Overseer of the Granaries of U and LE', 'Overseer of the Law Court' and 'Director of all Royal Works'.

TT29 - Amenemopet called Pairy

Amenemopet called Pairy succeeded Rekhmire and does not appear to be related to his predecessors but was probably appointed to this illustrious position by Amenhotep II as a result a childhood connection between the two men (Helck 1958: 294-95). He was Vizier during the latter part of the reign of Amenhotep II and into the reign of Tuthmosis IV. He constructed TT29, which is located in close proximity (60m to the west) to the tomb of his predecessor Rekhmire (see Figures 337 and 338). He also appears to have had the great honour of a second tomb in the Valley of the Kings, KV48. His brother, Sennefer-TT96 was buried nearby (see above), and his father, Ahmose called Humay-TT224, in Lower Qurna.

Both Rekhmire and Amenemopet called Pairy held office during the reign of Amenhotep II and are buried in close proximity (see Figure 339), so some tombs dating to Amenhotep II and discussed in relation to TT100 are also relevant here but are not discussed again. Three further tombs lie within a 100m radius of TT29 (see Figure 340). Kenamun-TT93 (AII), located 60m to the north west of TT29, was the 'Treasurer', making him the Vizier's closest colleague. He was also 'Chief Steward of the King' and 'Royal Scribe', so would have worked very closely with both Rekhmire and his successor, as all three titles are attested in both 'The Duties' and the Trauer Relief. Suemnut-TT92 (AII), located to the north of TT93, was a 'Royal Butler' and 'Royal Seal-bearer', who was also the 'Overseer' of the royal ships and stable. Although these titles are not attested in 'The Duties' or on the Trauer Relief, this

Figure 336: Courtyard of TT96 (Author's own)

Figure 337: The courtyard of TT29 (Author's own)

Figure 338: Entrance to TT29 (Author's own)

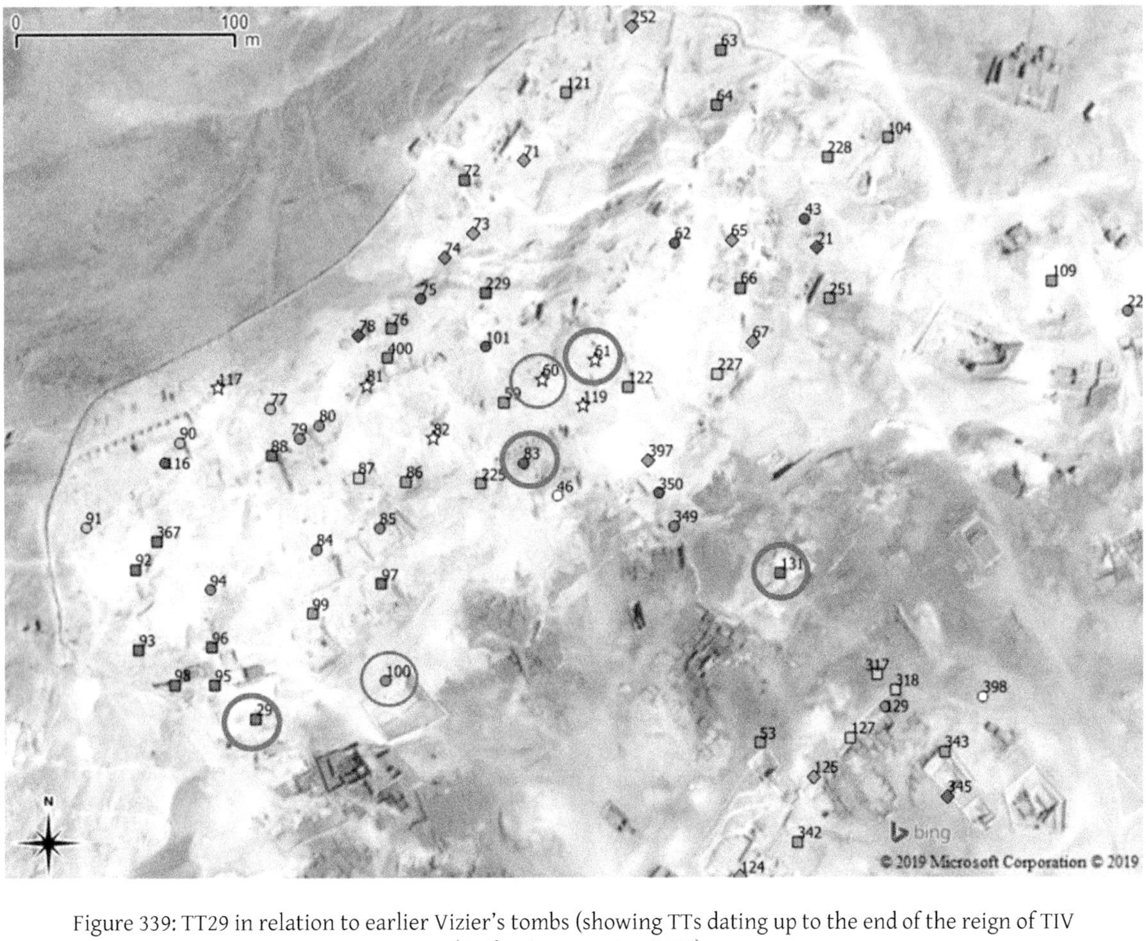

Figure 339: TT29 in relation to earlier Vizier's tombs (showing TTs dating up to the end of the reign of TIV (Author's own using QGIS)

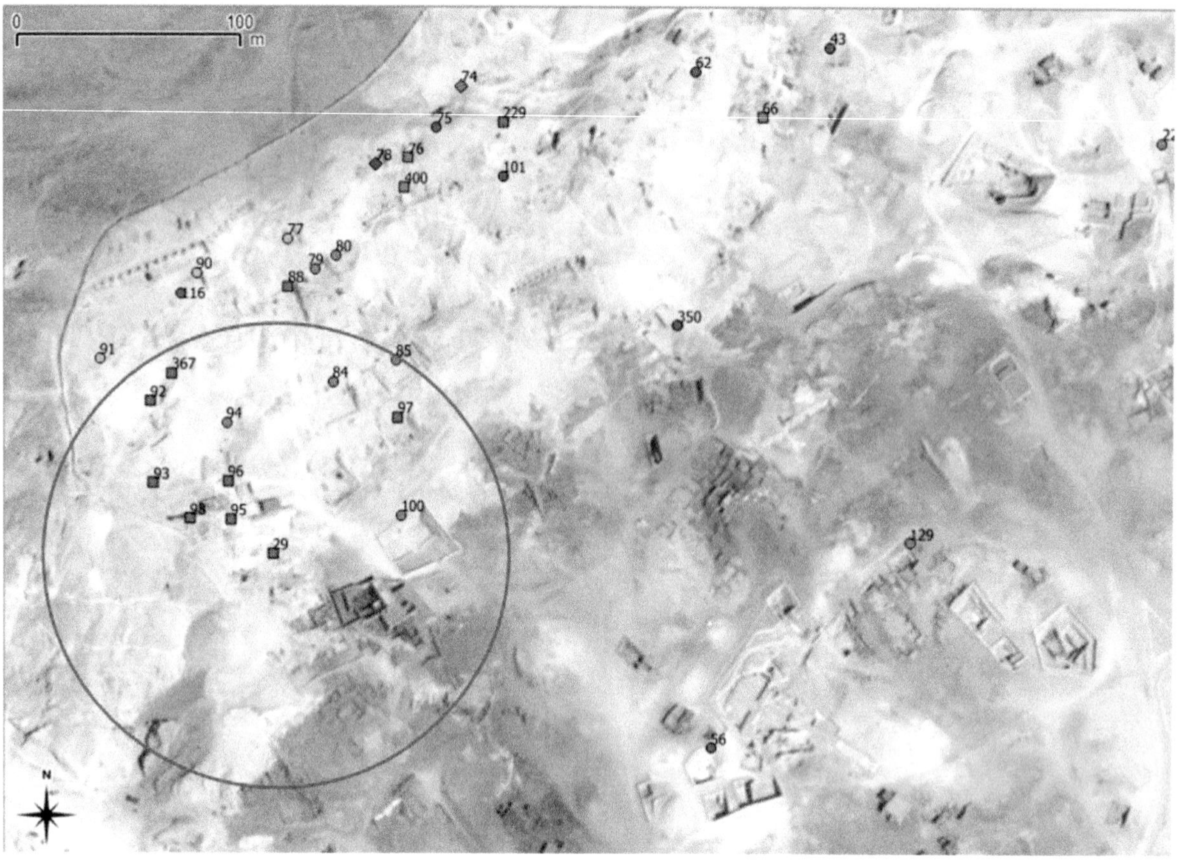

Figure 340: TT29 with contemporary TTs in a 100m radius (showing TTs dating to the reign of AII/TIV) (Author's own using QGIS)

Table 61: Contemporary TTs within a 100m radius of TT29

Tomb	Reign	Name	Title
TT84	TIII/AII	Iamunedjem	(See Table 60)
TT85	TIII/AII	Amenemhab called Mahu	(See Table 60)
TT92	AII	Suemnut	**Royal Butler**; Royal Seal-bearer; Overseer of the Priests of All the Gods; Overseer of Royal Ships; Chief of the Stable of the Lord of the Two Lands; etc...
TT93	AII	Kenamun	Treasurer; Chief Steward of the King; Royal Seal-bearer; Royal Scribe; etc...
TT94	TIII/AII	Ramose called Amay	(See Table 60)
TT95	AII	Mery	(See Table 60)
TT96	AII	Sennefer	(See Table 60)
TT97	AII	Amenemhet	(See Table 60)
TT98	AII	Kaemheribsen	(See Table 60)
TT100	TIII/AII	Rekhmire	(See Table 60)
TT367	AII	Paser	Captain of the Troops of the Lord of the Two Lands; etc...

individual must have been familiar with the Vizier on account of his relationship with the king. He was also 'Overseer of the Priests of all the Gods', and 'High Priests' are attested on the Trauer Relief, so a working relationship seems likely. Close to TT92 lies Paser-TT367 (AII), who was a 'Captain of Troops'. The relationship between Vizier and General has been established, so the Vizier did work with high-ranking members of the military, but this specific title does not appear in either of the aforementioned sources.

Hepu – TT66

The next Vizier with a known Theban tomb is Hepu who was buried in TT66. Hepu served as Vizier during the reign of Tuthmosis IV and is also buried in Upper Qurna, to the north east of the Viziers of the early Eighteenth Dynasty (see Figure 341).

There are only three relevant tombs located within 100m of TT66 (see Figure 342 and Table 62). Amenemwaskhet-TT62 (AII-TIV) was buried 30m to the north west. He was the 'Chamberlain', who had a close working relationship with the Vizier, as referenced in both 'The Duties' and the Trauer Relief. Neferrenpet-TT43 (AII-TIV), located 30m to the north east of TT66, was the 'Overseer of the Storehouse of the Lord of the Two Lands', who is not an attested colleague. TT350 (AII-TIV) is located 100m to the south and belonged to an unknown 'Scribe of Counting Bread'. This title is not used in connection to the Vizier in either source. Hekerneheh-TT64 (TIV) is located to the north of TT66 and was the 'Nurse' or 'Tutor of the King's Son Amenhotep' (Amenhotep III). In this role he may have had limited contact with the Vizier but would have been more of an acquaintance than a colleague.

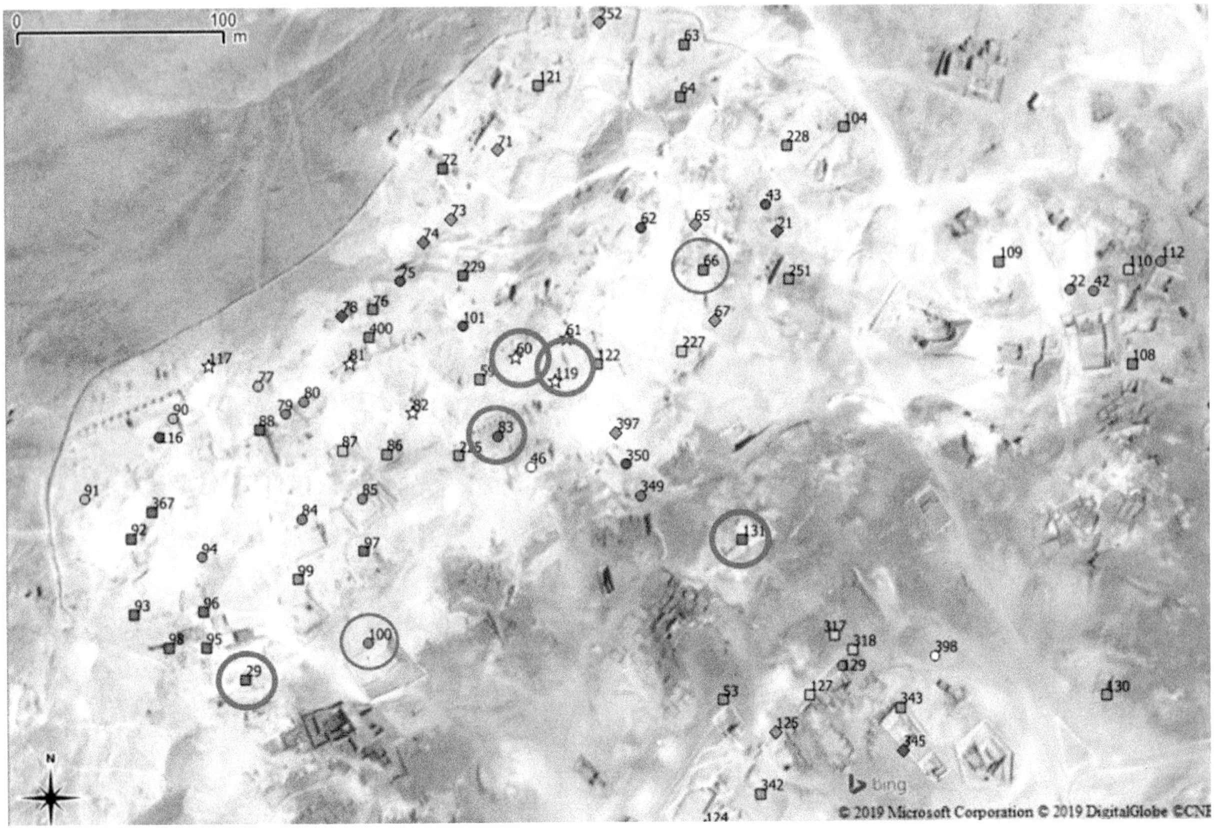

Figure 341: TT66 in relation to earlier Viziers' tombs (showing TTs dating up to the end of the reign of TIV) (Author's own using QGIS)

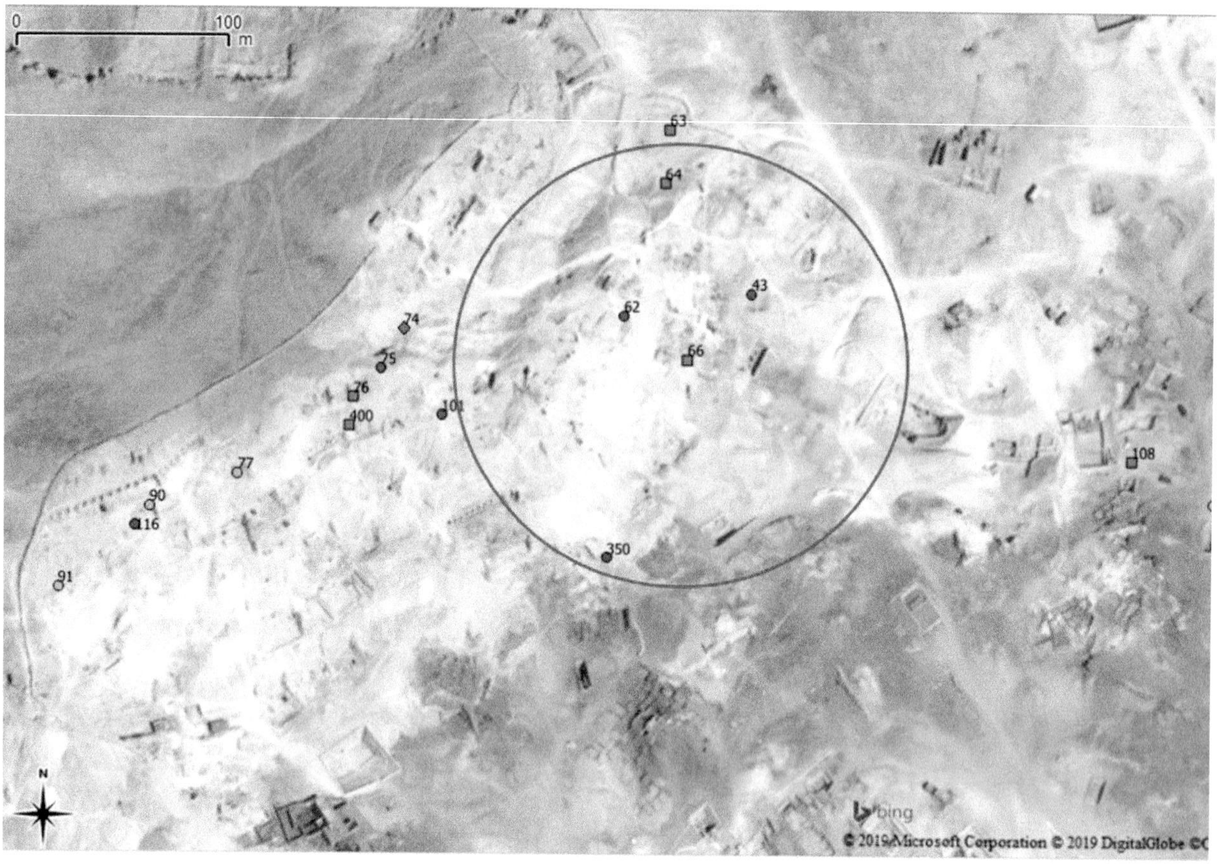

Figure 342: TT66 with contemporary tombs in a 100m radius (showing TTs dating to the reign of TIV) (Author's own using QGIS)

Table 62: Contemporary TTs within a 100m radius of TT66

Tomb	Reign	Name	Title
TT43	AII/TIV	Neferrenpet	Overseer of the Storehouse of the Lord of the Two Lands;
TT62	AII/TIV	Amenemwaskhet	Chamberlain; Royal Seal-bearer; ...Mayor;
TT64	TIV	Hekerneheh	Nurse/Tutor of the King's Son Amenhotep;
TT350	AII/TIV	Unknown	Scribe of Counting Bread;

Ramose - TT55

The next Vizier with a known TT is Ramose who was Vizier under Amenhotep III and into the reign of Amenhotep IV (Akhenaten). He was buried in TT55, which is approached by a monumental causeway leading to a large courtyard (see Figures 343 and 344). This tomb is located further down the slopes of Qurna than the tombs of previous Viziers, but still in roughly the same area (see Figure 345). This move was probably due to a combination of the lack of space on the upper slopes and the availability of better-quality limestone on the lower ground, as this more elaborate tomb chapel necessitated good quality stone for the construction of a hypostyle hall and carved decoration (see Figure 346). From an artistic point of view this tomb appears to have been built while the innovations of the Amarna period were being implemented, so presumably the court itself was also undergoing transition at this time. During the reign of Amenhotep III, fewer members of

Figure 343: View of the causeway leading to TT55 (Author's own)

Figure 344: Entrance to TT55 (Author's own)

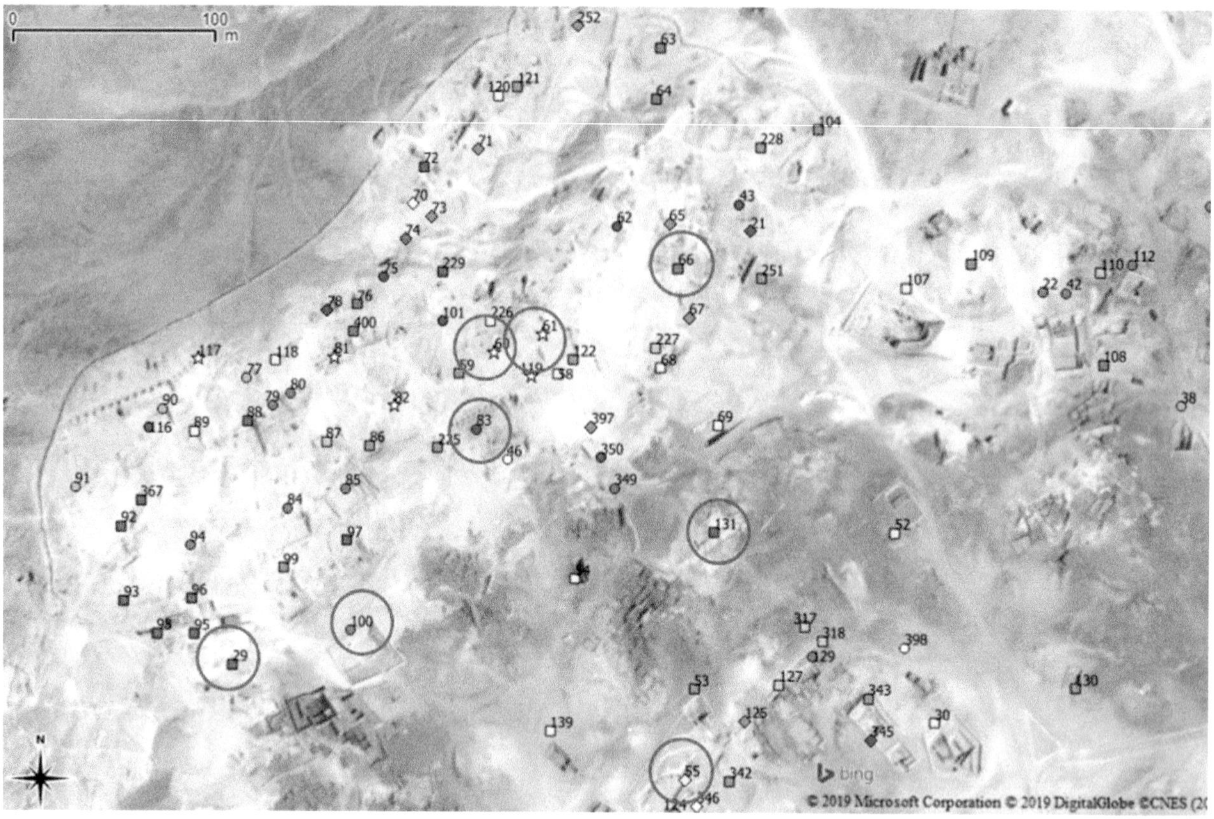

Figure 345: TT55 in relation to earlier Viziers' tombs (showing TTs dating up to the end of the reign of Amenhotep IV) (Author's own using QGIS)

Figure 346: The hypostyle hall of TT55 (Author's own)

the court were buried at Thebes, but those officials who were buried here also favoured the lower slopes of Qurna, Khokha or Asasif.

There are only two contemporary tombs in the vicinity of TT55 (AIII-AIV) (see Figure 347 and Table 63. The closest of these, Khaemhet called Mahu-TT57 (AIII), lies to the south-west of TT55, and was a 'Royal Scribe' and 'Overseer of the Granaries', so would have been a close colleague of the Vizier in both roles, as previously discussed. To the north of TT57 lies Pairy-TT139 (AIII), a '*wꜥb* priest in Front'. This individual does not hold a title specifically associating him with the Vizier.

Paser – TT106

Paser held the position of 'Southern Vizier' from the reign of Seti I until the reign of Ramesses II. He was the only definite Ramesside Vizier to be buried at Thebes and was well attested with a long list of titles and several monuments dedicated to him throughout Egypt. TT106 (see Figure 348) is located to the east of the tombs of the previous Viziers, closer to the earliest Viziers of the Eighteenth Dynasty (see Figure 349). His tomb was topped by a pyramid, located some distance away. The 'Duties of a Vizier' text also appears of the walls of his tomb, which alongside his decision to be

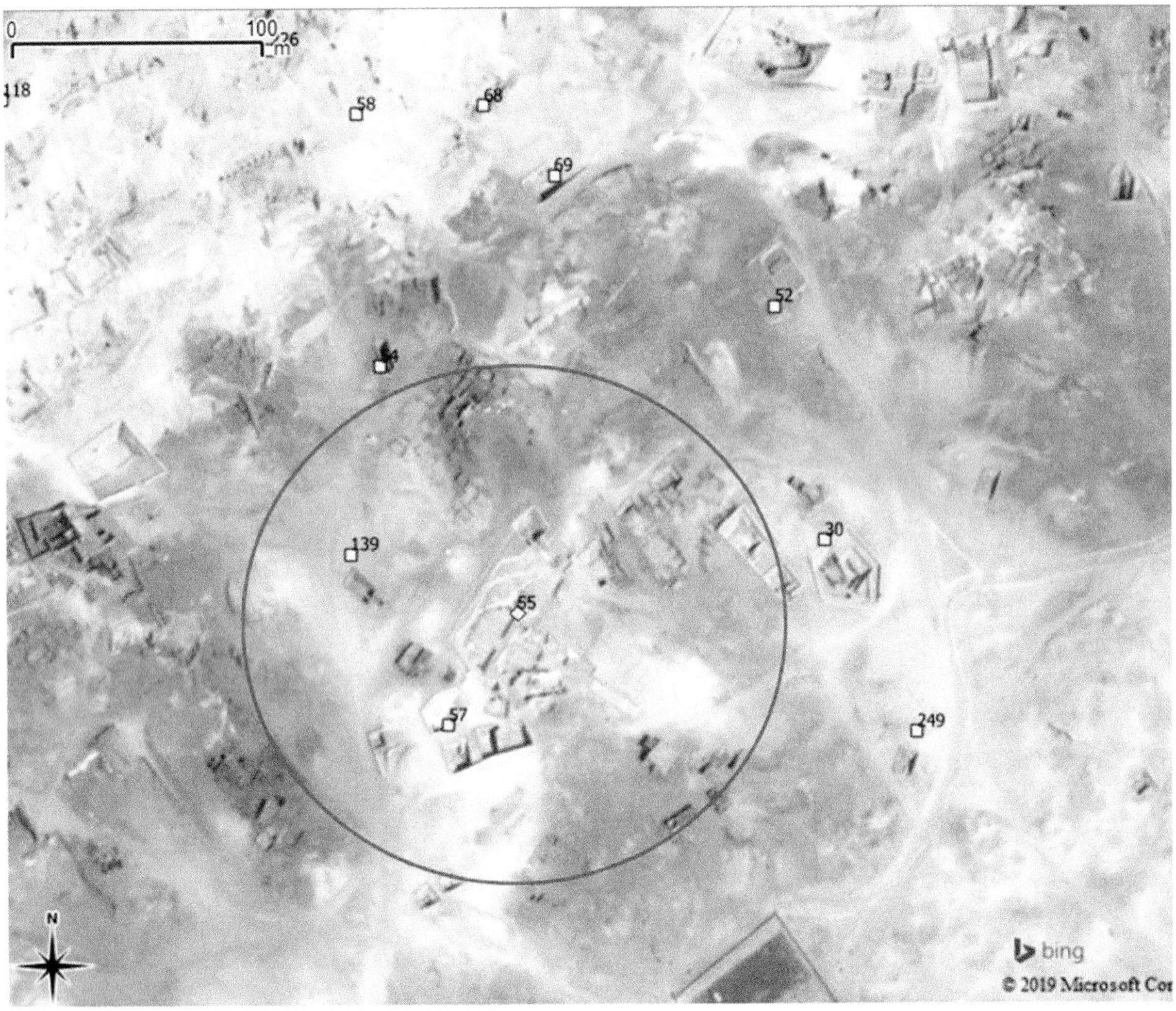

Figure 347: TT55 and contemporary tombs (showing TTs dating to the reign of AIII/IV) (Author's own using QGIS)

Table 63: Contemporary TTs within a 100m radius of TT55

Tomb	Reign	Name	Title
TT57	AIII	Khaemhet called Mahu	Royal Scribe; Overseer of the Granaries of the Lord of the Two Lands/Upper and Lower Egypt;
TT139	AIII	Pairy	*wꜥb* priest in Front;

Figure 348: Façade of TT106 (Hofmann 2018: Abb. 1- Courtesy of Dr Eva Hofmann: Ägyptologisches Institut Heidelberg)

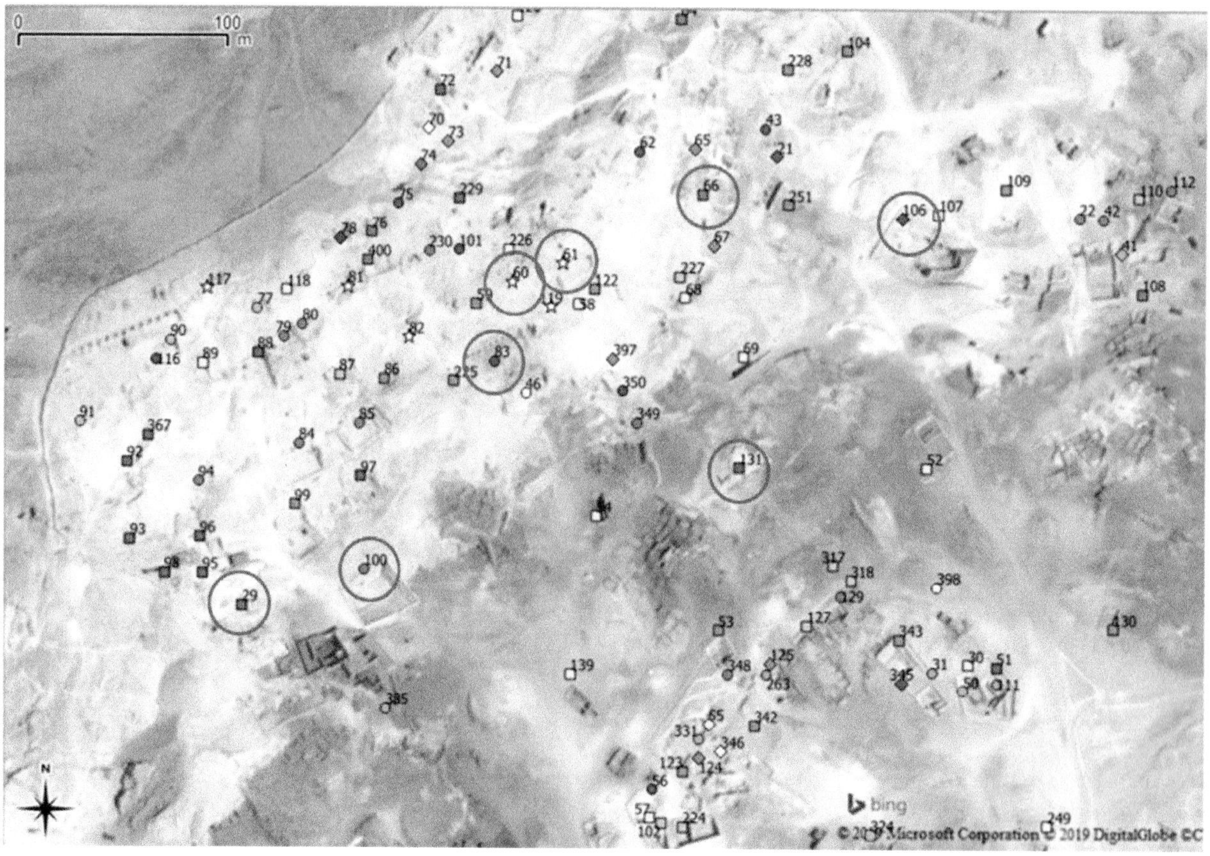

Figure 349: TT106 in relation to earlier Viziers' tombs (showing TTs dating up to the end of the reign of RII) (Author's own using QGIS)

buried at Thebes suggests a continuity of Eighteenth Dynasty Viziers' traditions. Paser also became 'High Priest of Amun' which may have influenced his choice of burial site.

TT106 (SI-RII) is in a relatively isolated position, with only one potentially contemporary TT within a 100m radius (see Figure 350). Amenemopet called Ipy-TT41 lies 100m to the east and is likely to predate TT106. If it was built during the reign of Seti I they could potentially be contemporary, and with a range of important titles, particularly that of 'Overseer of Granaries', these men would have been colleagues.

Problematic Viziers

Hapuseneb – TT67

Hapuseneb was buried in TT67 on the upper slopes of Qurna, which is dated to the reign of Hatshepsut. TT67 does fit the distribution pattern of Viziers' tombs as it is located close to the tombs of the earlier and contemporary Viziers, and within 100m of TT60 and TT61 (see Figure 351). In his tomb, Hapuseneb has the title 'High Priest of Amun', among others, but not 'Vizier'. However. on a block statue, Louvre A134, he is referred to also as 'Overseer of the Town' and 'Vizier',

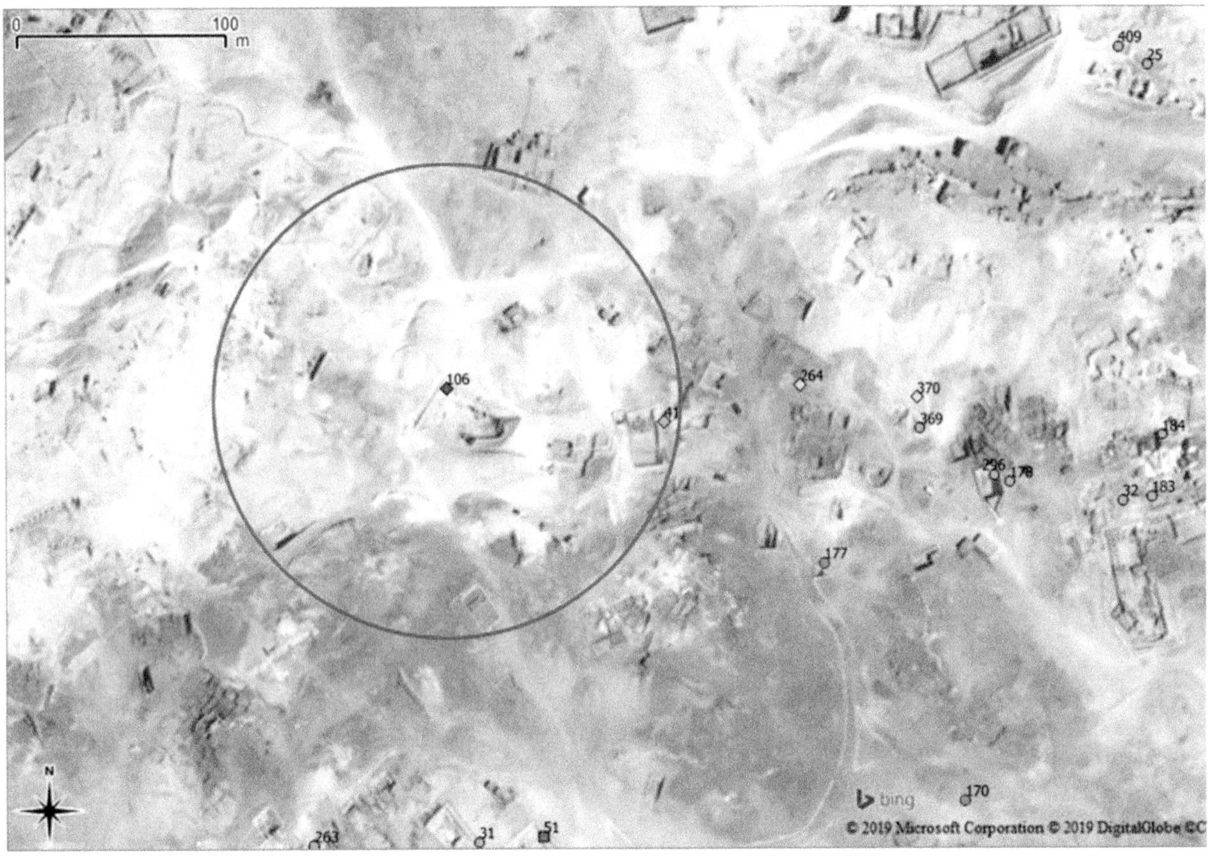

Figure 350: TT106 and contemporary TTs in a 100m radius (showing TTs dating to the reign of SI/RII) (Author's own using QGIS)

Table 64: Contemporary TTs within a 100m radius of TT106

Tomb	Reign	Name	Title
TT41	Hor-SI	Amenemopet called Ipy	**(Chief) Steward of Amun in the Southern City; Royal Scribe**; Overseer of the Granaries of U and LE / of All the Gods; Overseer of the Priests of Min and Isis; Overseer of the Cattle of Amun; Steward of the God's Wife; Royal Seal-bearer;

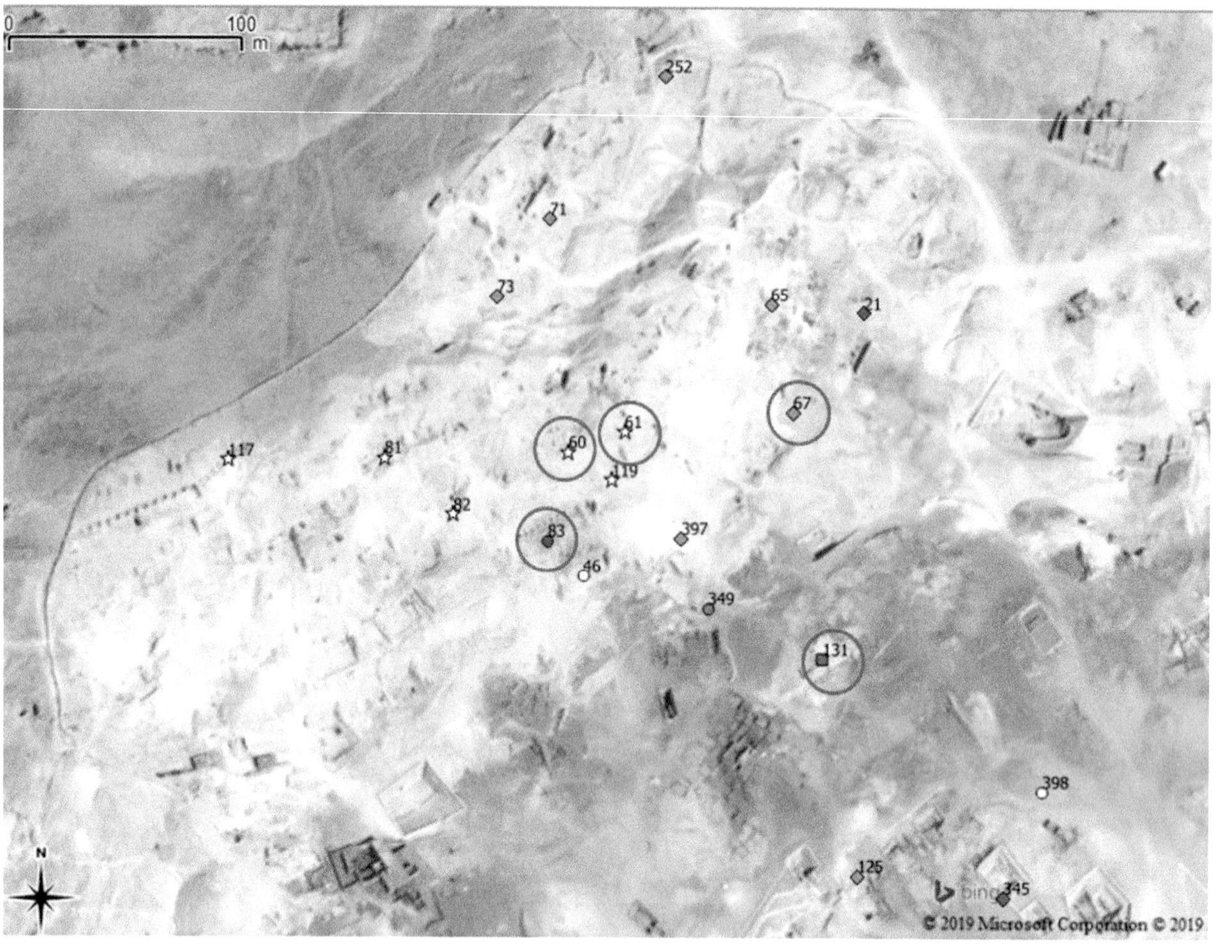

Figure 351: TT67 shown in relation to earlier Viziers' tombs (showing TTs dating up to the end of the reign of Hat) (Author's own using QGIS)

although these titles appear to have been added later (Delvaux 1988: 61). Ahmose served as Vizier during the reign of Hatshepsut and was succeeded by User, who held the position into the reign of Tuthmosis III. This would imply that if Hapuseneb was indeed a Vizier, he must have held this position at the same time as these men. As the title of Vizier is not attested in Hapuseneb's tomb or on any of his other monuments, this appears to have been an honorary title rather than a functional one (Helck 1977: 955), therefore Hapuseneb is not included in this study of Vizier's tombs.

Nebmarenakht (also called Sakhtnefer) - TT293

Several individuals were Vizier from the reign of Ramesses II onwards, but none have an identified TT. From the reign of Ramesses IX until Ramesses XI, Nebmarenakht held the title of Vizier. Khaemwaset temporarily replaced him as Vizier from year 14 to 17 of the reign of Ramesses IX, but Nebmarenakht was later reinstated. TT293 in Dra Abu el-Naga is accredited to Nebmarenakht, based on fragments found within the tomb (PM I: 236), which lies some distance away from all the other known Theban Viziers' tombs (see Figure 352).

This tomb was previously occupied by Ramessesnakht, the 'High Priest of Amun', during the reign of Ramesses IV, and reused in the reign of Ramesses X. Some debate surrounds the location of this tomb and the identity of its owner, as the original plan and description of the tomb (PM I: 370 and 376) do not match what is visible on the ground (Larkin and Van Siclen 1975: 134). Indeed Kampp (1996: 562) rather attributes TT293 to the scribe Huy.

There are no tombs in the vicinity of TT293 (or anywhere else in the necropolis) that can be securely dated to the reigns of Ramesses IX, X or XI. The non-royal mortuary landscape of the late Ramesside period is poorly understood as a result of the lack of securely dated tombs, classified only as Twentieth Dynasty or Ramesside and not to a specific reign (Bács 2011: 7).

It is unclear why Nebmaarenakht would have chosen to be buried so far away from the other New Kingdom Viziers, reusing a tomb in this area rather than Qurna. The lack of new burials accurately dated to the late Twentieth Dynasty and the increase in tomb reuse at this time suggests that the court was reusing existing

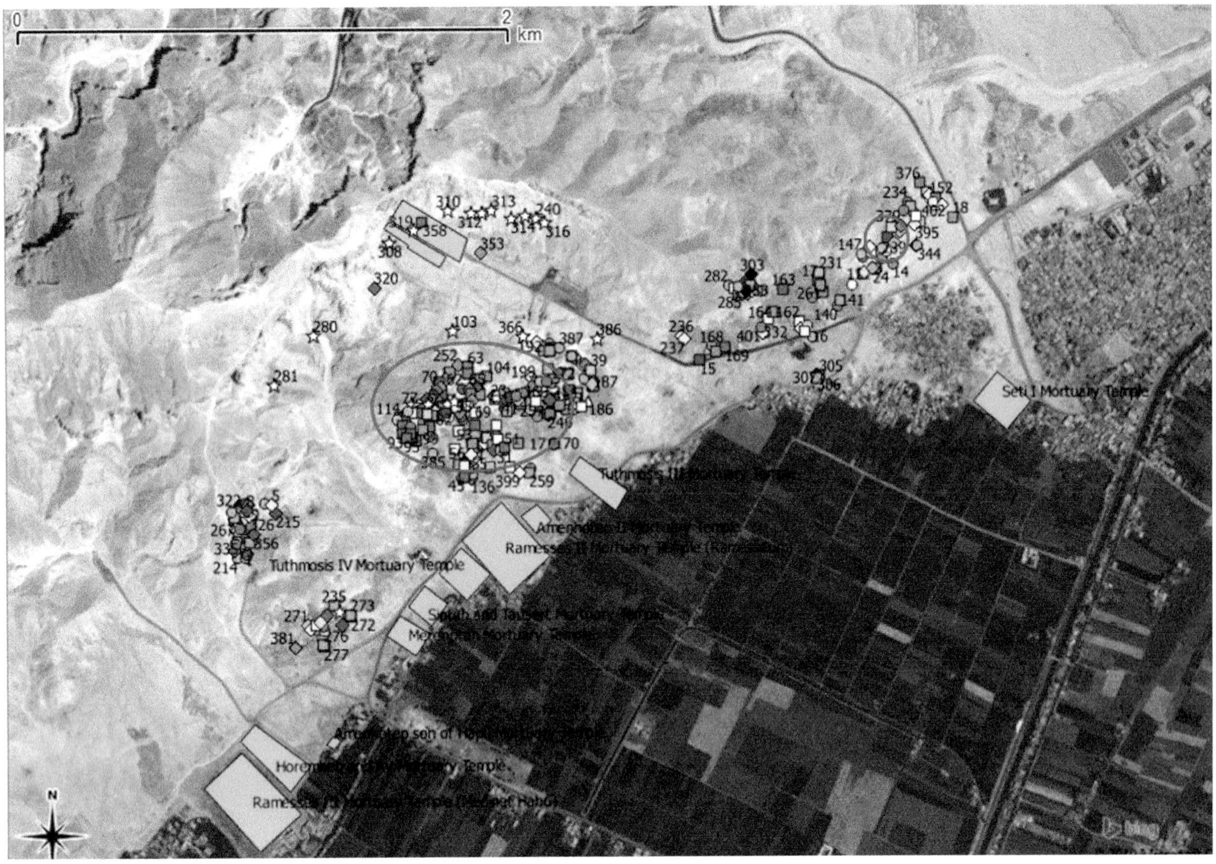

Figure 352: TT293 in relation to early Viziers' TTs (showing all TTs dating prior to the end of the New Kingdom) (Author's own using QGIS)

burials and possibly being buried elsewhere at this time. The relatively small, inconspicuous, usurped nature of the burial used by Nebmaarenkaht, and the lack of officials buried nearby may also reflect the declining power of the king and therefore the Vizier as the Ramesside period draws to a close. It also strengthens the case that this tomb never belonged to Nebmaarenakht but has been misidentified.

Conclusions

Viziers' tombs were important enough to act as a focal point for contemporary burials during the first part of the Eighteenth Dynasty. The office was held by one family for several reigns, resulting in close family burials on the upper slopes of Qurna (TT83, TT61 and TT131), with some of the court and other important individuals buried nearby. It is possible that this area was designated for these burials by the king, deliberately chosen to associate themselves with their illustrious Middle Kingdom ancestors (TT60), or simply that these upper slopes provided wonderful views towards the Nile and Karnak temple beyond. As the Dynasty went on the location of Viziers' tombs moved progressively southwards (TT100, TT29 and TT55) to the lower slopes of Qurna (with TT66 breaking this trend and returning to the upper slopes), but still in the same general area of the necropolis, and still surrounded by some of the most important officials of their Vizierate. This move to the lower slopes was probably due to the overcrowded nature of the best locations on the upper slopes and the superior rock quality lower down. Towards the end of the Dynasty, the king and court resided in the northern capital of Memphis. Although some officials were still buried at Thebes, there are fewer Viziers with Theban burials and fewer officials buried near to them.

During the Nineteenth Dynasty the majority of officials were buried in the north rather than at Thebes, which explains the shortage of Theban Vizier's tombs from the Nineteenth Dynasty onwards (see Chapter 3) The only definite exception, TT106, was located in the same locality as the early Eighteenth Dynasty Viziers, perhaps demonstrating a desire to associate himself with his Eighteenth Dynasty predecessors, as he also includes the 'Duties of the Vizier' text on the walls of his tomb. Paser's decision to be buried at Thebes could also be indicative of a particularly close connection to the city, as suggested by his attestations within Deir el-Medina tombs. By this time the tomb of the Vizier no longer acted as a focal point for elite burials, as demonstrated by the scarcity of contemporary tombs.

By the Twentieth Dynasty power had shifted from the Vizier to the local mayor(s), in a similar way to the power of the king decreasing in favour of the High Priest of Amun (Cooney 2018: 64-65).

Shirley (2008: 5-7) identified a spatial connection between the tombs of the earliest New Kingdom Viziers (TT83, TT61, TT100, TT131) and their families and close associates (TT81, TT82, TT100, TT122 and TT228), terming this a 'family complex' on the basis that these tombs lay along the same topographical contour line, in relatively close proximity to each other. However, Dorman (2003: 39) suggests that the fact that these tombs do not lie adjacent to each other, at a time when this would have been possible as these upper slopes were relatively unoccupied, shows that there was no necessity to create a 'family precinct', but rather that each tomb forms a discrete monument with family members commemorated in the tomb decoration rather than by connected tombs. Some compromise between the two seems more likely – that the tombs were deliberately spatially connected, but these connections could have been even stronger had this been the main factor when siting them. Proximity to the tombs of Middle Kingdom Viziers seems to have been the prime consideration for Amethu-TT83 and User-TT61, while different factors influenced User's southern burial (TT131), such as the desire for a larger tomb. Rekhmire-TT100 moved south-west along with the majority of officials from the reign of Amenhotep II (see Chapter 9), no longer concerned with a tomb adjacent to his family, although still easily accessible from their tombs.

Chapter 13:
High Priests of Amun

This chapter considers the locations of the known tombs in the Theban necropolis belonging to New Kingdom 'High Priests of Amun' (HPA), who were based at Karnak, and not those who performed this role at other temples. The surrounding tombs are also analysed for distributional patterns. A link has already been ascertained between the tombs of the 'Viziers', particularly those dating to the Eighteenth Dynasty located in Qurna (see Chapter 12). In the Old Kingdom distributional patterns existed between the tombs of the 'High Priests of Ptah' at Saqqara, when a clear cluster of nine tombs was identified, suggesting that high religious titles were a factor in determining tomb location (Reisner 1936: 393; Roth 1988: 203).

The High Priest of Amun

The HPA or '*ḥm nṯr tpy n 'Imn*' was an extremely important individual throughout the New Kingdom, who had responsibility for both religious activities and temple administration within the vast temple of Amun at Karnak. This led to him having considerable economic and political power as a result of the huge amount of resources controlled by the temple, and the influence of the god Amun on kingship in the New Kingdom (Kubisch 2018: 189). The role of the HPA was to lead the religious processions during the main festivals, to conduct cult ceremonies and to play a leading role when Amun was required to make an oracular decision (Kubisch 2018: 190). He was appointed by the king, and confirmed in his office by Amun himself, via oracle, from the reign of Ramesses II onwards (*LAe* II: 1242; Kubisch 2018: 196).

New Kingdom High Priests of Amun

The earliest occurrence of this title was during the reign of Ahmose at the beginning of the Eighteenth Dynasty. There are 29 known HPA dating to the New Kingdom (*LAe* II: 1241-1242), 11 of whom have known Theban tombs (see Figure 353 and Table 65). As the most important religious official of the New Kingdom, it seems likely that they were influential enough to have some input into the location of their tombs, and to potentially act as a focal point for other burials.

Six tombs of the HPA date to the Eighteenth Dynasty. TT67 belonged to Hapuseneb (Hat), TT86 and TT112

Figure 353: Google Earth image showing the tombs adapted by the HPA, K93.11 and K93.12 (Author's own using Google Earth)

Table 65: HPA with known TTs

TT	Dyn	Tomb Owner	Titles	Translit.
35	19	Bakenkhonsu	High Priest of Amun (in Karnak);	*ḥm-nṯr tpy n 'Imn (m ipt-swt);*
58	18 & 19 & 20	(1) Unknown (2) Unknown (3) Amenhotep	(1) Unknown (2) Unknown (3) Overseer of the Priests of Amun – HPA;	*(1) ?* *(2) ?* *(3)imy-r ḥmw-nṯr n 'Imn*
67	18	Hapuseneb	High Priest of Amun;	*ḥm-nṯr tpy n 'Imn;*
84	18	(2) Mery	(2) High Priest of Amun (TT95)	*(2) ḥm nṯr tpy n 'Imn*
86	18	Menkheperresoneb	High Priest of Amun;	*ḥm-nṯr tpy n 'Imn;*
95	18	Mery	High Priest of Amun (TT 84);	*ḥm-nṯr tpy n 'Imn;*
97	18	Amenemhet	High Priest of Amun;	*ḥm-nṯr tpy n 'Imn;*
112	18	Menkheperresoneb	High Priest of Amun;	*ḥm-nṯr tpy n 'Imn;*
157	19	Nebwenenef	High Priest of Amun;	*ḥm-nṯr tpy n 'Imn;*
283	19	Roma (Roy)	High Priest of Amun;	*ḥm-nṯr tpy n 'Imn;*
293	20	Ramessenakht	High Priest of Amun;	*ḥm-nṯr tpy n 'Imn;*

both belonged to individuals named Menkheperresoneb (TIII-AII), TT97 (AII) belongs to Amenemhat, while TT95 and TT84 (reused) both belong to Mery (AII). TT86 and TT112 have recently been identified as belonging to two different HPA, uncle and nephew, bearing the same name (Dorman 1993: 147-54). Three HPA tombs date to the Nineteenth Dynasty, with TT157 (RII) belonging to Nebwenef, and TT35 (RII) belonging to Bakenkhonsu. A third tomb, TT283 (RII-SII) belonging to Roma called Roy, is close in date. Bakenkhonsu may have been the father or brother of Roma called Roy (Rummel 2018: 260-262). Two further HPA burials date to the Twentieth Dynasty, in TT293 (RIV-RIX), belonging to Ramessesnakht, and TT58 (Dyn 18) reused by Amenhotep (RIX-RXI).

Another tomb potentially belonging to an HPA is TT106 (RII) belonging to Paser, which lies adjacent to the Upper Qurna cluster of Eighteenth Dynasty HPA, on the border with el-Khokha. There is some debate over whether Paser the 'Vizier' (TT106) and Paser the HPA were the same person. Both date to the reign of Ramesses II, but Paser the HPA never names his parents in his monuments whereas Paser the Vizier was the son of a former HPA (*LAe* II: 1243). It is also possible that if they were the same individual, that the title of HPA was purely honorary (Kubisch 2018: 199). As the title of HPA does not occur in TT106 (*KRI* I: 285-301; *KRI* III: 1-9; *KRI* VII: 16-18), this tomb has not been analysed further here. However, as all three other Nineteenth Dynasty HPA with Theban tombs are buried in Dra Abu el-Naga, one buried in Khokha would not fit this pattern.

Most Eighteenth Dynasty HPA were buried in Upper Qurna with one nearby in Khokha (TT112). Their tombs are not in extremely close proximity, but they were arranged in a loose cluster within 200m of each other. This cluster includes all of the HPA who held office during this period in chronological order (*LAe* II: 1241-1249). This cluster is located on the upper slopes with views towards the east bank, but it is not directly opposite Karnak temple, although this is visible from here (see Figure 354). The northernmost tombs of the cluster predate Amenhotep II, so are located closer to the causeway leading to Deir el-Bahri where both Hatshepsut and Tuthmosis III built temples which were the destination of Amun during the Beautiful Festival of the Valley. The southernmost tombs of this cluster date to the reign of Amenhotep II, when their tombs would also have overlooked the processional route taken by the god during the Beautiful Festival of the Valley from Deir el-Bahri heading southwards towards the mortuary temple of Amenhotep II. TT58 was an Eighteenth Dynasty tomb, dating to the reign of Amenhotep III, which was reused (for the second time) by a HPA during the Twentieth Dynasty. The original occupant (and the initial usurper) of the tomb is unknown, but the tomb's location amongst this cluster of Eighteenth Dynasty HPA, and in particularly close proximity to those who held this title during the reign of Amenhotep II, suggests that the tomb may have originally belonged to one of the missing HPA from this period.

There then appears to be a shift in the traditional burial site of the HPA to Dra Abu el-Naga West, as the majority of HPA seem to move north-east from Qurna after the Amarna Period. An additional tomb attributed to a HPA (not included on GIS maps as it is not a TT tomb), is Kampp-162-. This tomb is located in Dra Abu el-Naga

East and has been identified as belonging to the HPA Parennefer/ Wennenefer. It dates to the post-Amarna Period, to the reign of Tutankhamun or Horemheb (Kampp and Seyfried 1995: 334; Kampp 1996: 713-716; Kubisch 2018: 189). The next three HPA to be buried here are Nebwenef-TT157 (RII), Bakenkhonsu-TT35 (RII), and Roma called Roy-TT283 (RII-SII). These three Nineteenth Dynasty tombs form part of the so-called 'Ramesside Cluster' in Dra Abu el-Naga West (see Chapter 5) but lie some distance to the west of K-162-. TT35 and TT283 are in particularly close proximity, as the later TT283 is squeezed in next to TT35.

This shift from Qurna to Dra Abu el-Naga after the Eighteenth Dynasty appears to have happened with the tombs of the Viziers too, although there have not been enough TTs of Ramesside Viziers identified in the Theban necropolis to be sure. This move to Dra Abu el-Naga West coincides with the construction of the mortuary temple of Seti I at this end of the necropolis, which acted as a landing stage for the procession of the BFV when it reached the west bank, so the procession would have passed in front of these Nineteenth Dynasty tombs. This area is also directly opposite the east-west axis of Karnak temple (see Chapter 5). The HPA had moved to a less densely populated area of the necropolis, so there would definitely have been more space and choice when siting a tomb, in comparison to the crowded slopes of Upper Qurna, and they could also now align their tombs with a view of the god Amun crossing the Nile and beginning his procession (see Figure 354).

Of the two known Twentieth Dynasty HPA burials, the tomb of Ramessesnakht, TT293, is also located in Dra Abu el-Naga, but almost 100m further north than this Nineteenth Dynasty cluster. This may be due to lack of space, or a change in priority when siting a tomb. The second Twentieth Dynasty HPA with a known Theban tomb is Ramessesnakht's son, Amenhotep. Amenhotep returned to Qurna for burial, and the Eighteenth Dynasty tomb he reused, TT58, forms part of this earlier HPA cluster. TT58 may originally have been the burial of an earlier HPA, explaining the decision made by Amenhotep to choose this tomb to reuse at a time when tomb building was no longer a priority. It may also have been an attempt to associate himself with his Eighteenth Dynasty predecessors by reusing a tomb in the midst of them at the end of the Twentieth Dynasty, or a shortage of resources to build a new tomb at the end of the New Kingdom.

Both Ramessesnakht and Amenhotep appear to have built cult chapels in Dra Abu el-Naga East, remodelling the tombs of Amenhotep I and his mother Ahmose-Nefertari (Rummel 2018: 251). The monumental architecture of these remodelled tombs reveals the power and authority held by these Twentieth Dynasty HPA (Rummel 2018: 264). Ramessesnakht has been associated with K93.11, as he conducted some building activity in this Eighteenth Dynasty tomb but does not appear to have actually been buried here (Rummel 2014: 379; Rummel 2018: 257). An alternative suggestion for his burial place is TT148, the family tomb of his son-in-law, Amenemopet, 100m to the east of his

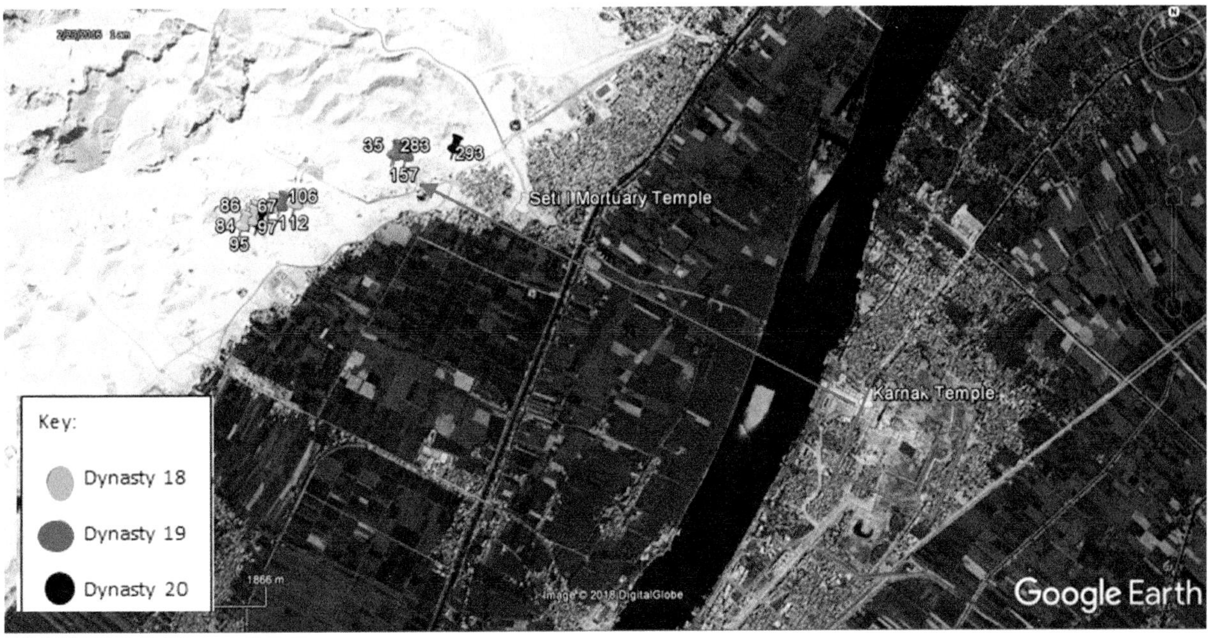

Figure 354: Google Earth image of the HPA tombs in relation to Karnak and Seti I temples (Author's own using Google Earth)

Figure 355: K93.11/K93.12 causeway in relation to Menisut in the background
(Rummel 2018: Figure 16 – Courtesy of Dr Ute Rummel)

Table 66: Table of New Kingdom HPA in Chronological Order (denotes those with TTs)

TT	HPA name	Reign
?	Djehuty	Ah
?	Minmontu called Senres	Ah?
?	Parennefer	AI?
?	Khonsuemheb	Early Dyn 18?
TT67	**Hapuseneb**	**Hat**
TT86	**Menkheperresoneb I ***	**TIII- AII**
TT112	**Menkheperresoneb II ***	**TIII-AII**
TT84 and TT95	**Mery**	**AII**
TT97	**Amenemhat**	**AII-TIV**
?	Ptahmose	AIII
?	Meryptah	AIII
K99.1	May	AIV
?	Amenemope	AIV?
K-162-	**Parennefer / Wenennefer ****	**Tut/Hor**
?	Wepwawetmose	Early Dyn 19?
?	Nebneteru	SI
TT157	**Nebwenef**	**RII**

TT	HPA name	Reign
(TT106?)	Paser	RII
TT35	**Bakenkhonsu**	**RII**
TT283	**Roma called Roy**	**RII/ Mer - SII**
?	Mahuhy	SII/ end Dyn 19
?	Minmose	End Dyn 19
?	Hori	End Dyn 19
?	Bakenkhonsu	Set - RIII
?	Usermaatrenakht	RIII
TT293 / K93.11?	**Ramessesnahkht**	**RIV-RIX**
?	Nesamun	RIX
TT58 / K93.12?	**Amenhotep**	**RIX-RXI (with gap)**
?	Ramessesnakht?	RX?
?	Herihor	RXI
?	Piankh	RXI

widely accepted burial in TT293 (Ockinga and Binder 2012: 209-219). The adjacent tomb, K93.12, has been identified as the cult chapel and potentially the burial place of Amenhotep (Rummel 2011: 429-431; Rummel 2014: 380), on the basis of the numerous remains of his burial equipment found in the burial chamber (Rummel 2018: 257). These tombs were potentially converted for ritual purposes as they were connected to Menisut via a causeway (see Figure 355), and in the case of Ramessesnakht may have been constructing his own private mortuary temple as he was not buried here (Rummel 2018: 264). Regardless of which of these tombs was the final resting place of Ramessesnakht and Amenhotep, the presence of these HPA in Dra Abu el-Naga East also reflects this shift north-eastwards away from Qurna after the Eighteenth Dynasty.

Conclusions

A definite pattern can be observed among the tombs of the HPA as the general trend shows that they were buried in Upper Qurna (and el-Khokha) during the Eighteenth Dynasty and moved northwards to Dra Abu el-Naga West during the Nineteenth Dynasty, to align their tombs with Karnak temple. During the Twentieth Dynasty, the role of the HPA changed enormously, as he grew in power as the king decreased. This may also reflect a change in burial practice which might explain the location of TT293 in Dra Abu el-Naga East followed by a return to Qurna. The conversion of K93.11 and K93.12 by these Twentieth Dynasty HPA also reflects the power they had to adapt royal tombs to potentially act as private mortuary temples.

Chapter 14: Final Observations

Conclusions based on Research Questions

- How did the Theban Necropolis evolve over time?

The evolution of the Theban Necropolis was a complex process, combining elements of gradual expansion in some areas, other areas which were used intensively until they were saturated with tombs, and areas which had relatively short periods of popularity. There was no single occupied area which gradually expanded to fill the entire necropolis, as suggested in the initial research questions, but rather different areas of the necropolis evolved in different ways, depending on a number of factors and their place among the wider sacred landscape of Western Thebes.

Upper Qurna was the most popular area in which to site a tomb in the early and mid-Eighteenth Dynasty, and was used intensively until the reign of Amenhotep III, when no space remained to build new tombs. Lower Qurna and el-Khokha were also popular in the early and mid-Eighteenth Dynasty, albeit less intensively, suggesting special permission was required to be buried in Upper Qurna at this time (see below). Within Upper Qurna trends can be observed dating to specific reigns, in particular to the reigns of Hatshepsut, Tuthmosis III and Amenhotep II. Space remained in Upper Qurna at this time allowing the occupied area to expand in specific directions during these reigns, apparently linked to views of royal mortuary temples. Lower Qurna appears to have been distinct from Upper Qurna, judging by the lower status of the majority of early to mid-Eighteenth Dynasty tomb owners here, becoming popular for higher status burials only once Upper Qurna was full at the end of the Eighteenth Dynasty. El-Khokha remained popular from the early Eighteenth Dynasty onwards but became more so for high status burials once Upper Qurna was full. The evolution of this central area of the necropolis, consisting of Upper and Lower Qurna and el-Khokha, could be described as a gradual expansion, but the titles of the tomb owners reveal a more complex situation.

Qurnet Murai developed in a more limited way, with a peak in popularity during the late Eighteenth Dynasty due to its proximity to contemporary royal mortuary temples, but it never expanded further, presumably as a result of its detachment from the rest of the necropolis. It was never occupied to the same extent as the central necropolis and the space between these areas rule out a gradual expansion. El-Asasif is another area which does not conform to the theory of natural expansion. Despite its location adjacent to royal mortuary temples, a processional causeway and Middle Kingdom tombs, this area is not used in the Eighteenth Dynasty, with the exception of two isolated burials. The increase in its popularity in the Ramesside Period appears to be the result of a change in permission, but its proximity to el-Khokha may also be a factor here as the occupied area expanded northwards. Dra Abu el-Naga remains in constant steady use throughout the New Kingdom, with a peak in high status burials in the Ramesside Period – specifically the 'Ramesside Cluster' in Dra Abu el-Naga West. The cemetery evolves here not as a result of natural expansion, but rather in response to cultic activity in the area relating to the wider funerary landscape. The presence of the probable tombs of Amenhotep I and Ahmose Nefertari, the causeway linking them to the mortuary temple of Menisut, the 'Forecourt of Amun' and the location of Karnak temple lying opposite the western end of this area, all played a part in the popularity of Dra Abu el-Naga.

- **Were individuals buried near their family or contemporaries – or perhaps even in friendship groups?**

There is limited evidence of familial relationships, but where such evidence exists it is possible to identify links between tombs belonging to members of the same family, particularly among high-status officials. Some of the most important examples are found among the closely linked tombs of the Eighteenth Dynasty 'dynasty' of Viziers, from Amethu called Ahmose (TT83) to Rekhmire (TT100) in Upper Qurna, and between the Vizier Amenemopet called Pairy (TT29) and his brother Sennefer (TT96). There is also a high proportion of tombs distributed in family clusters among the workmen at Deir el-Medina, but this is probably as a result of the unique nature of this community and the unusual amount of written evidence surviving at this site rather than being representative of the necropolis as a whole. Throughout the necropolis there are numerous examples of potential colleagues being buried close to each other. The most striking example of a collegial groups is found within the 'Amenhotep II Quarter' where a large group of contemporary high officials have built tombs within a distinct corner of Upper Qurna in close proximity to each other.

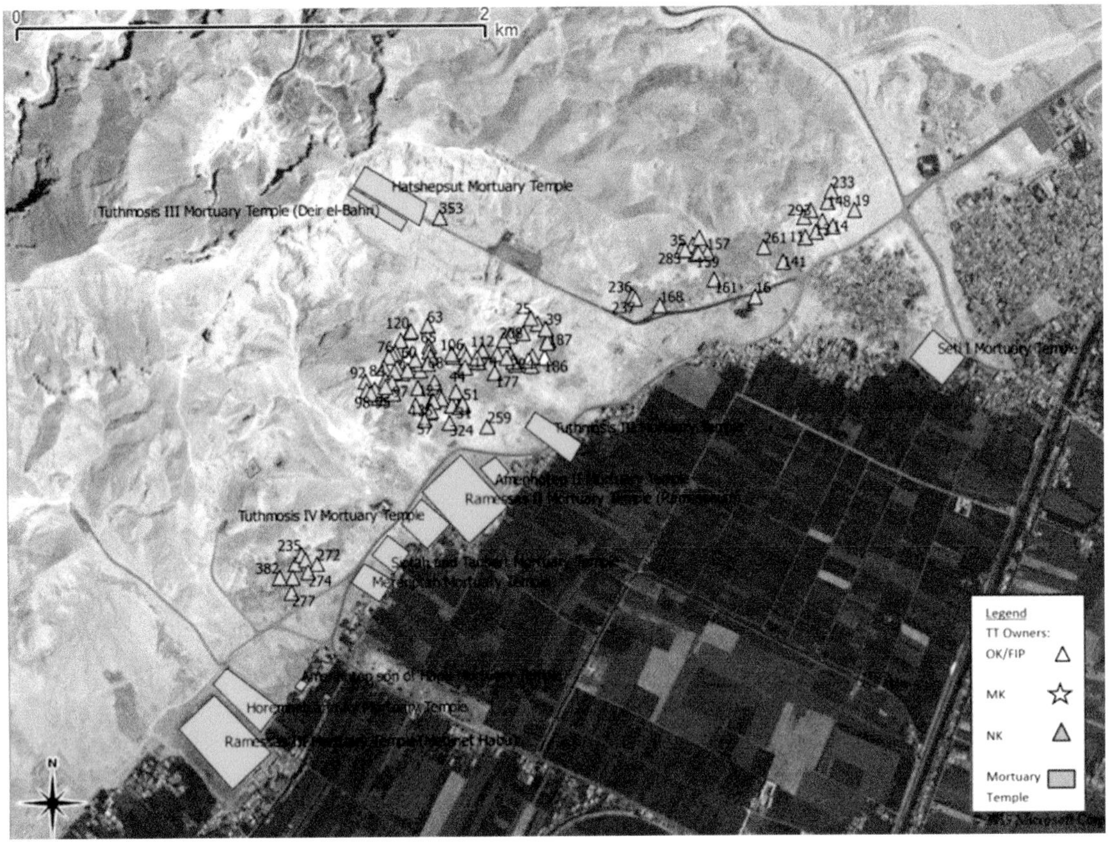

Figure 356: TTs belonging to Priests (Author's own using QGIS)

- Is there evidence of occupational clusters?

Tombs belonging to priests are distributed throughout the necropolis, with the highest concentration found in Upper Qurna (see Figure 356). The tombs of the Amun priesthood also follow this pattern, rather than a higher concentration being found in Dra Abu el-Naga West, opposite Karnak as may have been expected. This suggests that the priests did not have a designated area for burial and did not have preferential treatment in terms of tomb allocation (the HPA were an exception to this rule - see Chapter 13). The presence of priestly burials within Upper Qurna shows the status they must have had in order for them to have been afforded burial here among the state and royal officials.

The members of the temple administration were buried throughout the necropolis, with a number of tombs attested to them in all areas (see Figure 357). The highest concentration is found in Upper Qurna, Lower Qurna and el-Khokha. The most prestigious of these individuals were buried in Upper Qurna, but the lower members of the temple administration were buried in the less prestigious areas of Lower Qurna and el-Khokha predominantly, even in the Eighteenth Dynasty when there was plenty of space in Upper Qurna. This suggests that many administrative roles within the temple were less important within the hierarchy than those of the priests, and the general and royal administration. This also reinforces the idea that the state was responsible for tomb allocation.

The royal administration occupied positions throughout the necropolis but there was a particularly high density of tombs in Upper Qurna predominantly, and also to a lesser extent in Lower Qurna and el-Khokha (see Figure 358). The presence of royal administrators amongst the tombs of Upper Qurna suggests that the king may have had some influence on tomb allocation, granting the most desirable locations to his officials. This is particularly noticeable in the Eighteenth Dynasty when Upper Qurna was being developed as a cemetery.

The highest concentration of tombs belonging to the general state administration is found in Upper Qurna, showing the position of these individuals within the hierarchy (see Figure 359). There were fewer of these individuals buried in other popular areas such as Lower Qurna and el-Khokha. This apparent link between the most desirable locations and these individuals suggests state involvement in tomb allocation, as the best plots were available for state officials.

There are relatively few tombs belonging to the local administration (se Figure 360). They are found in all areas of the necropolis but there are only four found in

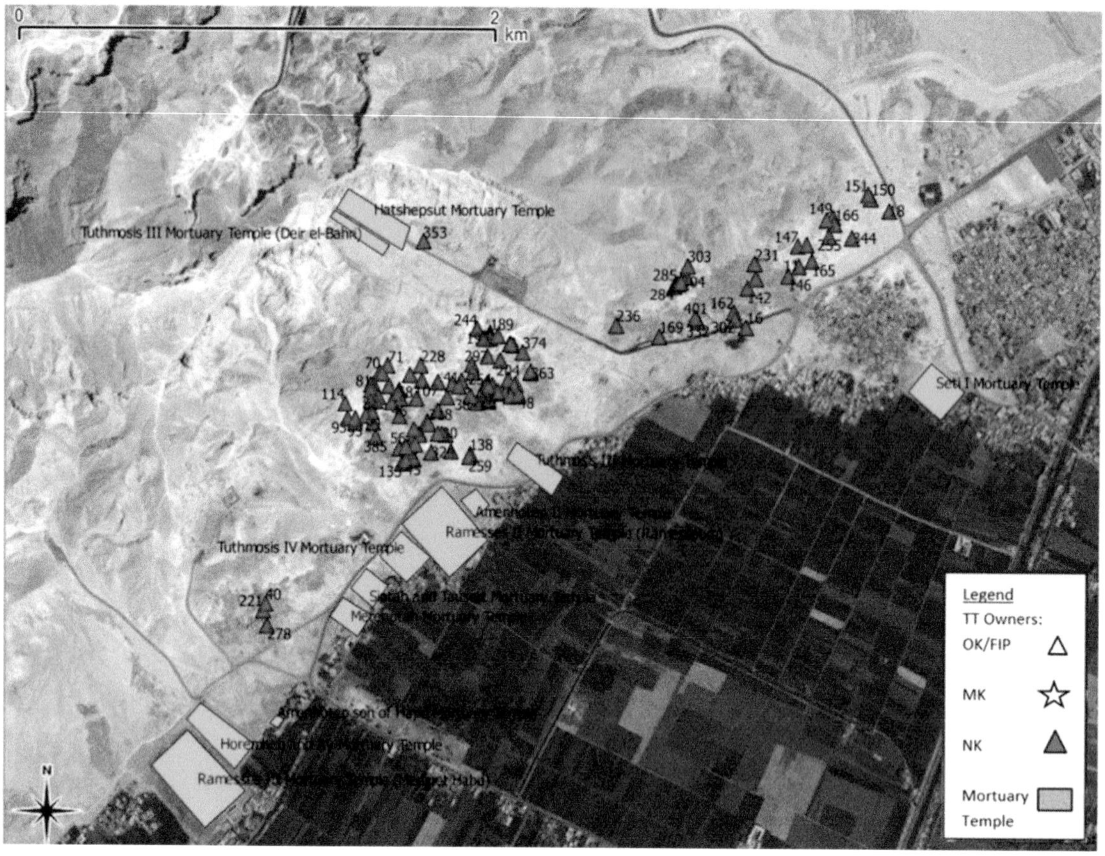

Figure 357: TTs belonging to the Temple Administration (Author's own using QGIS)

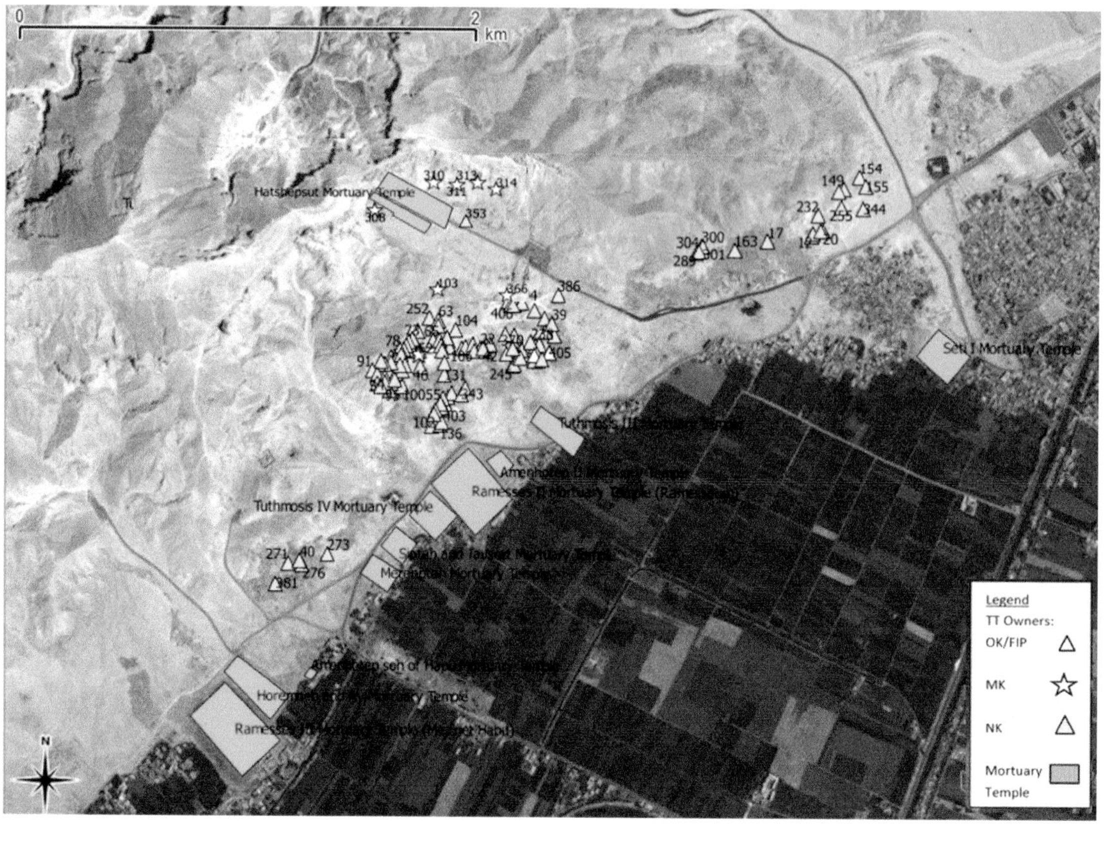

Figure 358: TTs belonging to the Royal Administration (Author's own using QGIS)

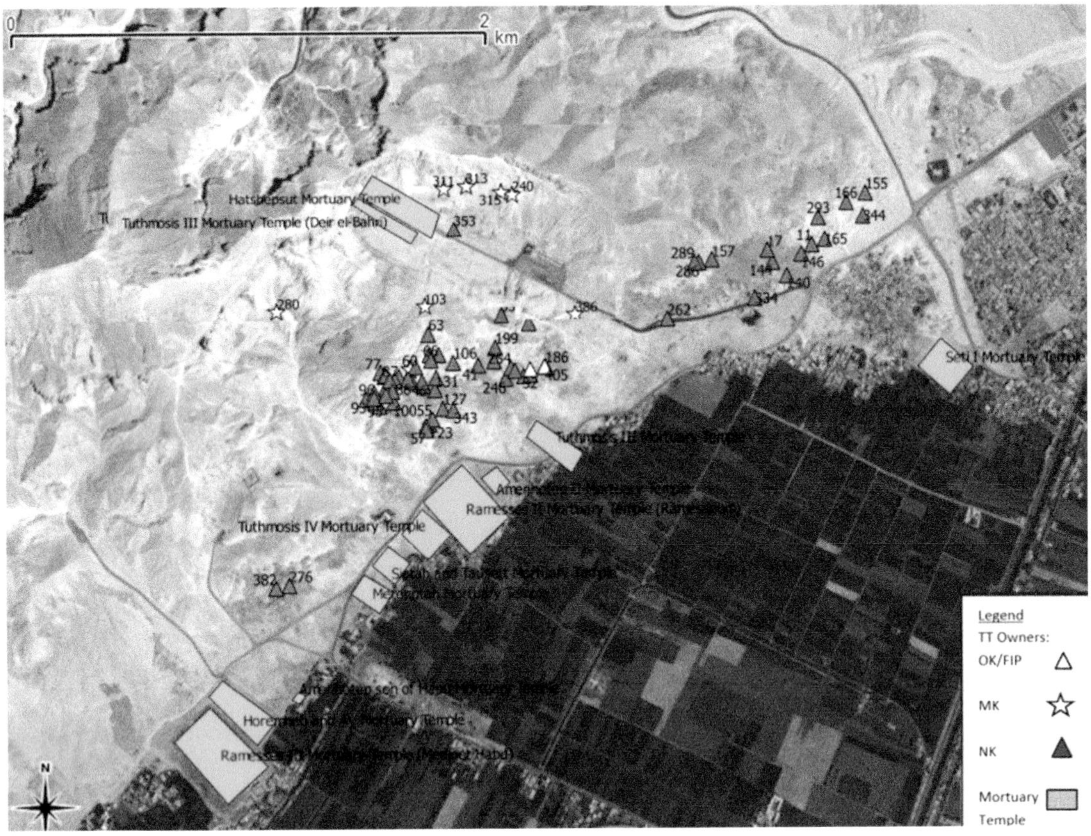

Figure 359: TTs belonging to the General Administration (Author's own using QGIS)

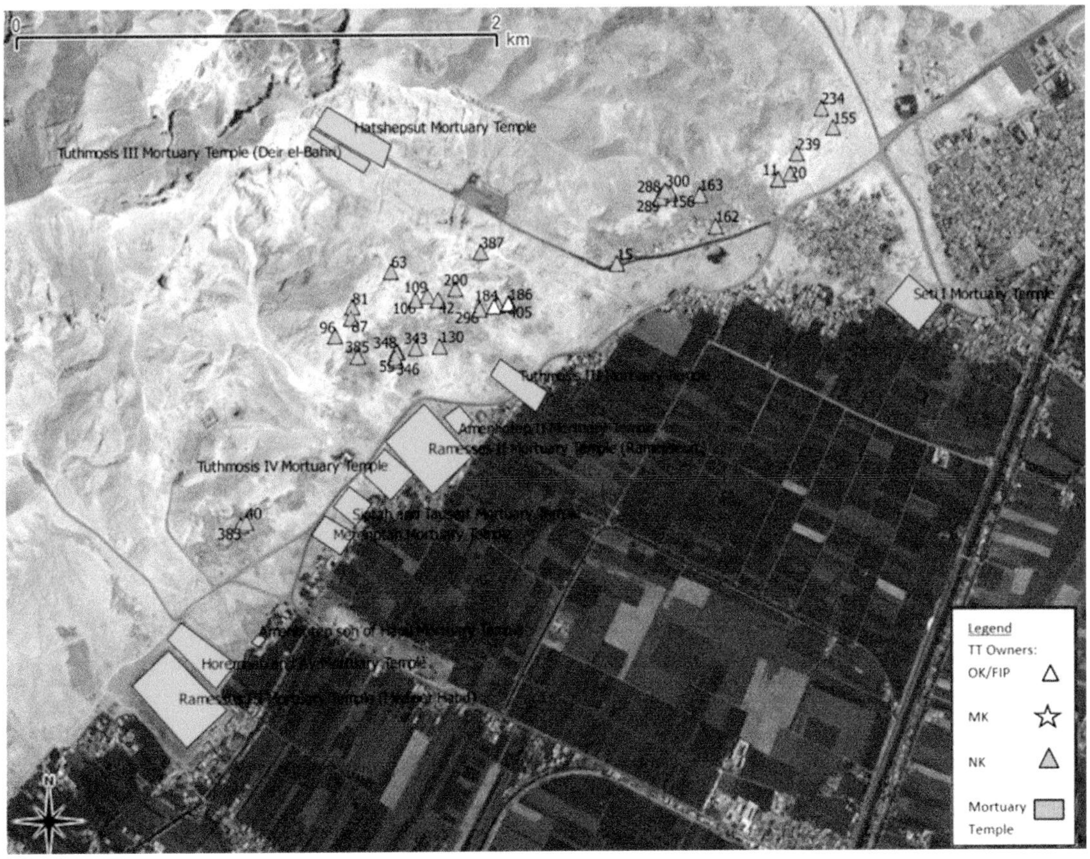

Figure 360: TTs belonging to the Local Administration (Author's own using QGIS)

Upper Qurna, who all held a range of other titles. This suggests that local officials were less important within the hierarchy than their state counterparts as Upper Qurna seems to have been reserved for state officials and priests.

The highest concentration of tombs belonging to those with military titles is within Upper Qurna, with very few military tombs found in other areas of the necropolis (see Figure 361). As the army was a state organisation, this again reinforces the idea that tombs, certainly in Upper Qurna, were allocated by the state. It also suggests that officials connected to the army were among the most important officials in Egypt, particularly in the Eighteenth Dynasty.

There is some evidence of clusters of tombs belonging to individuals with specific title, particularly among the highest status officials. The most remarkable of these clusters are the Eighteenth Dynasty Viziers in Upper Qurna, and the Eighteenth Dynasty and Ramesside HPA in Upper Qurna and Dra Abu el-Naga West respectively (see Chapters 12 and 13). There are also numerous other examples throughout the necropolis of individuals with similar titles being buried in close proximity to each other, but there is not a clear enough pattern to draw definite conclusions about areas of the necropolis being allocated to specific professions or groups.

- Were lower ranking individuals buried in the vicinity of their superior(s)?

Tomb placement deliberately emphasised the status of the tomb owner by attempting to attain proximity to the tombs of their illustrious predecessors, colleagues, friends or family members, whenever possible. The attraction of these important tombs as focal points for the tombs of people of lower rank was suggested by Taylor (2003: 139-41), as was the use of allotted areas of the necropolis by different social groups. This desire to be buried close to a high official seems to be true as in the case study of the Viziers and the 'Ramesside Cluster' that formed around the tombs of the Ramesside HPA, and also the use of some shared courtyards seemed to be an attempt to be associated with a high official, but this was limited by space constraints. Certainly, only the elite could command a position in the most prominent locations on the upper slopes, so the lower ranks of officials would have to make do with the lower slopes. These direct personal links between senior officials and their junior associates are hard to prove as the majority of examples cannot be proven to have held office at the same time. There are however several examples of individuals being buried in the vicinity of their direct superior, for example the 'Scribe' and 'Steward of the Vizier' Amenemhet (TT82), who was buried in close proximity to both 'Viziers' he served, Amethu called Ahmose (TT83) and User (TT61).

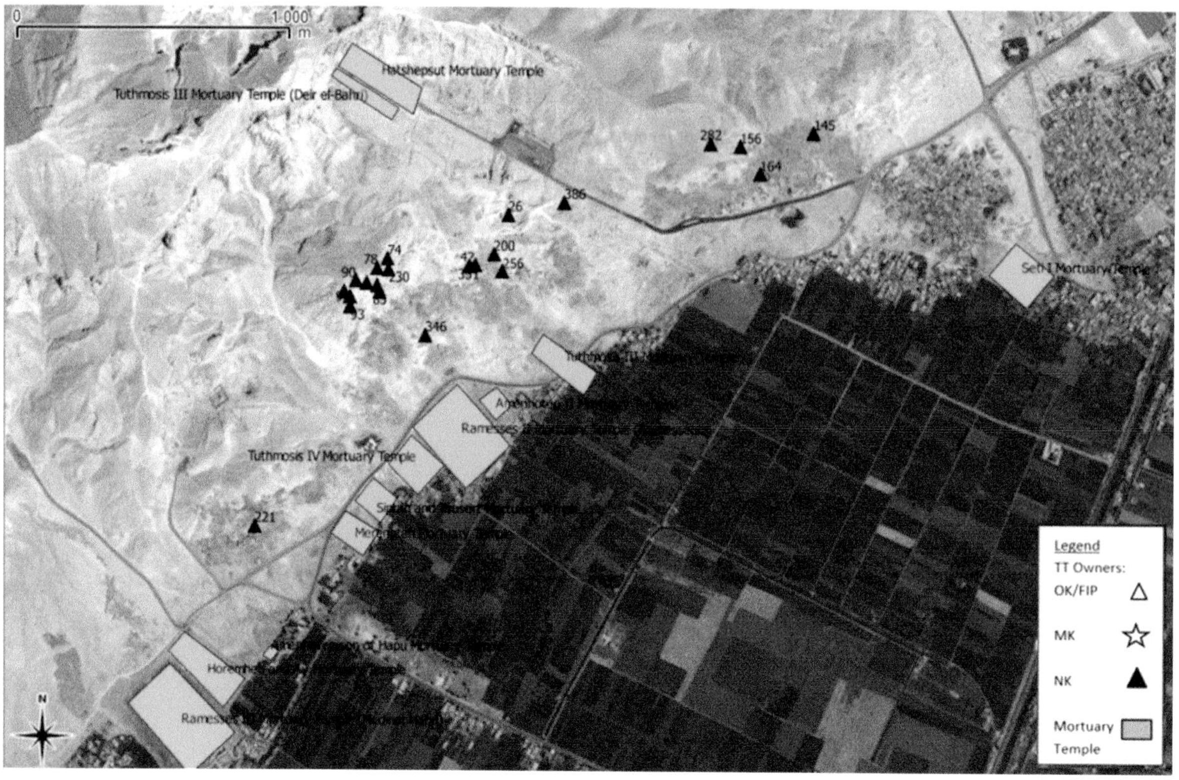

Figure 361: TTs belonging to the Military (Author's own using QGIS)

- Was tomb distribution influenced by proximity to the royal mortuary temple of the reigning king?
- Was tomb location influenced by the processional routes of the Beautiful Festival of the Valley and other festivals?

Views and orientation towards contemporary mortuary temples, and processional routes were desired in order to symbolically access necropolis festivals, cult activities and the associated visitors and offerings derived from them (as suggested by Kampp 1996: 120-122) and this can clearly be seen as a factor in tomb distribution, particularly in Dra Abu el-Naga (see Chapter 5) and the 'Amenhotep II Quarter' (see Chapter 9). This link between tomb orientation and royal mortuary temples was particularly important during the Eighteenth Dynasty, as suggested by Helck (1962: 225-43), when there is a clear correlation between tomb placement and contemporary mortuary temples. During the late Eighteenth Dynasty and Ramesside Period this seems to have been less of a concern, whether intentionally or due to restricted choice as the necropolis became fuller, although space, albeit flatter than ideal for tomb building, did remain behind the mortuary temples of Tuthmosis IV and Ramesses II, among others, suggesting a change in priority.

- Who was buried in the most desirable locations? Were they reserved for the wealthiest or most important individuals or those closest to the king?

The most desirable location for tomb building appears to have been the upper slopes of Qurna, providing superior views over contemporary mortuary temples and processional routes. Areas in close proximity to these important elements of the funerary landscape seem to have been less desirable than the upper slopes as they filled up more slowly with the tombs of lower status officials. The analysis of the titles of those buried in Upper Qurna reveal that high officials certainly seemed to favour this area in the Eighteenth Dynasty, as demonstrated not just by the distribution of the tombs of the Viziers and High Priests of Amun, but also the Overseers of the Granary and Treasurers. Tombs in Upper Qurna belonged to a combination of high-status priests, general state administrators and members of the royal administration, so this area was not reserved solely for those closest to the king but rather the most important individuals from all these groups. From the end of the Eighteenth Dynasty onwards these high-status officials had to relocate the focus of their tomb building either down the hill to Lower Qurna or east into el-Khokha, still close to the mortuary temples and processional routes but with less of a view, as the upper slopes were full. Meanwhile el-Asasif and Qurnet Murai saw less building activity for different reasons. Qurnet Murai was less popular as a result of its rather isolated position to the south of the more concentrated central areas of the necropolis, with the exception of the late Eighteenth Dynasty, and el-Asasif was apparently restricted for reasons relating to royal permission in the Eighteenth Dynasty. Dra Abu el-Naga does not fit neatly into a category as it was used steadily throughout the New Kingdom as a result of its position opposite Karnak, overlooking the processional route and hosting cultic activity. It peaked in popularity in the early Eighteenth Dynasty as a result of its proximity to Second Intermediate Period and early New Kingdom royal tombs and temples and attracted high profile burials once more in the Ramesside Period when central areas were full and a position opposite Karnak became more important than proximity to royal mortuary temples. This shift in tomb distribution reflected the shift in power at the end of the New Kingdom, as the priesthood of Amun rose to prominence over the king.

- Were certain locations popular during certain periods for a reason?

There was certainly a link between the popularity of specific areas and the view of contemporary mortuary temples from these areas during the Eighteenth Dynasty (for example the 'Amenhotep II Quarter' in Upper Qurna, and Qurnet Murai during the late Eighteenth Dynasty). During the Ramesside Period these spatial links with royal mortuary temples become less important but Dra Abu el-Naga West became more popular due to its alignment with the east-west axis of Karnak temple at a time when the cult of Amun was growing in power. Certain locations were also popular until they became full, such as Upper Qurna which was the most popular area for building the tombs of the high elite during the first half of the Eighteenth Dynasty due to its desirable location. When this area became full the focus of tomb building shifted to other areas such as Lower Qurna and el-Khokha as a result of natural expansion.

- Does this tell us anything about mortuary beliefs at different times?

The link between tomb distribution and the royal mortuary temples during the Eighteenth Dynasty suggests that there was a connection between private tombs and the contemporary royal mortuary temple at this time. One reason for this is the procession of the BFV and the importance of overlooking the procession in order to symbolically participate in the festival and share in the resulting offerings. This may also be connected to the idea of proximity to the king they served in life, in a similar way to building private tombs adjacent to royal tombs in earlier periods. This link is particularly visible during the reign of Amenhotep

II when the majority of tombs dating to his reign shift to the south-western corner of Upper Qurna, apparently in order to attain a spatial link with his mortuary temple as the tombs are also orientated in this direction. The movement away from this link with royal mortuary temples during the Ramesside Period may reflect a change in mortuary beliefs following the Amarna Period, with the rise of personal piety and the weakening of the royal cult towards the end of the New Kingdom. An example of this is the lack of private tombs built behind the Ramesseum, despite the longevity and divine status of Ramesses II.

More evidence of tomb distribution reflecting a change in private mortuary beliefs is found between tombs belonging to influential individuals such as the Viziers and other contemporary officials. In the Eighteenth Dynasty the tombs of the Viziers seem to act as a focal point for contemporary burials, but by the Ramesside Period this no longer seems to be a factor when locating a tomb. This may reflect the decreasing influence of state officials during the Ramesside Period. In contrast the tombs of the High Priests of Amun remain a focal point for the burials of lower-ranking priests and temple officials until the end of the New Kingdom. This relationship between high-ranking state officials and high-ranking priests also seems to be indicative of the evolving mortuary beliefs of private individuals following the Amarna Period.

- Why were some tombs located around a shared courtyard, or with shared access?

Overall, no definitive pattern can be established between tombs which shared courtyards or access. There seem to be familial or occupational links between some of the inhabitants of shared courtyards, while other courtyards seem to have been chosen on the basis of an impressive entrance, availability of space, or proximity to a venerated ancestor. The majority of connecting tombs seem to have been joined accidentally during the process of digging the later tomb.

- Which tombs were reused and who reused them? To what extent was this practice a result of lack of space and resources, or is there evidence of links between occupants of the same tomb?

The majority of tomb reusage occurred towards the end of the New Kingdom, reflecting a lack of space and resources required to build new tombs, necessitating the practice of reusing existing tombs. Trends are also observed in specific areas, most notably Upper Qurna, where reuse was more common, reinforcing the idea that this area was the most desirable for burial. There are also several examples of tombs being reused during periods of prosperity, suggesting a deliberate attempt by the later occupant to identify himself with the original tomb owner. This is especially seen in Upper Qurna during the Eighteenth Dynasty, which was a combination of early Eighteenth Dynasty reuse of Middle Kingdom tombs in an attempt by the tomb owners to associate themselves with their Middle Kingdom ancestors, and reuse of Eighteenth Dynasty tombs a short time after their construction, the majority of which had no clear link with the original occupant. There are isolated examples of familial and occupational links between owners of the same tomb, but not enough to draw wider conclusions.

- What does all this information tell us about how tomb plots were allocated?

There is certainly evidence from the Eighteenth Dynasty in particular, that Upper Qurna was reserved for the tombs of the most important individuals. The majority of these Eighteenth Dynasty tombs were owned by high-ranking members of the general and palace administration and also of the priesthood. This suggests that there was state involvement in tomb allocation at a time when the king had complete autonomy over his government and the Estate of Amun, so the king (or potentially this was delegated to the Vizier in the absence of a title relating to this role) had authority over the allocation of the best tomb plots to the most important or most favoured individuals, while those lower ranking individuals were granted plots on the lower slopes. The case study examining the distribution of the tombs of the Viziers also supports this theory, as these influential individuals occupy prime positions in close proximity to each other, as do the Eighteenth Dynasty High Priests of Amun.

By the end of the Ramesside Period as the king's authority over the Estate of Amun declined, a shift northward in the focus of tomb building towards Dra Abu el-Naga may reflect a change in the tomb allocation process, as the High Priests of Amun seem to decide upon a new area opposite Karnak in which to build their tombs, rather than building where they were told. These tombs attract other tomb owners to be buried here and the 'Ramesside Cluster' evolves, suggesting more of an element of personal choice based on beliefs rather that a hierarchical system of allocation.

The apparent special permission required to build adjacent to the causeway at el-Asasif during the Eighteenth Dynasty would also support the idea of a state system of tomb allocation at this time. As the New Kingdom progressed and the king became less powerful, more tombs were built in this area, suggesting a lack of centralised authority over tomb allocation, and more of an element of personal choice. The steady usage of Dra Abu el-Naga throughout the New Kingdom and apparent lack of organisation provides less evidence of a state-sponsored tomb allocation, but rather appears to have been a more natural evolution of an area used prior to the New Kingdom, with great cultic significance. It may be that only the area bordering the causeway of Deir el-Bahri and the areas of the necropolis to the south were controlled by this system, with Dra Abu el-Naga remaining distinct from the state necropolis.

General Conclusions

It seems clear that there was no prescriptive overall plan relating to tomb allocation in the Theban Necropolis as a whole, with designated areas used solely for particular professions or officials serving specific kings, partially confirming Rhind's hypothesis that it was more random than this (1862: 50-51), although some organisation can be identified. There are certainly areas, particularly in Upper Qurna, where the tombs of individuals from the same occupational group, affiliation, or family, who held similar titles or served specific kings, can be seen forming identifiable clusters. A broadly chronological pattern does emerge showing the necropolis loosely evolving from north to south, but it was far more complex a process than that suggested by Helck (1962: 225-43) and Dodson (1991: 33-42). The actual development of the necropolis, rather than being solely chronological, was influenced by a combination of factors, including status, titles, affiliation, desirable locations in terms of visibility and access, spatial connections with the wider funerary landscape, and the basic requirements of available resources and space.

Future Work

This work can be further developed by analysing specific areas in more detail, by collecting and considering additional data. The inclusion of tomb orientation data within the QGIS could enhance this study, allowing direct connections to be made between different tombs, between tombs and mortuary temples and between tombs and other natural and built features of the funerary landscape, including those on the east bank. Viewshed studies using QGIS would also be of benefit to this study, to ascertain precisely what is visible from each tomb and each area of the necropolis, in order to better understand links between them. It would also be interesting to obtain a fuller picture about each tomb, particularly those in identified areas of specific interest by considering tomb types as classified by Kampp (1996) and tomb decoration, along with undertaking prosopographical analysis of the tomb owners. It would also be beneficial to include the additional tombs numbered by Kampp (1996) in this more intensive analysis, as although inscriptional evidence from these tombs is limited, many of them have been dated so these tombs may help to confirm or disprove potential patterns. The inclusion of subsidiary burials within this analysis may also be of use, as this would provide a fuller picture of the use of the necropolis, and the popularity of tombs and areas of the necropolis, in a similar way to tomb reuse.

Areas of particular interest for this in-depth analysis include the 'Amenhotep II Quarter' in Upper Qurna, where a distinct group of tombs dating to a specific reign has been observed. The entirety of Upper Qurna would also benefit from further research employing these methods as a result of the number of high-profile burials dating to the Eighteenth Dynasty and general trends and patterns already identified. Another area of interest is Dra Abu el-Naga, particularly the potential links between tombs and cultic activity in the area. It would also be interesting to conduct further case studies focussing on tombs whose owners held specific titles and their relationship with surrounding tomb owners. For example, a potential link has been identified between several tombs in Upper Qurna belonging to 'Overseers of the Granary' and those belonging to their contemporary 'Overseer of the Treasury'. Further investigation would reveal if these were isolated cases or indicative of a wider pattern.

Appendices

Appendix 1 – Old Kingdom and First Intermediate Period Tomb Owners

TT	Kampp Date	Saleh Date	Tomb Owner	Occupation	Title	Transliteration	Connected tombs	References	GPS co-ordinates	
									X	Y
185	FIP	FIP	Senyiker	Temple admin	Hereditary Prince, Mayor; Divine Seal-bearer;	*ỉry-pꜥt ḥꜣty-ꜥ;* *ḫtmty-nṯr;*		Kampp 1996: 475; PM I: 291; Saleh 1977: 28; Soliman 2009: 16;	32.61282	25.73265
186	OK (Dyn 6)	Dyn 6	Iky	Local admin, royal admin, general admin & priesthood	Great Chieftain of the Nome/ District; Overseer of Granaries; Royal Chamberlain of the Great House; Overseer of the Phyles of the Nome; Chief of Secrets of Every Word that is Brought to the Nome /District; Staff of the People; Estate Manager; Lector Priest; Judge and Border Official of the pre-eminent place; Sole Companion;	*ḥry-tp ꜥꜣ n spꜣt;* *imy-r šnwt;* *ḥry-tp nsw pr-ꜥꜣ;* *imy-r sꜣw spꜣt;* *ḥry-sštꜣ n mdwt nbt štꜣt innt r spꜣt;* *mdw-rḫyt iwn-ḳnmwt;* *ḥkꜣ-ḥwt;* *ḫry-ḥbt;* *sꜣb ꜥḏ-mr ni nst ḫnnt;* *smr wꜥty;*	Father of TT405 –shared courtyard	Kampp 1996: 475; PM I: 291-293; Saleh 1977: 28; Soliman 2009: 22-25;	32.6132	25.73255
405	FIP	Dyn 6 (after TT186)	Khenti	Royal admin, local admin & priesthood	Royal Seal-bearer; Great Chieftain of the Nome/ District; Chief of Secrets of Every Word that is Brought to the Nome/ District; Lector Priest; Sole Companion; [Overseer of Granaries];	*ḫtmty-bity;* *ḥry-tp ꜥꜣ n spꜣt;* *ḥry-sštꜣ n mdwt nbt štꜣt innt r spꜣt;* *ḫry-ḥbt;* *smr wꜥty;* [*imy-r šnwty*];	Son of TT186 – shared courtyard	Kampp 1996: 610; PM I: 445; Saleh 1977: 28; Soliman 2009: 25-28;	32.61317	25.73254
413	OK/ FIP	Late Dyn 5-early 6	Ankhunas / Unasankh	Royal admin, local admin, general admin & priesthood?	The One who is at the Head of the King; Overseer of UE; Overseer of Granaries; Chief of Secrets of Every Word that is Brought to the Nome/district; [Great Chieftain of the Nome/ District; Lector Priest; Sole Companion; Chancellor of King of LE;]	*ḥry-tp nsw;* *imy-r šmꜥw;* *imy-r šnwty;* *ḥry-sštꜣ n mdwt nbt štꜣt innt r spꜣt;* [*ḥry-tp ꜥꜣ n spꜣt? ḫry-ḥbt?* *smr wꜥty?* *sḏꜣwty-bity?*]		Kampp 1996: 614; Saleh 1977: 28; Soliman 2009: 17-22;	32.61262	25.73245

[ ] denotes reconstructed titles (Saleh, 1997: 28)

Appendix 2: Middle Kingdom Tomb Owners

TT	Dynasty	Reign	Tomb Owner	Occupation	Title	Transliteration	Connected tombs	References	GPS co-ordinates	
									X	Y
60	11	(Mon II-III)	Antefoker and Senet (mother)	General admin, royal admin, local admin & priesthood (Maat)	Governor of the town and Vizier; Royal Seal-bearer; Hereditary Prince; Overseer of the 6 great Temples/ Law-courts; Priest of Maat; Mouth of Nekhen; Chief Justice; Sole Companion;	*imy-r niwt ṯ3ty;* *ḫtmty-bity;* *iry-pʿt;* *imy-r ḥwt ʿ3 6;* *ḥm-nṯr m3ʿt;* *r nḫn;* *s3b t3yty;* *smr wʿty;*		Gardiner and Weigall 1913: 22; Kampp 1996: 275-277; LD III, 258; PM I: 121-123; Soliman 2009: 131-133;	32.60805	25.73245
61	(1)12(2)18	(1) Sen I (2) TI-TIII	(1)? (2) User	(1) ? (2)	(1) ? (2) See Upper Qurna	*1) ?* *(2)*		Kampp 1996: 277-279; PM I: 123-125;	32.60827	25.73252
81	(1) MK (2) 18	(1) (2)AI-Hat	(1)? (2) Ineni	(1) ? (2)	(1) ? (2) See Upper Qurna	*1) ?* *(2)*	(2)	Davies 1963: 19-20; Dziobek 1992; Kampp 1996: 323-326; PM I: 159-163;	32.60734	25.73244
82	(1) MK (2)18	(1) (2)Hat/ TIII	(1) ? (2) Amenemhet	(1) ? (2)	(1) ? (2) See Upper Qurna	*(1) ?* *(2)*		Kampp 1996: 326-330; PM I: 163-167;	32.60761	25.73224
103	11		Dagi	General admin & royal admin	Overseer of the Pyramid Town and Vizier; Royal Seal-bearer; Overseer of the Double House of Silver and the Double House of Gold (=Treasurer); Overseer of Granaries; Overseer of all Temples of U and LE; Overseer of the Law Court; Mouth of Nekhen; Supreme Judge; Hereditary Prince and Mayor; Sole Companion;	*imy-r niwt ṯ3ty;* *ḫtmty-bity;* *imy-r pr.wy ḥḏ pr.wy nbw;* *imy-r šnwty;* *imy-r ḥwt nbw šmʿw mḥw;* *imy-r rwyt;* *r nḫn;* *s3b t3yty;* *iry-pʿt ḥ3ty-ʿ;* *smr wʿty;*		Arnold 1996: 13-15; Davies 1913: Pl. XXX, XXXI, XXXII, XXXVIII; Gardiner and Weigall 1913: 26; Kampp 1996: 377-378; PM I: 216-217; Soliman 2009: 108-112;	32.60824	25.73479
117	(1)11		?	?	?	*?*		Kampp 1996: 400-401; PM I: 233; Soliman 2009: 88-92;	32.60673	25.73243
119	(1) MK (2) 18	(1) (2)Hat-TIII	?	?	?	*?*		Kampp 1996: 406-407; PM I: 234;	32.60822	25.73236

TT	Dynasty	Reign	Tomb Owner	Occupation	Title	Transliteration	Connected tombs	References	GPS co-ordinates	
									X	Y
240	11	Mon II	Meru	General admin	Overseer of Sealers ;	*ỉmy-r ḫtmw;*		Arnold 1991: 21; Arnold 1996: 10; Kampp 1996: 516; LD III, 241; PM I: 330-331; Soliman 2009: 100-108;	32.61132	25.73839
270	(1) MK (2) 19/20			(2)	(1) ? (2) See Upper Qurna	*(1)?* *(2)*		Engelbach 1924: 20; Kampp 1996: 543; PM I: 350;	32.60402	25.72579
280	11	Mon III	Meketre	General admin	[Hereditary Prince] Mayor; Chief Steward in...; Overseer of the Seal (Chancellor);	*[ỉry-pꜥt];* *ḥꜣty-ꜥ;* *ỉmy-r pr wr m...;* *ỉmy-r ḫtmt;*	Adjoining tomb Antef (Overseer of Sealers)	Arnold 1991: 21; Arnold 1996: 1; Engelbach 1924: 20; Kampp 1996: 550; PM I: 359; Roehrig 2003: 11; Soliman 1996: 120-124;	32.60312	25.73465
281	11	Mon I	Unfinished temple of Mon I				Unfinished temple of Mon I	Kampp 1996: 550; PM I: 364;	32.60168	25.73307
308	11	Mon II	Kemsit	Royal & priesthood (Hathor)	Sole Royal Concubine; Priestess of Hathor;	*ḫkrt-nsw wꜥtt;* *ḥmt-nṯr ḥwt-ḥr;*		Engelbach 1924: 22; Kampp 1996: 572; PM I: 385-386; Soliman 2009: 53-54;	32.60595	25.73764
310	11		?	Royal admin	Royal Seal-bearer; Hereditary Prince, Mayor; Sole Companion;	*ḫtmty-bity;* *ỉry-pꜥt, ḥꜣty-ꜥ;* *smr-wꜥty;*		Engelbach 1924: 24; Kampp 1996: 572; PM I: 386;	32.6081	25.73865
311	11	Mon II	Khety	Royal admin, priesthood & general admin	Royal Seal-bearer; Overseer of the Seal (=Chancellor); Divine Father; Overseer of the Two Houses of Silver (=Treasury), Overseer of Silver together with Gold; Overseer of Lapis Lazuli and Turquoise; Overseer of Horn, Hoof, Scale and Feather; Hereditary Prince, Mayor; Sole Companion;	*ḫtmty bity;* *ỉmy-r ḫtm;* *ỉt-nṯr;* *ỉmy-r prwy-ḥḏ;* *ỉmy-r ḥḏ ḥnꜥ nbw; ỉmy-r ḫsbḏ mfkꜣ[t];* *ỉmy-r ꜥb wḥmw nšmt šw;* *ỉry-pꜥt ḥꜣty-ꜥ;* *smr-wꜥty;*		Arnold 1991: 21; Arnold 1996: 5; Chudzik 2016: 291; Engelbach 1924: 24; Kampp 1996: 572; PM I: 386; Soliman 2009: 95-99;	32.60895	25.73858
312	11		?	?	?	?		Engelbach 1924: 24; Kampp 1996: 572; PM I: 387-388;	32.60934	25.73857

TT	Dynasty	Reign	Tomb Owner	Occupation	Title	Transliteration	Connected tombs	References	GPS co-ordinates	
									X	Y
313	11	Mon II-III	Henunu	Royal admin & general admin	Royal Seal-bearer; Steward ; Overseer of the Great House; Overseer of Horn, Hoof, Scale and Feather; Overseer of Fowl that Swim, Fly and Land; Overseer of what is and is not; Sole Companion;	*ḫtmty-bity;* *imy-r pr;* *imy-r pr ꜥꜣ;* *imy-r ꜥb wḥmw nšmt šw;* *imy-r ḳbḥ pꜣwt ḫnnt; imy-r ntt iwtt;* *smr-wꜥty;*		Engelbach 1924: 24; Kampp 1996: 573; PM I: 388-389; Arnold 1996: 11; Soliman 2009: 112-114;	32.6097	25.73865
314	11		Horhotep	Royal admin	Royal Seal-bearer; Follower; Sole Companion;	*ḫtmty bity;* *šmsw;* *smr-wꜥty;*		Engelbach, 1924: 24; Kampp 1996: 573; PM I: 389; Soliman 2009: 128-129;	32.61042	25.7384
315	11	Mon II	Ipi	General admin	Governor of the Town and Vizier; Judge;	*imy-r niwt, ṯꜣty;* *sꜣb;*		Arnold 1996: 18; Engelbach 1924: 24; Kampp 1996: 573; PM I: 389-390; Soliman 2009: 115-119;	32.61094	25.73845
316	11/12		Neferhotep	Military	Bowman;	*iry-pḏt;*		Engelbach 1924: 24; Kampp 1996: 573; PM I: 390; Soliman 2009: 126-128;	32.61166	25.73826
319	11	Mon II	Neferu & Iah	Royal family	Daughter of the King (Mon I); Royal Wife (of Mon II); Hereditary Noble;	*sꜣt nsw;* *ḥmt nsw;* *iry-pꜥt;*		Engelbach 1924: 24; Kampp 1996: 573; PM I: 391-393; Soliman 2009: 67-75;	32.60681	25.73801
366	11	Mon II	Djar	Royal admin	Overseer of the King's Harem; Royal Seal-bearer; Sole Companion;	*imy-r ipt (nsw);* *ḫtmty bity;* *smr wꜥty;*		Fakhry 1947: 44; Kampp 1996: 592; Roehrig 1995: 255-269; PM I: 429-430; Soliman 2009: 85-88;	32.61083	25.7346
386	11		Intef	General admin & military	Royal Seal-bearer; Overseer of the Army;	*ḫtmty-bity;* *imy-r mšꜥ;*		Arnold 1991: 34; Kampp 1996: 604; PM I: 437; Soliman 2009: 92-95;	32.61352	25.73452

Appendix 3: Tomb Owners in Dra Abu el-Naga East

TT	Dyn	Reign (Kampp)	Tomb Owner	Occupation	Titles	Transliteration	Connected tombs / Notes	References	GPS co-ordinates	
									X	Y
11	18	Hat/TIII	Djehuty	General admin, royal admin, temple admin (Amun), priesthood (Hathor) & local admin.	Overseer of the (Double) House of Silver (=Treasury); Overseer of the Double House of Gold (=Treasury); Royal Seal-bearer; Overseer of Works; Overseer of the Cattle of Amun; Overseer of the Priests of Hathor, Mistress of Cusae (=el-Kusiyah –UE); Great Chief of Horus the Elder; Scribe; Hereditary Prince and Mayor; Sole Companion;	*ỉmy-r pr(.wy) ḥḏ;* *ỉmy-r pr.wy nbw;* *ḫtmw bity;* *ỉmy-r kꜣt;* *ỉmy-r iḥw n ỉmn;* *ỉmy-r ḥmw nṯr n ḥwt-ḥr nbt Ḳsy;* *ḥry-tp ꜥꜣ m ḥr wr;* *sš;* *iry-pꜥt ḥꜣty-ꜥ;* *smr wꜥty;*		Kampp 1996: 190-192; PM I: 21-24; *Urk.* IV: 432-449;	32.62333	25.73657
12	17/18	STII/AI	Hori	Royal admin	Overseer of the Granary of the King's Wife and King's Mother Aahhotep;	*ỉmy-r šnwty n ḥmt-nsw mwt-nsw Iꜥḥ-ḥtp;*		Gardiner and Weigall 1913: 16; Kampp 1996:192; LD III, 238; PM I: 24-25;	32.62338	25.73664
13	19	End Dyn 19	Shuroy	Priesthood (Amun)	Chief of the Brazier (Burners) of Amun	*ḥry ꜥḫ n ỉmn;*		Gardiner and Weigall 1913: 16; Kampp 1996: 192-193; PM I: 25-26;	32.62401	25.73708
14	19	End Dyn 19	Huy	Priesthood (Amun & AI)	*wab* priest of Amun; *wab* priest of 'Amenhotep (the Image of Amun') (=AI);	*wꜥb n ỉmn;* *wꜥb n ỉmn-ḥtp (pꜣ ibib n ỉmn);*		Betrò, Del Vesco and Miniaci 2009: Pl. 4, Fig. 86, 105, 107, 109; Kampp 1996: 193-194; KR*I* III, 399:8; PM I: 26;	32.62441	25.73692
18	18	TIII	Baki	Temple admin (Amun)	Chief Servant who Weighs the Silver and Gold of the Estate of Amun;	*sḏm ꜥš tp ḫꜣw ḥḏ nbw n pr ỉmn;*		Gardiner and Weigall 1913: 16; Kampp 1996: 199-200; PM I: 32;	32.62666	25.73839
19	19	SI/RII	Amenmose	Priesthood (AI)	High Priest of 'Amenhotep (of the Forecourt') (=AI); Lector Priest; Priest;	*ḥm-nṯr tpy n ỉmn-ḥtp (n pꜣ wbꜣ);* *ḫry-ḥbt;* *ḥm nṯr;*	SC TT344	Kampp 1996: 200-201; KR*I* III, 390-396; PM I: 32-34;	32.62527	25.73748

TT	Dyn	Reign (Kampp)	Tomb Owner	Occupation	Titles	Transliteration	Connected tombs / Notes	References	GPS co-ordinates	
									X	Y
20	18	TIII/(AII)	Montuher-khepeshef	Priesthood, royal admin, local admin, & honorary	Overseer of Priests; Royal Seal-bearer; Fan-bearer; Mayor of Thebu (=Aphroditopolis- capital of 10th nome); King's Son; Sole Companion; Hereditary Prince and Mayor;	*imy-r ḥm-nṯr;* *ḫtmty bity;* *ṯꜣy ḫw;* *ḥꜣty-ꜥ n ṯbw?* *sꜣ nsw;* *smr wꜥty;* *iry-pꜥt, ḥꜣty-ꜥ;* *etś....*	SC TT165	Davies 1913: Pl. IV, IX, VIII; Kampp 1996: 201-203; PM I: 34-35;	32.62378	25.73675
24	18	TII/(Hat) / TIII	Nebamun	Royal admin	Steward of the (Royal Wife) (Nebtu); Butler of the Palace; Chief of the Royal Ships; Overseer of (All) Royal Ships; Overseer of the Royal Office; Hereditary Prince and Mayor;	*imy-r pr n (ḥmt-nsw) (nbt-w);* *wdpw n stp-sꜣ;* *ḥry ꜥḥꜥw n nsw;* *imy-r ꜥḥꜥw (nb(w)) n nsw;* *imy-r ḫꜣ n nsw;* *iry-pꜥt ḥꜣty-ꜥ;*		Kampp 1996: 209-210; PM I: 41-42; *Urk.* IV: 151-153;	32.62368	25.73674
143	18	TIII/AII	Unknown		Unknown (Leader of an expedition?)	?		Kampp 1996: 428-429; PM I: 255-257; *Urk.* IV: 1472-1473;	32.62331	25.73711
146	17/18	End 17/ early 18	Nebamun	Temple admin (Amun) & general admin	Overseer of the Granary of Amun; Scribe; Counter of Grain;	*imy-r šnwty n ỉmn;* *sš;* *ḥsb it;*		Gardiner and Weigall , 1913:28; Kampp 1996: 430-432; PM I: 258;	32.62291	25.73624
147	18	TIV/AIII	Neferennpet *	Priesthood (Amun) & temple admin	Head of the Master of Ceremonies of Amun in Karnak; Scribe and Counter of Cattle of Amun in U and LE;	*ḥry smsw hꜣyt n ỉmn m ipt-swt;* *sš ḥsb iḥw n ỉmn m šmꜥw mḥw;*		Gardiner and Weigall 1913:28; Kampp 1996: 432-434; Ockinga 2008: 139-144; PM I: 258-259;	32.62329	25.73722
148	20	RIII/RV	Amenemopet	Priesthood (Amun (-Ra), Mut & Ra)	3rd Priest of Amun-Ra, King of the Gods; Priest of Amun; High Priest of Mut in Isheru; Divine Father; Chief of Secrets of Heaven, Earth and the Underworld; Greatest of Seers of Ra in Thebes;	*ḥm-nṯr 3 n ỉmn-Rꜥ nsw nṯrw;* *ḥm-nṯr n ỉmn;* *ḥm-nṯr tpy n Mwt m išrw;* *it-nṯr;* *ḥry sštꜣ m pt tꜣ dwꜣt;* *wr mꜣw n Rꜥ m Wꜣst;*	TT158= Father	Kampp 1996: 434-437; KR*I* V: 412-414; KR*I* VI: 90-94, 233-235; PM I: 259-260;	32.62421	25.73774
149	18 & 20	(1) (2)	(1) ? (2) Amenmose	(1)? (2) Royal admin & temple admin (Amun)	(1) ? (2) Royal Scribe of the Table of the Two Lands; Overseer of the Huntsmen of Amun;	*(1) ?* *(2) sš-nsw wdḥw n nb-tꜣwy; imy-r n nw n ỉmn;*		Gardiner and Weigall 1913: 30; Kampp 1996: 437-438; PM I: 260;	32.62458	25.73816

TT	Dyn	Reign (Kampp)	Tomb Owner	Occupation	Titles	Transliteration	Connected tombs / Notes	References	GPS co-ordinates	
									X	Y
150	18	AIII – Amarna?	Userhet	Temple admin (Amun)	Overseer of the Cattle of Amun;	*imy-r iḥw n ꞽImn*		Gaulthier 1908: 131; Kampp 1996: 438-439; PM I: 261;	32.62601	25.73879
151	18	TIV/AIII	Hety	Temple admin (Amun)	Scribe, Counter of Cattle of the God's Wife of Amun; Steward of the God's Wife;	*sš, ḥsb iḥw n ḥmt-nṯr nꞽImn; imy-r pr n ḥmt-nṯr;*		Gardiner and Weigall , 1913: 30; Kampp 1996: 439-440; PM I: 261-262;	32.62589	25.73891
152	18& 19/20	(1)AIII-Amarna (2) Ram?	(1)? (2)?		(1) Unknown (2) Unknown	*(1) ?* *(2) ?*		Gardiner and Weigall 1913: 30; Kampp 1996: 440; PM I: 262;	32.62578	25.73903
153	19/20	End Dyn 19/early Dyn 20	Unknown		Unknown	*?*		Gardiner and Weigall 1913: 30; Kampp 1996: 440-441; PM I: 262;	32.62567	25.7392
154	18	early Dyn 18-TIII	Teti	Royal admin	Butler	*wbꜣ*		Davies 1913: Pl. XXXIX; Kampp 1996: 441; PM I: 262;	32.62516	25.73858
155	18	Hat/TIII	Intef	Royal admin, local admin & general admin	(Chief)/(Great) Herald (of the King); Director of all Works of the Palace; Chief Steward Overseer of the Granaries; Great Chief of the Thinite nome; Mayor of Thinis; Great Chief of the Oasis in its Entirety; Excellent Scribe (of Reckoning)/ (Investigating Title-deeds); Hereditary Prince and Mayor; Great Companion; Sole Companion;	*wḥm (tpy)/(ꜥꜣ) (n nsw);* *ḫrp kꜣt nbt nt pr-nsw;* *imy-r pr wr;* *imy-r šnwty;* *ḥry-tp ꜥꜣ tꜣ-wr;* *ḥꜥty-ꜥ n ṯny;* *ḥry-tp n wḥꜣt mi-ḳdw=s;* *sš iḳr (n tp-ḥsb)/ (wḥꜥ drf);* *iry-pꜥt ḥꜥty-ꜥ;* *smr ꜥꜣ;* *smr wꜥty;*		Kampp 1996: 441-443; PM I: 263-265; Säve-Söderbergh 1957: 11-21, Pl. XI, XII, XIII, XIV, XIX; *Urk.* IV: 963-975;	32.62541	25.73825
165	18	TIV/AIII	Nehemaaway	General & temple admin (Amun)	Goldworker; Sculptor of Amun;	*nby;* *sꜥnḫ n ꞽImn;*	Shared Courtyard-TT20	Davies 1913: Pl. XXXIX; Kampp 1996: 454; PM I: 277; *Urk.* IV: 1607: 3;	32.62381	25.73672
166	18/19	Hor/SI	Ramose	Temple admin (Amun) & general admin	Overseer of Works in Karnak; Overseer of Cattle;	*imy-r kꜣt m ipt-swt;* *imy-r iḥw;*		Gardiner and Weigall 1913: 30; Kampp 1996: 454-455; PM I: 277-278;	32.62466	25.73795

TT	Dyn	Reign (Kampp)	Tomb Owner	Occupation	Titles	Transliteration	Connected tombs / Notes	References	GPS co-ordinates	
									X	Y
167	17/18	end Dyn 17/18	Unknown	?	Unknown	?		Gardiner and Weigall 1913: 30; Kampp 1996: 455-458; PM I: 278;	32.62419	25.73731
232	17/18 & 20	end Dyn 17/18 & Dyn 20	(1) Amenhotep (2) Tharwasa	(1) Temple admin (2) Temple admin (Amun)	(1) Secretary of the God's Wife (2)Scribe of the Divine Seal of the Estate of Amun;	*(1) sš šꜥt n ḥmt-nṯr* *(2)sš sḏꜣwt-nṯr n pr ꞽImn;*		Kampp 1996: 507 & 512; PM I: 328-329;	32.62361	25.73726
233	19/20	late Dyn 19/20	(1) Saroy & (2) Amenhotep Huy	(1) Royal admin, temple admin (Amun), priesthood (2) Royal admin	(1)Royal Scribe of the Offering Table of the Lord of the Two Lands; Keeper of the Royal Documents in the Presence of (the King); Festival Leader; Counter of Cattle in the Estate of Amun; Royal Messenger to Foreign Lands; Overseer of the Huntsmen of Amun; Royal Scribe (of the House of Rituals of the Lord of the Two Lands); Scribe of the *smA.y* (Archive?) of the Lord of the Two Lands; (2) Royal Scribe of the Offering Table of the Lord of the Two Lands;	*(1) sš-nsw wdḥw n nb-tꜣwy;* *iry sšw nsw m-bꜣh (nsw);* *sšmw ḥb;* *ḥsb iḥw m pr ꞽImn;* *wḥmw nsw n ḫꜣst;* *imy-r nw n ꞽImn* *sš nsw ḥwt iryw n nb tꜣwy;* *sš smꜣy n nb tꜣwy;* *(2) sš-nsw wdḥw n nb-tꜣwy;*		Gardiner and Weigall 1913: 36; Kampp 1996: 512-513; Ockinga 2000: 109; Ockinga and Binder 2012: 235; PM I: 329;	32.62437	25.73808
234	18	Dyn 18–Hat	Roy	Local admin	Mayor;	*ḥꜣty-ꜥ;*		Gardiner and Weigall 1913: 36; Kampp 1996: 512-513; PM I: 329;	32.62496	25.73889
239	18	TIV/AIII	Penhut	Local admin	Governor of All Northern Lands;	*imy-r ḫꜣswt nbt mḥyt;*		Gardiner and Weigall: 1913: 36; Kampp 1996: 516; PM I: 330;	32.62402	25.7374
255	18/19	Hor/SI	Roy	Royal admin & temple admin (Amun)	Royal Scribe; Steward in the Estate of Horemheb; Steward in the Estate of Amun;	*sš-nsw;* *imy-r pr m pr ḥr-m-ḥb;* *imy-r pr m pr ꞽImn*		Baud, M. & Drioton, E., 1935; Engelbach 1924: 18; Foucart 1928; Kampp 1996: 532-533; PM I: 339-340; Weeks 2005: 460-463;	32.62447	25.73755
293	19/20 & 20	(1)Ram (2) RIX/ RXI?	(1)Ramessenakht (2) Nebmaatrenakht?	(1)Priesthood (Amun) (2) General admin?	(1) High Priest of Amun; (2) Overseer of the Town, Vizier?	*(1) ḥm-nṯr tpy n ꞽImn;* *(2) imy-r niwt, ṯꜥty?*	From fragments only – tomb ID uncertain	Kampp 1996: 562-563; *KRI* VI:358: 16; *KRI* VI: 842: 2; PM I: 376;	32.62358	25.73745

TT	Dyn	Reign (Kampp)	Tomb Owner	Occupation	Titles	Transliteration	Connected tombs / Notes	References	GPS co-ordinates	
									X	Y
344	19	RII	Piay	Temple admin (Amun(-Ra) & AI) & royal admin	Overseer of the Cattle of Amun-Re in the Southern City; Overseer of the Cattle of Amun (in Karnak); Overseer of the Cattle of All the Gods; Royal Scribe; (Royal) Scribe of Counting the Cattle of Amun; Scribe of Counting the Cattle... of Amun; Scribe of Counting the Cattle and Herds; Scribe[of Counting the Cattle and] the Herds of Djeser-ka-re (=AI);	*imy-r iḥw n ʾImn-Rʿ m niwt rsyt;* *imy-r iḥw n ʾImn (m ipt-swt);* *ʾImy-r iḥw n nṯrw nbw;* *sš-nsw;* *sš (-nsw) n iḥw n ʾImn;* *sš ḥsb iḥw ...n ʾImn;* *šs ḥsb iḥw tꜣ mnmnt;* *sš ḥsb iḥw tꜣ mnmnt ḏsr-kꜣ-rʿ;*	Shared Courtyard-TT19	Gauthier 1908: 152-162; Kampp 1996: 584; Petrie 1909: 11, Pl. XXXIX; PM I: 412-413;	32.62532	25.73749
375	19/20	Ram	Unknown	?	Unknown	*?*		Kampp 1996: 597; PM I: 434;	32.62578	25.73912
376	18	TIV	Unknown	?	Unknown	*?*		Kampp 1996: 597-598; PM I: 434;	32.62544	25.73949
377	20	(end Dyn 19)/20	Unknown	?	Unknown	*?*		Kampp 1996: 598-599; PM I: 434;	32.62505	25.73872
378	18 & 19	Dyn 18(-TIII/AII) & 19	(1)Unknown (2) Unknown	?	(1) Unknown (2) Unknown	*(1) ?* *(2) ?*		Kampp 1996: 599-601; PM I: 435;	32.62485	25.7386
379	19	Dyn 19 (RII)	Unknown	?	Unknown	*?*		Kampp 1996: 601; PM I: 435;	32.6247	25.73812
393	18	TIV /(AIII)	Unknown	?	Unknown	*?*		Kampp 1996: 604-605; PM I: 442;	32.62603	25.73899
394	19/20	Ram (Dyn 20)	Unknown	?	Unknown	*?*		Kampp 1996: 605; PM I: 442;	32.62626	25.73881
395	19/20	Ram (Dyn 20)	Unknown	?	Unknown	*?*		Kampp 1996: 605; PM I: 442;	32.62524	25.73817
396	17/18	Dyn 17/18	Menumose	?	Unknown	*?*		Kampp 1996: 606; PM I: 442-443;	32.62527	25.73844
402	18	late Dyn 18-Tut	Unknown	?	Unknown	*?*		Kampp 1996: 610; PM I: 444;	32.62595	25.73888

Appendix 4: Tomb Owners in Dra Abu el-Naga West

TT	Dyn	Reign (Kampp)	Tomb Owner	Occupation	Titles	Transliteration	Connected tombs/ Notes	References	GPS co-ordinates X	GPS co-ordinates Y
15	18	Ah-AI	Tetiky	Local admin	Mayor in the Southern City; King's Son;	*ḥ3ty-ʿ m niwt rsyt;* *s3 nsw;*		Carnarvon and Carter 1912: 2-4, 12-21; Eaton-Krauss 1998: 205; Gardiner and Weigall 1913: 16; Kampp 1996: 194-196; PM I: 26-27;	32.61723	25.73384
16	19	RII / (Mer)	Panehesi	Priesthood (AI) & temple admin (Amun)	Priest of 'Amenhotep of the Forecourt'; Chief of the UE Offering Table (of Amun);	*ḥm-nṯr n ỉmn-ḥtp n p3 wb3;* *ḥry šmʿw wḏḥw (n ỉmn);*		Kampp 1996: 196-197; KR*I* III: 396-399; PM I:28-29;	32.62141	25.73456
17	18	(TIII)/AII	Nebamun	Royal admin & general admin	Physician (of the King) (in Thebes); Chief Physician; (Royal) Scribe (in Thebes);	*swnw (n nsw) (m w3st);* *wr swnw;* *sš (nsw) (m w3st);*	Connected to TT145	Kampp 1996: 198-199; PM I: 29-31; Save Sodenburgh 1957: Pl. XXI, XXII, XXVII; XXVIII,	32.62163	25.73637
35	19	RII	Bakenkhonsu	Priesthood (Amun)	High Priest of Amun (in Karnak); Overseer of the Priests of all the Gods of Thebes; Overseer of the Priests of Amun-Re; Chief of Secrets in Heaven, Earth and the Underworld; Divine Father; Hereditary Prince and Mayor;	*ḥm-nṯr tpy n ỉmn (m ipt-swt);* *imy-r ḥmw-nṯrw n nṯrw nbw W3st;* *imy-r ḥmw-nṯrw n ỉmn-Rʿ;* *ḥry sšt3 m pt t3 dw3t;* *it nṯr;* *iry-pʿt ḥ3ty-ʿ;*	Son/ brother owns TT283	Kampp 1996: 225-227; KR*I* III: 293-294; *LAe* II: 1243-1246; LD III: 241; PM I: 61-63;	32.61869	25.73617
140	18	TIII/AII	Neferrenpet called Kefia	Craftsman	Goldsmith; Sculptor;	*nby;* *sʿnḫ;*	Connected to TT141	Gardiner and Weigall 1913: 28; Kampp 1996: 427-428; PM I: 254;	32.62237	25.73555
141	20	Dyn 20	Bakenkhonsu	Priesthood (Amun)	*wab* priest of Amun;	*wʿb n ỉmn;*	Connected to TT140	Gardiner and Weigall 1913:28; Kampp 1996: 428; PM I: 254-255;	32.62248	25.73572

TT	Dyn	Reign (Kampp)	Tomb Owner	Occupation	Titles	Transliteration	Connected tombs/ Notes	References	GPS co-ordinates	
									X	Y
142	18	TIII/AII	Samut	Temple admin (Amun)	Overseer of the Works of Amen-Re in Karnak;	*ỉmy-r kꜣt n Ỉmn-Rꜥ m ỉpt-swt;*		Gardiner and Weigall 1913:8; Kampp 1996: 428; PM I: 255;	32.62142	25.73582
144	18	TIII?	Nu	General admin	Chief of the Field-labourers;	*ḥry ꜥḥwty;*		Gardiner and Weigall 1913:28; Kampp 1996: 429-430; PM I: 257;	32.62183	25.73598
145	18	Hat/TIII	Nebamun	Military	Captain of Troops;	*ḥry pḏt;*	Connected to TT17. Father of TT367.	Gardiner and Weigall 1913:28; Kampp 1996: 430; PM I: 257-258;	32.62168	25.73652
156	19	(Hor)/RII	Pennesuttawy	Military & local admin	Captain of Troops; Overseer of (Southern) Foreign Lands;	*ḥry pḏt; ỉmy-r ḫꜣswt (rsyt);*	Grandson/ son owns TT282	Kampp 1996: 443-445; KR*I* III: 113-114; PM I: 265-266;	32.61927	25.73613
157	19	RII	Nebwenenef	Priesthood (Amun) & general admin	High Priest of Amun; High Priest of Hathor, mistress of Iwnet (=Esna); Overseer of all the Priests of All the Gods; Overseer of the Priests of the Lords of Thebes; Divine Father; Greatest of Seers, (pure of hands) in Thebes; Overseer of Works; Overseer of the Double House (=Treasury) of Silver and Gold; Overseer of All Craftsmen in Thebes; Overseer of the Granary; Hereditary Prince and Mayor; Mayor;	*ḥm-nṯr tpy n Ỉmn; ḥm-nṯr tpy n ḥwt-ḥr nbt Ỉwnt; ỉmy-r ḥmw nṯr n nṯrw nbw; Ỉmy-r ḥmw nṯr n nbw Wꜣst; Ỉt nṯr, wr mꜣw (wꜥb ꜥwy) m Wꜣst; Ỉmy-r kꜣt; Ỉmy-r pr.wy ḥḏ nbw; Ỉmy-r ḥmwt nbt ḫnt Wꜣst; ỉmy-r šnwty; ỉry-pꜥt ḥꜣty-ꜥ; ḥꜣty-ꜥ;*		Kampp 1996: 445-447; KR*I* III: 282- 291; KR*I* VII: 131-133; LD III: 239; PM I: 266-268;	32.6195	25.73605
158	19	SII/Tau/ (RIII)	Tjanefer	Priesthood (Amun)	(3rd) Priest of Amun; Divine Father, *wab* priest of Amun in Karnak; Greatest of Seers of Ra (and Atum) in Thebes;	*ḥm-nṯr (3) n Ỉmn; Ỉt nṯr; wꜥb n Ỉmn m ỉpt-swt; wr mꜣw n Rꜥ (ỉtm) m Wꜣst;*	Son buried in TT148	Kampp 1996: 447-450; KR*I* V: 400-412; KR*I* VII: 280-281; LD III: 240; PM I: 268-271;	32.61896	25.73635

TT	Dyn	Reign (Kampp)	Tomb Owner	Occupation	Titles	Transliteration	Connected tombs/ Notes	References	GPS co-ordinates	
									X	Y
159	19/20	Late Dyn 19-early 20	Raia	Priesthood (Amun)	4th Priest of Amun;	*ḥm-nṯr 4 n ʾImn;*	Connected to TT286. Grandson of TT283? Father of TT284?	LAe II: 1243-1246; Kampp 1996: 450-451; KRI IV: 135: 5; PM I: 271-273;	32.61908	25.73603
161	18	AII	Nakht	Priesthood (Amun)	Bearer of the Floral Offerings of Amun;	*fꜣi ḥtpw ḥrrwt n ʾImn;*		Kampp 1996: 451-542; LD III, 241; Manniche 1986: 55-78; PM I: 274-275;	32.6198	25.73516
162	18	AIII	Kenamun	Local admin & temple admin (Amun)	Mayor in the Southern City; Overseer of the Granary of Amun;	*ḥꜣty-ʿ m niwt rsyt; imy-r šnwty n ʾImn;*		Davies 1963: 14-18, Pl. XV; Kampp 1996: 452; PM I: 275-276;	32.62095	25.73505
163	19	Mid-late Dyn 19	Amenemhet	Local admin & royal admin	Mayor of the Southern City; Royal Scribe;	*ḥꜣty-ʿ n niwt rsyt; sš-nsw;*		Gardiner and Weigall 1913: 30; Kampp 1996: 452; PM I: 276;	32.62035	25.73608
164	18	(Hat)/ TIII	Intef	Military	Scribe of Recruits;	*sš nfrw;*		Gardiner and Weigall 1913: 30; Kampp 1996: 453-454; PM I: 276-277;	32.61993	25.73535
168	19	RII	Any	Priesthood (Amun)	Divine Father of Amun in Karnak; Divine Father, Clean of Hands; Chosen Lector Priest of the Lord of Gods;	*it-nṯr n ʾImn m ʾIpt-swt; it-nṯr wʿb ʿwy; ḥry-ḥbt stp n nb nṯrw;*		Kampp 1996: 458; PM I: 278; KRI III: 300: 14-16;	32.61767	25.73427
169	18	AII	Senna	Temple craftsman (Amun)	Chief of the Goldsmiths of Amun;	*ḥry nbyw n ʾImn;*		Gardiner and Weigall 1913: 30; Kampp 1996: 458; PM I: 278-279;	32.61817	25.73425
231	18	Early Dyn 18	Nebamun	Temple admin (Amun)	Scribe; Counter of the Grain of Amun in the Granary of the Divine Offerings;	*sš; ḥsb bdt n ʾImn m šnwt nt ḥtp-nṯr;*		Gardiner and Weigall 1913: 36; Kampp 1996: 577; PM I: 328;	32.62168	25.73663

TT	Dyn	Reign (Kampp)	Tomb Owner	Occupation	Titles	Transliteration	Connected tombs/ Notes	References	GPS co-ordinates X	GPS co-ordinates Y
236	19/20	Ram	Hornakht	Priesthood (Amun) & temple admin (Amun)	2nd Priest of Amun; Overseer of the Treasury of Amun;	ḥm-nṯr 2 n Ỉmn; ỉmy-r pr-ḥḏ n Ỉmn;		Gardiner and Weigall 1913: 36; Kampp 1996: 579; PM I: 329;	32.61658	25.73461
237	19/20	Ram	Wennefer	Priesthood	Chief Lector Priest;	ẖry-ḥbt ḥry-tp;		Gardiner and Weigall 1913: 36; Kampp 1996: 579; PM I: 330;	32.6167	25.7345
260	18	TIII	User	Temple admin (Amun)	Measurer of [Amun]; Overseer of the Ploughed Lands of [Amun]; Overseer of the Field-labourers of Amun;	ḫꜣw n [Ỉmn]; ỉmy-r ḫbsw n [Ỉmn]; ỉmy-r ꜥḥwtỵ n Ỉmn;	Connected to TT261	Engelbach, 1924: 18; Kampp 1996: 538-539; Nasr 1993: 177; PM I: 343-344;	32.62173	25.73615
261	18	TIII/(AII)	Khaemwaset	Priesthood (AI)	wab priest of Amenhotep (=AI);	wꜥb n Ỉmn-ḥtp;	Connected to TT260	Kampp 1996: 539; Nasr 1988: 233; PM I: 344;	32.62175	25.73624
262	18	(Hat)/ TIII	Unknown	General admin	Overseer of the Arable Land (Fields);	ỉmy-r ꜣḥwt;		Engelbach 1924: 18; Kampp 1996: 540; PM I: 344;	32.61783	25.73409
282	19	RII	Nakht/ Menunakht	Military	Captain of Troops;	ḥry pḏt;	Grandfather/ father owns TT156	Kampp 1996: 550-552; KRI III: 115: 6; PM I: 364-365;	32.61831	25.73622
283	19	RII- SII	Roma (Roy)	Priesthood (Amun)	High Priest of Amun;	ḥm-nṯr tpy n Ỉmn;	Father/ brother owns TT35	KRI IV:127: 15; Kampp 1996: 553-554; LAe II: 1243-1246; PM I: 365-366;	32.61851	25.73615
284	19 & 20	(Dyn 18)/ 19 before RII & Dyn 20	(1) Unknown (2) Pahemneter	(1) ? (2) Temple admin	(1) Unknown (2) Scribe of the Offerings of All the Gods;	(1) ? (2) sš ḥtp n nṯrw nbw;	(2) Son of TT159?	Engelbach 1924: 20; Kampp 1996: 555-556; PM I: 366;	32.6187	25.73589
285	19 & 20	Dyn 19 & 20	(1)Iny (2) ?	(1) Temple admin (Mut) (2) ?	(1) Chief of the Storehouse of Mut; (2) ?	(1) ḥry šnꜥt n Mwt; (2) ?		EngelbacH 1924: 20; Kampp 1996: 556-557; PM I: 367-368;	32.61881	25.73596

TT	Dyn	Reign (Kampp)	Tomb Owner	Occupation	Titles	Transliteration	Connected tombs/ Notes	References	GPS co-ordinates	
									X	Y
286	19	(Late) Dyn 19	Niay	General admin	Scribe (of the Offering Table);	*sš (wdḥw);*	Connected to TT159	Engelbach 1924: 20; Kampp 1996: 557; PM I: 368;	32.61904	25.73596
287	19/20	Ram	Pendua	Priesthood (Amun)	*wab* priest of Amun;	*wꜥb n ꞽImn;*		Engelbach 1924: 20; Kampp 1996: 558; PM I: 369;	32.61916	25.73605
288	19	RII	(1) Setau	(1) ?	(1) TT 289?	*(1) ?*	SC with TT289 & TT304.	Engelbach 1924: 20; Kampp 1996: 558-561; PM I: 369;	32.61889	25.73604
289	19	RII	Setau	Local admin & general admin/ royal? & temple admin (Amun)	King's Son of Kush; Overseer of the Southern Foreign Lands; Steward; Overseer of the House of Silver (=Treasurer) of Amun;	*sꜣ-nsw n Kꜣš;* *imy-r ḫꜣswt rsyt;* *imy-r pr;* *imy-r pr-ḥḏ n ꞽImn;*	SC with TT288 & TT304.	Kampp 1996: 558-561; KR*I* III: 80: 15-16; PM I: 369-372;	32.61886	25.73598
300	19	RII/ Mer	Anhotep	Local admin & royal admin	King's Son of Kush; Overseer of the Southern Foreign Lands; Scribe of the Offering Table of the Lord of the Two Lands;	*sꜣ-nsw n Kꜣš;* *imy-r ḫꜣswt rsyt;* *sš wdḥw n nb tꜣwy;*	SC with TT301	Kampp 1996: 568-569; KR*I* III: 112: 4-5; PM I: 380-381;	32.61909	25.73622
301	20	(end Dyn 19) / Dyn 20	Hori	Royal admin & temple admin	Scribe of the Offering Table of the Lord of the Two Lands in the Estate of Amun;	*sš wdḥw n nb tꜣwy m pr ꞽImn;*	SC with TT300	Engelbach 1924: 22; Kampp 1996: 569; PM I: 381;	32.61913	25.73622
302	19/ 20	Ram	Paraemheb (or Userhet)	Temple admin (Amun)	Chief of the Magazine of Amun;	*ḥry šnꜥ n ꞽImn;*		Engelbach 1924: 22; Kampp 1996: 570; PM I: 381;	32.62099	25.73483
303	20/21	end Dyn 20/early 21	Paser	Temple admin (Amun) & priesthood (Amun)	Chief of the Magazine [of Amun?]; 3rd Priest of Amun;	*ḥry šnꜥ n ꞽImn;* *ḥm-nṯr 3 n ꞽImn;*		Engelbach 1924: 22; Kampp 1996: 570; PM I: 381;	32.6192	25.73657
304	20/21	Dyn 20/21	Piay	Temple admin (Amun) & royal admin	Scribe of the Offering Table of Amun; Scribe of the Offering Table of the Lord of the Two Lands;	*sš wdḥw n ꞽImn;* *sš wdḥw n nb tꜣwy;*	SC with TT288 & TT289.	Engelbach 1924: 22; Kampp 1996: 570-571; PM I: 383;	32.61898	25.73603
332	19/20	Ram	Penrennut	Temple admin (Amun)	Chief Guardian of the Granary of the Estate of Amun;	*ḥry sꜣwty n tꜣ šnwty pr ꞽImn;*		Engelbach 1924: 26; Kampp 1996: 577; PM I: 399;	32.61959	25.7347

TT	Dyn	Reign (Kampp)	Tomb Owner	Occupation	Titles	Transliteration	Connected tombs / Notes	References	GPS co-ordinates	
									X	Y
333	18	after Amarna/ (Ay)	Unknown	?	Unknown	?		Engelbach 1924: 26; Kampp 1996: 577-578; PM I: 399-401;	32.62121	25.73494
334	18	AIII	Unknown	General admin	Chief of Husbandmen;	ḥry iḥwtyw;		Engelbach 1924: 26; Kampp 1996: 579; PM I: 401;	32.62114	25.73475
401	18	TIII/AII	Nebseny	Temple craftsman (Amun)	Overseer of the Goldsmiths of Amun;	imy-r nbyw n ỉmn;		Fakhry 1947: 34; Kampp 1996: 609; PM I: 444;	32.61951	25.73486

Appendix 5: Outlying Tombs in Dra Abu el-Naga West

TT	Dyn	Reign (Kampp)	Tomb Owner	Occupation	Titles	Transliteration	Connected tombs / Notes	References	GPS co-ordinates	
									X	Y
305	20		Paser	Priesthood (Amun) & temple admin	wꜥb priest in front of Amun; Scribe of the Divine Offerings of Amun;	wꜥb n ḥꜣt ỉmn; sš ḥtp-nṯr n ỉmn;	Shared courtyard – TT306 & TT307	Engelbach 1924: 22; Kampp 1996: 571-572; PM I: 383;	32.62167	25.73332
306	20-21		Irdjanen	Temple admin (Amun)	Door-opener of the Estate of Amun;	wn n pr ỉmn;	Shared courtyard – TT305 & TT307	Engelbach 1924: 22; Kampp 1996: 572; PM I: 384;	32.6216	25.73332
307	20		Tjunefer	?	Unknown	?	Shared courtyard – TT305 & TT306	Engelbach 1924: 22; Kampp 1996: 572; PM I: 385;	32.62156	25.73325

Appendix 6: New Kingdom Tomb Owners in Deir el-Bahri

TT	Dynasty	PM date	Tomb Owner	Occupation	Title	Transliteration	Connected Tombs / Notes	References	GPS co-ordinates	
									X	Y
353	18	Hat	Senenmut (TT 71)	Royal admin	(Chief) Steward (of the king); (Chief) Steward of Amun; Overseer of the Audience-Chamber (=Chamberlain); Overseer of the Farmlands of Amun; Overseer of the Double House of Silver (=Treasury); Overseer of the Double House of Gold (=Treasury); Overseer of the House of the Morning (=Robing Room); Overseer of the Herds of Amun; Overseer of the Cattle of Amun; Overseer of the Priests of Montu of Heliopolis; Overseer of the Garden of Amun; Overseer of (all) Precious Things; Overseer of the Granary (of Amun); Overseer of the Works of Amun (in Djeser-Djeseru); Overseer of all the Works of the King in the Estate of Amun); Great One of the Tens of U and LE; (Hereditary Prince) Mayor; Priest of Amun-Userhat; Chief of Secrets in the House of the Morning (=Robing Room)/Chapels/of the West- side/ Colonnade; Chief of the Nobles of the King; Great Chief of the Palace; Director of the Great Ones of U and LE; Director of the Broad Court of Amun; Foster Child of the King;	*ỉmy-r pr (wr) (n nsw);* *ỉmy-r pr (wr) n ỉmn;* *ỉmy-r ˁẖnwty;* *ỉmy-r ˁḥwt n ỉmn;* *ỉmy-r pr.wy nbw;* *ỉmy-r pr.wy ḥḏ;* *ỉmy-r pr dwꜣt;* *ỉmy-r mnmnt n ỉmn;* *ỉmy-r ỉḥw n ỉmn;* *ỉmy-r ḥmw-nṯr n Mnṯw m ỉwny;* *ỉmy-r ḫnty-š n ỉmn;* *ỉmy-r sḏꜣwt (nb[t]);* *ỉmy-r šnwty (n ỉmn);* *ỉmy-r kꜣt n ỉmn (m ḏsr-ḏsrw);* *ỉmy-r kꜣt nbt nt nsw (m pr ỉmn);* *wr mḏw šmˁw mḥw;* *(ỉry-pˁt) ḥꜣty-ˁ;* *ḥm-nṯr n ỉmn-wsr-ḥꜣt;* *ḥry-sštꜣ m pr-dwꜣt/ m r-prw/n ỉmy-wrt;* */n wꜣḏty;* *ḥry-tp n sˁḥw-nsw;* *ḥry-tp ˁꜣ m pr-nsw;* *ḫrp wrw šmˁw mḥw;* *ḫrp wsḫt n ỉmn;* *sḏty- nsw;*	Owns TT71	Dorman 1988: 203-211; Kampp 1996: 588; PM I: 417-418;	32.60928	25.73729
358	18	AII	Ahmose Meritamun	Royal family	Daughter of TIII, Wife of AII	*sꜣ-nsw;* *ḥmt-nsw;*		Kampp 1996: 358; PM I: 421; Winlock 1929: 28.	32.60716	25.73831

Appendix 7: Outlying Tomb Owners in Deir el-Bahri

TT	Dyn	Reign (PM)	Tomb Owner	Occupation	Title	Transliteration	Connected Tombs / Notes	References	GPS co-ordinates	
									X	Y
280	MK	Amen I	Meketre		See Appendix 2			See Appendix 2	32.60312	25.73465
281	MK	Amen I	Unfinished Mortuary Temple / Royal Tomb – Amenemhat I		See Appendix 2			See Appendix 2	32.60168	25.73307
320	18	Ah (cachette -Dyn 21)	Inhapi	Royal family	Wife of Ahmose?	*ḥmt-nsw?*	DB320	Engelbach 1924: 24; Kampp 1996: 574; PM I: 393;	32.60536	25.73619

Appendix 8: Tomb Owners in el-Asasif

TT	Dynasty	Reign (Kampp)	Tomb Owner	Occupation	Title	Transliteration	Connected tombs / Notes	References	GPS co-ordinates	
									X	Y
25	19	RII	Amenemhab	Priesthood (Khonsu)	High Priest of Khonsu;	*ḥm-nṯr tpy n ḫnsw;*	Shared courtyard with TT28, TT408 & TT409	Kampp 1996: 211-212; KRI III:301: 15; KRI VII: 134-135; PM I: 42;	32.61272	25.7339
26	19	SII/Tau	Khnumemhab	Temple admin (Ramesseum), royal admin & military	Overseer of the House of Silver (=Treasury) [of] the (Temple of User-maat-re Setep-en-re in the Estate of Amun) (=Ramesseum); Royal Scribe; Overseer of the Army/ General of the Lord of the Two Lands;	*imy-r pr ḥḏ tꜣ ḥwt wsr-mꜣꜥt-Rꜥ stp-n-Rꜥ m pr-ỉmn; sš nsw; imy-r mšꜥ n nb tꜣwy;*	Shared courtyard with TT192, TT190, TT189, TT193, TT194, TT195, TT406 & TT364.	Kampp 1996: 212-213; KRI III:373: 15; KRI VII: 164: 3; LD III: 249; PM I: 43;	32.61168	25.73416
28	19/20	Ram	Hori	Temple admin (Amun)	Deputy of the Estate of Amun;	*idnw n pr-ỉmn;*	Shared courtyard with TT25, TT408 & TT409	Gardiner and Weigall 1913: 18; Kampp 1996: 214; PM I: 45;	32.6127	25.73393
39	18	Hat/TIII	Puyemra	Priesthood (Amun), royal admin	2nd priest of Amun; Royal Seal-bearer; Spokesman who Makes Peace in the Entire Land; Hereditary Prince (and Mayor); Sole Companion;	*ḥm-nṯr 2 n ỉmn; ḫtmty bity; r shrr m tꜣ r=ḏr=f; iry-pꜥt (ḥꜣty-ꜥ); smr wꜥty;*	Wife= daughter of high priest TT67	Davies 1923: Pl. XLVII, XLIX; Kampp 1996: 230-233; LD III: 243-244; PM I: 71-75; Urk. IV: 523-527;	32.61328	25.73353
188	18	AIII/AIV	Parennefer	Royal admin & priesthood	Royal Butler, Clean of Hands; Overseer of the Priests of all the Gods;	*wbꜣ-nsw wꜥb ꜥwy; imy-r ḥmw nṯr n nṯrw nbw;*	Shared courtyard with TT374	Kampp 1996: 475-478; PM I: 293-295; Urk. IV: 1996: 7, 18.	32.61299	25.7337
189	19	end RII/ (Mer)	Nakht-djehuty	Temple craftsman (Amun)	Overseer of Carpenters (of the Northern Lake (of Amun)); Chief of Goldworkers in the Estate of Amun;	*imy-r ḥmwt (n pꜣ š mḥyt (n ỉmn)); ḥry nbyw m pr ỉmn;*	Shared courtyard with TT192, TT190, TT193, TT194, TT195, TT406, TT26 and TT364	Kampp 1996: 478-480; KRI III: 348-353; PM I: 295-297;	32.61183	25.7343

TT	Dynasty	Reign (Kampp)	Tomb Owner	Occupation	Title	Transliteration	Connected tombs / Notes	References	GPS co-ordinates	
									X	Y
190	19	RII	(1) ?	(1) ?	(1)?	*(1) ?*	Shared courtyard with TT192, TT189, TT193, TT194, TT195, TT406, TT26 and TT364	Kampp 1996: 480; PM I: 297;	32.61176	25.73436
192	18	AIII/AIV	Kheruef called Senaa	Royal admin & General admin	Steward of the Great Royal Wife Tiye; (True) Royal Scribe; Controller of Monuments; Chief Royal Herald; Royal Seal-bearer; Overseer of Seal-bearers; Chief of Secrets of the Palace; Director of the Palace; Hereditary Prince and Mayor; Sole Companion;	*ỉmy-r pr n ḥmt-nsw wrt tiy; sš-nsw (mꜣˁ); ḫrp mnw; wḥmw-nsw tpy; ḫtmty bity; ỉmy-r ḫtmtyw; ḥry sštꜣ n pr-nsw; ḫrp ˁḥ; ỉry-pˁt ḥꜣty-ˁ; smr wˁty;*	Shared courtyard with TT190, TT189, TT193, TT194, TT195, TT406, TT26 and TT364	Kampp 1996: 480-483; PM I: 298-300; Urk. IV: 1858-1873;	32.61153	25.73427
193	20	(Dyn 19)/ 20	Ptahemheb	Temple admin (Amun)	Great One of the Seal in the House of Silver (=Treasury) of the Estate of Amun;	*ˁꜣ n ḫtm m pr-ḥḏ n pr ỉmn;*	Shared courtyard with TT192, TT190, TT189, TT194, TT195, TT406, TT26 and TT364	Gardiner and Weigall 1913: 34; Kampp 1996: 483; PM I: 300;	32.61182	25.73423
194	19	RII	Djehutyemheb	Temple admin (Amun) & royal admin	Overseer of Marshland Dwellers/ Peasants of the Estate of Amun; Scribe of the Divine Offerings of the Estate of Amun; Royal Scribe;	*ỉmy-r sḫty n pr ỉmn; sš ḥtp-nṯr n pr ỉmn; sš nsw;*	Shared courtyard with TT192, TT190, TT189, TT193, TT195, TT406, TT26 and TT364	Kampp 1996: 483-485; KRI VII: 153-158; PM I: 300-301;	32.61182	25.73419
195	20	Dyn 20	Bakenamun	Temple admin (Amun)	Scribe of the Treasury of the Estate of Amun;	*sš pr-ḥḏ n pr ỉmn;*	Shared courtyard with TT192, TT190, TT189, TT193, TT194, TT406, TT26 and TT364	Kampp 1996: 485; KRI VII: 144-145; PM I: 301;	32.6118	25.73414

TT	Dynasty	Reign (Kampp)	Tomb Owner	Occupation	Title	Transliteration	Connected tombs / Notes	References	GPS co-ordinates	
									X	Y
244	19/20	Ram	Pakaru	Temple craftsman (Amun)	Overseer of Craftsmen of the Temple of Amun;	*imy-r ḥmw(t) n ḥwt ꞽImn;*		Gardiner and Weigall 1913: 36; Kampp 1996: 520; Leclant 1954: 66; PM I: 332-333;	32.61133	25.73444
364	20	Dyn 20	Amenemhab	Temple admin (Amun & all)	Scribe of the Divine Offerings of All the Gods of Thebes; Scribe of the Granary of Amun;	*sš ḥtp-nṯr n nṯrw nbw n Wꜣst;* *sš šnwt n ꞽImn;*	Shared courtyard with TT192, TT190, TT189, TT193, TT194, TT195, TT406, and TT26.	Fakhry 1947: 44; Kampp 1996: 589-590; PM I: 345;	32.6116	25.73416
366	MK		Djar	Royal admin	See Appendix 2			See Appendix 2	32.61083	25.7346
374	19	after RII	Amenemopet	Temple admin (Ramesseum)	Scribe of the House of Silver (=Treasury) in the Temple of User-Maat-Re Setep-en-re (=Ramesseum);	*sš pr-ḥḏ m ḥwt Wsr-mꜣꜥt-rꜥ stp-n-rꜥ;*	Shared courtyard with TT188	Kampp 1996: 597; PM I: 434; KRI III: 374: 12-13;	32.61307	25.7337
386	MK		Intef	Royal admin & military	See Appendix 2			See Appendix 2	32.61352	25.73452
387	19	RII	Meryptah	Royal admin & local admin	Royal Scribe of the Offering Table of the Lord of the Two Lands (in the Estate of Amun); Overseer of the Foreign Lands of the Southern Hill-country/Desert;	*sš nsw n wdḥw n nb tꜣwy (m pr ꞽImn);* *imy-r ḫꜣswt n ḫꜣst rsyt;*		Kampp 1996: 604; PM I: 439; KRI III: 319-320; KRI VII: 143-144;	32.61212	25.73423
406	20	Dyn 20	Piay	Royal admin	Scribe of the Offering Table of the Lord of the Two Lands;	*sš wdḥw n nb tꜣwy;*	Shared courtyard with TT192, TT190, TT189, TT193, TT194, TT195, TT26 and TT364	Kampp 1996: 610-611; PM I: 446;	32.61177	25.73414
408	20	(end Dyn 19)/20	Bakenamun	Temple admin (Amun)	Head of Servants of the Estate of Amun;	*ḥry ḥmw n pr ꞽImn;*	Shared courtyard with TT25, TT28 & TT409	Kampp 1996: 611-612; PM I: 446;	32.61256	25.73398

TT	Dynasty	Reign (Kampp)	Tomb Owner	Occupation	Title	Transliteration	Connected tombs / Notes	References	GPS co-ordinates	
									X	Y
409	19	RII	Samut called Kyky	Temple admin (Amun & others), general admin & royal admin	(Royal) Scribe ([of] the Estate of Amun), True Scribe; Counter of the Cattle (of Amun); Overseer of Scribes; Counter of Cattle of the Estate of Amun; Counter of Cattle of the Lords of Thebes; Scribe of Counting the Cattle of All the Gods of Thebes; Counter in the Estate of Amun-Ra; Overseer of Counting the Cattle (of All the Gods of Thebes); (Great) Overseer of Counting the Cattle of Amun (and of Montu); Overseer of Counting the Cattle of Amun, of Mut and of Khonsu; Overseer of Counting the Cattle of all the gods [of] U and LE;	*sš (nsw) ([n] pr ꞽImn);* *sš mꜣꜥ;* *ḥsb iḥw (n ꞽImn);* *imy-r sš;* *ḥsb iḥw n pr ꞽImn;* *ḥsb iḥw n nbw Wꜣst;* *sš ḥsb iḥw n nṯrw nbw Wꜣst;* *ḥsb n pr ꞽImn-rꜥ;* *imy-r ḥsb iḥw (n nṯrw nbw Wꜣst);* *imy-r ḥsb iḥw (wr) n ꞽImn (n Mnṯw);* *imy-r ḥsb iḥw n ꞽImn n Mwt n ḫnsw,* *ḥsb iḥw n nṯrw nbw [n] šmꜥw mḥw,*	Shared courtyard with TT25, TT28 & TT408. Mentions Saroy (TT223? - chief of hunters of Amun) Amenemope (TT149 Amenmose? Hunter of Amun= son of Meryre - brother of Samut?	Kampp 1996: 612-613; KRI III: 331-345; Negm 1997: Pl. II, IV, VI, X, XII, XVI, XX, XXII, XXIV, XXVI, XXVIII, XXX, XXXVI, XXXVIII, XL, XLIV, LIV; PM I: 461-462;	32.6126	25.73396

Appendix 9: Tomb Owners in el-Khokha

TT	Dynasty	Reign (Kampp)	Tomb Owner	Occupation	Title	Transliteration	Connected tombs / Notes	References	GPS co-ordinates	
									X	Y
22	18	TIII/AII & AII/AIII	(1) Wah (2) partly Meryamun	(1)Royal admin (2) Royal family	(1)Royal Butler; (2) Eldest Son of the king;	*(1) wbꜣ-nsw;* *(2) sꜣ-nsw wr;*		Gardiner and Weigall 1913: 18; Kampp 1996: 205-206; PM I: 37-38;	32.61046	25.7327
23	19	Mer	Tjay called To	Royal admin, temple admin & priesthood (moon)	Royal Secretary of the Lord of the Two Lands; Secretary of Pharaoh; Fan-bearer on the Right of the King; (True) Royal Scribe; Chief Royal Scribe of his Lord; Scribe of Records of the Good God; Overseer of the Granaries of all the Gods of U and LE, High Priest of the Moon; Chief of his Office; Attendant of the Good God; Hereditary Prince and Mayor;	*sš-nsw šꜥt n nb tꜣwy;* *sš šꜥt n pr-ꜥꜣ;* *ṯꜣy ḫw ḥr imn n nsw;* *sš nsw (mꜣꜥ);* *sš nsw tpy n nb=f;* *sš sḥꜣw n nṯr nfr;* *imy-r šnwty n nṯrw nbw n šmꜥw mḥw,* *ḥm-nṯr tpy n iꜥḥ;* *wr iꜣt=f;* *iry rdwy n nṯr nfr;* *iry-pꜥt ḥꜣty-ꜥ;*		Kampp 1996: 206-209; KRI IV: 107-119; KRI VII: 221-225; 412-413; PM I: 38-41;	32.61023	25.73259
32	19	RII	Djehutymose	Temple admin (Amun), general admin & royal admin	(Chief) Steward of Amun; Overseer of the Granaries of U & LE; True Royal Scribe;	*imy-r pr (wr) n ꞽImn;* *imy-r šnwty n šmꜥw mḥw;* *sš nsw mꜣꜥ;*		Kampp 1996: 221-224; KRI III: 318-319; PM I: 49-50;	32.61262	25.73227
38	18	TIV/AIII	Djeserkarasoneb	Temple admin (Amun)	Steward of the Second Priest of Amun; Scribe of Counting the Grain of Amun; Counter of Grain in the Granary of the Divine Offerings of Amun;	*imy-r pr n ḥm nṯr 2 n ꞽImn;* *sš ḥsb it n ꞽImn;* *ḥsb it m šnwt nt ḥtpw-nṯr [n ꞽImn];*	Steward of TT75	Davies 1963: 1-8; Kampp 1996: 228-230; PM I: 69-70; Urk. IV: 1638-1640;	32.61108	25.73226
41	18/19	Hor-SI	Amenemopet called Ipy	Temple admin (Amun) priesthood (Min & Isis) royal admin & general admin	(Chief) Steward of Amun in the Southern City; Royal Scribe; Overseer of the Granaries of U and LE / of All the Gods; Overseer of the Priests of Min and Isis; Overseer of the Cattle of Amun; Steward of the God's Wife; Royal Seal-bearer; Hereditary Prince and Mayor;	*imy-r pr (wr) n ꞽImn (m niwt rsyt);* *sš nsw;* *imy-r šnwty n šmꜥw mḥw / n nṯrw nbw;* *imy-r ḥmw nṯrw n mnw ist;* *imy-r iḥw n ꞽImn;* *ꜥꜣ n pr n ḥmt-nṯr;* *ḫtmw-bity;* *iry-pꜥt ḥꜣty-ꜥ;*		Kampp 1996: 235-237; KRI III: 308-316; KRI VII: 135-139; PM I: 78-81;	32.61064	25.73257

TT	Dynasty	Reign (Kampp)	Tomb Owner	Occupation	Title	Transliteration	Connected tombs / Notes	References	GPS co-ordinates	
									X	Y
42	18	TIII/AII	Amenmose	Military, royal admin & local admin	Captain of Troops; Overseer of the Northern Foreign Lands; Royal Seal-bearer; Eyes of the King of UE, Ears of the king of LE upon the Foreign Land of the Wretched Retjenu; Chief of the Stable of the Lord of the Two Lands; King's Follower on the Foreign Land of Retjenu; Sole Companion;	*ḥry pḏt;* *ỉmy-r ḫꜣswt mḥty; ḫtmty bỉty;* *ỉrty nsw ꜥnḫwy n bỉty ḥr ḫꜣst rṯnw ḫst;* *ḥry ỉḥw n nb tꜣwy;* *šmsw nsw ḥr ḫꜣst rṯnw;* *smr wꜥty;*		Kampp 1996: 237-239; PM I: 82-83; Urk. IV: 1507-1508;	32.61057	25.7327
44	20	Dyn 20	Amenemhab	Priesthood (Amun) & temple admin (Amun)	wab priest (in front of Amun); Scribe of the Temple of Amun;	*wꜥb n ḥꜣt ꞽImn;* *sš ḥwt nṯr n ꞽImn;*		El-Saady 1997: 51-57; Kampp 1996: 241-242; PM I: 84-85;	32.61021	25.73222
47	18	AIII	Userhet	Royal admin	Overseer of the Royal Harem; Hereditary Prince and Mayor;	*ỉmy-r ỉpt nsw;* *ỉry-pꜥt ḥꜣty-ꜥ;*		Kampp 1996: 246-248; PM I: 87; Urk. IV: 1880: 5-7;	32.61128	25.73252
48	18	AIII	Amenemhat called Surere	Royal admin & temple admin (Amun)	Chief Steward (of the King); Royal Scribe; Divine Seal-bearer of Amun; Overseer of the Cattle of Amun; Overseer of the Arable Lands (fields) of Amun; Chief of Secrets in the Palace; Great Chief in the Palace; Chief of the House of the Morning; Overseer of Horns, Overseer of Hoofs and Overseer of Feathers; Overseer of the Recruits of Amun; Fan-bearer on the Right of the King; [Overseer of] all the [Craftsmen] of the King; Hereditary Prince and Mayor;	*ỉmy-r pr wr (n nsw);* *sš nsw;* *ḫtmty- nṯr n ꞽImn;* *ꞽImy-r ỉḥw n ꞽImn;* *ꞽImy-r ꜣḥwt n ꞽImn;* *ḥry sštꜣ n pr-nsw;* *ḥry-tp ꜥꜣ m pr-nsw;* *ḥry-tp n pr-dwꜣyt;* *ỉmy-r ꜥb ỉmy-r wḥmt ỉmy-r šwt;* *ỉmy-r nfrw ꞽImn;* *ṯꜣy ḫw ḥr ỉmn n nsw;* *[ỉmy-r ḥmwt] nbt nt nsw,* *ỉry-pꜥt ḥꜣty-ꜥ;*		Kampp 1996: 248-251; PM I: 87-91; Säve-Söderbergh 1957: Pl. XLIV, XLVII, LII, LV, LVII, LX; Urk. IV: 1906-1907;	32.61291	25.73233
49	18	Ay	Neferhotep	Temple admin (Amun)	Chief Scribe of Amun; Overseer of the Oxen and Heifers of Amun;	*sš wr n ꞽImn;* *ỉmy-r ỉwꜣ ỉmy-r nfrwt n ꞽImn;*	Shared courtyard with TT187, TT362 and TT363	Davies 1933: Pl. XXXVII; Desroches-Noblecourt 1985; Kampp 1996: 251-254; PM I: 91-95;	32.61334	25.73309

TT	Dynasty	Reign (Kampp)	Tomb Owner	Occupation	Title	Transliteration	Connected tombs / Notes	References	GPS co-ordinates	
									X	Y
105	20	Dyn 20	Khaemopet	Priesthood (Amun)	Priest of the Noble Ram-sceptre of Amun;	*ḥm-nṯr (sr ?) šps n ꞽImn;*	Shared courtyard with TT106 and TT107	Gardiner and Weigall 1913: 26; Kampp 1996: 380-381; PM I: 218-219;	32.60977	25.7326
106	19	SI/RII	Paser	General admin, royal admin & priesthood (Amun & Neith)	Governor of the Town and Vizier (of the town); Mouth of Nekhen; Fan-bearer on the Right of the King; Festival Leader of Amun; Overseer of Overseers of the Lord of the Two Lands; sab; Supreme Judge; High Priest of the Great of Magic; Priest of Maat; wab priest; Overseer of Chamberlains; Hereditary Prince and Mayor;	*imy-r niwt ṯꜣty (n niwt); r nḫn; ṯꜣw ḫw ḥr imnt n nsw; sšmw ḥb n ꞽImn; imy-r imyw n nb tꜣwy; sꜣb; sꜣb tꜣyty; ḥm-nṯr tpy n wrt ḥkꜣw; ḥm-nṯr Mꜣꜥt; wꜥb ; imy-r imy-ḫnwt; iry-pꜥt ḥꜣty-ꜥ;*	Shared courtyard with TT105 and TT107.	Kampp 1996: 382-385; KRI I: 285-301; KRI III: 1-9; KRI VII:16-18; PM I: 219-224; Säve-Söderbergh 1957: 11-21;	32.60971	25.7327
107	18	AIII	Nefersekheru	Royal admin & temple admin (Amun)	Royal Scribe, Steward of the Estate of Neb-maat-re (=AIII) 'Re is Gleaming'; Scribe of the Offering Table; Royal Seal-bearer; Steward of the Estate of 'The Sun-disc Gleams'; Overseer of the Granaries of Amun; Overseer of the Cattle of Amun; Overseer of the Works of the Great Nile Flood; Attendant of the Sovereign in his House; Hereditary Prince to the Limits of the Hall; Hereditary Prince and Mayor; Mayor in the Great House (=UE shrine); Controller of the Double Throne (in the Office of the first Sed Festival); Vigilant Director Sole Companion; King's Follower on all Foreign Lands;	*sš-nsw; imy-r pr n pr (nb-mꜣꜥt-Rꜥ) rꜥ-ṯḥn, sš wdḥw; ḫtmty bity; imy-r pr n itn ṯḥn, imy-r šnwty n ꞽImn, ꞽImy-r iḥw n ꞽImn; ꞽImy-r kꜣt m ḥꜥpy ꜥꜣ; iry-rdwy ity m pr=f; iry-pꜥt r-ḏrw wsḫt; iry-pꜥt ḥꜣty-ꜥ; ḥꜣty-ꜥ m pr-wr; ḫrp nsty (m iꜣt ḥb-sd tpy); ḫrp rs-tp; smr wꜥty; šmsw nsw ḥr ḫꜣswt nbt;*	Shared courtyard with TT105 and TT106	Kampp 1996: 386-387; LD III: 251-252; PM I: 224-225; Urk. IV: 1881-1883;	32.60987	25.73271
108	18	TIV	Nebseny	Priesthood (Onuris)	High Priest of Onuris (Inheret);	*ḥm-nṯr tpy n ꞽIn-ḥrt;*		Gardiner and Weigall 1913: 26; Kampp 1996: 387-388; PM I: 225-226;	32.61073	25.73242

TT	Dynasty	Reign (Kampp)	Tomb Owner	Occupation	Title	Transliteration	Connected tombs / Notes	References	GPS co-ordinates	
									X	Y
109	18	TIII/(AII)	Min	Local admin, priesthood (Onuris) & royal admin	Mayor (of Thinis); Mayor of the Oasis; Overseer of the Priests of Onuris; Steward of Onuris; Overseer of the Priests of Osiris; Festival Leader of Osiris; Overseer of the Expedition to the Western River; Nurse of Amenhotep (=AII); Royal Seal-bearer; Chief Overseer of UE; Vigilant Director of the Lord of the Two Lands; Director of the Secret Works of the neshmet-bark; Scribe; Great Companion; Hereditary Prince and Mayor;	*ḥ3ty-ʿ n ṯny;* *ḥ3ty-ʿ wḥ3t;* *imy-r ḥmw-nṯr (n in-ḥrt);* *imy-r pr n in-ḥrt;* *imy-r ḥmw nṯr n Wsir;* *sšmw ḥb n Wsir;* *imy-r mšʿ itrw imnty;* *mnʿy n s3-nsw ʾImn-ḥtp;* *ḫtmty bity;* *ḥry-tp imy-r šmʿw;* *ḫrp rs-tp n nb t3wy;* *ḫrp k3t sšt3 m nšmt;* *sš;* *smr ʿ3;* *iry-pʿt ḥ3ty-ʿ;*		Kampp 1996: 389-390; PM I: 226-227; Urk. IV: 976-982;	32.61015	25.73281
110	18	Hat/TIII	Djehuty	Royal admin & temple admin (Amun)	Royal Butler; Offerer (Maker of Offerings?) of Amun;	*wb3-nsw;* *wdnw n ʾImn;*		Engelmann von-Carnap 1995: 122; Gardiner and Weigall 1913: 26; Kampp 1996: 390-392; PM I: 227-228;	32.61072	25.73277
112	18 & 19/20	TIII/AII & Ram (Dyn 20?)	(1)Menkheper-resoneb (TT86) (2) Aashefytemwaset	(1) Priesthood (Amun) & royal admin (2) Priesthood (Amun)	(1) High Priest of Amun; Overseer of the Priests of U and LE; Head Divine Father of Amun; Royal Seal-bearer; Sole Companion; Hereditary Prince and Mayor; (2) wab Priest of Amun 'Great of Majesty';	*(1) ḥm-nṯr tpy n ʾImn;* *ʾImy-r ḥmw-nṯr nw šmʿw mḥw;* *it-nṯr tpy n ʾImn;* *ḫtmty bity;* *smr wʿty;* *iry-pʿt ḥ3ty-ʿ;* *(2) wʿb n ʾImn ʿ3 šsty?*	(1) Owns TT86	Davies and Gardiner 1933: Pl. XIX; Dorman 1995: 152; Kampp 1996: 392-394; PM I: 229-230;	32.61086	25.73281
113	20	RVIII	Kynebu	Priesthood (Amun & AII)	wab priest; Chief of Secrets (of Amun)/ (of the Estate of Amun); Priest in the Temple of Aa-kheperu-ra (=AII); Lector Priest; sem Priest in the Temple of Aa-khepru-ra (=AII);	*wʿb* *ḥry sšt3 (n ʾImn) /(n pr ʾImn;* *ḥm-nṯr m t3 ḥwt ʿ3-ḫprw-rʿ;* *ḥry ḥbt;* *stm m ḥwt nsw ʿ3-ḫprw-rʿ;*		Kampp 1996: 394-395; KRI VI: 441-446; PM I: 230-231;	32.61013	25.73229

TT	Dynasty	Reign (Kampp)	Tomb Owner	Occupation	Title	Transliteration	Connected tombs / Notes	References	GPS co-ordinates	
									X	Y
172	18	TIII/AII	Montuywy	Royal admin	Royal Butler; Royal Seal-bearer; Hereditary Prince; Sole Companion; Child of the Nursery;	*wbꜣ-nsw,* *ḫtmty bity;* *iry-pꜥt;* *smr wꜥty;* *ḫrd kꜣp;*		Gardiner and Weigall 1913: 32; Kampp 1996: 459-461; PM I: 279-280; Urk. IV: 1466-1468;	32.61181	25.73313
173	19	Dyn 19	Khay	Temple admin	Scribe of the Divine Offerings of all the Gods of Thebes;	*sš ḥtp-nṯr n nṯrw nbw Wꜣst;*		Gardiner and Weigall 1913: 32; Kampp 1996: 461; PM I: 281;	32.6115	25.73226
174	18 & 20	Dyn 18 & 20	(1) ? (2) Aashaket	(1) ? (2) Priesthood (Mut)	(1) ? (2) wab Priest in front of Mut;	*(1)* *(2)wꜥb n ḥꜣt n Mwt;*	Son owns TT187	Gardiner and Weigall 1913: 32; Kampp 1996: 461-462; PM I: 281;	32.61141	25.7327
175	18	TIV/AIII	Unknown		Unknown	*?*		Gardiner and Weigall 1913: 32; Kampp 1996: 462-464; PM I: 281;	32.61137	25.73233
176	18	AII/TIV	Amenuserhet		Servant, Clean of Hands;	*sḏm ꜥš wꜥb ꜥwy;*	Connected to TT177	Gardiner and Weigall 1913: 32; Kampp 1996: 464; PM I: 281-283;	32.61132	25.73211
177	19	RII- end Dyn 19	Amenemopet	Temple admin (Amun-Ramesseum) & priesthood (Amun-Ramesseum)	True Scribe in the Temple of User-maat-re Setep-en-re (=Ramesseum) in the Estate of Amun; wab Priest; Lector Priest (of Amun (in the Temple of User-maat-re Setep-en-re)) =Ramesseum;	*sš mꜣꜥt m t(ꜣ) ḥwt wsr-mꜣꜥt-Rꜥ stp-n-Rꜥ m pr ꞽImn;* *wꜥb;* *ḫry-ḥbt (n ꞽImn (m t(ꜣ) ḥwt Wsr-mꜣꜥt-rꜥ stp-n-rꜥ));*	Connected to TT176	Kampp 1996: 464-465; KRI III: 357-358; PM I: 283;	32.61133	25.73204
178	19	RII	Neferrenopet called Kenro	Temple admin (Amun(-Re) & priesthood	Scribe of the (Double) House of Silver (=Treasury) in/of the Estate of Amun-Re, King of the Gods; Scribe of the Divine Treasury [of] the Estate of Amun; Scribe of Divine Offerings (of the Estate of Amun); Scribe of the Mansion of Gold of Amun; wab Priest;	*sš pr(wy)-ḥḏ m/n pr ꞽImn-Rꜥ nsw-nṯrw;* *sš ḫtmt nṯr [n] pr ꞽImn;* *sš ḥtp[w]-nṯr (n pr ꞽImn);* *sš ḥwt-nbw n ꞽImn;* *wꜥb;*	Shared courtyard with TT295, TT296 & TT365	Kampp 1996: 465-466; KRI III: 321-331; PM I: 283-285;	32.61213	25.73234
179	18	Hat	Nebamun	Temple admin (Amun)	Scribe; Counter of Grain in the Granary of the Divine Offerings of Amun;	*sš;* *ḥsb it n šnwt nt ḥtp-nṯr n ꞽImn;*	Connected to TT180	Gardiner and Weigall 1913: 32; Kampp 1996: 466; PM I: 285-286;	32.6124	25.73241

TT	Dynasty	Reign (Kampp)	Tomb Owner	Occupation	Title	Transliteration	Connected tombs / Notes	References	GPS co-ordinates	
									X	Y
180	19/20	(Dyn 19/) Ram	Unknown		Unknown	?	Connected to TT179	Gardiner and Weigall 1913: 32; Kampp 1996: 466; PM I: 286;	32.61242	25.73241
181	18	AIII/AIV	(1)Nebamun and (2)Ipuky	(1&2) Royal admin & craftsman	(1) Chief Sculptor of the Lord of the Two Lands, Guardian of the Secret Place of Herihermeru; Keeper of the Balance in the Holy Place; Child of the Nursery; (2) Sculptor of the Lord of the Two Lands; Guardian of the Holy Place; Keeper of the Balance of the Lord of the Two Lands;	*(1) ḥry ṯȝy-mḏȝt (n) nb tȝwy;* *sȝwty n tȝ st sštȝ(t) m ḥr-ḥr-mr;* *iry mḫȝt m st ḏsrt;* *ḫrd n kȝp;* *(2) ṯȝy mḏȝt n nb-tȝwy;* *sȝwty n tȝ st ḏsrt;* *iry mḫȝt n nb tȝwy;*		Davies 1925: Pl. V, VIII, XV, XVII, XIX; Kampp 1996: 467-469; PM I: 286-289; Urk. IV: 1854-1855;	32.61209	25.73264
182	18	TIII	Amenemhet	General admin	Scribe of the Mat;	*sš n tmȝ;*		Gardiner and Weigall 1913: 32; Kampp 1996: 470-471; PM I: 289;	32.61238	25.73224
183	19	RII	Nebsumenu	Royal admin, priesthood (Amun) & temple admin (Amun(-Ra) & Re-Atum)	Chief Steward of the Lord of the Two Lands (in the Southern City); Chief Steward of Thebes; (True) Royal scribe; Chamberlain; Festival Leader of Amun; Festival Leader of the lords of Thebes; Overseer of the Double House of Silver of Amun (-Ra); Divine Father of Re-Atum;	*imy-r pr wr n nb tȝwy (m niwt rsyt);* *imy-r pr wr n Wȝst;* *sš nsw (mȝʿ);* *imy-ḫnt;* *sšmw ḥb n ʾImn;* *sšmw ḥb n nbw Wȝst;* *imy-r prwy ḥḏ n ʾImn (-rȝ);* *it nṯr n rʿ-itm;*	Brother owns TT385	Kampp 1996: 471-474; KRI III: 182-185; KRI VII: 114: 14; PM I: 289-290;	32.61274	25.73229
184	19	RII	Nefermenu	Local admin, royal admin & temple admin (AI & Amun)	Mayor in/of the Southern City; Royal Scribe; Chief Steward of the Temple of Djoser-k-are (AI); Overseer of the Granar(y/ies) of Amun;	*ḥȝty-ʿ m/n niwt rsyt;* *sš-nsw;* *imy-r pr wr n tȝ ḥwt ḏsr-kȝ-rʿ;* *imy-r šnwt(y) n ʾImn;*	Connected to TT412	Kampp 1996: 474-475; KRI III: 162-163; PM I: 290-291;	32.61278	25.73252
185	FIP		Senyiker	Temple admin	See Appendix 1			See Appendix 1	32.61282	25.73265
186	OK-FIP	Dyn 6?	Iky	Local admin, royal admin, general admin & priesthood	See Appendix 1			See Appendix 1	32.6132	25.73255

TT	Dynasty	Reign (Kampp)	Tomb Owner	Occupation	Title	Transliteration	Connected tombs / Notes	References	GPS co-ordinates	
									X	Y
187	19 & 20		(1) ? (2) Pakhyhet	(1) Priesthood & royal admin (2) Priesthood (Amun)	(1) High Priest; Royal Scribe; (2) wab Priest of Amun;	*(1) ḥm-nṯr tpy; sš nsw; (2) wʿb n ʾImn;*	Shared courtyard with TT49, TT362 and TT363. Father owns TT174	Davies 1933: 7, fig. 1; Gardiner and Weigall 1913: 32; Kampp 1996: 475; PM I: 293;	32.61337	25.73314
198	19/20	Ram	Rayia	Temple admin (Amun)	Chief of the Storehouse of Amun in Karnak;	*ḥry šnʿt n ʾImn m ipt-swt;*		Gardiner and Weigall 1913: 34; Kampp 1996: 485; PM I:303;	32.61115	25.73329
199	18	Dyn 18	Amenirnefer	General admin	Overseer of the Storehouse;	*imy-r šnʿw;*		Gardiner and Weigall 1913: 34; Kampp 1996: 485; PM I: 303;	32.61128	25.73318
200	18	TIII/AII	Dedi	Local admin, temple admin (Amun)& military	Overseer of the Deserts on the West of Thebes; Overseer of the Deserts on the West (of the town) (=Thebes); Captain of the neshmet bark 'Beloved of Amun'; Chief of the Regiment of Pharaoh; Chief of the Medjay (=Police); Standard-bearer of the Regiment of his Majesty;	*ʾImy-r ḫ3swt (ḥr)ʾImntt W3st; ʾImy-r ḫ3swt ḥr ʾImntt (niwt); w3ʿw n nšmt mry ʾImn; ḥry n p3 s3 n pr 3ʿ; ḥry mḏ3w; ṯ3y sryt n s3 n ḥm=f;*		Kampp 1996: 485-487; PM I: 303-304; Urk. IV: 995- 996;	32.6112	25.73303
201	18	TIV/AIII	Re	Royal admin	1st Royal Herald (of the Lord of the Two Lands);	*wḥm-nsw tpy (n nb t3wy);*		Kampp 1996: 487-488; PM I: 304-305; Urk. IV: 1640: 14;	32.61144	25.73316
202	20	Dyn 20	Nakhtamun	Priesthood (Ptah & Amun)	Priest of Ptah, Lord of Thebes; wab Priest in Front of Amun;	*ḥm-nṯr n ptḥ nb W3st; wʿb n ḥ3t ʾImn;*		Gardiner and Weigall 1913: 34; Kampp 1996: 488-489; PM I: 305;	32.61193	25.73329
203	18 & 19	Dyn 18 & RII	(1) ? (2) Wennefer	(1) ? (2) Priesthood (Mut)	(1)? (2) Divine Father (of Mut); Divine Father of the Lords of Thebes; Chief of Secrets of Mut;	*(1) ? (2) it-nṯr (n Mwt); it-nṯr n nbw w3st; ḥry sšt3 Mwt;*		KRI III: 301: 5-8; Kampp 1996: 489-490; PM I: 305;	32.61167	25.73316
204	18	Dyn 18	Nebanensu	Temple admin (Amun)	[Sailor of the High Priest] of Amun;	*[sḳd n ḥm-nṯr tpy] n ʾImn;*		Gardiner and Weigall 1913: 34; Kampp 1996: 490; PM I: 305;	32.61252	25.73281

TT	Dynasty	Reign (Kampp)	Tomb Owner	Occupation	Title	Transliteration	Connected tombs / Notes	References	GPS co-ordinates	
									X	Y
205	18	TIII/AII	Djehutymose	Royal admin	Royal Butler;	*wbꜣ-nsw;*		Gardiner and Weigall 1913: 34; Kampp 1996: 491; PM I: 305;	32.61266	25.73278
206	20	(Dyn 19)/ 20	Inpuemheb	Scribe (PoT)	Scribe in the Place of Truth;	*sš m st-mꜣꜥt;*		Davies 1999: 90; Kampp 1996: 491-492; KRI IV: 179: 14; PM I: 305-306;	32.6128	25.73282
207	20	RIII	Horemheb	Temple admin (Amun)	Scribe of the Divine Offerings of Amun;	*sš ḥtp-nṯr n ꞽImn;*		Gardiner and Weigall 1913: 34; Kampp 1996: 492-494; PM I: 306;	32.6122	25.73342
208	20	(Dyn 19)/ 20	Roma	Priesthood (Amun-Ra)	Divine Father of Amun-Re;	*it-nṯr n ꞽImn-Rꜥ;*		Gardiner and Weigall 1913: 34; Kampp 1996: 494; PM I: 306;	32.61241	25.73337
238	18	AII	Neferweben	Royal admin	Royal Butler, Clean of Hands;	*wbꜣ-nsw wꜥb-ꜥwy;*		Gardiner and Weigall 1913: 36; Kampp 1996: 515-516; PM I: 330;	32.61247	25.73288
241	18	Hat/TIII	Ahmose	Temple admin & priesthood	Scribe of the Divine Writings; Chief of Mysteries (in) the House of the Morning (=Robing Room); Child of the Nursery;	*šs mḏꜣt-nṯr;* *ḥry sštꜣ pr dwꜣt;* *ẖrd n kꜣp;*		Engelmann von-Carnap 1995: 122; Kampp 1996: 517-519; PM I: 331-332;	32.61275	25.73262
245	19	(Dyn 18)/ 19	Hor	Royal admin	Scribe; Steward of the Royal Wife;	*sš;* *imy-r pr n ḥmt-nsw;*	Shared courtyard with TT246, TT247, TT248 and TT258	Gardiner and Weigall 1913: 36; Kampp 1996: 520-521; PM I: 333;	32.61173	25.73209
246	18	(Hat)/ TIII	Senenre	General admin	Scribe;	*sš;*	Shared courtyard with TT245,TT247, TT248 and TT258	Gardiner and Weigall 1913: 36; Kampp 1996: 521-522; PM I: 333;	32.6117	25.73212
247	18	TIV/AIII	Samut	Temple admin (Amun)	Scribe; Counter of the Cattle of Amun;	*sš;* *ḥsb iḥw n ꞽImn;*	Shared courtyard with TT245, TT246, TT248 and TT258	Gardiner and Weigall 1913: 36; Kampp 1996: 522-523; PM I: 333;	32.61176	25.7321

TT	Dynasty	Reign (Kampp)	Tomb Owner	Occupation	Title	Transliteration	Connected tombs / Notes	References	GPS co-ordinates	
									X	Y
248	18	(TIII)/ AII	Djehutymose	Temple admin (TIII),	Offerer (Maker of Offerings?) of Men-kheper-re (=TIII);	*wdnw n Mn-ḫpr-rʿ;*	Shared courtyard with TT245, TT246, TT247 and TT258	Kampp 1996: 523-524; PM I: 335; Urk. IV: 1642: 5;	32.6118	25.73216
253	18	AIII	Khnummose	Temple admin (Amun)	Scribe; Counter of Grain in the Granary of Amun; Counter of Grain in the Granary of Divine Offerings;	*sš;* *ḥsb it m šnwty n ꞽImn;* *ḥsb it n šnwt nt ḥtp-nṯr;*	Shared courtyard with TT254 and TT294	Engelbach 1924: 18; Kampp 1996: 530; PM I: 337-338; Strudwick 1996: 24;	32.61194	25.73252
254	18	Tut-Ay	Mose	General admin & royal / temple admin	Scribe of the House of Silver (=Treasury); Keeper/Custodian of the Estate of Tiye in the Estate of Amun;	*sš pr-ḥḏ;* *iry pr tiy m pr-ꞽImn*	Shared courtyard with TT253 and TT294	Engelbach 1924: 18; Kampp 1996: 530-532; PM I: 338-339; Strudwick 1996: 57;	32.61189	25.73252
256	18	TIII/AII	Nebenkemet	Royal admin & military	Fan-bearer; Chief of the Stable; Follower of his Lord on his Expeditions on Water, on Land, and in all Foreign Countries; Hereditary Prince, Mayor; Child of the Nursery;	*ṯꜣy ḫw;* *ḥry iḥw;* *šmsw nb=f r iwt=f ḥr mw ḥr tꜣ ḥr ḫꜣswt nbt;* *iry-pʿt, ḥꜣty-ʿ;* *ḫrd n kꜣp;*	Connected to TT257	Kampp 1996: 533-535; LD III: 249; PM I: 340-341; Urk. IV: 997:3-8;	32.6115	25.73252
257	18 & 20	AIII-AIV & Dyn 20	(1)Neferhotep (2)Mahu	(1) Temple admin (Amun) (2) Temple admin (Amun)	(1) Scribe; Counter of the Grain of Amun; (2) Deputy in the Temple of User-maat-re Setep-en-re in the Estate of Amun on the West of Thebes (=Ramesseum); Scribe of Divine Offerings of the Lords of Thebes;	*(1) sš;* *ḥsb it n ꞽImn;* *(2)* *idnw n tꜣ ḥwt Wsr-mꜣʿt-rʿ stp-n-rʿ m pr ꞽImn-Rʿ ḥr ꞽImntt Wꜣst;* *sš ḥtp-nṯr n nbw Wꜣst;*	Connected to TT256	Engelbach 1924: 18; Kampp 1996: 535-536; KRI III: 377: 15-16; LD III: 250; PM I: 341-342;	32.61159	25.73249
258	18	TIV	Menkheper	Royal admin	Royal Scribe of the House of the Royal Children; Child of the Nursery;	*ḫrd n kꜣp,* *sš-nsw n pr ms(w) nsw;*	Shared courtyard with TT245, TT246, TT247 and TT248	Kampp 1996: 536; PM I: 342; Urk. IV: 1642-1643;	32.61179	25.73212
264	19	RII/ Mer	Ipy	General admin	Overseer of Cattle; Great One of the Lord of the Two Lands;	*imy-r iḥw;* *wr n nb tꜣwy;*		Engelbach 1924: 18; Kampp 1996: 541-542; PM I: 345;	32.61122	25.7327
294	18 & 19/20	TIII/AIII & Ram	(1) Amenhotep / Sen-djehuty (2) Roma	(1) Temple admin (Amun) (2) Priesthood (Amun)	(1) Overseer of the Granaries of Amun; (2) wab Priest of Amun;	*(1) imy-r šnwty n ꞽImn;* *(2) wʿb n ꞽImn;*	Shared courtyard with TT253 and TT254	Kampp 1996: 563-564; PM I: 376; Strudwick 1996: 8;	32.61192	25.73263

TT	Dynasty	Reign (Kampp)	Tomb Owner	Occupation	Title	Transliteration	Connected tombs / Notes	References	GPS co-ordinates	
									X	Y
295	18	TIV/ AIII	Djehutymose called Paroy	Royal admin, general admin, & priesthood (Anubis)	Chief of Secrets in the chest of Anubis; Chief in/of the Chest of Anubis; Chief of Secrets in the Place of Embalmment; sem Priest (in the Place of Embalmment); Scribe; Embalmer; Hereditary Prince, Mayor; Great Companion; Seal-bearer of the King of LE; Royal Scribe; Follower of the King...; Chief of the Library; Overseer of the Western House;	*ḥry sštȝ m hn inpw;* *ḥry-tp m/n hn ꞽInpw;* *ḥry sštȝ m pr-nfr;* *sm (m pr-nfr);* *sš; wt;* *iry-pꜥt, ḥȝty-ꜥ;* *smr ꜥȝ;* *ḫtmty-bity;* *sš nsw;* *šmsw nsw...;* *ḥry-tp m pr-mḏȝt;* *imy-r pr-imnt;*	Shared entrance through TT296 into 295; Shared courtyard TT178, TT295, TT296 & TT365	Hegazy and Tosi 1983: Pls. 2-7, 10; Kampp 1996: 564-565; PM I: 376-377;	32.61201	25.7324
296	19	RII	Nefersekheru	Temple admin & royal admin	Scribe of the Divine Offerings of all the Gods of Thebes; Deputy of the Treasury (of the Lord of the Two Lands in the (Southern) City); Scribe of the Treasury of the Lord of the Two Lands; Royal Scribe (of the Lord of the Two Lands);	*šs ḥtp-nṯr n nṯrw nbw wȝst;* *idnw n pr(.wy)-ḥḏ (n nb tȝwy m niwt (rsyt));* *sš n pr(.wy) ḥḏ n nb tȝwy;* *sš nsw (n nb tȝwy);*	Shared entrance through TT296 into 295; Shared courtyard TT178, TT295, TT296 and 365	Kampp 1996: 565-567; KRI VII: 145-153; PM I: 377-379;	32.61206	25.73237
297	18	Early Dyn 18	Amenemopet called Thanefer	Temple admin (Amun)	Scribe, Counter of the Grain of Amun; Overseer of the Fields [of Amun];	*sš, ḥsb it n ꞽImn;* *imy-r ȝḥt [n ꞽImn];*		Kampp 1996: 567-568; PM I: 379; Strudwick 2003: 31, Fig. 10.	32.61175	25.73355
351	19-20	Ram	Aabau	Military	Scribe of Horses;	*sš ssmwt;*		Fakhry 1947: 42; Kampp 1996: 588; PM I: 417;	32.61037	25.73266
352	19-20	Ram (after Mer)	Unknown	Temple admin (Amun)	Overseer of the Granary of Amun;	*imy-r šnwt n ꞽImn;*		Fakhry 1947: 42; Kampp 1996: 588; PM I: 417;	32.6104	25.73266
362	20	Dyn 20	Paanemwaset	Priesthood (Amun)	wab Priest of Amun;	*wꜥb n ꞽImn;*	Shared courtyard with TT49, TT187 and TT363	Kampp 1996: 589; PM I: 426;	32.61335	25.73304
363	20	Dyn 20	Paraemhab	Temple admin (Amun)	Chief of the Singers of Amun;	*ḥry ḥsw n ꞽImn;*	Shared courtyard with TT49, TT187 and TT362	Fakhry 1947: 44; Kampp 1996: 589; PM I: 427;	32.61338	25.73301

TT	Dynasty	Reign (Kampp)	Tomb Owner	Occupation	Title	Transliteration	Connected tombs / Notes	References	GPS co-ordinates	
									X	Y
365	18	TIII	Nefermenu	Temple admin (Amun)	Chief of the Hairdressers? of Amun in Karnak; Scribe of the House of Silver (=Treasury) of Amun;	*ḥry nbdw? n ʾImn n ỉpt-swt;* *sš pr-ḥḏ n ʾImn;*	Shared courtyard TT178, TT295, TT296 and TT365	Fakhry 1947: 44; Kampp 1996: 591; PM I: 427;	32.61212	25.7324
369	19	RII/(Dyn 19)	Khaemwaset	Priesthood (Ptah & Amun)	High Priest of Ptah; 2nd Priest of Amun; 4th Priest of Amun;	*ḥm-nṯr tpy n ptḥ;* *ḥm-nṯr 2 n ʾImn;* *ḥm-nṯr 4 n ʾImn;*		Holthoer 1984: 73-76, 84-85; Kampp 1996: 594; KRI VII: 158-159; PM I: 432;	32.61174	25.73254
370	19	RII/ Mer	Nebneshem	Royal admin & temple admin	Royal Scribe; Noble of the Estate of Amun; Overseer of [...] of Amun;	*sš-nsw;* *šps n pr ʾImn;* *ỉmy-r [?] n ʾImn;*		Holthoer 1984: 76-80, 86-89; Kampp 1996: 594-595; KRI VII: 159-160; PM I: 432;	32.61173	25.73266
371	19-20	Ram	Unknown		Unknown	?		Kamp, 1996: 595; PM I: 432;	32.61165	25.73265
372	20	RIII/RIV	Amenkhau	Temple admin	Overseer of Craftsmen of the Temple; Overseer of Craftsmen of the Temple of Millions of Years of the King of U and LE User-maat-re Mery-amun in the Estate of Amun on the West of Thebes (Medinet Habu);	*ỉmy-r ḥmww(tyw) m ḥwt-nsw;* *ỉmy-r ḥmww(tyw) n tꜣ ḥwt nt ḥḥ m rnpwt nsw bity Wsr-Mꜣʿt-Re Mry-ʾImn m pr ʾImn ḥr ỉmntt wꜣst;*		Kampp 1996: 595; KRI V: 419-420; PM I: 432-433;	32.61179	25.73257
373	19	RII	Amenmessu	Royal admin	(Royal) Scribe of the Offering Table (of the Lord of the Two Lands);	*sš (nsw) wdḥw (n nb tꜣwy);*		Kampp 1996: 595-596; KRI III: 216-218; KRI VII: 120-122; PM I: 433-434;	32.61306	25.73325
405	FIP		Khenti	Royal, local admin & priesthood	See Appendix 1			See Appendix 1	32.61317	25.73254
412	18	Hat/TIII	Kenamun	Royal admin	Royal Scribe;	*sš-nsw;*		Kampp 1996: 613-614; Saleh 1983; 15;	32.6127	25.73249
413	FIP		Ankhunas/ Unasankh	Royal admin, local admin, general admin & priesthood?	See Appendix 1			See Appendix 1	32.61262	25.73245

Appendix 10: Outlying Tomb Owners in el-Khokha

TT	Dyn	Reign (Kampp)	Tomb Owner	Occupation	Title	Transliteration	Connected Tombs / Notes	References	GPS co-ordinates	
									X	Y
170	19	RII- end Dyn 19	Nebmekhyt	Military & temple admin (Ramesseum)	Scribe of the Recruits of the Temple of User-maat-re Setep-en-re in the Estate of Amun (=Ramesseum);	*sš nfrw ḥwt wsr-mꜣꜥt-Rꜥ-stp-n-Rꜥ m pr ꞽImn*		Kampp 1996: 458-459; PM I: 279;	32.61194	25.73116
171	18	Dyn 18	Unknown		Unknown	?		Kampp 1996: 459; PM I: 279;	32.61194	25.73115

Appendix 11: Tomb Owners in Upper Qurna

TT	Dynasty	Reign (Kampp)	Tomb Owner	Occupation	Title	Transliteration	Connected tombs / Notes	References	GPS co-ordinates	
									X	Y
21	18	TI/Hat/ (TIII)	User	Royal admin (TI) & general admin	Scribe; (Chief) Steward of Aakheperkare (=TI); Hereditary Prince and Mayor;	*sš;* *ỉmy-r pr (wr) n ꜥꜣ-ḫpr-kꜣ-Rꜥ;* *ỉry-pꜥt ḥꜣty-ꜥ;*		Davies 1913: Pl. XIX; Kampp 1996: 203-205; PM I: 35-37; Urk. IV: 1497-1499;	32.60918	25.73292
29	18	(TIII)/ AII	Amenemopet called Pairi	General admin, priesthood (Maat), royal admin & local admin	Governor of the Town and Vizier, Priest of Maat; Divine Father; Sem priest; Mouth of Nekhen; Spokesman Who Makes Peace in the Entire Land; Chief of the Entire Land; Controller of Kilts; Royal Dignitary; Hereditary Prince and Mayor; Sole Companion;	*ỉmy-r nỉwt, ṯꜣty,* *ḥm-nṯr Mꜣꜥt;* *ỉt-nṯr;* *r nḫn;* *sm;* *r shrr m tꜣ r-ḏr=f;* *ḥry-tp n tꜣ r-ḏr=f;* *ḫrp šnḏwt;* *sꜥḥ nsw;* *ỉry-pꜥt ḥꜣty-ꜥ; smr wꜥty;*	Owner of KV48; son of TT224; brother of TT96	Kampp 1996: 214-215; PM I: 45-46; Urk. IV: 1439-1440;	32.60688	25.73125
43	18	AII/TIV	Neferrenpet	Royal admin	Overseer of the Storehouse of the Lord of the Two Lands	*ỉmy-r st n nb tꜣwy*		Gardiner and Weigall 1913: 20; Kampp 1996: 240; PM I: 83-84;	32.60913	25.73303
46	17/18 & 18	End Dyn 17/18 & AIII/AIV	(1) ? (2) Ramose	(1) ? (2) Royal admin, temple admin & general admin	(1) ? (2) Steward of the Temple of the Aten; True Royal Scribe; Overseer of the Granaries of U & LE; Fanbearer at the Right of the King; Hereditary Prince and Noble;	*ỉmy-r pr n tꜣ ḥwt pꜣ ỉtn;* *sš-nsw mꜣꜥ;* *ỉmy-r šnwty šmꜥw mḥw;* *ṯꜣw ḫw ḥr ỉmnt n nsw;* *ỉry-pꜥt ḥꜣty-ꜥ;*		Kampp 1996: 244-246; PM I: 86-87; Urk. IV: 1995: 10-14;	32.60811	25.73204
54	18 & 19	end AIII & RII	(1) Huy (2) Kenro	(1) Temple craftsman (Amun) (2) Priesthood & temple admin (Khonsu)	(1) Sculptor of Amun; (2) Chief of the Storehouse of Khonsu; wab priest;	*(1) ṯꜣy mḏꜣt n ỉmn;* *(2) ḥry šnꜥw n ḫnsw;* *wꜥb ;*		Gardiner and Weigall 1913: 20; Kampp 1996: 260-262; PM I: 104-105;	32.60841	25.73158
58	18 & 19 & 20	AIII & Dyn 19 & Dyn 20	(1)Unknown (2) Amenhotep (3) son -Amenemonet	(1)? (2) ? (3) Priesthood (Amun) & Temple admin (RII, Amun , Mut)	(1) Unknown (2) Unknown (3) Overseer of the Priests of Amun – HPA; Scribe (in) the Temple of Ramesses 'Beloved like Amun' (Abu Simbel); Temple Scribe in the Temple of Ramesses 'Beloved like Amun'; Scribe of the Divine Offerings of Amun; Scribe of the Temple of Mut;	*(1) ?* *(2) ?* *(3) ỉmy-r ḥmw-nṯr n ỉmn;* *sš (m) ḥwt-nṯr Rꜥ-ms-sw mr mỉ ỉmn;* *sš ḥwt-nṯr n tꜣ ḥwt Rꜥ-ms-sw mr mỉ ỉmn;* *sš ḥtp(w)-nṯr n ỉmn;* *sš ḥwt-nṯr n Mwt;*		Gardiner and Weigall 1913: 20; Kampp 1996: 269-272; KRI III: 346-347; PM I: 119-120;	32.60834	25.73237

TT	Dynasty	Reign (Kampp)	Tomb Owner	Occupation	Title	Transliteration	Connected tombs / Notes	References	GPS co-ordinates	
									X	Y
59	18	TIII	Ken	Priesthood (Mut)	High Priest of Mut, lady of Asher;	*ḥm-nṯr tpy n Mwt nbt Ỉšrw;*		Gardiner and Weigall 1913: 20; Kampp 1996: 272-275; PM I: 120-121;	32.6079	25.73237
60	MK		Antefoker (and Sent (mother))	General admin, Royal admin, Local admin & Priesthood (Maat)	See Appendix 2			See Appendix 2	32.60805	25.73245
61	MK & 18	MK & TI/ Hat/TIII	User (TT 131)	(2)General admin, local admin & priesthood (Maat)	(2) Governor of the town and Vizier; Overseer of the 6 Great Temples/Law-courts; Spokesman who Makes Peace in the Entire Land; Priest of Maat; Mouth of Nekhen; Hereditary Prince and Mayor;	(2) *imy-r niwt ṯ3ty;* *imy-r ḥwt wrt T;* *r shrr m nb r-ḏr=f;* *ḥm-nṯr m3ʿt;* *r nḫn;* *iry-pʿt ḥ3ty-ʿ;*	TT83 father; also owns TT131	Kampp 1996: 277-279; LD III: 287; PM I: 123-125; Urk. IV: 1039: 8-10;	32.60827	25.73252
62	18	AII/ TIV	Amenemwaskhet	Royal admin	Overseer of the Audience-chamber (=Chamberlain); Royal Seal-bearer; ...Mayor;	*imy-r ʿḫnwty;* *ḫtmty bity;* *...ḥ3ty-ʿ;*		Kampp 1996: 279-280; PM I: 125; Urk. IV: 1644:5;	32.60859	25.73294
63	18	TIV/ (AIII)	Sobekhotep	General admin, Royal admin, local admin & priesthood (Sobek)	Overseer of the Treasury; Royal Seal-bearer; Mayor of the Southern Lake (and of the Lake of Sobek) - Fayum; Great One of the Fayum; Mayor of Shedet (Fayum); Overseer of the Priests of Sobek of Shedet; Divine Father, Great One in the Palace; Great One in the Palace; Hereditary Prince and Mayor; Sole Companion; Great Companion; Fanbearer on the Right of the King; Eyes of the King;	*imy-r ḫtmt/ḫtmw;* *ḫtmw bity;* *ḥ3ty-ʿ n š rsy (n š n sbk);* *wr m ṯ3-š;* *ḥ3ty-ʿ n šdt;* *Ỉmy-r ḥmw nṯr n sbk šdt;* *it nṯr;* *ʿ3 m pr-nsw;* *wr m ʿḥ;* *iry-pʿt ḥ3ty-ʿ;* *smr wʿty;* *ʿ3 wʿty;* *ṯ3y ḫw ḥr imn n nsw;* *irty n nsw;*		Dziobek and Raziq 1990: Taf. 4b, 5b, 6a, 6b, 8, 14c, 14f, 15a, 22a, 22b, 27, 28, 34a, 34b, 35a, 38 a, 38b, 40a, 40b, 41a; Kampp 1996: 280-283; PM I: 125-128; Urk. IV: 1582-1584;	32.60878	25.73363
64	18	(AII)/ TIV/ (AIII)	Hekerneheh	Royal admin	Nurse/ Tutor of the King's Son Amenhotep (=AIII); Nurse /Tutor of the Royal Children; Hereditary Prince and Mayor; Child of the Nursery; King's Follower in Every Place; Fan-bearer on the Right of the King;	*mnʿy n s3-nsw Ỉmn-ḥtp;* *mnʿy n msw nsw;* *iry-pʿt ḥ3ty-ʿ;* *ḫrd n k3p;* *šmsw nsw m st nbt;* *ṯ3y ḫw ḥr Ỉmn n nsw;*		Kampp 1996: 283-285; LD III: 260-261; PM I: 128-129; Urk. IV: 1572-1574;	32.60876	25.73343

TT	Dynasty	Reign (Kampp)	Tomb Owner	Occupation	Title	Transliteration	Connected tombs / Notes	References	GPS co-ordinates	
									X	Y
65	18 & 20	Hat & RIX	(1) Nebamun (2) Imiseba	(1) Royal admin & general admin (2) Temple admin (Amun (-Ra)) & priesthood	(1) Overseer of the Granary; Royal Scribe of Accounts? in the Presence; (2) Chief Temple Scribe (of the Estate of Amun); Chief of the Altar; Temple Scribe in the Estate of Amun-Ra, King of the Gods; Deputy of the Double House of Silver (=Treasury) of the Estate of Amun in Karnak; wab Priest;	*(1)imy-r šnwty;* *sš-nsw r ꜥn n ḫft-ḥr;* *(2) ḥry sš ḥwt-nṯr (n pr ꞽImn);* *ḥry ḫꜣwt;* *sš ḥwt-nṯr n pr ꞽImn-rꜥ nsw nṯrw;* *ꞽIdnw n pr.wy ḥḏ n pr ꞽImn m ipt-swt;* *wꜥb;*		Gardiner and Weigall , 1913: 22; Kampp 1996: 285-287; KRI VI: 544-553; KRI VII: 373-378; LD III: 255-256; PM I: 129-132;	32.60882	25.73295
66	18	TIV	Hepu	General admin, local admin & priesthood	Vizier, Governor of the Town; Overseer of the Law-courts; Eyes of the King in the Southern City and his Ears in the Districts of LE; Divine Father; Hereditary Prince and Mayor; Spokesman who Makes Peace in the Entire Land; Sole Companion;	*ṯꜣty imy-r niwt;* *imy-r rwyt;* *irty n nsw m niwt šmꜥw ꜥnḫwy=f m spꜣt mḥw,* *it-nṯr,* *iry-pꜥt ḥꜣty-ꜥ;* *r shrr m tꜣ r ḏr=f;* *smr wꜥty;*		Davies 1963: 9-13, Pl. VIII, IX, XI; Kampp 1996: 287-289; PM I: 132-133; Urk. IV: 1576-1577;	32.60886	25.73278
67	18	Hat	Hapusoneb	Priesthood (Amun), Royal admin	High Priest of Amun; Overseer of all Works of the King; Overseer of the Priests of U & LE; 3rd Lector Priest of Amun in Karnak; Royal Seal-bearer; Hereditary Prince and Mayor; Great Companion;	*ḥm-nṯr tpy n ꞽImn;* *imy-r kꜣt nb n nsw;* *imy-r ḥmw-nṯrw nw šmꜥw mḥw;* *ḥry-ḥbt 3 n ꞽImn m ꞽIpt-swt;* *ḫtmty bity;* *iry-pꜥt ḥꜣty-ꜥ;* *smr ꜥꜣ;*	Daughter married TT39 owner	Kampp 1996: 289-292; LD III, 262; PM I: 133; Urk. IV: 488: 7, 489: 11-13;	32.60891	25.73259
68	18 & 20	AIII & Dyn 20 (RIII?)	(1) Meryptah (2)Perenkhnum	(1) Priesthood (Amun) (2) Priesthood (Amun & Mut)	(1) High Priest of Amun; (2)wab priest of Amun of Karnak; wab priest of Mut of Asher;	*(1) ḥm-nṯr tpy n ꞽImn;* *(2) wꜥb n ꞽImn m ipt-swt,* *wꜥb n Mwt m ꞽIšrw;*	Connected to TT227	Kampp 1996: 292-294; PM I: 133-134; Seyfried 1991: 116 & 118;	32.60879	25.7324
69	18	(TIV)/AIII	Menna	General admin, Royal admin & temple admin (Amun)	Scribe of the Arable Lands (fields) of the Lord of the Two Lands of U & LE; Scribe; Overseer of the Arable Land (fields) of the Lord of the Two Lands, Overseer of the Arable Land (fields) of Amun; Overseer of the Ploughed Fields of Amun;	*sš ꜣḥwt n nb-tꜣwy šmꜥw mḥw;* *sš;* *imy-r ꜣḥwt n nb tꜣwy;* *imy-r ꜣḥwt n ꞽImn;* *imy-r ḥbsw n ꞽImn;*		Kampp 1996: 294-297; PM I: 134-139; Urk. IV: 1608-1609;	32.60904	25.73218

TT	Dynasty	Reign (Kampp)	Tomb Owner	Occupation	Title	Transliteration	Connected tombs / Notes	References	GPS co-ordinates	
									X	Y
70	18 & 20/21	Dyn 18 & 20/21	(1) Unknown (2) Amenmose	(1) Unknown (2) Temple admin (Amun)	(1) Unknown (2) Overseer of the Craftsmen of the Estate of Amun	*(1)?* *(2)imy-r ḥmww n ʾImn*		Gardiner and Weigall1913: 22; Kampp 1996: 297-298; PM I: 139;	32.60769	25.73302
71	18	Hat	Senenmut	Royal admin & temple admin (Amun)	(Chief) Steward; Brave Chief Steward of the King, (Chief) Steward of Amun; Chief Steward of the God's Wife; Overseer of the Granaries of Amun; Overseer of the Works of Amun / in Karnak; Overseer of all Royal Works/ all Works of the King; Overseer of Works on the Two Great Obelisks in the Estate of Amun; Director of Works; Royal Seal-bearer; Great Chief of the Palace; Hereditary Prince and Mayor;	*imy-r pr (wr);* *imy-r pr wr ḳni n nsw;* *imy-r pr (wr) n ʾImn;* *imy-r pr wr n ḥmt-nṯr;* *imy-r šnwty n ʾImn;* *imy-r kꜣt n ʾImn/ m ʾIpt-swt;* *imy-r kꜣt nsw nb[t]/ nbt nt nsw,* *imy-r kꜣt ḥr nꜣ n tḫnwy wr(wy) m pr ʾImn;* *ḥrp kꜣt;* *ḫtmty bity;* *ḥry-tp ꜥꜣ m pr-nsw;* *iry-pꜥt ḥꜣty-ꜥ;*	Owns TT353	Dorman 1988: 203-211; Kampp 1996: 298-302; PM I: 139-142; Urk. IV: 398-402; 456: 9;	32.60798	25.73324
72	18	AII	Re	Priesthood (Amun, TIII & Hathor)	High Priest (of Amun); High Priest of Menkheperre (=TIII); High Priest of Amun in Henket-ankh; High Priest of Amun in Djeser-akhet (=TIII DelB temple); High Priest of Amun in Djeser-set; High Priest of Amun in Menisut (=Ahmose Nefertari temple); High Priest of Hathor, in the midst of Henket-ankh (=TIII temple);	*ḥm-nṯr tpy (n ʾImn);* *ḥm nṯr tpy Mn-ḫpr-Rꜥ;* *ḥm-nṯr tpy n ʾImn m ḥnkt-ꜥnḫ;* *ḥm-nṯr tpy n ʾImn m ḏsr-ꜣḫt;* *ḥm-nṯr tpy n ʾImn m ḏsr-st;* *ḥm-nṯr tpy n ʾImn m Mn-swt;* *ḥm-nṯr tpy n ḥwt-ḥr ḥr ib ḥnkt-ꜥnḫ;*		Kampp 1996: 303-306; LD III: 258-259; PM I: 142-143; Urk. IV: 1457-1459;	32.60774	25.73317
73	18	Hat	Amenhotep	Temple admin (Amun) & Royal admin	Overseer of Works on the Two Great Obelisks in the Estate of Amun; Chief Steward; Royal Steward; Brave One /Veteran of the King; Overseer of the Cattle of Amun; Royal Seal-bearer; Hereditary Prince and Noble, Sole Companion; Chief of the Entire Land;	*ʾImy-r kꜣt ḥr nꜣ tḫnwy wr(wy) m pr ʾImn;* *imy-r pr wr;* *imy-r pr n nsw;* *ḳn n nsw;* *imy-r iḥw n ʾImn;* *ḫtmw bity;* *iry-pꜥt ḥꜣty-ꜥ;* *smr wꜥty;* *ḥry-tp n tꜣ r-ḏr=f;*		Engelmann von-Carnap 1995: 122; Kampp 1996: 306-307; PM I: 143-144; Säve-Söderbergh 1957: Pl. II, IV, V, VI, VII;	32.60777	25.73298

TT	Dynasty	Reign (Kampp)	Tomb Owner	Occupation	Title	Transliteration	Connected tombs / Notes	References	GPS co-ordinates X	GPS co-ordinates Y
74	18	TIII/AII/TIV	Thanuny	Royal admin & military	Royal Scribe; Overseer of Royal Scribe; Overseer of Army Scribes; Overseer of the Scribes of the (Great) Royal Army; Scribe of the Army (in the Presence of his Majesty); Scribe of Recruits; Overseer of the Army – General; Royal Seal-bearer; Eyes of the King of UE, Ears of the King of LE; Official in Front of the Common People; Hereditary Prince and Mayor; Sole Companion;	*sš-nsw;* *imy-r sšw nsw;* *imy-r sšw mšʿ;* *imy-r sšw mšʿ (ʿꜣ) n nsw;* *sš-mšʿ (m-bꜣḥ ḥm=f);* *sš nfrw;* *imy-r mšʿ;* *ḫtmty bity;* *irty nsw ʿnḫwy n bity;* *sr m-ḥꜣt rḫyt;* *iry-pʿt ḥꜣty-ʿ;* *smr wʿty;*		Kampp 1996: 307-310; LD III: 264-265; PM I: 144-146; Urk. IV: 1003-1017;	32.60765	25.73289
75	18	AII/TIV	Amenhotep-saes	Priesthood (Amun) & Royal admin	2nd Priest of Amun; Royal Seal-bearer; Hereditary Prince and Mayor;	*ḥm-nṯr 2 n ʾImn;* *ḫtmty bity;* *iry-pʿt ḥꜣty-ʿ;*	TT38 - his Steward	Davies 1923: 1-18; Kampp 1996: 310-312; PM I: 146-149; Urk. IV: 1211-1212;	32.60755	25.73274
76	18	TIV	Thenuna	Royal admin, temple admin (Amun), priesthood & honorary title	Chief Steward of the King; Steward in the Estate of his Majesty; Fan-bearer on the Right of the King; Attendant of the Lord of the Two Lands (in Every Place which he has Trodden); Royal Seal-bearer; Overseer of the Cattle of Amun; Chief of Secrets of the Two Cobra Goddesses; Divine Father; Eyes of the King of UE, Ears of the King of LE; Hereditary Prince and Mayor; Great Chief in the Entire Land; Sole Companion; Official in Front of the Common People;	*ʾImy-r pr wr n nsw;* *ʾImy-r pr m pr ḥm=f;* *ṯꜣy ḫw ḥr ʾImn n nsw;* *iry rdwy n nb tꜣwy (m st nbt ḫnd n=f);* *ḫtmty bity;* *imy-r iḥw n ʾImn;* *ḥry sštꜣ n wꜣḏty;* *ʾIt-nṯr;* *irty n nsw ʿnḫwy n bity;* *iry-pʿt ḥꜣty-ʿ;* *ḥry wr m tꜣ r ḏr=f;* *smr wʿty;* *sr m-ḥꜣt rḫyt;*		Kampp 1996: 312-313; LD III: 266; PM I: 149-150; Urk. IV: 1577-1581;	32.60744	25.73264
77	18 & 18	TIV/AIII & AIII	(1)Ptahemhet (2) Roy	(1)Royal admin & general admin (2) Craftsman & Royal admin	(1) Fan- bearer of the Lord of the Two Lands; Eyes of the King of UE and Ears of the King of LE; Director of the Directors of Works; Child of the Nursery; (2) Overseer of Sculptors of the Lord of the Two Lands;	*(1)ṯꜣy ḫw n nb-tꜣwy;* *irty n nsw ʿnḫwy n bity;* *ḫrp ḫrpw m kꜣt;* *ḫrd n kꜣp;* *(2) imy-r gnwty n nb tꜣwy*		Kampp 1996: 313-315; LD III: 272; PM I: 150-152; Urk. IV: 1599- 1601;	32.60695	25.73235

TT	Dynasty	Reign (Kampp)	Tomb Owner	Occupation	Title	Transliteration	Connected tombs / Notes	References	GPS co-ordinates	
									X	Y
78	18	AII/TIV/AIII	Horemheb	Royal admin, military, temple admin (Amun) & priesthood	(True) Royal Scribe; Overseer of all Royal Scribes of the Army; Scribe of Recruits; Overseer of the Works of Amun; Overseer of Horses; Overseer of the Arable Land (fields) of Amun, Overseer of the Priests in U and LE; Overseer of the Cattle of Amun; Overseer of Cows, Calves and Bulls of Amun; Overseer of Horns, Overseer of Feathers and Scales; Attendant of the Lord of Power in the Southern and Northern Foreign Lands; Attendant of the Lord of the Two Lands in the Southern and Northern Foreign Lands; Eyes of the King in the Whole Land; Hereditary Prince and Mayor; Fan-bearer on the Right of the King;	*sš-nsw (mꜣꜥ); imy-r sš(w) nsw nb(w) n mšꜥ; sš nfrw; imy-r kꜣt n ꞽImn; imy-r ssmwt; imy-r ꜣḥwt n ꞽImn; imy-r ḥmw nṯr m šmꜥw mḥw; ꞽImy-r iḥw n ꞽImn; imy-r nfrw bḥsw iḥw n ꞽImn; ꞽImy-r ꜥb imy-r šwt nšmt; iry rdwy n nb ḫpš ḥr ḫꜣswt rsyt mḥty; iry rdwy n nb tꜣwy ḥr ḫꜣswt rsyt mḥty; irty nsw m tꜣ ḏr=f; iry-pꜥt ḥꜣty-ꜥ; ṯꜣy ḫw ḥr imn n nsw;*		Kampp 1996: 316-318; LD III: 269; PM I: 152-156; Urk. IV: 1589-1596;	32.6073	25.73262
79	18	TIII/AII	Menkheper(soneb)	General admin, Royal admin & priesthood (Amun)	Overseer of the Granary (of the Lord of the Two Lands)/ (of UE and LE) / (in Thebes); Royal Scribe; wab priest of Amun in Henket-ankh (=TIII); Hereditary Prince and Mayor;	*imy-r šnwty (n nb-tꜣwy)/ (nw šmꜥw mḥw) / (m iwnw šmꜥw); sš nsw; wꜥb n ꞽImn m ḥnkt-ꜥnḫ; iry-pꜥt ḥꜣty-ꜥ;*	TT87 father	Kampp 1996: 318-320; LD III: 271; PM I: 156-157; Urk. IV: 1191- 1204;	32.60706	25.73225
80	18	TIII/AII	Djehutynefer	General admin & Royal admin	Overseer of the House of Silver (=Treasury) (of the Lord of the Two Lands); Royal Scribe; Eyes of the King of UE, Ears of the King of LE; King's Follower on all His Expeditions in the Southern and Northern Foreign Lands; Hereditary Prince and Mayor; Sole Companion;	*imy-r pr ḥḏ (n nb tꜣwy); sš-nsw; irty nsw ꜥnḫwy n bity; šmsw nsw r iwt(w)=f ḥr ḫꜣswt rsy(t) mḥty(t); iry-pꜥt ḥꜣty-ꜥ; smr wꜥty;*	Owns TT104	Kampp 1996: 320-323; LD III: 271; PM I: 157-159; Urk. IV: 1475-1476;	32.60714	25.73229

TT	Dynasty	Reign (Kampp)	Tomb Owner	Occupation	Title	Transliteration	Connected tombs / Notes	References	GPS co-ordinates	
									X	Y
81	MK & 18	MK & Al-Hat	(2) Ineni	Temple admin (Amun), Royal admin & local admin	Overseer of the Granary (of Amun); Overseer of all Sealed Things in the Estate of Amun (=Treasurer); Seal-bearer of Every Seal in the Estate of Amun; Overseer of the Double House of Silver (and the Double House of Gold in Karnak); Overseer of Every Office in the Estate of Amun; Overseer of all the Works of Amun; Overseer of Works in Karnak; Director of all Work in Karnak; Overseer in Charge of/ concerning the Royal Tomb; Overseer of Works upon/in the Royal Tomb; Director of Work on the Royal Tomb; Scribe; Mayor in the City (Thebes); Hereditary Prince and Mayor; Dignitary;	*imy-r šnwty (n ʾImn);* *imy-r ḫtmt nbt m pr ʾImn;* *ḫtmw ḫtmwt nb(w)t m pr ʾImn;* *imy-r prwy ḥḏ (prwy nbw m ipt-swt);* *imy-r iꜣwt nbt m pr ʾImn;* *imy-r kꜣt nbt n ʾImn;* *imy-r kꜣt m ʾIpt-swt;* *ḫrp kꜣt nbt m ʾIpt-swt;* *imy-r ḫri ḥr/nt ḥrt nt nsw;* *ḫrp kꜣt ḥr/m ḥrt nt nsw;* *imy-r kꜣt m ḥrt nt nsw;* *sš;* *ḥꜣty-ʿ (m niwt);* *iry-pʿt ḥꜣty-ʿ;* *sꜣb;*	Brother-in-law of Amethu TT83	Dziobek 1992: 122-123, Taf. 60, 61, 63, 65. Kampp 1996: 323-326; PM I: 159-163; Urk. IV: 53-66; 67: 9-15;	32.60734	25.73244
82	MK & 18	MK & Hat/ TIII	(1) ? (2)Amenemhet	(1) ? (2)General admin & temple admin (Amun)	(1) ? (2) Steward (of the Vizier (of the Southern City)); Scribe (of the Vizier); Counter of Grain (in the Granary of the Divine Offerings) of Amun; Scribe of Counting the Grain of Amun; Chief of the Weavers of Amun; Steward of Counting Arable Lands (fields); Steward of Counting Everything which Exists, Steward of Counting People; Steward of Counting Metal; Overseer of Ploughed Lands; Master of Ceremonies -lit. Elder of the Forecourt [of the Estate of Amun] (Davies & Gardiner, 1973: 7);	*(1)?* *(2) imy-r pr (n ṯꜣty (n niwt rsy));* *sš (n ṯꜣty);* *ḥsb it (m šnwt nt ḥtpw-nṯr) n ʾImn;* *sš ḥsb it n ʾImn;* *ḥry mrw n ʾImn;* *imy-r pr ḥsb ꜣḥwt;* *imy-r pr ḥsb wnnt;* *imy-r pr ḥsb rmṯ;* *imy-r pr ḥsb ḥmty;* *imy-r ḥbsw;* *smsw hꜣyt[n pr ʾImn];*		Davies and Gardiner 1973 Pl. IV, VII, X-XIV, XXII, XXIII, XXVII, XXXI, XXXV, XXXVII, XXXVIII, XLIV. Engelmann von-Carnap 1995: 122; Kampp 1996: 326-330; PM I: 163-167; Urk. IV: 1050-1052;	32.60761	25.73224
83	18	Ah/(Hat)/ TIII	Ametju called Ahmose	General admin & priesthood (Maat)	Governor of the Town, Vizier; Priest of Maat; Mouth of Nekhen; Chief Justice; Great in his Office; Hereditary Prince and Mayor;	*imy-r niwt, ṯꜣty;* *ḥm-nṯr mꜣʿt;* *r nḫn;* *sꜣb tꜣyty;* *ʿꜣ m iꜣt=f;* *iry-pʿt ḥꜣty-ʿ;*	Father of TT61 & 131, grandfather of TT100, son mentioned in TT122; son owns TT228?	Kampp 1996: 330-332; PM I: 167; Urk. IV: 490-493;	32.60797	25.73216

TT	Dynasty	Reign (Kampp)	Tomb Owner	Occupation	Title	Transliteration	Connected tombs / Notes	References	GPS co-ordinates	
									X	Y
84	18 & 18	TIII/AII & AII	(1) Iamunedjem (2) Mery	(1) Royal admin & general admin (2) Priesthood (Amun)	(1)(1stt) Royal Herald; Royal Scribe; Overseer of the Granaries of U and LE; Overseer of the Law Court (of the King); Director of all Royal Works; Eyes of the King of UE, Ears of the King of LE; Follower (of his Lord to his Expeditions on Northern Foreign Lands) /(of the King on all Foreign Lands); Great one in the Palace; Hereditary Prince and Mayor; Vigilant Director; Great Official in the Palace; Warrior of the Good God; Sole Companion; (2) High Priest of Amun (TT95)	*(1) wḥm-nsw (tpy);* *sš nsw;* *imy-r šnwty n šmʿw mḥw;* *imy-r rwyt (nsw);* *ḫrp kꜣt nbt nt nsw;* *irty nsw ʿnḫwy n bity;* *šmsw (nb=f r iwt=f ḫr ḫꜣst nbt mḥyt)/ (nsw ḫr ḫꜣst nbt);* *ʿꜣ m pr-nsw;* *iry-pʿt ḥꜣty-ʿ;* *ḫrp rs-tp;* *sr ʿꜣ m pr nsw;* *kfʿw n nṯr nfr;* *smr wʿty;* *(2) ḥm nṯr tpy n ʾImn*	(2)owns TT95	Kampp 1996: 332-336; LD III: 278-279; PM I: 167-170; Urk. IV: 937-962;	32.60713	25.73185
85	18	TIII/AII	Amenemhab called Mahu	Military & Royal admin	Lieutenant Commander of the Army (of the Lord of the Two Lands); Captain of the Troops; Royal Seal-bearer; Attendant of the Lord of the Two Lands; Ears of the King; Mouth of the King; King's Follower (on his Expeditions)(on Water, on Land and in all Foreign Countries)/ (on his Expeditions on Northern and Southern Foreign Lands; Brave Warrior of the Lord of the Two Lands; Hereditary Prince and Mayor; Great Companion; Child of the Nursery;	*idnw n mšʿ (n nb tꜣwy);* *ḥry pḏt;* *ḫtmty bity;* *iry rdwy n nb tꜣwy;* *ʿnḫwy n nsw;* *r n nsw;* *šmsw nsw (r iwt(w)=f) (ḥr mw ḥr tꜣ ḥr ḫꜣswt nb(t))/ (r iwt=f ḥr ḫꜣswt šmʿw mḥyt);* *kfʿw ḳn n nb tꜣwy;* *iry-pʿt ḥꜣty-ʿ;* *smr ʿꜣ;* *ẖrd n kꜣp;*		Kampp 1996: 336-338; PM I: 170-175; Urk. IV: 898-906;	32.60739	25.73193

TT	Dynasty	Reign (Kampp)	Tomb Owner	Occupation	Title	Transliteration	Connected tombs / Notes	References	GPS co-ordinates X	Y
86	18	TIII	Menkheperesoneb	Priesthood (Amun), temple admin (Amun), Royal admin, general admin & craftsman	High Priest of Amun; Overseer of the Priests of U and LE; Overseer of the Granaries of Amun; Overseer of the Double House of Gold and Overseer of the Double House of Silver (=Treasury); Overseer of Works of Amun; Royal Seal-bearer; Chief of the Overseers of the Craftsmen; Overseer of the Foremost Offices; Hereditary Prince and Mayor; Chief of Secrets of the Two Cobra Goddesses; Great Chief in the Palace; Hereditary Prince and Mayor; Sole Companion;	ḥm-nṯr tpy n ʾImn; ỉmy-r ḥmw-nṯr nw šmʿw mḥw; ỉmy-r šnwty n ʾImn; ỉmy-r pr-wy nbw; ỉmy-r pr.wy ḥḏ; ỉmy-r kȝt n ʾImn; ḫtmty bỉty; ḥry-tp ỉmyw-r ḥmwt; ỉmy-r ỉȝwt ḫntt; ỉry-pʿt ḥȝty-ʿ; ḥry sštȝ n wȝḏty; ḥry-tp ʿȝ m pr nsw; ỉry-pʿt ḥȝty-ʿ; smr wʿty;	Owns TT112	Davies and Gardiner 1933: Pl. III; Dorman 1995: 152; Kampp 1996: 338–340; PM I: 175–178; Urk. IV: 926–928;	32.60749	25.73209
87	18 & 18	Hat/TIII & TIV–end Dyn 18	(1) Minnakht (2) ?	(1) General admin, temple admin (Amun) military & Royal admin (2) Unknown	(1) Overseer of the Granaries of U and LE; Overseer of the Granary (of Amun); Overseer of the Storehouse of Amun (and the King); Keeper of the Storehouse of Amun; Overseer of the Servants of Amun; Overseer of Horses of the Lord of the Two Lands; Royal Scribe; Overseer of the Foreign Lands of U and LE; Overseer of the Great Place; Overseer of the Department of the Wine Cellar; Hereditary Prince and Mayor; (2) Unknown	(1) ỉmy-r šnwty nw šmʿw mḥw; ỉmy-r šnwt (n ʾImn); ỉmy-r šnʿw n ʾImn; ỉry ʿt n ʾImn (nsw); ʾImy-r mrw n ʾImn; ỉmy-r ssmwt n nb tȝwy; sš-nsw; ỉmy-r ḫȝswt n šmʿw [prwy n]mḥw; ỉmy-r st wrt(t); ỉmy-r st ʿt ỉrp; ỉry-pʿt ḥȝty-ʿ; (2) ?	(1) TT79 son	Kampp 1996: 340–342; PM I: 178–179; Urk. IV: 1177–1180;	32.6073	25.73211

TT	Dynasty	Reign (Kampp)	Tomb Owner	Occupation	Title	Transliteration	Connected tombs / Notes	References	GPS co-ordinates X	GPS co-ordinates Y
88	18	(TIII)/ AII	Pehsukher called Thenunu	Military & Royal admin	Deputy of the King/his Majesty; Lieutenant Commander/Deputy of the (Numerous) Army of the Lord of the Two Lands; Royal Seal-bearer; Fan-bearer (of the Lord of the Two Lands); Attendant of the Lord of the Two Lands; Bowman of the Lord of the Two Lands; Attendant of the Lord of the Two Lands in the Southern and Northern Foreign Lands; Hereditary Prince and Mayor; Sole Companion; Official in Front of the Common People;	*idnw n nsw/ḥm=f;* *idnw n mšʿ (ʿšꜣ) n nb tꜣwy;* *ḫtmty bity;* *ṯꜣy ḫw n nb tꜣwy;* *iry rdwy n nb tꜣwy;* *iry pḏt n nb tꜣwy;* *iry rdwy n nb tꜣwy ḥr ḫꜣswt rsyt mḥty;* *iry-pʿt ḥꜣty-ʿ;* *smr wʿty;* *sr m-ḥꜣt rḫyt;*		Kampp 1996: 342-344; LD III: 272; PM I: 179-181; Urk. IV: 1459-1463;	32.60695	25.73219
89	18	AIII	Amenmose	Royal admin	Steward (in the Southern City); Royal Seal-bearer; Hereditary Prince and Mayor; Sole Companion;	*imy-r pr (m niwt rsyt);* *ḫtmty bity;* *iry-pʿt ḥꜣty-ʿ;* *smr wʿty;*		Kampp 1996: 344-348; PM I: 181-183; Urk. IV: 1022-1025;	32.60671	25.73215
90	18	TIV/ AIII	Nebamun	Military & Royal admin	Chief of Medjay (=police) on the West of Thebes; Captain of the Troops in western Thebes; Chief of Police of/in the Western City (Thebes); Chief of the Numerous Army; Commander of the Fleet of U and LE; Standard-bearer (of [the Royal Ship] 'Beloved of Amun'; Attendant of the Lord of the Two Lands in the Southern and Northern Foreign Lands; Hereditary Prince and Mayor;	*ḥry mḏꜣw ḥr imntt Wꜣst;* *ḥry-pḏt ḥr ꞽImntt Wꜣst;* *ḥry mḏꜣw n/ḥr ꞽImnt niwt;* *tp n mšʿ ʿšꜣ;* *ṯsw ʿḥʿw nw šmʿw mḥw;* *ṯꜣw sryt (n dpt nsw mry-ꞽImn);* *iry rdwy n nb tꜣwy; ḥr ḫꜣswt rsyt mḥty;* *iry-pʿt ḥꜣty-ʿ;*		Kampp 1996: 348-349; LD III: 273; PM I: 183-185; Urk. IV: 1618-1628;	32.60658	25.73223
91	18	TIV/AIII	Unknown	Military	Chief of Medjay (=police); Captain of the Troops of the Good God; Attendant of the Lord of the Two Lands (in Every Place which he has Trodden); Overseer of Horses; Hereditary Prince and Mayor;	*wr n mḏꜣw;* *ḥry pḏt n nṯr nfr;* *iry rdwy n nb tꜣwy (m st nbt ḫnd n=f);* *imy-r ssmwt;* *iry-pʿt ḥꜣty-ʿ;*		Kampp 1996: 349-350; PM I: 185-187; Urk. IV: 1598-1599;	32.60619	25.73193

TT	Dynasty	Reign (Kampp)	Tomb Owner	Occupation	Title	Transliteration	Connected tombs / Notes	References	GPS co-ordinates	
									X	Y
92	18	(TIII)/AII	Suemnut	Royal admin, priesthood (Amun) & military	Royal Butler, (clean of hands); Royal Seal-bearer; Overseer of the Priests of all the Gods; Divine Father, Festival Leader of Amun; Overseer of Royal Ships; Chief of the Stable of the Lord of the Two Lands; Attendant of the Lord of the Two Lands; King's Follower on all his Expeditions in the Southern and Northern Foreign Lands; King's Follower on Water and on Land; Fan-bearer (at the Right of the King); Hereditary Prince and Mayor; Sole Companion;	*wbꜣ-nsw (wʿb ʿwy);* *ḫtmty bity;* *imy-r ḥmw nṯr n nṯrw nbw;* *it nṯr;* *sšmw ḥb n ꞽImn;* *imy-r ʿḥʿw (n) nsw;* *ḥry iḥw n nb tꜣwy;* *(iry) rdwy n nb tꜣwy;* *šmsw nsw r iwt(w)=f ḥr ḫꜣswt rsy(t) mḥty(t);* *šmsw nsw ḥr mw ḥr tꜣ;* *ṯꜣy ḫw (ḥr imn nsw);* *iry-pʿt ḥꜣty-ʿ;* *smr wʿty;*		Kampp 1996: 350-352; PM I: 187-189; Urk. IV: 1449-1452;	32.60639	25.73178

TT	Dynasty	Reign (Kampp)	Tomb Owner	Occupation	Title	Transliteration	Connected tombs / Notes	References	GPS co-ordinates X	GPS co-ordinates Y
93	18	AII	Kenamun	Royal admin, general admin, priesthood, military & temple admin (Amun)	(Chief) Steward (of the King) (=AII); (Chief) Steward (of the King) in Peru-Nefer (=Memphite Estate); Royal Seal-bearer; Royal Scribe; Overseer of the Double House of Gold (=Treasury); Divine Father; Sem priest; Overseer of the (great) Overseers; Chief of Secrets of the Two Cobra Goddesses; Overseer of the Foremost Offices; Overseer of the Cattle of Amun; Overseer of Horns and overseer of Hooves; Overseer of Calves (of UE and LE)/ (of the Sovereign)/ (of Amun); Overseer of the Storehouse of Amun; Chief of the Stable; Eyes of the King of UE, Ears of the King of LE; Eyes of the King on the Roads Belonging to the Nine Bows; Attendant of the Lord of the Two Lands ; Great One of Great Ones; Hereditary Prince at the White Chapel of Geb; Chief of the Whole Land; Spokesman who Makes Peace in the Temple; Controller of Controllers; Dignitary of the Courtiers; Noble Dignitary among the Courtiers in very truth; Fan-bearer on the Right of the King; Sole Companion; Hereditary Prince and Mayor;	*imy-r pr (wr) (n nsw);* *imy-r pr (wr) (n nsw) m prw-nfr;* *ḫtmty bity;* *sš nsw;* *imy-r pr.wy nbw;* *it nṯr;* *sm;* *imy-r imyw-r (wrw);* *ḥry sštꜣ n wꜣḏty;* *imy-r iꜣwt ḫntt;* *'Imy-r iḥw n 'Imn;* *'Imy-r ꜥb imy-r wḥmt;* *'Imy-r bḥs (n šmꜥw mḥw)/ (ity)/ (n 'Imn);* *'Imy-r šnꜥt n 'Imn;* *ḥry iḥw;* *irty nsw ꜥnḫwy n bity;* *irty nsw r wꜣwꜣt psḏt 9;* *rdwy n nb tꜣwy;* *wr wrw;* *iry-pꜥt r ḥḏ n Gb;* *r shrr m rw-prw;* *ḥry-tp tꜣ r-ḏr=f;* *ḫrp ḫrpw;* *sꜥḥ smrw;* *sꜥḥ šps smrw n wn mꜣꜥ;* *ṯꜣy ḫw ḥr 'Imn n nsw;* *smr wꜥty;* *iry-pꜥt ḥꜣty-ꜥ;*	Mother was nurse of AII	Davies 1930 Pl. 8; Kampp 1996: 352-356; LD III: 274-275; PM I: 190-194; Urk. IV: 1385, 1403;	32.60641	25.73149

TT	Dynasty	Reign (Kampp)	Tomb Owner	Occupation	Title	Transliteration	Connected tombs / Notes	References	GPS co-ordinates	
									X	Y
94	18	TIII/AII	Ramose called Amay	Royal admin	1st Royal Herald; Fan-bearer (of the Lord of the Two Lands)/(on the Right of the King); Royal Seal-bearer; Judge in the Whole Land; Hereditary Prince and Mayor; Sole Companion;	*wḥmw-nsw tpy;* *ṯꜣy ḫw n nb tꜣwy/ ḥr imn n nsw;* *ḫtmty bity;* *wḏꜥ-rwt m tꜣ mi ḳd=f;* *iry-pꜥt ḥꜣty-ꜥ;* *smr wꜥty;*		Kampp 1996: 356-358; PM I: 194-195; Urk. IV: 1464-1465;	32.6067	25.73171
95	18	AII	Mery	Priesthood (Amun), temple admin (Amun) & Royal admin	High Priest of Amun (TT 84); Overseer of the Priests of U and LE; Steward of Amun; Overseer of the Double House of Silver (and the Double House of Gold) (=Treasurer) of Amun; Divine Father of the Great Place; Overseer of the Granary of Amun; Overseer of the Arable Land (fields) of Amun; Royal Seal-bearer; Overseer of Cattle (of Amun); Chief and Overseer of Singers; Chief Overseer of UE; Hereditary Prince and Mayor;	*ḥm-nṯr tpy n ꞽImn;* *imy-r ḥmw nṯr nw šmꜥw mḥw;* *imy-r pr ꞽImn;* *imy-r pr.wy ḥḏ (pr.wy nbw) n ꞽImn;* *it nṯr n st wrt;* *imy-r šnwty n ꞽImn;* *imy-r ꜣḥwt n ꞽImn;* *ḫtmty bity;* *imy-r iḥw (n ꞽImn);* *ḥry-tp (imy-r šmꜥw);* *iry-pꜥt ḥꜣty-ꜥ;*	Usurped TT84. Steward buried in TT45.	Kampp 1996: 358-360; LD III: 278; PM I: 195-197; Urk. IV: 1414: 8; 1570-1571;	32.60672	25.73137

TT	Dynasty	Reign (Kampp)	Tomb Owner	Occupation	Title	Transliteration	Connected tombs / Notes	References	GPS co-ordinates	
									X	Y
96	18	(TIII)/AII	Sennefer	Local admin, Royal admin, priesthood (Amun), temple admin (Amun & Horus)	Mayor (of the Southern city); Steward of Amun; Royal Seal-bearer; Overseer of the Granaries of Amun; Overseer of the Cattle of Amun; Overseer of the Garden of Amun; Director of the Cattle (of Amun in Djeser-djeseru); Steward (of the Lord of the Two Lands) Djeserkare (=AI); Overseer of the Arable Land (fields) of Amun; High Priest of Amun in Menisut; Overseer of the Priests of Ahmose Nefertari; Overseer of the Priests of the God's Wife; Overseer of the Priests of Horus, (the elder) lord of Apollinopolis (=Ashmunein); Festival Leader (of Amun); Master of Ceremonies of Akheperkare (=TI); Master of Ceremonies of Amun; Overseer of the Orchard of Amun; Overseer of Calves; Overseer of the Arable Land in the Record Department; Mouth of the King of UE, Ears of the King of LE; Royal Nurse; Hereditary Prince and Mayor; Foremost of Courtiers; Great Chief in the Southern City; Chief of the Courtiers of the Palace; Chief of U and LE; Sole Companion;	*ḥꜣty-ꜥ (n niwt rsy(t));* *imy-r pr ꞽImn;* *ḫtmty bity;* *ꞽImy-r šnwty n ꞽImn;* *ꞽImy-r iḥw n ꞽImn;* *ꞽImy-r ḫnt-š n ꞽImn;* *ꞽImy-r pr (n nb tꜣwy)ḏsr-kꜣ-rꜥ;* *ꞽImy-r ꜣḥwt n ꞽImn;* *ḫrp iḥw (nt ꞽImn m ḏsr-ḏsrw);* *ḥm-nṯr tpy n ꞽImn m Mn-swt;* *imy-r ḥm(w) nṯr n ꞽIꜥḥ-ms-nfrtiry;* *imy-r ḥmw nṯr n ḥmt nṯr;* *imy-r ḥmw nṯr n ḥr (smsw) nb Gsꜣ;* *sšmw ḥb (n ꞽImn);* *smsw hꜣyt n ꜥꜣ-ḫpr-kꜣ-rꜥ;* *smsw hꜣyt n ꞽImn;* *ꞽImy-r ꜥt nt ḥt nt ꞽImn;* *imy-r bḥsw;* *r nsw ꜥnḫwy n bity;* *mnꜥt nsw;* *iry-pꜥt ḥꜣty-ꜥ;* *ḥꜣty-ꜥ smrw; ḥry-tp ꜥꜣ m niwt rsy;* *ḥry-tp smrw ꜥḥ;* *ḥry-tp šmꜥw mḥw;* *smr wꜥty;*	Brother of TT29; Son of TT224	Kampp 1996: 360-364; LD III: 279; PM I: 197-203; Urk. IV: 1417-1434;	32.60671	25.7315

TT	Dynasty	Reign (Kampp)	Tomb Owner	Occupation	Title	Transliteration	Connected tombs / Notes	References	GPS co-ordinates	
									X	Y
97	18	AII	Amenemhet	Priesthood (Amun), general admin, Royal admin & temple admin (Amun)	High Priest of Amun; Overseer of the Priests of U and LE; (Chief) Divine Father (of Amun); Chief of Secrets in Karnak; wab priest; Steward of the Estate of Amun; Overseer of the Double House of Gold and Overseer of the Double House of Silver (=Treasurer); Royal Seal-bearer; Overseer of the Storehouse; Sandal Maker of the God; Eyes of the King of UE, Ears of the King of LE; Hereditary Prince and Mayor; Hereditary Prince in the White Chapel of Geb; Spokesman who Makes Peace in the Entire Land; Chief of the Whole Land; (Vigilant) Controller of the Double Throne as the Eyes of the King;	*ḥm-nṯr tpy n ʾImn;* *imy-r ḥmw nṯr nw šmʿw mḥw;* *it nṯr tpy n ʾImn;* *ḥry sštꜣ m ipt-swt;* *wʿb;* *ʾImy-r pr n pr ʾImn;* *ʾImy-r pr-wy nbw imy-r pr.wy ḥḏ;* *ḥtmty bity;* *imy-r st;* *ṯbw nṯr;* *irty nsw ʿnḫwy n bity;* *iry-pʿt ḥꜣty-ʿ;* *iry-pʿt ḥḏ n Gb;* *r shrr m tꜣ ḏr=f;* *ḥry-tp tꜣ r-ḏr=f;* *ḫrp (rs-tp) n nsty m irty n nsw;*		Kampp 1996: 364-367; PM I: 203-204; Urk. IV: 1408-1413;	32.60739	25.73173
98	18	AII/(TIV)	Kaemheribsen	Priesthood (Amun) & Royal admin	3rd Priest of Amun; Royal Seal-bearer;	*ḥm-nṯr 3 n ʾImn;* *ḥtmty bity;*		Kampp 1996: 367-368; LD III: 278; PM I: 204; Urk. IV: 1500: 6, 8;	32.60655	25.73137

TT	Dynasty	Reign (Kampp)	Tomb Owner	Occupation	Title	Transliteration	Connected tombs / Notes	References	GPS co-ordinates	
									X	Y
99	18	TIII	Sennefer	General admin, Royal admin, priesthood (many) & temple admin (Amun)	Overseer of Sealed Items (of Amun) – Treasurer; Royal Seal-bearer; Overseer of the Granary; Overseer of the Gold Lands of Amun; Overseer of all the Priests of all the Gods; Overseer of the Priests of Atum; Overseer of the Priests of Min of Koptos; Overseer of the Priests of Sobek and Anubis; Festival Leader of Atum; Festival Leader of all Gods of Heliopolis; Overseer of the Arable Land (fields) of Amun; Overseer of the Farm-lands of Amun; Overseer of Horned and Hoofed Livestock; Overseer of Feathered and Scaled Livestock; Royal Herald; Great One of the Great Ones in the Entire Land; Hereditary Prince and Mayor; Mayor; Mouth of the King of UE; Ears of the King of LE; Spokesman (who Makes Peace) in the Entire Land; Mouth which is in Charge of That Which Is [and That Which is Not]; Chief of Every Costly Stone; Chief of the Courtiers of the Palace; First Nobleman of Noblemen; Royal Steward; Chief of the Mayors; Overseer of Thousands of Everything (things); Royal Messenger; Sole Companion;	*imy-r ḫtmt(w) (n ꞽImn);* *ḫtmty bity;* *imy-r šnwty;* *imy-r ḫꜣswt nbw nt ꞽImn;* *imy-r ḥmw-nṯrw n nṯrw nbw;* *imy-r ḥmw-nṯrw n ꞽItm;* *imy-r ḥmw-nṯrw n mnw gbtyw;* *imy-r ḥmw-nṯrw n sbk n inpw;* *sšmw ḥb n ꞽItm;* *sšmw ḥb n nṯrw nbw ꞽIwnw;* *imy-r ꜣḫwt nt ꞽImn;* *imy-r ꜥḥwt nt ꞽImn;* *imy-r ꜥb wḥmt; imy-r šwt nšmt; wḥmw nsw;* *wr wrw m tꜣ r-ḏr=f;* *iry-pꜥt ḥꜣty-ꜥ;* *ḥꜣty-ꜥ;* *r n nsw;* *ꜥnḫwy n bity;* *r (shrr) m tꜣ r-ḏr=f;* *r ḥry m ntt iwtt...[n iwt];* *ḥry-tp n ꜥꜣt nbt;* *ḥry-tp smrw ꜥḥ;* *sr tpy n srwt;* *imy-r pr n nsw;* *ḥry-tp nw ḥꜣtyw-ꜥ;* *imy-r ḫꜣ m ḫt nbt;* *wpwty nsw;* *smr wꜥty;*		Kampp 1996: 368-370; PM I: 204-206; Strudwick 2016: Pl. 24-40; Urk. IV: 528 –532; 539-542;	32.60711	25.73162

TT	Dynasty	Reign (Kampp)	Tomb Owner	Occupation	Title	Transliteration	Connected tombs / Notes	References	GPS co-ordinates	
									X	Y
100	18	TIII/AII	Rekhmire	General admin, temple admin (Amun) & priesthood	Governor of the Town and Vizier; Overseer of the Stewards; Steward of Amun; Overseer of the Double House of Gold and Overseer of the Double House of Silver; Overseer of all Works of [Amun], Director of all Works in Karnak; Overseer of the 6 Great Mansions (of Justice?); Judge of the 6 Great Mansions; [Director] of all Ceremonial Aprons; Chief of Craftsmen; Overseer of Scribes; Chief Scribe of the Divine Offerings of Amun; Chief of Secrets (of the Palace); Greatest of Seers in the Great House; Chief of the Whole Land; sab; Supreme Judge; Follower of the King of LE; Royal Seal-bearer; Mouth of Nekhen; Priest of Maat; Divine Father; Sem priest in the 'House of Flame'; Attendant of Horus; Hereditary Prince and Mayor; Sole Companion; Foster Child of the King;	*imy-r niwt, ṯ3ty;* *imy-r imyw-r pr;* *imy-r pr n 'Imn;* *imy-r pr-wy nbw; imy-r pr.wy ḥḏ;* *imy-r k3t nbt n ['Imn];* *ḫrp k3t nbt m 'Ipt-swt;* *imy-r ḥwt-wryt 6;* *sḏmy ḥwt-wryt 6;* *[ḫrp] šndyt nbt;* *wr n ḥmw;* *imy-r sšw;* *sš ḥtp-nṯr tpy n 'Imn;* *ḥry sšt3 (n pr nsw);* *wr m3w m pr wr;* *ḥry-tp t3 r-ḏr=f;* *s3b;* *s3b t3yty;* *šmsw nsw bity* *ḥtmty bity;* *r nḫn;* *ḥm nṯr m3ˁt;* *it nṯr;* *sm m pr nsr;* *imt ḥt n ḥr;* *iry-pˁt ḥ3ty-ˁ;* *smr wˁty;* *sḏty nsw;*	TT83 is his grandfather	Davies 1943: Pls. XXIV, XXXVIII, LXXIV; Newberry 1900: Pls VII & VIII; Virey 1889: Pls II, XXVIII, XXIX, VVVIII; Kampp 1996: 370-373; PM I: 206-214; Urk. IV: 494; 1071-1093; 1119-1127; 1139-1142;	32.60741	25.73138
101	18	AII/ TIV?	Thanuro	Royal admin	The One who is Clean of Hands; King's Follower on Water, on Land, on Southern and Northern Foreign Lands; Hereditary Prince and Mayor;	*wˁb ˁwy;* *šmsw nsw ḥr mw ḥr t3 ḥr ḫ3swt rsy(t) mḥty(t);* *iry-pˁt ḥ3ty-ˁ;*		Kampp 1996: 373-375; PM I: 214-215; Urk. IV: 1474-1475;	32.60782	25.73257
104	18	(Hat)/ TIII	Djehutynefer (TT80)	Royal admin	(True)Royal Scribe; Follower of the King in all Foreign Lands; Attendant of the Good God;	*sš-nsw (m3ˁ);* *šmsw nsw ḥr ḫ3swt nbt;* *iry-rdwy nṯr nfr;*	Owns TT80	Dorman 1995: 146; Kampp 1996: 378-380; PM I: 217-218; Urk. IV: 1610: 18;	32.60947	25.73332
114	20		Unknown	Temple admin & craftsman (Amun)	Head of the Goldworkers of the Estate of Amun;	*ḥry nbyw n pr 'Imn;*		Gardiner and Weigall 1913:26; Kampp 1996: 395-396; PM I: 231-233;	32.60631	25.73202
115	19		Unknown		Unknown	?		Kampp 1996: 396; PM I: 233;	32.60642	25.73209

TT	Dynasty	Reign (Kampp)	Tomb Owner	Occupation	Title	Transliteration	Connected tombs / Notes	References	GPS co-ordinates	
									X	Y
116	18	AII/TIV	Unknown	Honorary	Hereditary Prince, Mayor;	*iry-pʿt ḥꜣty-ʿ;*		Kampp 1996: 396-398; LD III: 273; PM I: 233; Urk. IV: 1602: 5;	32.60652	25.73216
117	MK		(1)?	(1) ?	See Appendix 2			See Appendix 2	32.60673	25.73243
118	18	AIII	Amenmose	Royal admin	Fan-bearer on the Right of the King;	*ṯꜣy ḫw ḥr imn n nsw;*		Gardiner and Weigall 1913:26; Kampp 1996: 405-406; PM I: 233-234;	32.60708	25.73242
119	MK & 18	MK & Hat/ TIII	(1)Unknown (2) ?	?	Unknown	?		Kampp 1996: 406-407; PM I: 234;	32.60822	25.73236
120	18	AIII	Aanen	Priesthood (Amun)	2nd Priest of Amun;	*ḥm-nṯr 2 n ꞽImn;*	Parents: Yuya & Thuya (KV46); sister: Queen Tiye	Gardiner and Weigall 1913:26; Kampp 1996: 408-410; O'Connor and Cline 1998: 5-6; PM I: 234;	32.60807	25.73344
121	18	TIII	Aahmose	Priesthood (Amun & TIII)	Chief Lector Priest of Amun; 2nd Priest of Amun-Re, High Priest in Henket-ankh (=TIII temple); Divine Father,	*ḫry-ḥbt tpy n ꞽImn;* *ḥm-nṯr 2 n ꞽImn;* *ḥm-nṯr tpy n ꞽImn m ḥnkt-ʿnḫ;* *it-nṯr;*		Engelmann – von Carnap 1995: 122; Kampp 1996: 410-412; PM I: 235;	32.60815	25.73348
122	18	TIII	(1)Amenhotep with chapels of (2) Amenemhet	Temple admin (Amun)	(1) & (2) Overseer of the Storehouse of Amun;	*(1)&(2) imy-r šnʿw n ꞽImn;*	(1) son of TT83	Gardiner and Weigall 1913:26; Kampp 1996: 412; PM I: 235-236;	32.6084	25.73243
131	18	TI/ (Hat)/ TIII	Amenuser/ User (TT 61)	General admin, Royal admin & priesthood (Maat)	Governor of the Town and Vizier (TT61); Overseer of the Double House of Silver and the Double House of Gold (=Treasury); Royal Seal-bearer; Scribe; Overseer of the 6 Great Mansions; Supreme Judge; Mouth of Nekhen; Spokesman who Speaks the Truth in the Entire Land; Priest of Maat; Sole Companion; Hereditary Prince and Mayor;	*imy-r niwt, ṯꜣty;* *imy-r pr.wy ḥḏ pr.wy nbw;* *ḫtmty bity;* *sš;* *imy-r ḥwt wrt 6;* *sꜣb tꜣyty;* *r nḫn;* *r shrr m tꜣ r-ḏr=f;* *ḥm-nṯr mꜣʿt;* *smr wʿty;* *iry-pʿt ḥꜣty-ʿ;*	Owns TT61 Father owns TT83	Kampp 1996: 419-422; LD III: 287; PM I: 245-247; Urk. IV: 1039: 11-13 & 1382-1384;	32.60902	25.73176

TT	Dynasty	Reign (Kampp)	Tomb Owner	Occupation	Title	Transliteration	Connected tombs / Notes	References	GPS co-ordinates	
									X	Y
225	18	TIII	poss. Amenemhat	Priesthood (Hathor)	High Priest of Hathor;	*ḥm-nṯr tpy n ḥwt-ḥr;*		Gardiner and Weigall 1913: 36; Kampp 1996: 501-502; PM I: 325;	32.6078	25.73208
226	18	AIII	prob. Hekareshu	Royal admin, temple admin (Amun)	(True) Royal Scribe; Overseer of the Nurse(s) of the Royal Son; Overseer of all Works of the King; Steward of the King /of his Majesty; Steward of the Temple of Menkheperra in the Estate of Amun; Fan-bearer at the Right of the King; Door-keeper of Amun Lord of the Thrones of the Two Lands; Eyes of the King (of UE, Ears of the King of LE); Hereditary Prince and Mayor; Sole Companion;	*sš-nsw (mꜣꜥ);* *ỉmy-r mnꜥt n sꜣ-nsw;* *ỉmy-r kꜣ(t) nbt nt nsw;* *ỉmy-r pr n nsw/ n ḥm=f;* *ỉmy-r pr ḥwt mn-ḫpr-rꜥ m pr ỉmn;* *ṯꜣy ḫw ḥr imn n nsw;* *ỉry ꜥꜣ n ỉmn nb nswt n tꜣwy;* *ỉrty (n) nsw (ꜥnḫwy n bity);* *ỉry-pꜥt ḥꜣty-ꜥ;* *smr wꜥty;*		Davies and Gardiner 1933: Pls. XLII, XLIV; Kampp 1996: 502-503; PM I: 327; Urk. IV: 1877-1879;	32.60804	25.73257
227	18	Hat/TIII	poss. Siamun		Unknown (brother of TT 67?)	?		Gardiner and Weigall 1913: 36; Kampp 1996: 504-505; PM I: 327;	32.60877	25.73247
228	18	TIII	Amenmose (usurped Ram?)	Temple admin (Amun)	Scribe of the Treasury of Amun;	*sš pr-ḥḏ n ỉmn;*	Father owns TT83?	Gardiner and Weigall 1913: 36; Kampp 1996: 505-506; PM I: 327-328;	32.60922	25.73325
229	18	(TIII)/AII	Unknown		Unknown	?		Gardiner and Weigall 1913: 36; Kampp 1996: 506; PM I: 328;	32.60782	25.73276
230	18		Men?	Military	Scribe of the Army of the Lord of the Two Lands?	*sš-mšꜥ n nb-tꜣwy?*		Kampp 1996: 507; PM I: 328; Urk. IV: 1923: 3;	32.60769	25.73257
251	18	Early TIII	Amenmose	Royal admin & temple admin (Amun)	Royal Scribe; Overseer of the Storehouse of Amun; Overseer of the Cattle of Amun;	*sš-nsw;* *ỉmy-r šnꜥw n ỉmn;* *ỉmy-r ỉḥw n ỉmn;*		Engelmann von-Carnap, 1995: 122; Gardiner and Weigall 1913: 38; Kampp 1996: 526; PM I: 336-337;	32.60923	25.73274

TT	Dynasty	Reign (Kampp)	Tomb Owner	Occupation	Title	Transliteration	Connected tombs / Notes	References	GPS co-ordinates	
									X	Y
252	18	Hat	Senamun	Royal admin	Steward of the Royal Daughter; Nurse of the God's Wife Neferure; Nurse of the God's Wife Hatshepsut;	*ỉmy-r pr n sꜣt nsw; mnꜥy n ḥmt-nsw nfrw-rꜥ; mnꜥy n ḥmt-nsw ḥꜣt-špsw-t;*		Gardiner and Weigall 1913: 36; Kampp 1996: 527-530; PM I: 337; Urk. IV:418: 14-17;	32.60842	25.73371
349	18	early Dyn 18-Hat	Tjay	General admin	Overseer of Fowlhouses;	*ỉmy-r hꜣy;*		Fakhry 1947: 40; Kampp 1996: 586-587; PM I: 415;	32.60859	25.73193
350	18	AII/TIV	...y	General admin	Scribe of Counting Bread;	*sš ḥsb t;*		Fakhry 1947: 40; Kampp 1996: 587-588; PM I: 417;	32.60852	25.73205
367	18	AII	Paser	Military & honorary	Captain of the Troops (of the Lord of the Two Lands); Captain of Ttroops (of his Majesty); Chief Follower of his Majesty; Child of the Nursery; Follower of the King on his Expeditions (on Water, on Land and in all Foreign Countries); Follower of the King on all his Expeditions; Follower of the King in the Southern and Northern Foreign Lands;	*ḥry pḏt (n nb tꜣwy); ḥry pḏt n ḥm=f; ḥry šmsw n ḥm=f; ẖrd n kꜣp; šmsw nsw t ỉwt(w)=f (ḥr mw ḥr tꜣ ḥr ḫꜣswt nb(t)); šmsw nsw r ỉwt(w)=f; šmsw nsw ḥr ḫꜣswt rsy(t) mḥty(t);*	Son of TT145?	Kampp 1996: 592-593; LD III: 274; PM I: 347-349; Urk. IV: 1455-1457;	32.60648	25.73188
397	18	Hat/(TIII)	Nakht	Priesthood (Amun) & temple admin (Amun)	wab priest of Amun; Overseer of the Storehouse of Amun; 1st King's son of Amun;	*wꜥb n ỉmn; ỉmy-r šnꜥw n ỉmn; sꜣ nsw tpy n ỉmn;*		Kampp 1996: 606-608; PM I: 443;	32.60848	25.73217
400	18	(AII)/TIV	Panamun	?	Unknown	*?*		Kampp 1996: 609; PM I: 444;	32.60742	25.73253

Appendix 12: Tomb Owners in Lower Qurna

TT	Dynasty	Kampp Date	Tomb Owner	Occupation	Titles	Transliteration	Connected tombs / Notes	References	GPS co-ordinates	
									X	Y
30	18 & 20	AIII & RIII(?)	(1) ? (2) Khonsumose	(1) ? (2) Temple admin (Amun)	(1) ? (2) Scribe of the Treasury of the Estate of Amun;	*(1) ?* *(2) sš pr-ḥḏ n pr-ʾImn;*	Shared courtyard TT30, 50, 51 & 111.	Gardiner and Weigall 1913: 18; Kampp 1996: 215-219; PM I: 46-47;	32.61	25.73103
31	19	RII	Khonsu called To	Priesthood (TIII & Montu) & temple admin (TIV)	High Priest of Men-kheper-re(=TIII); Overseer of the Cattle of Men-kheperu-re (=TIV); High Priest of Montu;	*ḥm-nṯr tpy n mn-ḫpr-rʿ;* *imy-r iḥw n Mn-ḫprw-rʿ;* *ḥm-nṯr tpy n Mntw;*		Kampp 1996: 219-221; KRI III: 399-410; PM I: 47-49;	32.60985	25.73101
45	18 & 20	AII & RII/Dyn 20?	(1)Djehuty (2) Djehutemhab	(1) Temple admin (Amun) (2) Temple admin (Amun)	(1) Steward of the High Priest of Amun, Mery (TT95); Scribe (of the Offering Table of the HPA Mery); Overseer and Chief of the Servants/ Weavers of Amun; (2) Chief of the Makers of (Fine) Linen of the Estate of Amun;	*(1) imy-r pr n ḥm-nṯr tpy n ʾImn Mry;* *sš (wdḥw n ḥm-nṯr tpy n ʾImn Mry);* *imy-r ḥry mrw(t) n ʾImn;* *(2) ḥry irw (nfrw) sš n pr ʾImn;*	(1) Steward of TT95	Kampp 1996: 242-244; KRI III: 353-356; PM I: 85-86; Urk. IV: 1415-1416;	32.60864	25.73012
50	18	Hor	Neferhotep	Priesthood (Amun)	Divine Father (of Amun);	*it-nṯr (n ʾImn);*	Shared courtyard TT30, 50, 51 & 111.	Kampp 1996: 254-255; PM I: 95-97; Urk. IV: 2177-2179;	32.60998	25.73094
51	19	RI/SI	Userhet called Neferhebef	Priesthood (TI)	High Priest of the Royal ka of Aa-kheper-ka-re (TI); High Priest (of Aa-kheper-ka-re) (TI);	*ḥm-nṯr tpy n kȝ-nsw (ʿȝ-ḫpr-kȝ-Rʿ);* *ḥm-nṯr tpy (n ʿȝ-ḫpr-kȝ-rʿ);*	Shared courtyard TT30, 50, 51 & 111.	Kampp 1996: 255-257; KRI I: 333-341; PM I: 97-99;	32.61012	25.73103
52	18	(TIV)/AIII	Nakht	Temple admin (Amun)	Scribe; Astronomer of Amun;	*sš;* *wnwty n ʾImn;*		Kampp 1996: 257-258; PM I: 99-102; Urk. IV: 1603-1606;	32.60982	25.73177
53	18	(Hat)/TIII	Amenemhat	Temple admin (Amun)	Acolyte of Amun;	*imy-st-ʿ n ʾImn;*	Shared courtyard with TT134 and TT135	Engelmann von-Carnap 1995: 122; Kampp 1996: 258-260; PM I: 102-104;	32.60894	25.73116

TT	Dynasty	Kampp Date	Tomb Owner	Occupation	Titles	Transliteration	Connected tombs / Notes	References	GPS co-ordinates	
									X	Y
55	18	AIII /AIV	Ramose	General admin, priesthood, royal admin & local admin	Governor of the Town and Vizier; Royal Seal-bearer; Overseer of Works in the Great Monuments; Overseer of the Priests of U and LE,; Chief of Secrets of the Two Cobra Goddesses; Chief of Secrets of the Palace; Priest of Maat; Sem priest; Overseer of Scribes; Hereditary Prince and Mayor; Spokesman who Makes Peace in the Entire Land; Chief of the Entire Land; Controller of (all) Kilts; sab; Mouth of Nekhen; Great Companion of the Lord of the Two Lands; Sole Companion;	*imr-r niwt ṯ3ty;* *ḥtmty bity;* *imy-r k3t m mnw wrw;* *imy-r ḥmw nṯr nw šmꜥw mḥw;* *ḥry sšt3 n w3ḏty;* *ḥry sšt3 n pr-nsw;* *ḥm-nṯr M3ꜥt;* *sm;* *ỉmy-r sšw;* *iry-pꜥt ḥ3ty-ꜥ;* *r shrr m t3 r-ḏr=f;* *ḥry-tp n t3 r-ḏr=f;* *ḫrp šnḏwt (nbt);* *s3b;* *r nḫn;* *smr ꜥ3 n nb t3wy;* *smr wꜥty;*		Davies Pl. 22; Kampp 1996: 262-265; PM I: 105-111; Urk. IV :1776-1790;	32.6089	25.73081
56	18	(TIII)/AII/TIV	Userhet	Royal admin, general admin & temple admin (Amun)	Counter of Bread in U and LE; (True)(Royal) Scribe; Child of the Nursery; Overseer of the Cattle [of Amun]; Deputy of the Herald;	*ḥsb t m šmꜥw mḥw;* *sš(-nsw m3ꜥ);* *ḫrd n k3p;* *imy-r iḥw [n ỉmn];* *idnw n wḥmw;*		Kampp 1996: 265-267; LD III: 283; PM I: 111-113; Urk. IV: 1477-1480;	32.60866	25.73056
57	18	AIII	Khaemhet called Mahu	Royal admin, priesthood (Anubis) & general admin	Royal Scribe; Overseer of the Granaries (of the Lord of the Two Lands /U & LE); Eyes of the King in the Cities of UE, his Ears in the Districts of LE; Hereditary Prince and Mayor; Priest of Anubis; Chief of Secrets of the Granaries; Chief of Secrets (of the Chest of Anubis); Chief in the Funerary Workshop; Chief of the Coffin;	*sš-nsw;* *imy-r šnwty (n nb t3wy/ nw šmꜥw mḥw);* *irty n nsw m niwwt šmꜥw ꜥnḫwy=f m sp3t mḥw;* *iry-pꜥt ḥ3ty-ꜥ;* *ḥm-nṯr ỉnpw;* *ḥry sšt3 šnwty;* *ḥry sšt3(n hn inpw);* *ḥry-tp m pr-nfr;* *ḥry-tp n ḳrsw;*	Shared courtyard with TT102 – usurped by Father	Kampp 1996: 267-269; LD III: 283; PM I: 113-119; Urk. IV: 1841-1853;	32.60865	25.73046
102	18 & 18	Hat/TIII & AIII	(1) ? (2) Imhotep	Royal admin	(1) ? (2) Royal Scribe; Child of the Nursery;	*(1) ?* *(2) sš-nsw;* *ḫrd n k3p;*	Shared courtyard with TT57- son of Imhotep	Gardiner and Weigall 1913: 24; Kampp 1996: 375-377; PM I: 215-216;	32.6087	25.73044

TT	Dynasty	Kampp Date	Tomb Owner	Occupation	Titles	Transliteration	Connected tombs / Notes	References	GPS co-ordinates	
									X	Y
111	19 & Ram	RII & Ram	(1) Amenwahsu (2) Patkhy	(1) Priesthood (Amun & Sekhmet) & temple admin (Amun) (2) ?	(1) Divine Scribe (in the Estate of Amun); Scribe of the Divine Records (in the Estate of Amun); Festival Leader of all the Gods in their Festivals; Chief in the Estate of Amun; wab priest of Sekhmet; (2) ?	*(1) sš nṯr (m pr ỉmn);* *sš sš(w) nṯr (m pr ỉmn);* *sšmw ḥb n nṯrw nbw m ḥbw=sn;* *ḥry-tp m pr ỉmn;* *wꜥb sḫmt;* *(2)?*	Shared courtyard TT30, 50, 51 & 111	Kampp 1996: 392; KRI III:302-305; PM I: 229;	32.61012	25.73096
123	18	TIII	Amenemhet	General admin, royal admin & temple admin (Amun)	(Royal) Scribe; Overseer of the Granary of Amun; Counter of Bread (of U and LE); Overseer of Bread; Chief Scribe in the Palace;	*sš(- nsw);* *imy-r šnwty n ỉmn; ḥsb t (n šmꜥw mḥw);* *imy-r t;* *sš ꜥꜣ m pr-nsw;*		Kampp 1996: 412-414; PM I: 236-237; Urk. IV: 1026: 4-11;	32.60879	25.73063
124	18	(TI)/ Hat/ (TIII)	Ray	Royal admin	Overseer of the Storehouse of the Lord of the Two Lands; Steward of the Good God Aa-kheper-ka-re (=TI);	*imy-r šnꜥw n nb tꜣwy;* *imy-r pr n nṯr nfr (ꜥꜣ-ḫpr-kꜣ-rꜥ);*		Gardiner and Weigall 1913:26; Kampp 1996: 414-415; PM I: 237;	32.60886	25.73068
125	18	Hat	Duaerneheh	Royal admin & temple admin (Amun)	Chief Herald of the Lord of the Two Lands; Trusty Royal Herald; Royal Seal-bearer; Overseer of the Granaries of the Good God; Overseer of all the Craftsmen of the King; Overseer of all Works of the King; Overseer of the Administrative District (of Amun); Balance of the Lord of the Two Lands; Hereditary Prince, Mayor; Sole Companion;	*wḥmw tpy n nb tꜣwy;* *wḥmw mnḫ n nsw;* *ḫtmty bity;* *imy-r šnwty n nṯr nfr;* *ỉmy-r ḥmwt nbt nt nsw;* *imy-r kꜣt nbt nt nsw;* *imy-r gs-pr (n ỉmn);* *mḫꜣt n nb tꜣwy;* *iry-pꜥt ḥꜣty-ꜥ;* *smr wꜥty;*	Shared courtyard -TT263	Kampp 1996: 415-416; PM I: 237-241; Urk. IV: 453-454 & 1379-1380;	32.60916	25.73104

TT	Dynasty	Kampp Date	Tomb Owner	Occupation	Titles	Transliteration	Connected tombs / Notes	References	GPS co-ordinates	
									X	Y
127	18 & 19-20	Hat/TIII & Ram	(1) Senemiak (2) Pairy	(1) Royal admin & general admin (2) General admin & priesthood	(1) (Royal) Scribe; Overseer of the Double House of Silver (=Treasury); Royal Seal-bearer; Counter of Corn (of U and LE); Counter of Bread (of U & LE); Scribe of the Offering Table; Overseer of all Herbs/Vegetables; Ears of the King; Senior of the Good House (=Funerary Workshop); (2) Overseer of the Treasury; wab priest;	*(1) sš(-nsw); imy-r pr.wy ḥḏ; ḫtmty bity; ḥsb sšrw (n šmʿw mḥw); ḥsb t (n šmʿw mḥw); sš wdḥw; imy-r rnpwt nb(wt); ʿnḫwy n nsw; sȝb n pr-nfr; (2) imy-r pr ḥḏ; wʿb;*		Kampp 1996: 417-418; PM I: 241-243; Urk. IV: 513-514;	32.60932	25.73118
129	18	TIII/AII	Unknown	?	Unknown	*?*		Gardiner and Weigall 1913:28; Kampp 1996: 418; PM I: 244;	32.60946	25.73129
130	18	TIII	May	Local admin	Overseer of the Shore (=Harbourmaster) in the Southern City;	*imy-r mryt m niwt rsyt;*		Gardiner and Weigall 1913:28; Kampp 1996: 418-419; PM I: 244-245;	32.61061	25.73117
133	19	RII	Neferrenopet	Temple admin (Amun-Ramesseum) & royal admin	Chief of the Weavers in the Temple of User-maat-re Setep-en-re in the Estate of Amun (on the West of Thebes) (=Ramesseum); Chief of Weavers (of the Lord of the Two Lands);	*ḥry mrw (m t(ȝ) ḥwt wsr-mȝʿt-Rʿ-stp-n-Rʿ m pr ʾImn (ḥr ʾImntt Wȝst)); ḥry mrw (n nb tȝwy);*		Kampp 1996: 422; KRI III: 379: 3, 6, 11-13, 15-16; PM I: 249;	32.60852	25.73006
134	20	Dyn (19)/20	Thauenany called Any	Priesthood (AI)	Priest of Amenhotep who Rows on the Water of Amun;	*ḥm-nṯr n ʾImn-ḥtp pȝ ḫnt ḥr-bȝḥ mw ʾImn;*	Shared courtyard with TT53 and TT135	Kampp 1996: 422-423; LD III: 282; PM I: 249-250;	32.60893	25.73112
135	20	Dyn (19)/20	Bakenamun	Priesthood (Amun)	wab priest in front of Amun;	*wʿb n ḥȝt n ʾImn;*	Shared courtyard with TT53 and TT134	Gardiner and Weigall , 1913:28; Kampp 1996: 423; PM I: 250-251;	32.60897	25.73109
136	19		Unknown	Royal admin	Royal Scribe; [...] of the Lord of the Two Lands	*sš-nsw; [...]n nb tȝwy;*		Gardiner and Weigall 1913: 28; Kampp 1996: 424; PM I: 251;	32.60887	25.73007
137	19	RII	Mose	Royal admin & temple admin (Amun)	Chief of Works of the Lord of the Two Lands in Every Monument of Amun;	*ḥry kȝt n nb-tȝwy m mnw nb n ʾImn;*		Kampp 1996: 424; KRI III: 348: 10; PM I: 251;	32.60894	25.73019

TT	Dynasty	Kampp Date	Tomb Owner	Occupation	Titles	Transliteration	Connected tombs / Notes	References	GPS co-ordinates	
									X	Y
138	19	RII-end Dyn 19	Nedjemger	Temple admin (Amun-Ramesseum)	Overseer of the Garden (in the Temple of User-maat-re Setep-en-re in the Estate of Amun) (=Ramesseum);	*ỉmy-r ḫnty-š (m t(ꜣ) ḥwt wsr-mꜣꜥt-Rꜥ-stp-n-Rꜥ m pr ꞽImn);*	Shared courtyard with TT259	Kampp 1996: 424-426; KRI III: 383-387; PM I: 251-252;	32.61106	25.73036
139	18	AIII	Pairy	Priesthood	Priest in front;	*wꜥb n ḥꜣt;*		Gardiner and Weigall 1913:28; Kampp 1996: 426-427; PM I: 252-254;	32.60831	25.73099
224	18	Hat/TIII	Ahmose called Humay	Temple admin	Steward of the God's Wife;	*ỉmy-r pr n ḥmt-nṯr;*	Father of TT29 & TT96	Kampp 1996: 498-501; LD III: 286; PM I: 325; Urk. IV: 1432: 14;	32.60879	25.73043
249	18	(TIV)/AIII	Neferrenpet	Temple admin (AIII)	Keeper of Dates in the Temple of Neb-maat-re (=AIII);	*ỉry bnrt m ḥwt nb-mꜣꜥt-rꜥ;*		Gardiner and Weigall 1913: 36; Kampp 1996: 524; PM I: 335;	32.61034	25.73043
259	20		Hori	Priesthood, temple craftsman (Amun) & temple admin (Amun)	wab priest; Scribe in all the Monuments of the Estate of Amun; Chief of the Outline-draughtsmen in the House of Gold of the Estate of Amun;	*wꜥb;* *sš n mnw nbw n pr ꞽImn;* *ḥry sš-ḳdwt m ḥwt-nbw n pr ꞽImn;*	Shared courtyard with TT138	Engelbach, 1924: 18; Feucht 1995: 55; Kampp 1996: 537-538; PM I: 342-343;	32.61102	25.73025
263	19	RII	Piay	Temple admin (Amun-Ramesseum)	Scribe of the Storehouse (of) Amun-United-with Thebes; Scribe of the Storehouse in the Temple of User-Maat-re Setep-en-re in the Estate of Amun (=Ramesseum); Chief of the Storehouse of Amun-United-with Thebes in the Middle of the Temple of User-Maat-re Setep-en-re in [the Estate] of Amun (=Ramesseum);	*sš n šnꜥw (n) ꞽImn n ḥnmt Wꜣst;* *sš n šnꜥw m t(ꜣ) ḥwt wsr-mꜣꜥt-rꜥ stp-n-rꜥ m pr ꞽImn;* *ḥry šnꜥw n ꞽImn m ḥnmt wꜣst ḥr-ib ḥwt wsr-mꜣꜥt-rꜥ stp-n-rꜥ m [pr] ꞽImn;*	Shared courtyard with TT125	KRI III: 380-383; Kampp 1996: 540-541; PM I: 344-345;	32.60915	25.73099
269	19-21	Ram	Unknown	Unknown	Unknown			Engelbach 1924: 18; Kampp 1996: 543; PM I: 349;	32.60937	25.73118
309	19-21		Unknown	Unknown	Unknown			Engelbach 1924: 24; Kampp 1996; 572; PM I: 383;	32.60952	25.7314
317	18	Hat/TIII	Djehutynefer	Temple admin (Amun)	Scribe of Counting the Corn in the Granary of the Divine Offerings [of] Amun;	*sš ḥsb it m šnwt n ḥtp nṯr [n] ꞽImn*		Kampp 1996: 573; PM I: 390; Urk. IV: 135: 15;	32.60943	25.7314

TT	Dynasty	Kampp Date	Tomb Owner	Occupation	Titles	Transliteration	Connected tombs / Notes	References	GPS co-ordinates	
									X	Y
318	18	Hat/TIII	Amenmose	Temple craftsman (Amun)	Stonemason of Amun;	*ḥrty-nṯr n ỉmn;*		Engelbach 1924: 24; Kampp 1996: 573; PM I: 391;	32.6095	25.73135
324	18/19	Ay/SI (Ram)	Hatiay	Priesthood (all & Sobek & Montu) & temple admin (Montu)	High Priest of Montu; Overseer of Priests of all the Gods; High Priest of Sobek; Scribe of the Divine Offerings in the Estate of Montu;	*ḥm-nṯr tpy n Mnṯw; imy-r ḥmw-nṯr nṯrw nbw,* *ḥm-nṯr tpy n šbk;* *sš ḥtpw-nṯr m pr Mnṯw;*	Son owns TT331	Kampp 1996: 574-577; KRI VI: 359: 6, 11-12; PM I: 395-396;	32.60959	25.7304
331	19	RII	Penne called Sunero	Priesthood (Montu) & temple admin	High Priest of Montu; Overseer of the House of Gold and Silver (=Treasury) of all the Gods;	*ḥm-nṯr tpy n Mnṯw;* *ỉmy-r pr ḥḏ nbw n nṯrw nbw;*	Father owns TT324	Kampp 1996: 577; KRI VI: 418-421; PM I:399;	32.60885	25.73075
341	20	(RII)/Dyn 20	Nakhtamun	Temple admin	Chief of the Offering Table (in the Temple of User-maat-re Setep-en-re (in the Estate) of Amun (on the West of Thebes) =Ramesseum;	*ḥry ḫ3t (m ḥwt wsr-m3ʿt-rʿ-stp-n-rʿ m (pr) ỉmn (ḥr ỉmntt W3st);*		Kampp 1996: 579-581; KRI III, 359-364; PM I: 408-409;	32.60842	25.73052
342	18	TIII	Djehutymose	Royal admin	Deputy Chief Royal Herald;	*ỉdnw wḥm-nsw tpy;*		Engelmann von-Carnap 1995: 122; Fakhry 1947: 25-54; Kampp 1996: 581-582; PM I: 409-410;	32.60909	25.7308
343	18	TIII	Benia called Pahekamun	General admin, royal admin & local admin	Overseer of Works; Overseer of Works in Karnak; Overseer of Works in Thebes; Overseer of all Works of the King; Overseer of the Seal-bearers (=Chief Treasurer); Overseer of the Craftsmen of the Lord of the Two Lands; Child of the Nursery; Follower of the King; Attendant of the King;	*ỉmy-r k3t;* *ỉmy-r k3t m ỉpt-swt; ỉmy-r k3t m W3st;* *ỉmy-r k3t nbt n nsw;* *ỉmy-r ḫtmtyw;* *ỉmy-r ḥmwt n nb t3wy;* *ḫrd n k3p;* *šmsw nsw;* *ỉry rdwy=f);*		Kampp 1996: 582-584; LD III: 280; PM I: 410-412; Urk. IV: 1468- 1472;	32.60971	25.73113
345	18	TI-Hat	Amenhotep	Priesthood & royal family	Eldest King's Son of Aa-kheper-ka-re (=TI); wab priest,	*s3 nsw tpy n ʿ3-ḫpr-k3-rʿ; wʿb;*		Kampp 1996: 584-585; LD III: 280; PM I: 413-414; Urk. IV: 105: 15;	32.60972	25.73097
346	18 & 20	Dyn 18 –AIII (RII) & RIV	(1) Penre (2) Amenhotep	(1) Military & provincial admin (2) Royal admin	(1) Chief of the Medjay (=Police); Overseer of the Foreign Land of Retjenu (=Syria); (2) Overseer of the Women of the Royal Harem of the Adoratress Tentopet (=wife of RIV);	*(1) ḥry mḏ3w;* *ỉmy-r ḫ3st rṯnw;* *(2)ỉmy-r ipt nsw swt n ḏw3t ṯnt-ipt;*	Shared courtyard with TT403	Dodson and Hilton 2004: 190; Kampp 1996: 585; KRI VI: 86: 9-14; PM I: 414;	32.60895	25.73071

TT	Dynasty	Kampp Date	Tomb Owner	Occupation	Titles	Transliteration	Connected tombs / Notes	References	GPS co-ordinates	
									X	Y
347	Ram	Ram	Hori	Local admin	Scribe of the Nome/ District;	*sš n spꜣt;*		Fakhry 1947: 40; Kampp 1996: 586; PM I: 415;	32.60899	25.73097
348	18		(1) Unknown	(1) Royal admin & local admin	(1) Chief Steward; Sole Companion; Mayor;	*(1) imy-r pr wr;* *smr wꜥty;* *ḥꜣty-ꜥ;*		Fakhry 1947: 40; Kampp 1996: 586; PM I: 415;	32.60898	25.731
368	19/20	(Late 18)/Ram/ (Dyn 19)	Amenhotep called Huy	Temple craftsman (Amun)	Overseer of Sculptors of Amun in the Southern City;	*imy-r gnwty n Ỉmn m niwt rsyt;*		Kampp 1996: 593; PM I: 431;	32.60877	25.73056
384	19	Dyn 19	Nebmehyt	Priesthood (Amun)	wab priest in the Temple of User-maat-re- Setep-en-re (=Ramesseum); [...] of 'Amun-United-with Thebes' who Enters into the Temple of Sokar;	*wꜥb m tꜣ ḥwt wsr-mꜣꜥt-rꜥ stp-n-rꜥ m pr Ỉmn;* *[...] n Ỉmn m ḫnmt wꜣst ꜥḳ m ḥwt skr;*		Fakhry 1936: 124-126; Kampp 1996: 602-603; KRI III: 359; PM I: 384-385;	32.60983	25.73143
385	19	RII	Hunefer	Local admin & temple admin	Mayor in the (Southern) City; Overseer of the Granaries (of the Divine Offerings) of Amun;	*ḥꜣty-ꜥ m niwt (rsyt);* *imy-r šnwty (n ḥtpw-nṯrw) n Ỉmn;*	TT183 (brother?)	Kampp 1996: 603; KRI III, 163-164; PM I: 437;	32.6075	25.73086
398	17/18	Late 17/early 18	Kamose called Nentowaref	Honorary	Child of the Nursery;	*ẖrd n kꜣp;*		Kampp 1996: 608; PM I: 443;	32.60987	25.73132
399	19-20	Ram	Unknown		Unknown	*?*	Adjoining tomb TT399A.	PM I: 443-444; Kampp 1996: 609;	32.61069	25.73024
403	19-20	Ram	Merymaat	Temple admin & royal admin	Temple Scribe; Steward;	*sš ḥwt;* *imy-r pr;*	South side of courtyard of TT346	Kampp 1996: 610; PM I: 445;	32.60901	25.73067

Appendix 13: Tomb Owners in Qurnet Murai

TT	Dyn	Date	Tomb Owner	Occupation	Title	Transliteration	Connected tombs / Notes	References	GPS co-ordinates	
									X	Y
40	18	Tut	Amenhotep called Huy	Local admin, temple admin (Amun) & royal admin	King's Son of Kush; Overseer of the Southern Foreign Lands; (True)Royal Scribe; Messenger of the King upon every Foreign Land; Overseer of the Cattle of Amun; Hereditary Prince and Mayor; Fan-bearer on the Right of the King;	*sꜣ-nsw n Kꜣš;* *ỉmy-r ḫꜣswt rsyw;* *sš nsw (mꜣʿ);* *wpwt nsw ḥr ḫꜣswt nbt;* *ỉmy-r ỉḥw n ỉmn;* *ỉry-pʿt ḥꜣty-ʿ;* *ṯꜣy ḫw ḥr ỉmnt n nsw;*		Davies and Gardiner 1926: Pl. I, XI, XX, XXIX, XXXVII, XXXVIII; Kampp 1996: 233-235; LD III: 303-305; PM I: 75-78; *Urk. IV*: 2064-2072;	32.60335	25.72545
221	20	(RIII)	Horimin	Military & temple admin (Amun-Ramesseum)	Scribe of the army in the temple on the west of Thebes; Scribe of the temple [of] User-maat-re Setep-en-re of the estate of Amun;	*sš mšʿw m ḥwt-nsw ḥr ỉmntt Wꜣst;* *sš ḥwt-nṯr [n] wsr-mꜣʿt-rʿ stp-n-rʿ n pr ỉmn;*		Kampp 1996: 496; KR*I* V: 420: 8; KR*I* VII: 282: 8; PM I: 323;	32.60326	25.72524
222	20	RIII/RIV	Hekermaatre-nakht called Turo	Priesthood (Montu)	High Priest of Montu, Lord of Thebes; Overseer of Priests of all the Gods;	*ḥm-nṯr tpy n mnṯw nb Wꜣst;* *ỉmy-r ḥmw nṯrw n nṯrw nbw;*		Kampp 1996: 496-498; KR*I* V: 418: 16; KR*I* VI: 95-96; PM I: 323-324;	32.6036	25.72567
235	20		Userhet	Priesthood (Montu)	High Priest of Montu, Lord of Thebes;	*ḥm-nṯr tpy n Mnṯw nb Wꜣst;*		Gardiner and Weigall 1913: 36; Kampp 1996: 514; PM I: 329;	32.60383	25.72599
270	MK & 19/20	MK & Ram	(1)Unknown (2) Amenemwia	(1)? (2) Priesthood (Ptah-Sokar)	(1) ? (2) *wab* priest; Lector Priest of Ptah-Sokar;	*(1)?* *(2) wʿb;* *ḫry ḥbt n ptḥ-skr;*		Engelbach 1924: 20; Kampp 1996: 543; PM I: 350;	32.60402	25.72579
271	18	Ay	Nay	Royal admin	Royal Scribe	*šs-nsw*		Engelbach 1924: 20; Kampp 1996: 543-545; PM I: 350;	32.6029	25.72537
272	20		Khaemopet	Priesthood (Amun & Sokar)	Divine Father (of Amun in Thebes); *wab* priest; Lector Priest in the Temple of Sokar;	*ỉt nṯr (n ỉmn m Wꜣst);* *wʿb;* *ḫry ḥbt m ḥwt skr;*	Shared courtyard with TT273	Engelbach 1924: 20; Kampp 1996: 545; PM I: 350;	32.60445	25.72566

TT	Dyn	Date	Tomb Owner	Occupation	Title	Transliteration	Connected tombs / Notes	References	GPS co-ordinates	
									X	Y
273	20		Sayemitef	Royal admin	Scribe in the Estate of his Lord;	*sš m pr n nb=f;*	Shared courtyard with TT272	Engelbach, 1924: 20; Kampp 1996: 545-546; PM I: 351;	32.60443	25.72569
274	19	(RII)/Mer	Amenwahsu	Priesthood (Montu & Amun)	High Priest of Montu - Lord of Djeret (=Tod --5th UE nome) / Thebes; *sem* priest in the Temple of User-Maat-Re Setep-en-re (in) the Estate of Amun (=Ramesseum);	*ḥm nṯr tpy n mnṯw, nb ḏrt / nb Wꜣst;* *sm m ḥwt wsr-mꜣꜥt-rꜥ-stp-n-rꜥ pr-ʾImn;*		Kampp 1996: 546; *KRI* IV, 149: 12; PM I: 351-352;	32.60411	25.72537
275	18	Amarna-(Tut/Hor)	Sobekmose	Priesthood (AIII & Sokar)	*wab* priest; Chief Divine Father in the Temple of Nebmaatre (=AIII) / Sokar;	*wꜥb;* *ḥry it-nṯr m ḥwt nb-mꜣꜥt-rꜥ / skr;*		Engelbach 1924: 20; Kampp 1996: 546-547; PM I: 352;	32.60349	25.72519
276	18	TIII/AII	Amenemopet	Royal admin & general admin	Hereditary Prince, Mayor; Royal Seal-bearer; Overseer of the Double House of Gold (=Treasury); Overseer of the Double House of Silver (= Treasury); *sab* (=Judge?); Overseer of the Audience-Chamber (=Chamberlain); Sole Companion;	*iry-pꜥt; ḥꜣty-ꜥ;* *ḫtmty-bity;* *imy-r prwy nbw;* *imy-r prwy-ḥḏ;* *sꜣb;* *imy-r ꜥḫnwty;* *smr-wꜥty;*		Engelbach 1924: 20; Kampp 1996: 547-548; PM I: 352;	32.60346	25.72531
277	20		Ameneminet	Priesthood (Ptah (-Sokar) & AIII)	Divine Father of Ptah (-Sokar); Divine Father of the Temple of Neb-Maat-Ra (AIII) and of the Temple of Sokar; Divine Father in the Temple of Sokar; *wab* priest; Lector Priest; Chief of Secrets in the Temple of Eternity;	*it-nṯr n ptḥ (-skr);* *it-nṯr n ḥwt nb-mꜣꜥt-rꜥ n ḥwt skr;* *it-nṯr m ḥwt skr;* *wꜥb;* *ḫry-ḥbt;* *ḥry sštꜣ m pr-nḥḥ;*	Shared courtyard TT277 & 278;	Kampp 1996: 548-550; PM I: 353-355; Vandier D'Abbadie 1954: Pl. IV, V, IX, X, XIII, XVI, XIX;	32.60346	25.7247
278	20		Amenemhab	Temple admin (Amun-Re)	Herdsman of Amun-Re	*mniw n ʾImn-Rꜥ;*	Shared courtyard TT277 & 278	Kampp 1996: 550; PM I: 355-357; Vandier D'Abbadie 1954: Pl. XXIV, XXVI.	32.60343	25.72473

TT	Dyn	Date	Tomb Owner	Occupation	Title	Transliteration	Connected tombs / Notes	References	GPS co-ordinates X	Y
381	19	(RII)	Ameneminet?	Royal admin	Messenger of the King to Every Foreign Land;	wḥmw nsw n ḫꜣst nbt;		Bruyère 1934: 94; Kampp 1996: 601–602; PM I: 435;	32.60241	25.72467
382	19/20	Ram	Usermontu	General admin & priesthood (Montu)	High Priest of Montu, lord of Thebes; Chief Steward; Overseer of Cattle in the Granary; Overseer of the Double House of Silver (=Treasury);	ḥm-nṯr tpy Mnṯw nb Wꜣst; ỉmy-r pr wr; ỉmy-r ỉḥw m šnwt; ỉmy-r prwy-ḥḏ;		Kampp 1996: 602; KRI III: 302:3–4; PM I: 435–436;	32.60299	25.72522
383	18	AIII	Merymose	Local & royal family	King's son of Kush; King's son of AIII;	sꜣ nsw kꜣš; sꜣ nsw ỉmn-ḥtp;		Kampp 1996: 602; PM I: 436; Urk. IV: 723;	32.60319	25.72537

Appendix 14: Tomb Owners in Deir el-Medina

TT	Dyn	Reign	Tomb Owner	Occupation	Title	Transliteration	Connected Tombs/ Notes	References	GPS co-ordinates	
									X	Y
1	19	SI/RII	Sennedjem	Craftsman (PoT)	Servant in the Place of Truth (on the West of Thebes);	*sḏm ꜥš m st mꜣꜥt (ḥr ꞽImntt Wꜣst);*	Father of TT2; family Tomb inc. Sennedjem's son.	Bruyère 1959: Pl. XII, XIV, XV, XXII-XXXII; Kampp 1996: 188; KRI I: 411-412; PM I: 1-5;	32.60061	25.72776
2	19	RII	Khabekhnet	Craftsman (PoT)	Servant (of the Lord of the Two Lands) in the Place of Truth (on the West of Thebes);	*sḏm ꜥš (n nb tꜣwy) m st mꜣꜥt (ḥr ꞽImntt Wꜣst);*	Son of TT1; mentions: TT10/ TT7&TT360.	Kampp 1996: 188; KRI III: 800-816; PM I: 6-9;	32.60043	25.7277
3	19/ 20	Ram	Pashedu (TT326)	Craftsman (PoT & temple) & temple admin (Amun)	Servant in the Place of Truth (on the West of Thebes); Stone-mason of Amun in Karnak; Servant of the Storehouse of Amun in the Southern City;	*sḏm ꜥš m st mꜣꜥt (ḥr ꞽImntt Wꜣst); ḥrty-nṯr n ꞽImn m ꞽIpt-swt; bꜣk n šnꜥw n ꞽImn (m niwt rsy);*	Owns TT326– named chief workman there - Foreman? (Davies, 1999: 166);	Kampp 1996: 188; KRI I: 375-378; PM I: 9-11;	32.60046	25.72853
4	19	RII	Ken (TT337)	Craftsman (PoT & temple)	Sculptor (of Amun) (in the Place of Truth)/ (in Karnak); Servant in the Place of Truth;	*ṯꜣy mḏꜣt (n ꞽImn) (m st mꜣꜥt)/(m ꞽIpt-swt); sḏm ꜥš m st mꜣꜥt;*	Owns TT337. Mentions Paser (TT106) and Ramose (TT7); offered to in TT335	Kampp 1996: 188; KRI III: 675-681; PM I: 11-12;	32.60033	25.72807
5	19/20	Ram	Neferabet	Craftsman (PoT)	Servant in the Place of Truth (on the West of Thebes);	*sḏm ꜥš m st mꜣꜥt (ḥr imntt Wꜣst);*		Kampp 1996: 188; KRI III: 766-768; PM I: 12-14;	32.60159	25.72924
6	18/19	Hor-RII	Neferhotep & Nebnefer	(1) Craftsman (PoT) (2) Craftsman (PoT)	(1) Chief of the Gang (=Foreman) (in the Place of Truth); Foreman in the Place of Eternity; Great One of the Gang in the Place of Truth; (2) Foreman (in the Place of Truth)(on the West of Thebes); Great one of the Gang in the Place of Truth; Great one of [the Gang] in the Place of Truth on the West of Thebes;	*(1) ḥry ist (m st mꜣꜥt); ḥry ist m st r nḥḥ; ꜥꜣ n ist m st mꜣꜥt; (2) ḥry ist (m st mꜣꜥt)(ḥr imnt wꜣst); ꜥꜣ n ist m st mꜣꜥt; ꜥꜣ n [ist] ḥr imnt wꜣst;*	(1) Grandson / (2) son owns TT216	Kampp 1996: 188; KRI III: 576-581; LD III: 291; PM I: 14-15;	32.60024	25.72885
7	19	RII	Ramose	Scribe (PoT)	Scribe (in the Place of Truth); True Scribe in the Place of Truth;	*sš (m st mꜣꜥt); sš mꜣꜥ m st mꜣꜥt;*	Mentioned TT2/ TT4/ TT10	Kampp 1996: 188; KRI III: 612-614; LD III: 291; PM I: 15-16;	32.60016	25.72902

TT	Dyn	Reign	Tomb Owner	Occupation	Title	Transliteration	Connected Tombs/ Notes	References	GPS co-ordinates	
									X	Y
8	18	AII/AIII	Kha	Craftsman (PoT)	Chief in the Great Place; Overseer of Works (in the Place of Truth);	*ḥry m st ꜥꜣ;* *imy-r kꜣt (m st mꜣꜥt);*		Kampp 1996: 188-190; LD III: 289; PM I: 16-18; Vandier D'Abbadie 1939: 9-10;	32.60067	25.72906
9	20	RIII	Amenmose	Craftsman (PoT) & royal admin	Servant in the Place of Truth; Scorpion Controller of the Lord of the Two Lands;	*sḏm ꜥš m st mꜣꜥt;* *ḫrp srḳt n nb tꜣwy;*		Kampp 1996: 190; KRI VII: 40-44; PM I: 18-19;	32.60031	25.72798
10	19	RII	(1)Penbuy & (2) Kasa	(1) Craftsman & local admin (PoT) (2) Craftsman (PoT)	(1) Guardian in the Place Secretly (=Secret Place); Servant in the Place of Truth; (2) Servant in the Place of Truth (on the West of Thebes);	*(1) sꜣwty m st sštꜣw;* *sḏm ꜥš m st mꜣꜥt ḥr ꞽImntt Wꜣst* *(2) sḏm ꜥš m st mꜣꜥt (ḥr ꞽImntt Wꜣst);*	(1) Mentioned in TT2; (2) Grandson owns TT211. Mentions TT106 & TT7	Kampp 1996: 190; KRI III: 734-739; LD III: 290; PM I: 19-21;	32.60045	25.72923
210	19	RII	Ra	Craftsman (PoT)	Servant in the Place of Truth	*sḏm ꜥš m st mꜣꜥt*	Brother owns TT217	Kampp 1996: 494; KRI III: 782-784; PM I: 307;	32.60033	25.7279
211	19	SII/Sip	Paneb	Craftsman (PoT)	Servant of the Lord of the Two Lands in the Place of Truth (on the West of Thebes);	*sḏm ꜥš n nb-tꜣwy m st mꜣꜥt (ḥr imnt wꜣst);*	Grandfather owns TT10. Foreman from other sources – not inScribed in Tomb	Kampp 1996: 494; KRI IV: 189-193; PM I: 307-309;	32.60053	25.7292
212	19	RII	Ramose (TT7 & TT250)	Scribe (PoT)	(Royal) Scribe (in the Place of Truth);	*sš(-nsw) (m st mꜣꜥt);*	Owns TT7 & TT250	Kampp 1996: 494; KRI III: 614-615; LD III: 291; PM I: 309;	32.6004	25.72914
213	20	RIII?	Penamun	Craftsman (PoT)	Servant in the Place of Truth on the West of Thebes; Servant of the Lord of the Two Lands;	*sḏm ꜥš m st mꜣꜥt ḥr imntt wꜣst;* *sḏm ꜥš n nb tꜣwy;*	Father owns TT298;	Kampp 1996: 494; KRI III: 730-731; PM I: 310;	32.60031	25.72803
214	19	RII	Khawyheb	Local admin (PoT) & temple admin (Amun)	Guardian (of the Lord of the Two Lands) in the Place of Truth; Servant (of Amun);	*sꜣwty (n nb tꜣwy) m st mꜣꜥt;* *bꜣk (n ꞽImn);*		Kampp 1996: 494; KRI III, 695-697; PM I: 310-311;	32.60034	25.72751

TT	Dyn	Reign	Tomb Owner	Occupation	Title	Transliteration	Connected Tombs/ Notes	References	GPS co-ordinates	
									X	Y
215	19	SI/RII	Amenemopet	Scribe, craftsman & local admin (PoT)	(Royal) Scribe (in the Place of Truth); Overseer of Workmen in the Place of Eternity; Mayor in the Necropolis (lit. Desert of eternity); Scribe of the Cattle in the Place of Truth;	*sš(-nsw) (m st mꜣꜥt);* *imy-r ist m st nḥḥ;* *ḥꜣty-ꜥ m smyt nḥḥ;* *sš iḥw m st mꜣꜥt;*	Burial chamber is TT265	Kampp 1996: 494; KRI I: 381-385. PM I: 311-312;	32.60173	25.72899
216	19	RII/SII	Neferhotep	Craftsman (PoT)	Foreman (in the Place of Truth); Great One of the Gang; Overseer of Works;	*ḥry ist (m st mꜣꜥt); ꜥꜣ n ist (m st mꜣꜥt) /(n nb tꜣwy);* *imy-r kꜣt;*	Grandfather and father own TT6	Bruyère 1925: 36-46; Bruyère 1926: 35-42; Kampp 1996: 494-496; KRI III: 587-598; LD III: 291; PM I: 312-315;	32.60027	25.72892
217	19	RII	Ipuy	Craftsman (PoT)	Sculptor (in the Place of Truth(on the West of Thebes)); Sculptor of Amun in the Place of Truth on the West of Thebes; Servant (in the Place of Truth);	*ṯꜣy mḏꜣt (m st mꜣꜥt (ḥr ꞽmntt Wꜣst));* *ṯꜣy mḏꜣt n ꞽmn m st mꜣꜥt ḥr imnt wꜣst;* *sḏm ꜥš (m st mꜣꜥt);*	Brothers own TT210, TT335 & TT336	Davies 1927: Pl. XXX, XL; Kampp 1996: 496; KRI III: 660-663; PM I: 315-317;	32.60034	25.72864
218	19	RII	Amennakht	Craftsman (PoT)	Servant in the Place of Truth (on the West of Thebes);	*sḏm ꜥš m st mꜣꜥt (ḥr imnt wꜣst);*	Shared entrance TT218-220 - sons / son and grandson own TT219 & TT220	Kampp 1996: 496; KRI III: 708-710; KRI VII: 208-212; PM I: 317-320;	32.60061	25.72786
219	19	RII/Mer	Nebenmaat	Craftsman (PoT)	Servant (of the Lord of the Two Lands) in the Place of Truth (on the West of Thebes);	*sḏm ꜥš (n nb tꜣwy) m st mꜣꜥt (ḥr imntt Wꜣst);*	Shared entrance TT218-220 - father owns TT218, brother/ son owns TT220;	Kampp 1996: 496; KRI III: 758-764; PM I: 320-322;	32.60061	25.72786
220	19	RII/Mer	Khaemteri	Craftsman (PoT)	Servant in the Place of Truth;	*sḏm ꜥš m st mꜣꜥt;*	Shared entrance TT218-220 - father/ grandfather owns TT218, father/ brother owns TT219; depicted in TT335	Kampp 1996: 496; KRI III: 819: 11; PM I: 322;	32.60061	25.72786
250	19	RII	Ramose (TT7 & TT212)	Scribe (PoT)	Scribe in the Place of Truth;	*sš m st mꜣꜥt;*	Owns TT7 & TT212	Kampp 1996: 525; KRI III: 615-619; PM I: 366;	32.60078	25.72828
265	19	SI/RII	Amenemopet	Scribe (PoT)	Royal Scribe; Scribe in the Place of Truth on the West of Thebes;	*sš-nsw;* *sš n st mꜣꜥt ḥr ꞽmntt Wꜣst;*	Burial chamber of TT215	Engelbach 1924: 18; Kampp 1996: 542; PM I: 346;	32.60028	25.72901

TT	Dyn	Reign	Tomb Owner	Occupation	Title	Transliteration	Connected Tombs/ Notes	References	GPS co-ordinates	
									X	Y
266	20	(end Dyn 19)/ early 20	Amennakht	Craftsman (PoT)	Chief Craftsman in the Place of Truth;	*ḥmww wr m st mꜣꜥt;*	Parents shown in TT219	Kampp 1996: 543; KRI III: 689: 11, 16; PM I: 346-347;	32.60022	25.72879
267	20		Hay	Local admin & craftsman (PoT), temple admin (Amun)	Deputy of the Workmen in the Place of Truth (on the West of Thebes); [Maker] of the Images of all the Gods in the Mansion of Gold (=Sculptor's Workshop); Chief Craftsman of the Lord of the Two Lands in the House of Eternity; Outline Draughtsman of Amun in the Place of Truth on the West of Thebes; Temple Scribe of the Estate of Amun, lord of Karnak;	*idnw n tꜣ ist n st mꜣꜥt (ḥr ꞽImntt Wꜣst);* *[ms(t)] sšm(w) n nṯrw nbw m ḥwt-nbw;* *ḥmww wr n nb tꜣwy m pr ḏt;* *sš-ḳdwt n imn m st mꜣꜥt ḥr imntt wꜣst;* *sš ḥwt-nṯr m pr ꞽImn nb ipt-swt;*		Kampp 1996: 543; KRI V: 628-632; PM I: 347-349;	32.60025	25.72873
268	18/19		Nebnakht	Craftsman (PoT)	Servant (of the Lord of the Two Lands) in the Place of Truth;	*sḏm ꜥš (n nb tꜣwy) m st mꜣꜥt;*		Kampp 1996: 543; KRI III: 765: 14; PM I: 349;	32.60087	25.72805
269	19/20	Ram	Unknown	?	Unknown	?		Engelbach 1924: 18; Kampp 1996: 543; PM I: 349;	32.60937	25.73118
290	20	(RII)/Dyn 20	Irynefer	Craftsman (PoT)	Servant (in the Place of Truth);	*sḏm ꜥš (m st mꜣꜥt);*		Kampp 1996: 561; KRI III: 714-715; PM I: 372-373;	32.6009	25.72894
291	18	after Amarna/ Hor	(1) Nu & (2) Nakhtmin	(1) Craftsman (PoT) (2) Craftsman (PoT)	(1) Servant in the Great Place; (2) Servant in the Place of Truth;	*(1) sḏm ꜣs n st ꜥꜣt* *(2) sḏm ꜥš m st mꜣꜥt*		Engelbach 1924: 22; Kampp 1996: 561; PM I: 374;	32.6009	25.72893
292	19	SI/RII	Pashedu	Craftsman (PoT)	Servant in the Place of Truth;	*sḏm ꜥš m st mꜣꜥt;*	Parents of wife of TT335 - depicted in Tomb	Kampp 1996: 561; KRI I: 404-406; PM I: 374-376;	32.60036	25.72907
298	20	(1&2) (end Dyn 19)/20	(1) Baki & (2) Wennefer	(1) Craftsman (PoT) (2) Craftsman (PoT)	(1) Foreman in the Place of Truth; Great One of the Gang =Chief Workman; Servant in the Place of Truth; (2) Servant of the Lord of the Two Lands in the Place of Truth on the West of Thebes;	*(1) ḥry ist m st mꜣꜥt;* *ꜥꜣ n ist;* *sḏm ꜥš m st mꜣꜥt* *(2) sḏm ꜥš n nb tꜣwy n st mꜣꜥt ḥr ꞽImntt Wꜣst;*	Son owns TT213	Kampp 1996: 368; KRI I: 370-372; PM I: 379;	32.60062	25.72799

TT	Dyn	Reign	Tomb Owner	Occupation	Title	Transliteration	Connected Tombs/ Notes	References	GPS co-ordinates	
									X	Y
299	20	RIII/RIV	Inherkhau (TT359)	Craftsman (PoT)	Foreman (of the Lord of the Two Lands) in the Place of Truth on the West of Thebes; Overseer of Works of the Lord of the Two Lands in the Place of Truth; Overseer of Works in the Horizon of Eternity (=King's Tomb); Servant in the Place of Truth;	*ḥry ỉst (n nb tꜣwy) n st mꜣʿt ḥr ỉmntt wꜣst;* *ỉmy-r kꜣt n nb tꜣwy m st mꜣʿt;* *ỉmy-r kꜣt m ꜣḫt r nḥḥ;* *sḏm ʿš m st mꜣʿt;*	Also owns TT359; father owns TT360?	Bruyère 1927: 30-36; Kampp 1996: 368; KRI III: 609-611; LD III: 292-301; PM I: 380;	32.60024	25.72774
321	20	(end Dyn 19)/20	Khaemopet	Craftsman (PoT)	Servant in the Place of Truth (on the West of Thebes);	*sḏm ʿš m st mꜣʿt (ḥr ỉmntt Wꜣst);*		Kampp 1996: 574; KRI III: 817-818; PM I: 393;	32.60058	25.72925
322	19/20	Ram	Penshenabu	Craftsman (PoT)	Servant in the Place of Truth;	*sḏm ʿš m st mꜣʿt;*		Kampp 1996: 574; KRI III: 745: 7; PM I: 393-394;	32.60048	25.72909
323	19	SI	Pashedu	Craftsman (PoT & temple - Sokar)	Outline Draughtsman (of Amun) (in the Place of Truth); Outline Draughtsman in the Temple of Sokar;	*sš ḳdwt (n ỉmn) (m st mꜣʿt);* *sš ḳdwt m ḥwt-skr;*		Kampp 1996: 574; KRI I: 392-394; PM I: 394-395;	32.60063	25.72927
325	18		Smen	?	Unknown	?		Engelbach 1924: 24; Kampp 1996: 577; PM I: 396;	32.60082	25.72855
326	19/20	Ram	Pashedu (TT3)	Craftsman (PoT)	Foreman (in the Place of Truth); 'Great One of the Gang' =Chief Workman (in the Place of Truth);	*ḥry ỉst (m st mꜣʿt);* *ʿꜣ n ỉst (m st mꜣʿt);*	Owns TT3	Kampp 1996: 577; KRI I, 378-380; PM I: 396-397;	32.60078	25.72889
327	19/20	Ram	Turobay	Craftsman (PoT)	Servant in the Place of Truth;	*sḏm ʿš m st mꜣʿt;*		Kampp 1996: 577; KRI III, 835: 7-8, PM I: 397;	32.60028	25.72844
328	19/20	Ram (Dyn 20?)	Hay	Craftsman (PoT)	Servant in the Place of Truth;	*sḏm ʿš m st mꜣʿt;*		Kampp 1996: 577; KRI III: 787: 7, 12; PM I: 397;	32.6003	25.72848
329	19		(1) Mose & (2) annexe of Mose (grandson?) and Ipy (son?)	(1) Craftsman (PoT) (2) Craftsman & military (PoT)	(1) Servant in the Place of Truth; (2) Servant in the Place of Truth on the West of Thebes; Soldier of the Gang of the Place of Truth on the West of Thebes;	*(1)sḏm ʿš m st mꜣʿt;* *(2)sḏm ʿš m st mꜣʿt ḥr ỉmntt wꜣst;* *wʿw n ỉst m st mꜣʿt ḥr ỉmntt wꜣst;*	Family tomb with annexe	Kampp 1996: 577; KRI III: 749-750; PM I: 397-398;	32.60065	25.72818
330	19		Karo	Craftsman (PoT)	Servant in the Place of Truth;	*sḏm ʿš m st mꜣʿt*		Kampp 1996: 577; KRI III: 824: 8, 12; PM I: 398;	32.60072	25.72925

TT	Dyn	Reign	Tomb Owner	Occupation	Title	Transliteration	Connected Tombs/ Notes	References	GPS co-ordinates	
									X	Y
335	19	RII/Mer	Nakhtamun	Craftsman (PoT & temple - Amun) & priesthood (AI)	Sculptor of the Lord of the Two Lands (in the Place of Truth); Sculptor in the Place of Truth on the West of Thebes; Sculptor of Amun; Servant in the Place of Truth; Servant of the Lord of the Two Lands/ Good God; wab priest of the Lord of the Two Lands, Amenhotep (=AI);	*ṯ3y md3t n nb t3wy m st m3ʿt;* *ṯ3y md3t m st m3ʿt ḥr imnt w3st;* *ṯ3y md3t n ʾImn;* *sḏm ʿš m st m3ʿt;* *sḏm ʿš n nb t3wy / nṯr nfr;* *wʿb n nb t3wy ʾImn-ḥtp;*	Brothers own TT217 & TT336; TT4 offered to; depicted: wife's father-TT292; TT336, TT220.	Bruyère 1926: 113-178; Kampp 1996: 579; KRI III: 669-674; LD III: 292; PM I: 401-404;	32.60038	25.72812
336	19	RII/Mer	Neferenpet	Craftsman (PoT) & priesthood (Amun)	Sculptor (in the Place of Truth)/(of the Lord of the Two Lands); Servant in the Place of Truth; wab priest (of Amun);	*ṯ3y md3t (m st m3ʿt)/(n nb t3wy);* *sḏm ʿš m st m3ʿt;* *wʿb (n ʾImn);*	Brothers own TT217 & TT335; depicted in TT335	Kampp 1996: 579; KRI III: 666-669; PM I: 404-405;	32.60038	25.7282
337	19	RII	Ken (TT4)	Craftsman (PoT)	Sculptor (of Amun);	*ṯ3y md3t (n ʾImn);*	Owns TT4	Kampp 1996: 579; KRI III: 681: 8-9, 11; PM I: 405-406;	32.60041	25.72828
338	18	after Amarna (Tut/Hor)	May	Craftsman (PoT)	Outline Draughtsman of Amun;	*sš-ḳdwt m st m3ʿt;*		Kampp 1996: 579; PM I: 406; Rice 2002: 105-106;	32.60072	25.729
339	19	RII	(1) Huy & (2)Pashedu	Craftsman (PoT)	(1) Servant in the Place of Truth (2) Servant in the Place of Truth (on the West of Thebes); Stonemason of Amun in Karnak;	*(1) sḏm ʿš m st m3ʿt;* *(2) sḏm ʿš m st m3ʿt (ḥr imntt w3st);* *ḫrty-nṯr n ʾImn m ipt-swt;*		Kampp 1996: 579; KRI III: 748; 7, 10; 789-790; PM I: 406-407;	32.6005	25.729
340	18	early Dyn 18-Hat	Amenemhat (TT 354)	Craftsman (PoT)	Servant [in the Place of Truth];	*sḏm ʿš [m st m3ʿt].*		Cherpion 1999: Pl. 1-4; Kampp 1996: 579; PM I: 407-408;	32.60043	25.72849
354	18	AII/TIV	Amenemhat (TT 340)	Craftsman (PoT)	[Servant in the Place of Truth]?	*[sḏm ʿš m st m3ʿt]?*		Cherpion 1999: Pl.26-44; Kampp 1996: 588; PM I: 418-419;	32.60063	25.72817
355	20		Amenpahapi	Craftsman (PoT)	Servant in the Place of Truth;	*sḏm ʿš m st m3ʿt;*		Kampp 1996: 588; KRI VI: 435:5; PM I: 419;	32.60079	25.72804
356	19	SI/RII	Amenemwia	Craftsman (PoT)	Servant in the Place of Truth; Great One of the (Strong) Arm (of the Place of Truth) / (of the Lord of the Two Lands);	*sḏm ʿš m st m3ʿt;* *ʿ3 n ʿ (nḫt) (m st m3ʿt) / (n nb t3wy);*		Kampp 1996: 588; KRI III: 702-704; PM I: 419-420;	32.60094	25.72829
357	19	RII	Djehutyheremaktuef	Craftsman (PoT)	Servant in the Place of Truth (on the West of Thebes);	*sḏm ʿš m st m3ʿt (ḥr imntt w3st);*		Kampp 1996: 588; KRI III: 839-840; PM I: 420-421;	32.60132	25.72928

TT	Dyn	Reign	Tomb Owner	Occupation	Title	Transliteration	Connected Tombs/ Notes	References	GPS co-ordinates	
									X	Y
359	20	RIII/RIV	Inherkhau (TT 299?)	Craftsman (PoT)	Foreman in the Place of Truth ((on) the West of Thebes); Foreman in the Place of Eternity; Great One of the Gang in the Place of Truth on the West of Thebes; Overseer of Works in the Horizon of Eternity (=King's Tomb); Overseer of Works of the Lord of the Two Lands (in the Place of Truth); Overseer of Works in the place of Eternity; Overseer of Works of the Estate;	*ḥry ỉst m st mꜣꜥt ((ḥr) ỉmnt wꜣst);* *ḥry ỉst m st r nḥḥ;* *ꜥꜣ n ỉst m st mꜣꜥt ỉmnt wꜣst;* *ỉmy-r kꜣt m ꜣḫt r nḥḥ;* *ỉmy-r kꜣt n nb tꜣwy (m st mꜣꜥt);* *ỉmy-r kꜣt m st (r) nḥḥ;* *ỉmy-r kꜣt n pr-ḏt;*		Bruyère 1930: 32-70; Kampp 1996: 588; KRI VI: 184-195; KRI VII: 349-350; LD III: 292-301; PM I: 421-424;	32.60071	25.72765
360	19	RII	Kaha	Craftsman (PoT)	Foreman (of the Place of Truth); Great One of the Gang in the Place of Truth (on the West of Thebes) (of the Necropolis of Maat;	*ḥry ỉst (m st mꜣꜥt);* *ꜥꜣ n ỉst m st mꜣꜥt (ḥr ỉmntt wꜣst)(smt n mꜣꜥt);*	Son / grandson owns TT299? Mentioned in TT2. Father owns TT361.	Kampp 1996: 589; KRI III: 598-609; PM I: 424-425;	32.60066	25.72755
361	19	SI	Huy	Craftsman (PoT)	Great Carpenter in the Place of Truth; Servant in the Place of Truth;	*ḥmww wr m st mꜣꜥt (ḥr ỉmntt wꜣst);* *sḏm ꜥš m st mꜣꜥt;*	Son owns TT360. Grandson /son? Owns TT299	Bruyère 1930: 82-84; Kampp 1996: 589; KRI I: 397-398; PM I: 426;	32.60067	25.7276

Bibliography

Abdul-Qader Muhammed. A. 1966. *The Development of the Funerary Beliefs and Practices Displayed in the Private Tombs of the New Kingdom at Thebes.* Cairo: General Organisation for Government Printing Offices.

Al-Ayedi, A.R. 2006. *Index of Administrative, Religious and Military Titles of the New Kingdom.* Ismailia: Obelisk.

Allen, J. 1996a. Some Theban Officials of the Early Middle Kingdom, in P. Der Manuelian (ed.) *Studies in Honor of William Kelly Simpson: Volume I*: 1-26. Boston: Museum of Fine Arts.

Allen, J. 1996b. The Coffin Fragments of Meketra. *Metropolitan Museum Journal* 26: 39-40.

Allen, J. 2003. The high officials of the early Middle Kingdom, in N. Strudwick and J. Taylor (eds) *The Theban Necropolis: Past, Present and Future:* 14-29. London: British Museum Press.

Arnold, D. 1976. *Gräber des Alten und Mittleren Reiches in El-Tarif* (Archäologische Veröffentlichungen 17). Mainz am Rhein: Philipp von Zabern.

Arnold, D. 1991. Amenemhat I and the Early Twelfth Dynasty at Thebes. *Metropolitan Museum Journal 26:* 21-32.

Arnold, D. 1992. *Die Tempel* Ägyptens*: Götterwohnungen, Kultstätten, Baudenkmäler.* Zürich: Artemis and Winkler.

Arnold, D. 2005. The Temple of Hatshepsut at Deir el-Bahri, in C.H. Roehrig, R. Dreyfus and C. Keller (eds) *Hatshepsut from Queen to Pharaoh:* 135-140. New York: Metropolitan Museum of Art.

Assmann, J. 2005. *Death and Salvation in Ancient Egypt.* New York: Cornell University Press.

Auenmüller, J.S.G. 2013, Die Territorialitat der Agyptischen Elite(n) des Neuen Reiches. Eine Studie zu Raum und räumlichen Relationen im textlichen Diskurs, anhand prosopografischer Daten und im archäologischen Record. Unpublished PhD dissertation, University of Berlin. Viewed 27 June 2019, <http://diss.fu=berlin.de/diss/receive/FUDISS_thesis_0000000992520>

Auenmüller, J.S.G. 2014. The Location of New Kingdom Elite Tombs – Space, Place and Significance, in J. Dębowska-Ludwin, M.A. Jucha and P. Kolodziejczyk (eds) *Proceedings of the Sixth Central European Conference of Egyptologists. Egypt 2012: Perspectives of Research* (Studies in Ancient Art and Civilisation 18): 171-193. Krakow: Archeobooks.

Bács, T.A. 2011. The Last New Kingdom Tomb at Thebes: The End of a Great Tradition? *British Museum Studies in Ancient Egypt and Sudan* 16: 1-46.

Bács, T.A. 2018. Tombs and their Owners. Art and Identity in late Ramesside Thebes, in S. Kubisch and U. Rummel (eds) *The Ramesside Period in Egypt. Studies into Cultural and Historical Processes of the 19th and 20th Dynasties* (Sonderschrift des Deutschen Archäologischen Instituts 41): 15-32 Berlin: Der Gruyter.

Baud, M. and Drioton, E. 1935. *Tombes thébaines: Nécropole de Dirâ' Abû 'n-Nága, Le tombeau de Roy* (Mémoires publiés par les membres de l'Institut Français d'Archéologie Orientale du Cairo 57,1). Le Caire: l'Institut Français d'Archéologie Orientale.

Beinlich-Seeder, C. and Shedid, A. 1987. *Das Grab des Userhat (TT 56)* (Archäologische Veröffentlichungen, Deutschen Archäologisches Institut, Abteilung Kairo 50). Mainz: Philipp von Zabern.

Bierbrier, M. 1975. *The Late New Kingdom in Egypt (c. 1300-664 B.C.).* Warminster: Aris and Philips Ltd.

Bierbrier, M. 1982. *The Tomb Builders of the Pharaohs.* Cairo: The American University in Cairo Press.

Bietak, M. and Forstner-Müller, I. 2011. The Topography of New Kingdom Avaris and Per-Ramesses, in M. Collier and S. Snape (eds) *Ramesside Studies in Honour of K.A. Kitchen*: 23-50. Bolton: Rutherford Press.

Bruyère, B. 1925. *Rapport préliminaire sur les fouilles de Deir el-Médineh (1923-1924)* (Fouilles de l'Institute français d'archéologie orientale du Caire: Rapports préliminaires 2). Le Caire: Institut Français d'Archéologie Orientale.

Bruyère, B. 1926. *Rapport préliminaire sur les fouilles de Deir el-Médineh (1924-1925)* (Fouilles de l'Institute français d'archéologie orientale du Caire: Rapports préliminaires 3). Le Caire: Institut Français d'Archéologie Orientale.

Bruyère, B. 1927. *Rapport préliminaire sur les fouilles de Deir el-Médineh (1926)* (Fouilles de l'Institute français d'archéologie orientale du Caire: Rapports préliminaires 5). Le Caire: Institut Français d'Archéologie Orientale

Bruyère, B. 1930. *Rapport préliminaire sur les fouilles de Deir el-Médineh (1929)* (Fouilles de l'Institute français d'archéologie orientale du Caire: Rapports préliminaires 7). Le Caire: Institut Français d'Archéologie Orientale.

Bruyère, B. 1934. *Rapport préliminaire sur les fouilles de Deir el-Médineh (1931-32)* (Fouilles de l'Institute rançais d'archéologie orientale du Caire: Rapports préliminaires 10). Le Caire: Institut Français d'Archéologie Orientale.

Bruyère, B. 1952. *Tombes thébaines de Deir el-Médineh à decoration monochrome* (Mémoires publiés par les membres de l'Institut Français d'Archéology

Orientale du Cairo 86). Le Caire: Institut Français d'Archéologie Orientale.

Bruyère, B. 1959. *La tombe No 1 de Sen-nedjem à Deir el Médineh* (Mémoires publiés par les membres de l'Institut Français d'Archéology Orientale du Cairo 88). Le Caire: Institut Français d'Archéologie Orientale.

Cabrol, A. 2001. *Les voies processionnelles de Thèbes* (Orientalia Lovaniensia Analecta 97). Leuven: Leuven University Press.

Carnarvon, G. and Carter, H. 1912. *Five Years' Exploration at Thebes.* London: Oxford University Press.

Cĕrny, J. 2001. *A Community of Workmen at Thebes in the Ramesside Period* (Bibliothèque d'Étude 50). Le Caire: Institut Français d'Archéologie Orientale.

Cherpion, N. 1999. *Deux tombes de la XVIIIe dynastie à Deir el-Medina* (Mémoires publiés par les membres de l'Institut Français d'Archéology Orientale du Cairo 114). Le Caire: Institut Français d'Archéologie Orientale.

Cherpion, N. and Corteggiani, J.P. 2010. *La tombe d'Inherkhäouy (TT359) à Deir el-Medina*: Volume 1 and 2 (Mémoires publiés par les membres de l'Institut Français d'Archéology Orientale du Cairo 128). Le Caire: Institut Français d'Archéologie Orientale.

Chudzik, P. 2016. Middle Kingdom Tombs in Asasif: Archaeological Activities in 2015. *Polish Archaeology in the Mediterranean* 25: 289-302.

Cooney, K.M. 2008. Profit or Exploitation? The Production of Private Ramesside Tombs within the West Theban Funerary Economy. *Journal of Egyptian History* 1: 79-115.

Cooney, K.M. 2014. Private Sector Tomb Robbery and Funerary Arts Reuse according to West Theban Documentation, in J. Toivari-Vitala, T. Vartiainan and S. Uvanto (eds) *Deir el Médina Studies. Helsinki June 24-26 2009, Proceedings* (The Finnish Egyptological Society 2): 16-28. Helsinki: Finnish Egyptological Society.

Cooney, K.M. 2018. The End of the New Kingdom in Egypt. How Ancient Egyptian Funerary Materials Can Help Us Understand a Society in Crisis, in S. Kubisch and U. Rummel (eds) *The Ramesside Period in Egypt. Studies into Cultural and Historical Processes of the 19th and 20th Dynasties* (Sonderschrift des Deutschen Archäologischen Instituts 41): 63-88. Berlin: Der Gruyter.

Davies, B.G. 1999. *Who's Who at Deir el Medina: A Prosopographic Study of the Royal Workmen's Community* (Egyptologische Uitgaven XIII). Leiden: Nederlands Instituut voor het Nabije Oosten.

Davies, N. de G. 1923. *The Tomb of Puyemrê at Thebes: Volume 2* (Robb de Peyster Tytus Memorial Series 3). New York: The Metropolitan Museum of Art.

Davies, N de G. 1925a. *The Tomb of Two Sculptors at Thebes* (Robb de Peyster Tytus Memorial Series IV). New York: The Metropolitan Museum of Art.

Davies, N. de G. 1925b. The Tomb of Tetaky at Thebes (No. 15). *The The Journal of Egyptian Archaeology* 11: 10-17.

Davies, N. de G. 1927. *Two Ramesside Tombs at Thebes.* New York: The Metropolitan Museum of Art.

Davies, N. de G. 1933. *The Tomb of Nefer-Hotep at Thebes.* New York: The Metropolitan Museum of Art.

Davies, N. de G. 1935. *Paintings from the Tomb of Rekh-mi-Rē at Thebes.* New York: The Metropolitan Museum of Art.

Davies, N. de G. 1941. *The Tomb of the Vizier Ramose* (Mond Excavations at Thebes I). London: Egypt Exploration Society.

Davies, N. de G. 1943. *The Tomb of Rekh-mi-Rē: Volume I.* New York: The Metropolitan Museum of Art.

Davies, N. de G. 1963. *Private Tombs at Thebes: Volume IV. Scenes from Some Theban Tombs (Nos. 38, 66, 162, with excerpts from 81).* Oxford: Oxford University Press.

Davies, N. de G. and Davies, N.M. 1923. *The Tombs of Two Officials of Tuthmosis the Fourth (nos. 75 and 90)* (Theban Tombs Series 3). London: Egypt Exploration Society.

Davies, N. de G. and Gardiner, A.H. 1913. *Five Theban Tombs (being those of Mentuherkhepeshef, User, Daga, Nehemaway and Tati.* London: Egypt Exploration Society.

Davies, N de G. and Gardiner, A.H. 1915. *The Tombs of Amenemhet (No. 82)* (Theban Tombs Series 1). London: Egypt Exploration Society.

Davies, N de G. and Gardiner, A.H. 1926. *The Tomb of Huy: Viceroy of Nubia in the Reign of Tutankhamun (No. 40)* (Theban Tombs Series 4). London: Egypt Exploration Society.

Davies, N de G. and Gardiner, A.H. 1933. *The Tomb of Menkheperrasonb, Amenmose, and Another* (Theban Tombs Series 5). London: Egypt Exploration Society.

Davies, N. de G. Gardiner, A.H. and Davies, N. de G. 1920. *The Tomb of Antefoker, Vizier of Sésostris I and of his wife Senet* (Theban Tombs Series 2). London: Egypt Exploration Society.

Delvaux, L. 1988. La statue Louvre A 134 du premier prophète d'Amon. *Studien zur Altägyptischen Kultur* 15: 56-63.

Dodson, A. 1991. *Egyptian Rock-cut Tombs* (Shire Egyptology 14). Risborough: Shire Publications

Dodson, A. and Hilton, D. 2004. *The Complete Royal Families of Ancient Egypt.* London: Thames and Hudson.

Dodson, A. & Ikram, S. 2008. *The Tomb in Ancient Egypt: Royal and Private Sepulchres from the Early Dynastic Period to the Romans.* London: Thames and Hudson.

Dolińska, M. 2010. Temple of Tuthmosis III at Deir el-Bahari after 30 years of research, in M. Dolińska and H. Beinlich (eds) *Ägyptologische Tempeltagung: Interconnections between temples. Warschau, 22-25 September 2008* (Konigtum, Staat Und Gesellschaft Fruher Hochkulturen 3.3): 57-66. Wiesbaden: Harrassowitz.

Doncker, A.D. 2012. Theban Tomb Graffiti during the New Kingdom. Research on the Reception of Ancient Egyptian Images by Ancient Egyptians, in K. A. Kóthay (ed.) *Art and Society: Ancient and Modern Contexts of Egyptian Art. Proceedings of the International Conference Held at the Museum of Fine Arts, Budapest, 13-15 May 2010*: 23-34. Budapest: Museum of Fine Arts.

Dorman, P. 1988. *The Monuments of Senenmut: Problems in Historical Methodology.* London: Routledge.

Dorman, P. 1995. Two Tombs and One Owner, in J. Assmann, E. Dziobek, H. Guksch and F. Kampp (eds) *Thebanische Beamtennekropolen* (Studien zur Archäologie und Geschichte Altägyptens): 141-154. Heidelberg: Heidelberger Orientverlag.

Dorman, P. 2003. Family Burial and Commemoration in the Theban Necropolis, in N. Strudwick and J. Taylor (eds) *The Theban Necropolis: Past, Present and Future*: 30-41. London: British Museum Press.

Dziobek, E. 1992. *Das Grab des Ineni Theben Nr. 81* (Archäologische Veröffentlichungen 68). Mainz am Rhein: Philipp von Zabern.

Dziobek, E. 1995. Theban Tombs as a Source for Historical and Biographical Evaluation: The Case of User-Amun, in J. Assmann, E. Dziobek, H. Guksch and F. Kampp (eds) *Thebanische Beamtennekropolen* (Studien zur Archäologie und Geschichte Altägyptens): 129-140. Heidelberg: Heidelberger Orientverlag.

Dziobek, E. 1998. *Denkmäler des Vezirs User-Amun* (Studien zur Archäologie und Geschichte Altägyptens 18). Heidelberg: Heidelberger Orientverlag.

Dziobek, E. and Raziq, M.A. 1990. *Das Grab des Sobekhotep Theben Nr. 63* (Archäologische Veröffentlichungen 71). Mainz am Rhein: Philipp von Zabern.

Eaton-Krauss, M. 1998. Four Notes on the Early Eighteenth Dynasty. *The Journal of Egyptian Archaeology* 84: 205-210.

Edwards, I.E.S. 1965. Lord Dufferin's Excavations at Deir El-Bahri and the Clandeboye Collection. *The Journal of Egyptian Archaeology* 51: 25-26.

Eigner, D. 1983. Das thebanische Grab des Amenhotep, Wesir von Unterägypten: die Architektur. *Mitteilungen des Deutschen Archäologischen Instituts Abteilung Kairo* 39: 39-50.

El-Saady, H. 1997. *The Tomb of Amenemhab: No. 44 at Qurnah. The Tomb-chapel of a Priest Carrying the Shrine of Amun.* Warminster: Aris & Phillips Ltd.

El-Sabban, S. 2000. *The Festival Calendars of Ancient Egypt* (Liverpool Monographs in Archaeology and Oriental Studies). Liverpool: Liverpool University Press.

Engelbach, R. 1924. *A Supplement to The Topographical Catalogue of The Private Tombs of Thebes.* Le Caire: Institut Français d'Archéologie Orientale.

Engelmann von Carnap, E. 1995, Soziale Stellung und Grabanlage: Zur Struktur des Friedhofs der ersten Hälfe der 18. Dynastie in Scheich Abd el-Qurna und Chocha, in J. Assmann, E. Dziobek, H. Guksch and F. Kampp (eds) *Thebanische Beamtennekropolen* (Studien zur Archäologie und Geschichte Altägyptens): 107-128. Heidelberg: Heidelberger Orientverlag.

Eyre, C. 2013. *The Use of Documents in Pharaonic Egypt.* Oxford: Oxford University Press.

Fábián, Z. 2011. News from Old Kingdom Thebes, in E. Bechtold, A. Gulyás and A. Hasznos (eds) *From Illahun to Djeme. Papers Presented in Honour of Ulrich Luft* (British Archaeological Reports International Series 2311): 43-53. Oxford: British Archaeological Reports.

Fakhry, A. 1936. A Report on the Inspectorate of Upper Egypt. *Annales du Service des Antiquités de l'Égypte* 36

Fakhry, A. 1947. A Report on the Inspectorate of Upper Egypt. *Annales du Service des Antiquités de l'Égypte* 46.

Fantecchi, S.E and Zingarelli, A.P. 2002. Singers and Musicians in New Kingdom Egypt. *Göttinger Miszellen* 186: 36-69.

Faulkner, R.O. 1955. The Installation of the Vizier. *The Journal of Egyptian Archaeology* 41: 18-29.

Feucht, E. 1985. *Das Grab des Nefersecheru (TT296)* (Theben Band II). Mainz: Philipp von Zabern.

Feucht, E. 1995. Fragen an TT 259, in J. Assmann, E. Dziobek, H. Guksch and F. Kampp (eds) *Thebanische Beamtennekropolen* (Studien zur Archäologie und Geschichte Altägyptens): 55-61. Heidelberg: Heidelberger Orientverlag.

Feucht, E. 2006. *Die Gräber des Nedjemger (TT138) und des Hori (TT259)* (Theben Band XV). Mainz: Philipp von Zabern.

Fischer, H.G. 1997. *Egyptian Titles of the Middle Kingdom: A Supplement to Wm. Ward's Index.* 2nd Edition. New York: Metropolitan Museum of Art.

Desroches-Noblecourt, C. 1985. *Reconstitution du caveau de Sennefer dit 'tombe aux vignes', Thèbes-Ouest, Cheikh Abd el Gournah, XVIIIe Dynastie.* Paris: Fondation Kodak Pathé.

Foucart, G. 1924. Les précurseurs du Soleil. *Bulletin de l'Institut Français d'Archéologie Orientale* 24: 131-209.

Foucart, G., Baud, M. and Drioton, E. 1928-1935. *Tombes thébaines: Nécropole de Dirâ' Abû'n- Naga: Le tombeau de Roÿ (tombeau no. 255); Le tombeau de Panehsy (tombeau no. 16); Le tombeau d'Amonmos (tombeau no. 19); Le tombeau d'Amon-am-anit (tombeau no. 277)* (Mémoires publiés par les membres de l'Institut Français d'Archéology Orientale du Cairo 57). Le Caire: Institut Français d'Archéologie Orientale.

Franzmeier, F. and Moje, J. 2018. The Missing Dead? On the Question of the Burial Grounds in Pi-Ramesse, in S. Kubisch and U. Rummel (eds) *The Ramesside Period in Egypt: Studies into Cultural and Historical Processes of the 19th and 20th Dynasties* (Sonderschrift des Deutschen Archäologischen Instituts 41): 113-126. Berlin: Der Gruyter.

Gabolde, L. 1995. Autour de la tombe 276: pourquoi va-t-on se faire enterer à Gournet Mourai au début du Nouvel Empire?, in J. Assmann, E. Dziobek, H. Guksch and F. Kampp (eds) *Thebanische Beamtennekropolen*

(Studien zur Archäologie und Geschichte Altägyptens): 155-165. Heidelberg: Heidelberger Orientverlag.

Gardiner, A.H. 1925. The Autobiography of Rekhmere. *Zeitschrift für Ägyptische Sprache und Altertumskunde* 60: 62-76.

Gardiner, A.H. 1948a. *Ramesside Administrative Documents.* Oxford: Oxford University Press.

Gardiner, A.H. 1948b. *The Wilbour Papyrus: Volume II: Translation.* Oxford: Oxford University Press.

Gardiner, A. and Weigall, P. 1913. *A Topographical Catalogue of the Private Tombs of Thebes.* London: Bernard Quaritch.

Gauthier, H. 1908. Rapport sur une campagne de fouilles à Drah abou'l Neggah, en 1906. *Bulletin de l'Institut Français d'Archéologie Orientale* 6: 121-164.

Graefe, E. 1986. Talfest, in W. Helck and E. Otto (eds) *Lexikon der Ägyptologie: Volume VI*: 187-189. Wiesbaden: Harrassowitz.

Graham, A., Strutt, K.D., Hunter, M., Jones, S., Masson, A., Millet, M. and Pennington, B., 2012. Theban Harbours and Waterscapes Survey, 2012. *The Journal of Egyptian Archaeology* 98: 27–42.

Graham, A., Strutt, K.D., Hunter, M., Jones, S., Masson, A., Millet, M. and Pennington, B. 2013. Theban Harbours and Waterscapes Survey, 2013. *The Journal of Egyptian Archaeology* 99: 35–52.

Guksch, H. 1995. *Die Gräber des Nacht-Min und des Men-cheper-Ra-seneb: Theben Nr. 87 und 79* (Archäologische Veröffentlichungen 34). Mainz: Philipp von Zabern.

Habachi, L. and Anus, P. 1977. *Le tombeau de Nay à Gournet Mar'eï (No. 271)* (Mémoires publiés par les membres de l'Institut Français d'Archéology Orientale du Cairo 97). Le Caire: Institut Français d'Archéologie Orientale

Haeny, G. 1997. New Kingdom 'Mortuary Temples' and 'Mansions of Millions of Years', in B.E. Shafer (ed.) *Temples of Ancient* Egypt: 86-126. London: I.B. Tauri.

Hari, R. 1985. *La tombe thebaine du père divin Neferhotep (TT50)* (Collection epigraphica). Genève: Éditions de Belles-Lettres.

Hartwig, M. 2004. *Tomb Painting and Identity in Ancient Thebes, 1419-1372 BCE* (Monumenta Aegyptiaca 10). Brussels: Brepols Publishers.

Hartwig, M. 2013. *The Tomb Chapel of Menna (TT 69)* (American Research Center in Egypt Conservation Series 5). Cairo: The American University of Cairo Press.

Hayes, W.C. 1959. *The Scepter of Egypt: A Background for the Study of the Egyptian Antiquities in the Metropolitan Museum of Art: Volume 2: The Hyksos and the New Kingdom (1675-1080).* New York: The Metropolitan Museum of Art.

Hegazy, S. and Tosi, M. 1983. *A Theban Private Tomb No. 295* (Archäologische Veröffentlichungen, Deutschen Archäologisches Institut, Abteilung Kairo 45). Mainz: Philipp von Zabern.

Helck, W. 1955-1958. *Urkunden der 18. Dynastie Historich-biographische Urkunden. IV. Abteilung Band II.* Heft 17-22. Berlin: Akademie-Verlag.

Helck, W. 1958. *Zur Verwaltung des Mittleren und Neuen Reichs.* Leiden: Brill.

Helck, W. 1962. Soziale Stellung und Grablage: Bemerkungen Zur Thebanischen Nekropole. *Journal of the Economic and Social History of the Orient* 5.3: 225-243.

Hermann, A. 1940. *Die Stelen der thebanischen Felsgräber der 18. Dynastie* (*Ägyptologische* Forschungen 11). Glückstadt: J.J. Augustin.

Hodel-Hoenes, S. 2000. *Life and Death in Ancient Egypt: Scenes from Private Tombs in New Kingdom Thebes.* New York: Cornell University Press.

Hofmann, E. 1995. *Das Grab Des Neferrenpet Gen Kenro (TT178)* (Theben IX). Mainz: Philipp von Zabern.

Hofmann, E. 2018. Der Vorhof der Privatgräber – nur ein sakraler Ort?, in S. Kubisch and U. Rummel (eds) *The Ramesside Period in Egypt. Studies into Cultural and Historical Processes of the 19th and 20th Dynasties* (Sonderschrift des Deutschen Archäologischen Instituts 41): 149-174. Berlin: Der Gruyter.

Hölscher, U. 1939. *The Excavations at Medinet Habu II.* Oriental Institute Publications. Chicago: The Oriental Institute.

Holthoer, R. 1984. The Hamboula-Group Tombs at Khōkha, in R. Holthoer and T. Linders *Sundries in Honour of Säve-Söderbergh* (Boreas 13): 73-96. Uppsala: Institutionen för arkeologi och antik historia.

Hornung, E. 1975. Amunophis I, in W. Helck and E. Otto (eds) *Lexikon der* Ägyptologie: *Volume I*: 201-203. Wiesbaden: Harrassowitz.

Ikram, S. 2003. *Death and Burial in Ancient Egypt.* London: Longman.

James, T.G.H. 1985. *Pharaoh's People: Scenes from Life in Imperial Egypt.* Oxford: Oxford University Press.

Jimenez-Higueras, A. 2016. Development and Landscape of the Sacred Space at Dra Abu el-Naga: A case study within the Theban Necropolis. Unpublished PhD dissertation. University of Liverpool.

Kákosy, L. and Bács, T.A. (eds) 2004. *The Mortuary Monument of Djehutimes (TT 32)* (Studia Aegyptiaca Series Maior 1). Budapest: Archaeolingua.

Kampp, F. 1996. *Die Thebanische Nekropole. Zum Wandel des Grabgedankens von der XVIII. bis zur XX. Dynastie.* 2 Volumes (Theben XIII). Mainz: Philipp von Zabern.

Kampp-Seyfried, F. 2003. The Theban Necropolis: An Overview of Topography and Tomb Development from the Middle Kingdom to the Ramesside Period, in N. Strudwick and J. Taylor (eds) *The Theban Necropolis: Past, Present and Future*: 2-10. London: British Museum Press.

Kampp, F. and Seyfried, K.J. 1995. Eine Rückkehr Nach Theben: Das Grab des Pa-Ren-Nefer: Hoherpriester des Amun zur Zeit Tutanchamuns. *Antike Welt* 26.5: 325–342.

Karkowski, J. 1979. The Question of the Beautiful Feast of the Valley Representations in Hatshepsut's Temple at Deir el-Bahri, in W.F. Reineke (ed.) *First International Congress of Egyptology: Cairo, October 2-10, 1976* (Schriften zur Geschichte und Kultur des Alten Orients 14): 359-364. Berlin: De Gruyter.

Karkowski, J. 1992. Notes on the Beautiful Feast of the Valley as represented in Hatshepsut's temple at Deir el-Bahri, in S. Jakobielski and J. Karkowski (eds) *50 Years of Polish Expeditions in Egypt and the Near East: Acts of the Symposium of Warsaw University* 1986: 155-166. Varsovie: Centre d'Archéologie Méditerranéenne de l'Académie Polonaise des Sciences.

Kemp, B.J. 1989, *Ancient Egypt: Anatomy of a Civilization.* London: Routledge.

Kitchen, K. A. 1969-1990. *Ramesside Inscriptions, Historical and Biographical.* 8 Volumes. Oxford: Blackwell.

Kubisch, S. 2018. The Religious and Political Role of the High Priests of Amun, in S. Kubisch and U. Rummel (eds) *The Ramesside Period in Egypt. Studies into Cultural and Historical Processes of the 19th and 20th Dynasties* (Sonderschrift des Deutschen Archäologischen Instituts 41): 189-204. Berlin: Der Gruyter.

Kuhlmann K.P. and Schenkel, W. 1983, *Das Grab des Ibi. Theben Nr. 36. Obergutsverwalters der Gottesgemahlin des Amun* (Band I). Mainz: Philipp von Zabern.

Lacau, P. and Chevrier, H. 1977. *Une chapelle d'Hatshepsout à Karnak I.* Le Caire: l'Institut Français d'Archéologie Orientale.

Larché, F. and Burgos, F. 2006. *La chapelle Rouge: le sanctuaire de barque d'Hatshepsout.* Paris: Culturesfrance.

Larkin, D. and Van Siclen, C. 1975. Theban Tomb 293 and the Tomb of the Scribe Huy. *Journal of Near Eastern Studies* 34(2): 129-134.

Leclant, J. 1954. Fouilles et travaux en Egypte 1952-1953. *Orientalia Nova Series* 23: 64-79.

Lepsius, K.R. 1849. *Denkmäler aus Ägypten und Äthiopien nach den Zeichnungen der von Seiner Majestät dem Könige von Preußen Friedrich Wilhelm IV nach diesen Ländern gesendeten und in den Jahren 1842-1845. ausgeführten wissenschaftlichen Expedition auf Befehl Seiner Majestät herausgegeben und erläutert.* 13 Volumes. Berlin: Nicolaische Buchhandlung.

Lipińska, J. 1977. *Deir el-Bahari II: The Temples of Tuthmosis III.* Warsaw: Éditions scientifiques de Pologne.

Manniche, L. 1986. The Tomb of Nakht the Gardener, at Thebes, no. 161, as copied by Robert Hay. *The Journal of Egyptian Archaeology* 72: 55-78.

Manniche, L. 1987. *City of the Dead: Thebes in Egypt.* London: British Museum Press.

Manniche, L. 1988a. *The Wall Decoration of Three Theban Tombs (TT 77, 175 and 249).* Copenhagen: Museum Tusculanum Press.

Manniche, L. 1988b. *Lost Tombs: A Study of Certain Eighteenth Dynasty Monuments in the Theban Necropolis.* London: Kegan Paul International.

Manniche, L. 1997. Reflections on the Banquet Scene, in R. Tefnin (ed.) *La peinture égyptienne ancienne: Un monde de signes à préserver: Actes du Colloque international de Bruxelles, avril, 1994* (Monumenta Aegyptica 7): 29-36. Brussels: Fondation Egyptologique Reine Elisabeth.

Manniche, L. 2011. *Lost Ramesside and Post-Ramesside Private Tombs in the Theban Necropolis.* Copenhagen: Museum Tusculanum Press.

Marciniak, M. 1981. Une inscription commémorative de Deir el-Bahari. *Mitteilungen des Deutschen Archäologischen Instituts Abteilung Kairo 37:* 299-305.

Martin, G.T. 1991. *The Hidden Tombs of Memphis. New Discoveries from the Time of Tutankhamun and Ramesses the Great.* London: Thames and Hudson.

Miniaci, G. 2009. The Necropolis of Dra Abu el-Naga, in M. Betrò, P. Del Vesco and G. Miniaci *Seven Seasons at Dra Abu el-Naga. The Tomb of Huy (TT 14): Preliminary Results* (Progetti 3): 14-31. Pisa: Pisa University Press.

Mostafa, M.F. 1995. *Das Grab ds Neferhotep und des Meh (TT257)* (Theben VIII). Mainz am Rhein: Philipp von Zabern.

Nasr, M. 1988. The Theban Tomb 261 of Kha'emwese in Dra' Abu el-Naga. *Studien zur Altägyptischen Kultur 15:* 233-242.

Nasr, M. 1993. The Theban Tomb 260 of User. *Studien zur Altägyptischen Kultur* 20: 173-202.

Naunton, C. 2018. *Searching for the Lost Tombs of Egypt.* London: Thames and Hudson.

Negm, M. 1997. *The Tomb of Simut called Kyky: Theban Tomb 409 at Qurnah.* Warminster: Aris & Philips.

Neunert, G., Gabler, K. & Verbovsek, A. (eds.), 2013, *Nekropolen: Grab - Bild - Ritual,* Wiesbaden.

Newberry, P.E., 1900, *The Life of Rekhmara. Vezîr of Upper Egypt under Thothmes III and Amenhetep II (circa B.C. 1471-1448) with Twenty-Two Plates.* Westminster.

O'Connor, D., 1998, 'The City and the World: Worldview and Built Forms in the Reign of Amenhotep III', in O'Connor & Cline (eds.), 1998: 125-172.

O'Connor, D., 2009, *Abydos: Egypt's First Pharaohs and the Cult of Osiris.* London.

O'Connor, D. & Cline, E.H., 1998, *Amenhotep III: Perspectives on his Reign.* Michigan.

Ockinga, B.G., 2000, 'Theban Tomb 233 – Saroy Regains an Identity', *BACE* 11: 103-113.

Ockinga, B.G. 2006. Use, Reuse and Abuse of "Sacred Space": Observations of Dra Abu el-Naga, in P.F. Dorman and B.M. Bryan (eds) *Sacred Space and Sacred Function in Ancient Thebes* (Studies in Ancient Oriental Civilisations 61): 139-163. Chicago: The Oriental Institute.

Ockinga, B.G., 2008, 'Theban Tomb 147: Its Owners and Erasures Revisited', *BACE* 19: 139- 144.

Ockinga, B.G., 2009, *The Tomb of Amenemope (TT148) Volume I: Architecture, Texts and Decoration.* ACE Reports 27. Sydney.

Ockinga, B.G. & Binder, S., 2009, 'The Macquarie Theban Tombs Project: 20 years in Dra Abu El Naga', in *Ancient History: Resources for Teachers* 39.2: 205-247.

Otto, E., 1952, *Topographie des Thebanischen Gaues*, UGAAe 16. Leipzig.

Parkinson, R.B., 1991, *Voices from Ancient Egypt. An Anthology of Middle Kingdom Writings.* London.

Peden, A., 2001, *The Graffiti of Pharaonic Egypt. Scope and Roles of Informal Writings (c. 3100-332 B.G.).* Leiden.

Peden, A., 2011, 'The Community of Workmen at Deir el-Medina in the Ramesside Period: An Overview of Rank and Roles', in M. Collier and S. Snape (eds) *Ramesside Studies in Honour of K.A. Kitchen*: 381-386. Bolton: Rutherford Press.

Peet, T.E., 1930, *The Great Tomb Robberies of the Twentieth Egyptian Dynasty.* Oxford.

Pereyra, M.V. 2012. El palacio real en el umbral des Más Allá, in L.M. Araújo and J. C. Sales (eds) *Novos trabalhos de Egiptologia Iberica: IV* (Congress Iberico de Egiptologia 2): 909-921. Lisboa: Instituto Oriental.

Peterson, B.J. 1969. Some Reliefs from the Memphite Necropolis. *The Museum of Mediterranean and Near Eastern Antiquities Medelhavsmuseet Bulletin* 5: 3-15

Petrie, W.M., 1896, *Six Temples of Thebes, Naqada and Ballas.* Cambridge.

Petrie, W.M., 1909, *Qurneh*, London.

Pimpaud, A.B., 2014, 'Archaeological Map and Atlas of Western Thebes' Academia website,

Available at: https://www.academia.edu/6794288/Archaeological_Map_and_Atlas_of_Western_Thebes [Accessed 07 June 2019] 004).

Pinch, G., 2004, *Egyptian Mythology: A Guide to the Gods, Goddesses, and Traditions of Ancient Egypt.* Oxford.

Polz, D., 1990, 'Bemerkungen der Grabbenutzung in der thebanischen Nekropole', *MDAIK* 46: 301-336.

Polz, D., 1995a, 'The Location of the Tomb of Amenhotep I: A Reconsideration', in Wilkinson (ed.), 1995: 8-21.

Polz, D. 1995b. Dra' Abu el-Naga: Die thebanische Nekropole des frühen Neuen Reuches, in J. Assmann, E. Dziobek, H. Guksch and F. Kampp (eds), *Thebanische Beamtennekropolen* (Studien zur Archäologie und Geschichte Altägyptens): 25-42. Heidelberg: Heidelberger Orientverlag.

Polz, D., 1997, *Das Grab des Hui und des Kel. Theben Nr. 54.* Mainz.

Polz, D., 2007, 'Der Beginn des Neuen Reiches. Zur Vorgeschichte einer Zeitenwende', *SDAIK* 31: 104-111 & 172-197.

Polz, D., Rummel, U., Euchner, I. & Beckh, T., 2012, 'Topographical Archaeology in Dra' Abu el-Naga. Three Thousand Years of Cultural History', *MDAIK* 68: 115-134.

Porter, B. & Moss, R., 1960, *The Topographical Bibliography of Ancient Egyptian Hieroglyphic Texts, Statues, Reliefs and Paintings I: The Theban Necropolis: Part 1: Private Tombs: 2nd Edition*, Oxford.

Quirke, S., 2004, *Titles and Bureaux of Egypt 1850 - 1700 BC*, London.

Raven, M.J. 2018. The Saqqara Necropolis in the Ramesside Period. Between Tradition and Innovation, in S. Kubisch and U. Rummel (eds) *The Ramesside Period in Egypt. Studies into Cultural and Historical Processes of the 19th and 20th Dynasties* (Sonderschrift des Deutschen Archäologischen Instituts 41): 239-248. Berlin: Der Gruyter.

Reisner, G.A., 1936, *The Development of the Egyptian Tomb down to the Accession of Cheops.* Cambridge.

Rhind, A.H., 1862, *Thebes. Its Tombs and Their Tenants.* London.

Rice, M., 2002, *Who's Who in Ancient Egypt.* London.

Robins, G., 1993, *Women in Ancient Egypt*, London.

Roehrig, C. H. 1995. The Early Middle Kingdom Cemeteries at Thebes and the Tomb of Djari in J. Assmann, E. Dziobek, H. Guksch and F. Kampp (eds), *Thebanische Beamtennekropolen* (Studien zur Archäologie und Geschichte Altägyptens): 255-269. Heidelberg: Heidelberger Orientverlag.

Roehrig, C., 2003, 'The Middle Kingdom tomb of Wah at Thebes' in N. Strudwick and J. Taylor (eds) *The Theban Necropolis: Past, Present and Future:* 11-13. London: British Museum Press.

Romer, J., 1988, 'Who Made the Private Tombs of Thebes?', in B. Bryan and D. Lorton (eds) *Essays in Egyptology in Honour of Hans* Goedicke: 211-232. San Antonio: Van Siclen Books.

Roth, A.M., 1988, 'The Organization of Royal Cemeteries at Saqqara in the Old Kingdom', in *JARCE* 25: 201-214.

Rummel, U. 2011. Two Re-Used Blocks of the God's Wife Isis at Deir el-Bakhit/ Dra Abu el-Naga (Western Thebes), in M. Collier and S. Snape (eds) *Ramesside Studies in Honour of K.A. Kitchen*: 423-431. Bolton: Rutherford Press.

Rummel, U., 2013a, 'Gräber, Feste, Prozessionen: der Ritualraum Theben-West in der Ramessidenzeit', in Neunert, Gabler & Verbovsek (eds.), 2013: 207-232.

Rummel, U., 2013b, 'Ramesside Tomb-temples at Dra Abu el-Naga', *EA* 42: 14-17.

Rummel, U., 2014, 'War, Death and Burial of the High Priest Amenhotep: the Archaeological Record at Dra Abu el-Naga', *SAK 43*: 375-397.

Rummel, U. 2018, Ritual Space and Symbol of Power. Monumental Tomb Architecture in Thebes at the End of the New Kingdom, in S. Kubisch and U. Rummel (eds) *The Ramesside Period in Egypt. Studies into Cultural and Historical Processes of the 19th and 20th Dynasties* (Sonderschrift des Deutschen Archäologischen Instituts 41): 249-276. Berlin: Der Gruyter.

Rzepka, S. 2003. Old Kingdom Graffiti in Deir el-Bahri, in N. Kloth, K. Martin and E. Pardey (eds) *Es werde niedergelegt als Schriftstück: Festschrift für Hartwig*

Altenmüller (Studien zur Altägyptischen Kultur 9): 379-385. Hamburg: Helmut Buske.

Sakurai, K., Yoshimura, S., & Kondo, J., 1988, *Comparative Studies of Noble Tombs in Theban Necropolis*. Tokyo.

Saleh, M., 1977, *Three Old Kingdom Tombs at Thebes*. Mainz.

Saleh, M., 1983, 'The Tomb of the Royal Scribe Qen-amun at Khokha (Theban Necropolis No. 412)', *ASAE* 69: 15-28.

Säve-Söderbergh, T., 1957, *Four Eighteenth Dynasty Tombs*. Oxford.

Säve-Söderbergh, T., 1958, 'Eine Gastmahlsszene in Grabe des Schatzhauvorstehers Djehuti', *MDAIK* 16: 280-291.

Schott, S. 1934. The Feasts of Thebes, in H. Nelson and U. Holscher (eds) *Work in Western Thebes: 1931-33* (Oriental Institute Communications 18): 63-90. Chicago: The Oriental Institute.

Schott, S. 1953. *Das schöne Fest vom Wüstentale*. Wiesbaden: Franz Steiner Verlag.

Schreiber, G. 2008. *The Mortuary Monument of Djehutymes II. Finds from the New Kingdom to the Twenty-sixth Dynasty* (Studia Aegyptiaca Series Maior II). Budapest: Archaeolingua.

Sethe, K. 1906-1909. *Urkunden der 18. Dynastie: Historich-biographische Urkunden. IV. Heft 1-16. Abteilung Band II.* Leipzig: J.C. Hinrichs.

Seyfried, K-J. 1990. *Das Grab des Amonmose (TT373)* (Theben IV). Mainz: Philipp von Zabern.

Seyfried, K-J. 1991. *Das Grab des Paenkhemenu (TT68) und die Anlage TT227)* (Theben VI). Mainz: Philipp von Zabern.

Seyfried, K-J. 1995. *Das Grab des Djehutiemhab (TT194)* (Theben VII). Mainz: Philipp von Zabern.

Seyfried, K-J. 2013. Bemerkungen und Quellen zum HAb nfr n int, dem "Schönen Fest des Tales" in Theben. *Göttinger Miszellen* 13: 1-64.

Shedid, A.G. 1988. *Stil der Grabmalerein in der Zeit Amenophis' II: Untersucht an den thebanischen Gräbern Nr.104 und No.80* (Archäologische Veröffentlichungen, Deutschen Archäologisches Institut, Abteilung Kairo 66). Mainz: Philipp von Zabern.

Shedid, A.G. 1994. *Das Grab des Sennedjem: ein Künstlergrab der 19. Dynastie in Deir el-Medineh*. Mainz: Phillip von Zabern.

Shedid, A.G. and Seidel, M. 1996. *The Tomb of Nakht: The Art and History of an Eighteenth Dynasty Official's Tomb at Western Thebes*. Mainz: Phillip von Zabern.

Shirley, J.J. 2010. Viceroys, Viziers and the Amun Precinct: The Power of Heredity and Strategic Marriage in the Early 18th Dynasty. *Journal of Egyptian History* 3.1: 73-113.

Shirley, J.J. 2011. What's in a Title? Military and Civil Officials in the Egyptian 18th Dynasty Military Sphere, in S. Bar, D.E. Kahn and J.J. Shirley (eds) *Egypt, Canaan and Israel: History, Imperialism, Ideology and Literature*: 291-319. Leiden: Brill.

Shirley, J.J. 2014. The Power of the Elite: The Officials of Hatshepsut's Regency and Coregency, in J.M. Galán, B.M. Bryan and P. Dorman (eds) *Creativity and Innovation in the Reign of Hatshepsut* (Studies in Ancient Oriental Civilisations 69): 173-245. Chicago: The Oriental Institute.

Simpson, W.K. 1974. *The Terrace of The Great God at Abydos: The Offering Chapels of Dynasties 12 and 13* (Egyptology: The Pennsylvania-Yale expedition to Egypt). Milton Keynes: New Haven.

Slinger, K. 2015. Was the Orientation of Private Theban tombs Influenced by the Evolving Processional Route of the Beautiful Festival of the Valley in the 18th Dynasty? Unpublished MA dissertation. University of Liverpool.

Snape, S. 2011, *Ancient Egyptian Tombs: The Culture of Life and Death*. Oxford: Wiley-Blackwell.

Soliman, R. 2009. *Old and Middle Kingdom Theban Tombs*. London: Golden House Publications.

Staring, N.T.B. 2015. *Studies in the Saqqara New Kingdom Necropolis: From the Mid-19th Century Exploration of the Site to New Insights into the Life and Death of Memphite Officials, Their Tombs and the Use of Sacred Space*. PhD dissertation, University of Macquarie University. Viewed 27 June 2019, <*https://openaccess.leidenuniv.nl/bitstream/1887/51704/1/Staring_PhD2015_StudiesintheSaqqaraNewKingdomNecropolis.pdf*>

Strudwick, N. 1995. The Population of Thebes in the New Kingdom. Some Preliminary Thoughts, in J. Assmann, E. Dziobek, H. Guksch and F. Kampp (eds) *Thebanische Beamtennekropolen* (Studien zur Archäologie und Geschichte Altägyptens): 97-105. Heidelberg: Heidelberger Orientverlag.

Strudwick, N. 2003. *The Tomb of Amenemopet called Tjanefer at Thebes* (Abhandlungen des Deutschen Archäologischen Instituts Abteilung Kairo. *Ägyptologische* Reihe 19). Berlin: Achet.

Strudwick, N. 2010. Use and Re-use of Tombs in the Theban Necropolis: Patterns and Explanations, in J.C. Moreno Garcia (ed.) *Elites et pouvoir en Egypte ancienne: Cahiers de recherches de l'Institut de Papyrologie et d'Egyptologie de Lille* 28: 239-261. Lille: Université Charles de Gaulle-Lille 3.

Strudwick, N. (ed.) 2016. *The Tomb of Pharaoh's Chancellor Senneferi at Thebes (TT99). Part I: The New Kingdom*. Oxford: Oxbow Books.

Strudwick, N. and Strudwick, H. 1996. *The Tombs of Amenhotep, Khnummose, and Amenmose at Thebes (Nos. 294, 253 and 254)*. Oxford: The Griffith Institute.

Strudwick, N. and Strudwick, H. 1999. *Thebes in Egypt: A Guide to the Tombs and Temples of Luxor*. London: British Museum Press.

Taylor J.H. 2001. *Death and the Afterlife in Ancient Egypt*. London: British Museum Press.

Toonen, W. H. J., Graham, A., Pennington, B. T., Strutt, K. D., Hunter, M. A., Emery, V. L., Masson-Berghoff, A. and Barker, D. S. 2017. Holocene fluvial history of the Nile's west bank at ancient Thebes (Luxor, Egypt) and its relation with cultural dynamics and basin-wide hydroclimatic variability. *Geoarchaeology* 33.3: 273-290.

Ullmann, M. 2006. Thebes: Origins of a Ritual Landscape, in P.F. Dorman and B.M. Bryan (eds) *Sacred Space and Sacred Function in Ancient Thebes* (Studies in Ancient Oriental Civilisations 61): 3-13. Chicago: The Oriental Institute.

Van der Boorn, G.P.F. 1988. *The Duties of the Vizier: Civil Administration in the Early New Kingdom*. London: Kegan Paul International.

Vandier D'Abbadie, J. 1954. *Deux tombes ramessides à Gournet-Mourraï* (Mémoires publiés par les membres de l'Institut Français d'Archéology Orientale du Cairo 87). Le Caire: l'Institut Français d'Archéologie Orientale

Vandier D'Abbadie, J. and Jourdain, G. 1939. *Deux tombes de Deir el-Médineh*)(Mémoires publiés par les membres de l'Institut Français d'Archéology Orientale du Cairo 73). Le Caire: l'Institut Français d'Archéologie Orientale.

Virey, P. 1889. *Le tombeau de Rekhmara, préfet de Thèbes sous la XVIIIe dynastie* (Mémoires publiés par les membres de l'Institut Français d'Archéology Orientale du Cairo 5,1). Paris: Libraire de la Société Asiatique de l'École des Langues Orientales Vivantes.

Virey, P. 1891. *Sept tombeaux thébains de la XVIIIe dynastie* (Mémoires publiés par les membres de l'Institut Français d'Archéology Orientale du Cairo 5,2). Paris: Libraire de la Société Asiatique de l'École des Langues Orientales Vivantes.

Ward, W. 1982. *Index of Egyptian Administrative and Religious Titles of the Middle Kingdom: With a Glossary of Words and Phrases Used*. Beirut: American University of Beirut.

Weeks, K. 2005. *Illustrated Guide to Luxor: Tombs, Temples and Museums*. Cairo: The American University in Cairo Press

Wente, E.F. 1984. Some Graffiti from the Reign of Hatshepsut. *Journal of Near Eastern Studies* 4.1: 47-54.

Whale, S. 1989. *The Family in the Eighteenth Dynasty of Egypt: A Study of the Representation of Family in Private Tombs* (Australian Centre for Egyptology Studies I). Sydney: McQuarie Ancient History Association.

Wilkinson, C.K. and Hill, M. 1983. *Egyptian Wall Painting: The Metropolitan Museum of Art's Collection of Facsimiles*. New York: The Metropolitan Museum of Art.

Wilkinson, R. (ed.) 1995. *Valley of the Sun Kings: New Explorations in the Tombs of the Pharaohs*. Tucson: University of Arizona Egyptian Expedition.

Wilkinson, R. 2000. *The Complete Temples of Ancient Egypt*. London: Thames and Hudson.

Winlock, H.E. 1915. The Theban Necropolis in the Middle Kingdom. *The American Journal of Semitic Languages and Literatures* 32.1: 1-37.

Winlock, H.E. 1921. The Egyptian Expedition 1920-1921: III. Excavations at Thebes. *The Metropolitan Museum of Art Bulletin* 16.11 Part 2: Egyptian: 29-53.

Winlock, H.E. 1924. The Tombs of the Kings of the Seventeenth Dynasty at Thebes. *The Journal of Egyptian Archaeology* 10: 217-277.

Winlock, H.E. 1942. *Excavations at Deir el-Bahri (1911-1931)*. New York: The Macmillan Company.

Winlock, H.E. 1947. *The Rise and Fall of the Middle Kingdom in Thebes*. New York: The Macmillan Company.

Wüst, R.A.J. and J. McLane, J. 2000. Rock deterioration in the Royal Tomb of Seti I, Valley of the Kings, Luxor, Egypt. *Engineering Geology* 58: 163–190.

Zivie, A. 2007. *The Lost Tombs of Saqqara*. Toulouse: Cara Cara Editions.

Websites

Theban Mapping Project, 1997–2013, *Atlas of the Theban Necropolis*, viewed 10 December 2016,<http://thebanmappingproject.com/atlas/index_tn.asp>

Osirisnet, 2001, Osirisnet: Tombs of Egypt, viewed 10 September 2019, <https://osirisnet.net>

Staatliche Museen zu Berlin, 2017, viewed 12 June 2017, <http://www.smbdigital.de/eMuseumPlus?service=ExternalInterface&module=collection&objectId=606948&viewType=detailView>

Busing, M., 2017, Reliefblöcke aus dem Grab des Ptahemhat, Darstellung des Begräbniszuges mit Trauergefolge, viewed 12 June 2017, <http://www.smbdigital.de/eMuseumPlus?service=ExternalInterface&module=collection&objectId=606948&viewType=detailView>